TEXAS for the SOCIAL WORKER

A 2016 Sourcebook

EDITED BY

VICKI HANSEN AND J. RAY HAYS

N A S W, TEXAS CHAPTER
National Association of Social Workers
AUSTIN, TX

Bayou Publishing
HOUSTON, TX

This publication is designed to provide accurate and authoritative information in regard to the subject matter covered. It is sold with the understanding that the publisher is not engaged in rendering legal, accounting, psychotherapeutic or other professional service. If expert assistance is required, the services of a competent professional person should be sought. From a Declaration of Principles jointly adopted by a Committee of the American Bar Association and a Committee of Publishers.

Printed in the United States of America
Fourth Edition 10 9 8 7 6 5 4 3 2

Library of Congress Cataloging-in-Publication Data

Names: Hansen, Vicki, 1952- editor. | Hays, J. Ray (James Ray), 1942- editor.
    | National Association of Social Workers. Texas Chapter.
Title: Texas law for the social worker : a 2016 sourcebook / edited by Vicki
    Hansen and J. Ray Hays.
Description: Fourth edition. | Houston, TX : Bayou Publishing ; Austin, TX :
    NASW Texas Chapter, [2016] | Includes bibliographical references and index.
Identifiers: LCCN 2016014036 (print) | LCCN 2016014295 (ebook) | ISBN
    9781886298569 (pbk. : alk. paper) | ISBN 9781886298781 (ePUB) | ISBN
    9781886298736 (ePDF)
Subjects: LCSH: Social workers--Legal status, laws, etc.--Texas.
Classification: LCC KFT1549.5 .T49 2016 (print) | LCC KFT1549.5 (ebook) | DDC
    344.76403/13--dc23
LC record available at http://lccn.loc.gov/2016014036

Published by:

National Association of Social Workers
Texas Chapter
810 West 11th Street., Suite 410
Austin, TX 78701-2010
(512) 474-1454
http://www.naswtx.org

Bayou Publishing
2524 Nottingham
Houston, TX 77005-1412
713-526-4558
http://www.bayoupublishing.com

NOTE TO READER

CONTENTS AT A GLANCE

❏ STATUTES 37
  Occupations Code - Social Workers   39
  Administrative Code   63
  Civil Practice and Remedies Code   71
  Code of Criminal Procedure   86
  Education Code   93
  Family Code   106
  Government Code   144
  Health and Safety Code   151
  Human Resources Code   232
  Insurance Code   239
  Local Government Code   248
  Occupations Code — Other   249
  Penal Code   256
  Probate Code   262
  DSHS Rider 19   267

❏ CASE LAW 293
  Confidentiality of Psychotherapy Notes   295
    (Jaffee vs. Redmond)
  Duty to Warn/Protect   314
    (Thapar vs. Zezulka)
  Derived Judicial Immunity & Duty to Report 319
    (B.K. vs. Cox)
  Confidentiality of a Child's Mental Health Records   327
    (Abrams vs. Jones)

❏ HIPAA 339
  Texas Law and the Federal Health Insurance
  Portability and Accountability Act   340

❏ OPINIONS FROM THE ATTORNEY GENERAL 343
  Services Outside of Agency—Conflict of Interest?   345
  Court-Ordered Social Studies on Personal Time   347
  Political Activities of State Social Workers   351
  Discretion for Reporting Sexual Abuse   355
  Disclosure under Subpoena   358
  Parent's Access to School Counseling Records   364
  Sex Offender Treatment License Necessary?   371
  Grandparent Access to Children and Records   375
  Reporting Abuse during Childhood of Now-Adult Patient 384
  Reporting of Alleged Child Abuse   387
  Using Advocates in School for Counseling   389

❏ APPENDIX A: CODE OF ETHICS 393

❏   APPENDIX B: RULES & REGS—TEXAS STATE BOARD
     OF SOCIAL WORKER EXAMINERS 413
❏   APPENDIX C: NASW/TX RESOURCES 487
❏   INDEX. 499
❏   ORDERING INFORMATION. 513
❏   NATIONAL ASSOCIATION OF SOCIAL WORKERS
     TEXAS CHAPTER 514

CONTENTS

INTRODUCTION TO THE FOURTH EDITION ... 27

INTRODUCTION TO THIRD EDITION ... 29

INTRODUCTION TO FIRST AND SECOND EDITIONS ... 33

ABOUT THE EDITORS ... 35

❑ STATUTES 37

OCCUPATIONS CODE - SOCIAL WORKERS ... 39

   Chapter 505. Social Workers ... 39

   SubChapter A. General Provisions ... 39

      §505.001. Short Title ... 39

      §505.002. Definitions [(2011)] ... 39

      §505.0025. Practice of Social Work ... 39

      §505.003. Applications and Exemptions ... 39

      §505.004. Nondiscriminatory Actions and Decisions ... 40

      §505.005. Application of Sunset Act ... 40

   SubChapter B. Texas State Board of Social Worker Examiners ... 41

      §505.101. Board; Membership ... 41

      §505.201. General Rulemaking and Enforcement Authority ... 41

      §505.202. Rules Restricting Advertising or Competitive Bidding ... 41

      §505.203. Fees ... 41

      §505.204. Board Duties Regarding Complaints ... 42

      §505.205. Roster of License Holders ... 42

      §505.206. Roster of Independent Social Workers ... 42

      §505.207. Annual Report Regarding Licensing ... 42

      §505.208. Annual Report Regarding Funds ... 42

      §505.209. Rules on Consequences of Criminal Conviction ... 42

      §505.210. Use of Technology ... 43

      §505.211. Negotiated Rulemaking and Alternative Dispute Resolution Policy ... 43

   SubChapter E. Public Access Information and Complaint Procedures ... 43

      §505.251. Consumer Interest Information ... 43

      §505.252. Complaints ... 43

      §505.253. Records of Complaints ... 44

      §505.254. General Rules Regarding Complaint Investigation and Disposition ... 44

      §505.2545. Subpoenas ... 45

      §505.2547. Complaint Committee ... 46

§505.255. Public Participation   46
SubChapter F. Specialty Areas of Social Work   46
  §505.301. Establishment of Specialty Area   46
  §505.302. Regulation of Specialty Areas   46
  §505.303. Clinical Social Work Specialty   46
  §505.304. Order of Recognition of Specialty   47
  §505.305. Recognition of Specialty; Issuance of order   47
  §505.306. Prohibited Use of Specialty Area
             Identification or Title   47
  §505.307. Independent Practice Recognition; Minimum
             Qualifications.   47
SubChapter G. License Requirements   48
  §505.351. License Required   48
  §505.352. License Application   48
  §505.353. Eligibility   48
  §505.354. Examination   49
  §505.3545. Jurisprudence Examination   49
  §505.355. Examination Results   49
  §505.356. Reexamination   49
  §505.357. Temporary License   50
  §505.3575. Issuance of Licenses to Certain Out-of-State
             Applicants   50
  §505.358. Provisional License   50
  §505.359. Issuance of License to Provisional License Holder   51
  §505.360. Professional Identification [(d) Repealed 2003]   51
SubChapter H. Renewal of License and Order of Recognition of
Specialty   51
  §505.401. Staggered Expiration Dates   51
  §505.402. Renewal of License and order of Recognition of
             Specialty   52
  §505.403. Renewal of Expired License By Out-of-State
             Practitioner   52
  §505.404. Continuing Education   52
  §505.405. Grounds for Refusing Renewal   53
SubChapter I. Denial of License or Order and
Disciplinary Procedures   53
  §505.451. Grounds for Denial of License or order of
             Recognition of Specialty; Disciplinary Action   53
  §505.452. Conditions of Probation   54
  §505.453. Emergency Suspension   54
  §505.454. Sanctions for Holder of Expired License or order
             of Recognition of Specialty   54
  §505.455. Procedure; Hearing   54
  §505.456. Schedule of Sanctions   54
  §505.457. Informal Procedures   55
  §505.458. Refund   55
SubChapter J. Penalties and Enforcement Provisions   55
  §505.501. Monitoring of License Holder   55
  §505.502. Prohibited Conduct by Business
             or Professional Entity   55

§505.503. Injunction 56
§505.504. Civil Penalty 57
§505.505. Appeal Bond Not Required 57
§505.506. Representation by Attorney General 57
§505.507. Criminal Penalty 57
§505.508. Cease and Desist Order 57
SubChapter K. *Administrative Penalty* 57
§505.551. Imposition of Administrative Penalty 57
§505.552. Amount of Administrative Penalty 57
§505.553. Report and Notice of Violation and Penalty 58
§505.554. Penalty To Be Paid or Hearing Requested 58
§505.555. Hearing 58
§505.556. Decision by Board 59
§505.557. Options Following Decision: Pay or Appeal 59
§505.558. Collection of Penalty 59
§505.559. Determination by Court 60
§505.560. Remittance of Penalty and Interest 60
§505.561. Administrative Procedure 60
SubChapter L. *Reports of Certain Violations* 60
§505.601. Report of Violation. 60
§505.602. Reporting Immunity 60
§505.603. Cause of Action for Retaliation 61
Social Worker Rules & Regs 62

Rules Relating to the Licensing and Regulation of Social Workers 62
(Title 22—Examining Boards, Part 34, Chapter 781) 62

ADMINISTRATIVE CODE **63**

Rule 89.1053 Procedures for Use of Restraint and Time-Out 63
(A) Requirement to Implement 63
(B) Definitions 63
(C) Use of Restraint 63
(D) Training on Use of Restraint 63
(E) Documentation and Notification on Use of Restraint 64
(F) Clarification Regarding Restraint 64
(G) Use of Time-Out 65
(H) Training on Use of Time-Out 65
(I) Documentation on Use of Time-Out 66
(J) Student Safety 66
(K) Data Reporting 66
(L) Excluded Provisions 66
§411.653. Standards for Services to Persons with Co-Occurring
Psychiatric and Substance Use Disorders (COPSD) 66
§411.651. Purpose 66
§411.653. Definitions 66
§411.654. Services to Individuals with COPSD 68
§411.658. Specialty Competencies of Staff Providing
Services to Individuals with COPSD 69
§411.660. Screening, Assessment, and Treatment Planning 70

CIVIL PRACTICE AND REMEDIES CODE   71
Sexual Exploitation by Mental Health Provider—§81   71
§81.001. Definitions   71
§81.002. Sexual Exploitation Cause of Action   72
§81.003. Liability of Employer   72
§81.004. Damages   73
§81.005. Defenses   73
§81.006. Reporting Therapist-Client Sexual Relationship   74
§81.007. Limited Immunity from Liability   75
§81.008. Admission of Evidence   75
§81.009. Limitations   75
Declaration for Mental Health Treatment—§137   76
§137.001. Definition   76
§137.002. Eligible Persons; Period of validity   77
§137.003. Execution and Witnesses   77
§137.004. Health Care Provider   77
§137.005. Limitation on Liability   78
§137.006. Discrimination in Relation to Execution of
            Declaration for Mental Health Treatment   78
§137.007. Use and Effect of Declaration for Mental Health
            Treatment   78
§137.008. Disregard of Declaration for Mental Health
            Treatment   79
§137.009. Conflicting or Contrary Provisions   79
§137.010. Revocation   79
§137.011. Form of Declaration for Mental Health Treatment 80
    Declaration for Mental Health Treatment   80
    Psychoactive Medications   80
    Convulsive Treatment   80
    Preferences for Emergency Treatment   81
    Additional Preferences or Instructions   81
    Statement of Witnesses   81
    Notice to Person Making a Declaration for
            Mental Health Treatment   82
Subpoenas in Civil Cases—§176   82
§176.1 Form 82
§176.2 Required Actions   83
§176.3 Limitations   83
§176.4 Who May Issue   83
§176.5 Service   83
§176.6 Response   83
§176.7 Protection of Person from Undue Burden and Expense 84
§176.8 Enforcement of Subpoena   85

CODE OF CRIMINAL PROCEDURE   86
Incompetency to Stand Trial—§46B   86
Subchapter A.
    General Provisions   86
§46B.003. Incompetency; Presumptions   86

§46B.004. Raising the Issue of Incompetency to Stand Trial   *86*
§46B.005. Determining Incompetency to Stand Trial   *87*
§46B.007. Admissibility of Statements   *87*
Subchapter B.
Examination   *87*
§46B.021. Appointment of Experts   *87*
§46B.022. Experts: Qualifications   *88*
§46B.024. Factors Considered in Examination   *89*
§46B.025. Expert's Report   *89*
§46B.026. Report Deadline   *90*

Insanity Defense—§46C   *90*
Subchapter C.
Court-Ordered Examination & Report   *90*
§46C.101. Appointment of Experts   *90*
§46C.102. Expert's Qualifications   *91*
§46C.103. Competency to Stand Trail: Concurrent
      Appointment   *91*
§46C.104. Order Compelling Defendant to
      Submit to Examination   *91*
§46C.105. Reports Submitted by Experts   *92*
§46C.106. Compensation of Experts   *92*
§46C.107. Examination by Expert of Defendant's Choice   *92*

Education Code   **93**
Educators and School District Employees and Volunteers—§21   *93*
§21.003. Certification Required   *93*
Statewide Plan for Services to Children with Disabilities—§29   *93*
§29.001. Statewide Plan   *93*
§29.002. Definition   *94*
§29.003. Eligibility Criteria   *95*
§29.004. Full Individual and Initial Evaluation   *95*
§29.0041. Information & Consent for Certain Psychological
      Examinations or Tests   *96*
§29.005. Individualized Education Program   *97*
§30.001. Coordination of Services to
      Children with Disabilities   *97*
Alternative Settings for Behavior Management—§37   *98*
§37.0021. Use of Confinement, Restraint, Seclusion
      and Time-Out   *98*
Health and Safety—§38   *100*
§38.004. Child Abuse Reporting and Programs   *100*
§38.0041. Policies Addressing Sexual Abuse and Other
      Maltreatment of Children   *100*
§38.0042. Posting Child Abuse Hotline Telephone Number   *102*
§38.010. Outside Counselors   *102*
§38.016. Psychotropic Drugs and Psychiatric Evaluations or
      Examinations   *102*
Training Programs for Employees Regarding Sexual Abuse—§51   *103*
§51.976. Training Program Sexual Abuse Warning Signs   *103*

§51.9761. Child Abuse Reporting Policy and Training   104

FAMILY CODE   106

Court Ordered Counseling in Divorce—§6   106
    §6.505. Counseling   106
    §6.705. Testimony by Marriage Counselor   106
Consent to Treatment of Child by non-Parent or Child—§32   107
    §32.001. Consent by Non-Parent   107
    §32.002. Consent Form   107
    §32.003. Consent to Treatment by Child   108
    §32.004. Consent to Counseling   109
    §32.005. Examination without Consent of
                Abuse or Neglect of Child   109
    §32.1011. Consent to Immunization by Child   110
Waiver of Jurisdiction and Discretionary Transfer—§54.02   110
    §54.02. Waiver of Jurisdiction and Discretionary
                Transfer to Criminal Court   110
Family Violence—§71   114
    §71.0021. Dating Violence   114
    §71.003. Family   114
    §71.004. Family Violence   115
Protective Orders—§81   115
    §81.001. Entitlement to Protective Order   115
    §81.002. No Fee for Applicant   115
    §81.003. Fees and Costs Paid by Party Found to Have
                Committed Family Violence   115
Reporting Family Violence—§91   116
    §91.001. Definitions   116
    §91.002. Reporting by Witnesses Encouraged   116
    §91.003. Information Provided by Medical Professionals   116
    "Notice To Adult Victims of Family Violence"   117
Special Appointments and Social Studies—§107   117
    Subchapter D. Social Study   117
    § 107.0501. Definitions. In this subchapter: 117
    §107.051. Order for "Social Study"   117
    § 107.0511. Social Study Evaluator:
                Minimum Qualifications   118
    §107.0512. Social Study Evaluator:
                Conflicts of Interest and Bias   119
    §107.0513. General Provisions Applicable to Conduct
                of Social Study and Preparation of Report   120
    §107.0514. Elements of "Social Study"   120
    §107.05145. Social Study Evaluator Access to Investigative
                Records of Department of Family and
                Protective Services; Offense   121
    §107.0515. Reports of Certain Placements for Adoption   122
    §107.0519. Pre-Adoptive Social Study   122
    §107.052. Post-Placement Adoptive Social Study & Report   122
    §107.053. Prospective Adoptive Parents to Receive Copy   123

§107.054. Report Filed with Court   123
§107.055. Introduction of Report at Trial   123
§107.056. Preparation Fee   123
Texas Rules of Evidence and Privileges   123
Rule 510. Confidentiality of Mental
            Health Information in Civil Cases   123
Conservatorship, Possession, and Access—§153   125
§153.001. Public Policy   125
§153.002. Best Interest of Child   125
§153.0072. Collaborative Law   125
§153.073. Rights of Parent at All Times   126
§153.074. Rights and Duties During Period of Possession 126
§153.075. Duties of Parent not Appointed Conservator 127
§153.010. Order for Family Counseling   127
§153.132. Rights and Duties of Parent Appointed Sole
            Managing Conservator   127
§153.133. Parenting Plan for
            Joint Managing Conservatorship   128
§153.192. Right and Duties of Parent Appointed
            Possessory Conservator   129
§153.605. Appointment of Parenting Coordinator   129
Adoption—§162   129
§162.413. Counseling   129
Child Abuse or Neglect—§261   130
§261.001. Definitions   130
§261.101. Persons Required to Report; Time to Report 132
§261.102. Matters to be Reported   133
§261.103. Report Made to Appropriate Agency   133
§261.104. Contents of Report   133
§261.106. Immunities   133
§261.107. False Report; Penalty   133
§261.108. Frivolous Claims Against Person Reporting 134
§261.109. Failure to Report; Penalty   134
§261.201. Confidentiality and Disclosure of Information 135
§261.202. Privileged Communication   137
§261.203. Information Relating to Child Fatality   137
§261.301. Investigation of Report   139
§261.303. Interference with Investigation; Court Order 140
§261.305. Access to Mental Health Records   141
§261.316. Exemption From Fees for Medical Records   141
Medical Care and Educational Services for Children in Foster
Care—§266   141
§266.001. Definitions   141
§266.004. Consent For Medical Care   142

GOVERNMENT CODE   **144**
Texas Home Visiting Program (Social Worker)—§531   144
§531.981. Definitions   144
§531.982. Establishment of Texas Home Visiting Program 144

§531.983. Types of Home Visiting Programs 144
§531.985. Outcomes 145
Implementation of Medicaid Managed Care Program—§533 145
§533.0055. Provider Protection Plan 145
Provision of Social Services through Faith- and
Community-Based Organizations—§535 147
Subchapter A. *General Provisions* 147
§535.001. Definitions 147
§535.002. Purpose 147
§535.003. Construction 147
§535.004. Applicability of Certain Federal Law 148
Subchapter B. *Governmental Liaisons for Faith- and*
Community-Based Organizations 148
§535.051. Designation of Faith-
and Community-Based Liaisons 148
§535.052. General Duties of Liaisons 148
§535.053. Interagency Coordinating Group 149
§535.054. Reports 149
§535.055. TEXAS NONPROFIT COUNCIL 149
Confidentiality: Exceptions to Required Reporting—§552 150
§552.138. Exception: Confidentiality of Family Violence
Shelter Center, Victims of Trafficking Shelter
Center, Sexual Assault Program Information. 150

HEALTH AND SAFETY CODE 151
Task Force on Domestic Violence—§32.061 151
§32.061. Definition 151
§32.062. Establishment; Presiding Officer 151
§32.063. Duties Of Task Force 151
§32.064. Report 152
HIV Testing, Confidentiality, and Consent—§81 152
§81.103. Confidentiality; Criminal Penalty 152
§81.104. Injunction; Civil Liability 153
§81.105. Informed Consent 153
§81.106. General Consent 154
§81.107. Consent to Test for Accidental Exposures 154
§81.109. Counseling Required for Positive Test Results 154
Home and Community Support Services—§142 155
§142.001. Definitions 155
§142.0011. Scope, Purpose, and Implementation 158
§142.0012. Controlling Person 159
§142.002. License Required 159
§142.0025. Temporary License 160
§142.003. Exemptions from Licensing Requirement 160
§142.004. License Application 162
§142.005. Compliance Record in Other States 163
§142.006. License Issuance; Term 163
§142.0065. Display of License 163
§142.0085. Alternate Delivery Site License 164
§142.009. Surveys; Consumer Complaints 164

§142.0091. Training   166
§142.0092. Consumer Complaint Data   167
§142.0093. Retaliation Prohibited   167
§142.0105. License Renewal   167
§142.011. Denial, Suspension, or Revocation of License   168
§142.014. Civil Penalty   168
§142.0145. Violation Relating to Advance Directives   169
§142.015. Advisory Council   169
§142.017. Administrative Penalty   169
§142.0171. Notice; Request For Hearing   171
Treatment Facilities Marketing Practices Act—§164   172
§164.002. Legislative Purpose   172
§164.003. Definitions   172
§164.004. Exemptions   173
§164.005. Conditioning Employee or Agent
          Relationships on Patient Revenue   173
§164.006. Soliciting and Contracting with Certain
          Referral Sources   173
§164.007. Qualified Mental Health Referral Service:
          Definition and Standards   175
§164.008. Operating an Intervention & Assessment Service   176
§164.009. Disclosures and Representations   177
§164.010. Prohibited Acts   177
Medical Records Privacy—§181   178
§181.001. Definitions   178
§181.002. Applicability   179
§181.004. Applicability of State and Federal Law   180
§181.057. Information Relating to Offenders with Mental
          Impairments   180
§181.058. Educational Records   180
Subchapter C
Access to and Use of Protected Health Information   180
§181.101. Training Required   180
§181.102. Consumer Access to Electronic Health Records   180
§181.103. Consumer Information Website   181
§181.104. Consumer Complaint Report - Attorney General   181
Prohibited Acts   181
§181.151. Reidentified Information   181
§181.152. Marketing Uses of Information   182
§181.153. Sale of Protected Health Information Prohibited;
          Exceptions   182
§181.154. Notice and Authorization Required for Electronic
          Disclosure of Protected Health Information;
          Exceptions   183
Subchapter E
Enforcement   183
§181.201. Injunctive Relief; Civil Penalty   183
§181.202. Disciplinary Action   185
§181.203. Exclusion From State Programs   185

§181.205. Mitigation — *185*

§181.206. Audits of Covered Entities — *185*

§181.207. Funding — *186*

Death Records and Suicide Data Collection—§193 — *186*

§193.011. Memorandum on Suicide Data — *186*

Reports of Abuse, Neglect, and Exploitation of Residents of
Certain Facilities—§260A — *187*

§260A.001. Definitions. in this Chapter — *187*

§260A.002. Reporting of Abuse, Neglect, and Exploitation — *188*

§260A.003. Contents of Report — *188*

§260A.004. Anonymous Reports of Abuse, Neglect, or
Exploitation — *188*

§260A.005. Telephone Hotline; Processing of Reports — *189*

§260A.006. Notice — *189*

§260A.007. Investigation and Deport of Department — *189*

§260A.008. Confidentiality — *191*

§260A.009. Immunity — *192*

§260A.010. Privileged Communications — *192*

§260A.011. Central Registry — *192*

§260A.012. Failure to Report; Criminal Penalty — *192*

§260A.013. Bad Faith, Malicious, Or Reckless Reporting;
Criminal Penalty — *192*

§260A.014. Retaliation Against Employees Prohibited — *192*

§260A.015. Retaliation Against Volunteers, Residents, or
Family Members or Guardians of Residents — *193*

§260A.016. Reports Relating to Deaths of Residents of an
Institution — *194*

§260A.017. Duties of Law Enforcement; Joint Investigation — *195*

Nursing Home Residents Requiring MH or
MR Services—§242.158 — *195*

§242.158 Identification of Certain Nursing Home
Residents Requiring Mental Health or
Mental Retardation Services — *195*

Subchapter I.
Nursing Facility Administration — *196*

§242.301. Definitions — *196*

§242.302. Powers and Duties of Department — *196*

§242.303. Nursing Facility Administrators
Advisory Committee — *196*

Reports of Abuse or Neglect of Patients in Chemical Dependency
Treatment Facilities—§464 — *197*

§464.010. Reports of Abuse or Neglect — *197*

Voluntary Mental Health Services—§571 and 572 — *198*

§571.019. Limitation of Liability — *198*

§572.001. Request for Admission — *198*

§572.002. Admission — *199*

§572.0022. Information on Medications — *199*

§572.0025. Intake, Assessment, and Admission — *200*

§572.003. Rights of Patients — *201*

§572.004. Discharge   201
§572.005. Application for Court-Ordered Treatment   202
Court-Ordered Emergency Services—§573   203
§573.001. Apprehension by Peace Officer without Warrant   203
§573.011. Application for Emergency Detention   204
§573.021. Preliminary Examination   204
§573.022. Emergency Admission and Detention   205
§573.023. Release from Emergency Detention   206
§573.025. Rights of Persons Apprehended or Detained or
           Transported for Emergency Detention   206
Temporary and Extended Mental Health Services—§574   206
§574.010. Independent Psychiatric Evaluation and Expert
           Testimony   206
§574.034. Order for Temporary Mental Health Services   207
§574.035. Order for Extended Mental Health Services   208
§574.036. Order of Care or Commitment   210
§574.037. Court-Ordered Outpatient Services   211
§574.0415. Information on Medications   212
§574.042. Commitment to Private Facility   212
Rights of Patients—§574.105   212
§574.105. Rights of Patient   212
§574.106. Hearing on Patient's Capacity and Order
           Authorizing Psychoactive Medication   213
§574.109. Effect of Order   215
Voluntary Admission for Court-Ordered Services—§574.151   215
§574.151. Applicability   215
§574.152. Capacity to Consent to Voluntary Admission   215
§574.153. Rights of Person Admitted to Voluntary
           Inpatient Treatment   215
§574.154. Participation in Research Program   215
Rights of Patients—§576   216
§576.001. Rights Under Constitution and Law   216
§576.002. Presumption of Competency   216
§576.005. Confidentiality of Records   216
§576.006. Rights Subject to Limitation   216
§576.007. Notification of Release   217
§576.008. Notification of Protection / Advocacy System   217
§576.009. Notification of Rights   217
§576.021. General Rights Relating to Treatment   217
§576.022. Adequacy of Treatment   218
§576.023. Periodic Examination   218
§576.024. Use of Physical Restraint   218
§576.025. Administration of Psychoactive Medication   218
§576.026. Independent Evaluation   219
§576.027. List of Medications   220
Legally Adequate Consent—§591   220
§591.006. Consent   220
Mental Retardation—§592   221
§592.001. Purpose   221

§592.002. Rules   221
§592.011. Rights Guaranteed   221
§592.012. Protection from Exploitation and Abuse   221
§592.013. Least Restrictive Living Environment   221
§592.014. Education   221
§592.015. Employment   222
§592.016. Housing   222
§592.017. Treatment and Services   222
§592.018. Determination of Mental Retardation   222
§592.019. Administrative Hearing   222
§592.020. Independent Determination of
          Mental Retardation   222
§592.021. Additional Rights   222
§592.031. Rights in General   223
§592.032. Least Restrictive Alternative   223
§592.033. Individualized Plan   223
§592.034. Review and Reevaluation   223
§592.035. Participation in Planning   223
§592.036. Withdrawal from Voluntary Services   224
§592.037. Freedom from Mistreatment   224
§592.038. Freedom from Unnecessary Medication   224
§592.039. Grievances   224
§592.040. Information About Rights   224
§592.051. General Rights of Residents   224
§592.052. Medical and Dental Care and Treatment   225
§592.053. Standards of Care   225
§592.054. Duties of Superintendent or Director   225
§592.055. Unusual or Hazardous Treatment   225
Mental Retardation Records—§595   225
§595.001. Confidentiality of Records   225
§595.002. Rules   225
§595.003. Consent to Disclosure   225
§595.004. Right to Personal Record   226
§595.005. Exceptions   226
§595.006. Use of Record in Criminal Proceedings   226
§595.007. Confidentiality of Past Services   227
§595.008. Exchange of Records   227
§595.009. Receipt of Information by Persons other than
          Client or Patient   227
§595.010. Disclosure of Physical or Mental Condition   227
Mental Health Records—§611   227
§611.001. Definitions   227
§611.002. Confidentiality of Information and Prohibition
          Against Disclosure   227
§611.003. Persons Who May Claim
          Privilege of Confidentiality   228
§611.004. Authorized Disclosure of Confidential Information
          Other than in Administrative Proceeding   228
§611.0045. Right to Mental Health Record   229

§611.005. Legal Remedies for Improper Disclosure or
       Failure to Disclose   *230*

§611.006. Authorized Disclosure of Confidential
       Information in Judicial Proceeding   *230*

§611.007. Revocation of Consent   *231*

§611.008. Request by Patient   *231*

HUMAN RESOURCES CODE   **232**

Children's Policy Council and Mental Health Issues—§22.035   *232*

§22.035. Children's Policy Council   *232*

Regulation of Certain Child-Care Facilities—§42   *233*

Elder Abuse—§48   *233*

§48.001. Purpose   *233*

§48.002. Definitions   *233*

§48.051. Report of Abuse, Neglect, or Exploitation:
       Immunities   *235*

§48.052. Failure to Report; Penalty   *235*

§48.053. False Report; Penalty   *236*

§48.054. Immunity   *236*

§48.203. Voluntary Protective Services   *236*

Emergency Order for Protective Services—§48.208   *236*

§48.208. Emergency Order for Protective Services   *236*

INSURANCE CODE   **239**

Workers' Compensation Health Care Networks—§1305   *239*

Subchapter D. Contracting Provisions   *239*

§1305.151. Transfer of Risk   *239*

§1305.152. Network Contracts with Providers   *239*

§1305.153. Provider Reimbursement   *240*

§1305.154. Network-Carrier Contracts   *241*

§1305.1545. Restrictions on Payment and Reimbursement   *243*

Access to Certain Practitioners and Facilities—§1451   *243*

Subchapter A. General Provisions   *243*

§1451.001. Definitions; Health Care Practitioners   *243*

*Subchapter B. Designation of Practitioners under Accident
and Health Insurance Policy*   *245*

§1451.051. Applicability of Subchapter   *245*

§1451.052. Applicability of General Provisions   *245*

§1451.053. Practitioner Designation   *245*

§1451.054. Terms for Health Care Practitioners   *245*

Subchapter C. Selection of Practitioners   *245*

§1451.101. Definitions   *245*

§1451.102. Applicability of Subchapter   *245*

§1451.103. Conflicting Provisions Void   *246*

§1451.104. Nondiscriminatory Payment or
       Reimbursement; Exception   *246*

§1451.106. Selection of Advanced Practice Nurse   *247*

§1451.107. Selection of Audiologist   *247*

§1451.108. Selection of Chemical Dependency Counselor   *247*

§1451.109. Selection of Chiropractor   *247*

§1451.110. Selection of Dentist 247
§1451.111. Selection of Dietitian 247
§1451.113. Selection of Licensed Clinical Social Worker 247
§1451.114. Selection of Licensed Professional Counselor 247
§1451.116. Selection of Marriage and Family Therapist 247

LOCAL GOVERNMENT CODE 248
Provisions Relating to Public Safety—§370 248
§370.006. Assistance In Man-Made or Natural Disaster 248

OCCUPATIONS CODE — OTHER 249
Healing Art Practitioners—§104 249
§104.002. Healing Art 249
§104.003. Required Identification 249
§104.004. Other Persons Using Title "Doctor" 249
Unprofessional Conduct by Health Care Provider—§105 250
§105.001. Definition 250
§105.002. Unprofessional Conduct 250
Internet and Health Care—§106 251
General Regulatory Authority Regarding Health Care
Practitioners Use of Internet 251
§106.001. Effect of Internet Activity 251
Telemedicine And Telehealth—§111 251
§111.001. Definitions 251
§111.002. Informed Consent 251
§111.003. Confidentiality 251
§111.004. Rules 252
Mental Health Licenses and Use of Genetic Information—§58 252
Subchapter A. General Provisions 252
§58.001. Definitions 252
Subchapter B. Use and Retention of Genetic Information 253
§58.051. Certain Uses of Genetic Information Prohibited 253
§58.052. Destruction of Sample Material; Exceptions 253
Subchapter C. Disclosure of Genetic Information;
Confidentiality; Exceptions 254
§58.101. Disclosure of Test Results to Individual Tested 254
§58.102. Confidentiality of Genetic Information 254
§58.103. Exceptions to Confidentiality 254
§58.104. Authorized Disclosure 255
§58.105. Civil Penalty 255

PENAL CODE 256
Insanity—§8 256
§8.01. Insanity 256
Use of force on child, student, or incompetent—§9 256
§9.61. Parent — Child 256
§9.62. Educator — Student 256
§9.63. Guardian — Incompetent 256
Deviate sexual activity—§21 257
§21.01. Definitions 257

§21.02. Continuous Sexual Abuse of Young Child
or Children *257*
§21.06. Homosexual Conduct *258*
§21.07. Public Lewdness *258*
§21.08. Indecent Exposure *259*
§21.11. Indecency with a Child *259*
§21.12. Improper Relationship Between Educator and
Student *260*
Interference with child custody—§25 *260*
§25.03. Interference with Child Custody *260*

PROBATE CODE **262**
Guardianship Law —§659 *262*
Part G. Letters of Guardianship *262*
§659. Issuance of Letters of Guardianship *262*
§683. Court's Initiation of Guardianship Proceedings *262*
§683A. Information Letter *263*
§684. Findings Required *263*
§687. Examinations and Reports *264*
§690. Persons Appointed Guardian *265*
Part E. General Duties and Powers of Guardians *265*
§767. Powers and Duties of Guardians of the Person *265*
§768. General Powers and Duties of Guardian of Estate *266*
§769. Summary of Powers of Guardian *266*

DSHS RIDER 19 **267**
Reporting Child Abuse by DSHS Contractors/Providers *267*
FAQs: Frequently Asked Questions and Answers Concerning
DSHS Rider 19 *268*
I. Procedures *268*
II. Reporting Generally *271*
III. Reporting Suspected Sexual Abuse *272*
IV. Training *278*
V. Monitoring by DSHS *279*
Plan for Implementing DSHS Rider 19 *283*
Background *283*
Implementation Plan—Grant Contracted Services *283*
Medicaid Services *283*
Additional Requirements *284*
Sanctions *284*
Policies & Procedures *284*
DSHS Child Abuse Screening, Documenting, and Reporting *284*
Policy *284*
Procedures *285*
Reporting Generally *285*
Reporting Suspected Sexual Abuse *288*
Training *289*
Monitoring by DSHS *289*
Sanctions *289*
Quality Management Branch Policy and Procedures *289*
Policy *289*

Procedures   290
Child Abuse Reporting Form   292

❑   CASE LAW 293

CONFIDENTIALITY OF PSYCHOTHERAPY NOTES   295
Background   295
Opinion   296
Dissent   304

DUTY TO WARN/PROTECT   314
Background   314
Negligent Diagnosis and Treatment   315
Failure to Warn   316

DERIVED JUDICIAL IMMUNITY & DUTY TO REPORT   319
Background   319
I. Factual and Procedural Background   319
II. Issues Presented for Review   321
III. Standard of Review   321
IV. Analysis   321
   A. Did the Trial Court Err in Granting Summary Judgment
      Based on Derived Judicial Immunity?   321
      1. Rao, Baylor, and Cox were entitled to derived
         judicial immunity.   321
      2. Possible violation of statutes imposing criminal liability
         does not negate derived judicial immunity in
         a suit by a private citizen.   323
      3. Possible violation of a mandatory duty does not negate
         derived judicial immunity.   324
   B. Does the Statutory Immunity under Section 261.106 of
      the Texas Family Code Override the Common-Law
      Derived Judicial Immunity?   325
V. Conclusion   326

CONFIDENTIALITY OF A CHILD'S MENTAL HEALTH RECORDS   327
Background   327
Decision   329
Rights of Divorced Parents for Access to Records   329
Denying Parental Access to Records   330
Request for Records and "Acting on Behalf of the Child"   331
Recourse When a Child's Records Improperly Withheld   332
Conclusion and Dissenting Opinions   333

❑   HIPAA 339

TEXAS LAW AND THE FEDERAL HEALTH INSURANCE PORTABILITY
AND ACCOUNTABILITY ACT   340

❑   OPINIONS FROM THE ATTORNEY GENERAL 343
Services Outside of Agency—Conflict of Interest?   345
Court-Ordered Social Studies on Personal Time   347

Political Activities of State Social Workers   *351*
Discretion for Reporting Sexual Abuse   *355*
Disclosure under Subpoena   *358*
Parent's Access to School Counseling Records   *364*
Sex Offender Treatment License Necessary?   *371*
Grandparent Access to Children and Records   *375*
Reporting Abuse during Childhood of Now-Adult Patient   *384*
Reporting of Alleged Child Abuse   *387*
Using Advocates in School for Counseling   *389*

❏ Appendix A **393**
   Code of Ethics   **393**
   Code of Ethics of the National Association of Social Workers   *393*
   Preamble   *393*
   Purpose of the *NASW Code of Ethics*   *393*
   Ethical Principles   *396*
   Ethical Standards   *397*
     1. Social Workers' Ethical Responsibilities to Clients   *397*
       1.01 Commitment to Clients   *397*
       1.02 Self-Determination   *397*
       1.03 Informed Consent   *397*
       1.04 Competence   *398*
       1.05 Cultural Competence and Social Diversity   *398*
       1.06 Conflicts of Interest   *399*
       1.07 Privacy and Confidentiality   *399*
       1.08 Access to Records   *401*
       1.09 Sexual Relationships   *401*
       1.10 Physical Contact   *402*
       1.11 Sexual Harassment   *402*
       1.12 Derogatory Language   *402*
       1.13 Payment for Services   *402*
       1.14 Clients Who Lack Decision-Making Capacity   *402*
       1.15 Interruption of Services   *402*
       1.16 Termination of Services   *403*
     2. Social Workers' Ethical Responsibilities to Colleagues   *403*
       2.01 Respect *403*
       2.02 Confidentiality   *403*
       2.03 Interdisciplinary Collaboration   *403*
       2.04 Disputes Involving Colleagues   *404*
       2.05 Consultation   *404*
       2.06 Referral for Services   *404*
       2.07 Sexual Relationships   *404*
       2.08 Sexual Harassment   *405*
       2.09 Impairment of Colleagues   *405*
       2.10 Incompetence of Colleagues   *405*
       2.11 Unethical Conduct of Colleagues   *405*
     3. Social Workers' Ethical Responsibilities in Practice Settings   *405*
       3.01 Supervision and Consultation   *405*
       3.02 Education and Training   *406*

3.03 Performance Evaluation   406
3.04 Client Records   406
3.05 Billing   406
3.06 Client Transfer   407
3.07 Administration   407
3.08 Continuing Education and Staff Development   407
3.09 Commitments to Employers   407
3.10 Labor-Management Disputes   408
4. Social Workers' Ethical Responsibilities as Professionals   408
4.01 Competence   408
4.02 Discrimination   408
4.03 Private Conduct   408
4.04 Dishonesty, Fraud, and Deception   408
4.05 Impairment   409
4.06 Misrepresentation   409
4.07 Solicitations   409
4.08 Acknowledging Credit   409
5. Social Workers' Ethical Responsibilities to the Social Work Profession   409
5.01 Integrity of the Profession   409
5.02 Evaluation and Research   410
6. Social Workers' Ethical Responsibilities to the Broader Society   411
6.01 Social Welfare   411
6.02 Public Participation   411
6.03 Public Emergencies   411
6.04 Social and Political Action   411

❏ Appendix B 413

Rules & Regs
Texas State Board of Social Worker Examiners   413
Subchapter A: General Provisions   413
§781.101. Purpose and Scope   413
§781.102. Definitions   413
Subchapter B: Code of Conduct & Professional Standards   419
§781.201. Code of Conduct   419
§781.202. The Practice of Social Work   420
§781.203. General Standards of Practice   422
§781.204. Relationships with Clients   422
§781.205. Sexual Misconduct   424
§781.206. Professional Representation   425
§781.207. Testing   426
§781.208. Drug and Alcohol Use   426
§781.209. Client Records and Record Keeping   426
§781.210. Billing and Financial Relationships   427
§781.211. Client Confidentiality   427
§781.212. Licensees and the Board   428
§781.213. Corporations and Business Names   428
§781.214. Consumer Information   428
§781.215. Display of License Certificate   429
§781.216. Advertising and Announcements   429

§781.217. Research and Publications　　　　　　　　*429*
§781.218. Providing Social Studies　　　　　　　　*430*
§781.219. Licensed Sex Offender Treatment　　　　*430*
§781.220. Parent Coordination　　　　　　　　　　*430*
§781.221. Parenting Facilitation　　　　　　　　　*431*
Subchapter C: The Board　　　　　　　　　　　　*435*
§781.301. Board Rules　　　　　　　　　　　　　　*435*
§781.302. Board Meetings　　　　　　　　　　　　*435*
§781.303. Board Training　　　　　　　　　　　　*436*
§781.304. Transaction of Official Board Business　*436*
§781.305. Board Agendas　　　　　　　　　　　　*436*
§781.306. Board Minutes　　　　　　　　　　　　*436*
§781.307. Elections　　　　　　　　　　　　　　*437*
§781.308. Officers of the Board　　　　　　　　　*437*
§781.309. Committees of the Board　　　　　　　*437*
§781.310. Executive Director　　　　　　　　　　*437*
§781.311. Official Records of the Board　　　　　*438*
§781.312. Impartiality and Non-discrimination　　*438*
§781.313. Applicants with Disabilities　　　　　　*438*
§781.314. The License　　　　　　　　　　　　　*438*
§781.315. Roster of Licensees　　　　　　　　　*439*
§781.316. Fees　　　　　　　　　　　　　　　　*439*
§781.317. Criminal History Evaluation Letter　　*440*
Subchapter D: Licenses and Licensing Process　*440*
§781.401. Qualifications for Licensure　　　　　　*440*
§781.402. Supervision for LCSW & LMSW-AP and
　　　　　　Independent Practice Recognition　*442*
§781.403. Independent Practice Recognition (Non-Clinical)　*444*
§781.404. Board-approved Supervisor / Supervision Process　*446*
§781.405. Application for Licensure　　　　　　　*452*
§781.406. Required Documentation for Licensure　*453*
§781.407. Fitness of Applicants for Licensure　　*454*
§781.408. Materials Considered —Fitness Determination　*454*
§781.409. Finding of Non-fitness　　　　　　　　*454*
§781.410. Provisional Licenses　　　　　　　　　*454*
§781.411. Temporary License　　　　　　　　　　*455*
§781.412. Examination Requirement　　　　　　*455*
§781.413. Alternate Method of Examining Competency
　　　　　　(AMEC) Program　　　　　　　　*456*
§781.414. Issuance of License Certificates　　　*456*
§781.415. Application Denial　　　　　　　　　　*457*
§781.416. Required Reports to the Board　　　　*457*
§781.417. Surrender of License　　　　　　　　　*457*
§781.418. Issuance of Licenses to Out-of-State Applicants　*458*
§781.419. Military Spouse　　　　　　　　　　　*458*
Subchapter E　　　　　　　　　　　　　　　　*459*
License Renewal and Continuing Education　　*459*
§781.501. General　　　　　　　　　　　　　　*459*
§781.502. Renewal Cycles　　　　　　　　　　　*459*
§781.503. License Renewal　　　　　　　　　　*460*
§781.504. Late Renewal　　　　　　　　　　　　*461*

§781.505. Inactive Status   461
§781.506. Emeritus Status   462
§781.507. Active Military Duty   462
§781.508. Hour Requirements for Continuing Education   462
§781.509. Types of Acceptable Continuing Education   463
§781.510. Activities Unacceptable as Continuing Education 463
§781.511. Requirements for Continuing Education Providers 464
§781.512. Evaluation of Continuing Education Providers   465
§781.513. CE Hours Approved by Another Licensing Board 466
§781.514. Credit Hours Granted   466
§781.515. Continuing Education Documentation   466
§781.516. Supervisor Training Course Providers (Basics)   467
§781.517. Supervisor Training Course Providers (Evals)   468
Subchapter F: Complaints and Violations   469
§781.601. Purpose   469
§781.602. Disciplinary Action and Notices   469
§781.603. Complaint Procedures   470
§781.604. Ethics Committee Meetings and Policy   473
§781.605. Informal Conferences   474
§781.606. Licensing of Persons with Criminal Backgrounds 474
§781.607. Suspension, Revocation, or Non-renewal   474
§781.608. Informal Disposition   474
§781.609. Monitoring of Licensees   475
§781.610. Due Process Following Violation of an Order   476
Subchapter G: Formal Hearings   477
§781.701. Purpose   477
§781.702. Notice   477
§781.703. Default   477
§781.704. Action after Hearing   478
Subchapter H: Sanction Guidelines   478
§781.801. Purpose   478
§781.802. Relevant Factors   479
§781.803. Severity Level and Sanction Guide   479
§781.804. Other Disciplinary Actions   480
§781.805. State Office of Administrative Hearings   480
§781.806. Probation   481
§781.807. Release from Probation   485
§781.808. Peer Assistance Program   485

❏   APPENDIX C 487
     NASW/TX RESOURCES   487
        General Counsel Law Note Series   487
        Legal Issue of the Month   492

❏   ORDERING INFORMATION 513

❏   NATIONAL ASSOCIATION OF SOCIAL WORKERS—
     TEXAS CHAPTER. 514

Introduction to the Fourth Edition

This fourth edition of Texas Law for the Social Worker contains updated information from the 82nd and 83rd Legislative Sessions, most of which were implemented by November, 2013 or February, 2014. Some noteworthy changes were also implemented in the TSBSWE Rules and Regulations (effective March, 2013), which are now included. In addition, we've expanded the collection of Attorney General Opinions that relate to the practice of social work.

Regardless of setting, social workers will find information relevant to professional practice: academic professors; social work counselors in public education; workers and agency directors who provide child-care; clinicians doing court-evaluations, adoption studies, or home evaluations; directors and clinicians in training programs, governmental agencies, non-profit organizations, and private practice; any social worker dealing with confidentiality of records, issues regarding reporting of child abuse and/or neglect, social workers doing volunteer work or providing services to victims of human trafficking.

Three additional Attorney General Letters and Opinions relevant to the practice of social work have been included: whether parents may use the services of an advocate in dealing with matters of their child's education (GA-0813); whether a mental health professional is required by chapter 261, Family Code, to report abuse or neglect that occurred during the childhood of a now-adult patient (GA-0944); whether a law enforcement agency is required to furnish information about alleged child abuse or neglect by a person responsible for the child's care, custody, or welfare to the Department of Family and Protective Services (GA-0879), bringing the total to 11. This section contains selected letters from the archive of Attorney General Opinions and Open Records Opinions that are relevant to the practice of social work. These opinions are relatively difficult to research because of the way they are indexed on the website of the Texas Attorney General. We hope that this archive will assist practitioners who have questions related to these decisions. For a summary of all the Opinions, see page 344.

Four legal decisions important for the practice of social work are included in their entirety. We have opted to keep the complete presentation while at the same time highlighting the most relevant parts. When you find yourself facing one of these issues, we believe the legal decisions—and the background behind them—will be invaluable to you as a social worker.

Jaffee v. Redmond for the first time gave the right of privacy to psychotherapy notes in federal court. *Thapar v. Zezulka* provides an excellent discussion of the duty to warn and duty to protect doctrine in Texas. We waited over 20 years in Texas to know the status of these duties. The Texas Supreme Court has now given practitioners guidance when a patient threatens another person. In this case, the Texas Supreme Court takes the position that courts should not second-guess the decision by a practitioner to tell law enforcement personnel or medical personnel about the danger presented by a patient. This gives a good deal of discretion to practitioners who are faced with a difficult situation and the decision is certainly pro-therapist.

Abrams v. Jones concerns the privacy of information between a therapist, a child client, and the child's parents and provides a remedy for parents who request but are denied access to a child's records. Practitioners can draw guidance from this case about record keeping and the duty to parents and child clients. *B.K. vs Cox* evaluates the duty to report and derived judicial immunity.

Social work is bound by laws and rules under the over-arching NASW Code of Ethics. This social work sourcebook contains the laws and the Code of Ethics. While the law remains unchanged for a minimum of 2 years between legislative sessions, and the NASW Code of Ethics can change, at most, every 3 years, the "rules" can change much more frequently.

Please go to *http://www.dshs.state.tx.us/socialwork/default.shtm* regularly to check for updates.

For your convenience, in this Fourth edition of the Texas Law for the Social Worker we have included the most recent update to the Social Work Rules and Regulations (as of March 28, 2013). Please see Appendix B (page 413), and don't forget to check the website frequently for addtional updates.

For those desiring more in-depth coverage, we have continued to provide relevant Internet links for each of the topics. For instance, the NASW Legal Defense Fund (LDF) has funded in-depth research by the NASW General Counsel on hot legal topics. While not specific to the state of Texas, they are of exceptional quality. Appendix C contains relevant summary information which is free for eligible NASW members.

We have again collected for you up-to-date legal information informing the practice of social work in the state of Texas, saving you many long hours of cumbersome research. It is our hope you mark this volume up, refer to it often, and pass along a copy to colleagues. This fourth edition is timely in that many of the updated statutes and modified codes took effect November, 2013 or February, 2014.

—*Editors*

INTRODUCTION TO THIRD EDITION

We have worked hard to make this third edition as up-to-date as possible, complete and comprehensive, while filtering material we believe is directly related to the practice of social work. For your easy reference, we have included the newly revised *Code of Ethics of the National Association of Social Workers*. The changes were approved by the 2008 NASW Delegate Assembly, and officially updated January 1, 2009.

Social work is bound by laws and rules under the over-arching *NASW Code of Ethics*. The *NASW Code of Ethics* has been upheld in courts across the country to be applicable to members and nonmembers alike. This edition contains the Social Work Practice Act (the law) and the *Code of Ethics*. While the law remains unchanged for a minimum of 2 years between legislative sessions, and the *NASW Code of Ethics* can change, at most, every 3 years, the "rules" can change much more frequently. Please check regularly for updates to the rules by visiting *http://www.dshs.state.tx.us/socialwork/default.shtm*.

Three additional Attorney General Letters and Opinions relevant to the practice of social work have been included: on school counseling records kept by social workers (JC-0538), on whether a licensed social worker must also be licensed by the Council on Sex Offender Treatment to provide rehabilitation services or be a treatment provider for sex offenders (GA-423), and on grandparent access to client records (GA-260). One opinion (on relicensure without examination—JC-49) was deleted, bringing the total to eight. Again, the Attorney General Opinions are available on the web but are relatively difficult to research; we have saved you countless hours of work by filtering those relevant to social workers.

We continue to try to present HIPAA material in as simple yet up-to-date format as possible, highlighting in particular information that is directly relevant for social workers. Likewise, we have included the latest information (updated September 21, 2009) from DSHS on reporting child abuse as outlined in DSHS Rider 23 and the accompanying FAQs.

We have also abstracted information from the 81st Legislative Session. While no single issue surfaced as paramount, many changes were made that affect social workers in all areas of practice. The updates are included in the relevant statutes, codes, and rules. Consider, for instance, topics relating to:

• Mental health licenses and the use of genetic information, including disclosure, confidentiality and exceptions to confidentiality (§58.051 Occup Code)

• Reporting of abuse and neglect at nursing homes and convalescent homes (§224.122 Health & Safety Code), and the role of social workers in administrative decisions regarding mental health care in such institutions (§242.303 Health & Safety Code) and serving on the Nursing Facility Advisory Committee.

- Role of social workers in home and community support services for hospices (Health & Safety Code §142)

- Examinations by, reports by, and appropriate roles for social workers serving as court-appointed guardians and appropriate roles (§684 Probate Code)

- Unprofessional conduct by health care providers serving as healing art practitioners (§105 Occupations Code)

- Use of Internet and telehealth in the delivery of services by health care professionals (§111 Occupations Code)

- Appropriate credentials for social workers who are working or volunteering in a school district (§21.003 Education Code)

- Standards of care, including record-keeping, for social workers who are providing services to individuals with co-occurring psychiatric and substance use disorders (COPSD) (§411.660 Administrative Code)

- Update regarding the conservatorship, possession of, or access to, a child in a suit affecting the parent-child relationship (Fam Code §153)

- Newly introduced language regarding expansion of faith- and community-based health and human services and social services initiatives (Gov Code §535)

- Updated regulations for boarding homes that house three or more elderly people or people with disabilities and who are receiving non-medical services. Many such homes, previously managed or staffed by social workers, must now be appropriately licensed and regulated (Health & Safety Code § 254).

- To facilitate suicide prevention efforts, established guidelines for sharing suicide data between appropriate entities without identifying deceased individuals (Health & Safety Code §193.011).

- Eliminated mental health insurance plans ability to limit a person's direct access to licensed professional counselors and licensed marriage and family therapists by requiring that the person first obtain recommendations from his or her physician (§1451 Insurance Code)

- Updated clarifications on the specific timing of the 48-hour period for which a person may be detained in a mental health facility for a preliminary mental health examination (§573.021 Health & Safety Code).

- Social workers supporting violence prevention efforts with families, note the provisions for victims of family violence and sexual assault to terminate lease agreements early without incurring financial penalties (§92.016 Property Code) and the elimination of the 60-day waiting period before a divorce is granted in cases where a spouse has been convicted of an act of family violence against the petitioner or the petitioner has obtained a protective order against the other spouse for an act of family violence (§6.702 Family Code)

A host of pilot projects and other funding-related initiatives were addressed by the 81st Legislature. Since they are not specific to the practice of social work in Texas—and to keep this compendium somewhat manageable— we have not included them in this volume. If you are intrigued by them, we have provided on-line links.

These include establishing Health Information Exchange System for CHIP and Medicaid (HB1218), Medicaid Buy-in for Children with Significant Health Concerns (SB187), Preventable Adverse Event Reporting & Reimbursement (SB203), Obesity Prevention Pilot program for Medicaid & CHIP (SB870), Diabetes Self-Management Training Program (HB1990), and Home-based and community-based support services for Medicaid programs to persons who are deaf-blind with multiple disabilities (SB37); coordination of DADS with AAAs for informal care-giver support services (SB271); court-ordered administration of psychoactive medi-cation to certain criminal defendants (SB1233); TYC & CHIP funding for transition (HB1630); establishing comprehensive reentry and reintegration plan for offenders released or discharged from correctional facility (HB1711); ensuring continuity of care for mental health services for youth with mental illness or mental retardation who are transferred, discharged, or paroled from the TYC (HB4451); establishing a pretrial veterans assistance program for veteran's in the criminal justice system (SB1940); creation of Council on Children & Families to improve state services to kids (SB1646); prohibiting unnecessary restraints on pregnant inmates during labor and childbirth (HB3653); school districts considering mitigating factors, such as whether a child acted in self-defense or has a developmental disability, when disci-plining students under the "zero-tolerance" initiative (HB171); preventing health plans from denying coverage to children with autism under 10 (HB451); creation of interagency Task Force on Children with Special Needs to improve services provide to children with chronic illness (HB2196).

For those desiring more in-depth coverage, we have provided relevant Internet links for each of the topics. For instance, the NASW Legal Defense Fund (LDF) has funded in-depth research by the NASW General Counsel on hot legal topics. While not specific to the state of Texas, they are of exceptional quality. The Appendix contains relevant summary information which is free for eligible NASW members.

We have tried to collect for you up-to-date legal information informing the practice of social work in the state of Texas, saving you many long hours of cumber-some research. It is our hope you mark this volume up, refer to it often, and pass along a copy to colleagues. This third edition is timely in that many of the statutes and modified codes take effect September 1, 2009.

—*Editors*
Vicki Hansen
J. Ray Hays
Robert J. McPherson
October, 2010

Introduction to First and Second Editions

This book brings together into one source the legal rules that guide the practice of social work in Texas. We gathered those statutes that are most directly related to practice so that the practitioner can find in one place the guidance necessary for most legally related practice questions. In addition to statutory material, we included several other sources of legal guidance for the practitioner and student by adding case law, and a synopsis of the HIPAA security rule that came into effect in the spring of 2005.

The statutory material in this book follows the organization of the statutory codes; that is, we have kept the classification scheme used by the Texas Legislature instead of attempting to organize the material in a more user friendly way. For example, the concept of privacy of mental health information is covered primarily in Chapter 611 of the Health and Safety Code. However, there are several other Texas statutes that deal with privacy of information, such as the Communicable Disease Act, Family Code, and alcohol and drug statutes. The Social Work Practice Act is included with a link to the rules and regulations guiding the social work profession are derived, which can be changed at any time.

We have included four legal decisions in this book that are important for the practice of clinical social work. *Jaffee v. Redmond* for the first time gave the right of privacy to psychotherapy notes in federal court. We have also included two Texas legal decisions: *Thapar v. Zezulka* and *Abrams v. Jones*. *Thapar v. Zezulka* provides an excellent discussion of the duty to warn and duty to protect doctrine in Texas. We waited over 20 years in Texas to know the status of these duties. The Texas Supreme Court has now given practitioners guidance when a patient threatens another person. In this case, the Texas Supreme Court takes the position that courts should not second-guess the decision by a practitioner to tell law enforcement personnel or medical personnel about the danger presented by a patient. This gives a good deal of discretion to practitioners who are faced with a difficult situation and the decision is certainly pro-therapist. *Abrams v. Jones* concerns the privacy of information between a therapist, a child client, and the child's parents and provides a remedy for parents who request but are denied access to a child's records. Practitioners can draw guidance from this case about record keeping and the duty to parents and child clients. *B.K. vs Cox* evaluates the duty to report and derived judicial immunity.

Remember lawyers give opinions not answers. There are always "ifs," "ands," or "buts" in the law which most certainly keep lawyers fully employed. When you have a question about the legal aspects of practice use this text for reference but also get the consult from other professionals involved in your type of practice and do not hesitate to ask an attorney or your licensing board for advice. Your malpractice insurance carrier can provide consultation on matters that relate to many aspects of practice.

We are fortunate in Texas to be at the stage of professional development that we are. The continued growth of mental health practice is dependent not only on what we do in our offices but the shape of the laws that control practice. This volume represents the state of regulatory development. If you see areas where the rights and prerogatives of our patients and our profession can be enhanced, please take a pro-active stance of being involved in positive change by contacting the Texas Chapter of NASW or your local area society.

I am grateful to each person who has made suggestions about inclusion of material in this book and to my co-editors, Bob McPherson and Vicki Hansen. Finally, a portion of the proceeds from the sale of this book goes to the National Association of Social Workers Texas Chapter.

—*Ray Hays, Ph.D., J.D.*
Diplomate in Clinical and Forensic Psychology, ABPP
Houston, Texas
Nvember 2005

About the Editors

Vicki Hansen, LMSW-AP, ACSW, has served as the Executive Director of the Texas Chapter of the National Association of Social Workers since 1998. She is a Licensed Master Social Worker, Advanced Practitioner and a member of the NASW Academy of Certified Social Workers. She has participated in federal and foundation grants involving schools and service integration and developed parent participation materials used in Ohio and Florida. She was an organizer of a national symposium on the re-professionalization of public child welfare and was a contributing co-editor of a book of proceedings; was the Project Director of a 3-year grant from the Texas Cancer Council on developing cancer prevention materials for low-income, minority populations; served as an ombudsperson for the Texas Department of Health Strategic Health Partnership, as a participant for the TDH Bioterrorism Preparedness and Response Plan, and was a member of the Texas Social Work Licensing Revision Task Force. Vicki has served on the NASW national committee on Standards for Continuing Social Work Education and was recently appointed to the NASW Foundation Board of Directors. She has served as an adjunct faculty member of the University of Texas at San Antonio Social Work Program and Texas State Univerity, and has been an invited lecturer at many schools of social work across Texas. She was named the NASW Executive Director of the Year for 2005.

J. Ray Hays, Ph.D., J.D., is a member of the faculty of the Menninger Department of Psychiatry and Behavioral Sciences, Baylor College of Medicine, where he is Chief of the Psychology Service at Ben Taub General Hospital. He has edited this series since its inception in 1985 after proposing the idea for the book to the Texas Psychological Association Executive Committee. He is a Diplomate in both Clinical and Forensic Psychology from the American Board of Professional Psychology and the American Board of Forensic Psychology. His doctorate is from the University of Georgia with an internship at the Texas Research Institute of Mental Sciences. His law degree is from the South Texas College of Law. He is a former Chair of the Texas State Board of Examiners of Psychologists, serving as member from 1975 to 1982, and former President and one of the first Fellows of the American Association of State Psychology Boards, now the Association of State and Provincial Psychology Boards. He has written, edited, or compiled nine books, sixteen book chapters, and over 100 scientific articles on a variety of psychological topics. He is the recipient of the Texas Psychological Association Award for Outstanding Contribution to Education.

STATUTES

TEXAS STATUTES

OCCUPATIONS CODE - Social Workers 39

ADMINISTRATIVE CODE 63

CIVIL PRACTICE AND REMEDIES CODE 71

CODE OF CRIMINAL PROCEDURE 86

EDUCATION CODE 93

FAMILY CODE 106

GOVERNMENT CODE 144

HEALTH AND SAFETY CODE 151

HUMAN RESOURCES CODE 232

INSURANCE CODE 239

OCCUPATIONS CODE - - Other 249

PENAL CODE 256

PROBATE CODE 262

DSHS RIDER 19 267

OCCUPATIONS CODE - SOCIAL WORKERS

CHAPTER 505. SOCIAL WORKERS[1]

SUBCHAPTER A. GENERAL PROVISIONS

§505.001. SHORT TITLE

This chapter may be cited as the Social Work Practice Act.

§505.002. DEFINITIONS [(2011)]

In this chapter:[(1, 8, 9 repealed 2003)]

(2) *"Board"* means the Texas State Board of Social Worker Examiners.

(2-a) *"Commissioner"* means the commissioner of state health services.

(3) *"Council on Social Work Education"* means the national organization that is primarily responsible for the accreditation of schools of social work in the United States or its successor approved by the board.

(4) "Department" means the Department of State Health Services.

(4-a) *"Licensed baccalaureate social worker"* means a person who holds a baccalaureate social worker license issued by the board under this chapter.

(4-b) *"Licensed clinical social worker"* means a person who holds a clinical social worker license issued by the board under this chapter.

(5) *"Licensed master social worker"* means a person who holds a master social worker license issued by the board under this chapter.

(6) *"Licensed social worker"* means a person who holds a social worker license issued by the board under this chapter.

(9) *"Social worker"* means a person who holds any license issued by the board under this chapter.

§505.0025. PRACTICE OF SOCIAL WORK

(a) The practice of social work is the application of social work theory, knowledge, methods, ethics, and the professional use of self to restore or enhance social, psychosocial, or biopsychosocial functioning of individuals, couples, families, groups, organizations, or communities.

(b) The practice of social work may include the provision of individual, conjoint, family, and group psychotherapy using the Diagnostic and Statistical Manual of Mental Disorders, the International Classification of Diseases, and other diagnostic classification systems in assessment, diagnosis, treatment, and other activities by a person licensed under this chapter.

§505.003. APPLICATIONS AND EXEMPTIONS

(a) This chapter does not apply to:

(1) an activity conducted or a service performed by a person who is licensed, certified, or registered in a profession other than social work, including a physician, attorney, registered nurse, licensed vocational nurse,

---

1 (Occupations Code; Title 3. Health Professions; Subtitle I. Regulation of Psychology and Counseling; Chapter 505. Social Workers)

psychologist, occupational therapist, licensed marriage and family therapist, licensed chemical dependency counselor, or licensed professional counselor, if:

(A) the activity or service is conducted or performed within the scope of the person's license, certificate, or registration;

(B) the person does not use a title listed in Section 505.351; and

(C) the person does not:

    (i)   represent the service as social work;

    (ii) represent that the person is a social worker; or

    (iii) use a title that implies that the person is licensed in social work;

(2) a service performed by a person as a volunteer or staff member if the person does not:

(A) represent the service as social work;

(B) represent the person as a social worker; or

(C) use a title that implies that the person is licensed in social work;

(3) an activity conducted by a social work student, intern, or trainee in connection with an institution of higher education accredited by the Council on Social Work Education; or

(4) an activity conducted or a service performed by a pastoral care counselor who is acting within the person's ministerial capabilities and who does not use a title that implies that the counselor is licensed in social work, including:

(A) a Christian Science practitioner who is recognized by the Church of Christ Scientist as registered and published in the Christian Science Journal; and

(B) any other recognized religious practitioner.

(b) This chapter does not require a public agency or private employer, including a nonprofit corporation, to employ a person licensed under this chapter.

(c) A person who teaches social work at an institution of higher education or a private or independent institution of higher education as those terms are defined by Section 61.003, Education Code, is not required to hold a license under this chapter to the extent the person confines the person's activities to teaching and does not otherwise engage in the practice of social work.

§505.004. NONDISCRIMINATORY ACTIONS AND DECISIONS

An action taken or a decision made under this chapter, including an action or a decision relating to a license application, examination, regulation, or disciplinary proceeding, shall be taken or made without regard to sex, race, religion, national origin, color, or political affiliation.

§505.005. APPLICATION OF SUNSET ACT

The Texas State Board of Social Worker Examiners is subject to Chapter 325, Government Code (Texas Sunset Act). Unless continued in existence as provided by that chapter, the board is abolished and §505.101 expires September 1, 2017.

SubChapter B. Texas State Board of Social Worker Examiners

§505.101. Board; Membership

(a) The Texas State Board of Social Worker Examiners consists of nine members appointed by the governor with the advice and consent of the senate.

§505.201. General Rulemaking and Enforcement Authority

(a) The board may:

    (1) adopt and enforce rules necessary to perform the board's duties under this chapter;

    (2) establish standards of conduct and ethics for license holders; and

    (3) ensure strict compliance with and enforcement of this chapter.

(b) In adopting rules under this section, the board shall consider the rules and procedures of the Texas Board of Health and the department. The board shall adopt procedural rules, which may not be inconsistent with similar rules and procedures of the Texas Board of Health or the department.

(c) The board by rule may define a term not defined under Section 505.002 if a definition is necessary to administer or enforce this chapter.

(e) For each type of license issued under this chapter, the board shall establish:

    (1) the minimum eligibility requirements;

    (2) educational requirements;

    (3) professional experience criteria;

    (4) supervision requirements; and

    (5) independent practice criteria.

(f) The board shall establish procedures for recognition of independent practice.

§505.202. Rules Restricting Advertising or Competitive Bidding

(a) The board may not adopt rules restricting advertising or competitive bidding by a person regulated by the board except to prohibit false, misleading, or deceptive practices by that person.

(b) The board may not include in rules to prohibit false, misleading, or deceptive practices by a person regulated by the board a rule that:

    (1) restricts the use of any advertising medium;

    (2) restricts the person's personal appearance or the use of the person's voice in an advertisement;

    (3) relates to the size or duration of an advertisement by the person; or

    (4) restricts the use of a trade name in advertising by the person.

§505.203. Fees

(a) The board by rule shall set fees in amounts reasonable and necessary to cover the costs of administering this chapter.

(b) The board may not set a fee that existed on September 1, 1993, in an amount that is less than the amount of that fee on that date.

(c) Unless the board determines that the fees would not cover the costs associated with administering the renewal of licenses and orders of recognition of specialty under this chapter, the board shall set:

(1) the renewal fee for a license or order of recognition of specialty expired for 90 days or less in an amount that is 1-1/4 times the amount of the renewal fee for an unexpired license or order; and

(2) the renewal fee for a license or order of recognition of specialty expired for more than 90 days but less than one year in an amount that is 1-1/2 times the amount of the renewal fee for an unexpired license or order.

§505.204. BOARD DUTIES REGARDING COMPLAINTS

(a) The board by rule shall:

(1) adopt a form to standardize information concerning complaints made to the board; and

(2) prescribe information to be provided to a person when the person files a complaint with the board.

(b) The board shall provide reasonable assistance to a person who wishes to file a complaint with the board.

§505.205. ROSTER OF LICENSE HOLDERS

(a) The board shall prepare and publish at its discretion a roster that contains the name and address of each person licensed under this chapter.

(b) The board shall mail a copy of the roster to each license holder.

(c) The board may not include in the roster the name and address of a person who is delinquent in the payment of a fee required under this chapter on the date the roster is sent for printing.

§505.206. ROSTER OF INDEPENDENT SOCIAL WORKERS

The board shall publish a roster of persons recognized under Section 505.307 as qualified for the independent practice of social work.

§505.207. ANNUAL REPORT REGARDING LICENSING

Not later than November 1 of each year, the commissioner shall file with the governor and the presiding officer of each house of the legislature a written report regarding the licensing of social workers by the department during the preceding fiscal year.

§505.208. ANNUAL REPORT REGARDING FUNDS

(a) The department shall file annually with the governor and the presiding officer of each house of the legislature a complete and detailed written report accounting for all funds received and disbursed by the board during the preceding fiscal year.

(b) The report must be in the form and reported in the time provided by the General Appropriations Act.

§505.209. RULES ON CONSEQUENCES OF CRIMINAL CONVICTION

(a) The board shall adopt rules necessary to comply with Chapter 53.

(b) In its rules under this section, the board shall list the specific offenses for which a conviction would constitute grounds for the board to take action under Section

53.021.

§505.210. USE OF TECHNOLOGY

The board shall implement a policy requiring the board to use appropriate technological solutions to improve the board's ability to perform its functions. The policy must ensure that the public is able to interact with the board on the Internet.

§505.211. NEGOTIATED RULEMAKING AND ALTERNATIVE DISPUTE RESOLUTION POLICY

(a) The board shall develop and implement a policy to encourage the use of:

   (1) negotiated rulemaking procedures under Chapter 2008, Government Code, for the adoption of board rules; and

   (2) appropriate alternative dispute resolution procedures under Chapter 2009, Government Code, to assist in the resolution of internal and external disputes under the board's jurisdiction.

(b) The board's procedures relating to alternative dispute resolution must conform, to the extent possible, to any model guidelines issued by the State Office of Administrative Hearings for the use of alternative dispute resolution by state agencies.

(c) The department shall designate a trained person to:

   (1) coordinate the implementation of the policy adopted under Subsection (a);

   (2) serve as a resource for any training needed to implement the procedures for negotiated rulemaking or alternative dispute resolution; and

   (3) collect data concerning the effectiveness of those procedures, as implemented by the board.

SUBCHAPTER E. PUBLIC ACCESS INFORMATION AND COMPLAINT PROCEDURES

§505.251. CONSUMER INTEREST INFORMATION

(a) The board shall prepare information of consumer interest describing the regulatory functions of the board and the procedures by which consumer complaints are filed with and resolved by the board.

(b) The board shall make the information available to the public and appropriate state agencies.

§505.252. COMPLAINTS

(a) The board by rule shall establish methods by which consumers and service recipients are notified of the name, mailing address, and telephone number of the board for the purpose of directing complaints to the board. The board may provide for that notice:

   (1) on each registration form, application, or written contract for services of a person regulated by the board;

   (2) on a sign prominently displayed in the place of business of each person regulated by the board; or

   (3) in a bill for services provided by a person regulated by the board.

(b) The board shall list with its regular telephone number any toll-free telephone number established under other state law that may be called to present a complaint about a health professional.

§505.253. RECORDS OF COMPLAINTS

(a) The board shall maintain a system to promptly and efficiently act on complaints filed with the board. The board shall maintain:

    (1) information about the parties to the complaint and the subject matter of the complaint;

    (2) a summary of the results of the review or investigation of the complaint; and

    (3) information about the disposition of the complaint.

(b) The board shall make information available describing its procedures for complaint investigation and resolution.

(c) The board shall periodically notify the parties of the status of the complaint until final disposition of the complaint.

§505.254. GENERAL RULES REGARDING COMPLAINT INVESTIGATION AND DISPOSITION

(a) The board shall adopt rules concerning the investigation of a complaint filed with the department and referred to the board. The rules adopted under this subsection must:

    (1) distinguish among categories of complaints;

    (2) ensure that a complaint is not dismissed without appropriate consideration;

    (3) require that the board be advised of a complaint that is dismissed and that a letter be sent to the person who filed the complaint explaining the action taken on the dismissed complaint;

    (4) ensure that the person who filed the complaint has an opportunity to explain the allegations made in the complaint;

    (5) prescribe guidelines concerning the categories of complaints that require the use of a private investigator and the procedures for the board to obtain the services of a private investigator; and

    (6) prescribe the time after an act or omission during which a person may file a complaint with the board regarding the act or omission in order for the board to consider the complaint.

(b) The board shall:

    (1) dispose of each complaint in a timely manner; and

    (2) establish a schedule for conducting each phase of a complaint that is under the control of the board not later than the 30th day after the date the board receives the complaint.

(c) Each party to the complaint shall be notified of the projected time requirements for the complaint. Each party to the complaint shall be notified of any change in the schedule established under Subsection (b)(2) not later than the seventh day after the date the change is made.

(d) The executive director shall notify the board of a complaint that is not resolved within the time prescribed by the board for resolving the complaint so that the board may take necessary action on the complaint.

(e)   The board may conduct an investigation of a complaint and determine the validity of the complaint regardless of the status of the license or order of recognition of specialty of the person against whom the complaint is made.

§505.2545. SUBPOENAS

(a)   In an investigation of a complaint filed with the department and referred to the board, the board may request that the commissioner or the commissioner's designee approve the issuance of a subpoena. If the request is approved, the board may issue a subpoena to compel the attendance of a relevant witness or the production, for inspection or copying, of relevant evidence that is in this state.

(b)   A subpoena may be served personally or by certified mail.

(c)   If a person fails to comply with a subpoena, the board, acting through the attorney general, may file suit to enforce the subpoena in a district court in Travis County or in the county in which a hearing conducted by the board may be held.

(d)   On finding that good cause exists for issuing the subpoena, the court shall order the person to comply with the subpoena. The court may punish a person who fails to obey the court order.

(e)   The board may delegate the authority granted under Subsection (a) to the executive director or the secretary-treasurer of the board.

(f)   The board shall pay a reasonable fee for photocopies subpoenaed under this section in an amount not to exceed the amount the board may charge for copies of its records.

(g)   The reimbursement of the expenses of a witness whose attendance is compelled under this section is governed by Section 2001.103, Government Code.

(h)   All information and materials subpoenaed or compiled by the board in connection with a complaint and investigation are confidential and not subject to disclosure under Chapter 552, Government Code, and not subject to disclosure, discovery, subpoena, or other means of legal compulsion for their release to anyone other than the board or its employees or agents involved in discipline of the holder of a license or order of recognition, except that this information may be disclosed to:

(1)   persons involved with the board in a disciplinary action against the holder of a license or order of recognition;

(2)   social work licensing or disciplinary boards in other jurisdictions;

(3)   peer assistance programs approved by the board under Chapter 467, Health and Safety Code;

(4)   law enforcement agencies; and

(5)   persons engaged in bona fide research, if all individual-identifying information has been deleted.

(i)   The filing of formal charges against a holder of a license or order of recognition, the nature of those charges, disciplinary proceedings of the board, and final disciplinary actions, including warnings and reprimands, by the board are not confidential and are subject to disclosure in accordance with Chapter 552, Government Code.

§505.2547. COMPLAINT COMMITTEE

The board shall appoint at least one public member of the board to any board committee established to review a complaint filed with the board or review an enforcement action against a license holder related to a complaint filed with the board.

§505.255. PUBLIC PARTICIPATION

(a) The board shall develop and implement policies that provide the public with a reasonable opportunity to appear before the board and to speak on any issue under the board's jurisdiction.

(b) The board shall prepare and maintain a written plan that describes how a person who does not speak English may be provided reasonable access to the board's programs.

SUBCHAPTER F. SPECIALTY AREAS OF SOCIAL WORK

§505.301. ESTABLISHMENT OF SPECIALTY AREA

(a) The board may establish within the scope of social work practice and this chapter specialty areas of social work for license holders under this chapter who are licensed in good standing if establishment of the specialty areas:

(1) is necessary to promote the public interest; and

(2) assists the public in identifying qualified persons in a social work practice specialty.

(b) The board may not authorize a specialty area within the practice of social work unless the board sets the minimum qualifications for social work practice with appropriate supervision and examination, as determined by the board.

(c) The board may not establish a specialty area of social work or a specialty area identification that conflicts with a state licensing law.

§505.302. REGULATION OF SPECIALTY AREAS

(a) In establishing a specialty area of social work, the board shall:

(1) define the scope of the specialty;

(2) establish qualifications for specialty area practitioners that describe, in accordance with Subdivision (1), the scope of the specialty area;

(3) adopt rules of conduct to ensure strict compliance with and enforcement of this chapter; and

(4) adopt rules for the suspension or revocation of an order of recognition of specialty.

(b) A person who is not recognized as satisfying the qualifications for a specialty area may not practice in the specialty area.

§505.303. CLINICAL SOCIAL WORK SPECIALTY

(a) The board shall establish a specialty area for the practice of clinical social work that is available only to a licensed master social worker who satisfies the minimum number of years of active social work practice with appropriate supervision and clinical examination, as determined by the board.

(b) A person may not use the title *"Licensed Clinical Social Worker"* or the initials *"LCSW"* unless the person is recognized as qualified for the independent practice of clinical social work.

(c) For purposes of Subchapter C, Chapter 1451, Insurance Code:

(1) a person recognized as qualified for the independent practice of clinical social work may use the title *"Licensed Clinical Social Worker"* or another title approved by the board; and

(2) a board-approved title under this subsection has the same meaning and effect as the title *"Licensed Clinical Social Worker."*

§505.304. ORDER OF RECOGNITION OF SPECIALTY

(a) The board shall prescribe the name, design, and content of an order of recognition of specialty.

(b) An order of recognition of specialty must:

(1) state the full name of the person recognized in the order;

(2) state the official specialty serial number;

(3) include the presiding officer's signature; and

(4) include the board's official seal.

§505.305. RECOGNITION OF SPECIALTY; ISSUANCE OF ORDER

(a) The board shall recognize a social worker as qualified for the practice of a specialty area of social work if the social worker satisfies the recognition requirements established by the board and the board determines that the person is worthy of the public trust in performing services within the scope of the specialty area.

(b) The board shall issue an order of recognition of specialty to a social worker who is recognized as qualified for the practice of a specialty area of social work. The order of recognition of specialty evidences the state's recognition of the social worker as a specialty social work practitioner under the identification or title designated by the board.

§505.306. PROHIBITED USE OF SPECIALTY AREA IDENTIFICATION OR TITLE

If the board establishes a specialty area of social work, a social worker may not use the specialty area identification or title designated by the board unless the person is recognized as qualified for the practice of the specialty area under this chapter.

§505.307. INDEPENDENT PRACTICE RECOGNITION; MINIMUM QUALIFICATIONS.

(a) The board shall establish procedures for recognizing a social worker qualified for the independent practice of social work.

(b) A social worker may not be recognized as qualified for the independent practice of social work unless the person satisfies the requirements of social work education, experience, and supervision as determined by the board.

SubChapter G. License Requirements

§505.351. License Required

(a) A person may not use or cause to be used the title "social worker," "licensed baccalaureate social worker," "licensed master social worker," "licensed clinical social worker," or "licensed social worker," or any combination, variation, or abbreviation of those titles, as a professional or business identification, representation, asset, or means of obtaining a benefit unless the person holds an appropriate license issued under this chapter.

(b) A person may not use a title that implies that the person holds a license in social work unless the person holds an appropriate license issued under this chapter.

(c) A person who engages in or attempts to engage in conduct described by this section is considered to be engaged in the practice of social work.

§505.352. License Application

A person may apply for a license under this chapter by submitting an application to the board. The application must:

(1) be on a form prescribed by the board; and

(2) contain statements made under oath regarding the applicant's education and experience and any other information required by the board that qualifies the applicant for a license.

§505.353. Eligibility

(a) To be eligible for a license under this chapter, an applicant must:

(1) be at least 18 years of age;

(2) be worthy of the public trust and confidence;

(3) satisfy the education and experience requirements under this section; and

(4) pass the licensing examination conducted by the board under Section 505.354 and the jurisprudence examination conducted by the board under Section 505.3545.

(b) An applicant may take the licensing examination conducted by the board under Section 505.354 for:

(1) a master social worker license if the applicant possesses a doctoral or master's degree in social work from a graduate program that is accredited by or is in candidacy for the Council on Social Work Education;

(2) a baccalaureate social worker license if the applicant possesses a baccalaureate degree in social work from an educational program that is accredited by or is in candidacy for accreditation by the Council on Social Work Education; or

(3) a clinical social worker license if the applicant possesses a doctoral or master's degree in social work from an accredited graduate program approved by the board and meets the qualifications for clinical social work practice as determined by the board under this chapter

(c) The board may require an applicant to submit documentary evidence of the quality, scope, and nature of the applicant's experience and competence to:

(1) determine the credibility and acceptability of the applicant's professional

or technical experience or competence; and

(2) ensure the public safety, health, and welfare.

§505.354. EXAMINATION

(a) The board, at least once each calendar year, shall prepare and administer an examination to assess an applicant's qualifications for a license under this chapter.

(b) Each license examination shall be conducted in a manner that is determined by the board and is fair and impartial to each applicant and school or system of social work.

(c) Applicants may be known to the examiners only by numbers until after the general averages of the applicants' numbers in the class are determined and licenses are issued or denied.

(d) To maintain the highest standards in the social work profession, the scope and content of each examination must be sufficient to ensure professional efficacy and competence.

(e) The board shall have the written portion of the examination, if any, validated by an independent testing entity.

§505.3545. JURISPRUDENCE EXAMINATION

(a) The board shall develop and administer at least twice each calendar year a jurisprudence examination to determine an applicant's knowledge of this chapter, board rules, and any other applicable laws of this state affecting the applicant's social work practice.

(b) The board shall adopt rules to implement this section, including rules related to the development and administration of the examination, examination fees, guidelines for reexamination, grading the examination, and providing notice of examination results.

§505.355. EXAMINATION RESULTS

(a) The board shall notify each examinee of the examination results not later than the 30th day after the date the licensing examination is administered. If an examination is graded or reviewed by a national testing service, the board shall notify each examinee of the results of the examination not later than the 14th day after the date the board receives the results from the testing service.

(b) If the notice of the results of an examination graded or reviewed by a national testing service will be delayed for longer than 90 days after the examination date, the board shall notify the examinee of the reason for the delay before the 90th day.

(c) If requested by a person who fails an examination, the board shall provide to the person an analysis of the person's performance on the examination.

§505.356. REEXAMINATION

The board by rule shall establish:

(1) a limit on the number of times an applicant who fails an examination may retake the examination;

(2) the requirements for retaking an examination; and

(3)   alternative methods of examining applicants' competency.

§505.357. TEMPORARY LICENSE

(a)   The board shall issue a temporary license to an applicant who:

    (1)   has not taken the licensing examination under Section 505.354 or the jurisprudence examination under Section 505.3545; and

    (2)   satisfies the requirements for obtaining a license under this chapter other than passing the licensing and jurisprudence examinations.

(b)   A temporary license is valid until the results of the first appropriate licensing and jurisprudence examinations given after the date the license is issued are available.

§505.3575. ISSUANCE OF LICENSES TO CERTAIN OUT-OF-STATE APPLICANTS

(a)   Notwithstanding any other licensing requirement of this subchapter:

    (1)   the board may not require an applicant who is licensed in good standing in another state to pass a licensing examination conducted by the board under Section 505.354 if an applicant with substantially equivalent experience who resides in this state would not be required to take the licensing examination; and

    (2)   the board may issue a license to an applicant who is currently licensed in another state to independently practice social work if:

        (A)   after an assessment, the board determines that the applicant:

            (i)   demonstrates sufficient experience and competence;

            (ii)   has passed the jurisprudence examination conducted by the board under Section 505.3545; and

            (iii)   at the time of the application, is in good standing with the regulatory agency of the state in which the applicant is licensed; and

        (B)   the applicant presents to the board credentials that the applicant obtained from a national accreditation organization and the board determines that the requirements to obtain the credentials are sufficient to minimize any risk to public safety.

(b)   When assessing the experience and competence of an applicant for the purposes of this section, the board may take into consideration any supervision received by the applicant in another state or jurisdiction if the board determines that the supervision would be taken into consideration for the purpose of licensing or certification in the state or jurisdiction in which the applicant received the supervision.

§505.358. PROVISIONAL LICENSE

(a)   A person may apply for a provisional license as a social worker by paying the appropriate fee and filing an application with the board. The board may issue a provisional license to a person who meets the requirements of this section.

(b)   An applicant for a provisional license must:

    (1)   be licensed or certified in good standing as a social worker in another state that has licensing or certification requirements determined by the board to be substantially equivalent to the requirements of this chapter;

(2) have passed a national or other examination recognized by the board relating to the practice of social work; and

(3) be sponsored by a person licensed under this chapter with whom the provisional license holder may practice social work.

(c) An applicant is not required to comply with Subsection (b)(3) if the board determines that compliance constitutes a hardship to the applicant.

(d) A provisional license is valid until the date the board approves or denies the provisional license holder's application for a license under Section 505.359.

§505.359. ISSUANCE OF LICENSE TO PROVISIONAL LICENSE HOLDER

(a) The board shall issue an appropriate license to a provisional license holder:

(1) who passes the licensing examination under Section 505.354 and the jurisprudence examination under Section 505.3545;

(2) for whom the board verifies that the person satisfies the academic and experience requirements under Section 505.353; and

(3) who satisfies any other license requirements under this chapter.

(b) The board shall complete the processing of a provisional license holder's application for a license not later than the 180th day after the date the provisional license is issued or the date licenses are issued after successful completion of the next licensing and jurisprudence examinations, whichever date is later.

(c) The board may waive a license requirement for an applicant who is licensed or certified in another state if this state has entered into a reciprocity agreement with that state.

§505.360. PROFESSIONAL IDENTIFICATION [(d) Repealed 2003]

(a) A license holder shall use an identification provided by this section:

(1) in the professional use of the license holder's name; and

(2) in connection with any sign, directory, contract, document, pamphlet, stationery, advertisement, signature, or other means of written professional identification.

(b) A licensed master social worker shall use the identification "*licensed master social worker*" or the initials "*LMSW.*"

(c) A licensed baccalaureate social worker shall use the identification "*licensed baccalaureate social worker*" or the initials "*LBSW.*"

(e) A licensed clinical social worker shall use the identification "*licensed clinical social worker*" or the initials "*LCSW.*"

SUBCHAPTER H. RENEWAL OF LICENSE AND ORDER OF RECOGNITION OF SPECIALTY

§505.401. STAGGERED EXPIRATION DATES

(a) The board by rule shall adopt a system under which licenses and orders of recognition of specialty expire on various dates during the year.

(b) In the year in which the expiration date of an order of recognition of specialty is changed, the total renewal fee is payable.

§505.402. RENEWAL OF LICENSE AND ORDER OF RECOGNITION OF SPECIALTY

(a) A person may renew an unexpired license or order of recognition of specialty by paying the appropriate renewal fee required by the board to the department before the expiration date of the license or order.

(b) Not later than the 30th day before the expiration date of a person's license or order of recognition of specialty, the board shall send written notice of the impending license or order expiration to the person at the person's last known address according to the board's records.

(c) A person whose license or order of recognition of specialty has been expired for less than one year may renew the license or order by paying to the department the appropriate renewal fee required by the board for the expired license or order.

(d) Except as provided by Section 505.403, a person whose license or order of recognition of specialty has been expired for one year or more may not renew the license or order. The person may obtain a new license or order by submitting to reexamination.

§505.403. RENEWAL OF EXPIRED LICENSE BY OUT-OF-STATE PRACTITIONER

(a) The board may renew without reexamination an expired license or order of recognition of specialty of a person who was licensed in this state, moved to another state, and is currently licensed or certified and has been in practice in the other state for the two years preceding the date the person applied for a renewal license or order.

(b) The person must pay to the department a fee that is equal to the amount of the appropriate renewal fee for the license or order, as required by the board.

§505.404. CONTINUING EDUCATION

(a) The board by rule shall:

   (1) establish mandatory continuing education requirements for license holders under this chapter; and

   (2) establish a minimum number of hours of continuing education required to renew a license or an order of recognition of specialty.

(b) In establishing continuing education requirements, the board shall:

   (1) assess the continuing education needs of persons who hold licenses or orders of recognition of specialty;

   (2) adopt procedures to assess the participation of a person who holds a license or order of recognition of specialty in continuing education programs; and

   (3) identify the key factors for the competent performance of professional duties by a person who holds a license or order of recognition of specialty.

(c) The board by rule shall develop a process to evaluate and approve continuing education courses. The board may require persons who hold licenses or orders of recognition of specialty to attend continuing education courses specified by the board.

(d) For the purpose of establishing and maintaining continuing education programs, the board or department may take any action necessary to qualify for, accept, and receive funds and grants from any source, including the United

States, this state, or a private foundation.

§505.405. GROUNDS FOR REFUSING RENEWAL

The board may refuse to renew the license of a person who fails to pay an administrative penalty imposed under Subchapter K unless enforcement of the penalty is stayed or a court has ordered that the administrative penalty is not owed.

SUBCHAPTER I. DENIAL OF LICENSE OR ORDER AND DISCIPLINARY PROCEDURES

§505.451. GROUNDS FOR DENIAL OF LICENSE OR ORDER OF RECOGNITION OF SPECIALTY; DISCIPLINARY ACTION

The board shall deny an application for a license or order of recognition of specialty and shall revoke or suspend, including a suspension on an emergency basis, a license or order, place a holder of a license or order that has been suspended on probation, refuse to renew a person's license, or reprimand a holder of a license or order for:

(1) violating this chapter or a rule adopted by the board under this chapter;

(2) circumventing or attempting to circumvent the requirements of this chapter or a rule adopted by the board under this chapter;

(3) directly or indirectly participating in a scheme to evade the requirements of this chapter or a rule adopted by the board under this chapter;

(4) engaging in unethical conduct;

(5) engaging in conduct that discredits or tends to discredit the social work profession;

(6) performing an act, allowing an omission, or making an assertion or representation that is fraudulent, deceitful, or misleading or that tends to create a misleading impression;

(7) knowingly associating with or permitting the use of a license holder's professional services or identification in connection with an enterprise that the person knows or should have known in the exercise of reasonable diligence violates this chapter or a rule adopted by the board under this chapter;

(8) knowingly associating with or permitting the use of a license holder's name, professional services or identification, or endorsement in connection with an enterprise that the person knows or should have known in the exercise of reasonable diligence is a trade, business, or professional practice of a fraudulent, deceitful, or misleading nature;

(9) directly or indirectly revealing or causing to be revealed a confidential communication transmitted to the license holder by a client or other recipient of the license holder's services unless revealing the communication is required by law;

(10) having been denied an application for a license or certificate to practice social work in another jurisdiction for a reason that the board determines would be a violation of this chapter or a rule adopted by the board under this chapter;

(11) holding a license or certificate in another jurisdiction that is suspended or revoked for a reason that the board determines would be a violation of this chapter or a rule adopted by the board under this chapter;

(12) having been convicted of a felony in this state, another state, or the United States;

(13) refusing to perform an act or service within the scope of the license holder's license solely because of the recipient's age, sex, race, religion, national origin, color, or political affiliation; or

(14) committing an act for which liability exists under Chapter 81, Civil Practice and Remedies Code.

§505.452. CONDITIONS OF PROBATION

The board may require a person for whom a suspension of a license or order of recognition of specialty is probated to:

(1) report regularly to the board on matters that are the basis of the probation;

(2) limit practice to the areas prescribed by the board; or

(3) continue or review continuing professional education until the person attains a degree of skill satisfactory to the board in each area that is a basis of the probation.

§505.453. EMERGENCY SUSPENSION

The suspension by the board of a license or order of recognition of specialty on an emergency basis is effective immediately. The board shall provide an opportunity for a hearing to be held not later than the 20th day after the date of the emergency suspension.

§505.454. SANCTIONS FOR HOLDER OF EXPIRED LICENSE OR ORDER OF RECOGNITION OF SPECIALTY

(a) A person who holds an expired license or order of recognition of specialty under this chapter is subject to a sanction under this chapter if the board determines that the person violated this chapter or a rule adopted by the board under this chapter during the period in which the license or order was valid.

(b) Sections 505.455(b) and (c) and 505.456 apply to a disciplinary proceeding against a person under this section.

§505.455. PROCEDURE; HEARING

(a) A proceeding under Section 505.451 is initiated when a person files a written charge under oath with the department that is referred to the board. A charge may be filed by any person.

(b) A person subject to a sanction under Section 505.451 is entitled to notice and hearing before the State Office of Administrative Hearings before the sanction is imposed.

(c) Disciplinary proceedings and appeals from disciplinary proceedings of the board are governed by Chapter 2001, Government Code.

§505.456. SCHEDULE OF SANCTIONS

(a) The board by rule shall adopt a broad schedule of sanctions for violations of this chapter.

(b) The State Office of Administrative Hearings shall use the schedule of sanctions for any sanction imposed as a result of a hearing conducted by that office.

§505.457. INFORMAL PROCEDURES

(a) The board by rule shall adopt procedures governing:

    (1) informal disposition of a contested case under Section 2001.056, Government Code; and

    (2) an informal proceeding held in compliance with Section 2001.054, Government Code.

(b) Rules adopted under Subsection (a) must:

    (1) provide the complainant and the holder of a license or order of recognition of specialty an opportunity to be heard; and

    (2) require the presence of a representative of the attorney general or the department's legal staff to advise the board or the board's employees.

§505.458. REFUND

(a) Subject to Subsection (b), the board may order a license holder to pay a refund to a consumer as provided in an agreement resulting from an informal settlement conference instead of or in addition to imposing an administrative penalty under this chapter.

(b) The amount of a refund ordered as provided in an agreement resulting from an informal settlement conference may not exceed the amount the consumer paid to the license holder for a service regulated by this chapter. The board may not require payment of other damages or estimate harm in a refund order.

SUBCHAPTER J. PENALTIES AND ENFORCEMENT PROVISIONS

§505.501. MONITORING OF LICENSE HOLDER

The board by rule shall develop a system for monitoring compliance with this chapter by a person who holds a license or order of recognition of specialty. The rules under this section must include procedures to:

    (1) monitor for compliance a person who holds a license or order who is ordered by the board to perform certain acts; and

    (2) identify and monitor persons who hold licenses or orders of recognition of specialty who represent a risk to the public.

§505.502. PROHIBITED CONDUCT BY BUSINESS OR PROFESSIONAL ENTITY

(a) Except as provided by Subsection (b), a business or professional entity may not:

    (1) represent itself or another to the public as being engaged in the practice of social work or as offering social work services under an assumed, trade, business, professional, partnership, or corporate name or title;

    (2) directly or indirectly use or cause to be used the term *"social work," "social work services," "social work, inc.," "social workers," "licensed social workers," "licensed baccalaureate social workers," "licensed master social workers," "licensed clinical social workers," "LMSW," "LSW," "LBSW,"* or *"LCSW,"* or any combination, abbreviation, or variation of those terms; or

(3) directly or indirectly use or cause to be used a term listed in Subdivision (2)   in combination with any other word, letter, initial, sign, legend, or symbol on, in, or directly or indirectly as a part of:

   (A) any sign, directory, contract, pamphlet, stationery, advertisement, or other document;

   (B) a signature; or

   (C) a trade, assumed, corporate, or other business or professional name.

(b) A business or professional entity may engage in conduct described by Subsection (a) if:

   (1) the entity is actively engaged in the practice of social work; and

   (2) the social work services that constitute the entity's practice are:

      (A) personally performed by a social worker who is practicing in accordance with this chapter; or

      (B) performed under the supervision of a licensed baccalaureate social worker, licensed master social worker, or licensed clinical social worker.

§505.503. INJUNCTION

(a) In addition to any other action authorized by law, an action may be initiated in a district court to restrain a violation or threatened violation of this chapter, a rule adopted by the board under this chapter, or an order issued by the board or department under this chapter.

(b) Venue for an action brought under this section is in:

   (1) Travis County;

   (2) the county in which the defendant resides; or

   (3) the county in which any part of the alleged violation occurred.

(c) At the request of the board or department, the attorney general shall initiate and conduct an action in a district court in the state's name to obtain an injunction under this section.

(d) To obtain an injunction under this section, it is not necessary to allege or prove that:

    (1) an adequate remedy at law does not exist; or

    (2) substantial or irreparable damage would result from the continued violation.

(e) Any party in an action brought under this section may appeal.

§505.504. CIVIL PENALTY

(a) A person who violates or threatens to violate this chapter, a rule adopted by the board under this chapter, or an order issued by the board or department under this chapter is liable to the state for a civil penalty of not less than $50 or more than $500 for each day of violation.

(b) At the request of the board or department, the attorney general shall initiate and conduct an action in a district court in the state's name to obtain a civil penalty under this section.

§505.505. APPEAL BOND NOT REQUIRED

The board or department is not required to post an appeal bond in any action arising under this chapter.

§505.506. REPRESENTATION BY ATTORNEY GENERAL

The attorney general shall represent the board or department in an action brought to enforce this chapter.

§505.507. CRIMINAL PENALTY

(a) A person commits an offense if the person knowingly acts as a social worker without holding a license rquired under this chapter.

(b) An offense under Subsection (a) is a Class B misdemeanor.

§505.508. CEASE AND DESIST ORDER

If it appears to the board that a person who is not licensed under this chapter is violating this chapter, a rule adopted under this chapter, or another state statute or rule relating to the practice of social work, the board after notice and opportunity for a hearing may issue a cease and desist order prohibiting the person from engaging in the activity5.

SUBCHAPTER K. ADMINISTRATIVE PENALTY

§505.551. IMPOSITION OF ADMINISTRATIVE PENALTY

The board may impose an administrative penalty on:

    (1) a person licensed under this chapter who violates this chapter or a rule or order adopted under this chapter; and

    (2) a person who violates a cease and desist order issued by the board under Section 505.508.

§505.552. AMOUNT OF ADMINISTRATIVE PENALTY

(a) The amount of the administrative penalty may not be less than $50 or more than $5,000 for each violation. Each day a violation continues or occurs is a separate violation for the purpose of imposing a penalty.

(b)   The amount shall be based on:

    (1)   the seriousness of the violation, including the nature, circumstances, extent, and gravity of the violation;

    (2)   the economic harm caused by the violation;

    (3)   the history of previous violations;

    (4)   the amount necessary to deter a future violation;

    (5)   efforts to correct the violation; and

    (6)   any other matter that justice may require.

(c)   The board by rule shall adopt an administrative penalty schedule based on the criteria listed in Subsection (b) for violations of this chapter or board rules to ensure that the amounts of penalties imposed are appropriate to the violation. The board shall provide the administrative penalty schedule to the public on request.

§505.553. REPORT AND NOTICE OF VIOLATION AND PENALTY

(a)   If the executive director determines that a violation occurred, the director may issue to the board a report stating:

    (1)   the facts on which the determination is based; and

    (2)   the director's recommendation on the imposition of an administrative penalty, including a recommendation on the amount of the penalty.

(b)   Within 14 days after the date the report is issued, the executive director shall give written notice of the report to the person. The notice must:

    (1)   include a brief summary of the alleged violation;

    (2)   state the amount of the recommended administrative penalty; and

    (3)   inform the person of the person's right to a hearing on the occurrence of the violation, the amount of the penalty, or both.

§505.554. PENALTY TO BE PAID OR HEARING REQUESTED

(a)   Within 10 days after the date the person receives the notice, the person in writing may:

    (1)   accept the determination and recommended administrative penalty of the executive director; or

    (2)   make a request for a hearing on the occurrence of the violation, the amount of the penalty, or both.

(b)   If the person accepts the determination and recommended penalty of the executive director, the board by order shall approve the determination and impose the recommended penalty.

§505.555. HEARING

(a)   If the person requests a hearing or fails to respond in a timely manner to the notice, the executive director shall set a hearing and give written notice of the hearing to the person.

(b)   An administrative law judge of the State Office of Administrative Hearings shall hold the hearing.

(c)   The administrative law judge shall make findings of fact and conclusions of law and promptly issue to the board a proposal for a decision about the occurrence of the violation and the amount of a proposed administrative penalty.

§505.556. DECISION BY BOARD

(a)   Based on the findings of fact, conclusions of law, and proposal for decision, the board by order may determine that:

     (1)   a violation occurred and impose an administrative penalty; or

     (2)   a violation did not occur.

(b)   The notice of the board's order given to the person must include a statement of the right of the person to judicial review of the order.

§505.557. OPTIONS FOLLOWING DECISION: PAY OR APPEAL

(a)   Within 30 days after the date the board's order becomes final, the person shall:

     (1)   pay the administrative penalty; or

     (2)   file a petition for judicial review contesting the occurrence of the violation, the amount of the penalty, or both.

(b)   Within the 30-day period prescribed by Subsection (a), a person who files a petition for judicial review may:

     (1)   stay enforcement of the penalty by:

         (A)   paying the penalty to the court for placement in an escrow account; or

         (B)   giving the court a *supersedeas* bond approved by the court that:

             (i)   is for the amount of the penalty; and

             (ii)   is effective until all judicial review of the board's order is final; or

     (2)   request the court to stay enforcement of the penalty by:

         (A)   filing with the court a sworn affidavit of the person stating that the person is financially unable to pay the penalty and is financially unable to give the *supersedeas* bond; and

         (B)   giving a copy of the affidavit to the executive director by certified mail.

(c)   If the executive director receives a copy of an affidavit under Subsection (b)(2), the director may file with the court, within five days after the date the copy is received, a contest to the affidavit.

(d)   The court shall hold a hearing on the facts alleged in the affidavit as soon as practicable and shall stay the enforcement of the penalty on finding that the alleged facts are true. The person who files an affidavit has the burden of proving that the person is financially unable to pay the penalty and to give a *supersedeas* bond.

§505.558. COLLECTION OF PENALTY

(a)   If the person does not pay the administrative penalty and the enforcement of the penalty is not stayed, the penalty may be collected.

(b)   The attorney general may sue to collect the penalty.

§505.559. DETERMINATION BY COURT

(a) If the court sustains the determination that a violation occurred, the court may uphold or reduce the amount of the administrative penalty and order the person to pay the full or reduced amount of the penalty.

(b) If the court does not sustain the finding that a violation occurred, the court shall order that a penalty is not owed.

§505.560. REMITTANCE OF PENALTY AND INTEREST

(a) If the person paid the administrative penalty and if the amount of the penalty is reduced or the penalty is not upheld by the court, the court shall order, when the court's judgment becomes final, that the appropriate amount plus accrued interest be remitted to the person.

(b) The interest accrues at the rate charged on loans to depository institutions by the New York Federal Reserve Bank.

(c) The interest shall be paid for the period beginning on the date the penalty is paid and ending on the date the penalty is remitted.

(d) If the person gave a *supersedeas* bond and the penalty is not upheld by the court, the court shall order, when the court's judgment becomes final, the release of the bond.

(e) If the person gave a *supersedeas* bond and the amount of the penalty is reduced, the court shall order the release of the bond after the person pays the reduced amount.

§505.561. ADMINISTRATIVE PROCEDURE

A proceeding under this section is a contested case under Chapter 2001, Government Code.

SUBCHAPTER L. REPORTS OF CERTAIN VIOLATIONS

§505.601. REPORT OF VIOLATION.

In a written, signed report to the appropriate licensing board, agency, or facility, a person licensed under this chapter may report an incident that the person has reasonable cause to believe has exposed a client to substantial risk of harm, including:

(1) a failure to provide care that conforms to the minimum standards of acceptable and prevailing professional practice;

(2) illegal billing practices; or

(3) falsification of records.

§505.602. REPORTING IMMUNITY

A person who, without malice, makes a report authorized, or reasonably believed to be authorized, under this subchapter:

(1) is immune from civil liability; and

(2) may not be subjected by the person's employer to other retaliatory action as a result of making the report.

§505.603. CAUSE OF ACTION FOR RETALIATION

(a) A person named as a defendant in a civil action or subjected by the person's employer to other retaliatory action as a result of filing a report authorized, or reasonably believed to be authorized, under this subchapter may file a counterclaim in the pending action or prove a cause of action in a subsequent suit to recover defense costs, including reasonable attorney's fees and actual and punitive damages, if the suit or retaliatory action is determined to be frivolous, unreasonable, or taken in bad faith.

(b) A person may not suspend or terminate the employment of, or otherwise discipline or discriminate against, a person who makes a report, without malice, under this subchapter.

(c) A person who makes a report under this subchapter has a cause of action against a person who violates Subsection (b) and may recover:

  (1) the greater of:

    (A) actual damages, including damages for mental anguish even if no other injury is shown; or

    (B) $1,000;

  (2) exemplary damages;

  (3) court costs; and

  (4) reasonable attorney's fees.

(d) In addition to the amount recovered under Subsection (c), a person whose employment is suspended or terminated in violation of this section is entitled to:

  (1) reinstatement in the employee's former position or severance pay in an amount equal to three months of the employee's most recent salary; and

  (2) compensation for wages lost during the period of suspension or termination.

(e) A person who brings an action under this section has the burden of proof. It is a rebuttable presumption that the person's employment was suspended or terminated for making a report under this subchapter if:

  (1) the person was suspended or terminated within 60 days after the date the report was made; and

  (2) the person to whom the report that is the subject of the cause of action was made or the court determines that the report was:

    (A) authorized under this subchapter; and

    (B) made without malice.

(f) An action under this section may be brought in a district court of the county in which:

  (1) the plaintiff resides;

  (2) the plaintiff was employed by the defendant; or

  (3) the defendant conducts business.

SOCIAL WORKER RULES & REGS

RULES RELATING TO THE LICENSING AND REGULATION OF SOCIAL WORKERS[2]
(TITLE 22—EXAMINING BOARDS, PART 34, CHAPTER 781)

As noted in the Social Work Practice Act outlined above, The Texas State Board of Social Worker Examiners is charged with developing the rules and regulations for the practice of social work in the State of Texas. Visit the Texas State Board of Social Worker Examiners website for up-to-the minute information from the board:

http://www.dshs.state.tx.us/socialwork/default.shtm

ALERT: *Rules guiding the social work profession can be changed at any time. It is the licensee's responsibility to visit the Texas State Board of Social Worker Examiners website on a regular basis to check for any changes to the rules. http://www.dshs.state.tx.us/socialwork/default.shtm*

Social work is bound by laws and rules under the over-arching NASW Code of Ethics. This social work sourcebook contains the laws and the Code of Ethics. While the law remains unchanged for a minimum of 2 years between legislative sessions, and the NASW Code of Ethics can change, at most, every 3 years, the "rules" can change much more frequently.

Please go to *http://www.dshs.state.tx.us/socialwork/default.shtm* regularly to check for updates.

For your convenience, in this Fourth edition of the Texas Law for the Social Worker we have included the most recent update to the Social Work Rules and Regulations (as of March 28, 2013). Please see Appendix B (page 413), and don't forget to check the website frequently for addtional updates.

---

2   Texas State Board of Social Worker Examiners •Department of State Health Services •1100 West 49th Street •Austin, TX 78756-3183 •512/719-3521 •800/232-3162 •Fax: 512/834-6677 • lsw@dshs.state.tx.us • http://www.dshs.state.tx.us/socialwork/

Administrative Code

Rule 89.1053 Procedures for Use of Restraint and Time-Out[1]

(A) Requirement to Implement

In addition to the requirements of 34 Code of Federal Regulations (CFR), §300.346(a)(2)(i)and (c), school districts and charter schools must implement the provisions of this section regarding the use of restraint and time-out. In accordance with the provisions of Texas Education Code (TEC), §37.0021 (*Use of Confinement, Restraint, Seclusion, and Time-Out*), it is the policy of the state to treat with dignity and respect all students, including students with disabilities who receive special education services under TEC, Chapter 29, Subchapter A.

(B) Definitions

(1) *"Emergency"* means a situation in which a student's behavior poses a threat of:

    (A) imminent, serious physical harm to the student or others; or

    (B) imminent, serious property destruction.

(2) *"Restraint"* means use of physical force or a mechanical device to significantly restrict the free movement of all or a portion of the student's body.

(3) *"Time-out"* means a behavior management technique in which, to provide a student with an opportunity to regain self-control, the student is separated from other students for a limited period in a setting:

    (A) that is not locked; and

    (B) from which the exit is not physically blocked by furniture, a closed door held shut from the outside, or another inanimate object.

(C) Use of Restraint

A school employee, volunteer, or independent contractor may use restraint only in an emergency as defined in subsection (b) of this section and with the following limitations.

(1) Restraint shall be limited to the use of such reasonable force as is necessary to address the emergency.

(2) Restraint shall be discontinued at the point at which the emergency no longer exists.

(3) Restraint shall be implemented in such a way as to protect the health and safety of the student and others.

(4) Restraint shall not deprive the student of basic human necessities.

(D) Training on Use of Restraint

Training for school employees, volunteers, or independent contractors shall be provided according to the following requirements.

(1) Not later than April 1, 2003, a core team of personnel on each campus must be trained in the use of restraint, and the team must include a campus

---

1   (Texas Administrative Code; Title 19; Part 2, Chapter 89; Subchapter AA, Div 2; Rule 89.1053)

administrator or designee and any general or special education personnel likely to use restraint.

(2) After April 1, 2003, personnel called upon to use restraint in an emergency and who have not received prior training must receive training within 30 school days following the use of restraint.

(3) Training on use of restraint must include prevention and de-escalation techniques and provide alternatives to the use of restraint.

(4) All trained personnel shall receive instruction in current professionally accepted practices and standards regarding behavior management and the use of restraint.

(E) DOCUMENTATION AND NOTIFICATION ON USE OF RESTRAINT

In a case in which restraint is used, school employees, volunteers, or independent contractors shall implement the following documentation requirements.

(1) On the day restraint is utilized, the campus administrator or designee must be notified verbally or in writing regarding the use of restraint.

(2) On the day restraint is utilized, a good faith effort shall be made to verbally notify the parent(s) regarding the use of restraint.

(3) Written notification of the use of restraint must be placed in the mail or otherwise provided to the parent within one school day of the use of restraint.

(4) Written documentation regarding the use of restraint must be placed in the student's special education eligibility folder in a timely manner so the information is available to the ARD committee when it considers the impact of the student's behavior on the student's learning and/or the creation or revision of a behavioral intervention plan (BIP).

(5) Written notification to the parent(s) and documentation to the student's special education eligibility folder shall include the following:

(A) name of the student;

(B) name of the staff member(s) administering the restraint;

(C) date of the restraint and the time the restraint began and ended;

(D) location of the restraint;

(E) nature of the restraint;

(F) a description of the activity in which the student was engaged immediately preceding the use of restraint;

(G) the behavior that prompted the restraint;

(H) the efforts made to de-escalate the situation and alternatives to restraint that were attempted; and

(I) information documenting parent contact and notification.

(F) CLARIFICATION REGARDING RESTRAINT

The provisions adopted under this section do not apply to the use of physical force or a mechanical device which does not significantly restrict the free movement of all or a portion of the student's body. Restraint that involves significant restriction as referenced in subsection (b)(2) of this section does not include:

(1) physical contact or appropriately prescribed adaptive equipment to promote normative body positioning and/or physical functioning;

(2) limited physical contact with a student to promote safety (e.g., holding a student's hand), prevent a potentially harmful action (e.g., running into the street), teach a skill, redirect attention, provide guidance to a location, or provide comfort;

(3) limited physical contact or appropriately prescribed adaptive equipment to prevent a student from engaging in ongoing, repetitive self-injurious behaviors, with the expectation that instruction will be reflected in the individualized education program (IEP) as required by 34 CFR §300.346(a)(2)(i) and (c) to promote student learning and reduce and/or prevent the need for ongoing intervention; or

(4) seat belts / other safety equipment to secure students during transportation.

(G) USE OF TIME-OUT

A school employee, volunteer, or independent contractor may use time-out in accordance with subsection (b)(3) of this section with the following limitations.

(1) Physical force or threat of physical force shall not be used to place a student in time-out.

(2) Time-out may only be used in conjunction with an array of positive behavior intervention strategies and techniques and must be included in the student's IEP and/or BIP if it is utilized on a recurrent basis to increase or decrease a targeted behavior.

(3) Use of time-out shall not be implemented in a fashion that precludes the ability of the student to be involved in and progress in the general curriculum and advance appropriately toward attaining the annual goals specified in the student's IEP.

(H) TRAINING ON USE OF TIME-OUT

Training for school employees, volunteers, or independent contractors shall be provided according to the following requirements.

(1) Not later than April 1, 2003, general or special education personnel who implement time-out based on requirements established in a student's IEP and/or BIP must be trained in the use of time-out.

(2) After April 1, 2003, newly-identified personnel called upon to implement time-out based on requirements established in a student's IEP and/or BIP must receive training in the use of time-out within 30 school days of being assigned the responsibility for implementing time-out.

(3) Training on the use of time-out must be provided as part of a program which addresses a full continuum of positive behavioral intervention strategies, and must address the impact of time-out on the ability of the student to be involved in and progress in the general curriculum and advance appropriately toward attaining the annual goals specified in the student's IEP.

(4) All trained personnel shall receive instruction in current professionally accepted practices and standards regarding behavior management and the use of time-out.

(I) DOCUMENTATION ON USE OF TIME-OUT

Necessary documentation or data collection regarding the use of time-out, if any, must be addressed in the IEP or BIP. The admission, review, and dismissal (ARD) committee must use any collected data to judge the effectiveness of the intervention and provide a basis for making determinations regarding its continued use.

(J) STUDENT SAFETY

Any behavior management technique and/or discipline management practice must be implemented in such a way as to protect the health and safety of the student and others. No discipline management practice may be calculated to inflict injury, cause harm, demean, or deprive the student of basic human necessities.

(K) DATA REPORTING

Beginning with the 2003-2004 school year, with the exception of actions covered by subsection (f) of this section, data regarding the use of restraint must be electronically reported to the Texas Education Agency in accordance with reporting standards specified by the Agency.

(L) EXCLUDED PROVISIONS

The provisions adopted under this section do not apply to:

(1)   a peace officer while performing law enforcement duties;

(2)   juvenile probation, detention, or corrections personnel; or

(3)   an educational services provider with whom a student is placed by a judicial authority, unless the services are provided in an educational program of a school district.

§411.653. STANDARDS FOR SERVICES TO PERSONS WITH CO-OCCURRING PSYCHIATRIC AND SUBSTANCE USE DISORDERS (COPSD)[2]

§411.651. PURPOSE

The purpose of this subchapter is to improve existing mental health services provided by the entities defined in §411.653 of this title (relating to Definitions) by establishing standards to ensure the effective and coordinated provision of services to individuals who require specialized support or treatment due to co-occurring psychiatric and substance use disorders (COPSD).

§411.653. DEFINITIONS

The following words and terms, when used in this subchapter, have the following meanings, unless the context clearly indicates otherwise:

(1)   *Access*—An individual's ability to obtain the psychiatric and substance use disorder services needed.

(2)   *Adolescent*—A person who is 13 through 17 years of age.

(3)   *Adult*—A person who is 18 years of age or older.

(4)   *Child*—A person who is 3 through 12 years of age.

---

2   (Texas Administrative Code; Title 25. Health Services; Part 1. Department of State Health Services; Chapter 411. State Mental Health Authority Responsibilities; Subchapter N. Standards for Services to Individuals with CoOccurring Psychiatric and Substance Use Disorders (COPSD); Division 1. General Provisions; Rule §411.654)

(5) *Contract*—A legally enforceable written agreement for the purchase of services.

(6) *Co-occurring psychiatric and substance use disorders (COPSD)*—The co-occurring diagnoses of psychiatric disorders and substance use disorders.

(7) *Diagnostic and Statistical Manual of Mental Disorders (DSM)*—The most recent edition of the American Psychiatric Association's official classification of mental disorders.

(8) *Entity or entities*—The terms used to refer to the following:

    (A) Local mental health authorities (*LMHAs*);

    (B) Managed care organizations (*MCOs*);

    (C) State mental health facilities (*SMHF*); and

    (D) Medicaid providers who are required to comply with Chapter 419, Subchapter L of this title, governing Mental Health Rehabilitative Services, or Chapter 412, Subchapter I of this title, governing Mental Health Case Management Services.

(9) *Family member*—Anyone an individual identifies as being involved in the individual's life (e.g., the individual's parent, spouse, child, sibling, significant other, or friend).

(10) *Individual*—

    (A) For an LMHA—An adult with COPSD, adolescent with COPSD, or child with COPSD seeking or receiving services from or through the LMHA or its provider.

    (B) For an MCO—An enrolled adult with COPSD, adolescent with COPSD, or child with COPSD seeking or receiving services from or through the MCO or its provider.

    (C) For an SMHF—An adult with COPSD, adolescent with COPSD, or child with COPSD seeking or receiving services from or through the SMHF or its provider.

    (D) For a provider of rehabilitative services or a provider of mental health case managment services reimbursed by Medicaid—An adult with COPSD, adolescent with COPSD, or child with COPSD seeking or receiving rehabilitative services or mental health case managment services reimbursed by Medicaid.

(11) *Integrated assessment*—An assessment of an individual to gather both substance use and psychiatric information.

(12) *Legally authorized representative (LAR)*—A person authorized by law to act on behalf of an individual with regard to a matter (e.g., a parent, guardian, or managing conservator of a child or adolescent, a guardian of an adult, or a personal representative of a deceased individual).

(13) *Local mental health authority (LMHA)*—An entity designated as the local mental health authority by the DSHS in accordance with the Health and Safety Code, §533.035(a).

(14) *Managed care organization (MCO)*—An entity that has a current Department of Insurance certificate of authority to operate as a health

maintenance organization (HMO) under Insurance Code, Subchapter C of Chapter 843 or as an approved nonprofit health corporation under Insurance Code, Chapter 884.

(15) *Psychiatric disorder*—An emotional disturbance in a child or adolescent or a psychiatric disorder in an adult who is a member of the mental health priority population as defined in the Health and Human Services System Strategic Plan 2011 - 2015.

(16) *Readiness to change*—An individual's emotional and cognitive awareness of the need to change, coupled with a commitment to change.

(17) *Services*—Services provided to treat a psychiatric or substance use disorder.

(18) *Staff*—Full- or part-time employees, contractors, and interns of an entity.

(19) *Substance use disorder*—The use of one or more drugs, including alcohol, which significantly and negatively impacts one or more major areas of life functioning and which meets criteria described in the current Diagnostic and Statistical Manual of Mental Disorders for substance abuse or substance dependence.

(20) *Support services*—Services delivered to an individual, legally authorized representative (LAR) or family member(s) to assist the individual in functioning in the living, learning, working, and socializing environments.

(21) *Treatment plan*—A written document developed by the provider, in consultation with the individual (and LAR on the individual's behalf), that is based on assessments of the individual and which addresses the individual's strengths, needs, goals, and preferences regarding service delivery as referenced in §412.322 of this title (relating to Provider Responsibilities for Treatment Planning and Service Authorization) of Chapter 412, Subchapter G of this title, governing Mental Health Community Services Standards.

§411.654. Services to Individuals with COPSD

(a) Staff providing services to an individual with COPSD must ensure that services provided:

(1) address both psychiatric and substance use disorders;

(2) be provided within established practice guidelines for this population; and

(3) facilitate individuals or LARs in accessing available services they need and choose, including self-help groups.

(b) The services provided to an individual with COPSD must be provided:

(1) by staff who are competent in the areas identified in §411.658 of this title (relating to Specialty Competencies of Staff Providing Services to Individuals with COPSD);

(2) in an individual or small group setting;

(3) in an age, gender, and culturally appropriate manner; and

(4) in accordance with the individual's treatment plan.

§*411.658. SPECIALTY COMPETENCIES OF STAFF PROVIDING SERVICES TO INDIVIDUALS WITH COPSD*

(a) Entities must ensure that services to individuals are age and culturally appropriate and are provided by staff within their scope of practice who have the following minimum knowledge, technical, and interpersonal competencies prior to providing services:

   (1) Knowledge competencies:

      (A) knowledge of the fact that psychiatric and substance use disorders are potentially recurrent relapsing disorders; that although abstinence is the goal, relapses can be opportunities for learning and growth;

      (B) knowledge of the impact of substance use disorders on developmental, social, and physical growth and development of children and adolescents;

      (C) knowledge of interpersonal and family dynamics and their impact on individuals;

      (D) knowledge of the current Diagnostic and Statistical Manual of Mental Disorders diagnostic criteria for psychiatric disorders and substance use disorders and the relationship between psychiatric disorders and substance use disorders;

      (E) knowledge regarding the increased risks of self-harm, suicide, and violence in individuals;

      (F) knowledge of the elements of an integrated treatment plan and community support plan for individuals;

      (G) basic knowledge of pharmacology as it relates to individuals;

      (H) basic understanding of the neurophysiology of addiction;

      (I) basic knowledge of withdrawal symptoms and their potential risk factors to clients;

      (J) knowledge of the phases of recovery for individuals;

      (K) knowledge of the relationship between COPSD and Axis III disorders; and

      (L) basic knowledge of self-help in recovery.

   (2) Technical competencies:

      (A) ability to perform age-appropriate assessments of individuals; and

      (B) ability to formulate an individualized treatment plan and community support plan for individuals.

   (3) Interpersonal competencies:

      (A) ability to tailor interventions to the process of recovery for individuals;

      (B) ability to tailor interventions with readiness to change; and

      (C) ability to support individuals who choose to participate in 12-step recovery programs.

(b) Within 90 days of the effective date of this subchapter, entities must ensure that staff who provide services to individuals with COPSD, and who have not previously done so, have demonstrated the competencies described in subsection

(a) of this section. These competencies may be evidenced by compliance with current licensure requirements of the governing or supervisory boards for the respective disciplines involved in serving individuals with COPSD or by documentation regarding the attainment of the competencies described in subsection (a) of this section. For unlicensed staff delivering these services, these competencies are evidenced by documentation regarding their attainment as required in subsection (a) of this section.

§411.660. SCREENING, ASSESSMENT, AND TREATMENT PLANNING

(a) Screening and assessment. When a screening determines an assessment is necessary, an integrated assessment must be conducted to consider relevant past and current medical, psychiatric, and substance use information, including:

   (1) information from the individual (and LAR on the individual's behalf) regarding the individual's strengths, needs, natural supports, responsiveness to previous treatment, as well as preferences for and objections to specific treatments;

   (2) the needs and desire of the individual for family member involvement in treatment and services if the individual is an adult without an LAR; and

   (3) recommendations and conclusions regarding treatment needs and eligibility for services for individuals.

(b) Treatment plan development.

   (1) The individual (and LAR on the individual's behalf, if applicable) must be involved in all aspects of planning the individual's treatment. If the individual has requested the involvement of a family member, then the provider must attempt to involve the family member in all aspects of planning the individual's treatment.

   (2) The treatment plan must identify services to be provided and must include measurable outcomes that address COPSD.

   (3) The treatment plan must identify the LAR's or family members' need for education and support services related to the individual's mental illness and substance abuse and a method to facilitate the LAR's or family members' receipt of the needed education and support services.

   (4) The individual, LAR, and, if requested, family member, must be given a copy of the treatment plan.

(c) Treatment plan review. Each individual's treatment plan must be reviewed in accordance with TDMHMR-defined time frames and the review must be documented.

(d) Progress notes. The medical record notes must contain a description of the individual's progress towards goals identified in the treatment plan, as well as other clinically significant activities or events.

(e) Episode of care summary. Upon discharge or transfer of an individual from one entity to another, the individual's medical record must identify the services provided according to this subchapter and the items referenced in §412.322 (relating to Provider Responsibilities for Treatment Planning and Service Authorization) of Chapter 412, Subchapter G of this title, governing Mental Health Community Services Standards.

CIVIL PRACTICE AND REMEDIES CODE

SEXUAL EXPLOITATION BY MENTAL HEALTH PROVIDER—§81[3]

§81.001. DEFINITIONS

In this chapter:

(1) *"Mental health services"* means assessment, diagnosis, treatment, or counseling in a professional relationship to assist an individual or group in:

   (A) alleviating mental or emotional illness, symptoms, conditions, or disorders, including alcohol or drug addiction;

   (B) understanding conscious or subconscious motivations;

   (C) resolving emotional, attitudinal, or relationship conflicts; or

   (D) modifying feelings, attitudes, or behaviors that interfere with effective emotional, social, or intellectual functioning.

(2) *"Mental health services provider"* means an individual, licensed or unlicensed, who performs or purports to perform mental health services, including a:

   (A) licensed social worker as defined by §505.002, Occupations Code;

   (B) chemical dependency counselor as defined by §504.001, Occupations Code;

   (C) licensed professional counselor as defined by §503.002, Occupations Code;

   (D) licensed marriage and family therapist as defined by §505.002, Occupations Code;

   (E) member of the clergy;

   (F) physician who is practicing medicine as defined by §151.002, Occupations Code;

   (G) psychologist offering psychological services as defined by §501.003, Occupations Code; or

   (H) special officer for mental health assignment certified under §1701.404, Occupations Code.

(3) *"Patient"* means an individual who seeks or obtains mental health services. The term includes a person who has contact with a special officer for mental health assignment because of circumstances relating to the person's mental health.

(4) *" Sexual contact"* means:

   (A) *"deviate sexual intercourse"* as defined by Section 21.01, Penal Code;

   (B) *"sexual contact"* as defined by §21.01, Penal Code;

   (C) *"sexual intercourse"* as defined by §21.01, Penal Code; or

   (D) requests by the mental health services provider for conduct described

---

3   (Civil Practice and Remedies Code; Title 4. Liability in Tort; Chapter 81. Sexual Exploitation by Mental Health Services Provider)

by Paragraph (A), (B), or (C). "Sexual contact" does not include conduct described by Paragraph (A) or (B) that is a part of a professionally recognized medical treatment of a patient.

(5) *"Sexual exploitation"* means a pattern, practice, or scheme of conduct, which may include sexual contact, that can reasonably be construed as being for the purposes of sexual arousal or gratification or sexual abuse of any person. The term does not include obtaining information about a patient's sexual history within standard accepted practice while treating a sexual or marital dysfunction.

(6) *"Therapeutic deception"* means a representation by a mental health services provider that sexual contact with, or sexual exploitation by, the mental health services provider is consistent with, or a part of, a patient's or former patient's treatment.

(7) *"Mental health services,"* as defined by this section, provided by a member of the clergy does not include religious, moral, and spiritual counseling, teaching, and instruction.

§81.002. SEXUAL EXPLOITATION CAUSE OF ACTION

A mental health services provider is liable to a patient or former patient of the mental health services provider for damages for sexual exploitation if the patient or former patient suffers, directly or indirectly, a physical, mental, or emotional injury caused by, resulting from, or arising out of:

(1) sexual contact between the patient or former patient and the mental health services provider;

(2) sexual exploitation of the patient or former patient by the mental health services provider; or

(3) therapeutic deception of the patient or former patient by the mental health services provider.

§81.003. LIABILITY OF EMPLOYER

(a) An employer of a mental health services provider is liable to a patient or former patient of the mental health services provider for damages if the patient or former patient is injured as described by §81.002 and the employer:

(1) fails to make inquiries of an employer or former employer, whose name and address have been disclosed to the employer and who employed the mental health services provider as a mental health services provider within the five years before the date of disclosure, concerning the possible occurrence of sexual exploitation by the mental health services provider of patients or former patients of the mental health services provider; or

(2) knows or has reason to know that the mental health services provider engaged in sexual exploitation of a patient or former patient and the employer failed to:

(A) report the suspected sexual exploitation as required by §81.006; or

(B) take necessary action to prevent or stop the sexual exploitation by the mental health services provider.

(b) An employer or former employer of a mental health services provider is liable to a patient or former patient of the mental health services provider for damages if the patient or former patient is injured as described by §81.002 and the employer or former employer:

(1) knows of the occurrence of sexual exploitation by the mental health services provider of a patient or former patient;

(2) receives a specific request by an employer or prospective employer of the mental health services provider, engaged in the business of providing mental health services, concerning the possible existence or nature of sexual exploitation by the mental health services provider; and

(3) fails to disclose the occurrence of the sexual exploitation.

(c) An employer or former employer is liable under this section only to the extent that the failure to take the action described by Subsection (a) or (b) was a proximate and actual cause of damages sustained.

(d) If a mental health professional who sexually exploits a patient or former patient is a member of the clergy and the sexual exploitation occurs when the professional is acting as a member of the clergy, liability if any under this section is limited to the church, congregation, or parish in which the member of the clergy carried out the clergy member's pastoral duties:

(1) at the time the sexual exploitation occurs, if the liability is based on a violation of Subsection (a); or

(2) at the time of the previous occurrence of sexual exploitation, if the liability is based on a violation of Subsection (b).

(e) Nothing in Subsection (d) shall prevent the extension of liability under this section beyond the local church, congregation, or parish where the current or previous sexual exploitation occurred, as appropriate under Subsection (d), if the patient proves that officers or employees of the religious denomination in question at the regional, state, or national level:

(1) knew or should have known of the occurrences of sexual exploitation by the mental health services provider;

(2) received reports of such occurrences and failed to take necessary action to prevent or stop such sexual exploitation by the mental health services provider and that such failure was a proximate and actual cause of the damages; or

(3) knew or should have known of the mental health professional's propensity to engage in sexual exploitation.

§81.004. DAMAGES

(a) A plaintiff who prevails in a suit under this section may recover actual damages, including damages for mental anguish even if an injury other than mental anguish is not shown.

(b) In addition to an award under Subsection (a), a plaintiff who prevails in a suit under this section may recover exemplary damages and reasonable attorney fees.

§81.005. DEFENSES

(a) It is not a defense to an action brought under §81.002 or 81.003 that the sexual exploitation of the patient or former patient occurred:

(1) with the consent of the patient or former patient;

(2) outside the therapy or treatment sessions of the patient or former patient; or

(3) off the premises regularly used by the mental health services provider for the therapy or treatment sessions of the patient or former patient.

    (b) It is a defense to an action brought under §81.002 or 81.003 by a former patient that the person was not emotionally dependent on the mental health services provider when the sexual exploitation began and the mental health services provider terminated mental health services with the patient more than two years before the date the sexual exploitation began.

    (c) A person is considered not emotionally dependent for purposes of this chapter if the nature of the patient's or former patient's emotional condition and the nature of the treatment provided by the mental health services provider are not such that the mental health services provider knows or has reason to believe that the patient or former patient is unable to withhold consent to the sexual exploitation.

§81.006. REPORTING THERAPIST-CLIENT SEXUAL RELATIONSHIP

(a) If a mental health services provider or the employer of a mental health services provider has reasonable cause to suspect that a patient has been the victim of sexual exploitation by a mental health services provider during the course of treatment, or if a patient alleges sexual exploitation by a mental health services provider during the course of treatment, the mental health services provider or the employer shall report the alleged conduct not later than the 30th day after the date the person became aware of the conduct or the allegations to:

(1) the prosecuting attorney in the county in which the alleged sexual exploitation occurred; and

(2) any state licensing board that has responsibility for the mental health services provider's licensing.

(b) Before making a report under this section, the reporter shall inform the alleged victim of the reporter's duty to report and shall determine if the alleged victim wants to remain anonymous.

(c) A report under this section need contain only the information needed to:

(1) identify the reporter;

(2) identify the alleged victim, unless the alleged victim has requested anonymity; and

(3) express suspicion that sexual exploitation has occurred.

(d) Information in a report is privileged information and is for the exclusive use of the prosecuting attorney or state licensing board that receives the information. A person who receives privileged information may not disclose the information except to the extent that disclosure is consistent with the authorized purposes for which the person first obtained the information. The identity of an alleged victim of sexual exploitation by a mental health services provider may not be disclosed by the reporter, or by a person who has received or has access to a report or record, unless the alleged victim has consented to the disclosure in writing.

(e)   A person who intentionally violates Subsection (a) or (d) is subject to disciplinary action by that person's appropriate licensing board and also commits an offense. An offense under this subsection is a Class C misdemeanor.

§81.007. LIMITED IMMUNITY FROM LIABILITY

(a)   A person who, in good faith, makes a report required by §81.006 is immune from civil or criminal liability resulting from the filing of that report.

(b)   Reporting under this chapter is presumed to be done in good faith.

(c)   The immunity provided by this section does not apply to liability resulting from sexual exploitation by a mental health services provider of a patient or former patient.

§81.008. ADMISSION OF EVIDENCE

(a)   In an action for sexual exploitation, evidence of the plaintiff's sexual history and reputation is not admissible unless:

(1)   the plaintiff claims damage to sexual functioning; or

(2)   (A)   the defendant requests a hearing before trial and makes an offer of proof of the relevancy of the history or reputation; and

(B)   the court finds that the history or reputation is relevant and that the probative value of the evidence outweighs its prejudicial effect.

(b)   The court may allow the admission only of specific information or examples of the plaintiff's conduct that are determined by the court to be relevant. The court's order shall detail the information or conduct that is admissible and no other such evidence may be introduced.

§81.009. LIMITATIONS

(a)   Except as otherwise provided by this section, an action under this chapter must be filed before the third anniversary of the date the patient or former patient understood or should have understood the conduct for which liability is established under §81.002 or 81.003.

(b)   If a patient or former patient entitled to file an action under this chapter is unable to bring the action because of the effects of the sexual exploitation, continued emotional dependence on the mental health services provider, or threats, instructions, or statements by the mental health services provider, the deadline for filing an action under this chapter is tolled during that period, except that the deadline may not be tolled for more than 15 years.

(c)   This section does not apply to a patient or former patient who is a "child" or a "minor" as defined by §101.003, Family Code, until that patient or former patient has reached the age of 18. If the action is brought by a parent, guardian, or other person having custody of the child or minor, it must be brought within the period set forth in this section.

DECLARATION FOR MENTAL HEALTH TREATMENT—§137[4]

§137.001. DEFINITION

In this chapter:

(1) *"Adult"* means a person 18 years of age or older or a person under 18 years of age who has had the disabilities of minority removed.

(2) *"Attending physician"* means the physician, selected by or assigned to a patient, who has primary responsibility for the treatment and care of the patient.

(3) *"Declaration for mental health treatment"* means a document making a declaration of preferences or instructions regarding mental health treatment.

(4) *"Emergency"* means a situation in which it is immediately necessary to treat a patient to prevent:

   (A) probable imminent death or serious bodily injury to the patient because the patient:

      (i) overtly or continually is threatening or attempting to commit suicide or serious bodily injury to the patient; or

      (ii) is behaving in a manner that indicates that the patient is unable to satisfy the patient's need for nourishment, essential medical care, or self-protection; or

   (B) imminent physical or emotional harm to another because of threats, attempts, or other acts of the patient.

(5) *"Health care provider"* means an individual or facility licensed, certified, or otherwise authorized to administer health care or treatment, for profit or otherwise, in the ordinary course of business or professional practice and includes a physician or other health care provider, a residential care provider, or an inpatient mental health facility as defined by §571.003, Health and Safety Code.

(6) *"Incapacitated"* means that, in the opinion of the court in a guardianship proceeding under Chapter XIII, Texas Probate Code, or in a medication hearing under §574.106, Health and Safety Code, a person lacks the ability to understand the nature and consequences of a proposed treatment, including the benefits, risks, and alternatives to the proposed treatment, and lacks the ability to make mental health treatment decisions because of impairment.

(7) *"Mental health treatment"* means electroconvulsive or other convulsive treatment, treatment of mental illness with psychoactive medication as defined by §574.101, Health and Safety Code, or emergency mental health treatment.

(8) *"Principal"* means a person who has executed a declaration for mental health treatment.

---

4   (Civil Practice and Remedies Code; Title 6. Miscellaneous Provisions; Chapter 137. Declaration for Mental Health Treatment)

§137.002. ELIGIBLE PERSONS; PERIOD OF VALIDITY

Persons who may execute declaration for mental health treatment:

(a) An adult who is not incapacitated may execute a declaration for mental health treatment. The preferences or instructions may include consent to or refusal of mental health treatment.

(b) A declaration for mental health treatment is effective on execution as provided by this chapter. Except as provided by Subsection (c), a declaration for mental health treatment expires on the third anniversary of the date of its execution or when revoked by the principal, whichever is earlier.

(c) If the declaration for mental health treatment is in effect and the principal is incapacitated on the third anniversary of the date of its execution, the declaration remains in effect until the principal is no longer incapacitated.

§137.003. EXECUTION AND WITNESSES

(a) A declaration for mental health treatment must be signed by the principal in the presence of two or more subscribing witnesses.

(b) A witness may not, at the time of execution, be:

(1) the principal's health or residential care provider or an employee of that provider;

(2) the operator of a community health care facility providing care to the principal or an employee of an operator of the facility;

(3) a person related to the principal by blood, marriage, or adoption;

(4) a person entitled to any part of the estate of the principal on the death of the principal under a will, trust, or deed in existence or who would be entitled to any part of the estate by operation of law if the principal died intestate; or

(5) a person who has a claim against the estate of the principal.

(c) For a witness's signature to be effective, the witness must sign a statement affirming that, at the time the declaration for mental health treatment was signed, the principal:

(1) appeared to be of sound mind to make a mental health treatment decision;

(2) has stated in the witness's presence that the principal was aware of the nature of the declaration for mental health treatment and that the principal was signing the document voluntarily and free from any duress; and

(3) requested that the witness serve as a witness to the principal's execution of the document.

§137.004. HEALTH CARE PROVIDER

Health care provider is to act in accordance with declaration for mental health treatment.

A physician or other health care provider shall act in accordance with the declaration for mental health treatment when the principal has been found to be incapacitated. A physician or other provider shall continue to seek and act in accordance with the principal's informed consent to all mental health treatment decisions if the principal is capable of providing informed consent.

§137.005. LIMITATION ON LIABILITY

(a) An attending physician, health or residential care provider, or person acting for or under an attending physician's or health or residential care provider's control is not subject to criminal or civil liability and has not engaged in professional misconduct for an act or omission if the act or omission is done in good faith under the terms of a declaration for mental health treatment.

(b) An attending physician, health or residential care provider, or person acting for or under an attending physician's or health or residential care provider's control does not engage in professional misconduct for:

(1) failure to act in accordance with a declaration for mental health treatment if the physician, provider, or other person:

(A) was not provided with a copy of the declaration; and

(B) had no knowledge of the declaration after a good faith attempt to learn of the existence of a declaration; or

(2) acting in accordance with a directive for mental health treatment after the directive has expired or has been revoked if the physician, provider, or other person does not have knowledge of the expiration or revocation.

§137.006. DISCRIMINATION IN RELATION TO EXECUTION OF DECLARATION FOR MENTAL HEALTH TREATMENT

A health or residential care provider, health care service plan, insurer issuing disability insurance, self-insured employee benefit plan, or nonprofit hospital service plan may not:

(1) charge a person a different rate solely because the person has executed a declaration for mental health treatment;

(2) require a person to execute a declaration for mental health treatment before:

(A) admitting the person to a hospital, nursing home, or residential care home;

(B) insuring the person; or

(C) allowing the person to receive health or residential care;

(3) refuse health or residential care to a person solely because the person has executed a declaration for mental health treatment; or

(4) discharge the person solely because the person has or has not executed a declaration for mental health treatment.

§137.007. USE AND EFFECT OF DECLARATION FOR MENTAL HEALTH TREATMENT

(a) On being presented with a declaration for mental health treatment, a physician or other health care provider shall make the declaration a part of the principal's medical record. When acting in accordance with a declaration for mental health treatment, a physician or other health care provider shall comply with the declaration to the fullest extent possible.

(b) If a physician or other provider is unwilling at any time to comply with a declaration for mental health treatment, the physician or provider may withdraw from providing treatment consistent with the exercise of independent medical judgment and must promptly:

(1) make a reasonable effort to transfer care for the principal to a physician or provider who is willing to comply with the declaration;

(2) notify the principal, or principal's guardian, if appropriate, of the decision to withdraw; and

(3) record in the principal's medical record the notification and, if applicable, the name of the physician or provider to whom the principal is transferred.

§137.008. DISREGARD OF DECLARATION FOR MENTAL HEALTH TREATMENT

(a) A physician or other health care provider may subject the principal to mental health treatment in a manner contrary to the principal's wishes as expressed in a declaration for mental health treatment only:

(1) if the principal is under an order for temporary or extended mental health services under §574.034-574.035, Health and Safety Code, and treatment is authorized in compliance with §574.106, Health and Safety Code; or

(2) in case of emergency when the principal's instructions have not been effective in reducing the severity of the behavior that has caused the emergency.

(b) A declaration for mental health treatment does not limit any authority provided by Chapter 573 or 574, Health and Safety Code:

(1) to take a person into custody; or

(2) to admit or retain a person in a mental health treatment facility.

(c) This section does not apply to the use of electroconvulsive treatment or other convulsive treatment.

§137.009. CONFLICTING OR CONTRARY PROVISIONS

(a) Mental health treatment instructions contained in a declaration executed in accordance with this chapter supersede any contrary or conflicting instructions given by:

(1) a durable power of attorney under Chapter 135; or

(2) a guardian appointed under Chapter XIII, Texas Probate Code, after the execution of the declaration.

(b) Mental health treatment instructions contained in a declaration executed in accordance with this chapter shall be conclusive evidence of a declarant's preference in a medication hearing under §574.106, Health and Safety Code.

§137.010. REVOCATION

(a) A declaration for mental health treatment is revoked when a principal who is not incapacitated:

(1) notifies a licensed/certified health/residential care provider of the revocation;

(2) acts in a manner demonstrating specific intent to revoke the declaration; or

(3) executes a later declaration for mental health treatment.

(b) A principal's health/residential care provider who is informed of or provided with a revocation of a declaration for mental health treatment immediately shall:

(1) record the revocation in the principal's medical record; and

(2) give notice of the revocation to any other health or residential care provider the provider knows to be responsible for the principal's care.

§137.011. Form of Declaration for Mental Health Treatment

The declaration for mental health treatment must be in substantially the following form:

Declaration for Mental Health Treatment

I, _____, being an adult of sound mind, willfully and voluntarily make this declaration for mental health treatment to be followed if it is determined by a court that my ability to understand the nature and consequences of a proposed treatment, including the benefits, risks, and alternatives to the proposed treatment, is impaired to such an extent that I lack the capacity to make mental health treatment decisions. 'Mental health treatment' means electroconvulsive or other convulsive treatment, treatment of mental illness with psychoactive medication, and preferences regarding emergency mental health treatment.

(OPTIONAL PARAGRAPH) I understand that I may become incapable of giving or withholding informed consent for mental health treatment due to the symptoms of a diagnosed mental disorder. These symptoms may include::

Psychoactive Medications

If I become incapable of giving or withholding informed consent for mental health treatment, my wishes regarding psychoactive medications are as follows:

❏ I consent to the administration of the following medications:

❏ I do not consent to the administration of the following medications:

❏ I consent to the administration of a federal Food and Drug Administration approved medication that was only approved and in existence after my declaration and that is considered in the same class of psychoactive medications as stated below:

Conditions or limitations: _____

Convulsive Treatment

If I become incapable of giving or withholding informed consent for mental health treatment, my wishes regarding convulsive treatment are as follows:

❏ I consent to the administration of convulsive treatment.

❏ I do not consent to the administration of convulsive treatment.

Conditions or limitations: _____

PREFERENCES FOR EMERGENCY TREATMENT

In an emergency, I prefer the following treatment FIRST (circle one)

Restraint   Seclusion   Medication

In an emergency, I prefer the following treatment SECOND

Restraint   Seclusion   Medication

In an emergency, I prefer the following treatment THIRD

Restraint   Seclusion   Medication

I prefer a ☐ male ☐ female to administer restraint, seclusion, and/or medications.

Options for treatment prior to use of restraint, seclusion, and/or medications:

Conditions or limitations: _____

ADDITIONAL PREFERENCES OR INSTRUCTIONS

Conditions or limitations: _____

Signature of Principal/ Date: _____

STATEMENT OF WITNESSES

I declare under penalty of perjury that the principal's name has been represented to me by the principal, that the principal signed or acknowledged this declaration in my presence, that I believe the principal to be of sound mind, that the principal has affirmed that the principal is aware of the nature of the document and is signing it voluntarily and free from duress, that the principal requested that I serve as witness to the principal's execution of this document, and that I am not a provider of health or residential care to the principal, an employee of a provider of health or residential care to the principal, an operator of a community health care facility providing care to the principal, or an employee of an operator of a community health care facility providing care to the principal.

I declare that I am not related to the principal by blood, marriage, or adoption and that to the best of my knowledge I am not entitled to and do not have a claim against any part of the estate of the principal on the death of the principal under a will or by operation of law.

Signature: _____	Signature: _____
Print Name: _____	Print Name: _____
Date: _____	Date: _____
Address: _____	Address: _____
City/Zip: _____	City/Zip: _____

NOTICE TO PERSON MAKING A DECLARATION FOR MENTAL HEALTH TREATMENT

This is an important legal document. It creates a declaration for mental health treatment. Before signing this document, you should know these important facts:

This document allows you to make decisions in advance about mental health treatment and specifically three types of mental health treatment: psychoactive medication, convulsive therapy, and emergency mental health treatment. The instructions that you include in this declaration will be followed only if a court believes that you are incapacitated to make treatment decisions. Otherwise, you will be considered able to give or withhold consent for the treatments.

This document will continue in effect for a period of three years unless you become incapacitated to participate in mental health treatment decisions. If this occurs, the directive will continue in effect until you are no longer incapacitated.

You have the right to revoke this document in whole or in part at any time you have not been determined to be incapacitated. *You may not revoke this declaration when you are considered by a court to be incapacitated.* A revocation is effective when it is communicated to your attending physician or other health care provider.

If there is anything in this document that you do not understand, you should ask a lawyer to explain it to you. This declaration is not valid unless it is signed by two qualified witnesses who are personally known to you and who are present when you sign or acknowledge your signature.

SUBPOENAS IN CIVIL CASES—§176[5]

§176.1 FORM

Every subpoena must be issued in the name of "The State of Texas"[6] and must:

(a) state the style of the suit and its cause number;

(b) state the court in which the suit is pending;

(c) state the date on which the subpoena is issued;

(d) identify the person to whom the subpoena is directed;

(e) state the time, place, and nature of the action required by the person to whom the subpoena is directed, as provided in Rule 176.2;

(f) identify the party at whose instance the subpoena is issued, and the party's attorney of record, if any;

(g) state the text of Rule 176.8(a); and

(h) be signed by the person issuing the subpoena.

---

5   (Civil Practice & Remedies Code; Texas Rules of Civil Procedure; Part II - Rules of Practice in District and County Courts; Section 9. Evidence (and Discovery); A. Evidence; Rule 176. Subpoena)

6   Contact Information: Supreme Court Building • 201 West 14th, Room 104 • Austin, Texas 78701 • Telephone: (512) 463-1312 • Fax: (512)   463-1365

§176.2 REQUIRED ACTIONS

A subpoena must command the person to whom it is directed to do either or both of the following:

(a)　attend and give testimony at a deposition, hearing, or trial;

(b)　produce and permit inspection and copying of designated documents or tangible things in the possession, custody, or control of that person.

§176.3 LIMITATIONS

(a)　*Range.* A person may not be required by subpoena to appear or produce documents or other things in a county that is more than 150 miles from where the person resides or is served.

　　However, a person whose appearance or production at a deposition may be compelled by notice alone under Rules 199.3 or 200.2 may be required to appear and produce documents or other things at any location permitted under Rules 199.2(b)(2).

(b)　*Use for discovery.* A subpoena may not be used for discovery to an extent, in a manner, or at a time other than as provided by the rules of discovery.

§176.4 WHO MAY ISSUE

A subpoena may be issued by:

(a)　the clerk of the appropriate district, county, or justice court, who must provide the party requesting the subpoena with an original and a copy for each witness to be completed by the party;

(b)　an attorney authorized to practice in the State of Texas, as an officer of the court; or

(c)　an officer authorized to take depositions in this State, who must issue the subpoena immediately on a request accompanied by a notice to take a deposition under Rules 199 or 200, or a notice under Rule 205.3, and who may also serve the notice with the subpoena.

§176.5 SERVICE

(a)　*Manner of service.* A subpoena may be served at any place within the State of Texas by any sheriff or constable of the State of Texas, or any person who is not a party and is 18 years of age or older. A subpoena must be served by delivering a copy to the witness and tendering to that person any fees required by law. If the witness is a party and is represented by an attorney of record in the proceeding, the subpoena may be served on the witness's attorney of record.

(b)　*Proof of service.* Proof of service must be made by filing either:

　(1)　the witness's signed written memorandum attached to the subpoena showing that the witness accepted the subpoena; or

　(2)　a statement by the person who made the service stating the date, time, and manner of service, and the name of the person served.

§176.6 RESPONSE

(a)　*Compliance required.* Except as provided in this subdivision, a person served with a subpoena must comply with the command stated therein unless discharged by the court or by the party summoning such witness. A person commanded to appear and give testimony must remain at the place of deposition, hearing, or trial from day to day until discharged by the court or by the party summoning the witness.

(b) *Organizations.* If a subpoena commanding testimony is directed to a corporation, partnership, association, governmental agency, or other organization, and the matters on which examination is requested are described with reasonable particularity, the organization must designate one or more persons to testify on its behalf as to matters known or reasonably available to the organization.

(c) *Production of documents or tangible things.* A person commanded to produce documents or tangible things need not appear in person at the time and place of production unless the person is also commanded to attend and give testimony, either in the same subpoena or a separate one. A person must produce documents as they are kept in the usual course of business or must organize and label them to correspond with the categories in the demand.

A person may withhold material or information claimed to be privileged but must comply with Rule 193.3. A nonparty's production of a document authenticates the document for use against the nonparty to the same extent as a party's production of a document is authenticated for use against the party under Rule 193.7.

(d) *Objections.* A person commanded to produce and permit inspection or copying of designated documents and things may serve on the party requesting issuance of the subpoena - before the time specified for compliance - written objections to producing any or all of the designated materials. A person need not comply with the part of a subpoena to which objection is made as provided in this paragraph unless ordered to do so by the court. The party requesting the subpoena may move for such an order at any time after an objection is made.

(e) *Protective orders.* A person commanded to appear at a deposition, hearing, or trial, or to produce and permit inspection and copying of designated documents and things, and any other person affected by the subpoena, may move for a protective order under Rule 192.6(b)—before the time specified for compliance—either in the court in which the action is pending or in a district court in the county where the subpoena was served. The person must serve the motion on all parties in accordance with Rule 21a. A person need not comply with the part of a subpoena from which protection is sought under this paragraph unless ordered to do so by the court. The party requesting the subpoena may seek such an order at any time after the motion for protection is filed.

(f) *Trial subpoenas.* A person commanded to attend and give testimony, or to produce documents or things, at a hearing or trial, may object or move for protective order before the court at the time and place specified for compliance, rather than under paragraphs (d) and (e).

§176.7 PROTECTION OF PERSON FROM UNDUE BURDEN AND EXPENSE

A party causing a subpoena to issue must take reasonable steps to avoid imposing undue burden or expense on the person served. In ruling on objections or motions for protection, the court must provide a person served with a subpoena an adequate time for compliance, protection from disclosure of privileged material or information, and protection from undue burden or expense. The court may impose reasonable conditions on compliance with a subpoena, including compensating the witness for undue hardship.

§176.8 ENFORCEMENT OF SUBPOENA

(a) *Contempt.* Failure by any person without adequate excuse to obey a subpoena served upon that person may be deemed a contempt of the court from which the subpoena is issued or a district court in the county in which the subpoena is served, and may be punished by fine or confinement or both.

(b) *Proof of payment of fees required for fine or attachment.* A fine may not be imposed, nor a person served with a subpoena attached, for failure to comply with a subpoena without proof by affidavit of the party requesting the subpoena or the party's attorney of record that all fees due the witness by law were paid or tendered.

CODE OF CRIMINAL PROCEDURE

INCOMPETENCY TO STAND TRIAL—§46B[7]

SUBCHAPTER A.
GENERAL PROVISIONS

§46B.003. INCOMPETENCY; PRESUMPTIONS

(a) A person is incompetent to stand trial if the person does not have:

   (1) sufficient present ability to consult with the person's lawyer with a reasonable degree of rational understanding; or

   (2) a rational as well as factual understanding of the proceedings against the person.

(b) A defendant is presumed competent to stand trial and shall be found competent to stand trial unless proved incompetent by a preponderance of the evidence.

§46B.004. RAISING THE ISSUE OF INCOMPETENCY TO STAND TRIAL

(a) Either party may suggest by motion, or the trial court may suggest on its own motion, that the defendant may be incompetent to stand trial. A motion suggesting that the defendant may be incompetent to stand trial may be supported by affidavits setting out the facts on which the suggestion is made.

(b) If evidence suggesting the defendant may be incompetent to stand trial comes to the attention of the court, the court on its own motion shall suggest that the defendant may be incompetent to stand trial.

(c) On suggestion that the defendant may be incompetent to stand trial, the court shall determine by informal inquiry whether there is some evidence from any source that would support a finding that the defendant may be incompetent to stand trial.

(c-1) A suggestion of incompetency is the threshold requirement for an informal inquiry under Subsection (c) and may consist solely of a representation from any credible source that the defendant may be incompetent. A further evidentiary showing is not required to initiate the inquiry, and the court is not required to have a bona fide doubt about the competency of the defendant.   Evidence suggesting the need for an informal inquiry may be based on observations made in relation to one or more of the factors described by Article 46B.024 or on any other indication that the defendant is incompetent within the meaning of Article 46B.003.

(d) If the court determines there is evidence to support a finding of incompetency, the court, except as provided by Article 46B.005(d), shall stay all other proceedings in the case.

(e) At any time during the proceedings under this chapter after the issue of the defendant's incompetency to stand trial is first raised, the court on the motion of the attorney representing the state may dismiss all charges pending against the defendant, regardless of whether there is any evidence to support a finding

---

7   (Code of Criminal Procedure; Title 1 Code of Criminal Procedure; Chapter 46B. Incompetency to Stand Trial)

of the defendant's incompetency under Subsection (d) or whether the court has made a finding of incompetency under this chapter. If the court dismisses the charges against the defendant, the court may not continue the proceedings under this chapter, except that, if there is evidence to support a finding of the defendant's incompetency under Subsection (d), the court may proceed under Subchapter F. If the court does not elect to proceed under Subchapter F, the court shall discharge the defendant.

§46B.005. DETERMINING INCOMPETENCY TO STAND TRIAL

(a) If after an informal inquiry the court determines that evidence exists to support a finding of incompetency, the court shall order an examination under Subchapter B to determine whether the defendant is incompetent to stand trial.

(b) Except as provided by Subsection (c), the court shall hold a hearing under Subchapter C before determining whether the defendant is incompetent to stand trial.

(c) The court is not required to hold a hearing if:

  (1) neither party requests a jury trial on the issue of incompetency;

  (2) neither party opposes a finding of incompetency; and

  (3) the court does not, on its own motion, determine that a hearing is necessary to determine incompetency.

(d) If the issue of the defendant's incompetency to stand trial is raised after the trial begins, the court may determine the issue at any time before sentencing. If the determination is delayed until after the return of a verdict, the court shall make the determination as soon as reasonably possible after the return. If a verdict of not guilty is returned, the court may not determine the issue of incompetency.

§46B.007. ADMISSIBILITY OF STATEMENTS

A statement made by a defendant during an examination or hearing on the defendant's incompetency, the testimony of an expert based on that statement, and evidence obtained as a result of that statement may not be admitted in evidence against the defendant in any criminal proceeding, other than at:

  (1) a hearing on the defendant's incompetency; or

  (2) any proceeding at which the defendant first introduces into evidence a statement, testimony, or evidence described by this section.

SUBCHAPTER B.
EXAMINATION

§46B.021. APPOINTMENT OF EXPERTS

(a) On a suggestion that the defendant may be incompetent to stand trial, the court may appoint one or more disinterested experts to:

  (1) examine the defendant and report to the court on the competency or incompetency of the defendant; and

  (2) testify as to the issue of competency or incompetency of the defendant at any trial or hearing involving that issue.

(b) On a determination that evidence exists to support a finding of incompetency to stand trial, the court shall appoint one or more experts to perform the duties described by Subsection (a).

(c) An expert involved in the treatment of the defendant may not be appointed to examine the defendant under this article.

(d) The movant or other party as directed by the court shall provide to experts appointed under this article information relevant to a determination of the defendant's competency, including copies of the indictment or information, any supporting documents used to establish probable cause in the case, and previous mental health evaluation and treatment records.

(e) The court may appoint as experts under this chapter qualified psychiatrists or psychologists employed by the local mental health authority or local mental retardation authority. The local mental health authority or local mental retardation authority is entitled to compensation and reimbursement as provided by Article 46B.027.

(f) If a defendant wishes to be examined by an expert of the defendant's own choice, the court on timely request shall provide the expert with reasonable opportunity to examine the defendant.

§46B.022. EXPERTS: QUALIFICATIONS

(a) To qualify for appointment under this subchapter as an expert, a psychiatrist or psychologist must:

(1) as appropriate, be a physician licensed in this state or be a psychologist licensed in this state who has a doctoral degree in psychology; and

(2) have the following certification or training:

(A) as appropriate, certification by:

(i) the American Board of Psychiatry and Neurology with added or special qualifications in forensic psychiatry; or

(ii) the American Board of Professional Psychology in forensic psychology; or

(B) training consisting of:

(i) at least 24 hours of specialized forensic training relating to incompetency or insanity evaluations; and

(ii) at least eight hours of continuing education relating to forensic evaluations, completed in the 12 months preceding the appointment.

(b) In addition to meeting qualifications required by Subsection (a), to be appointed as an expert a psychiatrist or psychologist must have completed six hours of required continuing education in courses in forensic psychiatry or psychology, as appropriate, in either of the reporting periods in the 24 months preceding the appointment.

(c) A court may appoint as an expert a psychiatrist or psychologist who does not meet the requirements of Subsections (a) and (b) only if exigent circumstances require the court to base the appointment on professional training or experience of the expert that directly provides the expert with a specialized expertise to examine the defendant that would not ordinarily be possessed by a psychiatrist or psychologist who meets the requirements of Subsections (a) and (b).

§46B.024. FACTORS CONSIDERED IN EXAMINATION

During an examination under this subchapter and in any report based on that examination, an expert shall consider, in addition to other issues determined relevant by the expert, the following:

(1) the capacity of the defendant during criminal proceedings to:

   (A) rationally understand the charges against the defendant and the potential consequences of the pending criminal proceedings;

   (B) disclose to counsel pertinent facts, events, and states of mind;

   (C) engage in a reasoned choice of legal strategies and options;

   (D) understand the adversarial nature of criminal proceedings;

   (E) exhibit appropriate courtroom behavior; and

   (F) testify;

(2) as supported by current indications and the defendant's personal history, whether the defendant:

   (A) has a mental illness; or

   (B) is a person with mental retardation;

(3) whether the identified condition has lasted or is expected to last continuously for at least one year;

(4) the degree of impairment resulting from the mental illness or mental retardation, if existent, and the specific impact on the defendant's capacity to engage with counsel in a reasonable and rational manner; and

(5) if the defendant is taking psychoactive or other medication:

   (A) whether the medication is necessary to maintain the defendant's competency; and

   (B) the effect, if any, of the medication on the defendant's appearance, demeanor, or ability to participate in the proceedings.

§46B.025. EXPERT'S REPORT

(a) An expert's report to the court must state an opinion on a defendant's competency or incompetency to stand trial or explain why the expert is unable to state such an opinion and must also:

(1) identify and address specific issues referred to the expert for evaluation;

(2) document that the expert explained to the defendant the purpose of the evaluation, the persons to whom a report on the evaluation is provided, and the limits on rules of confidentiality applying to the relationship between the expert and the defendant;

(3) in specific terms, describe procedures, techniques, and tests used in the examination, the purpose of each procedure, technique, or test, and the conclusions reached;

(4) state the expert's clinical observations, findings, and opinions on each specific issue referred to the expert by the court, state the specific criteria supporting the expert's diagnosis, and state specifically any issues on which

the expert could not provide an opinion.

(a-1) The expert's opinion on the defendant's competency or incompetency may not be based solely on the defendant's refusal to communicate during the examination.

(b) If in the opinion of an expert appointed under Article 46B.021 the defendant is incompetent to proceed, the expert shall state in the report:

(1) the symptoms, exact nature, severity, and expected duration of the deficits resulting from the defendant's mental illness or mental retardation, if any, and the impact of the identified condition on the factors listed in Article 46B.024;

(2) an estimate of the period needed to restore the defendant's competency, including whether the defendant is likely to be restored to competency in the foreseeable future; and

(3) prospective treatment options, if any, appropriate for the defendant.

(c) An expert's report may not state the expert's opinion on the defendant's sanity at the time of the alleged offense, if in the opinion of the expert the defendant is incompetent to proceed.

§46B.026. REPORT DEADLINE

(a) Except as provided by Subsection (b), an expert examining the defendant shall provide the report on the defendant' s competency or incompetency to stand trial to the court, the attorney representing the state, and the attorney representing the defendant not later than the 30th day after the date on which the expert was ordered to examine the defendant and prepare the report.

(b) For good cause shown, the court may permit an expert to complete the examination and report and provide the report to the court and attorneys at a date later than the date required by Subsection (a).

INSANITY DEFENSE—§46C[8]

SUBCHAPTER C.
COURT-ORDERED EXAMINATION & REPORT

§46C.101. APPOINTMENT OF EXPERTS

(a) If notice of intention to raise the insanity defense is filed under Article 46C.051, the court may, on its own motion or motion by the defendant, the defendant's counsel, or the attorney representing the state, appoint one or more disinterested experts to:

(1) examine the defendant with regard to the insanity defense; and

(2) testify as to the issue of insanity at any trial or hearing involving that issue.

(b) The court shall advise an expert appointed under this article of the facts and circumstances of the offense with which the defendant is charged and the elements of the insanity defense.

---

8   (Code of Criminal Procedure; Title 1 Code of Criminal Procedure; Chapter 46C. Insanity Defensel)

§46C.102. EXPERT'S QUALIFICATIONS

(a) The court may appoint qualified psychiatrists or psychologists as experts under this chapter. To qualify for appointment under this subchapter as an expert, a psychiatrist or psychologist must:

(1) as appropriate, be a physician licensed in this state or be a psychologist licensed in this state who has a doctoral degree in psychology; and

(2) have the following certification or experience or training:

(A) as appropriate, certification by:

(i) the American Board of Psychiatry and Neurology with added or special qualifications in forensic psychiatry; or

(ii) the American Board of Professional Psychology in forensic psychology; or

(B) experience or training consisting of:

(i) at least 24 hours of specialized forensic training relating to incompetency or insanity evaluations;

(ii) at least five years of experience in performing criminal forensic evaluations for courts; and

(iii) eight or more hours of continuing education relating to forensic evaluations, completed in the 12 months preceding the appointment and documented with the court.

(b) In addition to meeting qualifications required by Subsection (a), to be appointed as an expert a psychiatrist or psychologist must have completed six hours of required continuing education in courses in forensic psychiatry or psychology, as appropriate, in the 24 months preceding the appointment.

(c) A court may appoint as an expert a psychiatrist or psychologist who does not meet the requirements of Subsections (a) and (b) only if exigent circumstances require the court to base the appointment on professional training or experience of the expert that directly provides the expert with a specialized expertise to examine the defendant that would not ordinarily be possessed by a psychiatrist or psychologist who meets the requirements of Subsections (a) and (b).

§46C.103. COMPETENCY TO STAND TRAIL: CONCURRENT APPOINTMENT

(a) An expert appointed under this subchapter to examine the defendant with regard to the insanity defense also may be appointed by the court to examine the defendant with regard to the defendant's competency to stand trial under Chapter 46B, if the expert files with the court separate written reports concerning the defendant's competency to stand trial and the insanity defense.

(b) Notwithstanding Subsection (a), an expert may not examine the defendant for purposes of determining the defendant's sanity and may not file a report regarding the defendant's sanity if in the opinion of the expert the defendant is incompetent to proceed.

§46C.104. ORDER COMPELLING DEFENDANT TO SUBMIT TO EXAMINATION

(a) For the purposes described by this chapter, the court may order any defendant to submit to examination, including a defendant who is free on bail. If the defendant fails or refuses to submit to examination, the court may order the defendant to custody for examination for a reasonable period not to exceed 21 days. Custody ordered by the court under this subsection may include custody at a facility operated by the department.

(b) If a defendant who has been ordered to a facility operated by the department for examination remains in the facility for a period that exceeds 21 days, the head of that facility shall cause the defendant to be immediately transported to the committing court and placed in the custody of the sheriff of the county in which the committing court is located. That county shall reimburse the facility for the mileage and per diem expenses of the personnel required to transport the defendant, calculated in accordance with the state travel rules in effect at that time.

(c) The court may not order a defendant to a facility operated by the department for examination without the consent of the head of that facility.

§46C.105. REPORTS SUBMITTED BY EXPERTS

(a) A written report of the examination shall be submitted to the court not later than the 30th day after the date of the order of examination. The court shall provide copies of the report to the defense counsel and the attorney representing the state.

(b) The report must include a description of the procedures used in the examination and the examiner's observations and findings pertaining to the insanity defense.

(c) The examiner shall submit a separate report stating the examiner's observations and findings concerning:

   (1) whether the defendant is presently a person with a mental illness and requires court-ordered mental health services under Subtitle C, Title 7, Health and Safety Code; or

   (2) whether the defendant is presently a person with mental retardation.

§46C.106. COMPENSATION OF EXPERTS

(a) The appointed experts shall be paid by the county in which the indictment was returned or information was filed.

(b) The county in which the indictment was returned or information was filed shall reimburse a facility operated by the department that accepts a defendant for examination under this subchapter for expenses incurred that are determined by the department to be reasonably necessary and incidental to the proper examination of the defendant.

§46C.107. EXAMINATION BY EXPERT OF DEFENDANT'S CHOICE

If a defendant wishes to be examined by an expert of the defendant's own choice, the court on timely request shall provide the examiner with reasonable opportunity to examine the defendant.

EDUCATION CODE

EDUCATORS AND SCHOOL DISTRICT EMPLOYEES AND VOLUNTEERS—§21[1]

§21.003. CERTIFICATION REQUIRED

(a) A person may not be employed as a teacher, teacher intern or teacher trainee, librarian, educational aide, administrator, educational diagnostician, or school counselor by a school district unless the person holds an appropriate certificate or permit issued as provided by Subchapter B.

(b) A person may not be employed by a school district as an audiologist, occupational therapist, physical therapist, physician, nurse, school psychologist, associate school psychologist, licensed professional counselor, marriage and family therapist, social worker, or speech language pathologist unless the person is licensed by the state agency that licenses that profession. A person may perform specific services within those professions for a school district only if the person holds the appropriate credential from the appropriate state agency.

STATEWIDE PLAN FOR SERVICES TO CHILDREN WITH DISABILITIES—§29[2]

§29.001. STATEWIDE PLAN

The agency shall develop, and modify as necessary, a statewide design, consistent with federal law, for the delivery of services to children with disabilities in this state that includes rules for the administration and funding of the special education program so that a free appropriate public education is available to all of those children between the ages of three and 21. The statewide design shall include the provision of services primarily through school districts and shared services arrangements, supplemented by regional education service centers. The agency shall also develop and implement a statewide plan with programmatic content that includes procedures designed to:

(1) ensure state compliance with requirements for supplemental federal funding for all state-administered programs involving the delivery of instructional or related services to students with disabilities;

(2) facilitate interagency coordination when other state agencies are involved in the delivery of instructional or related services to students with disabilities;

(3) periodically assess statewide personnel needs in all areas of specialization related to special education and pursue strategies to meet those needs through a consortium of representatives from regional education service centers, local education agencies, and institutions of higher education and through other available alternatives;

(4) ensure that regional education service centers throughout the state maintain a regional support function, which may include direct service delivery and a component designed to facilitate the placement of students with disabilities who cannot be appropriately served in their resident districts;

1   (Education Code; Title 2. Public Education; Subtitle D. Educators and School District Employees and Volunteers; Chapter 21. Educators)

2   (Education Code; Title 2. Public Education; Subtitle F. Curriculum, Programs, & Services; Chapter 29. Educational Programs; Subchapter A. Special Education Program)

(5) allow the agency to effectively monitor and periodically conduct site visits of all school districts to ensure that rules adopted under this section are applied in a consistent and uniform manner, to ensure that districts are complying with those rules, and to ensure that annual statistical reports filed by the districts and not otherwise available through the Public Education Information Management System under §42.006, are accurate and complete;

(6) ensure that appropriately trained personnel are involved in the diagnostic and evaluative procedures operating in all districts and that those personnel routinely serve on district admissions, review, and dismissal committees;

(7) ensure that an individualized education program for each student with a disability is properly developed, implemented, and maintained in the least restrictive environment that is appropriate to meet the student's educational needs;

(8) ensure that, when appropriate, each student with a disability is provided an opportunity to participate in career and technology and physical education classes, in addition to participating in regular or special classes; and

(9) ensure that each student with a disability is provided necessary related services;

(10) ensure that an individual assigned to act as a surrogate parent for a child with a disability, as provided by 20 U.S.C. §1415(b) is required to:

(A) complete a training program that complies with minimum standards established by agency rule;

(B) visit the child and the child's school;

(C) consult with persons involved in the child's education, including teachers, caseworkers, court-appointed volunteers, guardians ad litem, attorneys ad litem, foster parents, and caretakers;

(D) review the child's educational records;

(E) attend meetings of the child's admission, review, and dismissal committee;

(F) exercise independent judgment in pursuing the child's interests;

(G) and exercise the child's due process rights under applicable state and federal law, and

(11) ensure that each district develops a process to be used by a teacher who instructs a student with a disability in a regular classroom setting:

(A) to request a review of the student's individualized education program;

(B) that provides for a timely district response to the teacher's request; and

(C) that provides for notification to the student's parent or legal guardian of that response.

§29.002. DEFINITION

In this subchapter, "special services" means:

(1) special instruction, which may be provided by professional and

paraprofessional personnel in the regular classroom or in an instructional arrangement described by §42.151; or

(2) *related services*, which are developmental, corrective, supportive, or evaluative services, not instructional in nature, that may be required for the proper development and implementation of a student's individualized education program.

§29.003. ELIGIBILITY CRITERIA

(a) The agency shall develop specific eligibility criteria based on the general classifications established by this section with reference to contemporary diagnostic or evaluative terminologies and techniques. Eligible students with disabilities shall enjoy the right to a free appropriate public education, which may include instruction in the regular classroom, instruction through special teaching, or instruction through contracts approved under this subchapter. Instruction shall be supplemented by the provision of related services when appropriate.

(b) A student is eligible to participate in a school district's special education program if the student:

(1) is not more than 21 years of age and has a visual or auditory impairment that prevents the student from being adequately or safely educated in public school without the provision of special services; or

(2) is at least three but not more than 21 years of age and has one or more of the following disabilities that prevents the student from being adequately or safely educated in public school without the provision of special services:

(A) physical disability;   (E) autism;

(B) mental retardation;   (F) speech disability; or

(C) emotional disturbance;   (G) traumatic brain injury.

(D) learning disability;

§29.004. FULL INDIVIDUAL AND INITIAL EVALUATION

(a) A written report of a full individual and initial evaluation of a student for purposes of special education services shall be completed as follows, except as otherwise provided by this section:

(1) not later than the 45th school day following the date on which the school district, in accordance with 20 U.S.C. Section 1414(a), as amended, receives written consent for the evaluation, signed by the student's parent or legal guardian, except that if a student has been absent from school during that period on three or more days, that period must be extended by a number of school days equal to the number of school days during that period on which the student has been absent; or

(2) for students under five years of age by September 1 of the school year and not enrolled in public school and for students enrolled in a private or home school setting, not later than the 45th school day following the date on which the school district receives written consent for the evaluation, signed by a student's parent or legal guardian.

(a-1) If a school district receives written consent signed by a student's parent or legal guardian for a full individual and initial evaluation of a student at least 35 but less than 45 school days before the last instructional day of the school year, the evaluation must be completed and the written report of the evaluation must be provided to the parent or legal guardian not later than June 30 of that year. The student's admission, review, and dismissal committee shall meet not later than the 15th school day of the following school year to consider the evaluation. If a district receives written consent signed by a student's parent or legal guardian less than 35 school days before the last instructional day of the school year or if the district receives the written consent at least 35 but less than 45 school days before the last instructional day of the school year but the student is absent from school during that period on three or more days, Subsection (a)(1) applies to the date the written report of the full individual and initial evaluation is required.

(a-2) For purposes of this section, "school day" does not include a day that falls after the last instructional day of the spring school term and before the first instructional day of the subsequent fall school term. The commissioner by rule may determine days during which year-round schools are recessed that, consistent with this subsection, are not considered to be school days for purposes of this section.

(a-3) Subsection (a) does not impair any rights of an infant or toddler with a disability who is receiving early intervention services in accordance with 20 U.S.C. Section 1431.

(b)   The evaluation shall be conducted using procedures that are appropriate for the student's most proficient method of communication.

(c)   If a parent or legal guardian makes a written request to a school district's director of special education services or to a district administrative employee for a full individual and initial evaluation of a student, the district shall, not later than the 15th school day after the date the district receives the request:

   (1)   provide an opportunity for the parent or legal guardian to give written consent for the evaluation; or

   (2)   refuse to provide the evaluation and provide the parent or legal guardian with notice of procedural safeguards under 20 U.S.C. Section 1415(b).

§29.0041. INFORMATION & CONSENT FOR CERTAIN PSYCHOLOGICAL EXAMINATIONS OR TESTS

(a)   On request of a child's parent, before obtaining the parent's consent under 20 U.S.C. Section 1414 for the administration of any psychological examination or test to the child that is included as part of the evaluation of the child's need for special education, a school district shall provide to the child's parent:

   (1)   the name and type of the examination or test; and

   (2)   an explanation of how the examination or test will be used to develop an appropriate individualized education program for the child.

(b)   If the district determines that an additional examination or test is required for the evaluation of a child's need for special education after obtaining consent from the child's parent under Subsection (a), the district shall provide the information described by Subsections (a)(1) and (2) to the child's parent regarding the additional examination or test and shall obtain additional consent for the examination or test.

(c) The time required for the district to provide information and seek consent under Subsection (b) may not be counted toward the 60 calendar days for completion of an evaluation under Section 29.004. If a parent does not give consent under Subsection (b) within 20 calendar days after the date the district provided to the parent the information required by that subsection, the parent's consent is considered denied.

§29.005. INDIVIDUALIZED EDUCATION PROGRAM

(a) Before a child is enrolled in a special education program of a school district, the district shall establish a committee composed of the persons required under 20 U.S.C. Section 1401(11) to develop the child's individualized education program.

(b) The committee shall develop the individualized education program by agreement of the committee members or, if those persons cannot agree, by an alternate method provided by the agency. Majority vote may not be used to determine the individualized education program.

(c) If the individualized education program is not developed by agreement, the written statement of the program required under 20 U.S.C. Section 1401(11) must include the basis of the disagreement.

(d) If the child's parent is unable to speak English, the district shall:

   (1) provide the parent with a written or audiotaped copy of the child's individualized education program translated into Spanish if Spanish is the parent's native language; or

   (2) if the parent's native language is a language other than Spanish, make a good faith effort to provide the parent with a written or audiotaped copy of the child's individualized education program translated into the parent's native language.

(e) The commissioner by rule may require a school district to include in the individualized education program of a student with autism or another pervasive developmental disorder any information or requirement determined necessary to ensure the student receives a free appropriate public education as required under the Individuals with Disabilities Education Act (20 U.S.C. Section 1400 et seq.).

(f) The written statement of a student's individualized education program may be required to include only information included in the model form developed under Section 29.0051(a).

(g) The committee may determine that a behavior improvement plan or a behavioral intervention plan is appropriate for a student for whom the committee has developed an individualized education program. If the committee makes that determination, the behavior improvement plan or the behavioral intervention plan shall be included as part of the student's individualized education program and provided to each teacher with responsibility for educating the student.

§30.001. COORDINATION OF SERVICES TO CHILDREN WITH DISABILITIES

(a) In this section, *"children with disabilities"* means students eligible to participate in a school district's special education program under §29.003.

(b) The commissioner, with the approval of the State Board of Education, shall develop and implement a plan for the coordination of services to children with disabilities in each region served by a regional education service center. The plan must include procedures for:

(1) identifying existing public or private educational and related services for children with disabilities in each region;

(2) identifying and referring children with disabilities who cannot be appropriately served by the school district in which they reside to other appropriate programs;

(3) assisting school districts to individually or cooperatively develop programs to identify and provide appropriate services for children with disabilities;

(4) expanding and coordinating services provided by regional education service centers for children with disabilities; and

(5) providing for special services, including special seats, books, instructional media, and other supplemental supplies and services required for proper instruction.

(c) The commissioner may allocate appropriated funds to regional education service centers or may otherwise spend those funds, as necessary, to implement this section.

ALTERNATIVE SETTINGS FOR BEHAVIOR MANAGEMENT—§37[3]

§37.0021. USE OF CONFINEMENT, RESTRAINT, SECLUSION AND TIME-OUT

(a) It is the policy of this state to treat with dignity and respect all students, including students with disabilities who receive special education services under Subchapter A, Chapter 29. A student with a disability who receives special education services under Subchapter A, Chapter 29, may not be confined in a locked box, locked closet, or other specially designed locked space as either a discipline management practice or a behavior management technique.

(b) In this section:

(1) *"Restraint"* means the use of physical force or a mechanical device to significantly restrict the free movement of all/part of a student's body.

(2 *"Seclusion"* means a behavior management technique in which a student is confined in a locked box, locked closet, or locked room:

(A) that is designed solely to seclude a person; and

(B) that contains less than 50 square feet of space.

(3) *"Time-out"* means a behavior management technique in which, to provide a student with an opportunity to regain self-control, the student is separated from other students for a limited period in a setting:

(A) that is not locked; and

(B) from which the exit is not physically blocked by furniture, a closed door held shut from the outside, or another inanimate object.

(c) A school district employee or volunteer or an independent contractor of a district may not place a student in seclusion. This subsection does not apply to

---

3   (Education Code; Title 2. Public Education; Subtitle G. Safe Schools; Chapter 37. Discipline; Law and Order; Subchapter A. Alternative Settings for Behavior Management)

the use of seclusion in a court-ordered placement, other than a placement in an educational program of a school district, or in a placement or facility to which the following law, rules, or regulations apply:

(1) the Children's Health Act of 2000, Pub. L. No. 106-310, any subsequent amendments to that Act, any regulations adopted under that Act, or any subsequent amendments to those regulations;

(2) 40 T.A.C. Sections 720.1001-720.1013; or

(3) 25 T.A.C. Section 412.308(e).

(d) The commissioner by rule shall adopt procedures for the use of restraint and time-out by a school district employee or volunteer or an independent contractor of a district in the case of a student with a disability receiving special education services under Subchapter A, Chapter 29. A procedure adopted under this subsection must:

(1) be consistent with:

(A) professionally accepted practices and standards of student discipline and techniques for behavior management; and

(B) relevant health and safety standards; and

(2) identify any discipline management practice or behavior management technique that requires a district employee or volunteer or an independent contractor of a district to be trained before using that practice or technique.

(e) In the case of a conflict between a rule adopted under Subsection (d) and a rule adopted under Subchapter A, Chapter 29, the rule adopted under Subsection (d) controls.

(f) For purposes of this subsection, "weapon" includes any weapon described under Section 37.007(a)(1). This section does not prevent a student's locked, unattended confinement in an emergency situation while awaiting the arrival of law enforcement personnel if:

(1) the student possesses a weapon; and

(2) the confinement is necessary to prevent the student from causing bodily harm to the student or another person.

(g) This section and any rules or procedures adopted under this section do not apply to:

(1) a peace officer performing law enforcement duties , except as provided by Subsection (i);

(2) juvenile probation, detention, or corrections personnel; or

(3) an educational services provider with whom a student is placed by a judicial authority, unless the services are provided in an educational program of a school district.

(h) This section and any rules or procedures adopted under this section apply to a peace officer only if the peace officer:

(1) is employed or commissioned by a school district; or

(2) provides, as a school resource officer, a regular police presence on a school

district campus under a memorandum of understanding between the district and a local law enforcement agency.

(i) A school district shall report electronically to the agency, in accordance with standards provided by commissioner rule, information relating to the use of restraint by a peace officer performing law enforcement duties on school property or during a school-sponsored or school-related activity. A report submitted under this subsection must be consistent with the requirements adopted by commissioner rule for reporting the use of restraint involving students with disabilities.

HEALTH AND SAFETY—§38[4]

Addressing the role of social workers in school district programs for preventing, addressing, and creating awareness about sexual abuse; reporting child abuse and neglect and training regarding recognizing and reporting child abuse and neglect at schools, institutions of higher education, and other entities.

§38.004. CHILD ABUSE REPORTING AND PROGRAMS

(a) The agency shall develop a policy governing the reports of child abuse or neglect required by Chapter 261, Family Code, of school districts, open-enrollment charter schools, and their employees. The policy must provide for cooperation with law enforcement child abuse investigations without the consent of the child's parents if necessary, including investigations by the Department of Family and Protective Services. The policy must require each school district and open-enrollment charter school employee to report child abuse or neglect in the manner required by Chapter 261, Family Code. Each school district and open-enrollment charter school shall adopt the policy.

(a-1) The agency shall:

(1) maintain on the agency Internet website a list of links to websites that provide information regarding the prevention of child abuse; and

(2) develop and periodically update a training program on prevention of child abuse that a school district may use for staff development.

(b) Each school district shall provide child abuse antivictimization programs in elementary and secondary schools.

§38.0041. POLICIES ADDRESSING SEXUAL ABUSE AND OTHER MALTREATMENT OF CHILDREN

(a) Each school district and open-enrollment charter school shall adopt and implement a policy addressing sexual abuse and other maltreatment of children, to be included in the district improvement plan under Section 11.252 and any informational handbook provided to students and parents.

(b) A policy required by this section must address:

(1) methods for increasing staff, student, and parent awareness of issues regarding sexual abuse and other maltreatment of children, including prevention techniques and knowledge of likely warning signs indicating that a child may be a victim of sexual abuse or other maltreatment, using resources developed by the agency under Section 38.004;

---

4 (Education Code; Title 2. Public Education; Subtitle G. Safe Schools; Chapter 38. Health And Safety; Subchapter A. General Provisions)

    (2) actions that a child who is a victim of sexual abuse or other maltreatment should take to obtain assistance and intervention; and

    (3) available counseling options for students affected by sexual abuse or other maltreatment.

(c) The methods under Subsection (b)(1) for increasing awareness of issues regarding sexual abuse and other maltreatment of children must include training, as provided by this subsection, concerning prevention techniques for and recognition of sexual abuse and all other maltreatment of children. The training:

    (1) must be provided, as part of a new employee orientation, to all new school district and open-enrollment charter school employees and to existing district and open-enrollment charter school employees on a schedule adopted by the agency by rule until all district and open-enrollment charter school employees have taken the training; and

    (2) must include training concerning:

        (A) factors indicating a child is at risk for sexual abuse or other maltreatment;

        (B) likely warning signs indicating a child may be a victim of sexual abuse or other maltreatment;

        (C) internal procedures for seeking assistance for a child who is at risk for sexual abuse or other maltreatment, including referral to a school counselor, a social worker, or another mental health professional;

        (D) techniques for reducing a child's risk of sexual abuse or other maltreatment; and

        (E) community organizations that have relevant existing research-based programs that are able to provide training or other education for school district or open-enrollment charter school staff members, students, and parents.

(d) For any training under Subsection (c), each school district and open-enrollment charter school shall maintain records that include the name of each district or charter school staff member who participated in the training.

(e) If a school district or open-enrollment charter school determines that the district or charter school does not have sufficient resources to provide the training required under Subsection (c), the district or charter school shall work in conjunction with a community organization to provide the training at no cost to the district or charter school.

(f) The training under Subsection (c) may be included in staff development under Section 21.451.

(g) A school district or open-enrollment charter school employee may not be subject to any disciplinary proceeding, as defined by Section 22.0512(b), resulting from an action taken in compliance with this section. The requirements of this section are considered to involve an employee's judgment and discretion and are not considered ministerial acts for purposes of immunity from liability under Section 22.0511. Nothing in this section may be considered to limit the immunity from liability provided under Section 22.0511.

(h) For purposes of this section, "other maltreatment" has the meaning assigned by

Section 42.002, Human Resources Code.

§38.0042. POSTING CHILD ABUSE HOTLINE TELEPHONE NUMBER

(a) Each public school and open-enrollment charter school shall post in a clearly visible location in a public area of the school that is readily accessible to students a sign in English and in Spanish that contains the toll-free telephone number operated by the Department of Family and Protective Services to receive reports of child abuse or neglect.

(b) The commissioner may adopt rules relating to the size and location of the sign required by Subsection (a).

§38.010. OUTSIDE COUNSELORS

(a) A school district or school district employee may not refer a student to an outside counselor for care or treatment of a chemical dependency or an emotional or psychological condition unless the district:

   (1) obtains prior written consent for the referral from the student's parent;

   (2) discloses to the student's parent any relationship between the district and the outside counselor;

   (3) informs the student and the student's parent of any alternative public or private source of care or treatment reasonably available in the area;

   (4) requires the approval of appropriate school district personnel before a student may be referred for care or treatment or before a referral is suggested as being warranted; and

   (5) specifically prohibits any disclosure of a student record that violates state or federal law.

(b) In this section, "parent" includes a managing conservator or guardian.

§38.016. PSYCHOTROPIC DRUGS AND PSYCHIATRIC EVALUATIONS OR EXAMINATIONS

(a) In this section:

   (1) *"Parent"* includes a guardian or other person in parental relation.

   (2) *"Psychotropic drug"* means a substance that is:

      (A) used in the diagnosis, treatment, or prevention of a disease or as a component of a medication; and

      (B) intended to alter perception, emotion, or behavior.

(b) A school district employee may not:

   (1) recommend that a student use a psychotropic drug; or

   (2) suggest any particular diagnosis; or

   (3) use the refusal by a parent to consent to administration of a psychotropic drug to a student, or to a psychiatric evaluation or examination of a student as grounds, by itself, for prohibiting the child from attending a class or participating in a school-related activity.

(c) Subsection (b) does not:

   (1) prevent an appropriate referral under the child find system required under 20 U.S.C. Section 1412, as amended; or

(2) prohibit a school district employee who is a registered nurse, advanced nurse practitioner, physician, or certified or appropriately credentialed mental health professional from recommending that a child be evaluated by an appropriate medical practitioner; or

3) prohibit a school employee from discussing any aspect of a child's behavior or academic progress with the child's parent or another school district employee.

(d) The board of trustees of each school district shall adopt a policy to ensure implementation and enforcement of this section.

(e) An act in violation of Subsection (b) does not override the immunity from personal liability granted in §22.051 or other law or the district's sovereign and governmental immunity.

TRAINING PROGRAMS FOR EMPLOYEES REGARDING SEXUAL ABUSE— §51[5]

Addressing the role of social workers in training regarding recognizing and reporting child abuse and neglect at schools, institutions of higher education, and other entities.

§51.976. TRAINING AND EXAMINATION PROGRAM FOR EMPLOYEES OF CAMPUS PROGRAMS FOR MINORS ON WARNING SIGNS OF SEXUAL ABUSE AND CHILD MOLESTATION

(b) A program operator (i.e., a person who owns, operates, or supervises a campus program for minors, regardless of profit) may not employ an individual in a position involving contact with campers at a campus program for minors unless:

(1) the individual submits to the program operator or the campus program for minors has on file documentation that verifies the individual within the preceding two years successfully completed the training and examination program on sexual abuse and child molestation; or

(2) the individual successfully completes the campus program for minors training and examination program on sexual abuse and child molestation, which must be approved by the department, during the individual's first five days of employment by the campus program for minors and the campus program issues and files documentation verifying successful completion.

(c) Subsection (b) does not apply to an individual who is a student enrolled at the institution of higher education or private or independent institution of higher education that operates the campus program for minors or at which the campus program is conducted and whose contact with campers is limited to a single class of short duration.

(d) A program operator must:

(1) submit to the department:

(A) on the form and within the time prescribed by the department

---

5 (Education Code; Title 3. Higher Education; Subtitle A. Higher Education In General; Chapter 51. Provisions Generally Applicable To Higher Education; Subchapter Z. Miscellaneous Provisions)

verification that each employee of the campus program for minors has complied with the requirements of this section; and

 (B) the fee assessed by the department under Subsection (g); and

 (2) retain in the operator's records a copy of the documentation required or issued under Subsection (b) for each employee until the second anniversary of the examination date.

(e) A person applying for or holding an employee position involving contact with campers at a campus program for minors must successfully complete the training and examination program on sexual abuse and child molestation during the applicable period prescribed by Subsection (b).

(f) The executive commissioner of the Health and Human Services Commission by rule shall establish criteria and guidelines for the training and examination program on sexual abuse and child molestation required by this section. The program must include training and an examination on the topics listed in Section 141.0095(e), Health and Safety Code. The department may approve training and examination programs on sexual abuse and child molestation offered by trainers under contract with campus programs for minors or by online training organizations or may approve programs offered in another format authorized by the department.

(g) The department may assess a fee in the amount necessary to cover the costs of administering this section to:

 (1) each person that applies for the department's approval of a training and examination program on sexual abuse and child molestation under this section; and

 (2) each program operator who files with the department the verification form required under Subsection (d)(1)(A).

(h) The department at least every five years shall review each training and examination program on sexual abuse and child molestation approved by the department under Subsection (f) to ensure the program continues to meet the criteria and guidelines established by rule under that subsection.

(i) The department may investigate a person the department suspects of violating this section or a rule adopted under this section. A person who violates this section is subject to the enforcement provisions of Section 141.015, Health and Safety Code, as if the person violated Chapter 141, Health and Safety Code, or a rule adopted under that chapter.

(j) The program operator and the institution that operates the campus program for minors or at which the campus program is conducted are immune from civil or criminal liability for any act or omission of an employee for which the employee is immune under Section 261.106, Family Code.

(k) A program operator shall consider the costs of compliance with this section in determining any charges or fees imposed and collected for participation in the campus program for minors.

§51.9761. CHILD ABUSE REPORTING POLICY AND TRAINING

(a) In this section, "other maltreatment" has the meaning assigned by Section 42.002, Human Resources Code.

(b) Each institution of higher education shall adopt a policy governing the reporting of child abuse and neglect as required by Chapter 261, Family Code, for the institution and its employees. The policy must require each employee of the institution to report child abuse and neglect in the manner required by Chapter 261, Family Code.

(c) Each institution of higher education shall provide training for employees who are professionals as defined by Section 261.101, Family Code, in prevention techniques for and the recognition of symptoms of sexual abuse and other maltreatment of children and the responsibility and procedure of reporting suspected occurrences of sexual abuse and other maltreatment. The training must include:

  (1) techniques for reducing a child's risk of sexual abuse or other maltreatment;

  (2) factors indicating a child is at risk for sexual abuse or other maltreatment;

  (3) the warning signs and symptoms associated with sexual abuse or other maltreatment and recognition of those signs and symptoms; and

  (4) the requirements and procedures for reporting suspected sexual abuse or other maltreatment as provided by Chapter 261, Family Code.

FAMILY CODE

COURT ORDERED COUNSELING IN DIVORCE—§6[6]

§6.505. COUNSELING

(a) While a divorce suit is pending, the court may direct the parties to counsel with a person named by the court.

(b) The person named by the court to counsel the parties shall submit a written report to the court and to the parties before the final hearing. In the report, the counselor shall give only an opinion as to whether there exists a reasonable expectation of reconciliation of the parties and, if so, whether further counseling would be beneficial. The sole purpose of the report is to aid the court in determining whether the suit for divorce should be continued pending further counseling.

(c) A copy of the report shall be furnished to each party.

(d) If the court believes that there is a reasonable expectation of the parties' reconciliation, the court may by written order continue the proceedings and direct the parties to a person named by the court for further counseling for a period fixed by the court not to exceed 60 days, subject to any terms, conditions, and limitations the court considers desirable. In ordering counseling, the court shall consider the circumstances of the parties, including the needs of the parties' family and the availability of counseling services. At the expiration of the period specified by the court, the counselor to whom the parties were directed shall report to the court whether the parties have complied with the court's order. Thereafter, the court shall proceed as in a divorce suit generally.

(e) If the court orders counseling under this section and the parties to the marriage are the parents of a child under 18 years of age born or adopted during the marriage, the counseling shall include counseling on issues that confront children who are the subject of a suit affecting the parent-child relationship.

§6.705. TESTIMONY BY MARRIAGE COUNSELOR

(a) The report by the person named by the court to counsel the parties to a suit for divorce may not be admitted as evidence in the suit.

(b) The person named by the court to counsel the parties is not competent to testify in any suit involving the parties or their children.

(c) The files, records, and other work products of the counselor are privileged and confidential for all purposes and may not be admitted as evidence in any suit involving the parties or their children.

---

6   (Family Code; Title 1. The Marriage Relationship; Subtitle C. Dissolution of Marriage; Chapter 6. Suit for Dissolution of Marriage; Subchapter F. Temporary Orders)

CONSENT TO TREATMENT OF CHILD BY NON-PARENT OR CHILD—§32[7]

§32.001. CONSENT BY NON-PARENT

(a) The following persons may consent to medical, dental, psychological, and surgical treatment of a child when the person having the right to consent as otherwise provided by law cannot be contacted and that person has not given actual notice to the contrary:

   (1) a grandparent of the child;

   (2) an adult brother or sister of the child;

   (3) an adult aunt or uncle of the child;

   (4) an educational institution in which the child is enrolled that has received written authorization to consent from a person having the right to consent;

   (5) an adult who has actual care, control, and possession of the child and has written authorization to consent from a person having the right to consent;

   (6) a court having jurisdiction over a suit affecting the parent-child relationship of which the child is the subject;

   (7) an adult responsible for the actual care, control, and possession of a child under the jurisdiction of a juvenile court or committed by a juvenile court to the care of an agency of the state or county; or

   (8) a peace officer who has lawfully taken custody of a minor, if the peace officer has reasonable grounds to believe the minor is in need of immediate medical treatment.

(b) Except as otherwise provided by this subsection, the Texas Youth Commission may consent to the medical, dental, psychological, and surgical treatment of a child committed to the Texas Youth Commission under Title 3 when the person having the right to consent has been contacted and that person has not given actual notice to the contrary. Consent for medical, dental, psychological, and surgical treatment of a child for whom the Department of Family and Protective Services has been appointed managing conservator and who is committed to the Texas Youth Commission is governed by Sections 266.004, 266.009, and 266.010.

(c) This section does not apply to consent for the immunization of a child.

(d) A person who consents to the medical treatment of a minor under Subsection (a)(7) or (8) is immune from liability for damages resulting from the examination or treatment of the minor, except to the extent of the person's own acts of negligence. A physician or dentist licensed to practice in this state, or a hospital or medical facility at which a minor is treated is immune from liability for damages resulting from the examination or treatment of a minor under this section, except to the extent of the person's own acts of negligence.

§32.002. CONSENT FORM

(a) Consent to medical treatment under this subchapter must be in writing, signed by the person giving consent, and given to the doctor, hospital, or other medical facility that administers the treatment.

---

7 (Title 2. Child in Relation to the Family; Subtitle A. Limitations of Minority; Chapter 32. Consent to Treatment of Child by Non-Parent or Child; Subchapter A. Consent to Medical, Dental, Psychological, & Surgical Treatment)

(b)   The consent must include:

    (1)   the name of the child;

    (2)   the name of one or both parents, if known, and the name of any managing conservator or guardian of the child;

    (3)   the name of the person giving consent and the person's relationship to the child;

    (4)   a statement of the nature of the medical treatment to be given; and

    (5)   the date the treatment is to begin.

§32.003. CONSENT TO TREATMENT BY CHILD

(a)   A child may consent to medical, dental, psychological, and surgical treatment for the child by a licensed physician or dentist if the child:

    (1)   is on active duty with the armed services of the United States of America;

    (2)   is:

        (A)   16 years of age or older and resides separate and apart from the child's parents, managing conservator, or guardian, with or without the consent of the parents, managing conservator, or guardian and regardless of the duration of the residence; and

        (B)   managing the child's own financial affairs, regardless of the source of the income;

    (3)   consents to the diagnosis and treatment of an infectious, contagious, or communicable disease that is required by law or a rule to be reported by the licensed physician or dentist to a local health officer or the Texas Department of Health, including all diseases within the scope of §81.041, Health and Safety Code;

    (4)   is unmarried and pregnant and consents to hospital, medical, or surgical treatment, other than abortion, related to the pregnancy;

    (5)   consents to examination and treatment for drug or chemical addiction, drug or chemical dependency, or any other condition directly related to drug or chemical use; or

    (6)   is unmarried and has actual custody of the child's biological child and consents to medical, dental, psychological, or surgical treatment for the child.

(b)   Consent by a child to medical, dental, psychological, and surgical treatment under this section is not subject to disaffirmance because of minority.

(c)   Consent of the parents, managing conservator, or guardian of a child is not necessary in order to authorize hospital, medical, surgical, or dental care under this section.

(d)   A licensed physician, dentist, or psychologist may, with or without the consent of a child who is a patient, advise the parents, managing conservator, or guardian of the child of the treatment given to or needed by the child.

(e)   A physician, dentist, psychologist, hospital, or medical facility is not liable for the examination and treatment of a child under this section except for the provider's or the facility's own acts of negligence.

(f)   A physician, dentist, psychologist, hospital, or medical facility may rely on the written statement of the child containing the grounds on which the child has capacity to consent to the child's medical treatment.

§32.004. CONSENT TO COUNSELING

(a) A child may consent to counseling for:

    (1) suicide prevention;

    (2) chemical addiction or dependency; or

    (3) sexual, physical, or emotional abuse.

(b) A licensed or certified physician, psychologist, counselor, or social worker having reasonable grounds to believe that a child has been sexually, physically, or emotionally abused, is contemplating suicide, or is suffering from a chemical or drug addiction or dependency may:

    (1) counsel the child without the consent of the child's parents or, if applicable, managing conservator or guardian;

    (2) with or without the consent of the child who is a client, advise the child's parents or, if applicable, managing conservator or guardian of the treatment given to or needed by the child; and

    (3) rely on the written statement of the child containing the grounds on which the child has capacity to consent to the child's own treatment under this section.

(c) Unless consent is obtained as otherwise allowed by law, a physician, psychologist, counselor, or social worker may not counsel a child if consent is prohibited by a court order.

(d) A physician, psychologist, counselor, or social worker counseling a child under this section is not liable for damages except for damages resulting from the person's negligence or willful misconduct.

(e) A parent, or, if applicable, managing conservator or guardian, who has not consented to counseling treatment of the child is not obligated to compensate a physician, psychologist, counselor, or social worker for counseling services rendered under this section.

§32.005. EXAMINATION WITHOUT CONSENT OF ABUSE OR NEGLECT OF CHILD

(a) Except as provided by Subsection (c), a physician, dentist, or psychologist having reasonable grounds to believe that a child's physical or mental condition has been adversely affected by abuse or neglect may examine the child without the consent of the child, the child's parents, or other person authorized to consent to treatment under this subchapter.

(b) An examination under this section may include X-rays, blood tests, photographs, and penetration of tissue necessary to accomplish those tests.

(c) Unless consent is obtained as otherwise allowed by law, a physician, dentist, or psychologist may not examine a child:

    (1) 16 years of age or older who refuses to consent; or

    (2) for whom consent is prohibited by a court order.

(d) A physician, dentist, or psychologist examining a child under this section is not liable for damages except for damages resulting from the physician's or dentist's negligence.

§32.1011. CONSENT TO IMMUNIZATION BY CHILD

(a) Notwithstanding Section 32.003 or 32.101, a child may consent to the child's own immunization for a disease if:

    (1) the child:

        (A) is pregnant; or

        (B) is the parent of a child and has actual custody of that child; and

    (2) the Centers for Disease Control and Prevention recommend or authorize the initial dose of an immunization for that disease to be administered before seven years of age.

(b) Consent to immunization under this section must meet the requirements of Section 32.002(a).

(c) Consent by a child to immunization under this section is not subject to disaffirmance because of minority.

(d) A health care provider or facility may rely on the written statement of the child containing the grounds on which the child has capacity to consent to the child's immunization under this section.

(e) To the extent of any conflict between this section and Section 32.003, this section controls.

WAIVER OF JURISDICTION AND DISCRETIONARY TRANSFER—§54.02[8]

§54.02. WAIVER OF JURISDICTION AND DISCRETIONARY TRANSFER TO CRIMINAL COURT

(a) The juvenile court may waive its exclusive original jurisdiction and transfer a child to the appropriate district court or criminal district court for criminal proceedings if:

    (1) the child is alleged to have violated a penal law of the grade of felony;

    (2) the child was:

        (A) 14 years of age or older at the time he is alleged to have committed the offense, if the offense is a capital felony, an aggravated controlled substance felony, or a felony of the first degree, and no adjudication hearing has been conducted concerning that offense; or

        (B) 15 years of age or older at the time the child is alleged to have committed the offense, if the offense is a felony of the second or third degree or a state jail felony, and no adjudication hearing has been conducted concerning that offense; and

    (3) after a full investigation and a hearing, the juvenile court determines that there is probable cause to believe that the child before the court committed the offense alleged and that because of the seriousness of the offense alleged or the background of the child the welfare of the community requires criminal proceedings.

(b) The petition and notice requirements of Sections 53.04, 53.05, 53.06, and 53.07 of this code must be satisfied, and the summons must state that the hearing is

---

8 (Family Code; Title 3. Juvenile Justice; Chapter 54. Judicial Proceedings)

for the purpose of considering discretionary transfer to criminal court.

(c)   The juvenile court shall conduct a hearing without a jury to consider transfer of the child for criminal proceedings.

(d)   Prior to the hearing, the juvenile court shall order and obtain a complete diagnostic study, social evaluation, and full investigation of the child, his circumstances, and the circumstances of the alleged offense.

(e)   At the transfer hearing the court may consider written reports from probation officers, professional court employees, or professional consultants in addition to the testimony of witnesses. At least five days prior to the transfer hearing, the court shall provide the attorney for the child and the prosecuting attorney with access to all written matter to be considered by the court in making the transfer decision. The court may order counsel not to reveal items to the child or the child's parent, guardian, or guardian ad litem if such disclosure would materially harm the treatment and rehabilitation of the child or would substantially decrease the likelihood of receiving information from the same or similar sources in the future.

(f)   In making the determination required by Subsection (a) of this section, the court shall consider, among other matters:

(1)   whether the alleged offense was against person or property, with greater weight in favor of transfer given to offenses against the person;

(2)   the sophistication and maturity of the child;

(3)   the record and previous history of the child; and

(4)   the prospects of adequate protection of the public and the likelihood of the rehabilitation of the child by use of procedures, services, and facilities currently available to the juvenile court.

(g)   If the petition alleges multiple offenses that constitute more than one criminal transaction, the juvenile court shall either retain or transfer all offenses relating to a single transaction. Except as provided by Subsection (g-1), a child is not subject to criminal prosecution at any time for any offense arising out of a criminal transaction for which the juvenile court retains jurisdiction.

(g-1) A child may be subject to criminal prosecution for an offense committed under Chapter 19 or Section 49.08, Penal Code, if:

(1)   the offense arises out of a criminal transaction for which the juvenile court retained jurisdiction over other offenses relating to the criminal transaction; and

(2)   on or before the date the juvenile court retained jurisdiction, one or more of the elements of the offense under Chapter 19 or Section 49.08, Penal Code, had not occurred.

(h)   If the juvenile court waives jurisdiction, it shall state specifically in the order its reasons for waiver and certify its action, including the written order and findings of the court, and shall transfer the person to the appropriate court for criminal proceedings and cause the results of the diagnostic study of the person ordered under Subsection (d), including psychological information, to be transferred to the appropriate criminal prosecutor. On transfer of the person for criminal proceedings, the person shall be dealt with as an adult and in accordance with the Code of Criminal Procedure, except that if detention in a certified juvenile detention facility is authorized under Section 152.0015, Human Resources Code, the juvenile court may order the person to be detained in the facility pending trial or until the criminal court enters an order under Article 4.19, Code of Criminal Procedure. A transfer of custody made under this subsection is an arrest.

(h-1) If the juvenile court orders a person detained in a certified juvenile detention facility under Subsection (h), the juvenile court shall set or deny bond for the person as required by the Code of Criminal Procedure and other law applicable to the pretrial detention of adults accused of criminal offenses.

(i)   A waiver under this section is a waiver of jurisdiction over the child and the criminal court may not remand the child to the jurisdiction of the juvenile court.

(j)   The juvenile court may waive its exclusive original jurisdiction and transfer a person to the appropriate district court or criminal district court for criminal proceedings if:

(1)   the person is 18 years of age or older;

(2)   the person was:

(A)   10 years of age or older and under 17 years of age at the time the person is alleged to have committed a capital felony or an offense under Section 19.02, Penal Code;

(B)   14 years of age or older and under 17 years of age at the time the person is alleged to have committed an aggravated controlled substance felony or a felony of the first degree other than an offense under Section 19.02, Penal Code; or

(C)   15 years of age or older and under 17 years of age at the time the person is alleged to have committed a felony of the second or third degree or a state jail felony;

(3)   no adjudication concerning the alleged offense has been made or no adjudication hearing concerning the offense has been conducted;

(4)   the juvenile court finds from a preponderance of the evidence that:

(A)   for a reason beyond the control of the state it was not practicable to proceed in juvenile court before the 18th birthday of the person; or

(B)   after due diligence of the state it was not practicable to proceed in juvenile court before the 18th birthday of the person because:

(i)   the state did not have probable cause to proceed in juvenile court and new evidence has been found since the 18th birthday of the person;

(ii)   the person could not be found; or

(iii) a previous transfer order was reversed by an appellate court or set aside by a district court; and

(5)   the juvenile court determines that there is probable cause to believe that the child before the court committed the offense alleged.

(k)   The petition and notice requirements of Sections 53.04, 53.05, 53.06, and 53.07 of this code must be satisfied, and the summons must state that the hearing is for the purpose of considering waiver of jurisdiction under Subsection (j). The person's parent, custodian, guardian, or guardian ad litem is not considered a party to a proceeding under Subsection (j) and it is not necessary to provide the parent, custodian, guardian, or guardian ad litem with notice.

(l)   The juvenile court shall conduct a hearing without a jury to consider waiver of jurisdiction under Subsection (j). Except as otherwise provided by this subsection, a waiver of jurisdiction under Subsection (j) may be made without the necessity of conducting the diagnostic study or complying with the requirements of discretionary transfer proceedings under Subsection (d). If requested by the attorney for the person at least 10 days before the transfer hearing, the court shall order that the person be examined pursuant to Section 51.20(a) and that the results of the examination be provided to the attorney for the person and the attorney for the state at least five days before the transfer hearing.

(m) Notwithstanding any other provision of this section, the juvenile court shall waive its exclusive original jurisdiction and transfer a child to the appropriate district court or criminal court for criminal proceedings if:

   (1)   the child has previously been transferred to a district court or criminal district court for criminal proceedings under this section, unless:

      (A)   the child was not indicted in the matter transferred by the grand jury;

      (B)   the child was found not guilty in the matter transferred;

      (C)   the matter transferred was dismissed with prejudice; or

      (D)   the child was convicted in the matter transferred, the conviction was reversed on appeal, and the appeal is final; and

   (2)   the child is alleged to have violated a penal law of the grade of felony.

(n)   A mandatory transfer under Subsection (m) may be made without conducting the study required in discretionary transfer proceedings by Subsection (d). The requirements of Subsection (b) that the summons state that the purpose of the hearing is to consider discretionary transfer to criminal court does not apply to a transfer proceeding under Subsection (m). In a proceeding under Subsection (m), it is sufficient that the summons provide fair notice that the purpose of the hearing is to consider mandatory transfer to criminal court.

(o)   If a respondent is taken into custody for possible discretionary transfer proceedings under Subsection (j), the juvenile court shall hold a detention hearing in the same manner as provided by Section 54.01, except that the court shall order the respondent released unless it finds that the respondent:

   (1)   is likely to abscond or be removed from the jurisdiction of the court;

   (2)   may be dangerous to himself or herself or may threaten the safety of the public if released; or

   (3)   has previously been found to be a delinquent child or has previously been convicted of a penal offense punishable by a term of jail or prison and is likely to commit an offense if released.

(p)   If the juvenile court does not order a respondent released under Subsection (o), the court shall, pending the conclusion of the discretionary transfer hearing, order that the respondent be detained in:

   (1)   a certified juvenile detention facility as provided by Subsection (q); or

   (2) an appropriate county facility for the detention of adults accused of criminal offenses.

(q) The detention of a respondent in a certified juvenile detention facility must comply with the detention requirements under this title, except that, to the extent practicable, the person shall be kept separate from children detained in the same facility.

(r) If the juvenile court orders a respondent detained in a county facility under Subsection (p), the county sheriff shall take custody of the respondent under the juvenile court's order. The juvenile court shall set or deny bond for the respondent as required by the Code of Criminal Procedure and other law applicable to the pretrial detention of adults accused of criminal offenses.

(s) If a child is transferred to criminal court under this section, only the petition for discretionary transfer, the order of transfer, and the order of commitment, if any, are a part of the district clerk's public record.

FAMILY VIOLENCE—§71[9]

§71.0021. DATING VIOLENCE

(a) *"Dating violence"* means an act, other than a defensive measure to protect oneself, by an actor that:

   (1) is committed against a victim:

     (A) with whom the actor has or has had a dating relationship; or

     (B) because of the victim's marriage to or dating relationship with an individual with whom the actor is or has been in a dating relationship or marriage; and

   (2) is intended to result in physical harm, bodily injury, assault, or sexual assault or that is a threat that reasonably places the victim in fear of imminent physical harm, bodily injury, assault, or sexual assault.

(b) For purposes of this title, "dating relationship" means a relationship between individuals who have or have had a continuing relationship of a romantic or intimate nature. The existence of such a relationship shall be determined based on consideration of:

   (1) the length of the relationship;

   (2) the nature of the relationship; and

   (3) the frequency and type of interaction between the persons involved in the relationship.

(c) A casual acquaintanceship or ordinary fraternization in a business or social context does not constitute a "dating relationship" under Subsection (b).

§71.003. FAMILY

"Family" includes individuals related by consanguinity or affinity, as determined under Sections 573.022 and 573.024, Government Code, individuals who are former spouses of each other, individuals who are the biological parents of the same child, without regard to marriage, and a foster child and foster parent, without regard to whether those individuals reside together.

9 (Family Code; Title 4. Protective Orders and Family Violence; Subtitle A. General Provisions; Chapter 71. Definitions)

§71.004. FAMILY VIOLENCE

"Family violence" means:

(1) an act by a member of a family or household against another member of the family or household that is intended to result in physical harm, bodily injury, assault, or sexual assault or that is a threat that reasonably places the member in fear of imminent physical harm, bodily injury, assault, or sexual assault, but does not include defensive measures to protect oneself; or

(2) abuse, as that term is defined by §261.001(1)(C), (E), and (G) by a member of a family or household toward a child of the family or household.

PROTECTIVE ORDERS—§81[10]

§81.001. ENTITLEMENT TO PROTECTIVE ORDER

A court shall render a protective order as provided by §85.001(b) if the court finds that family violence has occurred and is likely to occur in the future.

§81.002. NO FEE FOR APPLICANT

An applicant for a protective order or an attorney representing an applicant may not be assessed a fee, cost, charge, or expense by a district or county clerk of the court or a sheriff, constable, or other public official or employee in connection with the filing, serving, or entering of a protective order or for any other service described by this subsection, including:

(1) a fee to dismiss, modify, or withdraw a protective order;

(2) a fee for certifying copies;

(3) a fee for comparing copies to originals;

(4) a court reporter fee;

(5) a judicial fund fee;

(6) a fee for any other service related to a protective order; or

(7) a fee to transfer a protective order.

§81.003. FEES AND COSTS PAID BY PARTY FOUND TO HAVE COMMITTED FAMILY VIOLENCE

(a) Except on a showing of good cause or of the indigence of a party found to have committed family violence, the court shall require in a protective order that the party against whom the order is rendered pay the $16 protective order fee, the standard fees charged by the clerk of the court in a general civil proceeding for the cost of serving the order, the costs of court, and all other fees, charges, or expenses incurred in connection with the protective order.

(b) The court may order a party against whom an agreed protective order is rendered under §85.005 to pay the fees required in Subsection (a).

---

10 (Family Code; Title 4. Protective Orders and Family Violence; Subtitle B. Protective Orders; Chapter 81. General Provisions)

REPORTING FAMILY VIOLENCE—§91[11]

§91.001. DEFINITIONS

In this subtitle:

(1) *"Family violence"* has the meaning assigned by §71.004.

(2) *"Medical professional"* means a licensed doctor, nurse, physician assistant, or emergency medical technician.

§91.002. REPORTING BY WITNESSES ENCOURAGED

A person who witnesses family violence is encouraged to report the family violence to a local law enforcement agency.

§91.003. INFORMATION PROVIDED BY MEDICAL PROFESSIONALS

A medical professional who treats a person for injuries that the medical professional has reason to believe were caused by family violence shall:

(1) immediately provide the person with information regarding the nearest family violence shelter center;

(2) document in the person's medical file:

(A) the fact that the person has received the information provided under Subdivision (1); and

(B) the reasons for the medical professional's belief that the person's injuries were caused by family violence; and

(3) give the person a written notice in substantially the following form, completed with the required information, in both English and Spanish:

"IT IS A CRIME FOR ANY PERSON TO CAUSE YOU ANY PHYSICAL INJURY OR HARM EVEN IF THAT PERSON IS A MEMBER OR FORMER MEMBER OF YOUR FAMILY OR HOUSEHOLD."

"A VIOLATION OF CERTAIN PROVISIONS OF COURT-ORDERED PROTECTION MAY BE A FELONY."

"CALL THE FOLLOWING VIOLENCE SHELTERS OR SOCIAL ORGANIZATIONS IF YOU NEED PROTECTION: _____."

---

11 (Family Code; Title 4. Protective Orders and Family Violence; Subtitle C. Reporting Family Violence; Chapter 91. Reporting Family Violence)

"NOTICE TO ADULT VICTIMS OF FAMILY VIOLENCE"

"You may report family violence to a law enforcement officer by calling the following telephone numbers: _____.

"If you, your child, or any other household resident has been injured or if you feel you are going to be in danger after a law enforcement officer investigating family violence leaves your residence or at a later time, you have the right to:

"Ask the local prosecutor to file a criminal complaint against the person committing family violence; and

"Apply to a court for an order to protect you. You may want to consult with a legal aid office, a prosecuting attorney, or a private attorney. A court can enter an order that:

"(1) prohibits the abuser from committing further acts of violence;

"(2) prohibits the abuser from threatening, harassing, or contacting you at home;

"(3) directs the abuser to leave your household; and

"(4) establishes temporary custody of the children or any property.

SPECIAL APPOINTMENTS AND SOCIAL STUDIES—§107[12]

SUBCHAPTER D. SOCIAL STUDY

§ 107.0501. DEFINITIONS. IN THIS SUBCHAPTER:

(1) "Social study" means an evaluative process through which information and recommendations regarding adoption of a child, conservatorship of a child, or possession of or access to a child may be made to a court, the parties, and the parties' attorneys. The term does not include services provided in accordance with the Interstate Compact on the Placement of Children adopted under Subchapter B, Chapter 162, or an evaluation conducted in accordance with §262.114 by an employee of or contractor with the Department of Family and Protective Services.

(2) "Social study evaluator" means an individual who conducts a social study under this subchapter.

§107.051. ORDER FOR "SOCIAL STUDY"

(a) The court may order the preparation of a social study into the circumstances and condition of:

(1) a child who is the subject of a suit or a party to a suit; and

(2) the home of any person requesting conservatorship of, possession of, or access to a child.

---

12 (Family Code; Title 5. The Parent-Child Relationship and the Suit Affecting the Parent-Child Relationship; Subtitle A. General Provisions; Chapter 107. Special Appointments & Social Studies; Subchapter D. Social Study)

(b) The social study may be made by a private entity, a person appointed by the court, a domestic relations office, or a state agency, including the Department of Family and Protective Services if the department is a party to the suit.

(c) In a suit in which adoption is requested or conservatorship of, possession of, or access to a child is an issue and in which a social study has been ordered and the Department of Family and Protective Services is not a party, the court shall appoint a private agency, another person, or a domestic relations office to conduct the social study.

(d) Except as provided by §107.0511(b), each individual who conducts a social study must be qualified under §107.0511.

§ 107.0511. SOCIAL STUDY EVALUATOR: MINIMUM QUALIFICATIONS

(a) In this section:

   (1) *"Full-time experience"* means a period during which an individual works at least 30 hours per week.

   (2) *"Human services field of study"* means a field of study designed to prepare an individual in the disciplined application of counseling, family therapy, psychology, or social work values, principles, and methods.

(b) The minimum qualifications prescribed by this section do not apply to an individual conducting a social study:

   (1) in connection with a suit pending before a court located in a county with a population of less than 500,000;

   (2) in connection with an adoption governed by rules adopted under §107.0519(a);

   (3) as an employee or other authorized representative of a licensed child-placing agency; or

   (4) as an employee or other authorized representative of the Department of Family and Protective Services.

(c) The executive commissioner of the Health and Human Services Commission shall adopt rules prescribing the minimum qualifications that an individual described by Subsection (b)(3) or (4) must possess in order to conduct a social study under this subchapter.

(d) To be qualified to conduct a social study under this chapter, an individual must:

   (1) have a bachelor's degree from an accredited college or university in a human services field of study and a license to practice in this state as a social worker, professional counselor, marriage and family therapist, or psychologist and:

      (A) have two years of full-time experience or equivalent part-time experience under professional supervision during which the individual performed functions involving the evaluation of physical, intellectual, social, and psychological functioning and needs and the potential of the social and physical environment, both present and prospective, to meet those needs; and

      (B) have participated in the performance of at least 10 court-ordered social studies under the supervision of an individual qualified under this section;

(2) meet the requirements of Subdivision (1)(A) and be practicing under the direct supervision of an individual qualified under this section in order to complete at least 10 court-ordered social studies under supervision; or

(3) be employed by a domestic relations office, provided that the individual conducts social studies relating only to families ordered by a court to participate in social studies conducted by the office.

(e) If an individual meeting the requirements of this section is not available in the county served by the court, the court may authorize an individual determined by the court to be otherwise qualified to conduct the social study.

(f) In addition to the qualifications prescribed by this section, an individual must complete at least eight hours of family violence dynamics training provided by a family violence service provider to be qualified to conduct a social study under this subchapter.

(g) Provides that the minimum qualifications prescribed by this section do not apply to an individual who, before September 1, 2007:

(1) lived in a county that has a population of 500,000 or more and is adjacent to two or more counties each of which has a population of 50,000 or more;

(2) received a four-year degree from an accredited institution of higher education;

(3) worked as a child protective services investigator for the Department of Family and Protective Services (DFPS) for at least four years;

(4) worked as a community supervision and corrections department officer; and

(5) conducted at least 100 social studies in the previous five years.

(h) Requires a person described by Subsection (g) who performs a social study to:

(1) complete at least eight hours of family violence dynamics training provided by a family violence service provider; and

(2) participate annually in at least 15 hours of continuing education for child custody evaluators that meets the Model Standards of Practice for Child Custody Evaluation adopted by the Association of Family and Conciliation Courts as those standards existed May 1, 2009, or a later version of those standards if adopted by rule of the executive commissioner of the Health and Human Services Commission.

(i) Provides that Subsections (g), (h) and this subsection expire Sept. 1, 2017.

§107.0512. SOCIAL STUDY EVALUATOR: CONFLICTS OF INTEREST AND BIAS

(a) A social study evaluator who has a conflict of interest with any party in a disputed suit or who may be biased on the basis of previous knowledge, other than knowledge obtained in a court-ordered evaluation, shall:

(1) decline to conduct a social study for the suit; or

(2) disclose any issue or concern to the court before accepting the appointment or assignment.

(b) A social study evaluator who has previously conducted a social study for a suit may conduct all subsequent evaluations in the suit unless the court finds that the evaluator is biased.

(c) This section does not prohibit a court from appointing an employee of the Department of Family and Protective Services to conduct a social study in a suit in which adoption is requested or possession of or access to a child is an issue and in which the department is a party or has an interest.

§107.0513. GENERAL PROVISIONS APPLICABLE TO CONDUCT OF SOCIAL STUDY AND PREPARATION OF REPORT

(a) Unless otherwise directed by a court or prescribed by a provision of this title, a social study evaluator's actions in conducting a social study shall be in conformance with the professional standard of care applicable to the evaluator's licensure and any administrative rules, ethical standards, or guidelines adopted by the state agency that licenses the evaluator.

(b) In addition to the requirements prescribed by this subchapter, a court may impose requirements or adopt local rules applicable to a social study or a social study evaluator.

(c) A social study evaluator shall follow evidence-based practice methods and make use of current best evidence in making assessments and recommendations.

(d) A social study evaluator shall disclose to each attorney of record any communication regarding a substantive issue between the evaluator and an attorney of record representing a party in a disputed suit. This subsection does not apply to a communication between a social study evaluator and an attorney ad litem or amicus attorney.

(e) To the extent possible, a social study evaluator shall verify each statement of fact pertinent to a social study and shall note the sources of verification and information in the report.

(f) A social study evaluator shall state the basis for the evaluator's conclusions or recommendations in the report. A social study evaluator who has evaluated only one side of a disputed case shall refrain from making a recommendation regarding conservatorship of a child or possession of or access to a child, but may state whether the party evaluated appears to be suitable for conservatorship.

(g) Each social study subject to this subchapter must be conducted in compliance with this subchapter, regardless of whether the study is conducted:

   (1) by a single social study evaluator or multiple evaluators working separately or together; or

   (2) within a county served by the court with continuing jurisdiction or at a geographically distant location.

(h) A social study report must include the name, license number, and basis for qualification under §107.0511 of each social study evaluator who conducted any portion of the social study.

§107.0514. ELEMENTS OF "SOCIAL STUDY"

(a) The basic elements of a social study under this subchapter consist of:

   (1) a personal interview of each party to the suit;

    (2)   an interview, conducted in a developmentally appropriate manner, of each child at issue in the suit who is at least four years of age;

    (3)   observation of each child at issue in the suit, regardless of the age of the child;

    (4)   the obtaining of information from relevant collateral sources;

    (5)   evaluation of the home environment of each party seeking conservatorship of a child at issue in the suit or possession of or access to the child, unless the condition of the home environment is identified as not being in dispute in the court order requiring the social study;

    (6)   for each individual residing in a residence subject to the social study, consideration of any criminal history information and any contact with the Department of Family and Protective Services or a law enforcement agency regarding abuse or neglect; and

    (7)   assessment of the relationship between each child at issue in the suit and each party seeking possession of or access to the child.

(b)   The additional elements of a social study under this subchapter consist of:

    (1)   balanced interviews and observation of each child at issue in the suit so that a child who is interviewed or observed while in the care of one party to the suit is also interviewed or observed while in the care of each other party to the suit;

    (2)   an interview of each individual residing in a residence subject to the social study; and

    (3)   evaluation of the home environment of each party seeking conservatorship of a child at issue in the suit or possession of or access to the child, regardless of whether the home environment is in dispute.

(c)   A social study evaluator may not offer an opinion regarding conservatorship of a child at issue in a suit or possession of or access to the child unless each basic element of a social study under Subsection (a) has been completed. A social study evaluator shall identify in the report any additional element of a social study under Subsection (b) that was not completed and shall explain the reasons that the element was not completed.

§107.05145. SOCIAL STUDY EVALUATOR ACCESS TO INVESTIGATIVE RECORDS OF DEPARTMENT OF FAMILY AND PROTECTIVE SERVICES; OFFENSE

(a)   A social study evaluator is entitled to obtain from the Department of Family and Protective Services a complete, unredacted copy of any investigative record regarding abuse or neglect that relates to any person residing in the residence subject to the social study.

(b)   Except as provided by this section, records obtained by a social study evaluator from the Department of Family and Protective Services under this section are confidential and not subject to disclosure under Chapter 552, Government Code, or to disclosure in response to a subpoena or a discovery request.

(c)   A social study evaluator may disclose information obtained under Subsection (a) in the social study report only to the extent the evaluator determines that the information is relevant to the social study or a recommendation made under this subchapter.

(d)   A person commits an offense if the person discloses confidential information obtained from the Department of Family and Protective Services in violation of this section. An offense under this subsection is a Class A misdemeanor.

§107.0515. REPORTS OF CERTAIN PLACEMENTS FOR ADOPTION

A social study evaluator shall report to the Department of Family and Protective Services any adoptive placement that appears to have been made by someone other than a licensed child-placing agency or the child's parents or managing conservator.

§107.0519. PRE-ADOPTIVE SOCIAL STUDY

(a)   This section does not apply to a study prepared by a licensed child-placing agency or the Department of Family and Protective Services. The procedures required in relation to a study prepared by a licensed child-placing agency or the Department of Family and Protective Services are governed by rules adopted by the executive commissioner of the Health and Human Services Commission, including rules adopted under Chapter 42, Human Resources Code.

(b)   A pre-adoptive social study shall be conducted as provided by this section to evaluate each party in a proceeding described by Subsection (c) who requests termination of the parent-child relationship or an adoption.

(c)   The social study under this section shall be filed in any suit for:

(1)   termination of the parent-child relationship in which a person other than a parent may be appointed managing conservator of a child; or

(2)   an adoption.

(d)   The social study under this section must be filed with the court before the court may sign the final order for termination of the parent-child relationship.

(e)   The costs of a social study in a suit for adoption under this section shall be paid by the prospective adoptive parent.

(f)   Unless otherwise agreed to by the court, the social study under this section must comply with the minimum requirements for the study under rules adopted by the executive commissioner of the Health and Human Services Commission.

(g)   In a suit filed after the child begins residence in the prospective adoptive home, the pre-adoptive social study under this section and the post-placement adoptive social study under §107.052 may be combined in a single report. Under this subsection, the pre-adoptive social study will be completed after the child is placed in the home.

§107.052. POST-PLACEMENT ADOPTIVE SOCIAL STUDY & REPORT

(a)   In a proceeding in which a pre-adoptive social study is required by §107.0519 for an adoption, a post-placement adoptive social study must be conducted and a report filed with the court before the court may render a final order in the adoption.

(b)   Unless otherwise agreed to by the court, the post-placement adoptive social study must comply with the minimum requirements for the study under rules adopted by the executive commissioner of the Health and Human Services Commission.

§107.053. PROSPECTIVE ADOPTIVE PARENTS TO RECEIVE COPY

In all adoptions a copy of the report shall be made available to the prospective adoptive parents prior to a final order of adoption.

§107.054. REPORT FILED WITH COURT

The agency or person making the social study shall file with the court on a date set by the court a report containing its findings and conclusions. The report shall be made a part of the record of the suit.

§107.055. INTRODUCTION OF REPORT AT TRIAL

(a) Disclosure to the jury of the contents of a report to the court of a social study is subject to the rules of evidence.

(b) In a contested case, the agency or person making the social study shall furnish copies of the report to the attorneys for the parties before the earlier of:

    (1) the seventh day after the date the social study is completed; or

    (2) the fifth day before the date of commencement of the trial.

(c) The court may compel the attendance of witnesses necessary for the proper disposition of the suit, including a representative of the agency making the social study, who may be compelled to testify.

§107.056. PREPARATION FEE

If the court orders a social study to be conducted, the court shall award the agency or other person a reasonable fee for the preparation of the study that shall be imposed in the form of a money judgment and paid directly to the agency or other person. The person or agency may enforce the judgment for the fee by any means available under law for civil judgments.

TEXAS RULES OF EVIDENCE AND PRIVILEGES[13]

RULE 510. CONFIDENTIALITY OF MENTAL HEALTH INFORMATION IN CIVIL CASES

(a) **Definitions.** As used in this rule:

    (1) "*Professional*" means any person:

        (A) authorized to practice medicine in any state or nation;

        (B) licensed or certified by the State of Texas in the diagnosis, evaluation or treatment of any mental or emotional disorder;

        (C) involved in the treatment or examination of drug abusers; or

        (D) reasonably believed by the patient to be included in any of the preceding categories.

    (2) "*Patient*" means any person who:

        (A) consults, or is interviewed by, a professional for purposes of diagnosis, evaluation, or treatment of any mental or emotional condition or disorder, including alcoholism and drug addiction; or

        (B) is being treated voluntarily or being examined for admission to voluntary treatment for drug abuse.

---

13 (Texas Rules of Evidence; Article 5. Privileges; Rule 510. Confidentiality of Mental Health Information in Civil Cases)

(3) A representative of the patient is:

  (A) any person bearing the written consent of the patient;

  (B) a parent if the patient is a minor;

  (C) a guardian if the patient has been adjudicated incompetent to manage the patient's personal affairs; or

  (D) the patient's personal representative if the patient is deceased.

(4) A communication is "*confidential*" if not intended to be disclosed to third persons other than those present to further the interest of the patient in the diagnosis, examination, evaluation, or treatment, or those reasonably necessary for the transmission of the communication, or those who are participating in the diagnosis, examination, evaluation, or treatment under the direction of the professional, including members of the patient's family.

(b) **General Rule of Privilege.**

  (1) Communication between a patient and a professional is confidential and shall not be disclosed in civil cases.

  (2) Records of the identity, diagnosis, evaluation, or treatment of a patient which are created or maintained by a professional are confidential and shall not be disclosed in civil cases.

  (3) Any person who received information from confidential communications or records as defined herein, other than a representative of the patient acting on the patient's behalf, shall not disclose in civil cases the information except to the extent that disclosure is consistent with the authorized purposes for which the information was first obtained.

  (4) The provisions of this rule apply even if the patient received the services of a professional prior to the enactment of Tex. Rev. Civ. Stat. art. 5561h (Vernon Supp. 1984)(now codified as Tex. Health & Safety Code §611.001-611.008).

(c) **Who May Claim the Privilege.**

  (1) The privilege of confidentiality may be claimed by the patient or by a representative of the patient acting on the patient's behalf.

  (2) The professional may claim the privilege of confidentiality but only on behalf of the patient. The authority to do so is presumed in the absence of evidence to the contrary.

(d) **Exceptions.** Exceptions to the privilege in court or administrative proceedings exist:

  (1) when the proceedings are brought by the patient against a professional, including but not limited to malpractice proceedings, and in any license revocation proceedings in which the patient is a complaining witness and in which disclosure is relevant to the claim or defense of a professional;

  (2) when the patient waives the right in writing to the privilege of confidentiality of any information, or when a representative of the patient acting on the patient's behalf submits a written waiver to the confidentiality privilege;

  (3) when the purpose of the proceeding is to substantiate and collect on a

claim for mental or emotional health services rendered to the patient;

(4) when the judge finds that the patient after having been previously informed that communications would not be privileged, has made communications to a professional in the course of a court-ordered examination relating to the patient's mental or emotional condition or disorder, providing that such communications shall not be privileged only with respect to issues involving the patient's mental or emotional health. On granting of the order, the court, in determining the extent to which any disclosure of all or any part of any communication is necessary, shall impose appropriate safeguards against unauthorized disclosure;

(5) as to a communication or record relevant to an issue of the physical, mental or emotional condition of a patient in any proceeding in which any party relies upon the condition as a part of the party's claim or defense;

(6) in any proceeding regarding the abuse or neglect, or the cause of any abuse or neglect, of the resident of an institution as defined in Tex. Health and Safety Code §242.002.

Notes and Comments: This rule only governs disclosures of patient-professional communications in judicial or administrative proceedings. Whether a professional may or must disclose such communications in other circumstances is governed by Tex. Health & Safety Code §611.001-611.008. Former paragraph (d)(6) of the Civil Evidence Rules, regarding disclosures in a suit affecting the parent-child relationship, is omitted.

CONSERVATORSHIP, POSSESSION, AND ACCESS—§153[14]

§153.001. PUBLIC POLICY

(a) The public policy of this state is to:

(1) assure that children will have frequent and continuing contact with parents who have shown the ability to act in the best interest of the child;

(2) provide a safe, stable, and nonviolent environment for the child; and

(3) encourage parents to share in the rights and duties of raising their child after the parents have separated or dissolved their marriage.

(b) A court may not render an order that conditions the right of a conservator to possession of or access to a child on the payment of child support.

§153.002. BEST INTEREST OF CHILD

The best interest of the child shall always be the primary consideration of the court in determining the issues of conservatorship and possession of and access to the child.

§153.0072. COLLABORATIVE LAW

(a) On a written agreement of the parties and their attorneys, a suit affecting the parent-child relationship may be conducted under collaborative law procedures.

(b) Collaborative law is a procedure in which the parties and their counsel agree

---

14 (Family Code; Title 5. The Parent-Child Relationship and the Suit Affecting the Parent-Child Relationship; Subtitle B. Suits Affecting the Parent-Child Relationship; Chapter 153. Conservatorship, Possession, & Access; Subchapter A. General Provisions)

in writing to use their best efforts and make a good faith attempt to resolve the suit affecting the parent-child relationship on an agreed basis without resorting to judicial intervention except to have the court approve the settlement agreement, make the legal pronouncements, and sign the orders required by law to effectuate the agreement of the parties as the court determines appropriate. The parties' counsel may not serve as litigation counsel except to ask the court to approve the settlement agreement.

(c)   A collaborative law agreement must include provisions for:

(1)   full and candid exchange of information between the parties and their attorneys as necessary to make a proper evaluation of the case;

(2)   suspending court intervention in the dispute while the parties are using collaborative law procedures;

(3)   hiring experts, as jointly agreed, to be used in the procedure;

(4)   withdrawal of all counsel involved in the collaborative law procedure if the collaborative law procedure does not result in settlement of the dispute; and

(5)   other provisions as agreed to by the parties consistent with a good faith effort to collaboratively settle the matter.

§153.073. RIGHTS OF PARENT AT ALL TIMES

(a)   Unless limited by court order, a parent appointed as a conservator of a child has at all times the right:

(1)   to receive information from any other conservator of the child concerning the health, education, and welfare of the child;

(2)   to confer with the other parent to the extent possible before making a decision concerning the health, education, and welfare of the child;

(3)   of access to medical, dental, psychological, and educational records of the child;

(4)   to consult with a physician, dentist, or psychologist of the child;

(5)   to consult with school officials concerning the child's welfare and educational status, including school activities;

(6)   to attend school activities;

(7)   to be designated on the child's records as a person to be notified in case of an emergency;

(8)   to consent to medical, dental, and surgical treatment during an emergency involving an immediate danger to the health and safety of the child; and

(9)   to manage the estate of the child to the extent the estate has been created by the parent or the parent's family.

(b)   The court shall specify in the order the rights that a parent retains at all times.

§153.074. RIGHTS AND DUTIES DURING PERIOD OF POSSESSION

Unless limited by court order, a parent appointed as a conservator of a child has the following rights and duties during the period that the parent has possession of the child:

(1)   the duty of care, control, protection, and reasonable discipline of the child;

(2) the duty to support the child, including providing the child with clothing, food, shelter, and medical and dental care not involving an invasive procedure;

(3) the right to consent for the child to medical and dental care not involving an invasive procedure; and

(4) the right to direct the moral and religious training of the child.

§153.075. Duties of Parent not Appointed Conservator

The court may order a parent not appointed as a managing or a possessory conservator to perform other parental duties, including paying child support.

§153.010. Order for Family Counseling

(a) If the court finds at the time of a hearing that the parties have a history of conflict in resolving an issue of conservatorship or possession of or access to the child, the court may order a party to:

(1) participate in counseling with a mental health professional who:

(A) has a background in family therapy;

(B) has a mental health license that requires as a minimum a master's degree; and

(C) has training in domestic violence if the court determines that the training is relevant to the type of counseling needed; and

(2) pay the cost of counseling.

(b) If a person possessing the requirements of Subsection (a)(1) is not available in the county in which the court presides, the court may appoint a person the court believes is qualified to conduct the counseling ordered under Subsection (a).

§153.132. Rights and Duties of Parent Appointed Sole Managing Conservator

Unless limited by court order, a parent appointed as sole managing conservator of a child has the rights and duties provided by Subchapter B and the following exclusive rights:

(1) the right to designate the primary residence of the child;

(2) the right to consent to medical, dental, and surgical treatment involving invasive procedures, and to consent to psychiatric and psychological treatment;

(3) the right to receive and give receipt for periodic payments for the support of the child and to hold or disburse these funds for the benefit of the child;

(4) the right to represent the child in legal action and to make other decisions of substantial legal significance concerning the child;

(5) the right to consent to marriage and to enlistment in the armed forces of the United States;

(6) the right to make decisions concerning the child's education;

(7) the right to the services and earnings of the child; and

(8) except when a guardian of the child's estate or a guardian or attorney *ad litem* has been appointed for the child, the right to act as an agent of the

child in relation to the child's estate if the child's action is required by a state, the United States, or a foreign government.

§153.133. PARENTING PLAN FOR JOINT MANAGING CONSERVATORSHIP

(a) If a written agreement of the parents is filed with the court, the court shall render an order appointing the parents as joint managing conservators only if the agreement:

(1) designates the conservator who has the exclusive right to designate the primary residence of the child and:

    (A) establishes, until modified by further order, the geographic area within which the conservator shall maintain the child's primary residence; or

    (B) specifies that the conservator may designate the child's primary residence without regard to geographic location;

(2) specifies the rights and duties of each parent regarding the child's physical care, support, and education;

(3) includes provisions to minimize disruption of the child's education, daily routine, and association with friends;

(4) allocates between the parents, independently, jointly, or exclusively, all of the remaining rights and duties of a parent provided by Chapter 151;

(5) is voluntarily and knowingly made by each parent and has not been repudiated by either parent at the time the order is rendered; and

(6) is in the best interest of the child.

(b) The agreement may contain an alternative dispute resolution procedure that the parties agree to use before requesting enforcement or modification of the terms and conditions of the joint conservatorship through litigation, except in an emergency.

(c) Requires the court, notwithstanding Subsection (a)(1) (relating to designating the conservator who has the exclusive right to designate the primary residence of the child), to render an order adopting the provisions of a written agreed parenting plan appointing the parents as joint managing conservators if the parenting plan:

(1) meets all the requirements of Subsections (a)(2) (relating to the parenting plan specifying the rights and duties of each parent regarding the child's physical care, support, and education), (3) (relating to the parenting plan including provisions in the parenting plan to minimize disruption of the child's education, daily routine, and association with friends), (4) (relating to the parenting plan allocating between the parents, independently, jointly, or exclusively, all of the remaining rights and duties of a parent), (5) (relating to the parenting plan being made voluntarily and knowingly by each parent and not repudiated by either at the time the order is rendered), and (6) (relating to the parenting plan being in the best interest of the child); and

(2) provides that the child's primary residence is required to be within a specified geographic area.

§153.192. Right and Duties of Parent Appointed Possessory Conservator

(a) Unless limited by court order, a parent appointed as possessory conservator of a child has the rights and duties provided by Subchapter B and any other right or duty expressly granted to the possessory conservator in the order.

(b) In ordering the terms and conditions for possession of a child by a parent appointed possessory conservator, the court shall be guided by the guidelines in Subchapter E.

§153.605. Appointment of Parenting Coordinator

(a) In a suit affecting the parent-child relationship, the court may, on its own motion or on a motion or agreement of the parties, appoint a parenting coordinator or assign a domestic relations office under Chapter 203 to appoint an employee or other person to serve as parenting coordinator.

(b) The court may not appoint a parenting coordinator unless, after notice and hearing, the court makes a specific finding that:

   (1) the case is a high-conflict case or there is good cause shown for the appointment of a parenting coordinator and the appointment is in the best interest of any minor child in the suit; and

   (2) the person appointed has the minimum qualifications required by §153.610, as documented by the person, unless those requirements have been waived by the court with the agreement of the parties in accordance with §53.610(c).

(c) Notwithstanding any other provision of this subchapter, a party may at any time file a written objection to the appointment of a parenting coordinator on the basis of family violence having been committed by another party against the objecting party or a child who is the subject of the suit. After an objection is filed, a parenting coordinator may not be appointed unless, on the request of a party, a hearing is held and the court finds that a preponderance of the evidence does not support the objection. If a parenting coordinator is appointed, the court shall order appropriate measures be taken to ensure the physical and emotional safety of the party who filed the objection. The order may provide that the parties not be required to have face-to-face contact and that the parties be placed in separate rooms during the parenting coordination.

(d) An individual appointed as a parenting coordinator may not serve in any non-confidential capacity in the same case, including serving as an amicus attorney, guardian ad litem, or social study evaluator under Chapter 107, as a friend of the court under Chapter 202, or as a parenting facilitator under this subchapter.

Adoption—§162[15]

§162.413. Counseling

The applicant must participate in counseling for not less than one hour with a social worker or mental health professional with expertise in postadoption counseling after the administrator has accepted the application for registration and before the release of confidential information.

---

15 (Family Code; Title 5. The Parent-Child Relationship and The Suit Affecting the Parent-Child Relationship; Subtitle B. Suits Affecting the Parent-Child Relationship; Chapter 162. Adoption; Subchapter E. Voluntary Adoption Registries)

CHILD ABUSE OR NEGLECT—§261[16]

§261.001. DEFINITIONS

In this chapter:

(1) *"Abuse"* includes the following acts or omissions by a person:

    (A) mental or emotional injury to a child that results in an observable and material impairment in the child's growth, development, or psychological functioning;

    (B) causing or permitting the child to be in a situation in which the child sustains a mental or emotional injury that results in an observable and material impairment in the child's growth, development, or psychological functioning;

    (C) physical injury that results in substantial harm to the child, or the genuine threat of substantial harm from physical injury to the child, including an injury that is at variance with the history or explanation given and excluding an accident or reasonable discipline by a parent, guardian, or managing or possessory conservator that does not expose the child to a substantial risk of harm;

    (D) failure to make a reasonable effort to prevent an action by another person that results in physical injury that results in substantial harm to the child;

    (E) sexual conduct harmful to a child's mental, emotional, or physical welfare;

    (F) failure to make a reasonable effort to prevent sexual conduct harmful to a child;

    (G) compelling or encouraging the child to engage in sexual conduct as defined by §43.01, Penal Code;

    (H) causing, permitting, encouraging, engaging in, or allowing the photographing, filming, or depicting of the child if the person knew or should have known that the resulting photograph, film, or depiction of the child is obscene as defined by Section 43.21, Penal Code, or pornographic;

    (I) the current use by a person of a controlled substance as defined by Chapter 481, Health and Safety Code, in a manner or to the extent that the use results in physical, mental, or emotional injury to a child; or

    (J) causing, expressly permitting, or encouraging a child to use a controlled substance as defined by Chapter 481, Health and Safety Code.

(2) *"Department"* means the Department of Protective and Regulatory Services.

(3) *"Designated agency"* means the agency designated by the court as responsible for the protection of children.

(4) *"Neglect"* includes:

---

16 (Family Code; Title 5. The Parent-Child Relationship and The Suit Affecting the Parent-Child Relationship; Subtitle E. Protection of the Child; Chapter 261. Investigation of Report of Child Abuse or Neglect; Subchapter A. General Provisions)

(A) the leaving of a child in a situation where the child would be exposed to a substantial risk of physical or mental harm, without arranging for necessary care for the child, and the demonstration of an intent not to return by a parent, guardian, or managing or possessory conservator of the child;

(B) the following acts or omissions by a person:

(i) placing a child in or failing to remove a child from a situation that a reasonable person would realize requires judgment or actions beyond the child's level of maturity, physical condition, or mental abilities and that results in bodily injury or a substantial risk of immediate harm to the child;

(ii) failing to seek, obtain, or follow through with medical care for a child, with the failure resulting in or presenting a substantial risk of death, disfigurement, or bodily injury or with the failure resulting in an observable and material impairment to the growth, development, or functioning of the child;

(iii) the failure to provide a child with food, clothing, or shelter necessary to sustain the life or health of the child, excluding failure caused primarily by financial inability unless relief services had been offered and refused; or

(iv) placing a child in or failing to remove the child from a situation in which the child would be exposed to a substantial risk of sexual conduct harmful to the child; or

(C) the failure by the person responsible for a child's care, custody, or welfare to permit the child to return to the child's home without arranging for the necessary care for the child after the child has been absent from the home for any reason, including having been in residential placement or having run away.

(5) *"Person responsible for a child's care, custody, or welfare"* means a person who traditionally is responsible for a child's care, custody, or welfare, including:

(A) a parent, guardian, managing or possessory conservator, or foster parent of the child;

(B) a member of the child's family or household as defined by Chapter 71;

(C) a person with whom the child's parent cohabits;

(D) school personnel or a volunteer at the child's school; or

(E) personnel or a volunteer at a public or private child-care facility that provides services for the child or at a public or private residential institution or facility where the child resides.

(6) *" Report"* means a report that alleged or suspected abuse or neglect of a child has occurred or may occur.

(7) *"Board"* means the Board of Protective and Regulatory Services.

(8) *"Born addicted to alcohol or a controlled substance"* means a child:

(A) who is born to a mother who during the pregnancy used a controlled substance, as defined by Chapter 481, Health and Safety Code, other than a controlled substance legally obtained by prescription, or alcohol; and

(B) who, after birth as a result of the mother's use of the controlled substance or alcohol:

(i) experiences observable withdrawal from the alcohol or controlled substance;

(ii) exhibits observable or harmful effects in the child's physical appearance or functioning; or

(iii) exhibits the demonstrable presence of alcohol or a controlled substance in the child's bodily fluids.

§261.101. PERSONS REQUIRED TO REPORT; TIME TO REPORT

(a) A person having cause to believe that a child's physical or mental health or welfare has been adversely affected by abuse or neglect by any person shall immediately make a report as provided by this subchapter.

(b) If a professional has cause to believe that a child has been abused or neglected or may be abused or neglected or that a child is a victim of an offense under §21.11, Penal Code, the professional shall make a report not later than the 48th hour after the hour the professional first suspects that the child has been or may be abused or neglected or is a victim of an offense under §21.11, Penal Code. A professional may not delegate to or rely on another person to make the report. In this subsection, "professional" means an individual who is licensed or certified by the state or who is an employee of a facility licensed, certified, or operated by the state and who, in the normal course of official duties or duties for which a license or certification is required, has direct contact with children. The term includes teachers, nurses, doctors, day-care employees, employees of a clinic or health care facility that provides reproductive services, juvenile probation officers, and juvenile detention or correctional officers.

(b-1) In addition to the duty to make a report under Subsection (a) or (b), a person or professional shall make a report in the manner required by Subsection (a) or (b), as applicable, if the person or professional has cause to believe that an adult was a victim of abuse or neglect as a child and the person or professional determines in good faith that disclosure of the information is necessary to protect the health and safety of:

(1) another child; or

(2) an elderly or disabled person as defined by Section 48.002, Human Resources Code.

(c) The requirement to report under this section applies without exception to an individual whose personal communications may otherwise be privileged, including an attorney, a member of the clergy, a medical practitioner, a social worker, a mental health professional, an employee or member of a board that licenses or certifies a professional, and an employee of a clinic or health care facility that provides reproductive services.

(d) Unless waived in writing by the person making the report, the identity of an individual making a report under this chapter is confidential and may be disclosed only:

(1)   as provided by §261.201; or

(2)   to a law enforcement officer for the purposes of conducting a criminal investigation of the report.

§261.102. MATTERS TO BE REPORTED

A report should reflect the reporter's belief that a child has been or may be abused or neglected or has died of abuse or neglect.

§261.103. REPORT MADE TO APPROPRIATE AGENCY

(a)   Except as provided by Subsection (b), a report shall be made to:

(1)   any local or state law enforcement agency;

(2)   the department if the alleged or suspected abuse involves a person responsible for the care, custody, or welfare of the child;

(3)   the state agency that operates, licenses, certifies, or registers the facility in which the alleged abuse or neglect occurred; or

(4)   the agency designated by the court to be responsible for the protection of children.

(b)   A report may be made to the Texas Youth Commission instead of the entities listed under Subsection (a) if the report is based on information provided by a child while under the supervision of the commission concerning the child's alleged abuse of another child.

§261.104. CONTENTS OF REPORT

The person making a report shall identify, if known:

(1)   the name and address of the child;

(2)   the name and address of the person responsible for the care, custody, or welfare of the child; and

(3)   any other pertinent information concerning the alleged or suspected abuse or neglect.

§261.106. IMMUNITIES

(a)   A person acting in good faith who reports or assists in the investigation of a report of alleged child abuse or neglect or who testifies or otherwise participates in a judicial proceeding arising from a report, petition, or investigation of alleged child abuse or neglect is immune from civil or criminal liability that might otherwise be incurred or imposed.

(b)   Immunity from civil and criminal liability extends to an authorized volunteer of the department or a law enforcement officer who participates at the request of the department in an investigation of alleged or suspected abuse or neglect or in an action arising from an investigation if the person was acting in good faith and in the scope of the person's responsibilities.

(c)   A person who reports the person's own abuse or neglect of a child or who acts in bad faith or with malicious purpose in reporting alleged child abuse or neglect is not immune from civil or criminal liability.

§261.107. FALSE REPORT; PENALTY

(a)   A person commits an offense if the person knowingly or intentionally makes a report as provided in this chapter that the person knows is false or lacks factual foundation. An offense under this section is a Class A misdemeanor unless it is shown on the trial of the offense that the person has previously been convicted under this section, in which case the offense is a state jail felony.

(b) A finding by a court in a suit affecting the parent-child relationship that a report made under this chapter before or during the suit was false or lacking factual foundation may be grounds for the court to modify an order providing for possession of or access to the child who was the subject of the report by restricting further access to the child by the person who made the report.

(c) The appropriate county prosecuting attorney shall be responsible for the prosecution of an offense under this section.

§261.108. FRIVOLOUS CLAIMS AGAINST PERSON REPORTING

(a) In this section:

(1) "*Claim*" means an action or claim by a party, including a plaintiff, counterclaimant, cross-claimant, or third-party plaintiff, requesting recovery of damages.

(2) "*Defendant*" means a party against whom a claim is made.

(b) A court shall award a defendant reasonable attorney's fees and other expenses related to the defense of a claim filed against the defendant for damages or other relief arising from reporting or assisting in the investigation of a report under this chapter or participating in a judicial proceeding resulting from the report if:

(1) the court finds that the claim is frivolous, unreasonable, or without foundation because the defendant is immune from liability under §261.106; and

(2) the claim is dismissed or judgment is rendered for the defendant.

(c) To recover under this section, the defendant must, at any time after the filing of a claim, file a written motion stating that:

(1) the claim is frivolous, unreasonable, or without foundation because the defendant is immune from liability under §261.106; and

(2) the defendant requests the court to award reasonable attorney's fees and other expenses related to the defense of the claim.

§261.109. FAILURE TO REPORT; PENALTY

(a) A person commits an offense if the person is required to make a report under Section 261.101(a) and knowingly fails to make a report as provided in this chapter.

(a-1) A person who is a professional as defined by Section 261.101(b) commits an offense if the person is required to make a report under Section 261.101(b) and knowingly fails to make a report as provided in this chapter.

(b) An offense under Subsection (a) is a Class A misdemeanor, except that the offense is a state jail felony if it is shown on the trial of the offense that the child was a person with an intellectual disability who resided in a state supported living center, the ICF-MR component of the Rio Grande State Center, or a facility licensed under Chapter 252, Health and Safety Code, and the actor knew that the child had suffered serious bodily injury as a result of the abuse or neglect.

(c)   An offense under Subsection (a-1) is a Class A misdemeanor, except that the offense is a state jail felony if it is shown on the trial of the offense that the actor intended to conceal the abuse or neglect.

§261.201. CONFIDENTIALITY AND DISCLOSURE OF INFORMATION

(a)   Except as provided by Section 261.203, the following information is confidential, is not subject to public release under Chapter 552, Government Code, and may be disclosed only for purposes consistent with this code and applicable federal or state law or under rules adopted by an investigating agency:

(1)   a report of alleged or suspected abuse or neglect made under this chapter and the identity of the person making the report; and

(2)   except as otherwise provided in this section, the files, reports, records, communications, audiotapes, videotapes, and working papers used or developed in an investigation under this chapter or in providing services as a result of an investigation.

(b)   A court may order the disclosure of information that is confidential under this section if:

(1)   a motion has been filed with the court requesting the release of the information;

(2)   a notice of hearing has been served on the investigating agency and all other interested parties; and

(3)   after hearing and an in camera review of the requested information, the court determines that the disclosure of the requested information is:

(A)   essential to the administration of justice; and

(B)   not likely to endanger the life or safety of:

(i)   a child who is the subject of the report of alleged or suspected abuse or neglect;

(ii)   a person who makes a report of alleged or suspected abuse or neglect; or

(iii)   any other person who participates in an investigation of reported abuse or neglect or who provides care for the child.

(b-1)   On a motion of one of the parties in a contested case before an administrative law judge relating to the license or certification of a professional, as defined by Section 261.101(b), or an educator, as defined by Section 5.001, Education Code, the administrative law judge may order the disclosure of information that is confidential under this section that relates to the matter before the administrative law judge after a hearing for which notice is provided as required by Subsection (b)(2) and making the review and determination required by Subsection (b)(3). Before the department may release information under this subsection, the department must edit the information to protect the confidentiality of the identity of any person who makes a report of abuse or neglect.

(c)   In addition to Subsection (b), a court, on its own motion, may order disclosure of information that is confidential under this section if:

(1)   the order is rendered at a hearing for which all parties have been given notice;

(2)   the court finds that disclosure of the information is:

   (A)   essential to the administration of justice; and

   (B)   not likely to endanger the life or safety of:

      (i)   a child who is the subject of the report of alleged or suspected abuse or neglect;

      (ii)   a person who makes a report of alleged or suspected abuse or neglect; or

      (iii)   any other person who participates in an investigation of reported abuse or neglect or who provides care for the child; and

(3)   the order is reduced to writing or made on the record in open court.

(d)   The adoptive parents of a child who was the subject of an investigation and an adult who was the subject of an investigation as a child are entitled to examine and make copies of any report, record, working paper, or other information in the possession, custody, or control of the state that pertains to the history of the child. The department may edit the documents to protect the identity of the biological parents and any other person whose identity is confidential, unless this information is already known to the adoptive parents or is readily available through other sources, including the court records of a suit to terminate the parent-child relationship under Chapter 161.

(e)   Before placing a child who was the subject of an investigation, the department shall notify the prospective adoptive parents of their right to examine any report, record, working paper, or other information in the possession, custody, or control of the state that pertains to the history of the child.

(f)   The department shall provide prospective adoptive parents an opportunity to examine information under this section as early as practicable before placing a child.

(f-1) The department shall provide to a relative or other individual with whom a child is placed any information the department considers necessary to ensure that the relative or other individual is prepared to meet the needs of the child. The information required by this subsection may include information related to any abuse or neglect suffered by the child.

(g)   Notwithstanding Subsection (b), the department, on request and subject to department rule, shall provide to the parent, managing conservator, or other legal representative of a child who is the subject of reported abuse or neglect information concerning the reported abuse or neglect that would otherwise be confidential under this section if the department has edited the information to protect the confidentiality of the identity of the person who made the report and any other person whose life or safety may be endangered by the disclosure.

(h)   This section does not apply to an investigation of child abuse or neglect in a home or facility regulated under Chapter 42, Human Resources Code.

(i)   Notwithstanding Subsection (a), the Texas Youth Commission shall release a report of alleged or suspected abuse or neglect made under this chapter if:

   (1)   the report relates to a report of abuse or neglect involving a child committed to the commission during the period that the child is committed to the commission; and

(2) the commission is not prohibited by Chapter 552, Government Code, or other law from disclosing the report.

(j) The Texas Youth Commission shall edit any report disclosed under Subsection (i) to protect the identity of:

(1) a child who is the subject of the report of alleged or suspected abuse or neglect;

(2) the person who made the report; and

(3) any other person whose life or safety may be endangered by the disclosure.

(k) Notwithstanding Subsection (a), an investigating agency, other than the department or the Texas Youth Commission, on request, shall provide to the parent, managing conservator, or other legal representative of a child who is the subject of reported abuse or neglect, or to the child if the child is at least 18 years of age, information concerning the reported abuse or neglect that would otherwise be confidential under this section. The investigating agency shall withhold information under this subsection if the parent, managing conservator, or other legal representative of the child requesting the information is alleged to have committed the abuse or neglect.

(l) Before a child or a parent, managing conservator, or other legal representative of a child may inspect or copy a record or file concerning the child under Subsection (k), the custodian of the record or file must redact:

(1) any personally identifiable information about a victim or witness under 18 years of age unless that victim or witness is:

(A) the child who is the subject of the report; or

(B) another child of the parent, managing conservator, or other legal representative requesting the information;

(2) any information that is excepted from required disclosure under Chapter 552, Government Code, or other law; and

(3) the identity of the person who made the report.

§261.202. PRIVILEGED COMMUNICATION

In a proceeding regarding the abuse or neglect of a child, evidence may not be excluded on the ground of privileged communication except in the case of communications between an attorney and client.

§261.203. INFORMATION RELATING TO CHILD FATALITY

(a) Not later than the fifth day after the date the department receives a request for information about a child fatality with respect to which the department is conducting an investigation of alleged abuse or neglect, the department shall release:

(1) the age and sex of the child;

(2) the date of death;

(3) whether the state was the managing conservator of the child at the time of the child's death; and

(4) whether the child resided with the child's parent, managing conservator, guardian, or other person entitled to possession of the child at the time of

the child's death.

(b) If, after a child abuse or neglect investigation is completed, the department determines a child's death was caused by abuse or neglect, the department shall promptly release the following information on request:

   (1) the information described by Subsection (a), if not previously released to the person requesting the information;

   (2) for cases in which the child's death occurred while the child was living with the child's parent, managing conservator, guardian, or other person entitled to possession of the child:

     (A) a summary of any previous reports of abuse or neglect of the deceased child or another child made while the child was living with that parent, managing conservator, guardian, or other person entitled to possession of the child;

     (B) the disposition of any report under Paragraph (A);

     (C) a description of the services, if any, that were provided by the department to the child or the child's family as a result of any report under Paragraph (A); and

     (D) the results of any risk or safety assessment completed by the department relating to the deceased child; and

   (3) for a case in which the child's death occurred while the child was in substitute care with the department or with a residential child-care provider regulated under Chapter 42, Human Resources Code, the following information:

     (A) the date the substitute care provider with whom the child was residing at the time of death was licensed or verified;

     (B) a summary of any previous reports of abuse or neglect investigated by the department relating to the substitute care provider, including the disposition of any investigation resulting from a report;

     (C) any reported licensing violations, including notice of any action taken by the department regarding a violation; and

     (D) records of any training completed by the substitute care provider while the child was placed with the provider.

(c) If the department is unable to release the information required by Subsection (b) before the 11th day after the date the department receives a request for the information or the date the investigation of the child fatality is completed, whichever is later, the department shall inform the person requesting the information of the date the department will release the information.

(d) After receiving a request for information required by Subsection (b), the department shall notify and provide a copy of the request to the attorney ad litem for the deceased child, if any.

(e) Before the department releases any information under Subsection (b), the department shall redact from the records any information the release of which would:

   (1) identify:

    (A) the individual who reported the abuse or neglect; or

    (B) any other individual other than the deceased child or an alleged perpetrator of the abuse or neglect;

(2) jeopardize an ongoing criminal investigation or prosecution;

(3) endanger the life or safety of any individual; or

(4) violate other state or federal law.

(f) The executive commissioner of the Health and Human Services Commission shall adopt rules to implement this section.

§261.301. INVESTIGATION OF REPORT

(a) With assistance from the appropriate state or local law enforcement agency, the department or designated agency shall make a prompt and thorough investigation of a report of child abuse or neglect allegedly committed by a person responsible for a child's care, custody, or welfare. The investigation shall be conducted without regard to any pending suit affecting the parent-child relationship.

(b) A state agency shall investigate a report that alleges abuse or neglect occurred in a facility operated, licensed, certified, or registered by that agency as provided by Subchapter E. In conducting an investigation for a facility operated, licensed, certified, registered, or listed by the department, the department shall perform the investigation as provided by:

(1) Subchapter E; and

(2) the Human Resources Code.

(c) The department is not required to investigate a report that alleges child abuse or neglect by a person other than a person responsible for a child's care, custody, or welfare. The appropriate state or local law enforcement agency shall investigate that report if the agency determines an investigation should be conducted.

(d) The department shall by rule assign priorities and prescribe investigative procedures for investigations based on the severity and immediacy of the alleged harm to the child. The primary purpose of the investigation shall be the protection of the child. The rules must require the department, subject to the availability of funds, to:

(1) immediately respond to a report of abuse and neglect that involves circumstances in which the death of the child or substantial bodily harm to the child would result unless the department immediately intervenes;

(2) respond within 24 hours to a report of abuse and neglect that is assigned the highest priority, other than a report described by Subdivision (1); and

(3) respond within 72 hours to a report of abuse and neglect that is assigned the second highest priority.

(e) As necessary to provide for the protection of the child, the department or designated agency shall determine:

(1) the nature, extent, and cause of the abuse or neglect;

(2) the identity of the person responsible for the abuse or neglect;

(3) the names and conditions of the other children in the home;

(4) an evaluation of the parents or persons responsible for the care of the child;

(5) the adequacy of the home environment;

(6) the relationship of the child to the persons responsible for the care, custody, or welfare of the child; and

(7) all other pertinent data.

(f) An investigation of a report to the department of serious physical or sexual abuse of a child shall be conducted jointly by an investigator from the appropriate local law enforcement agency and the department or agency responsible for conducting an investigation under Subchapter E.

(g) The inability or unwillingness of a local law enforcement agency to conduct a joint investigation under this section does not constitute grounds to prevent or prohibit the department from performing its duties under this subtitle. The department shall document any instance in which a law enforcement agency is unable or unwilling to conduct a joint investigation under this section.

(h) The department and the appropriate local law enforcement agency shall conduct an investigation, other than an investigation under Subchapter E, as provided by this section and Article 2.27, Code of Criminal Procedure, if the investigation is of a report that alleges that a child has been or may be the victim of conduct that constitutes a criminal offense that poses an immediate risk of physical or sexual abuse of a child that could result in the death of or serious harm to the child. Immediately on receipt of a report described by this subsection, the department shall notify the appropriate local law enforcement agency of the report.

§261.303. Interference with Investigation; Court Order

(a) A person may not interfere with an investigation of a report of child abuse or neglect conducted by the department or designated agency.

(b) If admission to the home, school, or any place where the child may be cannot be obtained, then for good cause shown the court having family law jurisdiction shall order the parent, the person responsible for the care of the children, or the person in charge of any place where the child may be to allow entrance for the interview, examination, and investigation.

(c) If a parent or person responsible for the child's care does not consent to release of the child's prior medical, psychological, or psychiatric records or to a medical, psychological, or psychiatric examination of the child that is requested by the department or designated agency, the court having family law jurisdiction shall, for good cause shown, order the records to be released or the examination to be made at the times and places designated by the court.

(d) A person, including a medical facility, that makes a report under Subchapter B1 shall release to the department or designated agency, as part of the required report under §261.103, records that directly relate to the suspected abuse or neglect without requiring parental consent or a court order. If a child is transferred from a reporting medical facility to another medical facility to treat the injury or condition that formed the basis for the original report, the transferee medical facility shall, at the department's request, release to the department records relating to the injury or condition without requiring parental consent or a court order.

(e)　A person, including a utility company, that has confidential locating or identifying information regarding a family that is the subject of an investigation under this chapter shall release that information to the department on request. The release of information to the department as required by this subsection by a person, including a utility company, is not subject to Section 552.352, Government Code, or any other law providing liability for the release of confidential information.

§261.305. ACCESS TO MENTAL HEALTH RECORDS

(a)　An investigation may include an inquiry into the possibility that a parent or a person responsible for the care of a child who is the subject of a report under Subchapter B1 has a history of medical or mental illness.

(b)　If the parent or person does not consent to an examination or allow the department or designated agency to have access to medical or mental health records requested by the department or agency, the court having family law jurisdiction, for good cause shown, shall order the examination to be made or that the department or agency be permitted to have access to the records under terms and conditions prescribed by the court.

(c)　If the court determines that the parent or person is indigent, the court shall appoint an attorney to represent the parent or person at the hearing. The fees for the appointed attorney shall be paid as provided by Chapter 107.

(d)　A parent or person responsible for the child's care is entitled to notice and a hearing when the department or designated agency seeks a court order to allow a medical, psychological, or psychiatric examination or access to medical or mental health records.

(e)　This access does not constitute a waiver of confidentiality.

§261.316. EXEMPTION FROM FEES FOR MEDICAL RECORDS

The department is exempt from the payment of a fee otherwise required or authorized by law to obtain a medical record from a hospital or health care provider if the request for a record is made in the course of an investigation by the department.

MEDICAL CARE AND EDUCATIONAL SERVICES FOR CHILDREN IN FOSTER CARE—§266[17]

Relating to the administration and monitoring of health care provided to foster children.

§266.001. DEFINITIONS

In this chapter:

(1)　"Advanced practice nurse" has the meaning assigned by Section 157.051, Occupations Code.

(1-a) "Commission" means the Health and Human Services Commission.

(2)　"Department" means the Department of Family and Protective Services.

---

17 (Family Code; Title 5. The Parent-Child Relationship and the Suit Affecting the Parent-Child Relationship; Subtitle E. Protection of the Child; Chapter 266. Medical Care and Educational Services for Children in Foster Care)

(2-a)"Drug research program" means any clinical trial, clinical investigation, drug study, or active medical or clinical research that has been approved by an institutional review board in accordance with the standards provided in the Code of Federal Regulations, 45 C.F.R. Sections 46.404 through 46.407, regarding:

(A) an investigational new drug; or

(B) the efficacy of an approved drug.

(3) "Executive commissioner" means the executive commissioner of the Health and Human Services Commission.

(4) "Foster child" means a child who is in the managing conservatorship of the department.

(4-a)"Investigational new drug" has the meaning assigned by 21 C.F.R. Section 312.3(b).

(5) "Medical care" means all health care and related services provided under the medical assistance program under Chapter 32, Human Resources Code, and described by Section 32.003(4), Human Resources Code.

(6) "Physician assistant" has the meaning assigned by Section 157.051, Occupations Code.

(7) "Psychotropic medication" means a medication that is prescribed for the treatment of symptoms of psychosis or another mental, emotional, or behavioral disorder and that is used to exercise an effect on the central nervous system to influence and modify behavior, cognition, or affective state. The term includes the following categories when used as described by this subdivision:

(A) psychomotor stimulants;

(B) antidepressants;

(C) antipsychotics or neuroleptics;

(D) agents for control of mania or depression;

(E) antianxiety agents; and

(F) sedatives, hypnotics, or other sleep-promoting medications.

§266.004. CONSENT FOR MEDICAL CARE

(a) Medical care may fot be provided to a child in foster care unless the person authorized by this section has provided consent.

(b) Except as provided by Section 266.010, the court may authorize the following persons to consent to medical care for a foster child:

(1) an individual designated by name in an order of the court, including the child's foster parent or the child's parent, if the parent's rights have not been terminated and the court determines that it is in the best interest of the parent's child to allow the parent to make medical decisions on behalf of the child; or

(2) the department or an agent of the department.

(h) Notwithstanding Subsection (b), a person may not be authorized to consent to medical care provided to a foster child unless the person has completed a department-approved training program related to informed consent and the provision of all areas of medical care as defined by Section 266.001. This subsection does not apply to a parent whose rights have not been terminated unless the court orders the parent to complete the training.

(h-1) The training required by Subsection (h) must include training related to informed consent for the administration of psychotropic medication and the appropriate use of psychosocial therapies, behavior strategies, and other non-pharmacological interventions that should be considered before or concurrently with the administration of psychotropic medications.

(h-2) Each person required to complete a training program under Subsection (h) must acknowledge in writing that the person:

(1)   has received the training described by Subsection (h-1);

(2)   understands the principles of informed consent for the administration of psychotropic medication; and

(3)   understands that non-pharmacological interventions should be considered and discussed with the prescribing physician, physician assistant, or advanced practice nurse before consenting to the use of a psychotropic medication.

(i)   The person authorized under Subsection (b) to consent to medical care of a foster child shall participate in each appointment of the child with the provider of the medical care.

GOVERNMENT CODE

TEXAS HOME VISITING PROGRAM (SOCIAL WORKER)—§531[18]

Establishing a Texas Home Visitation Program for at-risk families, with significant role by social workers.

§531.981. DEFINITIONS

In this subchapter:

(1) "Home visiting program" means a voluntary-enrollment program in which early childhood and health professionals such as nurses, social workers, or trained and supervised paraprofessionals repeatedly visit over a period of at least six months the homes of pregnant women or families with children under the age of six who are born with or exposed to one or more risk factors.

(2) "Risk factors" means factors that make a child more likely to experience adverse experiences leading to negative consequences, including preterm birth, poverty, low parental education, having a teenaged mother or father, poor maternal health, and parental underemployment or unemployment.

§531.982. ESTABLISHMENT OF TEXAS HOME VISITING PROGRAM

(a) The commission shall create a strategic plan to serve at-risk pregnant women and families with children under the age of six through home visiting programs that improve outcomes for parents and families.

(b) A pregnant woman or family is considered at-risk for purposes of this section and may be eligible for voluntary enrollment in a home visiting program if the woman or family is exposed to one or more risk factors.

(c) The commission may determine if a risk factor or combination of risk factors experienced by an at-risk pregnant woman or family qualifies the woman or family for enrollment in a home visiting program.

§531.983. TYPES OF HOME VISITING PROGRAMS

(a) A home visiting program is classified as either an evidence-based program or a promising practice program.

(b) An evidence-based program is a home visiting program that:

(1) is research-based and grounded in relevant, empirically based knowledge and program-determined outcomes;

(2) is associated with a national organization, institution of higher education, or national or state public health institute;

(3) has comprehensive standards that ensure high-quality service delivery and continuously improving quality;

(4) has demonstrated significant positive short-term and long-term outcomes;

(5) has been evaluated by at least one rigorous randomized controlled research trial across heterogeneous populations or communities, the results of at

---

18 (Government Code; Title 4. Executive Branch; Subtitle I. Health and Human Services; Chapter 531. Health and Human Services Commission; Subchapter X. Texas Home Visiting Program)

least one of which has been published in a peer-reviewed journal;

(6) follows with fidelity a program manual or design that specifies the purpose, outcomes, duration, and frequency of the services that constitute the program;

(7) employs well-trained and competent staff and provides continual relevant professional development opportunities;

(8) demonstrates strong links to other community-based services; and

(9) ensures compliance with home visiting standards.

(c) A promising practice program is a home visiting program that:

(1) has an active impact evaluation program or can demonstrate a timeline for implementing an active impact evaluation program;

(2) has been evaluated by at least one outcome-based study demonstrating effectiveness or a randomized controlled trial in a homogeneous sample;

(3) follows with fidelity a program manual or design that specifies the purpose, outcomes, duration, and frequency of the services that constitute the program;

(4) employs well-trained and competent staff and provides continual relevant professional development opportunities;

(5) demonstrates strong links to other community-based services; and

(6) ensures compliance with home visiting standards.

§531.985. Outcomes

The commission shall ensure that a home visiting program achieves favorable outcomes in at least two of the following areas:

(1) improved maternal or child health outcomes;

(2) improved cognitive development of children;

(3) increased school readiness of children;

(4) reduced child abuse, neglect, and injury;

(5) improved child safety;

(6) improved social-emotional development of children;

(7) improved parenting skills, including nurturing and bonding;

(8) improved family economic self-sufficiency;

(9) reduced parental involvement with the criminal justice system; and

(10) increased father involvement and support.

IMPLEMENTATION OF MEDICAID MANAGED CARE PROGRAM—§533[19]

Enacts provider protection plan that ensures efficiency and reduces administrative burdens on providers participating in a Medicaid managed care model or arrangement.

§533.0055. Provider Protection Plan

(a) The commission shall develop and implement a provider protection plan that is

19 (Government Code; Title 4. Executive Branch; Subtitle I. Health And Human Services; Chapter 533. Implementation of Medicaid Managed Care Program; Subchapter A. General Provisions)

designed to reduce administrative burdens placed on providers participating in a Medicaid managed care model or arrangement implemented under this chapter and to ensure efficiency in provider enrollment and reimbursement. The commission shall incorporate the measures identified in the plan, to the greatest extent possible, into each contract between a managed care organization and the commission for the provision of health care services to recipients.

(b)   The provider protection plan required under this section must provide for:

   (1)   prompt payment and proper reimbursement of providers by managed care organizations;

   (2)   prompt and accurate adjudication of claims through:

      (A)   provider education on the proper submission of clean claims and on appeals;

      (B)   acceptance of uniform forms, including HCFA Forms 1500 and UB-92 and subsequent versions of those forms, through an electronic portal; and

      (C)   the establishment of standards for claims payments in accordance with a provider's contract;

   (3)   adequate and clearly defined provider network standards that are specific to provider type, including physicians, general acute care facilities, and other provider types defined in the commission's network adequacy standards in effect on January 1, 2013, and that ensure choice among multiple providers to the greatest extent possible;

   (4)   a prompt credentialing process for providers;

   (5)   uniform efficiency standards and requirements for managed care organizations for the submission and tracking of preauthorization requests for services provided under the Medicaid program;

   (6)   establishment of an electronic process, including the use of an Internet portal, through which providers in any managed care organization's provider network may:

      (A)   submit electronic claims, prior authorization requests, claims appeals and reconsiderations, clinical data, and other documentation that the managed care organization requests for prior authorization and claims processing; and

      (B)   obtain electronic remittance advice, explanation of benefits statements, and other standardized reports;

   (7)   the measurement of the rates of retention by managed care organizations of significant traditional providers;

   (8)   the creation of a work group to review and make recommendations to the commission concerning any requirement under this subsection for which immediate implementation is not feasible at the time the plan is otherwise implemented, including the required process for submission and acceptance of attachments for claims processing and prior authorization requests through an electronic process under Subdivision (6) and, for any requirement that is not implemented immediately, recommendations regarding the expected:

(A) fiscal impact of implementing the requirement; and

(B) timeline for implementation of the requirement; and

(9) any other provision that the commission determines will ensure efficiency or reduce administrative burdens on providers participating in a Medicaid managed care model or arrangement.

PROVISION OF SOCIAL SERVICES THROUGH FAITH- AND COMMUNITY-BASED ORGANIZATIONS—§535[20]

SUBCHAPTER A. GENERAL PROVISIONS

§535.001. DEFINITIONS

In this chapter:

(1) "Community-based initiative" includes a social, health, human services, or volunteer income tax assistance initiative operated by a community-based organization.

(2) "Community-based organization" means a nonprofit corporation or association that is located in close proximity to the population the organization serves.

(3) "Faith-based initiative" means a social, health, or human services initiative operated by a faith-based organization.

(4) "Faith-based organization" means a nonprofit corporation or association that:

(A) is operated through a religious or denominational organization, including an organization that is operated for religious, educational, or charitable purposes and that is operated, supervised, or controlled, wholly or partly, by or in connection with a religious organization; or

(B) clearly demonstrates through the organization's mission statement, policies, or practices that the organization is guided or motivated by religion.

(5) "State Commission on National and Community Service" means the entity used as authorized by 42 U.S.C. Section 12638(a) to carry out the duties of a state commission under the National and Community Service Act of 1990 (42 U.S.C. Section 12501 et seq.).

§535.002. PURPOSE

The purpose of this chapter is to strengthen the capacity of faith- and community-based organizations and to forge stronger partnerships between those organizations and state government for the legitimate public purpose of providing charitable and social services to persons in this state.

§535.003. CONSTRUCTION

This chapter may not be construed to:

(1) exempt a faith- or community-based organization from any applicable state or federal law; or

---

20 (Government Code; Title 4. Executive Branch; Subtitle I. Health and Human Services; Chapter 535. Provision of Human Services and other Social Services through Faith- and Community-Based Organizations; Subchapter A. General Provisions)

(2) be an endorsement or sponsorship by this state of the religious character, expression, beliefs, doctrines, or practices of a faith-based organization.

§535.004. APPLICABILITY OF CERTAIN FEDERAL LAW

A power authorized or duty imposed under this chapter must be performed in a manner that is consistent with 42 U.S.C. Section 604a.

SUBCHAPTER B. GOVERNMENTAL LIAISONS FOR FAITH- AND COMMUNITY-BASED ORGANIZATIONS

§535.051. DESIGNATION OF FAITH- AND COMMUNITY-BASED LIAISONS .

(a) Requires the executive commissioner of the Health and Human Services Commission (executive commissioner), in consultation with the governor, to designate one employee from the Health and Human Services Commission (HHSC) and from each health and human services agency to serve as a liaison for faith- and community-based organizations.

(b) Requires the chief administrative officer of each of certain state agencies, in consultation with the governor, to designate one employee from the agency to serve as a liaison for certain faith- and community-based organizations.

(c) Requires that the commissioner of higher education, in consultation with the presiding officer of the interagency coordinating group, designate one employee from an institution of higher education to serve as a liaison for faith- and community-based organizations.

§535.052. GENERAL DUTIES OF LIAISONS

(a) A faith- and community-based liaison designated under Section 535.051 shall:

(1) identify and remove unnecessary barriers to partnerships between the state agency the liaison represents and faith- and community-based organizations;

(2) provide information and training, if necessary, for employees of the state agency the liaison represents regarding equal opportunity standards for faith- and community-based organizations seeking to partner with state government;

(3) facilitate the identification of practices with demonstrated effectiveness for faith- and community-based organizations that partner with the state agency the liaison represents;

(4) work with the appropriate departments and programs of the state agency the liaison represents to conduct outreach efforts to inform and welcome faith- and community-based organizations that have not traditionally formed partnerships with the agency;

(5) coordinate all efforts with the governor's office of faith-based and community initiatives and provide information, support, and assistance to that office as requested to the extent permitted by law and as feasible; and

(6) attend conferences sponsored by federal agencies and offices and other relevant entities to become and remain informed of issues and developments regarding faith- and community-based initiatives.

(b) A faith- and community-based liaison designated under Section 535.051 may coordinate and interact with statewide organizations that represent faith- or community-based organizations as necessary to accomplish the purposes of this chapter.

§535.053. INTERAGENCY COORDINATING GROUP

(a)   The interagency coordinating group for faith- and community-based initiatives is composed of each faith- and community-based liaison designated under Section 535.051 and a liaison from the State Commission on National and Community Service. The commission shall provide administrative support to the interagency coordinating group.

(b)   The liaison from the State Commission on National and Community Service is the presiding officer of the interagency coordinating group. If the State Commission on National and Community Service is abolished, the liaison from the governor's office is the presiding officer of the interagency coordinating group.

(c)   The interagency coordinating group shall:

(1)   meet periodically at the call of the presiding officer;

(2)   work across state agencies and with the State Commission on National and Community Service to facilitate the removal of unnecessary interagency barriers to partnerships between state agencies and faith- and community-based organizations; and

(3)   operate in a manner that promotes effective partnerships between those agencies and organizations to serve residents of this state who need assistance.

§535.054. REPORTS

(a)   Not later than December 1 of each year, the interagency coordinating group shall submit a report to the legislature that describes in detail the activities, goals, and progress of the interagency coordinating group.

(b)   The report made under Subsection (a) must be made available to the public through posting on the office of the governor's Internet website.

§535.055. TEXAS NONPROFIT COUNCIL

(a)   The Texas Nonprofit Council is established to help direct the interagency coordinating group in carrying out the group's duties under this section. The commission shall provide administrative support to the council.

(b)   The executive commissioner, in consultation with the presiding officer of the interagency coordinating group, shall appoint as members of the council two representatives from each of the following groups and entities: (1) statewide nonprofit organizations; (2) local governments; (3) faith-based groups; (4) community-based groups; (5) consultants to nonprofit corporations; and (6) statewide associations of nonprofit organizations.

(c)   The council, in coordination with the interagency coordinating group, shall:

(1)   make recommendations for improving contracting relationships between state agencies and faith- and community-based organizations;

(2)   develop best practices for cooperating and collaborating with faith- and community-based organizations;

(3)   identify and address duplication of services provided by the state and faith-and community-based organizations; and

(4)   identify and address gaps in state services that faith- and community-based organizations could fill.

(c-1) The council shall elect a chair or chairs and secretary from among its members and shall assist the executive commissioner in identifying individuals to fill vacant council positions that arise.

(c-2) Council members serve three-year terms. The terms expire on October 1 of every third year. A council member shall serve a maximum of two consecutive terms.

(d)   The council shall prepare a biennial report detailing the council's work, including in the report any recommendations relating to legislation necessary to address an issue identified under this section. The council shall present the report to the House Committee on Human Services or its successor, the House Committee on Public Health or its successor, and the Senate Health and Human Services Committee or its successor not later than December 1 of each even-numbered year.

(e)   Chapter 2110 does not apply to the Texas Nonprofit Council.

(f)   The Texas Nonprofit Council is subject to Chapter 325 (Texas Sunset Act). Unless continued in existence as provided by that chapter, the council is abolished and this section expires September 1, 2019.

CONFIDENTIALITY: EXCEPTIONS TO REQUIRED REPORTING—§5522[1]

Relates to the confidentiality of certain records maintained by a victims of trafficking shelter center and exception to reporting requirements. Confidentiality; provides an exception to the public information requirements for establishments that provide shelter to victims of human trafficking. Social workers do not need to disclose identity nor type of counseling services.

§552.138. EXCEPTION: CONFIDENTIALITY OF FAMILY VIOLENCE SHELTER CENTER, VICTIMS OF TRAFFICKING SHELTER CENTER, AND SEXUAL ASSAULT PROGRAM INFORMATION.

(a)   Information maintained by a family violence shelter center, victims of trafficking shelter center, or sexual assault program is excepted from the requirements of Section 552.021 if it is information that relates to: (1) the home address, home telephone number, or social security number of an employee or a volunteer worker, (2) the location or physical layout if center/shelter, (3) the name, home address, home telephone number, or numeric identifier of a current or former client, (4) the provision of services, including counseling and sheltering, to a current or former client, (5) the name, home address, or home telephone number of a private donor , (6) the home address or home telephone number of a member of the board of directors or the board of trustees.

(b)   The center may redact information maintained from any information the governmental body discloses under Section 552.021 without the necessity of requesting a decision from the attorney general under Subchapter G.

21 (Government Code; Title 5. Open Government; Ethics; Subtitle A. Open Government; Chapter 552. Public Information; Subchapter C. Information Excepted from Required Disclosure)

HEALTH AND SAFETY CODE

TASK FORCE ON DOMESTIC VIOLENCE—§32.061[22]

Creates a task force examining the impact of domestic violence on women and young children.

§32.061. DEFINITION

In this subchapter, "task force" means the task force on domestic violence.

§32.062. ESTABLISHMENT; PRESIDING OFFICER

(a) The task force is composed of 25 members appointed by the executive commissioner of the Health and Human Services Commission, with representatives, as follows: family violence centers (4); statewide family violence advocacy organization (1); statewide association of obstetricians and gynecologists (1); family and community health programs in the Department of State Health Services (2); statewide sexual assault advocacy organization (1); Health and Human Services Commission Texas Home Visiting Program (1); statewide association of midwifery (1); statewide family physician's association (1); statewide nursing association (1); statewide hospital association (1); statewide pediatric medical association (1); statewide medical association (1); The University of Texas School of Social Work Institute on Domestic Violence and Sexual Assault (1); The University of Texas School of Law Domestic Violence Clinic (1); the governor's EMS and Trauma Advisory Council (1); Department of Family and Protective Services prevention and early intervention program (1); statewide osteopathic medical association (1); statewide association of community health centers (1); the office of the attorney general (1); medical school or a teaching hospital in the state who is either an attending physician of the hospital or a faculty member of the medical school (1); and the Health and Human Services Commission's Family Violence Program (1).

(b) The executive commissioner of the Health and Human Services Commission shall appoint a task force member to serve as presiding officer of the task force.

§32.063. DUTIES OF TASK FORCE

The task force shall meet at the call of the presiding officer to:

(1) examine the impact of domestic violence on maternal and infant mortality, the health of mothers, and the health and development of fetuses, infants, and children;

(2) identify the health care services available to children age two and younger and mothers and explore opportunities for improving the ability of those services to address domestic violence;

(3) identify methods to effectively include domestic violence information and support in educational standards for educators and protocols for health care providers; and

(4) investigate and make recommendations relating to the coordination of health care services for children age two and younger and pregnant and

---

22 (Health and Safety Code; Title 2. Health; Subtitle B. Health Programs; Chapter 32. Maternal and Infant Health Improvement; Subchapter C. Task Force on Domestic Violence)

postpartum women who are victims of domestic violence, including recommendations for improving early screening and detection and public awareness efforts.

§32.064. REPORT

Not later than September 1, 2015, the task force shall submit a report to the governor, the lieutenant governor, the speaker of the house of representatives, the presiding officers of the standing committees of the legislature having primary jurisdiction over health and human services, the executive commissioner of the Health and Human Services Commission, and the commissioner of state health services containing:

(1)   the findings and legislative, policy, and research recommendations of the task force; and

(2)   a description of the activities of the task force.

(3)   The task force is abolished and this subchapter expires January 1, 2016.

HIV TESTING, CONFIDENTIALITY, AND CONSENT—§81[23]

§81.103. CONFIDENTIALITY; CRIMINAL PENALTY

(a)   A test result is confidential. A person that possesses or has knowledge of a test result may not release or disclose the test result or allow the test result to become known except as provided by this section.

(b)   A test result may be released to:

(1)   the department under this chapter;

(2)   a local health authority if reporting is required under this chapter;

(3)   the Centers for Disease Control and Prevention of the United States Public Health Service if reporting is required by federal law or regulation;

(4)   the physician or other person authorized by law who ordered the test;

(5)   a physician, nurse, or other health care personnel who have a legitimate need to know the test result in order to provide for their protection and to provide for the patient's health and welfare;

(6)   the person tested or a person legally authorized to consent to the test on the person's behalf;

(7)   the spouse of the person tested if the person tests positive for AIDS or HIV infection, antibodies to HIV, or infection with any other probable causative agent of AIDS;

(8)   a person authorized to receive test results under Article 21.31, Code of Criminal Procedure, concerning a person who is tested as required or authorized under that article;

(9)   a person exposed to HIV infection as provided by §81.050 ; and

(10) a county or district court to comply with this chapter or rules relating to the control and treatment of communicable diseases and health conditions.

(c)   The court shall notify persons receiving test results under Subsection (b)(8) of

23 (Health & Safety Code; Title 2. Health; Subtitle D. Prevention, Control, and Reports Of Diseases; Chapter 81. Communicable Diseases; Subchapter F. Tests for Acquired Immune Deficiency Syndrome and Related Disorders)

the requirements of this section.

(d) A person tested or a person legally authorized to consent to the test on the person's behalf may voluntarily release or disclose that person's test results to any other person, and may authorize the release or disclosure of the test results. An authorization under this subsection must be in writing and signed by the person tested or the person legally authorized to consent to the test on the person's behalf. The authorization must state the person or class of persons to whom the test results may be released or disclosed.

(e) A person may release or disclose a test result for statistical summary purposes only without the written consent of the person tested if information that could identify the person is removed from the report.

(j) A person commits an offense if, with criminal negligence and in violation of this section, the person releases or discloses a test result or other information or allows a test result or other information to become known. An offense under this subsection is a Class A misdemeanor.

(k) A judge of a county or district court may issue a protective order or take other action to limit disclosure of a test result obtained under this section before that information is entered into evidence or otherwise released in a court proceeding.

§81.104. INJUNCTION; CIVIL LIABILITY

(a) A person may bring an action to restrain a violation or threatened violation of §81.102 or 81.103.

(b) A person who violates §81.102 or who is found in a civil action to have negligently released or disclosed a test result or allowed a test result to become known in violation of §81.103 is liable for:

   (1) actual damages;

   (2) a civil penalty of not more than $5,000; and

   (3) court costs and reasonable attorney's fees incurred by the person bringing the action.

(c) A person who is found in a civil action to have willfully released or disclosed a test result or allowed a test result to become known in violation of §81.103 is liable for:

   (1) actual damages;

   (2) a civil penalty of not less than $5,000 nor more than $10,000; and

   (3) court costs and reasonable attorney's fees incurred by the person bringing the action.

(d) Each release or disclosure made, or allowance of a test result to become known, in violation of this subchapter constitutes a separate offense.

(e) A defendant in a civil action brought under this section is not entitled to claim any privilege as a defense to the action.

§81.105. INFORMED CONSENT

(a) Except as otherwise provided by law, a person may not perform a test designed to identify HIV or its antigen or antibody without first obtaining the informed consent of the person to be tested.

(b) Consent need not be written if there is documentation in the medical record that the test has been explained and the consent has been obtained.

§81.106. GENERAL CONSENT

(a) A person who has signed a general consent form for the performance of medical tests or procedures is not required to also sign or be presented with a specific consent form relating to medical tests or procedures to determine HIV infection, antibodies to HIV, or infection with any other probable causative agent of AIDS that will be performed on the person during the time in which the general consent form is in effect.

(b) Except as otherwise provided by this chapter, the result of a test or procedure to determine HIV infection, antibodies to HIV, or infection with any probable causative agent of AIDS performed under the authorization of a general consent form in accordance with this section may be used only for diagnostic or other purposes directly related to medical treatment.

§81.107. CONSENT TO TEST FOR ACCIDENTAL EXPOSURES

(a) In a case of accidental exposure to blood or other body fluids under §81.102(a)(4)(D), the health care agency or facility may test a person who may have exposed the health care worker to HIV without the person's specific consent to the test.

§81.109. COUNSELING REQUIRED FOR POSITIVE TEST RESULTS

(a) A positive test result may not be revealed to the person tested without giving that person the immediate opportunity for individual, face-to-face post-test counseling about:

(1) the meaning of the test result;

(2) the possible need for additional testing;

(3) measures to prevent the transmission of HIV;

(4) the availability of appropriate health care services, including mental health care, and appropriate social and support services in the geographic area of the person's residence;

(5) the benefits of partner notification; and

(6) the availability of partner notification programs.

(b) Post-test counseling should:

(1) increase a person's understanding of HIV infection;

(2) explain the potential need for confirmatory testing;

(3) explain ways to change behavior conducive to HIV transmission;

(4) encourage the person to seek appropriate medical care; and

(5) encourage the person to notify persons with whom there has been contact capable of transmitting HIV.

(c) Subsection (a) does not apply if:

(1) a report of a test result is used for statistical/research purposes only and any information that could identify the person is removed from the report;

(2) or, the test is conducted for the sole purpose of screening blood, blood products, bodily fluids, organs, or tissues to determine suitability for donation.

(d) A person who is injured by an intentional violation of this section may bring a civil action for damages and may recover for each violation from a person who violates this section:

(1) $1,000 or actual damages, whichever is greater; and

(2) reasonable attorney fees.

(e) This section does not prohibit disciplinary proceedings from being conducted by the appropriate licensing authorities for a health care provider's violation of this section.

(f) A person performing a test to show HIV infection, antibodies to HIV, or infection with any other probable causative agent of AIDS is not liable under Subsection (d) for failing to provide post-test counseling if the person tested does not appear for the counseling.

HOME AND COMMUNITY SUPPORT SERVICES—§142[24]

SUBCHAPTER A. HOME AND COMMUNITY SUPPORT SERVICES LICENSE

§142.001. DEFINITIONS

In this chapter:

(1) *"Administrative support site"* means a facility or site where a home and community support services agency performs administrative and other support functions but does not provide direct home health, hospice, or personal assistance services.

(2) *"Alternate delivery site"* means a facility or site, including a residential unit or an inpatient unit:

(A) that is owned or operated by a hospice;

(B) that is not the hospice's principal place of business;

(C) that is located in the geographical area served by the hospice; and

(D) from which the hospice provides hospice services.

(3) *"Bereavement"* means the process by which a survivor of a deceased person mourns and experiences grief.

(4) *"Bereavement services"* means support services offered to a family during bereavement.

(5) *"Branch office"* means a facility or site in the geographical area served by a home and community support agency where home health or personal assistance services are delivered or active client records are maintained.

(6) *"Certified agency"* means a home and community support services agency, or a portion of the agency, that:

(A) provides a home health service; and

(B) is certified by an official of the Department of Health and Human Services as in compliance with conditions of participation in Title XVIII, Social Security Act (42 U.S.C. §1395 et seq.).

(7) *"Certified home health services"* means home health services that are

---

24 (Health & Safety Code; Title 2. Health; Subtitle G. Licenses; Chapter 142. Home and Community Support Services; Subchapter A. Home and Community Support Services License)

provided by a certified agency.

(8) "*Chief financial officer*" means an individual who is responsible for supervising and managing all financial activities for a home and community support services agency.

(9) "*Controlling person*" means a person who controls a home and community support services agency or other person as described by §142.0012.

(10) "*Council*" means the Home and Community Support Services Advisory Council.

(11) "*Counselor*" means an individual qualified under Medicare standards to provide counseling services, including bereavement, dietary, spiritual, and other counseling services, to both the client and the family.

(11-a) "*Department*" means the Department of Aging and Disability Services.

(11-b) "*Executive commissioner*" means the executive commissioner of the Health and Human Services Commission.

(12) "*Home and community support services agency*" means a person who provides home health, hospice, or personal assistance services for pay or other consideration in a client's residence, an independent living environment, or another appropriate location.

(12-a) "*Home and community support services agency administrator*" or "*administrator*" means the person who is responsible for implementing and supervising the administrative policies and operations of the home and community support services agency and for administratively supervising the provision of all services to agency clients on a day-to-day basis.

(13) "*Home health service*" means the provision of one or more of the following health services required by an individual in a residence or independent living environment:

(A) nursing, including blood pressure monitoring and diabetes treatment;

(B) physical, occupational, speech, or respiratory therapy;

(C) medical social service;

(D) intravenous therapy;

(E) dialysis;

(F) service provided by unlicensed personnel under the delegation or supervision of a licensed health professional;

(G) the furnishing of medical equipment and supplies, excluding drugs and medicines; or

(H) nutritional counseling.

(14) "*Hospice*" means a person licensed under this chapter to provide hospice services, including a person who owns or operates a residential unit or an inpatient unit.

(15) "*Hospice services*" means services, including services provided by unlicensed personnel under the delegation of a registered nurse or physical therapist, provided to a client or a client's family as part of a coordinated program consistent with the standards and rules adopted under this chapter. These services include palliative care for terminally ill clients and

support services for clients and their families that:

(A)   are available 24 hours a day, seven days a week, during the last stages of illness, during death, and during bereavement;

(B)   are provided by a medically directed interdisciplinary team; and

(C)   may be provided in a home, nursing home, residential unit, or inpatient unit according to need. These services do not include inpatient care normally provided in a licensed hospital to a terminally ill person who has not elected to be a hospice client.

(16) *"Inpatient unit"* means a facility that provides a continuum of medical or nursing care and other hospice services to clients admitted into the unit and that is in compliance with:

(A)   the conditions of participation for inpatient units adopted under Title XVIII, Social Security Act (42 U.S.C. §1395 et seq.); and

(B)   standards adopted under this chapter.

(17) *"Independent living environment"* means:

(A)   a client's individual residence, which may include a group home or foster home; or

(B)   other settings where a client participates in activities, including school, work, or church.

(18) *"Interdisciplinary team"* means a group of individuals who work together in a coordinated manner to provide hospice services and must include a physician, registered nurse, social worker, and counselor.

(19) *"Investigation"* means an inspection or survey conducted by a representative of the department to determine if a licensee is in compliance with this chapter.

(20) *"Palliative care"* means intervention services that focus primarily on the reduction or abatement of physical, psychosocial, and spiritual symptoms of a terminal illness.

(21) *"Person"* means an individual, corporation, or association.

(22) *"Personal assistance service"* means routine ongoing care or services required by an individual in a residence or independent living environment that enable the individual to engage in the activities of daily living or to perform the physical functions required for independent living, including respite services. The term includes:

(A)   personal care;

(B)   health-related services performed under circumstances that are defined as not constituting the practice of professional nursing by the Texas Board of Nursing through a memorandum of understanding with the department in accordance with §142.016; and

(C)   health-related tasks provided by unlicensed personnel under the delegation of a registered nurse or that a registered nurse determines do not require delegation.

(22-a) *"Personal care"* means the provision of one or more of the following services required by an individual in a residence or independent living environment: (A) bathing; (B) dressing; (C) grooming; (D) feeding; (E) exercising; (F) toileting; (G) positioning; (H) assisting with self-administered medications; (I) routine hair and skin care; and (J) transfer or ambulation.

(23) *"Place of business"* means an office of a home and community support services agency that maintains client records or directs home health, hospice, or personal assistance services. The term does not include an administrative support site.

(24) *"Residence"* means a place where a person resides and includes a home, a nursing home, a convalescent home, or a residential unit.

(25) *"Residential unit"* means a facility that provides living quarters and hospice services to clients admitted into the unit and that is in compliance with standards adopted under this chapter.

(26) *"Respite services"* means support options that are provided temporarily for the purpose of relief for a primary caregiver in providing care to individuals of all ages with disabilities or at risk of abuse or neglect.

(27) *"Social worker"* means an individual licensed as a social worker under Chapter 505, Occupations Code.

(28) *"Support services"* means social, spiritual, and emotional care provided to a client and a client's family by a hospice.

(29) *"Terminal illness"* means an illness for which there is a limited prognosis if the illness runs its usual course.

(30) *"Volunteer"* means an individual who provides assistance to a home and community support services agency without compensation other than reimbursement for actual expenses.

§142.0011. Scope, Purpose, and Implementation

(a) The purpose of this chapter is to ensure that home and community support services agencies in this state deliver the highest possible quality of care. This chapter and the rules adopted under this chapter establish minimum standards for acceptable quality of care, and a violation of a minimum standard established or adopted under this chapter is a violation of law. For purposes of this chapter, components of quality of care include:

(1) client independence and self-determination;

(2) humane treatment;

(3) continuity of care;

(4) coordination of services;

(5) professionalism of service providers;

(6) quality of life; and

(7) client satisfaction with services.

(b) The department shall protect clients of home and community support services agencies by regulating those agencies and:

(1) adopting rules relating to quality of care and quality of life;

(2) strictly monitoring factors relating to the health, safety, welfare, and dignity of each client;

(3) imposing prompt and effective remedies for violations of this chapter and rules and standards adopted under this chapter;

(4) enabling agencies to provide services that allow clients to maintain the highest possible degree of independence and self-determination; and

(5) providing the public with helpful and understandable information relating to agencies in this state.

§142.0012. CONTROLLING PERSON

(a) A person is a controlling person if the person, acting alone or with others, has the ability to directly or indirectly influence, direct, or cause the direction of the management, expenditure of money, or policies of a home and community support services agency or other person.

(b) For purposes of this chapter, "controlling person" includes:

(1) a management company or other business entity that operates or contracts with others for the operation of a home and community support services agency;

(2) a person who is a controlling person of a management company or other business entity that operates a home and community support services agency or that contracts with another person for the operation of a home and community support services agency; and

(3) any other individual who, because of a personal, familial, or other relationship with the owner, manager, or provider of a home and community support services agency, is in a position of actual control or authority with respect to the agency, without regard to whether the individual is formally named as an owner, manager, director, officer, provider, consultant, contractor, or employee of the agency.

(c) A controlling person described by Subsection (b)(3)   does not include an employee, lender, secured creditor, or other person who does not exercise formal or actual influence or control over the operation of a home and community support services agency.

(d) The department may adopt rules that specify the ownership interests and other relationships that qualify a person as a controlling person.

§142.002. LICENSE REQUIRED

(a) Except as provided by §142.003, a person, including a health care facility licensed under this code, may not engage in the business of providing home health, hospice, or personal assistance services, or represent to the public that the person is a provider of home health, hospice, or personal assistance services for pay without a home and community support services agency license authorizing the person to perform those services issued by the department for each place of business from which home health, hospice, or personal assistance services are directed. A certified agency must have a license to provide certified home health services.

(b) A person who is not licensed to provide home health services under this chapter may not indicate or imply that the person is licensed to provide home health services by the use of the words "home health services" or in any other manner.

(c) A person who is not licensed to provide hospice services under this chapter may not use the word "hospice" in a title or description of a facility, organization, program, service provider, or services or use any other words, letters, abbreviations, or insignia indicating or implying that the person holds a license to provide hospice services under this chapter.

(d) A license to provide hospice services issued under this chapter authorizes a hospice to own or operate a residential unit or inpatient unit at the licensed site in compliance with the standards and rules adopted under this chapter.

(e) A license issued under this chapter may not be transferred to another person, but may be transferred from one location to another location. A change of ownership or location shall be reported to the department.

(f) A person who is not licensed to provide personal assistance services under this chapter may not indicate or imply that the person is licensed to provide personal assistance services by the use of the words "personal assistance services" or in any other manner.

§142.0025. TEMPORARY LICENSE

If a person is in the process of becoming certified by the United States Department of Health and Human Services to qualify as a certified agency, the department may issue a temporary home and community support services agency license to the person authorizing the person to provide certified home health services. A temporary license is effective as provided by rules adopted by the executive commissioner.

§142.003. EXEMPTIONS FROM LICENSING REQUIREMENT

(a) The following persons need not be licensed under this chapter:

(1) a physician, dentist, registered nurse, occupational therapist, or physical therapist licensed under the laws of this state who provides home health services to a client only as a part of and incidental to that person's private office practice;

(2) a registered nurse, licensed vocational nurse, physical therapist, occupational therapist, speech therapist, medical social worker, or any other health care professional as determined by the department who provides home health services as a sole practitioner;

(3) a registry that operates solely as a clearinghouse to put consumers in contact with persons who provide home health, hospice, or personal assistance services and that does not maintain official client records, direct client services, or compensate the person who is providing the service;

(4) an individual whose permanent residence is in the client's residence;

(5) an employee of a person licensed under this chapter who provides home health, hospice, or personal assistance services only as an employee of the license holder and who receives no benefit for providing the services, other than wages from the license holder;

(6) a home, nursing home, convalescent home, assisted living facility, special care facility, or other institution for individuals who are elderly or who have disabilities that provides home health or personal assistance services only to residents of the home or institution;

(7) a person who provides one health service through a contract with a person licensed under this chapter;

(8) a durable medical equipment supply company;

(9) a pharmacy or wholesale medical supply company that does not furnish services, other than supplies, to a person at the person's house;

(10) a hospital or other licensed health care facility that provides home health or personal assistance services only to inpatient residents of the hospital or facility;

(11) a person providing home health or personal assistance services to an injured employee under Title 5, Labor Code;

(12) a visiting nurse service that:

    (A) is conducted by and for the adherents of a well-recognized church or religious denomination; and

    (B) provides nursing services by a person exempt from licensing by §301.004, Occupations Code, because the person furnishes nursing care in which treatment is only by prayer or spiritual means;

(13) an individual hired and paid directly by the client or the client's family or legal guardian to provide home health or personal assistance services;

(14) a business, school, camp, or other organization that provides home health or personal assistance services, incidental to the organization's primary purpose, to individuals employed by or participating in programs offered by the business, school, or camp that enable the individual to participate fully in the business's, school's, or camp's programs;

(15) a person or organization providing sitter-companion services or chore or household services that do not involve personal care, health, or health-related services;

(16) a licensed health care facility that provides hospice services under a contract with a hospice;

(17) a person delivering residential acquired immune deficiency syndrome hospice care who is licensed and designated as a residential AIDS hospice under Chapter 248;

(18) the Texas Department of Criminal Justice;

(19) a person that provides home health, hospice, or personal assistance services only to persons receiving benefits under:

    (A) the home and community-based services (HCS) waiver program;

    (B) the Texas home living (TxHmL) waiver program; or

    (C) Section 534.152, Government Code; or

(20) an individual who provides home health or personal assistance services as the employee of a consumer or an entity or employee of an entity acting as a consumer's fiscal agent under §531.051, Government Code.

(b) A home and community support services agency that owns or operates an administrative support site is not required to obtain a separate license under this chapter for the administrative support site.

(c) A hospice that operates or provides hospice services to an inpatient unit under a contract with a licensed health care facility is not required to obtain an alternate delivery site license for that inpatient unit.

§142.004. LICENSE APPLICATION

(a) An applicant for a license to provide home health, hospice, or personal assistance services must:

    (1) file a written application on a form prescribed by the department indicating the type of service the applicant wishes to provide;

    (2) cooperate with any surveys required by the department for a license; and

    (3) pay the license fee prescribed by this chapter.

(b) In addition to the requirements of Subsection (a), if the applicant is a certified agency when the application for a license to provide certified home health services is filed, the applicant must maintain its Medicare certification. If the applicant is not a certified agency when the application for a license to provide certified home health services is filed, the applicant must establish that it is in the process of receiving its certification from the United States Department of Health and Human Services.

(c) The board by rule shall require that, at a minimum, before the department may approve a license application, the applicant must provide to the department:

    (1) documentation establishing that, at a minimum, the applicant has sufficient financial resources to provide the services required by this chapter and by the department during the term of the license;

    (2) a list of the management personnel for the proposed home and community support services agency, a description of personnel qualifications, and a plan for providing continuing training and education for the personnel during the term of the license;

    (3) documentation establishing that the applicant is capable of meeting the minimum standards established by the board relating to the quality of care;

    (4) a plan that provides for the orderly transfer of care of the applicant's clients if the applicant cannot maintain or deliver home health, hospice, or personal assistance services under the license;

    (5) identifying information on the home and community support services agency owner, administrator, and chief financial officer to enable the department to conduct criminal background checks on those persons;

    (6) identification of any controlling person with respect to the applicant; and

    (7) documentation relating to any controlling person identified under Subdivision (6), if requested by the department and relevant to the controlling person's compliance with any applicable licensing standard required or adopted by the board under this chapter.

(d) Information received by the department relating to the competence and financial resources of the applicant or a controlling person with respect to the applicant is confidential and may not be disclosed to the public.

(e) A home and community support services agency owned or operated by a state agency directly providing services is not required to provide the information described in Subsections (c)(1) and (5).

(f) The department shall evaluate and consider all information collected during the application process.

§142.005. COMPLIANCE RECORD IN OTHER STATES

The department may require an applicant or license holder to provide the department with information relating to compliance by the applicant, the license holder, or a controlling person with respect to the applicant or license holder with regulatory requirements in any other state in which the applicant, license holder, or controlling person operates or operated a home and community support services agency.

§142.006. LICENSE ISSUANCE; TERM

(a) The department shall issue a home and community support services agency license to provide home health, hospice, or personal assistance services for each place of business to an applicant if:

    (1) the applicant:

        (A) qualifies for the license to provide the type of service that is to be offered by the applicant;

        (B) submits an application and license fee as required by this chapter; and

        (C) complies with all applicable licensing standards required or adopted by the board under this chapter; and

    (2) any controlling person with respect to the applicant complies with all applicable licensing standards required or adopted by the board under this chapter.

(b) A license issued under this chapter expires two years after the date of issuance. The executive commissioner of the Health and Human Services Commission by rule may adopt a system under which licenses expire on various dates during the two-year period. For the year in which a license expiration date is changed, the department shall prorate the license fee on a monthly basis. Each license holder shall pay only that portion of the license fee allocable to the number of months for which the license is valid. A license holder shall pay the total license renewal fee at the time of renewal. The department may issue an initial license for a shorter term to conform expiration dates for a locality or an applicant. The department may issue a temporary license to an applicant for an initial license.

(c) The department may find that a home and community support services agency has satisfied the requirements for licensing if the agency is accredited by an accreditation organization, such as the Joint Commission on Accreditation of Healthcare Organizations or the Community Health Accreditation Program, and the department finds that the accreditation organization has standards that meet or exceed the requirements for licensing under this chapter. A license fee is required of the home and community support services agency at the time of a license application.

(d) The license must designate the types of services that the home and community support services agency is authorized to provide at or from the designated place of business.

§142.0065. DISPLAY OF LICENSE

A license issued under this chapter shall be displayed in a conspicuous place in the designated place of business and must show:

(1)   the name and address of the licensee;

(2)   the name of the owner or owners, if different from the information provided under Subdivision (1);

(3)   the license expiration date; and

(4)   the types of services authorized to be provided under the license.

§142.0085. Alternate Delivery Site License

(a)   The department shall issue an alternate delivery site license to a qualified hospice.

(b)   The board by rule shall establish standards required for the issuance of an alternate delivery site license.

(c)   An alternate delivery site license expires on the same date as the license to provide hospice services held by the hospice.

§142.009. Surveys; Consumer Complaints

(a)   The department or its representative may enter the premises of a license applicant or license holder at reasonable times to conduct a survey incidental to the issuance of a license and at other times as the department considers necessary to ensure compliance with this chapter and the rules adopted under this chapter.

(a-1) A license applicant or license holder must provide the department representative conducting the survey with a reasonable and safe workspace at the premises. The executive commissioner may adopt rules to implement this subsection.

(b)   A home and community support services agency shall provide each person who receives home health, hospice, or personal assistance services with a written statement that contains the name, address, and telephone number of the department and a statement that informs the recipient that a complaint against a home and community support services agency may be directed to the department.

(c)   The department or its authorized representative shall investigate each complaint received regarding the provision of home health, hospice, or personal assistance services, including any allegation of abuse, neglect, or exploitation of a child under the age of 18, and may, as a part of the investigation:

(1)   conduct an unannounced survey of a place of business, including an inspection of medical and personnel records, if the department has reasonable cause to believe that the place of business is in violation of this chapter or a rule adopted under this chapter;

(2)   conduct an interview with a recipient of home health, hospice, or personal assistance services, which may be conducted in the recipient's home if the recipient consents;

(3)   conduct an interview with a family member of a recipient of home health, hospice, or personal assistance services who is deceased or other person who may have knowledge of the care received by the deceased recipient of the home health, hospice, or personal assistance services; or

(4)   interview a physician or other health care practitioner, including a member of the personnel of a home and community support services agency, who cares for a recipient of home health, hospice, or personal assistance services.

(d) The reports, records, and working papers used or developed in an investigation made under this section are confidential and may not be released or made public except:

   (1) to a state or federal agency;

   (2) to federal, state, or local law enforcement personnel;

   (3) with the consent of each person identified in the information released;

   (4) in civil or criminal litigation matters or licensing proceedings as otherwise allowed by law or judicial rule;

   (5) on a form developed by the department that identifies any deficiencies found without identifying a person, other than the home and community support services agency;

   (6) on a form required by a federal agency if:

      (A) the information does not reveal the identity of an individual, including a patient or a physician or other medical practitioner;

      (B) the service provider subject to the investigation had a reasonable opportunity to review the information and offer comments to be included with the information released or made public; and

      (C) the release of the information complies with any other federal requirement; or

   (7) as provided by §142.0092.

(e) The department's representative shall hold a conference with the person in charge of the home and community support services agency before beginning the on-site survey to explain the nature and scope of the survey. When the survey is completed, the department's representative shall hold a conference with the person who is in charge of the agency and shall identify any records that were duplicated. Agency records may be removed from an agency only with the agency's consent.

(f) At the conclusion of a survey or complaint investigation, the department shall fully inform the person who is in charge of the home and community support services agency of the preliminary findings of the survey at an exit conference and shall give the person a reasonable opportunity to submit additional facts or other information to the department's authorized representative in response to those findings. The response shall be made a part of the record of the survey for all purposes. The department's representative shall leave a written list of the preliminary findings with the agency at the exit conference.

(g) After a survey of a home and community support services agency by the department, the department shall provide to the home and community support services agency administrator:

   (1) specific and timely written notice of the official findings of the survey, including:

      (A) the specific nature of the survey;

      (B) any alleged violations of a specific statute or rule;

      (C) the specific nature of any finding regarding an alleged violation or deficiency; and

(D) if a deficiency is alleged, the severity of the deficiency;

(2) information on the identity, including the name, of each department representative conducting, reviewing the results of the survey and the date on which the department representative acted on the matter; and

(3) if requested by the agency, copies of all documents relating to the survey maintained by the department or provided by the department to any other state or federal agency that are not confidential under state law.

(g-1)If the department or the department's authorized representative discovers any additional violations during the review of field notes or preparation of the official statement of deficiencies for a home and community support services agency, the department or the department's representative shall conduct an additional exit conference regarding the additional violations. The additional exit conference must be held in person and may not be held over the telephone, by e-mail, or by facsimile transmission.

(h) Except for the investigation of complaints, a home and community support services agency licensed by the department under this chapter is not subject to additional surveys relating to home health, hospice, or personal assistance services while the agency maintains accreditation for the applicable service from the Joint Commission for Accreditation of Healthcare Organizations, the Community Health Accreditation Program, or other accreditation organizations that meet or exceed the regulations adopted under this chapter. Each provider must submit to the department documentation from the accrediting body indicating that the provider is accredited when the provider is applying for the initial license and annually when the license is renewed.

(i) Except as provided by Subsection (h), the department may not renew an initial home and community support services agency license unless the department has conducted an initial on-site survey of the agency.

(j) Except as provided by Subsections (h) and (l), an on-site survey must be conducted within 18 months after a survey for an initial license. After that time, an on-site survey must be conducted at least every 36 months.

(k) If a person is renewing or applying for a license to provide more than one type of service under this chapter, the surveys required for each of the services the license holder or applicant seeks to provide shall be completed during the same surveyor visit.

(l) The department and other state agencies that are under the Health and Human Services Commission and that contract with home and community support services agencies to deliver services for which a license is required under this chapter shall execute a memorandum of understanding that establishes procedures to eliminate or reduce duplication of standards or conflicts between standards and of functions in license, certification, or compliance surveys and complaint investigations. The Health and Human Services Commission shall review the recommendation of the council relating to the memorandum of understanding before considering approval. The memorandum of understanding must be approved by the commission.

§142.0091. TRAINING

(a) The department shall provide specialized training to representatives of the department who survey home and community support services agencies. The training must include information relating to:

(1) the conduct of appropriate surveys that do not focus exclusively on medical standards under an acute care model; and

(2) acceptable delegation of nursing tasks.

(b) In developing and updating the training required by Subsection (a), the department shall consult with and include providers of home health, hospice, and personal assistance services, recipients of those services and their family members, and representatives of appropriate advocacy organizations.

(c) The department at least semiannually shall provide joint training for home and community support services agencies and surveyors on subjects that address the 10 most common violations of federal or state law by home and community support services agencies. The department may charge a home and community support services agency a fee, not to exceed $50 per person, for the training.

§142.0092. CONSUMER COMPLAINT DATA

(a) The department shall maintain records or documents relating to complaints directed to the department by consumers of home health, hospice, or personal assistance services. The department shall organize the records or documents according to standard, statewide categories as determined by the department. In determining appropriate categories, the department shall make distinctions based on factors useful to the public in assessing the quality of services provided by a home and community support services agency, including whether the complaint:

(1) was determined to be valid or invalid;

(2) involved significant physical harm or death to a patient;

(3) involved financial exploitation of a patient; or

(4) resulted in any sanction imposed against the agency.

(b) The department shall make the information maintained under this section available to the public in a useful format that does not identify individuals implicated in the complaints.

§142.0093. RETALIATION PROHIBITED

(a) A person licensed under this chapter may not retaliate against another person for filing a complaint, presenting a grievance, or providing in good faith information relating to home health, hospice, or personal assistance services provided by the license holder.

(b) This section does not prohibit a license holder from terminating an employee for a reason other than retaliation.

§142.0105. LICENSE RENEWAL

(a) A person who is otherwise eligible to renew a license may renew an unexpired license by submitting a completed application for renewal and paying the required renewal fee to the department not later than the 45th day before the expiration date of the license. A person whose license has expired may not engage in activities that require a license.

(b) An applicant for a license renewal who submits an application later than the

45th day before the expiration date of the license is subject to a late fee in accordance with department rules.

(c) Not later than the 120th day before the date a person's license is scheduled to expire, the department shall send written notice of the impending expiration to the person at the person's last known address according to the records of the department. The written notice must include an application for license renewal and instructions for completing the application.

§142.011. DENIAL, SUSPENSION, OR REVOCATION OF LICENSE

(a) The department may deny a license application or suspend or revoke the license of a person who:

    (1) fails to comply with the rules or standards for licensing required by this chapter; or

    (2) engages in conduct that violates Section 102.001, Occupations Code.

(b) The department may immediately suspend or revoke a license when the health and safety of persons are threatened. If the department issues an order of immediate suspension or revocation, the department shall immediately give the chief executive officer of the home and community support services agency adequate notice of the action taken, the legal grounds for the action, and the procedure governing appeal of the action. A person whose license is suspended or revoked under this subsection is entitled to a hearing not later than the seventh day after the effective date of the suspension or revocation.

(c) The department may suspend or revoke a home and community support services agency's license to provide certified home health services if the agency fails to maintain its certification qualifying the agency as a certified agency. A home and community support services agency that is licensed to provide certified home health services and that submits a request for a hearing as provided by Subsection (d) is subject to the requirements of this chapter relating to a home and community support services agency that is licensed to provide home health services, but not certified home health services, until the suspension or revocation is finally determined by the department or, if the license is suspended or revoked, until the last day for seeking review of the department order or a later date fixed by order of the reviewing court.

(d) A person whose application is denied or whose license is suspended or revoked is entitled to a hearing before the department if the person submits a written request to the department. Chapter 2001, Government Code and the department's rules for contested case hearings apply to hearings conducted under this section and to appeals from department decisions.

§142.014. CIVIL PENALTY

(a) A person who engages in the business of providing home health, hospice, or personal assistance service, or represents to the public that the person is a provider of home health, hospice, and personal assistance services for pay, without a license issued under this chapter authorizing the services that are being provided is liable for a civil penalty of not less than $1,000 or more than $2,500 for each day of violation. Penalties may be appropriated only to the department and to administer this chapter.

(b) An action to recover a civil penalty is in addition to an action brought for injunctive relief under §142.013 or any other remedy provided by law. The attorney general shall bring suit on behalf of the state to collect the civil penalty.

§142.0145. VIOLATION RELATING TO ADVANCE DIRECTIVES

(a) The department shall assess an administrative penalty against a home and community support services agency that violates §166.004.

(b) A penalty assessed under this section shall be $500.

(c) The penalty shall be assessed in accordance with department rules. The rules must provide for notice and an opportunity for a hearing.

§142.015. ADVISORY COUNCIL

(a) The Home and Community Support Services Advisory Council is composed of the following 13 members, appointed by the governor:

   (1) three consumer representatives;

   (2) two representatives of agencies that are licensed to provide certified home health services;

   (3) two representatives of agencies that are licensed to provide home health services but are not certified home health services;

   (4) three representatives of agencies that are licensed to provide hospice services, with one representative appointed from:

      (A) a community-based non-profit provider of hospice services;

      (B) a community-based proprietary provider of hospice services; and

      (C) a hospital-based provider of hospice services; and

   (5) three representatives of agencies that are licensed to provide personal assistance services.

(c) The council shall advise the department on licensing standards and on the implementation of this chapter. At each meeting of the council, the department shall provide an analysis of enforcement actions taken under this chapter, including the type of enforcement action, the results of the action, and the basis for the action. The council may advise the department on its implementation of the enforcement provisions of this chapter.

(d) Members of the council serve staggered two-year terms, with the terms of seven members expiring on January 31 of each even-numbered year and the terms of six members expiring on January 31 of each odd-numbered year.

(e) The council shall elect a presiding officer from among its members to preside at meetings and to notify members of meetings. The presiding officer shall serve for one year and may not serve in that capacity for more than two years.

(f) The council shall meet at least once a year and may meet at other times at the call of the presiding officer, any three members of the council, or the commissioner.

(g) Members of the council serve without compensation.

§142.017. ADMINISTRATIVE PENALTY

(a) The department may assess an administrative penalty against a person who violates:

   (1) this chapter or a rule adopted under this chapter; or

    (2) Section 102.001, Occupations Code, if the violation relates to the provision of home health, hospice, or personal assistance services.

(b) The penalty shall be not less than $100 or more than $1,000 for each violation. Each day of a violation that occurs before the day on which the person receives written notice of the violation from the department does not constitute a separate violation and shall be considered to be one violation. Each day of a continuing violation that occurs after the day on which the person receives written notice of the violation from the department constitutes a separate violation.

(c) The department by rule shall specify each violation for which an administrative penalty may be assessed. In determining which violations warrant penalties, the department shall consider:

    (1) the seriousness of the violation, including the nature, circumstances, extent, and gravity of the violation and the hazard of the violation to the health or safety of clients; and

    (2) whether the affected home and community support services agency had identified the violation as a part of its internal quality assurance process and had made appropriate progress on correction.

(d) The department by rule shall establish a schedule of appropriate and graduated penalties for each violation based on:

    (1) the seriousness of the violation, including the nature, circumstances, extent, and gravity of the violation and the hazard or safety of clients;

    (2) the history of previous violations by the person or a controlling person with respect to that person;

    (3) whether the affected home and community support services agency had identified the violation as a part of its internal quality assurance process and had made appropriate progress on correction;

    (4) the amount necessary to deter future violations;

    (5) efforts made to correct the violation; and

    (6) any other matters that justice may require.

(e) Except as provided by Subsection (j), the department by rule shall provide the home and community support services agency with a reasonable period of time following the first day of a violation to correct the violation before assessing an administrative penalty if a plan of correction has been implemented.

(f) An administrative penalty may not be assessed for minor violations unless those violations are of a continuing nature or are not corrected.

(g) The department shall establish a system to ensure standard and consistent application of penalties regardless of the home and community support services agency location.

(h) All proceedings for the assessment of an administrative penalty under this chapter are subject to Chapter 2001, Government Code.

(i) The department may not assess an administrative penalty against a state agency.

(j) The department may assess an administrative penalty without providing a reasonable period of time to the agency to correct the violation if the violation:

    (1) results in serious harm or death;

(2)   constitutes a serious threat to health or safety;

(3)   substantially limits the agency's capacity to provide care;

(4)   is a violation in which a person:

    (A)   makes a false statement, that the person knows or should know is false, of a material fact:

        (i)   on an application for issuance or renewal of a license or in an attachment to the application; or

        (ii)   with respect to a matter under investigation by the department;

    (B)   refuses to allow a representative of the department to inspect a book, record, or file required to be maintained by an agency;

    (C)   wilfully interferes with the work of a representative of the department or the enforcement of this chapter;

    (D)   wilfully interferes with a representative of the department preserving evidence of a violation of this chapter or a rule, standard, or order adopted or license issued under this chapter;

    (E)   fails to pay a penalty assessed by the department under this chapter not later than the 10th day after the date the assessment of the penalty becomes final; or

    (F)   fails to submit:

        (i)   a plan of correction not later than the 10th day after the date the person receives a statement of licensing violations; or

        (ii)   an acceptable plan of correction not later than the 30th day after the date the person receives notification from the department that the previously submitted plan of correction is not acceptable;

(5)   is a violation of §142.0145; or

(6)   involves the rights of the elderly under Ch. 102, Human Resources Code.

§142.0171. NOTICE; REQUEST FOR HEARING

(a)   If, after investigation of a possible violation and the facts surrounding that possible violation, the department determines that a violation has occurred, the department shall give written notice of the violation to the person alleged to have committed the violation. The notice shall include:

(1)   a brief summary of the alleged violation;

(2)   a statement of the amount of the proposed penalty based on the factors listed in §142.017(d); and

(3)   a statement of the person's right to a hearing on the occurrence of the violation, the amount of the penalty, or both the occurrence of the violation and the amount of the penalty.

(b)   Not later than the 20th day after the date on which the notice is received, the person notified may accept the determination of the department made under this section, including the proposed penalty, or may make a written request for a hearing on that determination.

(c)   If the person notified of the violation accepts the determination of the department or if the person fails to respond in a timely manner to the notice, the commissioner or the commissioner's designee shall issue an order approving the determination and ordering that the person pay the proposed penalty.

Treatment Facilities Marketing Practices Act—§164[25]

§164.002. Legislative Purpose

The purpose of this chapter is to safeguard the public against fraud, deceit, and misleading marketing practices and to foster and encourage competition and fair dealing by mental health facilities and chemical dependency treatment facilities by prohibiting or restricting practices by which the public has been injured in connection with the marketing and advertising of mental health services and the admission of patients. Nothing in this chapter should be construed to prohibit a mental health facility from advertising its services in a general way or promoting its specialized services. However, the public should be able to distinguish between the marketing activities of the facility and its clinical functions.

§164.003. Definitions

In this chapter:

(1) *"Advertising"* or *"advertise"* means a solicitation or inducement, through print or electronic media, including radio, television, or direct mail, to purchase the services provided by a treatment facility.

(2) *"Chemical dependency"* has the meaning assigned by §462.001.

(3) *"Chemical dependency facility"* means a treatment facility as that term is defined by §462.001.

(4) *"Intervention and assessment service"* means a service that offers assessment, counseling, evaluation, intervention, or referral services or makes treatment recommendations to an individual with respect to mental illness or chemical dependency.

(5) *"Mental health facility"* means:

(A) a *"mental health facility"* as defined by §571.003;

(B) a residential treatment facility, other than a mental health facility, in which persons are treated for emotional problems or disorders in a 24-hour supervised living environment; and

(C) an adult day-care facility or adult day health care facility as defined by §103.003, Human Resources Code.

(6) *"Mental health professional"* means a:

(A) *"physician"* as defined by §571.003;

(B) *"licensed professional counselor"* as defined by §503.002, Occupations Code;

(C) *"chemical dependency counselor"* as defined by §504.001, Occupations Code;

(D) *"psychologist"* offering *"psychological services"* as defined by §501.003, Occupations Code;

(E) *"registered nurse"* licensed under Chapter 301, Occupations Code;

25 (Health and Safety Code; Title 2. Health; Subtitle H. Public Health Provisions; Chapter 164. Treatment Facilities Marketing and Admission Practices)

(F)   *"vocational nurse"* licensed under Chapter 301, Occupations Code;

(G)   *"licensed marriage and family therapist"* as defined by §502.002, Occupations Code; and

(H)   *"social worker"* as defined by §505.002, Occupations Code.

(7)   *"Mental health services"* has the meaning assigned by §531.002.

(8)   *"Mental illness"* has the meaning assigned by §571.003.

(9)   *"Referral source"* means a person who is in a position to refer or who refers a person to a treatment facility. "Referral source" does not include a physician, an insurer, a health maintenance organization (HMO), a preferred provider arrangement (PPA), or other third party payor or discount provider organization (DPO) where the insurer, HMO, PPA, third party payor, or DPO pays in whole or in part for the treatment of mental illness or chemical dependency.

(10) *"Treatment facility"* means a chemical dependency facility and a mental health facility.

§164.004. EXEMPTIONS

This chapter does not apply to:

(1)   a treatment facility

(A)   operated by the Texas Department of Mental Health and Mental Retardation, a federal agency, or a political subdivision;

(B)   funded by the Texas Commission on Alcohol and Drug Abuse;

(2)   a community center established under Subchapter A, Chapter 534, or a facility operated by a community center; or

(3)   a facility owned and operated by a nonprofit or not-for-profit organization offering counseling concerning family violence, help for runaway children, or rape.

§164.005. CONDITIONING EMPLOYEE OR AGENT RELATIONSHIPS ON PATIENT REVENUE

A treatment facility may not permit or provide compensation or anything of value to its employees or agents, condition employment or continued employment of its employees or agents, set its employee or agent performance standards, or condition its employee or agent evaluations, based on:

(1)   the number of patient admissions resulting from an employee's or agent's efforts;

(2)   the number or frequency of telephone calls or other contacts with referral sources or patients if the purpose of the telephone calls or contacts is to solicit patients for the treatment facility; or

(3)   the existence of or volume of determinations made respecting the length of patient stay.

§164.006. SOLICITING AND CONTRACTING WITH CERTAIN REFERRAL SOURCES

A treatment facility or a person employed or under contract with a treatment facility, if acting on behalf of the treatment facility, may not:

(1) contact a referral source or potential client for the purpose of soliciting, directly or indirectly, a referral of a patient to the treatment facility without disclosing its soliciting agent's, employee's, or contractor's affiliation with the treatment facility;

(2) offer to provide or actually provide mental health or chemical dependency services to a public or private school in this state, on a part-time or full-time basis, the services of any of its employees or agents who make, or are in a position to make, a referral, if the services are provided on an individual basis to individual students or their families. Nothing herein prohibits a treatment facility from:

   (A) offering or providing educational programs in group settings to public schools in this state if the affiliation between the educational program and the treatment facility is disclosed;

   (B) providing counseling services to a public school in this state in an emergency or crisis situation if the services are provided in response to a specific request by a school; provided that, under no circumstances may a student be referred to the treatment facility offering the services; or

   (C) entering into a contract with the board of trustees of a school district with an alternative education program under §464.020, or with the board's designee, for the provision of chemical dependency treatment services;

(3) provide to an entity of state or local government, on a part-time or full-time basis, the mental health or chemical dependency services of any of its employees, agents, or contractors who make or are in a position to make referrals unless:

   (A) the treatment facility discloses to the governing authority of the entity:

      (i) the employee's, agent's, or contractor's relationship to the facility; and

      (ii) the fact that the employee, agent, or contractor might make a referral, if permitted, to the facility; and

   (B) the employee, agent, or contractor makes a referral only if:

      (i) the treatment facility obtains the governing authority's authorization in writing for the employee, agent, or contractor to make the referrals; and

      (ii) the employee, agent, or contractor discloses to the prospective patient the employee's, agent's, or contractor's relationship to the facility at initial contact; or

(4) in relation to intervention and assessment services, contract with, offer to remunerate, or remunerate a person who operates an intervention and assessment service that makes referrals to a treatment facility for inpatient treatment of mental illness or chemical dependency unless the intervention and assessment service is:

   (A) operated by a community mental health and mental retardation center funded by the Texas Department of Mental Health and Mental

Retardation;

(B)   operated by a county or regional medical society;

(C)   a qualified mental health referral service as defined by §164.007; or

(D)   owned and operated by a nonprofit or not-for-profit organization offering counseling concerning family violence, help for runaway children, or rape.

§164.007. QUALIFIED MENTAL HEALTH REFERRAL SERVICE: DEFINITION AND STANDARDS

(a)   A qualified mental health referral service means a service that conforms to all of the following standards:

(1)   the referral service does not exclude as a participant in the referral service an individual who meets the qualifications for participation and qualifications for participation cannot be based in whole or in part on an individual's or entity's affiliation or nonaffiliation with other participants in the referral service;

(2)   a payment the participant makes to the referral service is assessed equally against and collected equally from all participants, and is only based on the cost of operating the referral service and not on the volume or value of any referrals to or business otherwise generated by the participants of the referral service;

(3)   the referral service imposes no requirements on the manner in which the participant provides services to a referred person, except that the referral service may require that the participant charge the person referred at the same rate as it charges other persons not referred by the referral service, or that these services be furnished free of charge or at a reduced charge;

(4)   a referral made to a mental health professional or chemical dependency treatment facility is made only in accordance with Subdivision (1)   and the referral service does not make referrals to mental health facilities other than facilities maintained or operated by the Texas Department of Mental Health and Mental Retardation, community mental health and mental retardation centers, or other political subdivisions, provided that a physician may make a referral directly to any mental health facility;

(5)   the referral service is staffed by appropriately licensed and trained mental health professionals and a person who makes assessments for the need for treatment of mental illness or chemical dependency is a mental health professional as defined by this chapter;

(6)   in response to each inquiry or after personal assessment, the referral service makes referrals, on a clinically appropriate, rotational basis, to at least three mental health professionals or chemical dependency treatment facilities whose practice addresses or facilities are located in the county of residence of the person seeking the referral or assessment, but if there are not three providers in the inquirer's county of residence, the referral service may include additional providers from other counties nearest the inquirer's county of residence;

(7)   no information that identifies the person seeking a referral, such as name, address, or telephone number, is used, maintained, distributed, or provided

for a purpose other than making the requested referral or for administrative functions necessary to operating the referral service;

(8) the referral service makes the following disclosures to each person seeking a referral:

    (A) the manner in which the referral service selects the group of providers participating in the referral service;

    (B) whether the provider participant has paid a fee to the referral service;

    (C) the manner in which the referral service selects a particular provider from its list of provider participants to which to make a referral;

    (D) the nature of the relationship or any affiliation between the referral service and the group of provider participants to whom it could make a referral; and

    (E) the nature of any restriction that would exclude a provider from continuing as a provider participant;

(9) the referral service maintains each disclosure in a written record certifying that the disclosure has been made and the record certifying that the disclosure has been made is signed by either the person seeking a referral or by the person making the disclosure on behalf of the referral service; and

(10) if the referral service refers callers to a 1-900 telephone number or another telephone number that requires the payment of a toll or fee payable to or collected by the referral service, the referral service discloses the per minute charge.

(b) A qualified mental health referral service may not limit participation by a person for a reason other than:

(1) failure to have a current, valid license without limitation to practice in this state;

(2) failure to maintain professional liability insurance while participating in the service;

(3) a decision by a peer review committee that the person has failed to meet prescribed standards or has not acted in a professional or ethical manner;

(4) termination of the contract between the participant and the qualified mental health referral service by either party under the terms of the contract; or

(5) significant dissatisfaction of consumers that is documented and verifiable.

§164.008. OPERATING AN INTERVENTION AND ASSESSMENT SERVICE

A treatment facility may not own, operate, manage, or control an intervention and assessment service that makes referrals to a treatment facility for inpatient treatment of mental illness or chemical dependency unless the intervention and assessment service:

(1) is a qualified mental health referral service under Section 164.007;

(2) discloses in all advertising the relationship between the treatment facility and the intervention and assessment service; and

(3) discloses to each person contacting the service, at the time of initial contact, the relationship between the treatment facility and the intervention

and assessment service.

§164.009. DISCLOSURES AND REPRESENTATIONS

(a) A treatment facility may not admit a patient to its facilities without fully disclosing to the patient or, if the patient is a minor, the patient's parent, managing conservator, or guardian, in, if possible, the primary language of the patient, managing conservator, or guardian, as the case may be, the following information in writing before admission:

    (1) the treatment facility's estimated average daily charge for inpatient treatment with an explanation that the patient may be billed separately for services provided by mental health professionals;

    (2) the name of the attending physician, if the treatment facility is a mental health facility, or the name of the attending mental health professional, if the facility is a chemical dependency facility; and

    (3) the current "patient's bill of rights" as adopted by the Texas Department of Mental Health and Mental Retardation, the Texas Commission on Alcohol and Drug Abuse, or the Texas Department of Health that sets out restrictions to the patient's freedom that may be imposed on the patient during the patient's stay in a treatment facility.

(b) A treatment facility may not misrepresent to a patient or the parent, guardian, managing conservator, or spouse of a patient, the availability or amount of insurance coverage available to the prospective patient or the amount and percentage of a charge for which the patient will be responsible.

(c) A treatment facility may not represent to a patient who requests to leave a treatment facility against medical advice that:

    (1) the patient will be subject to an involuntary commitment proceeding or subsequent emergency detention unless that representation is made by a physician or on the written instruction of a physician who has evaluated the patient within 48 hours of the representation; or

    (2) the patient's insurance company will refuse to pay all or any portion of the medical expenses previously incurred.

(d) A mental health facility may not represent or recommend that a prospective patient should be admitted for inpatient treatment unless the representation is made by a licensed physician or, subsequent to evaluation by a licensed physician, by a mental health professional.

(e) A chemical dependency facility may not represent or recommend that a prospective patient should be admitted to a facility for treatment unless and until:

    (1) the prospective patient has been evaluated, in person, by a mental health professional; and

    (2) the mental health professional determines that the patient meets the facility's admission standards.

§164.010. PROHIBITED ACTS

It is a violation of this chapter, in connection with the marketing of mental health services, for a person to:

    (1) advertise, expressly or implied, the services of a treatment facility through

the use of:

   (A) promises of cure or guarantees of treatment results that cannot be substantiated; or

   (B) any unsubstantiated claims;

(2) advertise, expressly or implied, the availability of intervention and assessment services unless and until the services are available and are provided by mental health professionals licensed or certified to provide the particular service;

(3) fail to disclose before soliciting a referral source or prospective patient to induce a person to use the services of the treatment facility an affiliation between a treatment facility and its soliciting agents, employees, or contractors;

(4) obtain information considered confidential by state or federal law regarding a person for the purpose of soliciting that person to use the services of a treatment facility unless and until consent is obtained from the person or, in the case of a minor, the person's parent, managing conservator, or legal guardian or another person with authority to give that authorization; or

(5) represent that a referral service is a qualified mental health referral service unless and until the referral service complies with §164.007.

MEDICAL RECORDS PRIVACY—§181[26]

§181.001. DEFINITIONS

(a) Unless otherwise defined in this chapter, each term that is used in this chapter has the meaning assigned by the Health Insurance Portability and Accountability Act and Privacy Standards.

(b) In this chapter:

  (1) "*Commission*" means the Health and Human Services Commission.

  (2) "*Covered entity*" means any person who:

    (A) for commercial, financial, or professional gain, monetary fees, or dues, or on a cooperative, nonprofit, or pro bono basis, engages, in whole or in part, and with real or constructive knowledge, in the practice of assembling, collecting, analyzing, using, evaluating, storing, or transmitting protected health information. The term includes a business associate, health care payer, governmental unit, information or computer management entity, school, health researcher, health care facility, clinic, health care provider, or person who maintains an Internet site;

    (B) comes into possession of protected health information;

    (C) obtains or stores protected health information under this chapter; or

    (D) is an employee, agent, or contractor of a person described by Paragraph (A), (B), or (C) insofar as the employee, agent, or contractor creates, receives, obtains, maintains, uses, or transmits protected health information.

---

26 (Health And Safety Code; Title 2. Health; Subtitle I. Medical Records; Chapter 181. Medical Records Privacy; Subchapter A. General Provisions)

(2-a) "*Disclose*" means to release, transfer, provide access to, or otherwise divulge information outside the entity holding the information.

(2-b) "*Executive commissioner*" means the executive commissioner of the Health and Human Services Commission.

(3) "*Health Insurance Portability and Accountability Act and Privacy Standards*" means the privacy requirements in existence on September 1, 2011, of the Administrative Simplification subtitle of the Health Insurance Portability and Accountability Act of 1996 (Pub. L. No. 104-191) contained in 45 C.F.R. Part 160 and 45 C.F.R. Part 164, Subparts A and E.

(4) "*Marketing*" means:

  (A) making a communication about a product or service that encourages a recipient of the communication to purchase or use the product or service, unless the communication is made:

    (i) to describe a health-related product or service or the payment for a health-related product or service that is provided by, or included in a plan of benefits of, the covered entity making the communication, including communications about:

      (a) the entities participating in a health care provider network or health plan network;

      (b) replacement of, or enhancement to, a health plan; or

      (c) health-related products or services available only to a health plan enrollee that add value to, but are not part of, a plan of benefits;

    (ii) for treatment of the individual;

    (iii) for case management or care coordination for the individual, or to direct or recommend alternative treatments, therapies, health care providers, or settings of care to the individual; or

    (iv) by a covered entity to an individual that encourages a change to a prescription drug included in the covered entity's drug formulary or preferred drug list;

  (B) an arrangement between a covered entity and any other entity under which the covered entity discloses protected health information to the other entity, in exchange for direct or indirect remuneration, for the other entity or its affiliate to make a communication about its own product or service that encourages recipients of the communication to purchase or use that product or service; and

  (C) notwithstanding Paragraphs (A)(ii) and (iii), a product-specific written communication to a consumer that encourages a change in products.

  (5) "*Product*" means a prescription drug or prescription medical device.l.

§181.002. APPLICABILITY

(a) This chapter does not affect the validity of another statute of this state that provides greater confidentiality for information made confidential by this chapter.

(b) To the extent that this chapter conflicts with another law, other than Section 58.0052, Family Code, with respect to protected health information collected by a governmental body or unit, this chapter controls.

§181.004. APPLICABILITY OF STATE AND FEDERAL LAW

(a) A covered entity, as that term is defined by 45 C.F.R. Section 160.103, shall comply with the Health Insurance Portability and Accountability Act and Privacy Standards.

(b) Subject to Section 181.051, a covered entity, as that term is defined by Section 181.001, shall comply with this chapter.

§181.057. INFORMATION RELATING TO OFFENDERS WITH MENTAL IMPAIRMENTS

This chapter does not apply to an agency described by §614.017 with respect to the disclosure, receipt, transfer, or exchange of medical and health information and records relating to individuals in the custody of an agency or in community supervision.

§181.058. EDUCATIONAL RECORDS

In this chapter, protected health information does not include:

(1) education records covered by the Family Educational Rights and Privacy Act of 1974 (20 U.S.C. §1232g) and its subsequent amendments; or

(2) records described by 20 U.S.C. §1232g(a)(4)(B)(iv) and its subsequent amendments.

SUBCHAPTER C
ACCESS TO AND USE OF PROTECTED HEALTH INFORMATION

§181.101. TRAINING REQUIRED

(a) Each covered entity shall provide training to employees of the covered entity regarding the state and federal law concerning protected health information as necessary and appropriate for the employees to carry out the employees' duties for the covered entity.

(b) An employee of a covered entity must complete training described by Subsection (a) not later than the 90th day after the date the employee is hired by the covered entity.

(c) If the duties of an employee of a covered entity are affected by a material change in state or federal law concerning protected health information, the employee shall receive training described by Subsection (a) within a reasonable period, but not later than the first anniversary of the date the material change in law takes effect.

(d) A covered entity shall require an employee of the entity who receives training described by Subsection (a) to sign, electronically or in writing, a statement verifying the employee's completion of training. The covered entity shall maintain the signed statement until the sixth anniversary of the date the statement is signed.

§181.102. CONSUMER ACCESS TO ELECTRONIC HEALTH RECORDS

(a) Except as provided by Subsection (b), if a health care provider is using an electronic health records system that is capable of fulfilling the request, the health care provider, not later than the 15th business day after the date the health care provider receives a written request from a person for the person's electronic health record, shall provide the requested record to the person in electronic form unless the person agrees to accept the record in another form.

(b) A health care provider is not required to provide access to a person's protected health information that is excepted from access, or to which access may be denied, under 45 C.F.R. Section 164.524.

(c) For purposes of Subsection (a), the executive commissioner, in consultation with the Department of State Health Services, the Texas Medical Board, and the Texas Department of Insurance, by rule may recommend a standard electronic format for the release of requested health records. The standard electronic format recommended under this section must be consistent, if feasible, with federal law regarding the release of electronic health records.

§181.103. CONSUMER INFORMATION WEBSITE

The attorney general shall maintain an Internet website that provides:

(1) information concerning a consumer's privacy rights regarding protected health information under federal and state law;

(2) a list of the state agencies, including the Department of State Health Services, the Texas Medical Board, and the Texas Department of Insurance, that regulate covered entities in this state and the types of entities each agency regulates;

(3) detailed information regarding each agency's complaint enforcement process; and

(4) contact information, including the address of the agency's Internet website, for each agency listed under Subdivision (2) for reporting a violation of this chapter.

§181.104. CONSUMER COMPLAINT REPORT BY ATTORNEY GENERAL

(a) The attorney general annually shall submit to the legislature a report describing:

(1) the number and types of complaints received by the attorney general and by the state agencies receiving consumer complaints under Section 181.103; and

(2) the enforcement action taken in response to each complaint reported under Subdivision (1).

(b) Each state agency that receives consumer complaints under Section 181.103 shall submit to the attorney general, in the form required by the attorney general, the information the attorney general requires to compile the report required by Subsection (a).

(c) The attorney general shall de-identify protected health information from the individual to whom the information pertains before including the information in the report required by Subsection (a).

PROHIBITED ACTS

§181.151. REIDENTIFIED INFORMATION

A person may not reidentify or attempt to reidentify an individual who is the subject of any protected health information without obtaining the individual's consent or authorization if required under this chapter or other state or federal law.

§181.152. MARKETING USES OF INFORMATION

(a) A covered entity must obtain clear and unambiguous permission in written or electronic form to use or disclose protected health information for any marketing communication, except if the communication is:

  (1) in the form of a face-to-face communication made by a covered entity to an individual;

  (2) in the form of a promotional gift of nominal value provided by the covered entity;

  (3) necessary for administration of a patient assistance program or other prescription drug savings or discount program; or

  (4) made at the oral request of the individual.

(b) If a covered entity uses or discloses protected health information to send a written marketing communication through the mail, the communication must be sent in an envelope showing only the names and addresses of sender and recipient and must:

  (1) state the name and toll-free number of the entity sending the marketing communication; and

  (2) explain the recipient's right to have the recipient's name removed from the sender's mailing list.

(c) A person who receives a request under Subsection (b)(2) to remove a person's name from a mailing list shall remove the person's name not later than the 45th day after the date the person receives the request.

(d) A marketing communication made at the oral request of the individual under Subsection (a)(4) may be made only if clear and unambiguous oral permission for the use or disclosure of the protected health information is obtained. The marketing communication must be limited to the scope of the oral permission and any further marketing communication must comply with the requirements of this section.

§181.153. SALE OF PROTECTED HEALTH INFORMATION PROHIBITED; EXCEPTIONS

(a) A covered entity may not disclose an individual's protected health information to any other person in exchange for direct or indirect remuneration, except that a covered entity may disclose an individual's protected health information:

  (1) to another covered entity, as that term is defined by Section 181.001, or to a covered entity, as that term is defined by Section 602.001, Insurance Code, for the purpose of:

    (A) treatment;

    (B) payment;

    (C) health care operations; or

    (D) performing an insurance or health maintenance organization function described by Section 602.053, Insurance Code; or

  (2) as otherwise authorized or required by state or federal law.

(b) The direct or indirect remuneration a covered entity receives for making a disclosure of protected health information authorized by Subsection (a)(1)(D) may not exceed the covered entity's reasonable costs of preparing or transmitting the protected health information.

§181.154. NOTICE AND AUTHORIZATION REQUIRED FOR ELECTRONIC DISCLOSURE OF PROTECTED HEALTH INFORMATION; EXCEPTIONS

(a) A covered entity shall provide notice to an individual for whom the covered entity creates or receives protected health information if the individual's protected health information is subject to electronic disclosure. A covered entity may provide general notice by:

(1) posting a written notice in the covered entity's place of business;

(2) posting a notice on the covered entity's Internet website; or

(3) posting a notice in any other place where individuals whose protected health information is subject to electronic disclosure are likely to see the notice.

(b) Except as provided by Subsection (c), a covered entity may not electronically disclose an individual's protected health information to any person without a separate authorization from the individual or the individual's legally authorized representative for each disclosure. An authorization for disclosure under this subsection may be made in written or electronic form or in oral form if it is documented in writing by the covered entity.

(c) The authorization for electronic disclosure of protected health information described by Subsection (b) is not required if the disclosure is made:

(1) to another covered entity, as that term is defined by Section 181.001, or to a covered entity, as that term is defined by Section 602.001, Insurance Code, for the purpose of:

(A) treatment;

(B) payment;

(C) health care operations; or

(D) performing an insurance or health maintenance organization function described by Section 602.053, Insurance Code; or

(2) as otherwise authorized or required by state or federal law.

(d) The attorney general shall adopt a standard authorization form for use in complying with this section. The form must comply with the Health Insurance Portability and Accountability Act and Privacy Standards and this chapter.

(e) This section does not apply to a covered entity, as defined by Section 602.001, Insurance Code, if that entity is not a covered entity as defined by 45 C.F.R. Section 160.103.

SUBCHAPTER E
ENFORCEMENT

§181.201. INJUNCTIVE RELIEF; CIVIL PENALTY

(a) The attorney general may institute an action for injunctive relief to restrain a violation of this chapter.

(b) In addition to the injunctive relief provided by Subsection (a), the attorney general may institute an action for civil penalties against a covered entity for a violation of this chapter. A civil penalty assessed under this section may not exceed:

   (1) $5,000 for each violation that occurs in one year, regardless of how long the violation continues during that year, committed negligently;

   (2) $25,000 for each violation that occurs in one year, regardless of how long the violation continues during that year, committed knowingly or intentionally; or

   (3) $250,000 for each violation in which the covered entity knowingly or intentionally used protected health information for financial gain.

(b-1) The total amount of a penalty assessed against a covered entity under Subsection (b) in relation to a violation or violations of Section 181.154 may not exceed $250,000 annually if the court finds that the disclosure was made only to another covered entity and only for a purpose described by Section 181.154(c) and the court finds that:

   (1) the protected health information disclosed was encrypted or transmitted using encryption technology designed to protect against improper disclosure;

   (2) the recipient of the protected health information did not use or release the protected health information; or

   (3) at the time of the disclosure of the protected health information, the covered entity had developed, implemented, and maintained security policies, including the education and training of employees responsible for the security of protected health information.

(c) If the court in which an action under Subsection (b) is pending finds that the violations have occurred with a frequency as to constitute a pattern or practice, the court may assess a civil penalty not to exceed $1.5 million annually.

(d) In determining the amount of a penalty imposed under Subsection (b), the court shall consider:

   (1) the seriousness of the violation, including the nature, circumstances, extent, and gravity of the disclosure;

   (2) the covered entity's compliance history;

   (3) whether the violation poses a significant risk of financial, reputational, or other harm to an individual whose protected health information is involved in the violation;

   (4) whether the covered entity was certified at the time of the violation as described by Section 182.108;

   (5) the amount necessary to deter a future violation; and

   (6) the covered entity's efforts to correct the violation.

(e) The attorney general may institute an action against a covered entity that is licensed by a licensing agency of this state for a civil penalty under this section only if the licensing agency refers the violation to the attorney general under Section 181.202(2).

(f) The office of the attorney general may retain a reasonable portion of a civil penalty recovered under this section, not to exceed amounts specified in the General Appropriations Act, for the enforcement of this subchapter.

§181.202. DISCIPLINARY ACTION

In addition to the penalties prescribed by this chapter, a violation of this chapter by a covered entity that is licensed by an agency of this state is subject to investigation and disciplinary proceedings, including probation or suspension by the licensing agency. If there is evidence that the violations of this chapter are egregious and constitute a pattern or practice, the agency may:

(1)   revoke the covered entity's license; or

(2)   refer the covered entity's case to the attorney general for the institution of an action for civil penalties under Section 181.201(b).

§181.203. EXCLUSION FROM STATE PROGRAMS

In addition to the penalties prescribed by this chapter, a covered entity shall be excluded from participating in any state-funded health care program if a court finds the covered entity engaged in a pattern or practice of violating this chapter.

§181.205. MITIGATION

(a)   In an action or proceeding to impose an administrative penalty or assess a civil penalty for actions related to the disclosure of individually identifiable health information, a covered entity may introduce, as mitigating evidence, evidence of the entity's good faith efforts to comply with:

(1)   state law related to the privacy of individually identifiable health information; or

(2)   the Health Insurance Portability and Accountability Act and Privacy Standards.

(b)   In determining the amount of a penalty imposed under other law in accordance with Section 181.202, a court or state agency shall consider the following factors:

(1)   the seriousness of the violation, including the nature, circumstances, extent, and gravity of the disclosure;

(2)   the covered entity's compliance history;

(3)   whether the violation poses a significant risk of financial, reputational, or other harm to an individual whose protected health information is involved in the violation;

(4)   whether the covered entity was certified at the time of the violation as described by Section 182.108;

(5)   the amount necessary to deter a future violation; and

(6)   the covered entity's efforts to correct the violation.

(c)   On receipt of evidence under Subsections (a) and (b), a court or state agency shall consider the evidence and mitigate imposition of an administrative penalty or assessment of a civil penalty accordingly.

§181.206. AUDITS OF COVERED ENTITIES

(a)   The commission, in coordination with the attorney general, the Texas Health Services Authority, and the Texas Department of Insurance:

(1) may request that the United States secretary of health and human services conduct an audit of a covered entity, as that term is defined by 45 C.F.R. Section 160.103, in this state to determine compliance with the Health Insurance Portability and Accountability Act and Privacy Standards; and

(2) shall periodically monitor and review the results of audits of covered entities in this state conducted by the United States secretary of health and human services.

(b) If the commission has evidence that a covered entity has committed violations of this chapter that are egregious and constitute a pattern or practice, the commission may:

(1) require the covered entity to submit to the commission the results of a risk analysis conducted by the covered entity if required by 45 C.F.R. Section 164.308(a)(1)(ii)(A); or

(2) if the covered entity is licensed by a licensing agency of this state, request that the licensing agency conduct an audit of the covered entity's system to determine compliance with the provisions of this chapter.

(c) The commission annually shall submit to the appropriate standing committees of the senate and the house of representatives a report regarding the number of federal audits of covered entities in this state and the number of audits required under Subsection (b).

§181.207. FUNDING

The commission and the Texas Department of Insurance, in consultation with the Texas Health Services Authority, shall apply for and actively pursue available federal funding for enforcement of this chapter.

DEATH RECORDS AND SUICIDE DATA COLLECTION—§193[27]

Section 1. The purpose of this Act is to encourage the prompt reporting of suicide data that does not name a deceased individual and to encourage use of the data for instructive and preventive purposes.

§193.011. MEMORANDUM ON SUICIDE DATA

The purpose of this Act is to encourage the prompt reporting of suicide data that does not name a deceased individual and to encourage use of the data for instructive and preventive purposes.

(a) In this section, "authorized entity" means a medical examiner, a local registrar, a local health authority, a local mental health authority, a community mental health center, a mental health center that acts as a collection agent for the suicide data reported by community mental health centers, or any other political subdivision of this state.

(b) An authorized entity may enter into a memorandum of understanding with another authorized entity to share suicide data that does not name a deceased individual. The shared data may include:

(1) the deceased individual's date of birth, race or national origin, gender, and zip code of residence;

---

27 (Health & Safety Code; Title 3. Vital Statistics; Chapter 193. Death Records; Section 1. Death Records and Suicide Data Collection)

(2) any school or college the deceased individual was attending at the time of death;

(3) the suicide method used by the deceased individual;

(4) the deceased individual's status as a veteran or member of the armed services; and

(5) the date of the deceased individual's death.

(c) The suicide data an authorized entity receives or provides under Subsection (b) is not confidential.

(d) An authorized entity that receives suicide data under a memorandum of understanding authorized by this section may periodically release suicide data that does not name a deceased individual to an agency or organization with recognized expertise in suicide prevention. The agency or organization may use suicide data received by the agency or organization under this subsection only for suicide prevention purposes.

(e) An authorized entity or an employee or agent of an authorized entity is not civilly or criminally liable for receiving or providing suicide data that does not name a deceased individual and that may be shared under a memorandum of understanding authorized by this section.

(f) This section does not prohibit the sharing of data as authorized by other law.

REPORTS OF ABUSE, NEGLECT, AND EXPLOITATION OF RESIDENTS OF CERTAIN FACILITIES—§260A[28]

§260A.001. DEFINITIONS. IN THIS CHAPTER

(1) "*Abuse*" means:

    (a) the negligent or wilful infliction of injury, unreasonable confinement, intimidation, or cruel punishment with resulting physical or emotional harm or pain to a resident by the resident's caregiver, family member, or other individual who has an ongoing relationship with the resident; or

    (b) sexual abuse of a resident, including any involuntary or nonconsensual sexual conduct that would constitute an offense under section 21.08, penal code (indecent exposure), or chapter 22, penal code (assaultive offenses), committed by the resident's caregiver, family member, or other individual who has an ongoing relationship with the resident.

(2) "*Department*" means the department of aging and disability services.

(3) "*Executive commissioner*" means the executive commissioner of the health and human services commission.

(4) "*Exploitation*" means the illegal or improper act or process of a caregiver, family member, or other individual who has an ongoing relationship with the resident using the resources of a resident for monetary or personal benefit, profit, or gain without the informed consent of the resident.

(5) "*Facility*" means:

---

28 (Health & Safety Code; Title 4. Health Facilities; Subtitle B. Licensing of Health Facilities; Chapter 260A. Reports of Abuse, Neglect, and Exploitation of Residents of Certain Facilities)

(a)   an institution as that term is defined by section 242.002;

(b)   an assisted living facility as that term is defined by section 247.002; and

(c)   a prescribed pediatric extended care center as that term is defined by section 248a.001.

(6)   "*Neglect*" means the failure to provide for one's self the goods or services, including medical services, which are necessary to avoid physical or emotional harm or pain or the failure of a caregiver to provide such goods or services.

(7)   "*Resident*" means an individual, including a patient, who resides in or receives services from a facility.

§260A.002. REPORTING OF ABUSE, NEGLECT, AND EXPLOITATION

(a)   A person, including an owner or employee of a facility, who has cause to believe that the physical or mental health or welfare of a resident has been or may be adversely affected by abuse, neglect, or exploitation caused by another person shall report the abuse, neglect, or exploitation in accordance with this chapter.

(b)   Each facility shall require each employee of the facility, as a condition of employment with the facility, to sign a statement that the employee realizes that the employee may be criminally liable for failure to report those abuses.

(c)   A person shall make an oral report immediately on learning of the abuse, neglect, or exploitation and shall make a written report to the department not later than the fifth day after the oral report is made.

§260A.003. CONTENTS OF REPORT

(a)   A report of abuse, neglect, or exploitation is nonaccusatory and reflects the reporting person's belief that a resident has been or will be abused, neglected, or exploited or has died of abuse or neglect.

(b)   The report must contain:

(1)   the name and address of the resident;

(2)   the name and address of the person responsible for the care of the resident, if available; and

(3)   other relevant information.

(c)   Except for an anonymous report under section 260a.004, a report of abuse, neglect, or exploitation under section 260a.002 should also include the address or phone number of the person making the report so that an investigator can contact the person for any necessary additional information. The phone number, address, and name of the person making the report must be deleted from any copy of any type of report that is released to the public, to the facility, or to an owner or agent of the facility.

§260A.004. ANONYMOUS REPORTS OF ABUSE, NEGLECT, OR EXPLOITATION

(a)   An anonymous report of abuse, neglect, or exploitation, although not encouraged, shall be received and acted on in the same manner as an acknowledged report.

(b)   An anonymous report about a specific individual that accuses the individual of abuse, neglect, or exploitation need not be investigated.

§260A.005. TELEPHONE HOTLINE; PROCESSING OF REPORTS

(a) The department shall operate the department's telephone hotline to:

  (1) receive reports of abuse, neglect, or exploitation; and

  (2) dispatch investigators.

(b) A report of abuse, neglect, or exploitation shall be made to the department's telephone hotline or to a local or state law enforcement agency. A report made relating to abuse, neglect, or exploitation or another complaint described by section 260a.007(c)(1) shall be made to the department's telephone hotline and to the law enforcement agency described by section 260a.017(a).

(c) Except as provided by section 260a.017, a local or state law enforcement agency that receives a report of abuse, neglect, or exploitation shall refer the report to the department.

§260A.006. NOTICE

(a) Each facility shall prominently and conspicuously post a sign for display in a public area of the facility that is readily available to residents, employees, and visitors.

(b) The sign must include the statement: Cases of suspected abuse, neglect, or exploitation shall be reported to the texas department of aging and disability services by calling (insert telephone hotline number).

(c) A facility shall provide the telephone hotline number to an immediate family member of a resident of the facility upon the resident's admission into the facility.

§260A.007. INVESTIGATION AND DEPORT OF DEPARTMENT

(a) The department shall make a thorough investigation after receiving an oral or written report of abuse, neglect, or exploitation under section 260a.002 or another complaint alleging abuse, neglect, or exploitation.

(b) The primary purpose of the investigation is the protection of the resident.

(c) The department shall begin the investigation:

  (1) within 24 hours after receipt of the report or other allegation, if the report of abuse, neglect, exploitation, or other complaint alleges that:

    (a) a resident's health or safety is in imminent danger;

    (b) a resident has recently died because of conduct alleged in the report of abuse, neglect, exploitation, or other complaint;

    (c) a resident has been hospitalized or been treated in an emergency room because of conduct alleged in the report of abuse, neglect, exploitation, or other complaint;

    (d) a resident has been a victim of any act or attempted act described by section 21.02, 21.11, 22.011, or 22.021, penal code; or

    (e) a resident has suffered bodily injury, as that term is defined by section 1.07, penal code, because of conduct alleged in the report of abuse, neglect, exploitation, or other complaint; or

(2) before the end of the next working day after the date of receipt of the report of abuse, neglect, exploitation, or other complaint, if the report or complaint alleges the existence of circumstances that could result in abuse, neglect, or exploitation and that could place a resident's health or safety in imminent danger.

(d) The department shall adopt rules governing the conduct of investigations, including procedures to ensure that the complainant and the resident, the resident's next of kin, and any person designated to receive information concerning the resident receive periodic information regarding the investigation.

(e) In investigating the report of abuse, neglect, exploitation, or other complaint, the investigator for the department shall:

    (1) make an unannounced visit to the facility to determine the nature and cause of the alleged abuse, neglect, or exploitation of the resident;

    (2) interview each available witness, including the resident who suffered the alleged abuse, neglect, or exploitation if the resident is able to communicate or another resident or other witness identified by any source as having personal knowledge relevant to the report of abuse, neglect, exploitation, or other complaint;

    (3) personally inspect any physical circumstance that is relevant and material to the report of abuse, neglect, exploitation, or other complaint and that may be objectively observed;

    (4) make a photographic record of any injury to a resident, subject to subsection (n); and

    (5) write an investigation report that includes:

        (a) the investigator's personal observations;

        (b) a review of relevant documents and records;

        (c) a summary of each witness statement, including the statement of the resident that suffered the alleged abuse, neglect, or exploitation and any other resident interviewed in the investigation; and

        (d) a statement of the factual basis for the findings for each incident or problem alleged in the report or other allegation.

(f) An investigator for an investigating agency shall conduct an interview under subsection (e)(2) in private unless the witness expressly requests that the interview not be private.

(g) Not later than the 30th day after the date the investigation is complete, the investigator shall prepare the written report required by subsection (e). The department shall make the investigation report available to the public on request after the date the department's letter of determination is complete. The department shall delete from any copy made available to the public:

    (1) the name of:

        (a) any resident, unless the department receives written authorization from a resident or the resident's legal representative requesting the resident's name be left in the report;

        (b) the person making the report of abuse, neglect, exploitation, or other complaint; and

    (c) an individual interviewed in the investigation; and

  (2) photographs of any injury to the resident.

(h) In the investigation, the department shall determine:

    (1) the nature, extent, and cause of the abuse, neglect, or exploitation;

    (2) the identity of the person responsible for the abuse, neglect, or exploitation;

    (3) the names and conditions of the other residents;

    (4) an evaluation of the persons responsible for the care of the residents;

    (5) the adequacy of the facility environment; and

    (6) any other information required by the department.

(i) If the department attempts to carry out an on-site investigation and it is shown that admission to the facility or any place where the resident is located cannot be obtained, a probate or county court shall order the person responsible for the care of the resident or the person in charge of a place where the resident is located to allow entrance for the interview and investigation.

(j) Before the completion of the investigation, the department shall file a petition for temporary care and protection of the resident if the department determines that immediate removal is necessary to protect the resident from further abuse, neglect, or exploitation.

(k) The department shall make a complete final written report of the investigation and submit the report and its recommendations to the district attorney and, if a law enforcement agency has not investigated the report of abuse, neglect, exploitation, or other complaint, to the appropriate law enforcement agency.

(l) Within 24 hours after receipt of a report of abuse, neglect, exploitation, or other complaint described by subsection (c)(1), the department shall report the report or complaint to the law enforcement agency described by section 260a.017(a). The department shall cooperate with that law enforcement agency in the investigation of the report or complaint as described by section 260a.017.

(m) The inability or unwillingness of a local law enforcement agency to conduct a joint investigation under section 260a.017 does not constitute grounds to prevent or prohibit the department from performing its duties under this chapter. The department shall document any instance in which a law enforcement agency is unable or unwilling to conduct a joint investigation under section 260a.017.

(n) If the department determines that, before a photographic record of an injury to a resident may be made under subsection (e), consent is required under state or federal law, the investigator:

    (1) shall seek to obtain any required consent; and

    (2) may not make the photographic record unless the consent is obtained.

§260A.008. CONFIDENTIALITY

A report, record, or working paper used or developed in an investigation made under this chapter and the name, address, and phone number of any person making a report under this chapter are confidential and may be disclosed only for purposes consistent with rules adopted by the executive commissioner. The report, record, or working paper and the name, address, and phone number of the person making the report shall be disclosed to a law enforcement agency as necessary to permit the law enforcement agency to investigate a report of abuse, neglect, exploitation, or other complaint in accordance with section 260a.017.

§260A.009. IMMUNITY

(a) A person who reports as provided by this chapter is immune from civil or criminal liability that, in the absence of the immunity, might result from making the report.

(b) The immunity provided by this section extends to participation in any judicial proceeding that results from the report.

(c) This section does not apply to a person who reports in bad faith or with malice.

§260A.010. PRIVILEGED COMMUNICATIONS

In a proceeding regarding the abuse, neglect, or exploitation of a resident or the cause of any abuse, neglect, or exploitation, evidence may not be excluded on the ground of privileged communication except in the case of a communication between an attorney and client.

§260A.011. CENTRAL REGISTRY

(a) The department shall maintain in the city of austin a central registry of reported cases of resident abuse, neglect, or exploitation.

(b) The executive commissioner may adopt rules necessary to carry out this section.

(c) The rules shall provide for cooperation with hospitals and clinics in the exchange of reports of resident abuse, neglect, or exploitation.

§260A.012. FAILURE TO REPORT; CRIMINAL PENALTY

(a) A person commits an offense if the person has cause to believe that a resident's physical or mental health or welfare has been or may be further adversely affected by abuse, neglect, or exploitation and knowingly fails to report in accordance with section 260a.002.

(b) An offense under this section is a class a misdemeanor.

§260A.013. BAD FAITH, MALICIOUS, OR RECKLESS REPORTING; CRIMINAL PENALTY

(a) A person commits an offense if the person reports under this chapter in bad faith, maliciously, or recklessly.

(b) An offense under this section is a class a misdemeanor.

(c) The criminal penalty provided by this section is in addition to any civil penalties for which the person may be liable.

§260A.014. RETALIATION AGAINST EMPLOYEES PROHIBITED

(a) In this section, "employee" means a person who is an employee of a facility or any other person who provides services for a facility for compensation, including a contract laborer for the facility.

(b) An employee has a cause of action against a facility, or the owner or another employee of the facility, that suspends or terminates the employment of the person or otherwise disciplines or discriminates or retaliates against the employee for reporting to the employee's supervisor, an administrator of the facility, a state regulatory agency, or a law enforcement agency a violation of law, including a violation of chapter 242 or 247 or a rule adopted under chapter 242 or 247, or for initiating or cooperating in any investigation or proceeding of a governmental entity relating to care, services, or conditions at the facility.

(c) The petitioner may recover:

(1) the greater of $1,000 or actual damages, including damages for mental anguish even if an injury other than mental anguish is not shown, and damages for lost wages if the petitioner's employment was suspended or terminated;

(2) exemplary damages;

(3) court costs; and

(4) reasonable attorney's fees.

(d) In addition to the amounts that may be recovered under subsection (c), a person whose employment is suspended or terminated is entitled to appropriate injunctive relief, including, if applicable:

(1) reinstatement in the person's former position; and

(2) reinstatement of lost fringe benefits or seniority rights.

(e) The petitioner, not later than the 90th day after the date on which the person's employment is suspended or terminated, must bring suit or notify the texas workforce commission of the petitioner's intent to sue under this section. A petitioner who notifies the texas workforce commission under this subsection must bring suit not later than the 90th day after the date of the delivery of the notice to the commission. On receipt of the notice, the commission shall notify the facility of the petitioner's intent to bring suit under this section.

(f) The petitioner has the burden of proof, except that there is a rebuttable presumption that the person's employment was suspended or terminated for reporting abuse, neglect, or exploitation if the person is suspended or terminated within 60 days after the date on which the person reported in good faith.

(g) A suit under this section may be brought in the district court of the county in which:

(1) the plaintiff resides;

(2) the plaintiff was employed by the defendant; or

(3) the defendant conducts business.

(h) Each facility shall require each employee of the facility, as a condition of employment with the facility, to sign a statement that the employee understands the employee's rights under this section. The statement must be part of the statement required under section 260a.002. If a facility does not require an employee to read and sign the statement, the periods under subsection (e) do not apply, and the petitioner must bring suit not later than the second anniversary of the date on which the person's employment is suspended or terminated.

§260A.015. RETALIATION AGAINST VOLUNTEERS, RESIDENTS, OR FAMILY MEMBERS OR GUARDIANS OF RESIDENTS

(a) A facility may not retaliate or discriminate against a volunteer, resident, or family member or guardian of a resident because the volunteer, resident, resident's family member or guardian, or any other person:

(1) makes a complaint or files a grievance concerning the facility;

(2) reports a violation of law, including a violation of chapter 242 or 247 or a rule adopted under chapter 242 or 247; or

(3) initiates or cooperates in an investigation or proceeding of a governmental entity relating to care, services, or conditions at the facility.

(b) A volunteer, resident, or family member or guardian of a resident who is retaliated or discriminated against in violation of subsection (a) is entitled to sue for:

(1) injunctive relief;

(2) the greater of $1,000 or actual damages, including damages for mental anguish even if an injury other than mental anguish is not shown;

(3) exemplary damages;

(4) court costs; and

(5) reasonable attorney's fees.

(c) A volunteer, resident, or family member or guardian of a resident who seeks relief under this section must report the alleged violation not later than the 180th day after the date on which the alleged violation of this section occurred or was discovered by the volunteer, resident, or family member or guardian of the resident through reasonable diligence.

(d) A suit under this section may be brought in the district court of the county in which the facility is located or in a district court of travis county.

§260A.016. REPORTS RELATING TO DEATHS OF RESIDENTS OF AN INSTITUTION

(a) In this section, "institution" has the meaning assigned by section 242.002.

(b) An institution shall submit a report to the department concerning deaths of residents of the institution. The report must be submitted not later than the 10th day after the last day of each month in which a resident of the institution dies. The report must also include the death of a resident occurring within 24 hours after the resident is transferred from the institution to a hospital.

(c) The institution must make the report on a form prescribed by the department. The report must contain the name and social security number of the deceased.

(d) The department shall correlate reports under this section with death certificate information to develop data relating to the:

(1) name and age of the deceased;

(2) official cause of death listed on the death certificate;

(3) date, time, and place of death; and

(4) name and address of the institution in which the deceased resided.

(e) Except as provided by subsection (f), a record under this section is confidential and not subject to the provisions of chapter 552, government code.

(f) The department shall develop statistical information on official causes of death to determine patterns and trends of incidents of death among residents and in specific institutions. Information developed under this subsection is public.

(g) A licensed institution shall make available historical statistics on all required information on request of an applicant or applicant's representative.

§260A.017. DUTIES OF LAW ENFORCEMENT; JOINT INVESTIGATION

(a) The department shall investigate a report of abuse, neglect, exploitation, or other complaint described by section 260a.007(c)(1) jointly with:

    (1) the municipal law enforcement agency, if the facility is located within the territorial boundaries of a municipality; or

    (2) the sheriff's department of the county in which the facility is located, if the facility is not located within the territorial boundaries of a municipality.

(b) The law enforcement agency described by subsection (a) shall acknowledge the report of abuse, neglect, exploitation, or other complaint and begin the joint investigation required by this section within 24 hours after receipt of the report or complaint. The law enforcement agency shall cooperate with the department and report to the department the results of the investigation.

(c) The requirement that the law enforcement agency and the department conduct a joint investigation under this section does not require that a representative of each agency be physically present during all phases of the investigation or that each agency participate equally in each activity conducted in the course of the investigation.

NURSING HOME RESIDENTS REQUIRING MH OR MR SERVICES—§242.158[29]

§242.158 IDENTIFICATION OF CERTAIN NURSING HOME RESIDENTS REQUIRING MENTAL HEALTH OR MENTAL RETARDATION SERVICES

(a) Each resident of a nursing home who is considering making a transition to a community-based care setting shall be identified to determine the presence of a mental illness or mental retardation, regardless of whether the resident is receiving treatment or services for a mental illness or mental retardation.

(b) In identifying residents having a mental illness or mental retardation, the department shall use an identification process that is at least as effective as the mental health and mental retardation identification process established by federal law. The results of the identification process may not be used to prevent a resident from remaining in the nursing home unless the nursing home is unable to provide adequate care for the resident.

(c) The department shall compile and provide to the Texas Department of Mental Health and Mental Retardation information regarding each resident identified as having a mental illness or mental retardation before the resident makes a transition from the nursing home to a community-based care setting.

(d) The Texas Department of Mental Health and Mental Retardation shall use the information provided under Subsection (c) solely for the purposes of:

    (1) determining the need for and funding levels of mental health and mental retardation services for residents making a transition from a nursing home to a community-based care setting;

    (2) providing mental health or mental retardation services to an identified resident after the resident makes that transition; and

---

29 (Health & Safety Code; Title 4. Health Facilities; Subtitle B. Licensing of Health Facilities; Chapter 242. Convalescent and Nursing Homes and Related Institutions; Subchapter F. Medical, Nursing, and Dental Services other than Administration of Medication)

(3) referring an identified resident to a local mental health or mental retardation authority or private provider for additional mental health or mental retardation services.

(e) This section does not authorize the department to decide for a resident of a nursing home that the resident will make a transition from the nursing home to a community-based care setting.

Subchapter I.
Nursing Facility Administration

§242.301. Definitions

In this subchapter:

(1) *"Nursing facility"* means an institution or facility that is licensed as a nursing home, nursing facility, or skilled nursing facility by the department under this chapter.

(2) *"Nursing facility administrator"* or *"administrator"* means a person who engages in the practice of nursing facility administration, without regard to whether the person has an ownership interest in the facility or whether the functions and duties are shared with any other person.

(3) *"Practice of nursing facility administration"* means the performance of the acts of administering, managing, supervising, or being in general administrative charge of a nursing facility.

§242.302. Powers and Duties of Department

(a) The board may adopt rules consistent with this subchapter.

(b) The department shall:

(1) adopt and publish a code of ethics for nursing facility administrators;

(2) establish the qualifications of applicants for licenses and the renewal of licenses issued under this subchapter;

(3) spend funds necessary for the proper administration of the department's assigned duties under this subchapter;

(4) establish reasonable and necessary fees for the administration and implementation of this subchapter; and

(5) establish a minimum number of hours of continuing education required to renew a license issued under this subchapter and periodically assess the continuing education needs of license holders to determine whether specific course content should be required.

(c) The department is the licensing agency for the healing arts, as provided by 42 U.S.C. §1396g.

§242.303. Nursing Facility Administrators Advisory Committee

(a) The Nursing Facility Administrators Advisory Committee is appointed by the governor.

(b) Members of the committee serve for staggered terms of six years, with the terms of three members expiring on February 1 of each odd-numbered year.

(c) The committee shall consist of:

(1) three licensed nursing facility administrators, at least one of whom shall represent a not-for-profit nursing facility;

(2) one physician with experience in geriatrics who is not employed by a nursing facility;

(3) one registered nurse with experience in geriatrics who is not employed by a nursing facility;

(4) one social worker with experience in geriatrics who is not employed by a nursing facility; and

(5) three public members with experience working with the chronically ill and infirm as provided by 42 U.S.C. §1396g.

(d) The committee shall advise the board on the licensing of nursing facility administrators, including the content of applications for licensure and of the examination administered to license applicants under §242.306.

The committee shall review and recommend rules and minimum standards of conduct for the practice of nursing facility administration. The committee shall review all complaints against administrators and make recommendations to the department regarding disciplinary actions. Failure of the committee to review complaints and make recommendations in a timely manner shall not prevent the department from taking disciplinary action.

(e) Appointments to the committee shall be made without regard to the race, color, disability, sex, religion, or national origin of the person appointed.

(f) A member of the committee receives no compensation but is entitled to reimbursement for actual and necessary expenses incurred in performing the member's duties under this section.

(g) The department shall pay the expenses of the committee and shall supply necessary personnel and supplies.

(h) A vacancy in a position on the committee shall be filled in the same manner in which the position was originally filled and shall be filled by a person who meets the qualifications of the vacated position.

REPORTS OF ABUSE OR NEGLECT OF PATIENTS IN CHEMICAL DEPENDENCY TREATMENT FACILITIES—§464[30]

§464.010. REPORTS OF ABUSE OR NEGLECT

(a) A person, including treatment facility personnel, who believes that a client's physical or mental health or welfare has been, is, or will be adversely affected by abuse or neglect caused by any person shall report the facts underlying that belief to the commission. This requirement is in addition to the requirements prescribed by Chapter 261, Family Code, and Chapter 48, Human Resources Code.

(b) The commission shall prescribe procedures for the investigation of reports under Subsection (a) and for coordination with law enforcement agencies or other agencies.

---

30 (Health & Safety Code; Title 6. Food, Drugs, Alcohol, and Hazardous Substances; Subtitle B. Alcohol and Substance Abuse Programs; Chapter 464. Facilities Treating Alcoholics and Drug-Dependent Persons; Subchapter A. Regulation of Chemical Dependency Treatment Facilities)

(c) An individual who in good faith reports to the commission under this section is immune from civil or criminal liability based on the report. That immunity extends to participation in a judicial proceeding resulting from the report but does not extend to an individual who caused the abuse or neglect.

(d) The commission may request the attorney general's office to file a petition for temporary care and protection of a client of a residential treatment facility if it appears that immediate removal of the client is necessary to prevent further abuse.

(e) All records made by the commission during its investigation of alleged abuse or neglect are confidential and may not be released except that the release may be made:

   (1) on court order;

   (2) on written request and consent of the person under investigation or that person's authorized attorney; or

   (3) as provided by §464.011.

VOLUNTARY MENTAL HEALTH SERVICES—§571 AND 572[31]

§571.019. LIMITATION OF LIABILITY

(a) A person who participates in the examination, certification, apprehension, custody, transportation, detention, treatment, or discharge of any person or in the performance of any other act required or authorized by this subtitle and who acts in good faith, reasonably, and without negligence is not criminally or civilly liable for that action.

(b) A physician performing a medical examination and providing information to the court in a court proceeding held under this subtitle or providing information to a peace officer to demonstrate the necessity to apprehend a person under Chapter 573 is considered an officer of the court and is not liable for the examination or testimony when acting without malice.

(c) A physician or inpatient mental health facility that discharges a voluntary patient is not liable for the discharge if:

   (1) a written request for the patient's release was filed and not withdrawn; and

   (2) the person who filed the written request for discharge is notified that the person assumes all responsibility for the patient on discharge.

§572.001. REQUEST FOR ADMISSION

(a) A person 16 years of age or older may request admission to an inpatient mental health facility or for outpatient mental health services by filing a request with the administrator of the facility where admission or outpatient treatment is requested. The parent, managing conservator, or guardian of a person younger than 18 years of age may request the admission of the person to an inpatient mental health facility or for outpatient mental health services by filing a request with the administrator of the facility where admission or outpatient treatment is requested.

(a-1) Except as provided by Subsection (c), an inpatient mental health facility may

---

31 (Health & Safety Code; Title 7. Mental Health and Mental Retardation; Subtitle C. Texas Mental Health Code; Chapter 572. Voluntary Inpatient Mental Health Services)

admit or provide services to a person 16 years of age or older and younger than 18 years of age if the person's parent, managing conservator, or guardian consents to the admission or services, even if the person does not consent to the admission or services.

(b) An admission request must be in writing and signed by the person requesting the admission.

(c) A person or agency appointed as the guardian or a managing conservator of a person younger than 18 years of age and acting as an employee or agent of the state or a political subdivision of the state may request admission of the person younger than 18 years of age only with the person's consent. If the person does not consent, the person may be admitted for inpatient services only pursuant to an application for court-ordered mental health services or emergency detention or an order for protective custody.

(c-1) A person younger than 18 years of age may not be involuntarily committed unless provided by this chapter, other state law, or department rule.

(d) The administrator of an inpatient or outpatient mental health facility may admit a minor who is 16 years of age or older to an inpatient or outpatient mental health facility as a voluntary patient without the consent of the parent, managing conservator, or guardian.

(e) A request for admission as a voluntary patient must state that the person for whom admission is requested agrees to voluntarily remain in the facility until the person's discharge and that the person consents to the diagnosis, observation, care, and treatment provided until the earlier of:

   (1) the person's discharge; or

   (2) the period prescribed by §572.004.

§572.002. ADMISSION

The facility administrator or the administrator's authorized, qualified designee may admit a person for whom a proper request for voluntary inpatient or outpatient services is filed if the administrator or the designee determines:

   (1) from a preliminary examination that the person has symptoms of mental illness and will benefit from the inpatient or outpatient services;

   (2) that the person has been informed of the person's rights as a voluntary patient; and

   (3) that the admission was voluntarily agreed to:

      (A) by the person, if the person is 16 years of age or older; or

      (B) by the person's parent, managing conservator, or guardian, if the person is younger than 18 years of age.

§572.0022. INFORMATION ON MEDICATIONS

(a) A mental health facility shall provide to a patient in the patient's primary language, if possible, and in accordance with board rules information relating to prescription medication ordered by the patient's treating physician.

(b) The facility shall also provide the information to the patient's family on request, but only to the extent not otherwise prohibited by state or federal confidentiality laws.

§572.0025. INTAKE, ASSESSMENT, AND ADMISSION

(a) The board shall adopt rules governing the voluntary admission of a patient to an inpatient mental health facility, including rules governing the intake and assessment procedures of the admission process.

(b) The rules governing the intake process shall establish minimum standards for:

  (1) reviewing a prospective patient's finances and insurance benefits;

  (2) explaining to a prospective patient the patient's rights; and

  (3) explaining to a prospective patient the facility's services and treatment process.

(c) The assessment provided for by the rules may be conducted only by a professional who meets the qualifications prescribed by board rules.

(d) The rules governing the assessment process shall prescribe:

  (1) the types of professionals who may conduct an assessment;

  (2) the minimum credentials each type of professional must have to conduct an assessment; and

  (3) the type of assessment that professional may conduct.

(e) In accordance with board rule, a facility shall provide annually a minimum of eight hours of inservice training regarding intake and assessment for persons who will be conducting an intake or assessment for the facility. A person may not conduct intake or assessments without having completed the initial and applicable annual inservice training.

(f) A prospective voluntary patient may not be formally accepted for treatment in a facility unless:

  (1) the facility has a physician's order admitting the prospective patient, which order may be issued orally, electronically, or in writing, signed by the physician, provided that, in the case of an oral order or an electronically transmitted unsigned order, a signed original is presented to the mental health facility within 24 hours of the initial order; the order must be from:

    (A) an admitting physician who has conducted an in-person physical and psychiatric examination within 72 hours of the admission; or

    (B) an admitting physician who has consulted with a physician who has conducted an in-person examination within 72 hours of the admission; and

  (2) the facility administrator or a person designated by the administrator has agreed to accept the prospective patient and has signed a statement to that effect.

(g) An assessment conducted as required by rules adopted under this section does not satisfy a statutory or regulatory requirement for a personal evaluation of a patient or a prospective patient by a physician before admission.

(h) In this section:

  (1) *"Admission"* means the formal acceptance of a prospective patient to a facility.

  (2) *"Assessment"* means the administrative process a facility uses to gather

information from a prospective patient, including a medical history and the problem for which the patient is seeking treatment, to determine whether a prospective patient should be examined by a physician to determine if admission is clinically justified.

(3) *"Intake"* means the administrative process for gathering information about a prospective patient and giving a prospective patient information about the facility and the facility's treatment and services.

§572.003. RIGHTS OF PATIENTS

(a) A person's voluntary admission to an inpatient mental health facility under this chapter does not affect the person's civil rights or legal capacity or affect the person's right to obtain a writ of habeas corpus.

(b) In addition to the rights provided by this subtitle, a person voluntarily admitted to an inpatient mental health facility under this chapter has the right:

(1) to be reviewed periodically to determine the person's need for continued inpatient treatment; and

(2) to have an application for court-ordered mental health services filed only as provided by §572.005.

(c) A person admitted to an inpatient mental health facility under this chapter shall be informed of the rights provided under this section and §572.004:

(1) orally in simple, nontechnical terms, within 24 hours after the time the person is admitted, and in writing in the person's primary language, if possible; or

(2) through the use of a means reasonably calculated to communicate with a hearing impaired or visually impaired person, if applicable.

(d) The patient's parent, managing conservator, or guardian shall also be informed of the patient's rights as required by this section if the patient is a minor.

§572.004. DISCHARGE

(a) A voluntary patient is entitled to leave an inpatient mental health facility in accordance with this section after a written request for discharge is filed with the facility administrator or the administrator's designee. The request must be signed, timed, and dated by the patient or a person legally responsible for the patient and must be made a part of the patient's clinical record. If a patient informs an employee of or person associated with the facility of the patient's desire to leave the facility, the employee or person shall, as soon as possible, assist the patient in creating the written request and present it to the patient for the patient's signature.

(b) The facility shall, within four hours after a request for discharge is filed, notify the physician responsible for the patient's treatment. If that physician is not available during that period, the facility shall notify any available physician of the request.

(c) The notified physician shall discharge the patient before the end of the four-hour period unless the physician has reasonable cause to believe that the patient might meet the criteria for court-ordered mental health services or emergency detention.

(d) A physician who has reasonable cause to believe that a patient might meet the criteria for court-ordered mental health services or emergency detention shall examine the patient as soon as possible within 24 hours after the time the request for discharge is filed. The physician shall discharge the patient on completion of the examination unless the physician determines that the person meets the criteria for court-ordered mental health services or emergency detention. If the physician makes a determination that the patient meets the criteria for court-ordered mental health services or emergency detention, the physician shall, not later than 4 p.m. on the next succeeding business day after the date on which the examination occurs, either discharge the patient or file an application for court-ordered mental health services or emergency detention and obtain a written order for further detention. The physician shall notify the patient if the physician intends to detain the patient under this subsection or intends to file an application for court-ordered mental health services or emergency detention. A decision to detain a patient under this subsection and the reasons for the decision shall be made a part of the patient's clinical record.

(e) If extremely hazardous weather conditions exist or a disaster occurs, the physician may request the judge of a court that has jurisdiction over proceedings brought under Chapter 574 to extend the period during which the patient may be detained. The judge or a magistrate appointed by the judge may by written order made each day extend the period during which the patient may be detained until 4 p.m. on the first succeeding business day. The written order must declare that an emergency exists because of the weather or the occurrence of a disaster.

(f) The patient is not entitled to leave the facility if before the end of the period prescribed by this section:

(1) a written withdrawal of the request for discharge is filed; or

(2) an application for court-ordered mental health services or emergency detention is filed and the patient is detained in accordance with this subtitle.

(g) A plan for continuing care shall be prepared in accordance with §574.081 for each patient discharged. If sufficient time to prepare a continuing care plan before discharge is not available, the plan may be prepared and mailed to the appropriate person within 24 hours after the patient is discharged.

(h) The patient or other person who files a request for discharge of a patient shall be notified that the person filing the request assumes all responsibility for the patient on discharge.

§572.005. APPLICATION FOR COURT-ORDERED TREATMENT

(a) An application for court-ordered mental health services may not be filed against a patient receiving voluntary inpatient services unless:

(1) a request for release of the patient has been filed with the facility administrator; or

(2) in the opinion of the physician responsible for the patient's treatment, the patient meets the criteria for court-ordered mental health services and:

(A) is absent from the facility without authorization;

(B) is unable to consent to appropriate and necessary psychiatric treatment; or

(C) refuses to consent to necessary and appropriate treatment recommended by the physician responsible for the patient's treatment and that physician completes a certificate of medical examination for mental illness that, in addition to the information required by §574.011, includes the opinion of the physician that:

  (i) there is no reasonable alternative to the treatment recommended by the physician; and

  (ii) the patient will not benefit from continued inpatient care without the recommended treatment.

(b) The physician responsible for the patient's treatment shall notify the patient if the physician intends to file an application for court-ordered mental health services.

COURT-ORDERED EMERGENCY SERVICES—§573[32]

§573.001. APPREHENSION BY PEACE OFFICER WITHOUT WARRANT

(a) A peace officer, without a warrant, may take a person into custody if the officer:

  (1) has reason to believe and does believe that:

    (A) the person is mentally ill; and

    (B) because of that mental illness there is a substantial risk of serious harm to the person or to others unless the person is immediately restrained; and

  (2) believes that there is not sufficient time to obtain a warrant before taking the person into custody.

(b) A substantial risk of serious harm to the person or others under Subsection (a)(1)(B) may be demonstrated by:

  (1) the person's behavior; or

  (2) evidence of severe emotional distress and deterioration in the person's mental condition to the extent that the person cannot remain at liberty.

(c) The peace officer may form the belief that the person meets the criteria for apprehension:

  (1) from a representation of a credible person; or

  (2) on the basis of the conduct of the apprehended person or the circumstances under which the apprehended person is found.

(d) A peace officer who takes a person into custody under Subsection (a) shall immediately transport the apprehended person to:

  (1) the nearest appropriate inpatient mental health facility; or

  (2) a mental health facility deemed suitable by the local mental health authority, if an appropriate inpatient mental health facility is not available.

(e) A jail or similar detention facility may not be deemed suitable except in an extreme emergency.

---

32 (Health & Safety Code; Title 7. Mental Health and Mental Retardation; Subtitle C. Texas Mental Health Code; Chapter 573. Emergency Detention)

(f)   A person detained in a jail or a nonmedical facility shall be kept separate from any person who is charged with or convicted of a crime.

(g)   A peace officer who takes a person into custody under Subsection (a) may immediately seize any firearm found in possession of the person. After seizing a firearm under this subsection, the peace officer shall comply with the requirements of Article 18.191, Code of Criminal Procedure. The peace officer shall immediately inform the person orally in simple, nontechnical terms:

   (1)   of the reason for the detention; and

   (2)   that a staff member of the facility will inform the person of the person's rights within 24 hours after the time the person is admitted to a facility, as provided by Section

§573.011. APPLICATION FOR EMERGENCY DETENTION

(a)   An adult may file a written application for the emergency detention of another person.

(b)   The application must state:

   (1)   that the applicant has reason to believe and does believe that the person evidences mental illness;

   (2)   that the applicant has reason to believe and does believe that the person evidences a substantial risk of serious harm to himself or others;

   (3)   a specific description of the risk of harm;

   (4)   that the applicant has reason to believe and does believe that the risk of harm is imminent unless the person is immediately restrained;

   (5)   that the applicant's beliefs are derived from specific recent behavior, overt acts, attempts, or threats;

   (6)   a detailed description of the specific behavior, acts, attempts, or threats; and

   (7)   a detailed description of the applicant's relationship to the person whose detention is sought.

(c)   The application may be accompanied by any relevant information.

§573.021. PRELIMINARY EXAMINATION

(a)   A facility shall temporarily accept a person for whom an application for detention is filed or for whom a peace officer files a notification of detention under Section 573.002(a).

(b)   A person accepted for a preliminary examination may be detained in custody for not longer than 48 hours after the time the person is presented to the facility unless a written order for protective custody is obtained. The 48-hour period allowed by this section includes any time the patient spends waiting in the facility for medical care before the person receives the preliminary examination. If the 48-hour period ends on a Saturday, Sunday, legal holiday, or before 4 p.m. on the first succeeding business day, the person may be detained until 4 p.m. on the first succeeding business day. If the 48-hour period ends at a different time, the person may be detained only until 4 p.m. on the day the 48-hour period ends. If extremely hazardous weather conditions exist or a disaster occurs, the presiding judge or magistrate may, by written order made each day, extend by an additional 24 hours the period during which the person may be detained. The written order must declare that an emergency exists because of the weather or the occurrence of a disaster.

(c)   A physician shall examine the person as soon as possible within 12 hours after the time the person is apprehended by the peace officer or transported for emergency detention by the person's guardian.

(d)   A facility must comply with this section only to the extent that the commissioner determines that a facility has sufficient resources to perform the necessary services under this section.

(e)   A person may not be detained in a private mental health facility without the consent of the facility administrator.

§573.022. EMERGENCY ADMISSION AND DETENTION

(a)   A person may be admitted to a facility for emergency detention only if the physician who conducted the preliminary examination of the person makes a written statement that:

(1)   is acceptable to the facility;

(2)   states that after a preliminary examination it is the physician's opinion that:

(A)   the person is mentally ill;

(B)   the person evidences a substantial risk of serious harm to himself or others;

(C)   the described risk of harm is imminent unless the person is immediately restrained; and

(D)   emergency detention is the least restrictive means by which the necessary restraint may be accomplished; and

(3)   includes:

(A)   a description of the nature of the person's mental illness;

(B)   a specific description of the risk of harm the person evidences that may be demonstrated either by the person's behavior or by evidence of severe emotional distress and deterioration in the person's mental condition to the extent that the person cannot remain at liberty; and

(C)   the specific detailed information from which the physician formed the opinion in Subdivision (2).

(b)   A county mental health facility that has admitted a person for emergency detention under this section may transport the person to:

(1)   a facility of the single portal authority for the area;

(2)   an appropriate inpatient mental health facility, if no single portal authority serves the area; or

(3)   a facility deemed suitable by the county's mental health authority, if no single portal authority serves the area and an appropriate inpatient mental health facility is not available.

(c)   A facility that has admitted a person for emergency detention under Subsection (a) or to which a person has been transported under Subsection (b) may transfer the person to an appropriate mental hospital with the written consent of the hospital administrator.

§573.023. RELEASE FROM EMERGENCY DETENTION

(a) A person apprehended under Subchapter A or detained under Subchapter B shall be released on completion of the preliminary examination unless the person is admitted to a facility under §573.022.

(b) A person admitted to a facility under §573.022 shall be released if the facility administrator determines at any time during the emergency detention period that one of the criteria prescribed by §573.022(2) no longer applies.

§573.025. RIGHTS OF PERSONS APPREHENDED OR DETAINED OR TRANSPORTED FOR EMERGENCY DETENTION

(a) A person apprehended, detained or transported for emergency detention under this chapter has the right:

(1) to be advised of the location of detention, the reasons for the detention, and the fact that the detention could result in a longer period of involuntary commitment;

(2) to a reasonable opportunity to communicate with and retain an attorney;

(3) to be transported to a location as provided by §573.024 if the person is not admitted for emergency detention, unless the person is arrested or objects;

(4) to be released from a facility as provided by §573.023;

(5) to be advised that communications with a mental health professional may be used in proceedings for further detention;

(6) to be transported in accordance with Sections 573.026 and 574.045, if the person is detained under §573.022 or transported under an order of protective custody under §574.023; and

(7) to a reasonable opportunity to communicate with a relative or other responsible person who has a proper interest in the person's welfare.

(b) A person apprehended or detained under this subtitle shall be informed of the rights provided by this section and this subtitle:

(1) orally in simple, nontechnical terms, within 24 hours after the time the person is admitted to a facility, and in writing in the person's primary language if possible; or

(2) through the use of a means reasonably calculated to communicate with a hearing or visually impaired person, if applicable.

(c) The executive commissioner of the Health and Human Services Commission by rule shall prescribe the manner in which the person is informed of the person's rights under this section and this subtitle.

TEMPORARY AND EXTENDED MENTAL HEALTH SERVICES—§574[33]

§574.010. INDEPENDENT PSYCHIATRIC EVALUATION AND EXPERT TESTIMONY

(a) The court may order an independent evaluation of the proposed patient by

---

33 (Health & Safety Code; Title 7. Mental Health and Mental Retardation; Subtitle C. Texas Mental Health Code; Chapter 574. Court-Ordered Mental Health Services; Subchapter A. Application for Commitment and Prehearing Procedures)

a psychiatrist chosen by the proposed patient if the court determines that the evaluation will assist the finder of fact. The psychiatrist may testify on behalf of the proposed patient.

(b) If the court determines that the proposed patient is indigent, the court may authorize reimbursement to the attorney ad litem for court-approved expenses incurred in obtaining expert testimony and may order the proposed patient's county of residence to pay the expenses.

§574.034. ORDER FOR TEMPORARY MENTAL HEALTH SERVICES

(a) The judge may order a proposed patient to receive court-ordered temporary inpatient mental health services only if the judge or jury finds, from clear and convincing evidence, that:

(1) the proposed patient is mentally ill; and

(2) as a result of that mental illness the proposed patient:

(A) is likely to cause serious harm to himself;

(B) is likely to cause serious harm to others; or

(C) is:

(i) suffering severe and abnormal mental, emotional, or physical distress;

(ii) experiencing substantial mental or physical deterioration of the proposed patient's ability to function independently, which is exhibited by the proposed patient's inability, except for reasons of indigence, to provide for the proposed patient's basic needs, including food, clothing, health, or safety; and

(iii) unable to make a rational and informed decision as to whether or not to submit to treatment.

(b) The judge may order a proposed patient to receive court-ordered temporary outpatient mental health services only if:

(1) the judge finds that appropriate mental health services are available to the patient; and

(2) the judge or jury finds, from clear and convincing evidence, that:

(A) the proposed patient is mentally ill;

(B) the nature of the mental illness is severe and persistent;

(C) as a result of the mental illness, the proposed patient will, if not treated, continue to:

(i) suffer severe and abnormal mental, emotional, or physical distress; and

(ii) experience deterioration of the ability to function independently to the extent that the proposed patient will be unable to live safely in the community without court-ordered outpatient mental health services; and

(D) the proposed patient has an inability to participate in outpatient treatment services effectively and voluntarily, demonstrated by:

(i) any of the proposed patient's actions occurring within the two-year period which immediately precedes the hearing; or

(ii) specific characteristics of the proposed patient's clinical condition that make impossible a rational and informed decision whether to submit to voluntary outpatient treatment.

(c) If the judge or jury finds that the proposed patient meets the commitment criteria prescribed by Subsection (a), the judge or jury must specify which criterion listed in Subsection (a)(2) forms the basis for the decision.

(d) To be clear and convincing under Subsection (a), the evidence must include expert testimony and, unless waived, evidence of a recent overt act or a continuing pattern of behavior that tends to confirm:

(1) the likelihood of serious harm to the proposed patient or others; or

(2) the proposed patient's distress and the deterioration of the proposed patient's ability to function.

(e) To be clear and convincing under Subdivision (b)(2), the evidence must include expert testimony and, unless waived, evidence of a recent overt act or a continuing pattern of behavior that tends to confirm:

(1) the proposed patient's distress;

(2) the deterioration of ability to function independently to the extent that the proposed patient will be unable to live safely in the community; and

(3) the proposed patient's inability to participate in outpatient treatment services effectively and voluntarily.

(f) The proposed patient and the proposed patient's attorney, by a written document filed with the court, may waive the right to cross-examine witnesses, and, if that right is waived, the court may admit, as evidence, the certificates of medical examination for mental illness. The certificates admitted under this subsection constitute competent medical or psychiatric testimony, and the court may make its findings solely from the certificates. If the proposed patient and the proposed patient's attorney do not waive in writing the right to cross-examine witnesses, the court shall proceed to hear testimony. The testimony must include competent medical or psychiatric testimony. In addition, the court may consider the testimony of a nonphysician mental health professional as provided by §574.031(f).

(g) An order for temporary inpatient or outpatient mental health services shall state that treatment is authorized for not longer than 90 days. The order may not specify a shorter period.

(h) A judge may not issue an order for temporary inpatient or outpatient mental health services for a proposed patient who is charged with a criminal offense that involves an act, attempt, or threat of serious bodily injury to another person.

§574.035. ORDER FOR EXTENDED MENTAL HEALTH SERVICES

(a) The judge may order a proposed patient to receive court-ordered extended inpatient mental health services only if the jury, or the judge if the right to a jury is waived, finds, from clear and convincing evidence, that:

(1) the proposed patient is mentally ill;

(2) as a result of that mental illness the proposed patient:

    (A) is likely to cause serious harm to himself;

    (B) is likely to cause serious harm to others; or

    (C) is:

       (i) suffering severe and abnormal mental, emotional, or physical distress;

      (ii) experiencing substantial mental or physical deterioration of the proposed patient's ability to function independently, which is exhibited by the proposed patient's inability, except for reasons of indigence, to provide for the proposed patient's basic needs, including food, clothing, health, or safety; and

     (iii) unable to make a rational and informed decision as to whether or not to submit to treatment;

(3) the proposed patient's condition is expected to continue for more than 90 days; and

(4) the proposed patient has received court-ordered inpatient mental health services under this subtitle or under Article 46.02, Code of Criminal Procedure, for at least 60 consecutive days during the preceding 12 months.

(b) The judge may order a proposed patient to receive court-ordered extended outpatient mental health services only if:

(1) the judge finds that appropriate mental health services are available to the patient; and

(2) the jury, or the judge if the right to a jury is waived, finds from clear and convincing evidence that:

    (A) the proposed patient is mentally ill;

    (B) the nature of the mental illness is severe and persistent;

    (C) as a result of the mental illness, the proposed patient will, if not treated, continue to:

       (i) suffer severe and abnormal mental, emotional, or physical distress; and

      (ii) experience deterioration of the ability to function independently to the extent that the proposed patient will be unable to live safely in the community without court-ordered outpatient mental health services;

    (D) the proposed patient has an inability to participate in outpatient treatment services effectively and voluntarily, demonstrated by:

       (i) any of the proposed patient's actions occurring within the two-year period which immediately precedes the hearing; or

      (ii) specific characteristics of the proposed patient's clinical condition that make impossible a rational and informed decision whether to submit to voluntary outpatient treatment;

    (E) the proposed patient's condition is expected to continue for more than 90 days; and

      (F) the proposed patient has received:

          (i) court-ordered inpatient mental health services under this subtitle or under Subchapter D or E, Chapter 46B, Code of Criminal Procedure, for a total of at least 60 days during the preceding 12 months; or

          (ii) court-ordered outpatient mental health services under this subtitle or under Subchapter D or E, Chapter 46B, Code of Criminal Procedure, during the preceding 60 days.

(c) If the jury or judge finds that the proposed patient meets the commitment criteria prescribed by Subsection (a), the jury or judge must specify which criterion listed in Subsection (a)(2) forms the basis for the decision.

(d) The jury or judge is not required to make the finding under Subsection (a)(4) or (b)(2)(F) if the proposed patient has already been subject to an order for extended mental health services.

(e) To be clear and convincing under Subsection (a), the evidence must include expert testimony and evidence of a recent overt act or a continuing pattern of behavior that tends to confirm:

    (1) the likelihood of serious harm to the proposed patient or others; or

    (2) the proposed patient's distress and the deterioration of the proposed patient's ability to function.

(f) To be clear and convincing under Subdivision (b)(2), the evidence must include expert testimony and evidence of a recent overt act or a continuing pattern of behavior that tends to confirm:

    (1) the proposed patient's distress;

    (2) the deterioration of ability to function independently to the extent that the proposed patient will be unable to live safely in the community; and

    (3) the proposed patient's inability to participate in outpatient treatment services effectively and voluntarily.

(g) The court may not make its findings solely from the certificates of medical examination for mental illness but shall hear testimony. The court may not enter an order for extended mental health services unless appropriate findings are made and are supported by testimony taken at the hearing. The testimony must include competent medical or psychiatric testimony.

(h) An order for extended inpatient or outpatient mental health services shall state that treatment is authorized for not longer than 12 months. The order may not specify a shorter period.

(i) A judge may not issue an order for extended inpatient or outpatient mental health services for a proposed patient who is charged with a criminal offense that involves an act, attempt, or threat of serious bodily injury to another person.

§574.036. ORDER OF CARE OR COMMITMENT

(a) The judge shall dismiss the jury, if any, after a hearing in which a person is found to be mentally ill and to meet the criteria for court-ordered temporary or extended mental health services.

(b) The judge may hear additional evidence relating to alternative settings for care before entering an order relating to the setting for the care the person will receive.

(c) The judge shall consider in determining the setting for care the recommendation for the most appropriate treatment alternative filed under §574.012.

(d) The judge shall order the mental health services provided in the least restrictive appropriate setting available.

(e) The judge may enter an order:

   (1) committing the person to a mental health facility for inpatient care if the trier of fact finds that the person meets the commitment criteria prescribed by §574.034(a) or 574.035(a); or

   (2) committing the person to outpatient mental health services if the trier of fact finds that the person meets the commitment criteria prescribed by §574.034(b) or 574.035(b).

§574.037. COURT-ORDERED OUTPATIENT SERVICES

(a) The court, in an order that directs a patient to participate in outpatient mental health services, shall designate the person identified under Section 574.0125 as responsible for those services or may designate a different person if necessary. The person designated must be the facility administrator or an individual involved in providing court-ordered outpatient services. A person may not be designated as responsible for the ordered services without the person's consent unless the person is the facility administrator of a department facility or the facility administrator of a community center that provides mental health services in the region in which the committing court is located.

(b) The person responsible for the services shall submit to the court a general program of the treatment to be provided as required by this subsection and Subsection (b-2). The program must be incorporated into the court order. The program must include:

   (1) services to provide care coordination; and

   (2) any other treatment or services, including medication and supported housing, that are available and considered clinically necessary by a treating physician or the person responsible for the services to assist the patient in functioning safely in the community.

(b-1) If the patient is receiving inpatient mental health services at the time the program is being prepared, the person responsible for the services under this section shall seek input from the patient's inpatient treatment providers in preparing the program.

(b-2) The person responsible for the services shall submit the program to the court before the hearing under Section 574.034 or 574.035 or before the court modifies an order under Section 574.061, as appropriate.

(c) The person responsible for the services shall inform the court of:

   (1) the patient's failure to comply with the court order; and

   (2) any substantial change in the general program of treatment that occurs before the order expires.

(c-1) A patient subject to court-ordered outpatient services may petition the court for specific enforcement of the court order.

(c-2) A court may, on its own motion, set a status conference with the person responsible for the services, the patient, and the patient's attorney.

(c-3) The court shall order the patient to participate in the program but may not compel performance. If a court receives information under Subsection (c)(1) that a patient is not complying with the court's order, the court may:

   (1) set a modification hearing under Section 574.062; and

   (2) issue an order for temporary detention if an application is filed under Section 574.063.

(c-4) The failure of a patient to comply with the program incorporated into a court order is not grounds for punishment for contempt of court under Section 21.002, Government Code.

(d) A facility must comply with this section to the extent that the commissioner determines that the designated mental health facility has sufficient resources to perform the necessary services.

(e) A patient may not be detained in a private mental health facility without the consent of the facility administrator.

§574.0415. INFORMATION ON MEDICATIONS

(a) A mental health facility shall provide to a patient in the patient's primary language, if possible, and in accordance with board rules information relating to prescription medication ordered by the patient's treating physician.

(b) The facility shall also provide the information to the patient's family on request, but only to the extent not otherwise prohibited by state or federal confidentiality laws.

§574.042. COMMITMENT TO PRIVATE FACILITY

The court may order a patient committed to a private mental hospital at no expense to the state if the court receives:

   (1) an application signed by the patient or the patient's guardian or next friend requesting that the patient be placed in a designated private mental hospital at the patient's or applicant's expense; and

   (2) written agreement from the hospital administrator of the private mental hospital to admit the patient and to accept responsibility for the patient in accordance with this subtitle.

RIGHTS OF PATIENTS—§574.105[34]

§574.105. RIGHTS OF PATIENT

A patient for whom an application for an order to authorize the administration of a psychoactive medication is filed is entitled to:

   (1) representation by a court-appointed attorney who is knowledgeable about issues to be adjudicated at the hearing;

---

34 (Health & Safety Code; Title 7. Mental Health and Mental Retardation; Subtitle C. Texas Mental Health Code; Chapter 574. Court-Ordered Mental Health Services; Subchapter G. Administration of Medication to Patient under Order for Inpatient Mental Health Services)

(2)　meet with that attorney as soon as is practicable to prepare for the hearing and to discuss any of the patient's questions or concerns;

(3)　receive, immediately after the time of the hearing is set, a copy of the application and written notice of the time, place, and date of the hearing;

(4)　be told, at the time personal notice of the hearing is given, of the patient's right to a hearing and right to the assistance of an attorney to prepare for the hearing and to answer any questions or concerns;

(5)　be present at the hearing;

(6)　request from the court an independent expert; and

(7)　oral notification, at the conclusion of the hearing, of the court's determinations of the patient's capacity and best interests.

§574.106. HEARING ON PATIENT'S CAPACITY AND ORDER AUTHORIZING PSYCHOACTIVE MEDICATION

(a)　The court may issue an order authorizing the administration of one or more classes of psychoactive medication to a patient who:

(1)　is under a court order to receive inpatient mental health services; or

(2)　is in custody awaiting trial in a criminal proceeding and was ordered to receive inpatient mental health services in the six months preceding a hearing under this section.

(a-1)　The court may issue an order under this section only if the court finds by clear and convincing evidence after the hearing:

(1)　that the patient lacks the capacity to make a decision regarding the administration of the proposed medication and treatment with the proposed medication is in the best interest of the patient; or

(2)　if the patient was ordered to receive inpatient mental health services by a criminal court with jurisdiction over the patient, that treatment with the proposed medication is in the best interest of the patient and either:

(A)　the patient presents a danger to the patient or others in the inpatient mental health facility in which the patient is being treated as a result of a mental disorder or mental defect as determined under Section 574.1065; or

(B)　the patient:

(i)　has remained confined in a correctional facility, as defined by Section 1.07, Penal Code, for a period exceeding 72 hours while awaiting transfer for competency restoration treatment; and

(ii)　presents a danger to the patient or others in the correctional facility as a result of a mental disorder or mental defect as determined under Section 574.1065.

(b)　In making the finding that treatment with the proposed medication is in the best interest of the patient, the court shall consider:

(1)　the patient's expressed preferences regarding treatment with psychoactive medication;

(2)　the patient's religious beliefs;

(3)   the risks and benefits, from the perspective of the patient, of taking psychoactive medication;

(4)   the consequences to the patient if the psychoactive medication is not administered;

(5)   the prognosis for the patient if the patient is treated with psychoactive medication;

(6)   alternative, less intrusive treatments that are likely to produce the same results as treatment with psychoactive medication; and

(7)   less intrusive treatments likely to secure the patient's agreement to take the psychoactive medication.

(c)   A hearing under this subchapter shall be conducted on the record by the probate judge or judge with probate jurisdiction, except as provided by Subsection (d).

(d)   A judge may refer a hearing to a magistrate or court-appointed associate judge who has training regarding psychoactive medications. The magistrate or associate judge may effectuate the notice, set hearing dates, and appoint attorneys as required in this subchapter. A record is not required if the hearing is held by a magistrate or court-appointed associate judge.

(e)   A party is entitled to a hearing *de novo* by the judge if an appeal of the magistrate's or associate judge's report is filed with the court within three days after the report is issued. The hearing de novo shall be held within 30 days of the filing of the application for an order to authorize psychoactive medication.

(f)   If a hearing or an appeal of an associate judge's or magistrate's report is to be held in a county court in which the judge is not a licensed attorney, the proposed patient or the proposed patient's attorney may request that the proceeding be transferred to a court with a judge who is licensed to practice law in this state. The county judge shall transfer the case after receiving the request, and the receiving court shall hear the case as if it had been originally filed in that court.

(g)   As soon as practicable after the conclusion of the hearing, the patient is entitled to have provided to the patient and the patient's attorney written notification of the court's determinations under this section. The notification shall include a statement of the evidence on which the court relied and the reasons for the court's determinations.

(h)   An order entered under this section shall authorize the administration to a patient, regardless of the patient's refusal, of one or more classes of psychoactive medications specified in the application and consistent with the patient's diagnosis. The order shall permit an increase or decrease in a medication's dosage, restitution of medication authorized but discontinued during the period the order is valid, or the substitution of a medication within the same class.

(i)   The classes of psychoactive medications in the order must conform to classes determined by the department.

(j)   An order issued under this section may be reauthorized or modified on the petition of a party. The order remains in effect pending action on a petition for reauthorization or modification. For the purpose of this subsection, "modification" means a change of a class of medication authorized in the order.

(k)   This section does not apply to a patient who receives services under an order of protective custody under Section 574.021.

(l)   For a patient described by Subsection (a-1)(2)(B), an order issued under this section:

   (1)   authorizes the initiation of any appropriate mental health treatment for the patient awaiting transfer; and

   (2)   does not constitute authorization to retain the patient in a correctional facility for competency restoration treatment.

§574.109. EFFECT OF ORDER

(a)   A person's consent to take a psychoactive medication is not valid and may not be relied on if the person is subject to an order issued under §574.106.

(b)   The issuance of an order under §574.106 is not a determination or adjudication of mental incompetency and does not limit in any other respect that person's rights as a citizen or the person's property rights or legal capacity.

VOLUNTARY ADMISSION FOR COURT-ORDERED SERVICES—§574.151

Voluntary Admission for Certain Persons for Whom Motion for Court-Ordered Services Has Been Filed

§574.151. APPLICABILITY

This subchapter applies only to a person for whom a motion for court-ordered mental health services is filed under §574.001, for whom a final order on that motion has not been entered under §574.034 or 574.035, and who requests voluntary admission to an inpatient mental health facility:

   (1)   while the person is receiving at that facility involuntary inpatient services under Subchapter B or under Chapter 573; or

   (2)   before the 31st day after the date the person was released from that facility under §573.023 or 574.028.

§574.152. CAPACITY TO CONSENT TO VOLUNTARY ADMISSION

A person described by §574.151 is rebuttably presumed to have the capacity to consent to admission to the inpatient mental health facility for voluntary inpatient mental health services.

§574.153. RIGHTS OF PERSON ADMITTED TO VOLUNTARY INPATIENT TREATMENT

(a)   A person described by §574.151 who is admitted to the inpatient mental health facility for voluntary inpatient mental health services has all of the rights provided by Chapter 576 for a person receiving voluntary or involuntary inpatient mental health services.

(b)   A right assured by §576.021 may not be waived by the patient, the patient's attorney or guardian, or any other person acting on behalf of the patient.

§574.154. PARTICIPATION IN RESEARCH PROGRAM

Notwithstanding any other law, a person described by §574.151 may not participate in a research program in the inpatient mental health facility unless:

   (1)   the patient provides written consent to participate in the research program

under a protocol that has been approved by the facility's institutional review board; and

(2) the institutional review board specifically reviews the patient's consent under the approved protocol.

RIGHTS OF PATIENTS—§576[35]

§576.001. RIGHTS UNDER CONSTITUTION AND LAW

(a) A person with mental illness in this state has the rights, benefits, responsibilities, and privileges guaranteed by the constitution and laws of the United States and this state.

(b) Unless a specific law limits a right under a special procedure, a patient has:

(1) the right to register and vote at an election;

(2) the right to acquire, use, and dispose of property, including contractual rights;

(3) the right to sue and be sued;

(4) all rights relating to the grant, use, and revocation of a license, permit, privilege, or benefit under law;

(5) the right to religious freedom; and

(6) all rights relating to domestic relations.

§576.002. PRESUMPTION OF COMPETENCY

(a) The provision of court-ordered, emergency, or voluntary mental health services to a person is not a determination or adjudication of mental incompetency and does not limit the person's rights as a citizen, or the person's property rights or legal capacity.

(b) There is a rebuttable presumption that a person is mentally competent unless a judicial finding to the contrary is made under the Texas Probate Code.

§576.005. CONFIDENTIALITY OF RECORDS

Records of a mental health facility that directly or indirectly identify a present, former, or proposed patient are confidential unless disclosure is permitted by other state law.

§576.006. RIGHTS SUBJECT TO LIMITATION

(a) A patient in an inpatient mental health facility has the right to:

(1) receive visitors;

(2) communicate with a person outside the facility by telephone and by uncensored and sealed mail; and

(3) communicate by telephone and by uncensored and sealed mail with legal counsel, the department, the courts, and the state attorney general.

(b) The rights provided in Subsection (a) are subject to the general rules of the facility. The physician ultimately responsible for the patient's treatment may also restrict a right only to the extent that the restriction is necessary to the

---

35   (Health & Safety Code; Title 7. Mental Health and Mental Retardation; Subtitle C. Texas Mental Health Code; Chapter 576. Rights of Patients; Subchapter A. General Rights)

patient's welfare or to protect another person but may not restrict the right to communicate with legal counsel, the department, the courts, or the state attorney general.

(c)   If a restriction is imposed under this section, the physician ultimately responsible for the patient's treatment shall document the clinical reasons for the restriction and the duration of the restriction in the patient's clinical record. That physician shall inform the patient and, if appropriate, the patient's parent, managing conservator, or guardian of the clinical reasons for the restriction and the duration of the restriction.

§576.007. NOTIFICATION OF RELEASE

(a)   The department or facility shall make a reasonable effort to notify an adult patient's family before the patient is discharged or released from a facility providing voluntary or involuntary mental health services if the patient grants permission for the notification.

(b)   The department shall notify each adult patient of the patient's right to have his family notified under this section.

§576.008. NOTIFICATION OF PROTECTION / ADVOCACY SYSTEM

A patient shall be informed in writing, at the time of admission and discharge, of the existence, purpose, telephone number, and address of the protection and advocacy system established in this state under the federal Protection and Advocacy for Mentally Ill Individuals Act of 1986 (42 U.S.C. Sec. 10801, et seq.).

§576.009. NOTIFICATION OF RIGHTS

A patient receiving involuntary inpatient mental health services shall be informed of the rights provided by this subtitle:

(1)   orally, in simple, nontechnical terms, and in writing that, if possible, is in the person's primary language; or

(2)   through the use of a means reasonably calculated to communicate with a hearing impaired or visually impaired person, if applicable.

§576.021. GENERAL RIGHTS RELATING TO TREATMENT

(a)   A patient receiving mental health services under this subtitle has the right to:

(1)   appropriate treatment for the patient's mental illness in the least restrictive appropriate setting available;

(2)   not receive unnecessary or excessive medication;

(3)   refuse to participate in a research program;

(4)   an individualized treatment plan and to participate in developing the plan; and

(5)   a humane treatment environment that provides reasonable protection from harm and appropriate privacy for personal needs.

(b)   participation in a research program does not affect a right provided by this chapter.

(c)   A right provided by this section may not be waived by the patient, the patient's attorney or guardian, or any other person behalf of the patient.

§576.022. ADEQUACY OF TREATMENT

(a) The facility administrator of an inpatient mental health facility shall provide adequate medical and psychiatric care and treatment to every patient in accordance with the highest standards accepted in medical practice.

(b) The facility administrator of an inpatient mental health facility may give the patient accepted psychiatric treatment and therapy.

§576.023. PERIODIC EXAMINATION

The facility administrator is responsible for the examination of each patient of the facility at least once every six months and more frequently as practicable.

§576.024. USE OF PHYSICAL RESTRAINT

(a) A physical restraint may not be applied to a patient unless a physician prescribes the restraint.

(b) A physical restraint shall be removed as soon as possible.

(c) Each use of a physical restraint and the reason for the use shall be made a part of the patient's clinical record. The physician who prescribed the restraint shall sign the record.

§576.025. ADMINISTRATION OF PSYCHOACTIVE MEDICATION

(a) A person may not administer a psychoactive medication to a patient receiving voluntary or involuntary mental health services who refuses the administration unless:

  (1) the patient is having a medication-related emergency;

  (2) the patient is younger than 16 years of age and the patient's parent, managing conservator, or guardian consents to the administration on behalf of the patient;

  (3) the refusing patient's representative authorized by law to consent on behalf of the patient has consented to the administration;

  (4) the administration of the medication regardless of the patient's refusal is authorized by an order issued under §574.106; or

  (5) the patient is receiving court-ordered mental health services authorized by an order issued under:

    (A) Article 46.02 or 46.03, Code of Criminal Procedure; or

    (B) Chapter 55, Family Code.

(b) Consent to the administration of psychoactive medication given by a patient or by a person authorized by law to consent on behalf of the patient is valid only if:

  (1) the consent is given voluntarily and without coercive or undue influence;

  (2) the treating physician or a person designated by the physician provided the following information, in a standard format approved by the department, to the patient and, if applicable, to the patient's representative authorized by law to consent on behalf of the patient:

    (A) the specific condition to be treated;

    (B) the beneficial effects on that condition expected from the medication;

  (C) the probable health and mental health consequences of not consent-
       ing to the medication;

  (D) the probable clinically significant side effects and risks associated with
       the medication;

  (E) the generally accepted alternatives to the medication, if any, and why
       the physician recommends that they be rejected; and

  (F) the proposed course of the medication;

  (3) the patient and, if appropriate, the patient's representative authorized by
       law to consent on behalf of the patient is informed in writing that consent
       may be revoked; and

  (4) the consent is evidenced in the patient's clinical record by a signed form
       prescribed by the facility or by a statement of the treating physician or a
       person designated by the physician that documents that consent was given
       by the appropriate person and the circumstances under which the consent
       was obtained.

(c) If the treating physician designates another person to provide the information
     under Subsection (b), then, not later than two working days after that person
     provides the information, excluding weekends and legal holidays, the physician
     shall meet with the patient and, if appropriate, the patient's representative who
     provided the consent, to review the information and answer any questions.

(d) A patient's refusal or attempt to refuse to receive psychoactive medication,
     whether given verbally or by other indications or means, shall be documented
     in the patient's clinical record.

(e) In prescribing psychoactive medication, a treating physician shall:

  (1) prescribe, consistent with clinically appropriate medical care, the medica-
       tion that has the fewest side effects or the least potential for adverse side
       effects, unless the class of medication has been demonstrated or justified
       not to be effective clinically; and

  (2) administer the smallest therapeutically acceptable dosages of medication
       for the patient's condition.

(f) If a physician issues an order to administer psychoactive medication to a patient
     without the patient's consent because the patient is having a medication-related
     emergency:

  (1) the physician shall document in the patient's clinical record in specific med-
       ical or behavioral terms the necessity of the order and that the physician
       has evaluated but rejected other generally accepted, less intrusive forms of
       treatment, if any; and

  (2) treatment of the patient with the psychoactive medication shall be provid-
       ed in the manner, consistent with clinically appropriate medical care, least
       restrictive of the patient's personal liberty.

(g) In this section, "medication-related emergency" and "psychoactive medica-
     tion" have the meanings assigned by §574.101.

§576.026. INDEPENDENT EVALUATION

(a) A patient receiving inpatient mental health services under this subtitle is entitled to obtain at the patient's cost an independent psychiatric, psychological, or medical examination or evaluation by a psychiatrist, physician, or nonphysician mental health professional chosen by the patient. The facility administrator shall allow the patient to obtain the examination or evaluation at any reasonable time.

(b) If the patient is a minor, the minor and the minor's parent, legal guardian, or managing or possessory conservator is entitled to obtain the examination or evaluation. The cost of the examination or evaluation shall be billed by the professional who performed the examination or evaluation to the person responsible for payment of the minor's treatment as a cost of treatment.

§576.027. LIST OF MEDICATIONS

(a) The facility administrator of an inpatient mental health facility shall provide to a patient, a person designated by the patient, and the patient's legal guardian or managing conservator, if any, a list of the medications prescribed for administration to the patient while the patient is in the facility. The list must include for each medication:

   (1) the name of the medication;

   (2) the dosage and schedule prescribed for the administration of the medication; and

   (3) the name of the physician who prescribed the medication.

(b) The list must be provided within four hours after the facility administrator receives a written request for the list from the patient, a person designated by the patient, or the patient's legal guardian or managing conservator and on the discharge of the patient. If sufficient time to prepare the list before discharge is not available, the list may be mailed within 24 hours after discharge to the patient, a person designated by the patient, and the patient's legal guardian or managing conservator.

(c) A patient or the patient's legal guardian or managing conservator, if any, may waive the right of any person to receive the list of medications while the patient is participating in a research project if release of the list would jeopardize the results of the project.

LEGALLY ADEQUATE CONSENT—§591[36]

§591.006. CONSENT

(a) Consent given by a person is legally adequate if the person:

   (1) is not a minor and has not been adjudicated incompetent to manage the person's personal affairs by an appropriate court of law;

   (2) understands the information; and

   (3) consents voluntarily, free from coercion or undue influence.

(b) The person giving the consent must be informed of and understand:

   (1) the nature, purpose, consequences, risks, and benefits of and alternatives to the procedure;

   (2) that the withdrawal or refusal of consent will not prejudice the future

---

36 (Health & Safety Code; Title 7. Mental Health and Mental Retardation; Subtitle D. Persons with Mental Retardation Act; Chapter 591. General Provisions; Subchapter A. General Provisions)

provision of care and services; and

(3) the method used in the proposed procedure if the person is to receive unusual or hazardous treatment procedures, experimental research, organ transplantation, or nontherapeutic surgery.

MENTAL RETARDATION—§592[37]

§592.001. PURPOSE

The purpose of this chapter is to recognize and protect the individual dignity and worth of each person with mental retardation.

§592.002. RULES

The board by rule shall ensure the implementation of the rights guaranteed in this chapter.

§592.011. RIGHTS GUARANTEED

(a) Each person with mental retardation in this state has the rights, benefits, and privileges guaranteed by the constitution and laws of the United States and this state.

(b) The rights specifically listed in this subtitle are in addition to all other rights that persons with mental retardation have and are not exclusive or intended to limit the rights guaranteed by the constitution and laws of the United States and this state.

§592.012. PROTECTION FROM EXPLOITATION AND ABUSE

Each person with mental retardation has the right to protection from exploitation and abuse because of the person's mental retardation.

§592.013. LEAST RESTRICTIVE LIVING ENVIRONMENT

Each person with mental retardation has the right to live in the least restrictive setting appropriate to the person's individual needs and abilities and in a variety of living situations, including living:

(1) alone;

(2) in a group home;

(3) with a family; or

(4) in a supervised, protective environment.

§592.014. EDUCATION

Each person with mental retardation has the right to receive publicly supported educational services, including those services provided under the Education Code, that are appropriate to the person's individual needs regardless of the person's:

(1) chronological age;

(2) degree of retardation;

(3) accompanying disabilities or handicaps; or

(4) admission or commitment to mental retardation services.

---

37   (Health & Safety Code; Title 7. Mental Health and Mental Retardation; Subtitle D. Persons with Mental Retardation Act; Chapter 592. Rights of Persons with Mental Retardation; Subchapter A. General Provisions)

§592.015. EMPLOYMENT

An employer, employment agency, or labor organization may not deny a person equal opportunities in employment because of the person's mental retardation, unless:

(1)   the person's mental retardation significantly impairs the person's ability to perform the duties and tasks of the position for which the person has applied; or

(2)   the denial is based on a bona fide occupational qualification reasonably necessary to the normal operation of the particular business or enterprise.

§592.016. HOUSING

An owner, lessee, sublessee, assignee, or managing agent or other person having the right to sell, rent, or lease real property, or an agent or employee of any of these, may not refuse to sell, rent, or lease to any person or group of persons solely because the person is a person with mental retardation or a group that includes one or more persons with mental retardation.

§592.017. TREATMENT AND SERVICES

Each person with mental retardation has the right to receive for mental retardation adequate treatment and habilitative services that:

(1)   are suited to the person's individual needs;

(2)   maximize the person's capabilities;

(3)   enhance the person's ability to cope with the person's environment; and

(4)   are administered skillfully, safely, and humanely with full respect for the dignity and personal integrity of the person.

§592.018. DETERMINATION OF MENTAL RETARDATION

A person thought to be a person with mental retardation has the right promptly to receive a determination of mental retardation using diagnostic techniques that are adapted to that person's cultural background, language, and ethnic origin to determine if the person is in need of mental retardation services as provided by Subchapter A, Chapter 593.

§592.019. ADMINISTRATIVE HEARING

A person who files an application for a determination of mental retardation has the right to request and promptly receive an administrative hearing under Subchapter A, Chapter 593, to contest the findings of the determination of mental retardation.

§592.020. INDEPENDENT DETERMINATION OF MENTAL RETARDATION

A person for whom a determination of mental retardation is performed or a person who files an application for a determination of mental retardation under §593.004 and who questions the validity or results of the determination of mental retardation has the right to an additional, independent determination of mental retardation performed at the person's own expense.

§592.021. ADDITIONAL RIGHTS

Each person with mental retardation has the right to:

(1)   presumption of competency;

(2) due process in guardianship proceedings; and

(3) fair compensation for the person's labor for the economic benefit of another, regardless of any direct or incidental therapeutic value to the person.

§592.031. RIGHTS IN GENERAL

(a) Each client has the same rights as other citizens of the United States and this state unless the client's rights have been lawfully restricted.

(b) Each client has the rights listed in this subchapter in addition to the rights guaranteed by Subchapter B.

§592.032. LEAST RESTRICTIVE ALTERNATIVE

Each client has the right to live in the least restrictive habilitation setting and to be treated and served in the least intrusive manner appropriate to the client's individual needs.

§592.033. INDIVIDUALIZED PLAN

(a) Each client has the right to a written, individualized habilitation plan developed by appropriate specialists.

(b) The client, and the parent of a client who is a minor or the guardian of the person, shall participate in the development of the plan.

(c) The plan shall be implemented as soon as possible but not later than the 30th day after the date on which the client is admitted or committed to mental retardation services.

(d) The content of an individualized habilitation plan is as required by the department.

§592.034. REVIEW AND REEVALUATION

(a) Each client has the right to have the individualized habilitation plan reviewed at least:

(1) once a year if the client is in a residential care facility; or

(2) quarterly if the client has been admitted for other services.

(b) The purpose of the review is to:

(1) measure progress;

(2) modify objectives and programs if necessary; and

(3) provide guidance and remediation techniques.

(c) Each client has the right to a periodic reassessment.

§592.035. PARTICIPATION IN PLANNING

(a) Each client, and parent of a client who is a minor or the guardian of the person, have the right to:

(1) participate in planning the client's treatment and habilitation; and

(2) be informed in writing at reasonable intervals of the client's progress.

(b) If possible, the client, parent, or guardian of the person shall be given the opportunity to choose from several appropriate alternative services available to the client from a service provider.

§592.036. WITHDRAWAL FROM VOLUNTARY SERVICES

(a) Except as provided by §593.030, a client, the parent if the client is a minor, or a guardian of the person may withdraw the client from mental retardation services.

(b) This section does not apply to a person who was committed to a residential care facility as provided by Subchapter C, Chapter 593.

§592.037. FREEDOM FROM MISTREATMENT

Each client has the right not to be mistreated, neglected, or abused by a service provider.

§592.038. FREEDOM FROM UNNECESSARY MEDICATION

(a) Each client has the right to not receive unnecessary or excessive medication.

(b) Medication may not be used:

    (1) as punishment;

    (2) for the convenience of the staff;

    (3) as a substitute for a habilitation program; or

    (4) in quantities that interfere with the client's habilitation program.

(c) Medication for each client may be authorized only by prescription of a physician and a physician shall closely supervise its use.

(d) Each client has the right to refuse psychoactive medication, as provided by Subchapter F.

§592.039. GRIEVANCES

A client, or a person acting on behalf of a person with mental retardation or a group of persons with mental retardation, has the right to submit complaints or grievances regarding the infringement of the rights of a person with mental retardation or the delivery of mental retardation services against a person, group of persons, organization, or business to the appropriate public responsibility committee for investigation and appropriate action.

§592.040. INFORMATION ABOUT RIGHTS

(a) On admission for mental retardation services, each client, and the parent if the client is a minor or the guardian of the person of the client, shall be given written notice of the rights guaranteed by this subtitle. The notice shall be in plain and simple language.

(b) Each client shall be orally informed of these rights in plain and simple language.

(c) Notice given solely to the parent or guardian of the person is sufficient if the client is manifestly unable to comprehend the rights.

§592.051. GENERAL RIGHTS OF RESIDENTS

Each resident has the right to:

    (1) a normal residential environment;

    (2) a humane physical environment;

    (3) communication and visits; and

    (4) possess personal property.

§592.052. MEDICAL AND DENTAL CARE AND TREATMENT

Each resident has the right to prompt, adequate, and necessary medical and dental care and treatment for physical and mental ailments and to prevent an illness or disability.

§592.053. STANDARDS OF CARE

Medical and dental care and treatment shall be performed under the appropriate supervision of a licensed physician or dentist and shall be consistent with accepted standards of medical and dental practice in the community.

§592.054. DUTIES OF SUPERINTENDENT OR DIRECTOR

(a)   Except as limited by this subtitle, the superintendent or director shall provide without further consent necessary care and treatment to each court-committed resident and make available necessary care and treatment to each voluntary resident.

(b)   Notwithstanding Subsection (a), consent is required for :

 (1)   all surgical procedures; and

 (2)   as provided by Section 592.153, the administration of psychoactive medications.

§592.055. UNUSUAL OR HAZARDOUS TREATMENT

This subtitle does not permit the department to perform unusual or hazardous treatment procedures, experimental research, organ transplantation, or nontherapeutic surgery for experimental research.

MENTAL RETARDATION RECORDS—§595[38]

§595.001. CONFIDENTIALITY OF RECORDS

Records of the identity, diagnosis, evaluation, or treatment of a person that are maintained in connection with the performance of a program or activity relating to mental retardation are confidential and may be disclosed only for the purposes and under the circumstances authorized under Sections 595.003 and 595.004.

§595.002. RULES

The board shall adopt rules to carry out this chapter that the department considers necessary or proper to:

(1)   prevent circumvention or evasion of the chapter; or

(2)   facilitate compliance with the chapter.

§595.003. CONSENT TO DISCLOSURE

(a)   The content of a confidential record may be disclosed in accordance with the prior written consent of:

 (1)   the person about whom the record is maintained;

 (2)   the person's parent if the person is a minor;

 (3)   the guardian if the person has been adjudicated incompetent to manage the person's personal affairs; or

---

38   (Health & Safety Code; Title 7. Mental Health and Mental Retardation; Subtitle D. Persons with Mental Retardation Act; Chapter 595. Records)

(4) if the person is dead:

    (A) the executor or administrator of the deceased's estate; or

    (B) if an executor or administrator has not been appointed, the deceased's spouse or, if the deceased was not married, an adult related to the deceased within the first degree of consanguinity.

(b) Disclosure is permitted only to the extent, under the circumstances, and for the purposes allowed under department rules.

§595.004. RIGHT TO PERSONAL RECORD

(a) The content of a confidential record shall be made available on the request of the person about whom the record was made unless:

(1) the person is a client; and

(2) the qualified professional responsible for supervising the client's habilitation states in a signed written statement that having access to the record is not in the client's best interest.

(b) The parent of a minor or the guardian of the person shall be given access to the contents of any record about the minor or person.

§595.005. EXCEPTIONS

(a) The content of a confidential record may be disclosed without the consent required under §595.003 to:

(1) medical personnel to the extent necessary to meet a medical emergency;

(2) qualified personnel for management audits, financial audits, program evaluations, or research approved by the department; or

(3) personnel legally authorized to conduct investigations concerning complaints of abuse or denial of rights of persons with mental retardation.

(b) A person who receives confidential information under Subsection (a)(2) may not directly or indirectly identify a person receiving services in a report of the audit, evaluation, or research, or otherwise disclose any identities.

(c) The department may disclose without the consent required under §595.003 a person's educational records to a school district that provides or will provide educational services to the person.

(d) If authorized by an appropriate order of a court of competent jurisdiction granted after application showing good cause, the content of a record may be disclosed without the consent required under §595.003. In determining whether there is good cause, a court shall weigh the public interest and need for disclosure against the injury to the person receiving services. On granting the order, the court, in determining the extent to which any disclosure of all or any part of a record is necessary, shall impose appropriate safeguards against unauthorized disclosure.

§595.006. USE OF RECORD IN CRIMINAL PROCEEDINGS

Except as authorized by a court order under §595.005, a confidential record may not be used to:

(1) initiate or substantiate a criminal charge against a person receiving services; or

(2) conduct an investigation of a person receiving services.

§595.007. C ONFIDENTIALITY OF P AST S ERVICES

The prohibition against disclosing information in a confidential record applies regardless of when the person received services.

§595.008. E XCHANGE OF R ECORDS

The prohibitions against disclosure apply to an exchange of records between government agencies or persons, except for exchanges of information necessary for:

(1) delivery of services to clients; or

(2) payment for mental retardation services as defined in this subtitle.

§595.009. R ECEIPT OF I NFORMATION BY P ERSONS OTHER THAN C LIENT OR P ATIENT

(a) A person who receives information that is confidential under this chapter may not disclose the information except to the extent that disclosure is consistent with the authorized purposes for which the information was obtained.

(b) This section does not apply to the person about whom the record is made, or the parent, if the person is a minor, or the guardian of the person.

§595.010. D ISCLOSURE OF P HYSICAL OR M ENTAL C ONDITION

This chapter does not prohibit a qualified professional from disclosing the current physical and mental condition of a person with mental retardation to the person's parent, guardian, relative, or friend.

M ENTAL H EALTH R ECORDS—§611[39]

§611.001. D EFINITIONS

In this chapter:

(1) *"Patient"* means a person who consults or is interviewed by a professional for diagnosis, evaluation, or treatment of any mental or emotional condition or disorder, including alcoholism or drug addiction.

(2) *"Professional"* means:

   (A) a person authorized to practice medicine in any state or nation;

   (B) a person licensed or certified by this state to diagnose, evaluate, or treat any mental or emotional condition or disorder; or

   (C) a person the patient reasonably believes is authorized, licensed, or certified as provided by this subsection.

§611.002. C ONFIDENTIALITY OF I NFORMATION AND P ROHIBITION A GAINST D ISCLOSURE

(a) Communications between a patient and a professional, and records of the identity, diagnosis, evaluation, or treatment of a patient that are created or maintained by a professional, are confidential.

(b) Confidential communications or records may not be disclosed except as provided by §611.004 or 611.0045.

---

39 (Health & Safety Code; Title 7. Mental Health and Mental Retardation; Subtitle E. Special Provisions Relating to Mental Illness and Mental Retardation; Chapter 611. Mental Health Records)

(c)   This section applies regardless of when the patient received services from a professional.

§611.003. Persons Who May Claim Privilege of Confidentiality

(a)   The privilege of confidentiality may be claimed by:

(1)   the patient;

(2)   a person listed in §611.004(a)(4) or (a)(5) who is acting on the patient's behalf; or

(3)   the professional, but only on behalf of the patient.

(b)   The authority of a professional to claim the privilege of confidentiality on behalf of the patient is presumed in the absence of evidence to the contrary.

§611.004. Authorized Disclosure of Confidential Information Other than in Administrative Proceeding

(a)   A professional may disclose confidential information only:

(1)   to a governmental agency if the disclosure is required or authorized by law;

(2)   to medical or law enforcement personnel if the professional determines that there is a probability of imminent physical injury by the patient to the patient or others or there is a probability of immediate mental or emotional injury to the patient;

(3)   to qualified personnel for management audits, financial audits, program evaluations, or research, in accordance with Subsection (b);

(4)   to a person who has the written consent of the patient, or a parent if the patient is a minor, or a guardian if the patient has been adjudicated as incompetent to manage the patient's personal affairs;

(5)   to the patient's personal representative if the patient is deceased;

(6)   to individuals, corporations, or governmental agencies involved in paying or collecting fees for mental or emotional health services provided by a professional;

(7)   to other professionals and personnel under the professionals' direction who participate in the diagnosis, evaluation, or treatment of the patient;

(8)   in an official legislative inquiry relating to a state hospital or state school as provided by Subsection (c);

(9)   to designated persons or personnel of a correctional facility in which a person is detained if the disclosure is for the sole purpose of providing treatment and health care to the person in custody;

(10) to an employee or agent of the professional who requires mental health care information to provide mental health care services or in complying with statutory, licensing, or accreditation requirements, if the professional has taken appropriate action to ensure that the employee or agent:

(A)   will not use or disclose the information for any other purposes; and

(B)   will take appropriate steps to protect the information; or

(11) to satisfy a request for medical records of a deceased or incompetent person

pursuant to §4.01(e), Medical Liability and Insurance Improvement Act of Texas (Article 4590i, Vernon's Texas Civil Statutes).

(b)   Personnel who receive confidential information under Subsection (a)(3) may not directly or indirectly identify or otherwise disclose the identity of a patient in a report or in any other manner.

(c)   The exception in Subsection (a)(8) applies only to records created by the state hospital or state school or by the employees of the hospital or school. Information or records that identify a patient may be released only with the patient's proper consent.

(d)   A person who receives information from confidential communications or records may not disclose the information except to the extent that disclosure is consistent with the authorized purposes for which the person first obtained the information. This subsection does not apply to a person listed in Subsection (a)(4) or (a)(5) who is acting on the patient's behalf.

§611.0045. RIGHT TO MENTAL HEALTH RECORD

(a)   Except as otherwise provided by this section, a patient is entitled to have access to the content of a confidential record made about the patient.

(b)   The professional may deny access to any portion of a record if the professional determines that release of that portion would be harmful to the patient's physical, mental, or emotional health.

(c)   If the professional denies access to any portion of a record, the professional shall give the patient a signed and dated written statement that having access to the record would be harmful to the patient's physical, mental, or emotional health and shall include a copy of the written statement in the patient's records. The statement must specify the portion of the record to which access is denied, the reason for denial, and the duration of the denial.

(d)   The professional who denies access to a portion of a record under this section shall redetermine the necessity for the denial at each time a request for the denied portion is made. If the professional again denies access, the professional shall notify the patient of the denial and document the denial as prescribed by Subsection (c).

(e)   If a professional denies access to a portion of a confidential record, the professional shall allow examination and copying of the record by another professional if the patient selects the professional to treat the patient for the same or a related condition as the professional denying access.

(f)   The content of a confidential record shall be made available to a person listed by §611.004(a)(4) or (5) who is acting on the patient's behalf.

(g)   A professional shall delete confidential information about another person who has not consented to the release, but may not delete information relating to the patient that another person has provided, the identity of the person responsible for that information, or the identity of any person who provided information that resulted in the patient's commitment.

(h)   If a summary or narrative of a confidential record is requested by the patient or other person requesting release under this section, the professional shall prepare the summary or narrative.

(i)   The professional or other entity that has possession or control of the record shall grant access to any portion of the record to which access is not specifically denied under this section within a reasonable time and may charge a reasonable fee.

(j)   Notwithstanding §5.08, Medical Practice Act (Article 4495b, Vernon's Texas Civil Statutes), this section applies to the release of a confidential record created or maintained by a professional, including a physician, that relates to the diagnosis, evaluation, or treatment of a mental or emotional condition or disorder, including alcoholism or drug addiction.

(k)   The denial of a patient's access to any portion of a record by the professional or other entity that has possession or control of the record suspends, until the release of that portion of the record, the running of an applicable statute of limitations on a cause of action in which evidence relevant to the cause of action is in that portion of the record.

§611.005. LEGAL REMEDIES FOR IMPROPER DISCLOSURE OR FAILURE TO DISCLOSE

(a)   A person aggrieved by the improper disclosure of or failure to disclose confidential communications or records in violation of this chapter may petition the district court of the county in which the person resides for appropriate relief, including injunctive relief. The person may petition a district court of Travis County if the person is not a resident of this state.

(b)   In a suit contesting the denial of access under §611.0045, the burden of proving that the denial was proper is on the professional who denied the access.

(c)   The aggrieved person also has a civil cause of action for damages.

§611.006. AUTHORIZED DISCLOSURE OF CONFIDENTIAL INFORMATION IN JUDICIAL PROCEEDING

(a)   A professional may disclose confidential information in:

  (1)   a judicial or administrative proceeding brought by the patient or the patient's legally authorized representative against a professional, including malpractice proceedings;

  (2)   a license revocation proceeding in which the patient is a complaining witness and in which disclosure is relevant to the claim or defense of a professional;

  (3)   a judicial or administrative proceeding in which the patient waives the patient's right in writing to the privilege of confidentiality of information or when a representative of the patient acting on the patient's behalf submits a written waiver to the confidentiality privilege;

  (4)   a judicial or administrative proceeding to substantiate and collect on a claim for mental or emotional health services rendered to the patient;

  (5)   a judicial proceeding if the judge finds that the patient, after having been informed that communications would not be privileged, has made communications to a professional in the course of a court-ordered examination relating to the patient's mental or emotional condition or disorder, except that those communications may be disclosed only with respect to issues involving the patient's mental or emotional health;

(6) a judicial proceeding affecting the parent-child relationship;

(7) any criminal proceeding, as otherwise provided by law;

(8) a judicial or administrative proceeding regarding the abuse or neglect, or the cause of abuse or neglect, of a resident of an institution, as that term is defined by Chapter 242;

(9) a judicial proceeding relating to a will if the patient's physical or mental condition is relevant to the execution of the will;

(10) an involuntary commitment proceeding for court-ordered treatment or for a probable cause hearing under:

(A) Chapter 462;

(B) Chapter 574; or

(C) Chapter 593; or

(11) a judicial or administrative proceeding where the court or agency has issued an order or subpoena.

(b) On granting an order under Subsection (a)(5), the court, in determining the extent to which disclosure of all or any part of a communication is necessary, shall impose appropriate safeguards against unauthorized disclosure.

§611.007. REVOCATION OF CONSENT

(a) Except as provided by Subsection (b), a patient or a patient's legally authorized representative may revoke a disclosure consent to a professional at any time. A revocation is valid only if it is written, dated, and signed by the patient or legally authorized representative.

(b) A patient may not revoke a disclosure that is required for purposes of making payment to the professional for mental health care services provided to the patient.

(c) A patient may not maintain an action against a professional for a disclosure made by the professional in good faith reliance on an authorization if the professional did not have notice of the revocation of the consent.

§611.008. REQUEST BY PATIENT

(a) On receipt of a written request from a patient to examine or copy all or part of the patient's recorded mental health care information, a professional, as promptly as required under the circumstances but not later than the 15th day after the date of receiving the request, shall:

(1) make the information available for examination during regular business hours and provide a copy to the patient, if requested; or

(2) inform the patient if the information does not exist or cannot be found.

(b) Unless provided for by other state law, the professional may charge a reasonable fee for retrieving or copying mental health care information and is not required to permit examination or copying until the fee is paid unless there is a medical emergency.

(c) A professional may not charge a fee for copying mental health care information under Subsection (b) to the extent the fee is prohibited under Subchapter M, Chapter 161.

HUMAN RESOURCES CODE

CHILDREN'S POLICY COUNCIL AND MENTAL HEALTH ISSUES—§22.035[40]

Specifically targets mental health and mental health services as for the Children's Policy Council to study.

§22.035. CHILDREN'S POLICY COUNCIL

(a) A work group to be known as the Children's Policy Council shall assist the Department of Aging and Disability Services, the Health and Human Services Commission, the Department of State Health Services, the Department of Assistive and Rehabilitative Services, and the Department of Family and Protective Services in developing, implementing, and administering family support policies for children with disabilities relating to:

   (1) long-term services and supports;

   (2) health services; and

   (3) mental health services.

(b) The executive commissioner of the Health and Human Services Commission shall appoint the members of the work group, which must include the following: consumers (under age 22) and relatives of consumers of long-term care and health programs for children; consumers (under 25) and relatives of consumers of mental health services; health-care advocates; public and private agencies providing long-term care and mental health to children; community businesses; faith-based organizations.

(j) The work group may study and make recommendations in the following areas:

   (1) access of a child or a child's family to effective case management services, including case management services with a single case manager, parent case managers, or independent case managers;

   (2) the transition needs of children who reach an age at which they are no longer eligible for services at the Department of State Health Services, the Texas Education Agency, and other applicable state agencies;

   (3) the blending of funds, including case management funding, for children needing long-term care, health services, and mental health services;

   (4) collaboration and coordination of children's services between the Department of Aging and Disability Services, the Department of State Health Services, the Department of Assistive and Rehabilitative Services, the Department of Family and Protective Services, and any other agency determined to be applicable by the work group;

   (5) budgeting and the use of funds appropriated for children's long-term care services, health services, and mental health services;

   (6) services and supports for families providing care for children with disabilities;

---

40 (Human Resources Code; Title 2. Department of Human Services and Department of Protective and Regulatory Services; Subtitle B. Structure and Functions of Department of Human Services; Chapter 22. General Functions of Department of Human Services)

(7) effective permanency planning for children who reside in institutions or who are at risk of placement in an institution;

(8) barriers to enforcement of regulations regarding institutions that serve children with disabilities; and

(9) the provision of services under the medical assistance program to children younger than 23 years of age with disabilities or special health care needs under a waiver granted under Section 1915(c) of the federal Social Security Act (42 U.S.C. Section 1396n(c)).

(k) Not later than September 1 of each even-numbered year, the work group shall report on its findings and recommendations to the legislature and the executive commissioner of the Health and Human Services Commission.

(l) After evaluating and considering recommendations reported under Subsection (k), the executive commissioner of the Health and Human Services Commission shall adopt rules to implement guidelines for providing long-term care, health services, and mental health services to children with disabilities.

Regulation of Certain Child-Care Facilities—§42[41]

Outlines targeted goals, special rules and standards, and exemptions for certain emergency shelters that provide sheter, care, or servides to alleged victims of human trafficking (see in particular §42.042.(g-2) and §42.01.23B)

Elder Abuse—§48[42]

§48.001. Purpose

The purpose of this chapter is to provide for the authority to investigate the abuse, neglect, or exploitation of an elderly or disabled person and to provide protective services to that person.

§48.002. Definitions

(a) Except as otherwise provided under §48.251, in this chapter:

(1) *"Elderly person"* means a person 65 years of age or older.

(2) *"Abuse"* means:

(A) the negligent or willful infliction of injury, unreasonable confinement, intimidation, or cruel punishment with resulting physical or emotional harm or pain to an elderly or disabled person by the person's caretaker, family member, or other individual who has an ongoing relationship with the person; or

(B) sexual abuse of an elderly or disabled person, including any involuntary or nonconsensual sexual conduct that would constitute an offense under §21.08, Penal Code (indecent exposure) or Chapter 22, Penal Code (assaultive offenses), committed by the person's caretaker,

---

41 (Human Resources Code; Title 2. Department of Human Services and Department of Protective and Regulatory Services; Subtitle D. Department of Family and Protective Services; Child Welfare And Protective Services; Chapter 42. Regulation of Certain Facilities, Homes, and Agencies that Provide Child-Care Services; Subchapter C. Regulation)

42 (Human Resources Code; Title 2. Department of Human Services and Department of Protective and Regulatory Services; Subtitle D. Department of Family and Protective Services; Child Welfare and Protective Services; Chapter 48. Investigations and Protective Services for Elderly and Disabled Persons; Subchapter A. General Provisions)

family member, or other individual who has an ongoing relationship with the person.

(3) *"Exploitation"* means the illegal or improper act or process of a caretaker, family member, or other individual who has an ongoing relationship with an elderly or disabled person that involves using, or attempting to use, the resources of the elderly or disabled person, including the person's social security number or other identifying information, for monetary or personal benefit, profit, or gain without the informed consent of the elderly or disabled person.

(4) *"Neglect"* means the failure to provide for one's self the goods or services, including medical services, which are necessary to avoid physical or emotional harm or pain or the failure of a caretaker to provide such goods or services.

(5) *"Protective services"* means the services furnished by the department or by a protective services agency to an elderly or disabled person who has been determined to be in a state of abuse, neglect, or exploitation or to a relative or caretaker of an elderly or disabled person if the department determines the services are necessary to prevent the elderly or disabled person from returning to a state of abuse, neglect, or exploitation. These services may include social casework, case management, and arranging for psychiatric and health evaluation, home care, day care, social services, health care, respite services, and other services consistent with this chapter. The term does not include the services of the department or another protective services agency in conducting an investigation regarding alleged abuse, neglect, or exploitation of an elderly or disabled person.

(6) *"Protective services agency"* means a public or private agency, corporation, board, or organization that provides protective services to elderly or disabled persons in the state of abuse, neglect, or exploitation.

(7) *"Department"* means the Department of Protective and Regulatory Services.

(8) *"Disabled person"* means a person with a mental, physical, or developmental disability that substantially impairs the person's ability to provide adequately for the person's care or protection and who is:

(A) 18 years of age or older; or

(B) under 18 years of age and who has had the disabilities of minority removed.

(9) *"Legal holiday"* means a state holiday listed in Subchapter B, Chapter 662, Government Code, or an officially declared county holiday.

(10) *"Volunteer"* means a person who:

(A) performs services for or on behalf of the department under the supervision of a department employee; and

(B) does not receive compensation that exceeds the authorized expenses the person incurs in performing those services.

(b) The definitions of "abuse," "neglect," and "exploitation" adopted by the department as prescribed by §48.251 apply to an investigation of abuse, neglect, or exploitation in a facility subject to Subchapters F & H.

§48.051. REPORT OF ABUSE, NEGLECT, OR EXPLOITATION: IMMUNITIES

(a) Except as prescribed by Subsection (b), a person having cause to believe that an elderly or disabled person is in the state of abuse, neglect, or exploitation, including a disabled person receiving services as described by Section 48.252, shall report the information required by Subsection (d) immediately to the department.

(b) If a person has cause to believe that an elderly or disabled person, other than a disabled person receiving services as described by Section 48.252, has been abused, neglected, or exploited in a facility operated, licensed, certified, or registered by a state agency, the person shall report the information to the state agency that operates, licenses, certifies, or registers the facility for investigation by that agency.

(c) The duty imposed by Subsections (a) and (b) applies without exception to a person whose knowledge concerning possible abuse, neglect, or exploitation is obtained during the scope of the person's employment or whose professional communications are generally confidential, including an attorney, clergy member, medical practitioner, social worker, employee or member of a board that licenses or certifies a professional, and mental health professional.

(d) The report may be made orally or in writing. It shall include:

(1) the name, age, and address of the elderly or disabled person;

(2) the name and address of any person responsible for the elderly or disabled person's care;

(3) the nature and extent of the elderly or disabled person's condition;

(4) the basis of the reporter's knowledge; and

(5) any other relevant information.

(e) If a person who makes a report under this section chooses to give self-identifying information, the caseworker who investigates the report shall contact the person if necessary to obtain any additional information required to assist the person who is the subject of the report.

§48.052. FAILURE TO REPORT; PENALTY

(a) A person commits an offense if the person has cause to believe that an elderly or disabled person has been abused, neglected, or exploited or is in the state of abuse, neglect, or exploitation and knowingly fails to report in accordance with this chapter. An offense under this subsection is a Class A misdemeanor, except that the offense is a state jail felony if it is shown on the trial of the offense that the disabled person was a person with mental retardation who resided in a state supported living center, the ICF-MR component of the Rio Grande State Center, or a facility licensed under Chapter 252, Health and Safety Code, and the actor knew that the disabled person had suffered serious bodily injury as a result of the abuse, neglect, or exploitation.

(b) This section does not apply if the alleged abuse, neglect, or exploitation occurred in a facility licensed under Chapter 242, Health and Safety Code. Failure to report abuse, neglect, or exploitation that occurs in a facility licensed under that chapter is governed by that chapter.

§48.053. FALSE REPORT; PENALTY

A person commits an offense if the person knowingly or intentionally reports information as provided in this chapter that the person knows is false or lacks factual foundation. An offense under this section is a Class A misdemeanor.

§48.054. IMMUNITY

(a) A person filing a report under this chapter or testifying or otherwise participating in any judicial proceeding arising from a petition, report, or investigation is immune from civil or criminal liability on account of his or her petition, report, testimony, or participation, unless the person acted in bad faith or with a malicious purpose.

(b) A person, including an authorized department volunteer, medical personnel, or law enforcement officer, who at the request of the department participates in an investigation required by this chapter or in an action that results from that investigation is immune from civil or criminal liability for any act or omission relating to that participation if the person acted in good faith and, if applicable, in the course and scope of the person's assigned responsibilities or duties.

(c) A person who reports the person's own abuse, neglect, or exploitation of another person or who acts in bad faith or with malicious purpose in reporting alleged abuse, neglect, or exploitation is not immune from civil or criminal liability.

§48.203. VOLUNTARY PROTECTIVE SERVICES

(a) An elderly or disabled person may receive voluntary protective services if the person requests or consents to receive those services.

(b) The elderly or disabled person who receives protective services shall participate in all decisions regarding his or her welfare, if able to do so.

(c) The least restrictive alternatives should be made available to the elderly or disabled person who receives protective services.

(d) Except as provided by Section 48.208, if an elderly or disabled person withdraws from or refuses consent to voluntary protective services, the services may not be provided.

EMERGENCY ORDER FOR PROTECTIVE SERVICES—§48.208[43]

Relating to the assessment of an elderly or disabled person's psychological status for purposes of an emergency order authorizing protective services.

§48.208. EMERGENCY ORDER FOR PROTECTIVE SERVICES

(a) For purposes of this section, a person lacks the capacity to consent to receive protective services if, because of mental or physical impairment, the person is incapable of understanding the nature of the services offered and agreeing to receive or rejecting protective services.

(b) If the department determines that an elderly or disabled person is suffering from abuse, neglect, or exploitation presenting a threat to life or physical safety, that the person lacks capacity to consent to receive protective services, and that no consent can be obtained, the department may petition the probate or statutory

43 (Human Resources Code; Title 2. Department f Human Services and Department of Protective and Regulatory Services; Subtitle D. Department of Family and Protective Services; Child Welfare and Protective Services; Chapter 48. Investigations and Protective Services for Elderly and Disabled Persons; Subchapter E. Provision of Services; Emergency Protection)

or constitutional county court that has probate jurisdiction in the county in which the elderly or disabled person resides for an emergency order authorizing protective services.

(c) The petition shall be verified and shall include:

    (1) the name, age, and address of the elderly or disabled person who needs protective services;

    (2) the nature of the abuse, neglect, or exploitation;

    (3) the services needed; and

    (4) a medical report signed by a physician stating that the person is suffering from abuse, neglect, or exploitation presenting a threat to life or physical safety and stating that the person is physically or mentally incapable of consenting to services unless the court finds that an immediate danger to the health or safety of the elderly or disabled person exists and there is not sufficient time to obtain the medical report.

(c-1) Notwithstanding Subsection (c)(4), in lieu of a medical report described by Subsection (c)(4), the petition may include an assessment of the elderly or disabled person's health status as described by Subsection (c-2) or psychological status as described by Subsection (c-3), or a medical opinion of the elderly or disabled person's health status as described by Subsection (c-4), if the department determines, after making a good faith effort, that a physician from whom the department may obtain the medical report is unavailable. The department shall ensure that the person who performs an assessment of the elderly or disabled person's health or psychological status has training and experience in performing the applicable assessment.

(c-3) An assessment of the elderly or disabled person's psychological status must be performed by a licensed professional counselor, licensed psychologist, or master social worker who has training and expertise in issues related to abuse, neglect, and exploitation. The person performing the assessment shall sign a report stating:

    (1) that the elderly or disabled person is reported to be suffering from abuse, neglect, or exploitation, which may present a threat to the person's life or physical safety; and

    (2) that in the professional opinion of the licensed professional counselor, licensed psychologist, or master social worker, as applicable, the issuance of an emergency order authorizing protective services without the elderly or disabled person's consent is necessary under the circumstances.

(d) On finding that there is reasonable cause to believe that abuse, neglect, or exploitation presents a threat to life or physical safety for the elderly or disabled person and that the elderly or disabled person lacks capacity to consent to services, the court may:

    (1) order removal of the elderly or disabled person to safer surroundings;

    (2) order medical services; and

    (3) order other available services necessary to remove conditions creating the threat to life or physical safety, including the services of law enforcement officers or emergency medical services personnel.

(d-1) If the court renders an order that is based on a petition including an assessment under Subsection (c-2) or (c-3) or a medical opinion under Subsection (c-4), the court shall order that the elderly or disabled person be examined by a physician not later than 72 hours after the time the provision of protective services begins. After performing the examination, the physician shall sign and submit to the court a medical report stating the physician's opinion whether the elderly or disabled person is:

(1)   suffering from abuse, neglect, or exploitation presenting a threat to life or physical safety; and

(2)   physically or mentally incapable of consenting to services.

(e-1) An emergency order that was rendered based on a petition that included an assessment under Subsection (c-2) or (c-3) or a medical opinion under Subsection (c-4) immediately terminates if the medical report issued under Subsection (d-1) states the physician's opinion that the elderly or disabled person:

(1)   is not suffering from abuse, neglect, or exploitation presenting a threat to life or physical safety; or

(2)   is physically or mentally capable of consenting to services.

(f)   Any medical facility, emergency medical services provider, or physician who provides treatment to or who transports an elderly or disabled person pursuant to an emergency order under Subsection (d) or an emergency authorization under Subsection (h) is not liable for any damages arising from the treatment or transportation, except those damages resulting from the negligence of the facility, provider, or physician.

INSURANCE CODE

WORKERS' COMPENSATION HEALTH CARE NETWORKS—§1305[44]

SUBCHAPTER D. CONTRACTING PROVISIONS

§1305.151. TRANSFER OF RISK

A contract under this subchapter may not involve a transfer of risk.

§1305.152. NETWORK CONTRACTS WITH PROVIDERS

(a)   A network shall enter into a written contract with each provider or group of providers that participates in the network. A provider contract under this section is confidential and is not subject to disclosure as public information under Chapter 552, Government Code.

(b)   A network is not required to accept an application for participation in the network from a health care provider who otherwise meets the requirements specified in this chapter for participation if the network determines that the network has contracted with a sufficient number of qualified health care providers.

(c)   Provider contracts and subcontracts must include, at a minimum, the following provisions:

   (1)   a hold-harmless clause stating that the network and the network's contracted providers are prohibited from billing or attempting to collect any amounts from employees for health care services under any circumstances, including the insolvency of the insurance carrier or the network, except as provided by §1305.451(b)(6);

   (2)   a statement that the provider agrees to follow treatment guidelines adopted by the network under §1305.304, as applicable to an employee's injury;

   (3)   a continuity of treatment clause that states that if a provider leaves the network, the insurance carrier or network is obligated to continue to reimburse the provider for a period not to exceed 90 days at the contracted rate for care of an employee with a life-threatening condition or an acute condition for which disruption of care would harm the employee;

   (4)   a clause regarding appeal by the provider of termination of provider status and applicable written notification to employees regarding such a termination, including provisions determined by the commissioner; and

   (5)   any other provisions required by the commissioner by rule.

(d)   Continued care as described by Subsection (c)(3) must be requested by a provider. A dispute involving continuity of care is subject to the dispute resolution process under Subchapter I.

(e)   An insurance carrier and a network may not use any financial incentive or make a payment to a health care provider that acts directly or indirectly as an inducement to limit medically necessary services.

---

44 (Insurance Code; Title 8. Health Insurance and other Health Coverages; Subtitle D. Provider Plans; Chapter 1305. Workers' Compensation Health Care Networks; Subchapter D. Contracting Provisions)

§1305.153. PROVIDER REIMBURSEMENT

(a) The amount of reimbursement for services provided by a network provider is determined by the contract between the network and the provider or group of providers.

(b) If an insurance carrier or network has preauthorized a health care service, the insurance carrier or network or the network's agent or other representative may not deny payment to a provider except for reasons other than medical necessity.

(c) Out-of-network providers who provide care as described by §1305.006 shall be reimbursed as provided by the Texas Workers' Compensation Act and applicable rules of the commissioner of workers' compensation.

(d) Subject to Subsection (a), billing by, and reimbursement to, contracted and out-of-network providers is subject to the requirements of the Texas Workers' Compensation Act and applicable rules of the commissioner of workers' compensation, as consistent with this chapter. This subsection may not be construed to require application of rules of the commissioner of workers' compensation regarding reimbursement if application of those rules would negate reimbursement amounts negotiated by the network.

(e) An insurance carrier shall notify in writing a network provider if the carrier contests the compensability of the injury for which the provider provides health care services. A carrier may not deny payment for health care services provided by a network provider before that notification on the grounds that the injury was not compensable. Payment for medically necessary health care services provided prior to written notification of a compensability denial is not subject to denial, recoupment, or refund from a network provider based on compensability. If the insurance carrier successfully contests compensability, the carrier is liable for health care provided before issuance of the notification required by this subsection, up to a maximum of $7,000.

(f) If, for the purposes of credentialing and contracting with health care providers on behalf of the certified network, a person is serving as both a management contractor under Section 1305.102 or a third party to which the network delegates a function and as an agent of the health care provider, the contract between the management contractor or third party and the health care provider must specify:

(1) the certified network's contract rate for health care services; and

(2) the amount of reimbursement the health care provider will be paid after the health care provider agent's fee for providing administrative services is applied.

(g) If a management contractor or third party to which the network delegates a function is serving as an agent for health care providers in the certified network, the management contractor or third party must disclose that relationship in its contract with the certified network.

(h) A contract described by Subsection (f), or a contract between a management contractor or third party to which the network delegates a function and a certified network, must comply with the requirements of this chapter.

(i) If a contract described by Subsection (f) complies with the requirements of this chapter, the health care provider shall be reimbursed in accordance with the terms of the contract. If a contract described by Subsection (f) does not comply with the requirements of this chapter, the health care provider shall be reimbursed in accordance with the certified network's contracted rate.

(j) A certified network, management contractor, or third party to which the network delegates a function may not require a health care provider, as a condition for contracting with the certified network, to utilize as a health care provider agent the management contractor or the third party.

§1305.154. NETWORK-CARRIER CONTRACTS

(a) Except for emergencies and out-of-network referrals, a network may provide health care services to employees only through a written contract with an insurance carrier. A network-carrier contract under this section is confidential and is not subject to disclosure as public information under Chapter 552, Government Code.

(b) A carrier and a network may negotiate the functions to be provided by the network, except that the network shall contract with providers for the provision of health care, and shall perform functions related to the operation of a quality improvement program and credentialing in accordance with the requirements of this chapter.

(c) A network's contract with a carrier must include:

   (1) a description of the functions that the carrier delegates to the network, consistent with the requirements of Subsection (b), and the reporting requirements for each function;

   (2) a statement that the network and any management contractor or third party to which the network delegates a function will perform all delegated functions in full compliance with all requirements of this chapter, the Texas Workers' Compensation Act, and rules of the commissioner or the commissioner of workers' compensation;

   (3) a provision that the contract:

      (A) may not be terminated without cause by either party without 90 days' prior written notice; and

      (B) must be terminated immediately if cause exists;

   (4) a hold-harmless provision stating that the network, a management contractor, a third party to which the network delegates a function, and the network's contracted providers are prohibited from billing or attempting to collect any amounts from employees for health care services under any circumstances, including the insolvency of the carrier or the network, except as provided by §1305.451(b)(6);

   (5) a statement that the carrier retains ultimate responsibility for ensuring that all delegated functions and all management contractor functions are performed in accordance with applicable statutes and rules and that the contract may not be construed to limit in any way the carrier's responsibility, including financial responsibility, to comply with all statutory and regulatory requirements;

   (6) a statement that the network's role is to provide the services described under Subsection (b) as well as any other services or functions delegated by

the carrier, including functions delegated to a management contractor, subject to the carrier's oversight and monitoring of the network's performance;

(7) a requirement that the network provide the carrier, at least monthly and in a form usable for audit purposes, the data necessary for the carrier to comply with reporting requirements of the department and the division of workers' compensation with respect to any services provided under the contract, as determined by commissioner rules;

(8) a requirement that the carrier, the network, any management contractor, and any third party to which the network delegates a function comply with the data reporting requirements of the Texas Workers' Compensation Act and rules of the commissioner of workers' compensation;

(9) a contingency plan under which the carrier would, in the event of termination of the contract or a failure to perform, reassume one or more functions of the network under the contract, including functions related to:

(A) payments to providers and notification to employees;

(B) quality of care;

(C) utilization review;

(D) continuity of care, including a plan for identifying and transitioning employees to new providers;

(10) a provision that requires that any agreement by which the network delegates any function to a management contractor or any third party be in writing, and that such an agreement require the delegated third party or management contractor to be subject to all the requirements of this subchapter;

(11) a provision that requires the network to provide to the department the license number of a management contractor or any delegated third party who performs a function that requires a license as a utilization review agent under Article 21.58A or any other license under this code or another insurance law of this state;

(12) an acknowledgment that:

(A) any management contractor or third party to whom the network delegates a function must perform in compliance with this chapter and other applicable statutes and rules, and that the management contractor or third party is subject to the carrier's and the network's oversight and monitoring of its performance; and

(B) if the management contractor or the third party fails to meet monitoring standards established to ensure that functions delegated to the management contractor or the third party under the delegation contract are in full compliance with all statutory and regulatory requirements, the carrier or the network may cancel the delegation of one or more delegated functions;

(13) a requirement that the network and any management contractor or third party to which the network delegates a function provide all necessary information to allow the carrier to provide information to employees as required by §1305.451; and

(14) a provision that requires the network, in contracting with a third party directly or through another third party, to require the third party to permit the commissioner to examine at any time any information the commissioner believes is relevant to the third party's financial condition or the ability of the network to meet the network's responsibilities in connection with any function the third party performs or has been delegated.

§1305.1545. RESTRICTIONS ON PAYMENT AND REIMBURSEMENT

(a) An insurance carrier or third-party administrator may not reimburse a doctor or other health care provider, an institutional provider, or an organization of doctors and health care providers on a discounted fee basis for services that are provided to an injured employee unless:

(1) the carrier or third-party administrator has contracted with either:

(A) the doctor or other health care provider, institutional provider, or organization of doctors and health care providers; or

(B) a network that has contracted with the doctor or other health care provider, institutional provider, or organization of doctors and health care providers; and

(2) the doctor or other health care provider, institutional provider, or organization of doctors and health care providers has agreed to the contract and has agreed to provide health care services under the terms of the contract.

(b) A party to a carrier-network contract may not sell, lease, or otherwise transfer information regarding the payment or reimbursement terms of the contract without the express authority of and prior adequate notification to the other contracting parties. This subsection does not affect the authority of the commissioner under this code to request and obtain information.

(c) An insurance carrier or third-party administrator who violates this section:

(1) commits an unfair claim settlement practice in violation of Subchapter A, Chapter 542, Insurance Code; and

(2) is subject to administrative penalties under Chapters 82 and 84, Insurance Code.

ACCESS TO CERTAIN PRACTITIONERS AND FACILITIES—§1451[45]

SUBCHAPTER A. GENERAL PROVISIONS

§1451.001. DEFINITIONS; HEALTH CARE PRACTITIONERS

In this chapter:

(1) *"Acupuncturist"* means an individual licensed to practice acupuncture by the Texas State Board of Medical Examiners.

(2) *"Advanced practice nurse"* means an individual licensed by the Board of Nurse Examiners as a registered nurse and recognized by that board as an advanced practice nurse.

(3) *"Audiologist"* means an individual licensed to practice audiology by the

---

45 (Insurance Code; Title 8. Health Insurance and other Health Coverages; Subtitle F. Physicians and Health Care Providers; Chapter 1451. Access to Certain Practitioners and Facilities; Subchapter A. General Provisions)

State Board of Examiners for Speech-Language Pathology and Audiology.

(4) *"Chemical dependency counselor"* means an individual licensed by the Texas Commission on Alcohol and Drug Abuse.

(5) *"Chiropractor"* means an individual licensed by the Texas Board of Chiropractic Examiners.

(6) *"Dentist"* means an individual licensed to practice dentistry by the State Board of Dental Examiners.

(7) *"Dietitian"* means an individual licensed by the Texas State Board of Examiners of Dietitians.

(8) *"Hearing instrument fitter and dispenser"* means an individual licensed by the State Committee of Examiners in the Fitting and Dispensing of Hearing Instruments.

(9) *"Licensed clinical social worker"* means an individual licensed by the Texas State Board of Social Worker Examiners as a licensed clinical social worker.

(10) *"Licensed professional counselor"* means an individual licensed by the Texas State Board of Examiners of Professional Counselors.

(11) *"Marriage and family therapist"* means an individual licensed by the Texas State Board of Examiners of Marriage and Family Therapists.

(12) *"Occupational therapist"* means an individual licensed as an occupational therapist by the Texas Board of Occupational Therapy Examiners.

(13) *"Optometrist"* means an individual licensed to practice optometry by the Texas Optometry Board.

(14) *"Physical therapist"* means an individual licensed as a physical therapist by the Texas Board of Physical Therapy Examiners.

(15) *"Physician"* means an individual licensed to practice medicine by the Texas State Board of Medical Examiners. The term includes a doctor of osteopathic medicine.

(16) *"Physician assistant"* means an individual licensed by the Texas State Board of Physician Assistant Examiners.

(17) *"Podiatrist"* means an individual licensed to practice podiatry by the Texas State Board of Podiatric Medical Examiners.

(18) *"Psychological associate"* means an individual licensed as a psychological associate by the Texas State Board of Examiners of Psychologists who practices solely under the supervision of a licensed psychologist.

(19) *"Psychologist"* means an individual licensed as a psychologist by the Texas State Board of Examiners of Psychologists.

(20) *"Speech-language pathologist"* means an individual licensed to practice speech-language pathology by the State Board of Examiners for Speech-Language Pathology and Audiology.

(21) *"Surgical assistant"* means an individual licensed as a surgical assistant by the Texas State Board of Medical Examiners.

SUBCHAPTER B. DESIGNATION OF PRACTITIONERS UNDER ACCIDENT AND HEALTH INSURANCE POLICY

§1451.051. APPLICABILITY OF SUBCHAPTER

(a) This subchapter applies to an .accident and health insurance policy, including an individual, blanket, or group policy.

(b) This subchapter applies to an accident and health insurance policy issued by a stipulated premium company subject to Chapter 884.

§1451.052. APPLICABILITY OF GENERAL PROVISIONS

The provisions of Chapter 1201, including provisions relating to the applicability, purpose, and enforcement of that chapter, the construction of policies under that chapter, rulemaking under that chapter, and definitions of terms applicable in that chapter, apply to this subchapter.

§1451.053. PRACTITIONER DESIGNATION

(a) An accident and health insurance policy may not make a benefit contingent on treatment or examination by one or more particular health care practitioners listed in §1451.001 unless the policy contains a provision that designates the practitioners whom the insurer will and will not recognize.

(b) The insurer may include the provision anywhere in the policy or in an endorsement attached to the policy.

§1451.054. TERMS FOR HEALTH CARE PRACTITIONERS

A provision of an accident and health insurance policy that designates the health care practitioners whom the insurer will and will not recognize must use the terms defined by §1451.001 with the meanings assigned by that section.

SUBCHAPTER C. SELECTION OF PRACTITIONERS

§1451.101. DEFINITIONS

In this subchapter:

(1) *"Health insurance policy"* means a policy, contract, or agreement described by §1451.102.

(2) *"Insured"* means an individual who is issued, is a party to, or is a beneficiary under a health insurance policy.

(3) *"Insurer"* means an insurer, association, or organization described by §1451.102.

(4) *"Nurse first assistant"* has the meaning assigned by §301.1525, Occupations Code.

§1451.102. APPLICABILITY OF SUBCHAPTER

Except as provided by this subchapter, this subchapter applies only to an individual, group, blanket, or franchise insurance policy, insurance agreement, or group hospital service contract that provides health benefits, accident benefits, or health and accident benefits for medical or surgical expenses incurred as a result of an accident or sickness and that is delivered, issued for delivery, or renewed in this state by any incorporated or unincorporated insurance company, association, or organization, including:

(1) a fraternal benefit society operating under Chapter 885;

(2) a general casualty company operating under Chapter 861;

(3) a life, health, or accident insurance company operating under Ch 841 or 982;

(4) a Lloyd's plan operating under Chapter 941;

(5) a local mutual aid association operating under Chapter 886;

(6) a mutual insurance company writing insurance other than life insurance operating under Chapter 883;

(7) a mutual life insurance company operating under Chapter 882;

(8) a reciprocal exchange operating under Chapter 942;

(9) a statewide mutual assessment company, mutual assessment company, or mutual assessment life, health, and accident association operating under Chapter 881 or 887; and

(10) a stipulated premium company operating under Chapter 884.

§1451.103. CONFLICTING PROVISIONS VOID

(a) A provision of a health insurance policy that conflicts with this subchapter is void to the extent of the conflict.

(b) The presence in a health insurance policy of a provision void under Subsection (a) does not affect the validity of other policy provisions.

(c) An insurer shall bring each approved policy form that contains a provision that conflicts with this subchapter into compliance with this subchapter by use of:

(1) a rider or endorsement approved by the commissioner; or

(2) a new or revised policy form approved by the commissioner.

§1451.104. NONDISCRIMINATORY PAYMENT OR REIMBURSEMENT; EXCEPTION

(a) An insurer may not classify, differentiate, or discriminate between scheduled services or procedures provided by a health care practitioner selected under this subchapter and performed in the scope of that practitioner's license and the same services or procedures provided by another type of health care practitioner whose services or procedures are covered by a health insurance policy, in regard to:

(1) the payment schedule or payment provisions of the policy; or

(2) the amount or manner of payment or reimbursement under the policy.

(b) An insurer may not deny payment or reimbursement for services or procedures in accordance with the policy payment schedule or payment provisions solely because the services or procedures were performed by a health care practitioner selected under this subchapter.

(c) Notwithstanding Subsection (a), a health insurance policy may provide for a different amount of payment or reimbursement for scheduled services or procedures performed by an advanced practice nurse, nurse first assistant, licensed surgical assistant, or physician assistant if the methodology used to compute the amount is the same as the methodology used to compute the amount of payment or reimbursement when the services or procedures are provided by a physician.

§1451.106. SELECTION OF ADVANCED PRACTICE NURSE

An insured may select an advanced practice nurse to provide the services scheduled in the health insurance policy that are within the scope of the nurse's license.

§1451.107. SELECTION OF AUDIOLOGIST

An insured may select an audiologist to measure hearing to determine the presence or extent of the insured's hearing loss or provide aural rehabilitation services to the insured if the insured has a hearing loss and the services or procedures are scheduled in the health insurance policy.

§1451.108. SELECTION OF CHEMICAL DEPENDENCY COUNSELOR

An insured may select a chemical dependency counselor to provide services or procedures scheduled in the health insurance policy that are within the scope of the counselor's license.

§1451.109. SELECTION OF CHIROPRACTOR

An insured may select a chiropractor to provide the medical services scheduled in the health insurance policy that are within the scope of the chiropractor's license.

§1451.110. SELECTION OF DENTIST

An insured may select a dentist to provide the medical or surgical services or procedures scheduled in the health insurance policy that are within the scope of the dentist's license.

§1451.111. SELECTION OF DIETITIAN

An insured may select a licensed dietitian or a provisionally licensed dietitian acting under the supervision of a licensed dietitian to provide the services scheduled in the health insurance policy that are within the scope of the dietitian's license.

§1451.113. SELECTION OF LICENSED CLINICAL SOCIAL WORKER

An insured may select a licensed clinical social worker to provide the services or procedures scheduled in the health insurance policy that:

(1) are within the scope of the social worker's license, including the provision of direct, diagnostic, preventive, or clinical services to individuals, families, and groups whose functioning is threatened or affected by social or psychological stress or health impairment; and

(2) are specified as services under the terms of the health insurance policy.

§1451.114. SELECTION OF LICENSED PROFESSIONAL COUNSELOR

An insured may select a licensed professional counselor to provide services scheduled in the health insurance policy that are within the scope of the counselor's license.[46]

§1451.116. SELECTION OF MARRIAGE AND FAMILY THERAPIST

An insured may select a marriage and family therapist to provide services scheduled in the health insurance policy that are within the scope of the therapist's license.[47]

---

46 Please note: Insurance policy no longer able to require the recommendation of a physician in order to secure services . 9/1/09 deleted the phrase "The health insurance policy may require that services of a licensed professional counselor must be recommended by a physician."

47 Please note: Insurance policy no longer able to require the recommendation of a physician in order to secure services . 9/1/09 deleted the phrase "The health insurance policy may require that services of a marriage and family therapist must be recommended by a physician."

Local Government Code

Provisions Relating to Public Safety—§370[1]

Gives liability protection for volunteers in disasters if requested by county authorities.

§370.006. Assistance In Man-Made or Natural Disaster

(a) The governing body of a municipality, the chief of the fire department, or an emergency management director or coordinator designated for the municipality under Section 418.1015, Government Code, may request or accept any care, assistance, or advice described by Section 79.003(a), Civil Practice and Remedies Code, including the loan or operation of construction equipment or other heavy equipment by the owner or operator of the equipment, as applicable, or the donation of resources to the extent the governing body, chief, or emergency management director or coordinator believes necessary to address a man-made or natural disaster.

(b) The commissioners court of a county, the county judge, the county fire marshal, an incorporated volunteer fire department under contract with a county under Section 352.001, a volunteer fire department described by Section 352.005, as applicable, or an emergency management director or coordinator designated for the county under Section 418.1015, Government Code, may request or accept any care, assistance, or advice described by Section 79.003(a), Civil Practice and Remedies Code, including the loan or operation of construction equipment or other heavy equipment by the owner or operator of the equipment, as applicable, or the donation of resources to the extent the commissioners court, county judge, county fire marshal, volunteer fire department, or emergency management director or coordinator believes necessary to address a man-made or natural disaster.

(c) A person as defined by Section 79.001, Civil Practice and Remedies Code, who provides care, assistance, or advice to a municipality or county in the manner described by this section is immune from civil liability as provided by Section 79.003, Civil Practice and Remedies Code.

(d) Subsection (a) or (b) does not authorize the acceptance of care, assistance, or advice in violation of any other law or contractual agreement that prohibits the acceptance of that care, assistance, or advice.

---

1   (Local Government Code; Title 11. Public Safety; Subtitle C. Public Safety Provisions Applying to More Than One Type of Local Government; Chapter 370. Miscellaneous Provisions Relating To Municipal And County Health And Public Safety)

OCCUPATIONS CODE — OTHER

HEALING ART PRACTITIONERS—§104[2]

§104.001. Short Title. This chapter may be cited as the Healing Art Identification Act.

§104.002. HEALING ART

The healing art includes any system, treatment, operation, diagnosis, prescription, or practice to ascertain, cure, relieve, adjust, or correct a human disease, injury, or unhealthy or abnormal physical or mental condition.

§104.003. REQUIRED IDENTIFICATION

(a)   A person subject to this section who uses the person's name on a written or printed professional identification, including a sign, pamphlet, stationery, or letterhead, or who uses the person's signature as a professional identification shall designate as required by this section the healing art the person is licensed to practice.

(b)   A person who is licensed by the Texas State Board of Medical Examiners and holds a doctor of medicine degree shall use: (1) physician or surgeon, M.D.; (2) doctor, M.D.; or (3) doctor of medicine, M.D.

(c)   A person who is licensed by the Texas State Board of Medical Examiners and holds a doctor of osteopathy degree shall use: (1) physician or surgeon, D.O.; (2) osteopathic physician or surgeon; (3) doctor, D.O.; (4) doctor of osteopathy; (5) doctor of osteopathic medicine; (6) osteopath; or (7) D.O.

(d)   A person who is licensed by the State Board of Dental Examiners shall use: (1) dentist; (2) doctor, D.D.S.; (3) doctor of dental surgery; (4) D.D.S.; or (5) doctor of dental medicine, D.M.D.

(e)   A person who is licensed by the Texas Board of Chiropractic Examiners shall use: (1) chiropractor; (2) doctor, D.C.; (3) doctor of chiropractic; or (4) D.C.

(f)   A person who is licensed by the Texas Optometry Board shall use: (1) optometrist; (2) doctor, optometrist; (3) doctor of optometry; or (4) O.D.

(g)   A person who is licensed by the Texas State Board of Podiatric Medical Examiners shall use: (1) chiropodist; (2) doctor, D.S.C.; (3) doctor of surgical chiropody; 4) D.S.C.; (5) podiatrist; (6) doctor, D.P.M.; (7) doctor of podiatric medicine; or (8) D.P.M.

§104.004. OTHER PERSONS USING TITLE "DOCTOR"

In using the title "*doctor*" as a trade or professional asset or on any manner of professional identification, including a sign, pamphlet, stationery, or letterhead, or as a part of a signature, a person other than a person described by Section 104.003 shall designate the authority under which the title is used or the college or honorary degree that gives rise to the use of the title.

---

2   (Occupations Code; Title 3. Health Professions; Subtitle A. Provisions Applying to Health Professions Generally; Chapter 104. Healing Art Practitioners)

UNPROFESSIONAL CONDUCT BY HEALTH CARE PROVIDER—§105[3]

§105.001. DEFINITION

In this chapter, "*health care provider*" means a person who furnishes services under a license, certificate, registration, or other authority issued by this state or another state to diagnose, prevent, alleviate, or cure a human illness or injury.

§105.002. UNPROFESSIONAL CONDUCT

(a) A health care provider commits unprofessional conduct if the health care provider, in connection with the provider's professional activities:

    (1) knowingly presents or causes to be presented a false or fraudulent claim for the payment of a loss under an insurance policy;

    (2) knowingly prepares, makes, or subscribes to any writing, with intent to present or use the writing, or to allow it to be presented or used, in support of a false or fraudulent claim under an insurance policy; or

    (3) knowingly directs or requires a patient to obtain health care goods or services from a niche hospital in which the health care provider or an immediate family member of the provider has a financial interest, unless the provider:

        (A) discloses to the patient, in writing, that the provider or the provider's family member has a financial interest in the niche hospital; and

        (B) informs the patient that the patient has the option of using an alternative health care facility.

(b) In addition to other provisions of civil or criminal law, commission of unprofessional conduct under Subsection (a) constitutes cause for the revocation or suspension of a provider's license, permit, registration, certificate, or other authority or other disciplinary action.

(c) Subsection (a)(3) does not apply to a financial interest in publicly available shares of a registered investment company, such as a mutual fund, that owns publicly traded equity securities or debt obligations issued by a niche hospital or an entity that owns the niche hospital.

(d) In this section:

    (1) "*Diagnosis-related group*" means the classification system mandated by Medicare regulations for reimbursement purposes that groups patients according to principal diagnosis, presence of a surgical procedure, age, presence or absence of significant complications, and other relevant criteria.

    (2) "*Niche hospital*" means a hospital that:

        (A) classifies at least two-thirds of the hospital's Medicare patients or, if data is available, all patients:

            (i) in not more than two major diagnosis-related groups; or

            (ii) in surgical diagnosis-related groups;

        (B) specializes in one or more of the following areas:

---

3   (Occupations Code; Title 3. Health Professions; Subtitle A. Provisions Applying to Health Professions Generally; Chapter 105. Unprofessional Conduct by Health Care Provider)

(i) cardiac; (ii) orthopedics; (iii) surgery; or (iv) women's health; and

(C) is not:

(i) a public hospital;

(ii) a hospital for which the majority of inpatient claims are for major diagnosis-related groups relating to rehabilitation, psychiatry, alcohol and drug treatment, or children or newborns; or

(iii) a hospital with fewer than 10 claims per bed per year.

INTERNET AND HEALTH CARE—§106[4]

GENERAL REGULATORY AUTHORITY REGARDING HEALTH CARE PRACTITIONERS USE OF INTERNET

§106.001. EFFECT OF INTERNET ACTIVITY

(a) In this section:

(1) *"Licensing authority"* means a department, commission, board, office, or other agency of the state or a political subdivision of the state that regulates activities and persons under this title.

(2) *"Internet"* has the meaning assigned by §2002.001, Government Code.

(b) The fact that an activity occurs through the use of the Internet does not affect a licensing authority's power to regulate an activity or person that would otherwise be regulated under this title.

TELEMEDICINE AND TELEHEALTH—§111[5]

§111.001. DEFINITIONS

In this chapter:

(1) *"Health professional"* and *"physician"* have the meanings assigned by Section 1455.001, Insurance Code.

(2) *"Telehealth service"* and *"telemedicine medical service"* have the meanings assigned by §57.042, Utilities Code.

§111.002. INFORMED CONSENT

A treating physician or health professional who provides or facilitates the use of telemedicine medical services or telehealth services shall ensure that the informed consent of the patient, or another appropriate individual authorized to make health care treatment decisions for the patient, is obtained before telemedicine medical services or telehealth services are provided.

§111.003. CONFIDENTIALITY

A treating physician or health professional who provides or facilitates the use of telemedicine medical services or telehealth services shall ensure that the confidentiality of the patient's medical information is maintained as required by Chapter 159 or other applicable law.

---

4   (Occupations Code; Title 3. Health Professions; Subtitle A. Provisions Applying to Health Professions Generally; Chapter 106. General Regulatory Authority Regarding Health Care Practitioners' Use of Internet)

5   (Occupations Code; Title 3. Health Professions; Subtitle A. Provisions Applying to Health Professions Generally; Chapter 111. Telemedicine and Telehealth)

§111.004. RULES

The Texas State Board of Medical Examiners, in consultation with the commissioner of insurance, as appropriate, may adopt rules necessary to:

(1) ensure that patients using telemedicine medical services receive appropriate, quality care;

(2) prevent abuse and fraud in the use of telemedicine medical services, including rules relating to the filing of claims and records required to be maintained in connection with telemedicine medical services;

(3) ensure adequate supervision of health professionals who are not physicians and who provide telemedicine medical services;

(4) establish the maximum number of health professionals who are not physicians that a physician may supervise through a telemedicine medical service; and

(5) require a face-to-face consultation between a patient and a physician providing a telemedicine medical service within a certain number of days following an initial telemedicine medical service only if the physician has never seen the patient.

MENTAL HEALTH LICENSES AND USE OF GENETIC INFORMATION—§58[6]

SUBCHAPTER A. GENERAL PROVISIONS

§58.001. DEFINITIONS

In this chapter:

(1) *"DNA"* means deoxyribonucleic acid.

(2) *"Family health history"* means a history taken by a physician or genetic professional to ascertain genetic or medical information about an individual's family.

(3) *"Genetic characteristic"* means a scientifically or medically identifiable genetic or chromosomal variation, composition, or alteration that:

   (A) is scientifically or medically believed to:

      (i) predispose an individual to a disease, disorder, or syndrome; or

      (ii) be associated with a statistically significant increased risk of developing a disease, disorder, or syndrome; and

   (B) may or may not be associated with any symptom of an ongoing disease, disorder, or syndrome affecting an individual on the date the genetic information is obtained regarding the individual.

(4) *"Genetic information"* means information that is:

   (A) obtained from or based on a scientific or medical determination of the presence or absence in an individual of a genetic characteristic; or

   (B) derived from the results of a genetic test performed on, or a family health history obtained from, an individual.

(5) *"Genetic test"* means a presymptomatic laboratory test of an individual's

---

6   (Occupations Code; Title 2. General Provisions Relating to Licensing; Chapter 58. Use of Genetic Information)

genes, gene products, or chromosomes that:

(A) analyzes the individual's DNA, RNA, proteins, or chromosomes; and

(B) is performed to identify any genetic variation, composition, or alteration that is associated with the individuals having a statistically increased risk of:

   (i) developing a clinically recognized disease, disorder, or syndrome; or

   (ii) being a carrier of a clinically recognized disease, disorder, or syndrome.

The term does not include a blood test, cholesterol test, urine test, or other physical test used for a purpose other than determining a genetic or chromosomal variation, composition, or alteration in a specific individual.

(6) "*Licensing authority*" means a state agency or political subdivision that issues an occupational license.

(7) "*Occupational license*" means a license, certificate, registration, permit, or other form of authorization required by law or rule that must be obtained by an individual to engage in a particular business or occupation.

(8) "*Political subdivision*" means a municipality, county, or special district or authority. The term includes a school district.

(9) "*RNA*" means ribonucleic acid.

(10) "*State agency*" means a department, board, bureau, commission, committee, division, office, council, or agency in the executive or judicial branch of state government.

SUBCHAPTER B. USE AND RETENTION OF GENETIC INFORMATION

§58.051. CERTAIN USES OF GENETIC INFORMATION PROHIBITED

A licensing authority may not deny an application for an occupational license, suspend, revoke, or refuse to renew an occupational license, or take any other disciplinary action against a license holder based on the refusal of the license applicant or license holder to:

(1) submit to a genetic test;

(2) submit a family health history;

(3) disclose whether the applicant or holder has submitted to a genetic test; or

(4) disclose the results of any genetic test to which the applicant or holder has submitted.

§58.052. DESTRUCTION OF SAMPLE MATERIAL; EXCEPTIONS

A sample of genetic material obtained from an individual for a genetic test shall be destroyed promptly after the purpose for which the sample was obtained is accomplished unless:

(1) the sample is retained under a court order;

(2) the individual authorizes retention of the sample for medical treatment or scientific research;

(3) the sample was obtained for research that is cleared by an institutional review board and retention of the sample is:

    (A) under a requirement the institutional review board imposes on a specific research project; or

    (B) authorized by the research participant with institutional review board approval under federal law; or

(4) the sample was obtained for a screening test established by the Texas Department of Health under §33.011, Health & Safety Code, and performed by that department or a laboratory approved by that department.

SUBCHAPTER C. DISCLOSURE OF GENETIC INFORMATION; CONFIDENTIALITY; EXCEPTIONS

§58.101. DISCLOSURE OF TEST RESULTS TO INDIVIDUAL TESTED

An individual who submits to a genetic test has the right to know the results of the test. On written request by the individual, the entity that performed the test shall disclose the test results to:

(1) the individual; or

(2) a physician designated by the individual.

§58.102. CONFIDENTIALITY OF GENETIC INFORMATION

(a) Except as provided by Section 58.103, genetic information is confidential and privileged regardless of the source of the information.

(b) A person who holds genetic information about an individual may not disclose or be compelled to disclose, by subpoena or otherwise, that information unless the disclosure is specifically authorized as provided by §58.104.

(c) This section applies to a redisclosure of genetic information by a secondary recipient of the information after disclosure of the information by an initial recipient.

§58.103. EXCEPTIONS TO CONFIDENTIALITY

(a) Subject to Subchapter G, Chapter 411, Government Code, genetic information may be disclosed without an authorization under §58.104 if the disclosure is:

(1) authorized under a state or federal criminal law relating to:

    (A) the identification of individuals; or

    (B) a criminal or juvenile proceeding, an inquest, or a child fatality review by a multidisciplinary child-abuse team;

(2) required under a specific order of a state or federal court;

(3) for the purpose of establishing paternity as authorized under a state or federal law;

(4) made to provide genetic information relating to a decedent and the disclosure is made to the blood relatives of the decedent for medical diagnosis; or

(5) made to identify a decedent.

(b) Genetic information may be disclosed without an authorization under § 58.104

if:

(1) the disclosure is for information from a research study in which the procedure for obtaining informed written consent and the use of the information is governed by national standards for protecting participants involved in research projects, including guidelines issued under 21 C.F.R. Part 50 and 45 C.F.R. Part 46;

(2) the information does not identify a specific individual; and

(3) the information is provided to the Texas Department of Health to comply with Chapter 87, Health and Safety Code.

§58.104. AUTHORIZED DISCLOSURE

An individual or the legal representative of an individual may authorize disclosure of genetic information relating to the individual by a written authorization that includes:

(1) a description of the information to be disclosed;

(2) the name of the person to whom the disclosure is made; and

(3) the purpose for the disclosure.

§58.105. CIVIL PENALTY

(a) A person who discloses genetic information in violation of Sections 58.102-58.104 is liable for a civil penalty not to exceed $10,000.

(b) The attorney general may bring an action in the name of the state to recover a civil penalty under this section, plus reasonable attorney's fees and court costs.

PENAL CODE

INSANITY—§8[7]

§8.01. INSANITY

(a)   It is an affirmative defense to prosecution that, at the time of the conduct charged, the actor, as a result of severe mental disease or defect, did not know that his conduct was wrong.

(b)   The term *"mental disease or defect"* does not include an abnormality manifested only by repeated criminal or otherwise antisocial conduct.

USE OF FORCE ON CHILD, STUDENT, OR INCOMPETENT—§9[8]

§9.61. PARENT — CHILD

(a)   The use of force, but not deadly force, against a child younger than 18 years is justified:

(1)   if the actor is the child's parent or stepparent or is acting in loco parentis to the child; and

(2)   when and to the degree the actor reasonably believes the force is necessary to discipline the child or to safeguard or promote his welfare.

(b)   For purposes of this section, *"in loco parentis"* includes grandparent and guardian, any person acting by, through, or under the direction of a court with jurisdiction over the child, and anyone who has express or implied consent of the parent or parents.

§9.62. EDUCATOR — STUDENT

The use of force, but not deadly force, against a person is justified:

(1)   if the actor is entrusted with the care, supervision, or administration of the person for a special purpose; and

(2)   when and to the degree the actor reasonably believes the force is necessary to further the special purpose or to maintain discipline in a group.

§9.63. GUARDIAN — INCOMPETENT

The use of force, but not deadly force, against a mental incompetent is justified:

(1)   if the actor is the incompetent's guardian or someone similarly responsible for the general care and supervision of the incompetent; and

(2)   when and to the degree the actor reasonably believes the force is necessary:

(A)   to safeguard and promote the incompetent's welfare; or

(B)   if the incompetent is in an institution for his care and custody, to maintain discipline in the institution.

---

7   (Penal Code; Title 2. General Principles of Criminal Responsibility; Chapter 8. General Defenses to Criminal Responsibility)

8   (Penal Code; Title 2. General Principles of Criminal Responsibility; Chapter 9. Justification Excluding Criminal Responsibility; Subchapter F. Special Relationships)

Deviate sexual activity—§21[9]

§21.01. Definitions

In this chapter:

(1) *"Deviate sexual intercourse"* means:

    (A) any contact between any part of the genitals of one person and the mouth or anus of another person; or

    (B) the penetration of the genitals or the anus of another person with an object.

(2) *"Sexual contact"* means any touching of the anus, breast, or any part of the genitals of another person with intent to arouse or gratify the sexual desire of any person.

(3) *"Sexual intercourse"* means any penetration of the female sex organ by the male sex organ.

§21.02. Continuous Sexual Abuse of Young Child or Children

(a) In this section, "child" has the meaning assigned by Section 22.011(c).

(b) A person commits an offense if:

    (1) during a period that is 30 or more days in duration, the person commits two or more acts of sexual abuse, regardless of whether the acts of sexual abuse are committed against one or more victims; and

    (2) at the time of the commission of each of the acts of sexual abuse, the actor is 17 years of age or older and the victim is a child younger than 14 years of age.

(c) For purposes of this section, "act of sexual abuse" means any act that is a violation of one or more of the following penal laws:

    (1) aggravated kidnapping under Section 20.04(a)(4), if the actor committed the offense with the intent to violate or abuse the victim sexually;

    (2) indecency with a child under Section 21.11(a)(1), if the actor committed the offense in a manner other than by touching, including touching through clothing, the breast of a child;

    (3) sexual assault under Section 22.011;

    (4) aggravated sexual assault under Section 22.021;

    (5) burglary under Section 30.02, if the offense is punishable under Subsection (d) of that section and the actor committed the offense with the intent to commit an offense listed in Subdivisions (1)-(4);

    (6) sexual performance by a child under Section 43.25;

    (7) trafficking of persons under Section 20A.02(a)(7) or (8); and

    (8) compelling prostitution under Section 43.05(a)(2).

(d) If a jury is the trier of fact, members of the jury are not required to agree unanimously on which specific acts of sexual abuse were committed by the defendant or the exact date when those acts were committed. The jury must agree unanimously that the defendant, during a period that is 30 or more days in duration,

[9] (Penal Code; Title 5. Offenses against the Person; Chapter 21. Sexual Offenses)

committed two or more acts of sexual abuse.

(e) A defendant may not be convicted in the same criminal action of an offense listed under Subsection (c) the victim of which is the same victim as a victim of the offense alleged under Subsection (b) unless the offense listed in Subsection (c):

(1) is charged in the alternative;

(2) occurred outside the period in which the offense alleged under Subsection (b) was committed; or

(3) is considered by the trier of fact to be a lesser included offense of the offense alleged under Subsection (b).

(f) A defendant may not be charged with more than one count under Subsection (b) if all of the specific acts of sexual abuse that are alleged to have been committed are alleged to have been committed against a single victim.

(g) It is an affirmative defense to prosecution under this section that the actor:

(1) was not more than five years older than:

(A) the victim of the offense, if the offense is alleged to have been committed against only one victim; or

(B) the youngest victim of the offense, if the offense is alleged to have been committed against more than one victim;

(2) did not use duress, force, or a threat against a victim at the time of the commission of any of the acts of sexual abuse alleged as an element of the offense; and

(3) at the time of the commission of any of the acts of sexual abuse alleged as an element of the offense:

(A) was not required under Chapter 62, Code of Criminal Procedure, to register for life as a sex offender; or

(B) was not a person who under Chapter 62 had a reportable conviction or adjudication for an offense under this section or an act of sexual abuse as described by Subsection (c).

(h) An offense under this section is a felony of the first degree, punishable by imprisonment in the Texas Department of Criminal Justice for life, or for any term of not more than 99 years or less than 25 years.

§21.06. HOMOSEXUAL CONDUCT

(a) A person commits an offense if he engages in deviate sexual intercourse with another individual of the same sex.

(b) An offense under this section is a Class C misdemeanor.

§21.07. PUBLIC LEWDNESS

(a) A person commits an offense if he knowingly engages in any of the following acts in a public place or, if not in a public place, he is reckless about whether another is present who will be offended or alarmed by his:

(1) act of sexual intercourse;

(2) act of deviate sexual intercourse;

(3) act of sexual contact; or

(4) act involving contact between the person's mouth or genitals and the anus or genitals of an animal or fowl.

(b) An offense under this section is a Class A misdemeanor.

§21.08. INDECENT EXPOSURE

(a) A person commits an offense if he exposes his anus or any part of his genitals with intent to arouse or gratify the sexual desire of any person, and he is reckless about whether another is present who will be offended or alarmed by his act.

(b) An offense under this section is a Class B misdemeanor.

§21.11. INDECENCY WITH A CHILD

(a) A person commits an offense if, with a child younger than 17 years of age, whether the child is of the same or opposite sex, the person:

   (1) engages in sexual contact with the child or causes the child to engage in sexual contact; or

   (2) with intent to arouse or gratify the sexual desire of any person:

      (A) exposes the person's anus or any part of the person's genitals, knowing the child is present; or

      (B) causes the child to expose the child's anus or any part of the child's genitals.

(b) It is an affirmative defense to prosecution under this section that the actor:

   (1) was not more than three years older than the victim and of the opposite sex;

   (2) did not use duress, force, or a threat against the victim at the time of the offense; and

   (3) at the time of the offense:

      (A) was not required under Chapter 62, Code of Criminal Procedure, to register for life as a sex offender; or

      (B) was not a person who under Chapter 62 had a reportable conviction or adjudication for an offense under this section.

(b-1) It is an affirmative defense to prosecution under this section that the actor was the spouse of the child at the time of the offense.

(c) In this section, "sexual contact" means the following acts, if committed with the intent to arouse or gratify the sexual desire of any person:

   (1) any touching by a person, including touching through clothing, of the anus, breast, or any part of the genitals of a child; or

   (2) any touching of any part of the body of a child, including touching through clothing, with the anus, breast, or any part of the genitals of a person.

(d) An offense under Subsection (a)(1) is a felony of the second degree and an offense under Subsection (a)(2) is a felony of the third degree.

§21.12. IMPROPER RELATIONSHIP BETWEEN EDUCATOR AND STUDENT

(a)   An employee of a public or private primary or secondary school commits an offense if the employee:

   (1)   engages in sexual contact, sexual intercourse, or deviate sexual intercourse with a person who is enrolled in a public or private primary or secondary school at which the employee works;

   (2)   holds a certificate or permit issued as provided by Subchapter B, Chapter 21, Education Code, or is a person who is required to be licensed by a state agency as provided by Section 21.003(b), Education Code, and engages in sexual contact, sexual intercourse, or deviate sexual intercourse with a person the employee knows is:

      (A)   enrolled in a public primary or secondary school in the same school district as the school at which the employee works; or

      (B)   a student participant in an educational activity that is sponsored by a school district or a public or private primary or secondary school, if:

         (i)   students enrolled in a public or private primary or secondary school are the primary participants in the activity; and

         (ii)   the employee provides education services to those participants; or

   (3)   engages in conduct described by Section 33.021, with a person described by Subdivision (1), or a person the employee knows is a person described by Subdivision (2)(A) or (B), regardless of the age of that person.

(b)   An offense under this section is a felony of the second degree.

(b-1)   It is an affirmative defense to prosecution under this section that:

   (1)   the actor was the spouse of the enrolled person at the time of the offense; or

   (2)   the actor was not more than three years older than the enrolled person and, at the time of the offense, the actor and the enrolled person were in a relationship that began before the actor's employment at a public or private primary or secondary school.

(c)   If conduct constituting an offense under this section also constitutes an offense under another section of this code, the actor may be prosecuted under either section or both sections.

(d)   The name of a person who is enrolled in a public or private primary or secondary school and involved in an improper relationship with an educator as provided by Subsection (a) may not be released to the public and is not public information under Chapter 552, Government Code.

INTERFERENCE WITH CHILD CUSTODY—§25[10]

§25.03. INTERFERENCE WITH CHILD CUSTODY

(a)   A person commits an offense if the person takes or retains a child younger than 18 years of age:

   (1)   when the person knows that the person's taking or retention violates the express terms of a judgment or order, including a temporary order, of a

---

10   (Penal Code; Title 6. Offenses against the Family; Chapter 25. Offenses against the Family)

court disposing of the child's custody;

(2)   when the person has not been awarded custody of the child by a court of competent jurisdiction, knows that a suit for divorce or a civil suit or application for habeas corpus to dispose of the child's custody has been filed, and takes the child out of the geographic area of the counties composing the judicial district if the court is a district court or the county if the court is a statutory county court, without the permission of the court and with the intent to deprive the court of authority over the child; or

(3)   outside of the United States with the intent to deprive a person entitled to possession of or access to the child of that possession or access and without the permission of that person.

(b)   A noncustodial parent commits an offense if, with the intent to interfere with the lawful custody of a child younger than 18 years, the noncustodial parent knowingly entices or persuades the child to leave the custody of the custodial parent, guardian, or person standing in the stead of the custodial parent or guardian of the child.

(c)   It is a defense to prosecution under Subsection (a)(2) that the actor returned the child to the geographic area of the counties composing the judicial district if the court is a district court or the county if the court is a statutory county court, within three days after the date of the commission of the offense.

(c-1) It is an affirmative defense to prosecution under Subsection (a)(3) that:

(1)   the taking or retention of the child was pursuant to a valid order providing for possession of or access to the child; or

(2)   notwithstanding any violation of a valid order providing for possession of or access to the child, the actor's retention of the child was due only to circumstances beyond the actor's control and the actor promptly provided notice or made reasonable attempts to provide notice of those circumstances to the other person entitled to possession of or access to the child.

(c-2) Subsection (a)(3) does not apply if, at the time of the offense, the person taking or retaining the child:

(1)   was entitled to possession of or access to the child; and

(2)   was fleeing the commission or attempted commission of family violence, as defined by Section 71.004, Family Code, against the child or the person.

(d)   An offense under this section is a state jail felony.

PROBATE CODE

GUARDIANSHIP LAW —§659[11]

PART G. LETTERS OF GUARDIANSHIP

§659. ISSUANCE OF LETTERS OF GUARDIANSHIP

(a) When a person who is appointed guardian has qualified under Section 699 of this code, the clerk shall issue to the guardian a certificate under seal, stating the fact of the appointment, of the qualification, the date of the appointment and qualification, and the date the letters of guardianship expire. The certificate issued by the clerk constitutes letters of guardianship.

(b) All letters of guardianship expire one year and four months after the date of issuance unless renewed.

(c) The clerk may not renew letters of guardianship relating to the appointment of a guardian of the estate until the court receives and approves the guardian's annual accounting. The clerk may not renew letters of guardianship relating to the appointment of a guardian of the person until the court receives and approves the annual report. If the guardian's annual accounting or annual report is disapproved or not timely filed, the clerk may not issue further letters of guardianship to the delinquent guardian unless ordered by the court.

(d) Regardless of the date the court approves an annual accounting or annual report for purposes of this section, a renewal relates back to the date the original letters of guardianship are issued, unless the accounting period has been changed as provided by this chapter, in which case a renewal relates back to the first day of the accounting period.

§683. COURT'S INITIATION OF GUARDIANSHIP PROCEEDINGS

(a) If a court has probable cause to believe that a person domiciled or found in the county in which the court is located is an incapacitated person, and the person does not have a guardian in this state, the court shall appoint a guardian ad litem or court investigator to investigate and file an application for the appointment of a guardian of the person or estate, or both, of the person believed to be incapacitated.

(b) To establish probable cause under this section, the court may require:

(1) an information letter about the person believed to be incapacitated that is submitted by an interested person and satisfies the requirements of Section 683A of this code; or

(2) a written letter or certificate from a physician who has examined the person believed to be incapacitated that satisfies the requirements of Section 687(a) of this code, except that the letter must be dated not earlier than the 120th day before the date of the filing of an application under Subsection (a) of this section and be based on an examination the physician performed not earlier than the 120th day before that date.

(c) A court that creates a guardianship for a ward under this chapter may authorize

---

11 (Probate Code; Chapter XIII. Guardianship; Part 1. General Provisions Subpart G. Letters of Guardianship)

compensation of a guardian ad litem who files an application under Subsection (a) of this section from available funds of the ward's estate. If after examining the ward's assets the court determines the ward is unable to pay for services provided by the guardian ad litem, the court may authorize compensation from the county treasury.

§683A. Information Letter

An information letter under Section 683(b)(1) of this code about a person believed to be incapacitated may:

(1) include the name, address, telephone number, county of residence, and date of birth of the person;

(2) state whether the residence of the person is a private residence, health care facility, or other type of residence;

(3) describe the relationship between the interested person and the person;

(4) contain the names and telephone numbers of any known friends and relatives of the person;

(5) state whether a guardian of the person or estate of the person has been appointed in this state;

(6) state whether the person has executed a power of attorney and, if so, the designee's name, address, and telephone number;

(7) describe any property of the person, including the estimated value of that property;

(8) list any amount and source of monthly income of the person; and

(9) describe the nature and degree of the person's alleged incapacity and include a statement of whether the person is in imminent danger of serious impairment to the person's physical health, safety, or estate.

§684. Findings Required

(a) Before appointing a guardian, the court must find by clear and convincing evidence that:

(1) the proposed ward is an incapacitated person;

(2) it is in the best interest of the proposed ward to have the court appoint a person as guardian of the proposed ward; and

(3) the rights of the proposed ward or the proposed ward's property will be protected by the appointment of a guardian.

(b) Before appointing a guardian, the court must find by a preponderance of the evidence that:

(1) the court has venue of the case;

(2) the person to be appointed guardian is eligible to act as guardian and is entitled to appointment, or, if no eligible person entitled to appointment applies, the person appointed is a proper person to act as guardian;

(3) if a guardian is appointed for a minor, the guardianship is not created for the primary purpose of enabling the minor to establish residency for enrollment in a school or school district for which the minor is not otherwise eligible for enrollment; and

(4) the proposed ward is totally without capacity as provided by this code to care for himself or herself and to manage the individual's property, or the proposed ward lacks the capacity to do some, but not all, of the tasks necessary to care for himself or herself or to manage the individual's property.

(c) The court may not grant an application to create a guardianship unless the applicant proves each element required by this code. A determination of incapacity of an adult proposed ward, other than a person who must have a guardian appointed to receive funds due the person from any governmental source, must be evidenced by recurring acts or occurrences within the preceding six-month period and not by isolated instances of negligence or bad judgment.

(d) A court may not appoint a guardian of the estate of a minor when a payment of claims is made under Section 887 of this code.

(e) A certificate of the executive head or a representative of the bureau, department, or agency of the government, to the effect that the appointment of a guardian is a condition precedent to the payment of any funds due the proposed ward from that governmental entity, is prima facie evidence of the necessity for the appointment of a guardian.

§687. EXAMINATIONS AND REPORTS

(a) The court may not grant an application to create a guardianship for an incapacitated person, other than a minor, person whose alleged incapacity is mental retardation, or person for whom it is necessary to have a guardian appointed only to receive funds from a governmental source, unless the applicant presents to the court a written letter or certificate from a physician licensed in this state that is dated not earlier than the 120th day before the date of the filing of the application and based on an examination the physician performed not earlier than the 120th day before the date of the filing of the application. The letter or certificate must:

(1) describe the nature and degree of incapacity, including the medical history if reasonably available;

(2) provide a medical prognosis specifying the estimated severity of the incapacity;

(3) state how or in what manner the proposed ward's ability to make or communicate responsible decisions concerning himself or herself is affected by the person's physical or mental health;

(4) state whether any current medication affects the demeanor of the proposed ward or the proposed ward's ability to participate fully in a court proceeding;

(5) describe the precise physical and mental conditions underlying a diagnosis of senility, if applicable;

(6) state whether in the physician's opinion the proposed ward:

(A) has the mental capacity to vote in a public election; and

(B) has the ability to safely operate a motor vehicle; and

(7) include any other information required by the court.

(b) Except as provided by Subsection (c) of this section, if the court determines it is necessary, the court may appoint the necessary physicians to examine the proposed ward. The court must make its determination with respect to the necessity for a physician's examination of the proposed ward at a hearing held for that purpose. Not later than the fourth day before the date of the hearing, the applicant shall give to the proposed ward and the proposed ward's attorney ad litem written notice specifying the purpose and the date and time of the hearing. A physician who examines the proposed ward, other than a physician or psychologist who examines the proposed ward under Subsection (c) of this section, shall make available to an attorney ad litem appointed to represent the proposed ward, for inspection, a written letter or certificate from the physician that complies with the requirements of Subsection (a) of this section.

(c) If the basis of the proposed ward's alleged incapacity is mental retardation, the proposed ward shall be examined by a physician or psychologist licensed in this state or certified by the Texas Department of Mental Health and Mental Retardation to perform the examination, unless there is written documentation filed with the court that shows that the proposed ward has been examined according to the rules adopted by the Texas Department of Mental Health and Mental Retardation not earlier than 24 months before the date of a hearing to appoint a guardian for the proposed ward. The physician or psychologist shall conduct the examination according to the rules adopted by the Texas Department of Mental Health and Mental Retardation and shall submit written findings and recommendations to the court.

§690. PERSONS APPOINTED GUARDIAN

Only one person may be appointed as guardian of the person or estate, but one person may be appointed guardian of the person and another of the estate, if it is in the best interest of the ward. Nothing in this section prohibits the joint appointment, if the court finds it to be in the best interest of the ward, of:

(1) a husband and wife;

(2) joint managing conservators;

(3) coguardians appointed under the laws of a jurisdiction other than this state; or

(4) both parents of an adult who is incapacitated if the incapacitated person:

   (A) has not been the subject of a suit affecting the parent-child relationship; or

   (B) has been the subject of a suit affecting the parent-child relationship and both of the incapacitated person's parents were named as joint managing conservators in the suit but are no longer serving in that capacity.

PART E. GENERAL DUTIES AND POWERS OF GUARDIANS

§767. POWERS AND DUTIES OF GUARDIANS OF THE PERSON

(a) The guardian of the person is entitled to take charge of the person of the ward, and the duties of the guardian correspond with the rights of the guardian. A guardian of the person has:

(1) the right to have physical possession of the ward and to establish the ward's legal domicile;

(2) the duty to provide care, supervision, and protection for the ward;

(3) the duty to provide the ward with clothing, food, medical care, and shelter;

(4) the power to consent to medical, psychiatric, and surgical treatment other than the in-patient psychiatric commitment of the ward; and

(5) on application to and order of the court, the power to establish a trust in accordance with 42 U.S.C. Section 1396p(d)(4)(B), as amended, and direct that the income of the ward as defined by that section be paid directly to the trust, solely for the purpose of the ward's eligibility for medical assistance under Chapter 32, Human Resources Code.

(b) Notwithstanding Subsection (a)(4) of this section, a guardian of the person of a ward has the power to transport the ward to an inpatient mental health facility for a preliminary examination in accordance with Subchapters A and C, Chapter 573, Health and Safety Code.

§768. GENERAL POWERS AND DUTIES OF GUARDIAN OF ESTATE

The guardian of the estate of a ward is entitled to the possession and management of all property belonging to the ward, to collect all debts, rentals, or claims that are due to the ward, to enforce all obligations in favor of the ward, and to bring and defend suits by or against the ward; but, in the management of the estate, the guardian is governed by the provisions of this chapter. It is the duty of the guardian of the estate to take care of and manage the estate as a prudent person would manage the person's own property, except as otherwise provided by this chapter. The guardian of the estate shall account for all rents, profits, and revenues that the estate would have produced by such prudent management.

§769. SUMMARY OF POWERS OF GUARDIAN

The guardian of both the person of and estate of a ward has all the rights and powers and shall perform all the duties of the guardian of the person and of the guardian of the estate.

DSHS RIDER 19[1]

REPORTING CHILD ABUSE BY DSHS CONTRACTORS/PROVIDERS[2]

The DSHS policy to implement DSHS Rider 19 affects contractors/providers in the following DSHS funded programs, unless the contract provides otherwise:

* Title V Maternal and Child Health including Case Management
* Family Planning
* Primary Health Care
* HIV/STD
* Women, Infants and Children (WIC)
* Mental Health and Substance Abuse

When a report to the Department of Family and Protective Services (DFPS) is indicated and the situation is not an emergency, contractors/providers are encouraged to use the DFPS Statewide Abuse, Neglect and Exploitation Reporting System found on the DFPS web site at: https://www.txabusehotline.org/Default.asp.

NOTE to Contractors/Providers: Please consult your own attorney for any *legal advice* on what constitutes abuse and what your reporting obligations are under the Family Code, Chapter 261. Under Rider 19, DSHS enforces only a "good faith effort" to report child abuse; however the Family Code requires that you not knowingly fail to report any case where a child may be adversely affected by abuse. In particular, there have been some misunderstanding of the criminal laws relating to offenses against children. Sexual abuse, including sexual assault and indecency with a child, can occur even when there is no force, duress, or coercion; in other words when the minor and his or her partner are both willing sexual partners. Your own attorney can explain these criminal laws to you so that you can then report when required by law.

Contact Information:

HIV/STD Contractor Contact: HIV Consultant
HIV/STD Services Program
ph. 512-533-3000 • Email: hivstd@dshs.state.tx.us

Mental Health Services Contractor Contact: Mike Hastie
Community Mental Health Lead Program Services Unit •
ph. 512-419-2254 • Email: michael.hastie@dshs.state.tx.us

Substance Abuse Services Contractor Contact: Calvin Holloway
DSHS/MHSA Community MH and SA Services
ph. 512-206-5877 • Email: calvin.holloway@dshs.state.tx.us

Community Health Services Contractor Contact: Quality Management Branch (QMB) (Family Planning, Primary Care, WIC, Title V MCH)
ph. 512-776-7111 Ext. 6250 • Email: QMB@dshs.state.tx.us

Family & Community Health Services Division
1100 West 49th Street • Austin, TX 78756
(512) 458-7321 • Fax: (512) 458-7446 • Email: childabuse@dshs.state.tx.us

---

1   Previously Rider 23, 33, 11, 18, 14 and 27
2   Revised Effective September 1, 2011; updated August 28, 2012

This section contains:
(1) FAQs
(2) Plan for Implementing
(3) Policies and Procedures

FAQs: FREQUENTLY ASKED QUESTIONS AND ANSWERS CONCERNING DSHS RIDER 19

The Q&As are arranged to coincide with the sections of the DSHS Child Abuse Screening, Documenting and Reporting Policy for Contractors/Providers. The footnote after each question indicates when the Q and A was placed on the DSHS website and when it was subsequently revised.

I. PROCEDURES

1. *Question: Although it would be best if minors under age 17 abstained from sexual activity, as a professional I believe I have the discretion to determine if abuse has occurred. Why is DSHS requiring me to do something that is beyond the law?*[3]

Answer: The DSHS policy to implement the Rider imposes no additional requirement to report child abuse than what is required by §261.101(b), Family Code, which states that a professional must make a report of abuse when the professional has cause to believe that a child has been abused or neglected or when the child is a victim of an offense under §21.11, Penal Code, Indecency With a Child, and the professional has reason to believe the child has been abused as defined in §261.001(1).

Section 261.101(b) defines *"professional"* as an individual who is licensed or certified by the state, or who is an employee of a facility licensed, certified, or operated by the state and who, in the normal course of official duties (or duties for which a license or certification is required), has direct contact with children. "Professionals" include teachers, nurses, doctors, day-care employees, employees of a clinic or health care facility that provides reproductive services, juvenile probation officers, and juvenile detention or correctional officers. Although other persons who are not professionals have different reporting responsibilities (they must report suspected child abuse immediately rather than the 48-hour time frame allowed for professionals), DSHS will not review or question a contractor's/provider's good-faith designation of staff as a professional or a non-professional. Contractors/providers are responsible for making those determinations.

Section 261.001(1)(E) defines child abuse as sexual conduct harmful to a child's mental, emotional, or physical welfare, including conduct that constitutes the offense of indecency with a child under §21.11, Penal Code, sexual assault under §22.011, Penal Code, or aggravated sexual assault under §22.021, Penal Code. The victim of a crime, by definition, suffers mental, emotional, or physical harm.

2. *Question: Many stakeholders expressed a concern about a potential breach of confidentiality of information relating to a minor, especially in the case of a sexually transmitted disease and HIV.*[4]

3　(1-01; updated 9-01 to reflect revisions to Chapter 261, Family Code, and rider number; updated 9-07 to delete the rider number; updated 12-08 to add definition of "professional.")

4　(8-00; revised 1-01; revised 4-03 to address concerns about breach of confidentiality in general terms applicable to all professionals; added citations in Health and Safety Code relating to confidentiality related to HIV and STD; clarified that federal grantors expect states to comply with

Answer: Nothing in the policy imposes any obligation to report child abuse on the part of the provider that does not already exist. Licensing laws and rules generally provide that there is not breach of confidentiality in releasing information as required or authorized by law or they expressly require abuse to be reported by licensees. For example, §159.004, Occupations Code, allows a physician to release confidential medical records or information to a governmental agency if required or allowed by law.

Section 261.101, Family Code, states that reporting requirements apply regardless of professional confidentiality. It is not a breach of confidentiality to report child abuse.

There are very few restrictions on the type of information that may be reported. For example, HIV status cannot be reported unless the child is under the age of 13 years and such test result or diagnosis is relevant to the report of abuse. Communicable disease information held by DSHS, a local health department, or local health authority cannot be released except in limited circumstances. (See §81.046(d), Health & Safety Code, for STD information which may be released on a child under 13 years of age and §81.103, Health & Safety Code, for confidentiality protection related to HIV). These restrictions do not prevent the reporting of abuse or the victim's identity.

The DSHS Child Abuse Reporting Form is a record used by DSHS to ensure that its contractors/providers are making a good faith effort to comply with child abuse reporting requirements. The information on that form is subject to the same protection of confidentiality as other client records but is also just as releasable as any other information relating to the abuse as stated above.

For those programs also governed by federal laws, regulations, and policies, the federal grantors do not consider it a breach of confidentiality to follow state laws on the reporting of child abuse. They expect states and the states' contractors/providers to follow the laws on reporting child abuse.

3. Question: One commenter noted that reporting abuse could result in notification of a parent in disregard of the child's right to confidentiality to obtain medical services for contraception and an STD under §32.003, Family Code. Another commenter believes there is a conflict between DSHS implementation policy and Chapter 32, Family Code, which allows a minor to self-consent to certain services.[5]

Answer: Section 32.003, Family Code, permits an unmarried, unemancipated minor to self-consent to treatment for specific communicable diseases and pregnancy but not contraceptive services. The section goes on to say that the provider may inform the parents of treatment given to the minor, so confidentiality is not guaranteed under this section. In addition, DSHS policy does not change any existing requirements to report abuse of a minor. Therefore, there is no conflict between DSHS policy and Chapter 32, Family Code.

4. Question: One commenter noted that the proposed DSHS policy would hinder the HIV partner notification program.[6]

state laws on child abuse reporting; revised 12-08 to ensure consistency with statutory language, policy and reporting form)
5   (8-00)
6   (8-00)

Answer: The proposed DSHS policy does not impose any reporting obligation on employees of the Partner Notification Program that does not already exist. The identity of the partner is confidential under §81.051, Health & Safety Code.

5. *Question: Several commenters stated that the proposed DSHS policy would interfere with the professional relationship between patient and health care provider in that these providers "should be empowered to determine the best method of determining sexual abuse and how to encourage the victim to voluntarily talk to law enforcement authorities."*[7]

Answer: See Answer to Question No. 1 in this Section.

6. *Question: Several commenters noted that since DSHS requires its contractors/providers to implement and enforce a written policy and train its staff on reporting requirements, DSHS needs to provide more detailed instructions on how contractors/providers should meet these requirements.*[8]

Answer: DSHS has established a basic policy and a DSHS Child Abuse Reporting Form for use by its contractors/providers. DSHS recognizes that contractors/providers may need updated technical assistance as a result of the new reporting form and the modifications to the DSHS Policy. DSHS staff will provide this assistance as requested. Contractors/Providers have always been expected to ensure their staff is adequately trained to comply with laws and rules that affect clients served by both the provider and their staff. The details of training staff to comply with child abuse reporting will vary according to the contractor/provider, and the contractor/provider is in the best position to determine how training should be carried out.

7. *Question: One commenter stated that by using only pregnancy or confirmed STD (as mechanisms for monitoring providers), DSHS would not be able to identify other cases of abuse not related to sexual activity.*[9]

Answer: The DSHS policy, on which monitoring is focused on minors under age 14 who are pregnant or who have a confirmed STD, in no way diminishes or negates the provider's obligation to report all abuse as required by the law. This expectation is clearly stated in the policy and is noted on the DSHS Child Abuse Reporting Form.

8. *What will DSHS consider an acceptable basis for determining a report of abuse is not required?*[10]

Answer: This is addressed in several other answers to the FAQs; however, the answer will be repeated here. For DSHS monitoring purposes, documentation that an affirmative defense exists will be an acceptable basis for determining a report of abuse is not required for any client under the age of 17 who was determined to have been abused as defined by the Family Code §261.001, including but not limited to, victims of an offense under the Penal Code §21.11, or §22.011. An acceptable affirmative defense for abuse as defined in the Penal Code §21.11 (indecency with a child) may be: 1) the actor was not more than three years older than the victim and of the opposite sex and 2) the actor did not use duress, force, or a threat against the victim at the time of the offense; or (3) the actor was the spouse of the child at the time of the offense.

---

7   (8-00)
8   (8-00; revised 12-08 to add language regarding technical assistance).
9   (8-00; revised 12-08 to add reference to reporting form).
10 (4-03; revised 12-08 to update statutory references; revised 9/10/09 to update statutory references).

An acceptable affirmative defense for abuse as defined in the Penal Code §22.011 (sexual assault) may be: 1) the actor was not more than three years older than the victim at the time of the offense; 2) that the victim was 14 years or older and 3) the victim was not a person whom the actor was prohibited from marrying, purporting to marry or living with under the appearance of being married under Penal Code 25.01 concerning bigamy; or the actor was the spouse of the child at the time of the offense. In both cases, if the perpetrator is the spouse of the minor at the time of the offense, no report is required under DSHS policy. There is no acceptable affirmative defense applicable for abuse of children under the age of 14 because a child under 14 cannot consent to sexual activity under Texas law. .

9. Question: One commenter asked why DSHS did not plan to monitor for minors under age 14 receiving family planning services.[11]

Answer: DSHS has focused its monitoring efforts on the most clearly evident and easily confirmed manifestations of sexual activity, i.e., pregnancy or confirmed STD. In addition to reviewing the records of minors under age 14 who are pregnant or with a confirmed diagnosis of STD, DSHS will continue to randomly review records of clients aged 14 and older for compliance with Chapter 261, Family Code—although the contractor is not required to use a checklist for these records. DSHS monitoring practices in no way diminishes or negates reporting required by Chapter 261. DSHS will also monitor to ensure the contractor has a written policy in place and trains staff for reporting all abuse.

II. REPORTING GENERALLY

1. Question: Is there a way to contact DPRS other than a phone call?[12]

Answer: Yes, reports can be faxed toll free to DFPS in Austin at (800) 647-7410 or submitted via the DFPS online reporting system found on the DFPS web site at: https://www.txabusehotline.org/Default.aspx

The law does not require you to report online. However, DFPS prefers this method of reporting, so DSHS encourages contractors/providers to do so whenever feasible.

2. Question: One commenter asked who would determine the definition of "any other pertinent information" to be reported to the agency receiving a child abuse report.[13]

Answer: The DSHS policy does not change the requirements or interpretation of §261.104, Family Code. What is "pertinent" is based on the contractor/provider's judgment and/or request for information from the agency receiving the report. Examples of what DFPS considers to be pertinent information are listed on the DSHS Child Abuse Reporting Form.

---

11 (8-00; revised 12-08 to remove outdated reference)
12 (1-01; revised 11/01 to change DPRS to DFPS; revised 12-08 to reference the online reporting system).
13 (8-00; revised 12-08 to reference new form).

3. Question: One commenter stated that DSHS should communicate with law enforcement agencies regarding implementation.[14]

Answer: All agencies identified in §261.105, Family Code, are charged with accepting reports of suspected abuse. The four associations for law enforcement agencies were provided with information on the Rider and its implementation in November 2000.

4. Question: One commenter noted that a non-professional should be given 72 hours to report suspected abuse.[15]

Answer: The obligation of a non-professional to report suspected child abuse immediately is set forth in §261.101, Family Code. DSHS requires its providers to train all staff—both professional and non-professional—on how the law defines abuse and on the obligations of the person reporting.

5. Question: One commenter noted that use of the words "suspect" and "cause to believe" in DSHS Policy under "Reporting Generally" was confusing since each word implies a different standard of reporting.[16]

Answer: These terms are derived directly from Chapter 261, Family Code.

6. Question: Is it acceptable to report all suspected abuse to DPRS?[17]

Answer: The Family Code requires that "...a report shall be made to:

(1) any local or state law enforcement agency;

(2) the department [DFPS];

(3) the state agency that operates, licenses, certifies, or registers the facility in which the alleged abuse or neglect occurred; or

(4) the agency designated by the court to be responsible for the protection of children."

However, the laws further states that a report must [emphasis added] be made to the department [DFPS] if the alleged or suspected abuse or neglect involves a person responsible for the care, custody, or welfare of the child. Although the law allows any report to be submitted to DFPS, that agency recommends that reports of abuse involving an alleged abuser who is not the parent or caregiver should be reported to the appropriate law enforcement agency whenever possible.

III. REPORTING SUSPECTED SEXUAL ABUSE

1. Question: Does the contractor/provider have to keep the DSHS Child Abuse Reporting Form in the client's record, or can all the forms be kept in a separate file?[18]

Answer: DSHS Child Abuse Reporting Forms may be kept in either the client's record or a separate file.

2. Question: Define "sexually transmitted disease." Are only reportable

---

14 (8-00, revised 1-01)

15 (8-00)

16 (8-00)

17 ((4-03; revised 9-07 to reflect changes to the Family Code that eliminated the language limiting reports to DFPS to those where the person responsible for the care, custody or welfare of the child is involved; revised 11-07 to change DPRS to DFPS and to match changes in the Family Code; revised 12-08 to clarify reporting guidelines). .

18 (1-01)

sexually transmitted diseases to be used as evidence of sexual activity?[19]

Answer: Any disease that is transmitted as a result of any sexual activity as described in Sections 21.01, 21.11, and 22.011 of the Penal Code, whether reportable or not, should be considered a "sexually transmitted disease" if not acquired through perinatal transmission or transfusion.

3. Question: One commenter noted the DSHS policy was not clear as to what level of certainty a provider must attain to "confirm" a diagnosis of STD.[20]

Answer: For the purposes of this policy, DSHS considers "confirmation" of a diagnosis as that point at which the provider recommends treatment. Confirmation of a diagnosis of STD in a minor under 14 years of age will trigger the requirement for use of the DSHS Child Abuse Reporting Form; however, a contractor/provider must report all abuse if required by Chapter 261, Family Code, without regard to confirmation of the diagnosis of any disease.

4. Question: One commenter asked if the DSHS Child Abuse Reporting Form is legal since it requires persons wishing to report anonymously to identify themselves on the form.[21]

Answer: Use of the DSHS Child Abuse Reporting Form does not prohibit a person from reporting child abuse anonymously. The purpose of the DSHS Child Abuse Reporting Form is to facilitate monitoring by DSHS to ensure compliance by its contractors/providers and to facilitate reporting to law enforcement and DFPS. The DSHS Child Abuse Reporting Form, which is submitted to law enforcement or DFPS, makes optional the name of the person or agency reporting abuse.

5. Question: In regard to the issue of reporting sexual activity involving a minor under age 14, one commenter asked if a Texas minor could be married at age 13 or below.[22]

Answer: A minor in Texas must have a parent's consent to be married if the minor is age 16 or 17. A minor aged 15 or younger can only be married pursuant to judicial order or could have been married in another state or country.

6. Question: A pregnant 13 year old girl requesting services states she is married. Is the contractor/provider required to request documentation from the girl to verify marital status?[23]

Answer: The contractor/provider may, but is not required, to request documentation. However, if the client discloses information that causes the provider to suspect abuse has occurred, further questioning may be warranted.

7. Question: Does DSHS expect contractors/providers to report child abuse if the minor involved has been emancipated?[24]

Answer: Emancipation of a minor by a court does not in and of itself exempt the contractor/provider from child abuse reporting requirements. DSHS would

---

19 (1-01)
20 (8-00)
21 (8-00; revised 12-08 to clarify reporting guidelines).
22 (08-00; Revised 04-08 to incorporate change legal age for marriage and the legal age for minors to marry with parental consent)
23 (6-01; revised 12-08 to include additional guidance)
24 (7-01)

expect its contractors/providers to treat the emancipated minor just like any other minor and report child abuse, if required, unless the contractor/provider has reason to believe the emancipation order exempts the minor from Chapter 261 reporting requirements. "Reason to believe" could be based on the contractor's/provider's actual review of the court order or a statement by the minor that they are specifically exempt from child abuse reporting requirements under the court order—much the same as a contract/provider or may rely on statements by a minor that he or she is married.

8. Question: One commenter suggested that interchangeable use of "sexual activity" and "minors who are pregnant or have a confirmed STD" was confusing and should be clarified.[25]

Answer: These two phrases have two separate meanings as used in the DSHS policy, DSHS Child Abuse Reporting Form, and Quality Management Policy/Procedures materials. "Sexual activity" includes any activity that indicates a person is sexually active. For monitoring purposes, DSHS will focus on records of minors under age 14 who are pregnant or have a confirmed STD. The wording will be clarified where appropriate.

9. Question: If a female client is 17 years old but was 16 when pregnant with a 23 year old male, they are living together as husband and wife, and together for a year, is the contractor/provider required to report?[26]

Answer: "Living together as husband and wife" does not necessarily create a legally recognized marriage, especially if it involves someone under age 18. However, under the circumstances stated above, neither the contractor/provider nor DSHS is required to determine whether or not the couple is legally married. DSHS would look at the age and circumstances of the minor when he or she presented to the contractor/provider and whether or not presentation was on or after your program's implementation date. If the minor was age 17 at the time presenting to the contractor/provider and it was on or after your program's implementation date, DSHS would not expect the contractor/provider to report suspected abuse based on sexual activity alone because neither Indecency with a Child, §21.11, Penal Code, nor Sexual Assault (as statutory rape) under §22.011, Penal Code, applies to a 17 year old. If the minor was age 16 at the time presenting to the contractor/provider and it was on or after your program's implementation date, a report of suspected abuse should be made. The agency receiving the report of suspected abuse (e.g., DFPS or a local law enforcement agency) would determine whether the couple was legally married if that agency chose to investigate.

---

25 (8-00)
26 (2-01)

10. *Question: A 15 year old client says she is pregnant by a 17 year old but the contractor/provider knew he had moved by the time of conception and suspects the father is an older man aged 26. Should the contractor/provider report this as abuse?*[27]

Answer: DSHS does not believe sexual activity alone between a 15-year-old and a 17-year-old is Indecency with a Child, Sexual Assault, or child abuse under Chapter 261. DSHS does believe that sexual activity alone between an unmarried 15-year-old and a 26-year-old is abuse and should be reported. The contractor/provider should report the situation as abuse based on the level of certainty of their suspicion that the minor was involved sexually with a 26-year-old adult. The law does not require perfect certainty to report abuse. It does require information sufficient to lead the contractor/provider to have "cause to believe" that abuse is occurring. In other words, if abuse is suspected based on known information, the contractor/provider should report.

11. *Question: A 15-year-old client is pregnant by an 18-year-old male (contractor/provider does not have proof of his age) and they do not live together. Should the contractor/provider report this as abuse?*[28]

Answer: Contractor/Provider may use affirmative defense as appropriate and if allowed by the contractor's/provider's policy. Otherwise, a report should be made.

12. *Question: Can the DSHS Child Abuse Reporting Form be modified by a contractor/provider?*[29]

Answer: DSHS Policy does not allow modification of an official DSHS form by anyone other than the DSHS owner of the form. In addition, the purpose of the DSHS Child Abuse Reporting Form is to facilitate monitoring by DSHS to ensure compliance by its contractors/providers as well as facilitate reporting. DSHS monitoring would become more confusing and time consuming if there were multiple versions of the form even if all DSHS required information were still included. However, contractors/providers may add to the form below the information DSHS requires. This is not considered modifying the form.

13. *Question: Contractors/providers collect medical history information on whether the client has any infectious diseases. If the client self-reports she has an STD, does the client need to be reported under the provisions of the DSHS policy?*[30]

Answer: In the absence of a medically confirmed diagnosis (i.e., a record of test results from a physician or someone working under a physician's orders), no reporting is required by DSHS policy because the contractor/provider has no knowledge that the client has a confirmed diagnosis of an STD. However, if the contractor/provider receives subsequent information to indicate that a minor of any age has been abused, e.g., been the victim of sexual assault by engaging in voluntary or involuntary sexual intercourse with a person more than three years older or of any other type of abuse, then a report is required by law and under the DSHS policy.

14. *Question: A contractor/provider reported that an irate parent*

---

27 (2-01)
28 (2-01; revised 9-08 to provide further reporting guidance)
29 (6-02; revised 12-08 for consistency with new reporting form and policy)
30 (4-03)

visited the contractor/provider to complain that his child had been reported as a victim of suspected child abuse. The agency staff felt threatened by the parent. In addition, the contractor's/provider's staff was very concerned that confidentiality had been breached by the agency that received the report and provided it to local law enforcement. Evidently, local law enforcement revealed the identity of the reporter in the course of their dealings with the parent. Isn't the agency receiving the report required to keep the identity of the person who reported confidential?[31]

Answer: The Rider does not affect how reports of suspected child abuse are handled or investigated. Family Code §261.201 provides that the report itself as well as the identity of the person making the report is confidential and may be disclosed only for purposes consistent with the Family Code and applicable state or federal law or regulations. Law enforcement may also have the same discretion to disclose the identity of the person making the report when a report is referred by DFPS, but the law is not absolutely clear on this point. Agencies may wish to consult with their own legal counsel and/or talk to local law enforcement about how this will be handled. Local law enforcement often welcomes a dialogue with contractors/providers on how agencies are dealing with reporting suspected child abuse.

Contractors/providers are allowed by law to report anonymously and may wish to do so in order to avoid these situations. Further, Chapter 261 of the Family Code states that a person acting in good faith who reports or assists in an investigation of a report of alleged child abuse or neglect is immune from civil or criminal prosecution. We point this out in case persons who are the subject of reports threaten to sue.

15. Question: A counselor at one of our clinics had a client age 14 who became sexually active at the age of 13, but reported she had not had a partner in the last three months. Should we have asked for the age of her previous partner?[32]

Answer: The client was a victim of sexual abuse of a minor and must be reported. There is no affirmative defense for the sexual partner of a minor under age 14 so the age of the partner is not legally relevant.

16. Question: Do contractors/providers have to ask males who come to the clinic for condoms and treatment of an STD the age of their partner?[33]

Answer: DSHS has no requirement that you ask the age of the partner(s) of a male in the circumstances described. A minor of either sex requesting condoms does not alone trigger the need to report or determine the affirmative defense which, under DSHS policy, would allow the contractor/provider not to report. If, however, during your routine treatment of the minor, you discover that he or she is or has been sexually active, you should report the minor or determine whether an affirmative defense exists. Also, if it comes to your attention that a male or female client has a sexual partner under age 17 and more than three years younger than the client, a report must be filed concerning abuse of the partner by the client; the partner would be under age 14 in this case and no affirmative defense applies.

17. Question: Do all teens 16 years of age and younger who are sexually

31 (4-03)
32 (04-03)
33 (4-03)

active have to be reported? Or, do they just have to be reported if their partner is more than three years older, if they are more than three years older than their partner, or if they refuse to give the age of the partner?[34]

Answer: For teens under age 17 who are not married, the contractor/provider must either 1) report them all if they are or have been sexually active or 2) determine if an affirmative defense to prosecution exists which, under DSHS policy, would allow the contractor/provider not to report. If the client is not willing to provide the age of the partner, a report must be made because you do not have sufficient information to document an affirmative defense. Clients under age 17 who are married may be victims of child abuse if the actor is not the client's spouse. Contractor/providers are expected to report such situations only if such information is presented to the contractor/provider (in other words, DSHS does not expect contractors/providers to ask any questions about sexual activity by a married minor). Suspected sexual abuse of a client under the age of 17 by his or her spouse is not subject to DSHS monitoring or documenting.

18. Question: Is every child conceived under the age of 17 considered a separate event? Example: A client has a child at age 13 and she is reported. She later comes back to the contractor's/provider's clinic at age 15 pregnant with her second child. Is the initial DSHS Child Abuse Reporting Form enough for the whole file?[35]

Answer: Every event is considered separately. In the example above, the contractor/provider must either 1) report a 15 year old who is pregnant or 2) determine if an affirmative defense to prosecution exists which would allow the contractor/provider not to report under DSHS policy.

19. Question: Where is the "cut-off" for reporting? Example: An 18 year old mother walks in to apply for services and her child was conceived before age 17. Do we need to report her?[36]

Answer: There is no "cut-off" under the provisions of the law. However, DSHS does not monitor for instances such as described in the example above.

20. Question: The DSHS Child Abuse Reporting Form says "optional" where contact information for the staff person or reporting agency is to be listed. What do we do if DFPS says it is not optional and will not take our report unless we give our name?[37]

Answer: You may report anonymously as stated in the DSHS policy. The Family Code at §261.104 does not require your name to be given. The contractor/provider might cite the law to the caseworker in explaining why he/she is not providing his/her name. The DSHS requirement for a "good faith effort" would be satisfied if the reporter attempts to report to DFPS when appropriate, is asked for his/her identity (perhaps even before any other information can be offered), and then DFPS declines to accept or enter the report if the reporter declines to identify himself/herself. The reporter may then either attempt to report to law enforcement, or may document their unsuccessful attempt to report to DFPS and end the matter as far as compliance

---

34 (4-03; revised 12-08 to clarify policy related to marital status; revised 9/10/09 to reflect policy changes)
35 (04-3; revised 12-08 to delete reference to marital status)
36 (4-03)
37 (4-03; revised 11-07 to change DPRS to DFPS; revised 12-08 to reflect new reporting form)

278 TEXAS LAW FOR THE SOCIAL WORKER

with DSHS policy. DSHS will call this a good faith effort. As to whether that will suffice to avoid prosecution for knowingly failing to report under Family Code §261.109, the contractor/provider should seek advice from their agency counsel.

21. Question: If a case has been reported once and there is no new information about the case (pregnancy or STI), do we have to report it again if the client returns to the clinic?

Answer: DSHS will accept one report as evidence the contractor made a good faith effort for each case/incident of abuse for a client being seen repeatedly at a particular clinic. Unless the contractor has new information that a new incident has occurred with a different partner, once a report has been made and documented in the client record, DSHS does not require another report to meet our standard of a good faith effort. The DSHS monitoring staff only looks for one report in the scenario you describe. Please be advised that contractors should allow any staff member to make another report if the staff member wants to report. Further, because the DSHS policy reflects only what DSHS requires for a good faith effort; the agency is advised to review the law for themselves with their own counsel and decide if the law requires them to make multiple reports. An agency, however, should always allow any staff person to report if the person feels obligated to do so.

22. Question: If a 13 year old previously received services at a clinic and was reported for potential sexual abuse, does the case need to be reported again each time he/she comes in for an exam or other services? For example, if the 13 year old comes in for pills only, does it have to be reported?

Answer: Unless the contractor has new information that a new incident has occurred with a different partner, once a report has been made and documented in the client record, DSHS does not require another report to meet our standard of a good faith effort. The DSHS monitoring staff only looks for one report in the scenario you describe. Please be advised that contractors should allow any staff member to make another report if the staff member wants to report. Further, because the DSHS policy reflects only what DSHS requires for a good faith effort; the agency is advised to review the law for themselves with their own counsel and decide if the law requires them to make multiple reports.

IV. TRAINING

1. Question: One commenter suggested that training be focused on non-professional staff—especially those who conduct screens during a face-to-face interview with clients—since professional staff is trained by way of their licensing process.[38]

Answer: DSHS has the obligation to ensure its contractors make a good faith effort to comply with Chapter 261, Family Code, regardless of their professional or non-professional status. Contractors, regardless of their professional or non-professional status, will be responsible for ensuring a policy is in place, appropriate training of professional and non-professional staff is conducted, and the DSHS Child Abuse Reporting Form is used as required. Therefore, training of the persons responsible for the contracting entity is particularly necessary to ensure the contractor meets DSHS requirements. Contractors are responsible for determining the level

---

38 (8-00)

and manner of training considering factors such as a staff person's level of contact with clients and the staff person's professional status.

V. MONITORING BY DSHS

1. Question: By what standard will DSHS monitor its contractors/ providers for good faith efforts to comply with Chapter 261, Family Code?[39]

Answer: For contractors/providers currently monitored by the DSHS Quality Management Branch (QM), QM will review all records of unmarried minors under age 14 who are pregnant or who have a confirmed STD acquired other than by perinatal transmission to ensure the DSHS Child Abuse Reporting Form was used to report those cases as abuse. QM will continue its routine, random review of records for all other clients. If, during that review, instances of abuse are identified, QM will review the record to ensure a report was made. This process will be incorporated into the QM Core Tool.

Review of the contractor/provider's process for ensuring staff complies with Chapter 261 and for staff training will also be incorporated into the QM Core Tool. To some extent, this will be primarily an educational process. Sanctions against a contractor/provider are not expected to be imposed until the contractor/provider has a second citation for failure to comply.

2. Question: If I report suspected abuse to DFPS or local law enforcement and they do not believe the information indicates reportable abuse, will I be cited by DSHS for failure to report?[40]

Answer: Under these circumstances, DSHS believes the contractor/provider has demonstrated he/she has made a good faith effort to comply with Chapter 261 as long as the contractor/provider documents the contact with DFPS or local law enforcement.

3. Question: What records will be monitored besides those for minors under age 14 who are pregnant or have a confirmed STD?[41]

Answer: A sample of all client records is routinely reviewed during QM monitoring visits. While under DSHS policy all client records of minors under age 14 who are pregnant or have a confirmed STD will be reviewed, a sample of all other records will also be reviewed. If during that review instances of failure to report abuse are noted, they will be included in the site visit report.

---

39 (1-01; 4-03 to clarify sanctions occur after the second incident of noncompliance; revised 11-07 to change Quality Assurance Division to Quality Management Branch)
40 (1-01; revised 11-07 to change DPRS to DFPS)
41 (1-01; 4-03 to clarify that the records chosen are a sample of records; revised 12-08 to delete reference to marital status)

4. Question: There seems to be a conflict in the information provided by different DSHS programs whose contractors/providers are covered by the DSHS Rider Implementation Plan. Are there different expectations for different programs?[42]

Answer: DSHS programs whose contractors/providers are subject to rider compliance use the Child Abuse Screening, Documentation and Reporting Policy, but some have their own rules and some have different operational criteria based on the services they deliver. Although some programs provide more or somewhat differently worded materials, expectations for reporting child abuse are the same across all DSHS programs.

5. Issue: One commenter recommended that the Texas Medical Board, not DSHS, be authorized to review cases of possible non-compliance with child abuse reporting requirements.[43]

Answer: The sanctions permissible under DSHS contracts are holds on funds, loss of funds and/or cancellation of the contract. Only DSHS, not a licensing board, has the authority to impose sanctions under a DSHS contract. The sanctions permissible under contracts with DSHS do not include disciplinary action against a practitioner. Only state licensing boards have that authority.

6. Question: How should a contractor chart in the charts to cover their liability? What needs to be covered and how?[44]

Answer: Charts should contain enough information to allow a DSHS determination during monitoring as to whether or not a report of abuse was required. The requirements are contained in materials available to the contractor/provider. DSHS can only address a possible liability under DSHS policy; other questions of liability should be addressed to the contractor's/provider's attorney.

7. Question: What does DSHS consider a good faith effort by contractors/providers in issuing their internal policy on child abuse reporting?[45]

Answer: DSHS will consider that contractors/providers who follow these steps when creating their internal policy are making a good faith effort if the contractor/provider 1) clearly describes in their internal policy that they adopt the DSHS Policy; 2) clearly describes the process they will use to determine if a report of abuse is required for minor clients 3) clearly describes what "abuse" is to match the provisions of the laws on reporting child abuse; 4) clearly describes the time frames for reporting (professionals must report within 48 hours and nonprofessionals must report immediately); 5) clearly describes that staff must include a statement in the client's file or the centralized tracking system that either a report was not required and the basis for that determination or a report was required; and 6) the policy clearly describes what additional, if any, documentation the staff must include in the client file or the centralized tracking system. If a report was required, DSHS reviewers will expect the record to reflect the documentation requirements the contractor/provider outlined in their internal policy. DSHS will not review or correct a contractor's/provider's designation of staff as professional or non-professional. Contractors/

---

42 (8-00; revised 12-08 for clarification purposes)
43 (8-00; 4-03 add that holds on funds is a permissible sanction)
44 (2-01)
45 (4-03; revised 12-08 to delete reference to marital status and to clarify issue related to professional and non-professional staff)

providers are responsible for making those determinations.

8. *Question: What will DSHS consider an acceptable basis for determining a report of abuse is not required?*[46]

Answer: This is addressed in several other answers to the FAQs; however, the answer will be repeated here. For DSHS monitoring purposes, documentation that an affirmative defense exists will be an acceptable basis for determining a report of abuse is not required for any client under the age of 17 who was determined to have been abused as defined by the Family Code §261.001, including but not limited to, victims of an offense under the Penal Code §21.11, or §22.011. An acceptable affirmative defense for abuse as defined in the Penal Code §21.11 (indecency with a child) may be: 1) the actor was not more than three years older than the victim and of the opposite sex; and 2) the actor did not use duress, force, or a threat against the victim at the time of the offense. An acceptable affirmative defense for abuse as defined in the Penal Code §22.011 (sexual assault) may be: 1) the actor was not more than three years older than the victim at the time of the offense; 2) that the victim was 14 years or older and 3) the victim was not a person whom the actor was prohibited from marrying, purporting to marry or living with under the appearance of being married under Penal Code 25.01 concerning bigamy. There is no acceptable affirmative defense applicable for abuse of children under the age of 14 because a child under 14 cannot consent to sexual activity under Texas law.

9. *Question: What circumstances other than a minor under age 14 who is pregnant or has an STD acquired other than through perinatal transmission trigger the responsibility to determine if a report of abuse is required?*[47]

Answer: DSHS cannot describe all the possible situations that might trigger the responsibility to determine if a report of abuse is required. Certain circumstances by themselves do not necessarily trigger the responsibility to report. The sole fact that a minor has made a request for birth control does not mean the minor has been abused or neglected as defined in the Family Code §261 or the victim of the offenses of indecency with a child, sexual assault or aggravated sexual assault. If that is all the contractor/provider knows, there is nothing to ask about. However, if the contractor in its routine handling of the request for birth control determines that acts have occurred which constitute abuse or sexual abuse, the responsibility to determine if a report is needed has been triggered. For a minor who is postpartum, who is pregnant, or who has a child, the responsibility to determine if a report of abuse is required has already been triggered by the minor's situation. In the case of a minor requesting a pregnancy test, DSHS believes the contractor/provider has enough information that the minor is sexually active and must determine whether or not a report is required.

---

46 (4-03; revised 12-08 to update statutory references)
47 (4-03)

10. *Question: Does DSHS monitoring include reviewing whether or not a contractor/provider reported within the time frames specified in the law? Specifically, will noncompliance be found if the contractor/provider failed to report within 48 hours for professionals and immediately for nonprofessionals?*[48]

Answer: Yes, the DSHS policy reiterates the requirements of the law on time frames for reporting and DSHS expects contractors/providers to meet these time frames and address them in their internal policy.

11. *Question: Many contractors/providers have reported that staff at the Department of Family and Protective Services (DFPS) is asking for more information than the contractor/provider has collected regarding the suspected abuse. For example, DFPS staff often asks for the names of all persons involved or how often the incidents have occurred to assist them in their investigation. Are contractors/providers required to obtain this information before reporting to DFPS?*[49]

Answer: The only information required by law, if known, is stated in the law as follows: the name and address of the child; the name and address of the person responsible for the care, custody or welfare of the child; and any other information concerning the alleged or suspected abuse or neglect. If all the contractor/provider knows or suspects is that a crime has been committed, the previously mentioned information, if known, is all they have to report. If a contractor/provider does not routinely collect the other kinds of information DFPS needs, the contractor/provider is not required by law to ask the client for that information. However, if a contractor/provider wishes to ask for further information that is pertinent to the investigation of abuse, the contractor/provider may do so. For cases in which a contractor/provider is seriously concerned about a potential abuse situation, additional details can assist DFPS or law enforcement in determining whether to pursue an investigation.

12. *Question: When DSHS monitors a contractor/provider, what does DSHS expect in order for the contractor/provider to meet Procedures I and III of the DSHS Child Abuse Screening, Documenting and Reporting Policy for Contractors/Providers? These procedures state, respectively, "Each contractor/provider shall adopt this policy as its own" and "Each contractor/provider shall develop on internal policy and procedures which describe how it will determine, document, and report instances of abuse, sexual or nonsexual, in accordance with the Texas Family Code, Chapter 261."*[50]

Answer: A statement to the effect of "Agency X adopts the DSHS Child Abuse Screening, Documenting and Reporting Policy for Contractors/Providers by reference in our agency internal policy and will comply with all provisions of the DSHS policy" would be sufficient to meet Procedure I. However, adoption of the DSHS policy alone is not sufficient to meet the requirements of Procedure III. The contractor/provider must have an internal policy and it must describe the internal agency process for determining, documenting and reporting.

---

48 (4-03)
49 (4-03; revised 11-07 to change DPRS to DFPS; revised 9-08 to clarify reporting guidelines)
50 (4-03)

PLAN FOR IMPLEMENTING DSHS RIDER 19
REPORTING CHILD ABUSE BY DSHS SERVICES CONTRACTORS

BACKGROUND

Article II of the General Appropriations Act for fiscal years (FYs) 2008-2009 includes the Texas Department of State Health Services (DSHS) Rider 19 relating to the reporting of child abuse. The rider states that DSHS "may distribute or provide appropriated funds only to recipients which show good faith efforts to comply with all child abuse reporting guidelines and requirements set forth in Chapter 261, Texas Family Code." Provisions of the General Appropriations Act became effective on September 1, 2007.

DSHS has always had the understanding and expectation that its providers/contractors report child abuse according to the law. To emphasize that expectation, DSHS has incorporated the requirements of Rider 19 into its contracts.

IMPLEMENTATION PLAN—GRANT CONTRACTED SERVICES

Grant contractors and their subcontractors are required to implement and enforce the DSHS Child Abuse Screening, Documenting, and Reporting Policy for Contractors/Providers reporting all suspected instances of child abuse consistent with all requirements of Chapter 261, Texas Family Code. The contractor must train staff on all reporting requirements and use the Checklist for DSHS Monitoring for any client under 14 years of age who is pregnant or has a confirmed sexually transmitted disease acquired in a manner other than through perinatal transmission or transfusion. DSHS expectations for "good faith effort" will be met if a contractor and its subcontractors comply with these requirements.

DSHS staff will monitor to determine compliance by reviewing all contractor records relating to services to minors under age 14 who are pregnant or have a confirmed diagnosis of a sexually transmitted disease acquired in a manner other than through perinatal transmission or transfusion, including HIV, to determine if the Checklist was used and if child abuse was reported. For specific monitoring procedures, see attached Quality Assurance Monitoring Division Policy and Procedures for Compliance with Child Abuse Screening, Documenting, and Reporting for Contractors/Providers.

Use of the checklist for DSHS monitoring of reporting of abuse of children younger than 14 who are pregnant or have STDs acquired in a manner other than through perinatal transmission or transfusion does not relieve contractors or subcontractors of the requirements in Chapter 261,Texas Family Code, to report any other instance of suspected abuse of other children.

MEDICAID SERVICES

Medicaid provider agreements incorporate all directives published in the Medicaid Provider Procedures Manual and the bimonthly Texas Medicaid Bulletin. Directives have been published in the Texas Medicaid Bulletin to require providers to make a good faith effort to comply with all child abuse reporting guidelines and requirements in Chapter 261, Texas Family Code. The directive requires the provider to implement and enforce a written policy and train its staff on reporting requirements. The language is also included in the Medicaid Provider Procedures Manual.

The DSHS Checklist for Monitoring may be used by Medicaid providers. While there is no on-site quality assurance process under which the provider's files are routinely reviewed, record reviews may be conducted during compliance activities required by other funding sources.

Additional Requirements

DSHS requires a report of child abuse to include the following items as required by the Texas Family Code: name and address of the child; name and address of the person responsible for the care, custody, or welfare of the child; and any other pertinent information. The Texas Family Code requires these items only if known by the reporter. Minors tested anonymously for HIV/STD cannot be reported.

DSHS informs and provides technical assistance to its contractors on reporting requirements. DSHS expectations for its contractors/providers and clarification of its policy through Frequently Asked Questions are available through the DSHS website at http://www.dshs.state.tx.us/childabusereporting. This website is updated as needed and every affected program website is linked to the updated site.

Section 261.103, Texas Family Code, requires a person to make a report of abuse to one of four agencies, depending on the circumstances in which the abuse occurred. Reports are to be made to any local or state law enforcement agency; the Texas Department of Protective and Regulatory Services if the alleged or suspected abuse involves a person responsible for the care, custody or welfare of the child; the state agency that operates, licenses, certifies or registers the facility in which the alleged abuse or neglect occurred; or the agency designated by the court to be responsible for the protection of children. A report may be made to the Texas Youth Commission instead of the above-mentioned agencies if the report is based on information provided by a child while under the supervision of the commission concerning the child's alleged abuse of another child.

Sanctions

Failure by a contractor/provider to develop, implement, enforce a policy, or train staff can result in withholding of funds payable to the contractor/provider until the contractor/provider has corrected the failure. Failure by a contractor to complete the Checklist for clients under age 14 who are pregnant or have a confirmed diagnosis of sexually transmitted disease acquired in a manner other than through perinatal transmission or transfusion, when required, or failure by contractors/providers to report suspected child abuse can also result in the temporary withholding of funds until the contractor/provider complies.

Policies & Procedures

DSHS Child Abuse Screening, Documenting, and Reporting Policy for Contractors/Providers[51]

Policy

Each contractor/provider shall comply with the provisions of state law as set

---

51 [Revised effective January 1, 2009 ; last updated 9/21/2009. Revised 9/1/01 to update statutory language in Chapter 261, Family Code; Revised effective 5/15/03 to add 1) Sanctions section, 2) clarifications on: requirements for contractor's internal policy and adoption of the DSHS Policy, 3) reporting and what triggers the need to determine if a report is required, 4) confidentiality; reporting anonymously, 5) emancipated and divorced minors, 6) modification of the Checklist, 7) clarifications on training; and 8) description of minors under age 14 who must be reported using the Checklist. Revised items I and IV in the "Reporting Generally" §9/1/05 to reflect changes in language in Chapter 261, Family Code. Revised 03/16/09 to provide clarification on treatment

forth in Chapter 261 of the Texas Family Code relating to reporting suspected child abuse and the provisions of the Texas Department of State Health Services (DSHS) policy. DSHS shall distribute funds only to a contractor/provider who has demonstrated a good faith effort to comply with child abuse reporting guidelines and requirements in Chapter 261 and this DSHS policy. Contractor/provider staff shall respond to disclosures or suspicions of abuse of minors by reporting to appropriate agencies as required by law.

PROCEDURES

I. Each contractor/provider shall adopt this policy as its own.

    A. A statement in the contractor/provider's internal policy to the effect of "Agency X adopts the DSHS Child Abuse Screening, Documenting, and Reporting Policy for Contractors/Providers by reference in our internal policy and will comply with all provisions of the DSHS policy" is sufficient.

    B. Adoption of the DSHS policy alone is not sufficient to meet the requirements of Procedure III of this policy.

II. Each contractor/provider shall report suspected sexual abuse of a child as described in this policy and as required by law.

III. Each contractor/provider shall develop an internal policy and procedures that describe how it will determine, document, and report instances of abuse, sexual or nonsexual, in accordance with the Texas Family Code, Chapter 261.

    A. The contractor/provider's internal policy must clearly describe:

        1. the process that will be used to determine if a report of abuse is required for minor clients;

        2. what constitutes abuse to match the provisions of the laws on reporting child abuse;

        3. the proper time frames for reporting;

        4. the requirement that staff must include a statement in the individual client's file or a centralized tracking system that either a report was required and the basis for that determination, or a report was not required; and

        5. what additional documentation, if any, the staff must include in the client file or the centralized tracking system.

    B. When a report is required, the client record or centralized tracking system must reflect the documentation requirements outlined in the internal policy.

REPORTING GENERALLY

I. A professional as defined in the law is required to report not later than the 48th hour after the hour the professional has cause to believe the child

---

of divorced minors and to allow documentation using a print-out or confirmation from the DFPS online reporting system Revised 9/10/09 to reflect the changes in the Penal Code, Sections 21 and 22. Revised items in Reporting Generally, XII to reflect the changes in the language in the Penal Code, §21.11, Indecency with a Child and §22.011, Sexual Assault relating to affirmative defense to prosecution for certain sex offenses and §22.011 regarding the definition of a child.]

has been or may be abused as defined in §261.001(1) or 261.401, Family Code, or is the victim of the offense of indecency with a child and the professional has cause to believe the child has been abused as defined in §261.001(1), Family Code.

II.   A non-professional shall make a report immediately after the non-professional has cause to believe that the child's physical or mental health or welfare has been adversely affected by abuse.

III. A report shall be made regardless of whether the contractor/provider staff suspects or knows that a report may have previously been made.

IV.   Reports of abuse or indecency with a child shall be made to:

A.   Texas Department of Family and Protective Services (DFPS):

1   Texas Abuse Hotline at 1-800-252-5400 operated 24 hours a day, 7 seven days a week,

2.   by DFPS fax at 1-800-647-7410,

3.   online at https://www.txabusehotline.org/Default.aspx; or

B.   any local or state law enforcement agency; or

C.   the state agency that operates, licenses, certifies, or registers the facility in which the alleged abuse occurred; or

D.   the agency designated by the court to be responsible for the protection of children.

When the alleged or suspected abuse involves a person responsible for the care, custody, or welfare of the child, the report must be made to DFPS.

V. The law requires that the following information, if known, be reported:

A.   name and address of minor;

B.   name and address of the minor's parent or person responsible for the care, custody, or welfare of the child if not the parent; and

C. any other pertinent information concerning the alleged or suspected abuse, such as the child's school, name and age of the alleged abuser, and description of the child's condition or injury. If a contractor does not routinely collect other kinds of information that DFPS or local law enforcement may request, the contractor/provider is not required by law or the DSHS policy to ask the client for that information. Additional information included in the report, however, can be helpful to DFPS or law enforcement in investigating the situation.

VI.   Reports can be made anonymously; however, contractors/providers are encouraged to provide their contact information so that the receiving agency can conduct a thorough investigation, including follow-up with the contractor/provider, if necessary.

VII. Confidentiality

A.   A contractor/provider may not reveal whether or not the child has been tested for or diagnosed with HIV or AIDS, unless the child is under the age of 13 years and such test result or diagnosis is relevant to the report of abuse.

B. §261.001, Family Code, states that reporting requirements apply regardless of professional confidentiality and licensing laws and rules for professionals. It is not a breach of confidentiality to report child abuse.

C. For those programs also governed by federal laws, regulations, and policies, the federal grantors do not consider it a breach of confidentiality to follow state laws on reporting of child abuse.

D. Family Code §261.201 provides that reports of abuse to DFPS as well as the identity of the person making the report are confidential and may be disclosed only for purposes consistent with the Family Code and applicable state or federal law or regulations. The law is not absolutely clear on what discretion law enforcement has regarding disclosure of the identity of the person making the report. DSHS recommends contractors/providers discuss this with their own legal counsel and/or local law enforcement about how this will be handled.

VIII. If the identity of the minor is unknown (e.g., the minor is at the contractor/provider's office to anonymously receive testing for HIV or an STD), no report is required.

IX. For DSHS monitoring purposes, contractors shall document that an affirmative defense as defined for purposes of compliance with this policy exists concerning a minor who is under the age of 17 and who was determined to have been abused as defined by the Family Code §261.101, including but not limited to, victims of an offense under Penal Code §21.11 or §22.011.

A. There is no affirmative defense for abuse of a minor under the age of 14.

B. An acceptable affirmative defense for abuse as defined in the Penal Code §21.11 (sexual indecency with a child) may be that the actor was not more than three years older than the victim, and of the opposite sex, and the actor did not use duress, force or a threat against the victim at the time of the offense.

C. An acceptable affirmative defense for abuse as defined in the Penal Code §22.011 (sexual assault) may be that the actor was not more than three years older than the victim at the time of the offense and the victim was a child 14 years of age or older.

X. Circumstances which trigger the responsibility of the contractor/provider to determine if a report of abuse is required include but are not limited to:

A. Minors who are postpartum, pregnant, or have a child; and

B. Minors who request a pregnancy test.

XI. Circumstances which may trigger the responsibility to determine if a report of abuse is required include but are not limited to:

A. Minor seeking birth control: DSHS does not require a contractor/provider to report abuse based solely on a minor's request for birth control. The contractor/provider must determine whether acts have occurred which constitute abuse and may determine whether any affirmative defense applies, based on all information available from the contractor/provider's routine treatment of the minor.

B. Minor who self-reports that he or she has a sexually transmitted disease (STD): DSHS does not require a contractor/provider to report abuse based solely on the statement of a minor that he or she has an STD. If test results from a physician or someone working under a physician's orders confirms a diagnosis of an STD, the contractor/provider must report or determine an affirmative defense to prosecution. However, without a medically confirmed diagnosis of an STD, the contractor/provider must determine whether acts have occurred which constitute abuse and may determine whether any affirmative defense applies, based on all the information available from the contractor/provider's routine treatment of the minor.

C. Minor who is married and is the subject of a report of sexual contact with a person who is not her or his spouse.

XII. If the perpetrator is the spouse of the married minor at the time of the sexual contact, no report is required under DSHS policy.

A. Contractors/providers may, but are not required to, request documentation that a minor is married or divorced. The contractor/provider may choose to rely on statements by the minor as to his/her marital status.

XIII. A court order for emancipation of a minor for general purposes makes the person who is otherwise 16 years old an adult for all legal purposes under Texas law. A court order of emancipation for limited purposes means the 16-year old person has certain legal capacities, such as the ability to own and/or manage property, to sue and be sued in court, or to execute contracts, but not others exercised by adults, such as voting.

A. If a contractor/provider has reason to believe that a 16-year old minor is the subject of an order of emancipation for general or all purposes, based on review of the order itself and/or a statement from the minor, no report of child abuse should be made.

B. If a contractor/provider has reason to believe that a 16-year old minor is the subject of an order of emancipation for limited purposes, based on review of the order itself and/or a statement from the minor, a report of child abuse should be made if supported by the facts.

REPORTING SUSPECTED SEXUAL ABUSE

I. Each contractor/provider shall ensure that its employees, volunteers, or other staff reports a minor under 14 years of age who is pregnant or has a confirmed STD acquired in a manner other than through perinatal transmission or transfusion. A sexually transmitted disease is any disease that is transmitted by any sexual activity as described in §§21.01, 21.11, and 22.011 of the Penal Code, whether reportable or not.

II. The Texas Family Code, Chapter 261, requires reporting of various types of sexual abuse. Instances of reportable abuse include but are not limited to, the actions described in: Penal Code, §21.11(a) relating to indecency with a child; Penal Code, §21.01(2) defining "sexual contact"; Penal Code, §43.01(1) or (3) – (5); or Penal Code, §22.011(a)(2) relating to sexual assault of a child; or Penal Code, §22.021(a)(2) relating to aggravated sexual assault of a child.

III. The DSHS Child Abuse Reporting Form shall be used in the following manner: (1) to fax reports of abuse to DFPS or law enforcement and to document the report in the client record; (2) to document reports made by telephone; and (3) to document decisions not to report based on the existence of an affirmative defense. When making an online report to DFPS, contractor/providers may use a print-out of that report, rather than the Child Abuse Reporting Form, for documentation in the client record. All forms or online print-outs shall be retained by the contractor/provider in a manner required by the program and are subject to DSHS monitoring. All forms or online print-outs concerning clients less than 14 years of age as described in item I. of this section will be examined during monitoring and must be readily available to the DSHS monitoring staff.

A. The DSHS Child Abuse Reporting Form is an official DSHS form and may not be modified by the contractor/provider.

B. Contractors/providers may add information to the bottom of the form below the DSHS required information. This is not considered modifying the form.

TRAINING

I. Each contractor/provider shall develop training for all staff on the policies and procedures in regard to reporting child abuse. New staff shall receive this training as part of their initial training/orientation. Training shall be documented.

II. As part of the training, staff shall be informed that the staff person who conducts screening and has cause to suspect abuse has occurred is legally responsible for reporting. A joint report may be made with the supervisor.

III. Each contractor/provider is responsible for determining the level and manner of training for employees considering factors such as the staff person's level of contact with clients and the staff person's professional status.

MONITORING BY DSHS

Monitoring of contractors/providers for compliance with the law and policy shall be conducted in accordance with program policies and procedures.

SANCTIONS

Upon a contractor/provider's second and any subsequent failure to comply with the child abuse reporting requirements in the Family Code, Chapter 261, and/or this Policy, DSHS shall temporarily withhold all advances or reimbursements for proper charges or obligations incurred for all contract attachments subject to the Policy until all compliance issues are resolved.

QUALITY MANAGEMENT BRANCH POLICY AND PROCEDURES FOR COMPLIANCE WITH CHILD ABUSE SCREENING, DOCUMENTING AND REPORTING FOR CONTRACTORS/PROVIDERS[52]

POLICY

Contractors/providers will be monitored to ensure compliance with screening for child abuse and reporting according to Chapter 261 of the Texas Family Code and the DSHS Child Abuse Screening, Documenting, and Reporting Policy for

---

52 (Updated May 21, 2003)

Contractors/Providers.

PROCEDURES

During site monitoring of contractors/providers by the Quality Management Branch the following procedures will be utilized to evaluate compliance.

1) The contractor's/provider's process used to ensure that staff are reporting according to Chapter 261 and the DSHS Child Abuse Screening, Documenting and Reporting Policy for Contractors/Providers will be reviewed as part of the Core Tool, Section I, B. Laws, Regulations, and Policies (Clinical), item # 2. To verify compliance with this item, monitors must review: a) that the contractor/provider adopted the DSHS Policy; b) the contractor's/provider's internal policy which details how the contractor/provider will determine, document and report instances of abuse, sexual or non-sexual for all clients who have never been married and are under the age of 17 in compliance with the Texas Family Code, Chapter 261 and the DSHS Policy; c) the contractor/provider followed their internal policy and the DSHS Policy; and d) the contractor/provider's documentation of staff training on child abuse reporting requirements and procedures.

2) All clinical/case management records of clients under 14 years of age who are pregnant or have a confirmed diagnosis of an STD acquired in a manner other than through perinatal transmission or transfusion will be reviewed for appropriate screening and reporting documentation as required in the clinic or site being visited during a site monitoring visit. The review of the records will involve reviewing that the Checklist for DSHS Monitoring was utilized; a report was made; and the report was made in the proper time frames required by law. The records to be reviewed for compliance are only those for services provided. Results of the record reviews will be summarized on the Core Tool .

3) If during the record review process, noncompliance is identified, the staff person responsible will be notified and asked to make a report as required by law. The contractor/provider Director will be notified of the problem (or WIC Director for contractors that are WIC only contractors). Noncompliance will again be identified during the Exit Conference with the contractor/provider. One incidence constitutes noncompliance.

4) If it is found during routine record review of other records for services that a report should have been made as evidenced by the age of the client and evidence of sexual activity, the failure to appropriately screen and report will be identified as lack of compliance with the DSHS Policy; and the DSHS Quality Management Branch will identify the need for the contractor/provider to train staff. Failure to report will be brought to the attention of the staff person who should have made the report or the appropriate supervisor with a request to immediately report. This failure to report will also be discussed with the contractor/provider Director (or if a WIC only contractor, the WIC Director). Results of the record review will be summarized on the Core Tool.

5) The report sent to the contractor/provider will also indicate the number of records reviewed in each clinic that were found to be out of compliance. This report will be sent to the contractor/provider 4 to 6 weeks from the date of the review, which is the usual process for Site Monitoring Reports.

6) The contractor/provider will then be given 6 weeks to respond with written corrective actions to all findings. If the contractor/provider has other findings that warrant technical assistance, accelerated monitoring or probation, either regional or central office staff will make the necessary contacts. Records and/or policies will again be reviewed to ensure compliance with Chapter 261 and the DSHS Policy requirements. Only records created or amended since the last visit will be reviewed during subsequent monitoring. If any subsequent finding of noncompliance is identified during a subsequent monitoring or technical assistance visit, the contractor/provider will be referred for financial sanctioning.

7) If the contractor/provider does not provide corrective actions during the required time period, the contractor/provider will be sent a past due letter with a time period of 10 days to submit the corrective actions. If the corrective actions are not submitted during the time period given, failure to submit the corrective action is considered a subsequent finding of noncompliance and the contractor/provider will be referred for financial sanctioning due to noncompliance with Chapter 261 and the DSHS Policy.

8) If a contractor/provider is found to have minimal findings overall but did have findings of noncompliance with Chapter 261 and the DSHS Policy, an additional sanction (accelerated monitoring or probation) visit solely to review child abuse reporting will not be conducted. For agencies that receive technical assistance visits as a result of a quality assurance review, the agency will again be reviewed for compliance with child abuse reporting for the requirements with which the agency did not comply. In all cases, the corrective actions submitted by the contractor/provider will be reviewed to ensure that the issues have been addressed. Agencies who do not receive a sanction or technical assistance visit will be required to complete the DSHS Progress Report, Compliance with Child Abuse Reporting within 3 months after the corrective actions are begun (no later than 6 months from the initial visit). Failure to submit a Progress Report within the required time period or submission of a report that is not adequate, constitutes a subsequent finding of noncompliance with the DSHS Child Abuse Screening, Documenting, and Reporting Policy for Contractors/Providers and the contractor/provider will be referred for financial sanctions.

Child Abuse Reporting Form[53]
Department of State Health Services (DSHS)

DSHS monitors for reporting of abuse based on the factors described on this form and in the DSHS Screening, Documenting & Reporting Policy. You must use this form when:

- faxing reports of abuse to DFPS (800-647-7410) or law enforcement and documenting the report in the client record;
- documenting reports made by telephone to DFPS (800-252-5400, 24/7) or law enforcement; and
- documenting decisions not to report based on existence of an affirmative defense.

You may report abuse online at *www.txabusehotline.org/Default.aspx* and use a print-out of the report or a copy of the confirmation from DFPS with the client's name and date of birth written on it, instead of this form, as documentation in the client record.

For DSHS monitoring purposes: You must report all situations involving a minor under 14 years of age who is pregnant or has a confirmed diagnosis of a sexually transmitted disease acquired in a manner other than through perinatal transmission or transfusion. This form or the printed online report will be examined by DSHS monitoring staff and must be made available for review. For minors under age 14:

Confirmed HIV/STD via sexual contact or IV drug abuse: Yes___ No___ Pregnant? Yes___ No___

Additionally, this form may be used as documentation of reporting other cases of potential child abuse and may be provided to the DSHS monitoring staff during a review to show evidence of reporting.

Date:_____Child/Minor's name:_____Child/Minor's Age:_____

In accordance with DSHS policy, an affirmative defense for sexual assault or indecency with a child may be established for clients ages 14, 15, and 16 years. All instances of sexual activity of clients under 14 years of age must be reported. Check below if using the optional affirmative defense language for clients ages 14, 15, and 16 years of age:

- ☐ The actor was not more than three years older than the victim
- ☐ And no duress or force was used
- ☐ And partner is of the opposite sex

Using the criteria above or any other information provided by the client, did you determine that a report of child abuse is required? Yes _____ No_____

Reported to (if indicated): DFPS ☐ Case number: _____ Local Law enforcement ☐ (optional)

The law requires you to report, if known, the name and address of the child, the name and address of the parent or caregiver, and any other pertinent information. You are not required to report information not routinely collected, but any known details can assist DFPS or law enforcement in investigating suspected abuse:

1. Client's address or some other way to locate (name of school or directions to home if rural or P.O. Box): _____

2. Name of parent or caregiver and address (or directions to home if rural or P.O. Box): _____ _____

3. Name and age of alleged abuser: _____

4. Address or some other way to locate alleged abuser: _____

5. Explanation of why abuse is believed to have occurred (could include description of injury or condition, how the harm occurred or why the child appears to be at risk, explanation by child or parent, parents' involvement in the abuse/neglect situation, or when and where the incident occurred): _____ _____

Contact information for staff person or agency submitting report (optional): _____

CASE LAW

Four legal decisions important for the practice of social work are included in this Section:

Jaffee v. Redmond for the first time gave the right of privacy to psychotherapy notes in federal court. *Thapar v. Zezulka* provides an excellent discussion of the duty to warn and duty to protect doctrine in Texas. We waited over 20 years in Texas to know the status of these duties. The Texas Supreme Court has now given practitioners guidance when a patient threatens another person. In this case, the Texas Supreme Court takes the position that courts should not second-guess the decision by a practitioner to tell law enforcement personnel or medical personnel about the danger presented by a patient. This gives a good deal of discretion to practitioners who are faced with a difficult situation and the decision is certainly pro-therapist.

Abrams v. Jones concerns the privacy of information between a therapist, a child client, and the child's parents and provides a remedy for parents who request but are denied access to a child's records. Practitioners can draw guidance from this case about record keeping and the duty to parents and child clients. *B.K. vs Cox* evaluates the duty to report and derived judicial immunity.

Confidentiality of Psychotherapy Notes

(Jaffee vs. Redmond)[1]

Background

Petitioner, the administrator of decedent Allen's estate, filed this action alleging that Allen's constitutional rights were violated when he was killed by respondent Redmond, an on-duty police officer employed by respondent village. The court ordered respondents to give petitioner notes made by Karen Beyer, a licensed clinical social worker, during counseling sessions with Redmond after the shooting, rejecting their argument that a psychotherapist-patient privilege protected the contents of the conversations. Neither Beyer nor Redmond complied with the order. At trial, the jury awarded petitioner damages after being instructed that the refusal to turn over the notes was legally unjustified and the jury could presume that the notes would have been unfavorable to respondents. The Court of Appeals reversed and remanded, finding that "reason and experience," the touchstones for acceptance of a privilege under Federal Rule of Evidence 501, compelled recognition of a psychotherapist-patient privilege. However, it found that the privilege would not apply if in the interests of justice, the evidentiary need for disclosure outweighed the patient's privacy interests. Balancing those interests, the court concluded that Beyer's notes should have been protected.

Held: The conversations between Redmond and her therapist and the notes taken during their counseling sessions are protected from compelled disclosure under Rule 501.[2]

(a) Rule 501 authorizes federal courts to define new privileges by interpreting "the principles of the common law . . . in the light of reason and experience." The Rule thus did not freeze the law governing privileges at a particular point in history, but rather directed courts to "continue the evolutionary development of testimonial privileges."[3] An exception from the general rule disfavoring testimonial privileges

---

1   *Jaffee, Special Administrator For Allen, Deceased v. Redmond et al.*518 U.S. 1 (1996)
2   Pp. 5-17
3   Trammel v. United States, 445 U.S. 40, 47

is justified when the proposed privilege "promotes sufficiently important interests to outweigh the need for probative evidence . . . ."[4]

(b) Significant private interests support recognition of a psychotherapist privilege. Effective psychotherapy depends upon an atmosphere of confidence and trust, and therefore the mere possibility of disclosure of confidential communications may impede development of the relationship necessary for successful treatment. The privilege also serves the public interest, since the mental health of the Nation's citizenry, no less than its physical health, is a public good of transcendent importance. In contrast, the likely evidentiary benefit that would result from the denial of the privilege is modest. That it is appropriate for the federal courts to recognize a psychotherapist privilege is confirmed by the fact that all 50 States and the District of Columbia have enacted into law some form of the privilege,[5] and reinforced by the fact that the privilege was among the specific privileges recommended in the proposed privilege rules that were rejected in favor of the more open-ended language of the present Rule 501.[6]

(c) The federal privilege, which clearly applies to psychiatrists and psychologists, also extends to confidential communications made to licensed social workers in the course of psychotherapy. The reasons for recognizing the privilege for treatment by psychiatrists and psychologists apply with equal force to clinical social workers, and the vast majority of States explicitly extend a testimonial privilege to them. The balancing component implemented by the Court of Appeals and a few States is rejected, for it would eviscerate the effectiveness of the privilege by making it impossible for participants to predict whether their confidential conversations will be protected. Because this is the first case in which this Court has recognized a psychotherapist privilege, it is neither necessary nor feasible to delineate its full contours in a way that would govern all future questions.[7]

Stevens, J., delivered the opinion of the Court, in which O'Connor, Kennedy, Souter, Thomas, Ginsburg, and Breyer, JJ., joined. Scalia, J., filed a dissenting opinion, in which Rehnquist, C. J., joined as to Part III.

OPINION

(Justice Stevens delivered the opinion of the Court.) After a traumatic incident in which she shot and killed a man, a police officer received extensive counseling from a licensed clinical social worker. The question we address is whether statements the officer made to her therapist during the counseling sessions are protected from compelled disclosure in a federal civil action brought by the family of the deceased. Stated otherwise, the question is whether it is appropriate for federal courts to recognize a "psychotherapist privilege" under Rule 501 of the Federal Rules of Evidence.

I. Petitioner is the administrator of the estate of Ricky Allen. Respondents are Mary Lu Redmond, a former police officer, and the Village of Hoffman Estates, Illinois, her employer during the time that she served on the police force.[8] Petitioner commenced this action against respondents after Redmond shot and killed Allen while on patrol duty.

On June 27, 1991, Redmond was the first officer to respond to a "fight in

4   *Id.*, at 51. Pp. 5-7
5   see Trammel v. United States, 445 U.S., at 48 -50
6   Pp. 7-13
7   Pp. 13-16. 51 F. 3d 1346, affirmed
8   Redmond left the police department after the events at issue in this lawsuit.

progress" call at an apartment complex. As she arrived at the scene, two of Allen's sisters ran toward her squad car, waving their arms and shouting that there had been a stabbing in one of the apartments. Redmond testified at trial that she relayed this information to her dispatcher and requested an ambulance. She then exited her car and walked toward the apartment building. Before Redmond reached the building, several men ran out, one waving a pipe. When the men ignored her order to get on the ground, Redmond drew her service revolver. Two other men then burst out of the building, one, Ricky Allen, chasing the other. According to Redmond, Allen was brandishing a butcher knife and disregarded her repeated commands to drop the weapon. Redmond shot Allen when she believed he was about to stab the man he was chasing. Allen died at the scene. Redmond testified that before other officers arrived to provide support, "people came pouring out of the buildings," and a threatening confrontation between her and the crowd ensued.

Petitioner filed suit in Federal District Court alleging that Redmond had violated Allen's constitutional rights by using excessive force during the encounter at the apartment complex. The complaint sought damages under Rev. Stat. Section(s) 1979, 42 U. S. C. Section(s) 1983 and the Illinois wrongful death statute, Ill. Comp. Stat., ch. 740, Section(s) 180/1 et seq. (1994). At trial, petitioner presented testimony from members of Allen's family that conflicted with Redmond's version of the incident in several important respects. They testified, for example, that Redmond drew her gun before exiting her squad car and that Allen was unarmed when he emerged from the apartment building.

During pretrial discovery petitioner learned that after the shooting Redmond had participated in about 50 counseling sessions with Karen Beyer, a clinical social worker licensed by the State of Illinois and employed at that time by the Village of Hoffman Estates. Petitioner sought access to Beyer's notes concerning the sessions for use in cross-examining Redmond. Respondents vigorously resisted the discovery. They asserted that the contents of the conversations between Beyer and Redmond were protected against involuntary disclosure by a psychotherapist-patient privilege. The district judge rejected this argument. Neither Beyer nor Redmond, however, complied with his order to disclose the contents of Beyer's notes. At depositions and on the witness stand both either refused to answer certain questions or professed an inability to recall details of their conversations.

In his instructions at the end of the trial, the judge advised the jury that the refusal to turn over Beyer's notes had no "legal justification" and that the jury could therefore presume that the contents of the notes would have been unfavorable to respondents.[9] The jury awarded petitioner $45,000 on the federal claim and $500,000 on her state-law claim.

The Court of Appeals for the Seventh Circuit reversed and remanded for a new trial. Addressing the issue for the first time, the court concluded that "reason and experience," the touchstones for acceptance of a privilege under Rule 501 of the Federal Rules of Evidence, compelled recognition of a psychotherapist-patient privilege.[10] "Reason tells us that psychotherapists and patients share a unique relationship,

9   App. to Pet. for Cert. 67.
10   51 F. 3d 1346, 1355 (1995). Rule 501 provides as follows: "Except as otherwise required by the Constitution of the United States or provided by Act of Congress, or in rules prescribed by the Supreme Court pursuant to statutory authority, the privilege of a witness, person, government, State, or political subdivision thereof shall be governed by the principles of the common law as they may be interpreted by the courts of the United States in the light of reason and experience. However, in civil actions and proceedings, with respect to an element of a claim or defense as

in which the ability to communicate freely without the fear of public disclosure is the key to successful treatment."[11] As to experience, the court observed that all 50 States have adopted some form of the psychotherapist-patient privilege. The court attached particular significance to the fact that Illinois law expressly extends such a privilege to social workers like Karen Beyer.[12] The court also noted that, with one exception, the federal decisions rejecting the privilege were more than five years old and that the "need and demand for counseling services has skyrocketed during the past several years."[13]

The Court of Appeals qualified its recognition of the privilege by stating that it would not apply if "in the interests of justice, the evidentiary need for the dis-closure of the contents of a patient's counseling sessions outweighs that patient's privacy interests." Balancing those conflicting interests, the court observed, on the one hand, that the evidentiary need for the contents of the confidential conversa-tions was diminished in this case because there were numerous eyewitnesses to the shooting, and, on the other hand, that Officer Redmond's privacy interests were substantial.[14] Based on this assessment, the court concluded that the trial court had erred by refusing to afford protection to the confidential communications between Redmond and Beyer.

The United States courts of appeals do not uniformly agree that the federal courts should recognize a psychotherapist privilege under Rule 501.[15] Because of the conflict among the courts of appeals and the importance of the question, we granted certiorari. 516 U. S. (1995). We affirm.

II. Rule 501 of the Federal Rules of Evidence authorizes federal courts to define new privileges by interpreting "common law principles . . . in the light of reason and experience." The authors of the Rule borrowed this phrase from our opinion in Wolfle v. United States, 291 U. S. 7, 12 (1934),[16] which in turn referred to the oft-repeated observation that "the common law is not immutable but flexible,

---

to which State law supplies the rule of decision, the privilege of a witness, person, government, State or political subdivision thereof shall be determined in accordance with State law."

11 *Id.*, at 1355-1356

12 See Illinois Mental Health and Developmental Disabilities Confidentiality Act, Ill. Comp. Stat., ch. 740, Section(s) 110/1-110/17 (1994).

13 *Id.*, at 1355-1356

14 "Her ability, through counseling, to work out the pain and anguish undoubtedly caused by Al-len's death in all probability depended to a great deal upon her trust and confidence in her coun-selor Karen Beyer. Officer Redmond, and all those placed in her most unfortunate circumstances, are entitled to be protected in their desire to seek counseling after mortally wounding another human being in the line of duty. An individual who is troubled as the result of her participation in a violent and tragic event, such as this, displays a most commendable respect for human life and is a person well-suited 'to protect and to serve.'" 51 F. 3d, at 1358. *Id.*, at 1357-1358..

15 Compare In re Doe, 964 F. 2d 1325 (CA2 1992) (recognizing privilege); In re Zuniga, 714 F. 2d 632 (CA6), cert. denied, 464 U.S. 983 (1983) (same), with United States v. Burtrum, 17 F. 3d 1299 (CA10), cert. denied, 513 U. S. ___ (1994) (declining to recognize privilege); In re Grand Jury Proceedings, 867 F. 2d 562 (CA9), cert. denied sub nom. Doe v. United States, 493 U.S. 906 (1989) (same); United States v. Corona, 849 F. 2d 562 (CA11 1988), cert. denied, 489 U.S. 1084 (1989) (same); United States v. Meagher, 531 F. 2d 752 (CA5), cert. denied, 429 U.S. 853 (1976) (same)

16 "[T]he rules governing the competence of witnesses in criminal trials in the federal courts are not necessarily restricted to those local rules in force at the time of the admission into the Union of the particular state where the trial takes place, but are governed by common law principles as interpreted and applied by the federal courts in the light of reason and experience. Funk v. United States, 290 U. S. 371." Wolfle v. United States, 291 U. S., at 12-13.

and by its own principles adapts itself to varying conditions."[17] The Senate Report accompanying the 1975 adoption of the Rules indicates that Rule 501 "should be understood as reflecting the view that the recognition of a privilege based on a confidential relationship . . . should be determined on a case-by-case basis." [18] The Rule thus did not freeze the law governing the privileges of witnesses in federal trials at a particular point in our history, but rather directed federal courts to "continue the evolutionary development of testimonial privileges."[19]

The common-law principles underlying the recognition of testimonial privileges can be stated simply. "`For more than three centuries it has now been recognized as a fundamental maxim that the public . . . has a right to every man's evidence. When we come to examine the various claims of exemption, we start with the primary assumption that there is a general duty to give what testimony one is capable of giving, and that any exemptions which may exist are distinctly exceptional, being so many derogations from a positive general rule.'"[20] Exceptions from the general rule disfavoring testimonial privileges may be justified, however, by a "'public good transcending the normally predominant principle of utilizing all rational means for ascertaining the truth.'"[21]

Guided by these principles, the question we address today is whether a privilege protecting confidential communications between a psychotherapist and her patient "promotes sufficiently important interests to outweigh the need for probative evidence . . . ."[22] Both "reason and experience" persuade us that it does.

III.   Like the spousal and attorney-client privileges, the psychotherapist-patient privilege is "rooted in the imperative need for confidence and trust."[23] Treatment by a physician for physical ailments can often proceed successfully on the basis of a physical examination, objective information supplied by the patient, and the results of diagnostic tests. Effective psychotherapy, by contrast, depends upon an atmosphere of confidence and trust in which the patient is willing to make a frank and complete disclosure of facts, emotions, memories, and fears. Because of the sensitive nature of the problems for which individuals consult psychotherapists, disclosure of confidential communications made during counseling sessions may cause embarrassment or disgrace. For this reason, the mere possibility of disclosure may impede development of the confidential relationship necessary for successful

17 Funk v. United States, 290 U. S. 371, 383 (1933). See also Hawkins v. United States, 358 U.S. 74, 79 (1958) (changes in privileges may be "dictated by 'reason and experience'")
18 S. Rep. No. 93- 1277, p. 13 (1974). In 1972 the Chief Justice transmitted to Congress proposed Rules of Evidence for United States Courts and Magistrates. 56 F. R. D. 183 (hereinafter Proposed Rules). The rules had been formulated by the Judicial Conference Advisory Committee on Rules of Evidence and approved by the Judicial Conference of the United States and by this Court. Trammel v. United States, 445 U.S. 40, 47 (1980). The proposed rules defined nine specific testimonial privileges, including a psychotherapist-patient privilege, and indicated that these were to be the exclusive privileges absent constitutional mandate, Act of Congress, or revision of the Rules. Proposed Rules 501-513, 56 F. R. D., at 230-261. Congress rejected this recommendation in favor of Rule 501's general mandate. Trammel, 445 U.S., at 47 .
19 Trammel v. United States, 445 U.S. 40, 47 (1980); see also University of Pennsylvania v. EEOC, 493 U.S. 182, 189 (1990)
20 United States v. Bryan, 339 U.S. 323, 331 (1950) (quoting J. Wigmore, Evidence Section(s) 2192, p. 64 (3d ed. 1940)). 8 See also United States v. Nixon, 418 U.S. 683, 709 (1974)
21 Trammel, 445 U.S., at 50 , quoting Elkins v. United States, 364 U.S. 206, 234 (1960) (Frankfurter, J., dissenting)
22 445 U.S., at 51
23 Trammel, 445 U.S., at 51

treatment.[24] As the Judicial Conference Advisory Committee observed in 1972 when it recommended that Congress recognize a psychotherapist privilege as part of the Proposed Federal Rules of Evidence, a psychiatrist's ability to help her patients "is completely dependent upon [the patients'] willingness and ability to talk freely. This makes it difficult if not impossible for [a psychiatrist] to function without being able to assure . . . patients of confidentiality and, indeed, privileged communication. Where there may be exceptions to this general rule . . ., there is wide agreement that confidentiality is a sine qua non for successful psychiatric treatment."[25]

By protecting confidential communications between a psychotherapist and her patient from involuntary disclosure, the proposed privilege thus serves important private interests.

Our cases make clear that an asserted privilege must also "serve public ends."[26] Thus, the purpose of the attorney-client privilege is to "encourage full and frank communication between attorneys and their clients and thereby promote broader public interests in the observance of law and administration of justice." And the spousal privilege, as modified in Trammel, is justified because it "furthers the important public interest in marital harmony."[27] The psychotherapist privilege serves the public interest by facilitating the provision of appropriate treatment for individuals suffering the effects of a mental or emotional problem. The mental health of our citizenry, no less than its physical health, is a public good of transcendent importance.[28]

In contrast to the significant public and private interests supporting recognition of the privilege, the likely evidentiary benefit that would result from the denial of the privilege is modest. If the privilege were rejected, confidential conversations between psychotherapists and their patients would surely be chilled, particularly when it is obvious that the circumstances that give rise to the need for treatment will probably result in litigation. Without a privilege, much of the desirable evidence to which litigants such as petitioner seek access-for example, admissions against interest by a party-is unlikely to come into being. This unspoken "evidence" will therefore serve no greater truth-seeking function than if it had been spoken and privileged.

That it is appropriate for the federal courts to recognize a psychotherapist privilege under Rule 501 is confirmed by the fact that all 50 States and the District of Columbia have enacted into law some form of psychotherapist privilege.[29] We

---

24 See studies and authorities cited in the Brief for American Psychiatric Association et al. as Amici Curiae 14-17, and the Brief for American Psychological Association as Amicus Curiae 12-17.
25 Advisory Committee's Notes to Proposed Rules, 56 F. R. D. 183, 242 (1972) (quoting Group for Advancement of Psychiatry, Report No. 45, Confidentiality and Privileged Communication in the Practice of Psychiatry 92 (June 1960))
26 Upjohn Co. v. United States, 449 U.S. 383, 389 (1981)
27 445 U.S., at 53 . See also United States v. Nixon, 418 U.S., at 705 ; Wolfle v. United States, 291 U. S., at 14
28 This case amply demonstrates the importance of allowing individuals to receive confidential counseling. Police officers engaged in the dangerous and difficult tasks associated with protecting the safety of our communities not only confront the risk of physical harm but also face stressful circumstances that may give rise to anxiety, depression, fear, or anger. The entire community may suffer if police officers are not able to receive effective counseling and treatment after traumatic incidents, either because trained officers leave the profession prematurely or because those in need of treatment remain on the job.
29 Ala. Code Section(s) 34-26-2 (1975); Alaska Rule Evid. 504; Ariz. Rev. Stat. Section(s) 32-2085 (1992); Ark. Rule Evid. 503; Cal. Evid. Code Ann. Section(s) 1010, 1012, 1014 (1995); Colo. Rev. Stat. Section(s) 13-90-107(g)(1) (1987); Conn. Gen. Stat. Section(s) 52-146c (1995); Del. Uniform Rule Evid. 503; D. C. Code Ann. Section(s) 14-307 (1995); Fla. Stat. Section(s) 90.503 (Supp. 1992); Ga. Code Ann. Section(s) 24-9-21 (1995); Haw. Rules Evid. 504, 504.1;

have previously observed that the policy decisions of the States bear on the question whether federal courts should recognize a new privilege or amend the coverage of an existing one.[30] Because state legislatures are fully aware of the need to protect the integrity of the fact-finding functions of their courts, the existence of a consensus among the States indicates that "reason and experience" support recognition of the privilege. In addition, given the importance of the patient's understanding that her communications with her therapist will not be publicly disclosed, any State's promise of confidentiality would have little value if the patient were aware that the privilege would not be honored in a federal court.[31] Denial of the federal privilege therefore would frustrate the purposes of the state legislation that was enacted to foster these confidential communications.

It is of no consequence that recognition of the privilege in the vast majority of States is the product of legislative action rather than judicial decision. Although common-law rulings may once have been the primary source of new developments in federal privilege law, that is no longer the case. In Funk v. United States, 290 U. S. 371 (1933), we recognized that it is appropriate to treat a consistent body of policy determinations by state legislatures as reflecting both "reason" and "experience."[32] That rule is properly respectful of the States and at the same time reflects the fact that once a state legislature has enacted a privilege there is no longer an opportunity for common-law creation of the protection. The history of the psychotherapist privilege illustrates the latter point. In 1972 the members of the Judicial Conference Advisory Committee noted that the common law "had indicated a disposition to recognize a psychotherapist-patient privilege when legislatures began moving into the field."[33] The present unanimous acceptance of the privilege shows that the state lawmakers moved quickly. That the privilege may have developed faster legislatively than it would have in the courts demonstrates only that the States rapidly recognized the wisdom of the rule as the field of psychotherapy developed.[34]

Idaho Rule Evid. 503; Ill. Comp. Stat., ch. 225 Section(s) 15/5 (1994); Ind. Code Section(s) 25-33-1-17 (1993); Iowa Code Section(s) 622.10 (1987); Kan. Stat. Ann. Section(s) 74-5323 (1985); Ky. Rule Evid. 507; La. Code Evid. Ann., Art. 510 (West 1995); Me. Rule Evid. 503; Md. Cts. & Jud. Proc. Section(s) 9-109 (1995); Mass. Gen. Laws Section(s) 233:20B (1995); Mich. Comp. Laws Ann. Section(s) 333.18237 (Supp. 1996); Minn. Stat. Ann. Section(s) 595.02 (1988 and Supp. 1996); Miss. Rule Evid. 503; Mo. Rev. Stat. Section(s) 491.060 (1994); Mont. Code Ann. Section(s) 26-1-807 (1995); Neb. Rev. Stat. Section(s) 27-504 (1995); Nev. Rev. Stat. Ann. Section(s) 49.209 (Supp. 1995); N. H. Rule Evid. 503; N. J. Stat. Ann. Section(s) 45:14B-28 (West 1995); N. M. Rule Evid. 11-504; N. Y. Civ. Prac. Law Section(s) 4507 (McKinney 1992); N. C. Gen. Stat. Section(s) 8-53.3 (Supp. 1995); N. D. Rule Evid. Section(s) 503; Ohio Rev. Code Ann. Section(s) 2317.02 (1995); Okla. Stat., Tit. 12 Section(s) 2503 (1991); Ore. Rules Evid. 504, 504.1; 42 Pa. Cons. Stat. Section(s) 5944 (1982) R. I. Gen. Laws Section(s) 5-37.3-3, 5-37.3-4 (1995); S. C. Code Ann. Section(s) 19-11-95 (Supp. 1995); S. D. Codified Laws Section(s) 19-13-6 to 19-13-11 (1995); Tenn. Code Ann. Section(s) 24-1-207 (1980); Tex. Rules Civ. Evid. 509, 510; Utah Rule Evid. 506; Vt. Rule Evid. 503; Va. Code Ann. Section(s) 8.01-400.2 (1992); Wash. Rev. Code Section(s) 18.83.110 (1994); W. Va. Code Section(s) 27-3-1 (1992); Wis. Stat. Section(s) 905.04 (1993-1994); Wyo. Stat. Section(s) 33-27-123 (Supp. 1995). ;

30 See Trammel, 445 U.S., at 48 -50; United States v. Gillock, 445 U.S. 360, 368 , n. 8 (1980)

31 At the outset of their relationship, the ethical therapist must disclose to the patient "the relevant limits on confidentiality." See American Psychological Association, Ethical Principles of Psychologists and Code of Conduct, Standard 5.01 (Dec. 1992). See also National Federation of Societies for Clinical Social Work, Code of Ethics V(a) (May 1988); American Counseling Association, Code of Ethics and Standards of Practice A.3.a (effective July 1995).

32 Id., at 376-381

33 Proposed Rules, 56 F. R. D., at 242 (citation omitted)

34 Petitioner acknowledges that all 50 state legislatures favor a psychotherapist privilege. She nevertheless discounts the relevance of the state privilege statutes by pointing to divergence among

The uniform judgment of the States is reinforced by the fact that a psychotherapist privilege was among the nine specific privileges recommended by the Advisory Committee in its proposed privilege rules. In United States v. Gillock,[35] our holding that Rule 501 did not include a state legislative privilege relied, in part, on the fact that no such privilege was included in the Advisory Committee's draft. The reasoning in Gillock thus supports the opposite conclusion in this case. In rejecting the proposed draft that had specifically identified each privilege rule and substituting the present more open-ended Rule 501, the Senate Judiciary Committee explicitly stated that its action "should not be understood as disapproving any recognition of a psychiatrist-patient . . . privileg[e] contained in the [proposed] rules."[36]

Because we agree with the judgment of the state legislatures and the Advisory Committee that a psychotherapist-patient privilege will serve a "public good transcending the normally predominant principle of utilizing all rational means for ascertaining truth,"[37] we hold that confidential communications between a licensed psychotherapist and her patients in the course of diagnosis or treatment are protected from compelled disclosure under Rule 501 of the Federal Rules of Evidence.[38]

IV. All agree that a psychotherapist privilege covers confidential communications made to licensed psychiatrists and psychologists. We have no hesitation in concluding in this case that the federal privilege should also extend to confidential communications made to licensed social workers in the course of psychotherapy. The reasons for recognizing a privilege for treatment by psychiatrists and psychologists apply with equal force to treatment by a clinical social worker such as Karen Beyer.[39] Today, social workers provide a significant amount of mental health

---

the States concerning the types of therapy relationships protected and the exceptions recognized. A small number of state statutes, for example, grant the privilege only to psychiatrists and psychologists, while most apply the protection more broadly. Compare Haw. Rules Evid. 504, 504.1 and N. D. Rule Evid. 503 (privilege extends to physicians and psychotherapists), with Ariz. Rev. Stat. Ann. Section(s) 32-3283 (1992) (privilege covers "behavioral health professional[s]"); Tex. Rule Civ. Evid. 510(a)(1) (privilege extends to persons "licensed or certified by the State of Texas in the diagnosis, evaluation or treatment of any mental or emotional disorder" or "involved in the treatment or examination of drug abusers"); Utah Rule Evid. 506 (privilege protects confidential communications made to marriage and family therapists, professional counselors, and psychiatric mental health nurse specialists). The range of exceptions recognized by the States is similarly varied. Compare Ark. Code Ann. Section(s) 17-46-107 (1987) (narrow exceptions); Haw. Rules Evid. 504, 504.1 (same), with Cal. Evid. Code Ann. Section(s) 1016-1027 (West 1995) (broad exceptions); R. I. Gen. Laws Section(s) 5-37.3-4 (1956) (same). These variations in the scope of the protection are too limited to undermine the force of the States' unanimous judgment that some form of psychotherapist privilege is appropriate.

35 445 U.S. 360, 367 -368 (1980)
36 S. Rep. No. 93-1277, at 13
37 Trammel, 445 U.S., at 50
38 Like other testimonial privileges, the patient may of course waive the protection.
39 If petitioner had filed her complaint in an Illinois state court, respondents' claim of privilege would surely have been upheld, at least with respect to the state wrongful death action. An Illinois statute provides that conversations between a therapist and her patients are privileged from compelled disclosure in any civil or criminal proceeding. Ill. Comp. Stat., ch. 740, Section(s) 110/10 (1994). The term "therapist" is broadly defined to encompass a number of licensed professionals including social workers. Ch. 740, Section(s) 110/2. Karen Beyer, having satisfied the strict standards for licensure, qualifies as a clinical social worker in Illinois. 51 F. 3d 1346, 1358, n. 19 (CA7 1995). Indeed, if only a state-law claim had been asserted in federal court, the second sentence in Rule 501 would have extended the privilege to that proceeding. We note that there is disagreement concerning the proper rule in cases such as this in which both federal and state claims are asserted in federal court and relevant evidence would be privileged under state

treatment.[40] Their clients often include the poor and those of modest means who could not afford the assistance of a psychiatrist or psychologist, but whose counseling sessions serve the same public goals.[41] Perhaps in recognition of these circumstances, the vast majority of States explicitly extend a testimonial privilege to licensed social workers.[42] We therefore agree with the Court of Appeals that "[d]rawing a distinction between the counseling provided by costly psychotherapists and the counseling provided by more readily accessible social workers serves no discernible public purpose."[43]

We part company with the Court of Appeals on a separate point. We reject the balancing component of the privilege implemented by that court and a small number of States.[44] Making the promise of confidentiality contingent upon a trial judge's later evaluation of the relative importance of the patient's interest in privacy and the evidentiary need for disclosure would eviscerate the effectiveness of the privilege. As

law but not under federal law. See C. Wright & K. Graham, 23 Federal Practice and Procedure Section(s) 5434 (1980). Because the parties do not raise this question and our resolution of the case does not depend on it, we express no opinion on the matter.

40 See, e.g., U. S. Dept. of Health and Human Services, Center for Mental Health Services, Mental Health, United States, 1994 pp. 85-87, 107-114; Brief for National Association of Social Workers et al. as Amici Curiae 5-7 (citing authorities)

41 The Judicial Conference Advisory Committee's proposed psychotherapist privilege defined psychotherapists as psychologists and medical doctors who provide mental health services. Proposed Rules, 56 F.R.D., at 240. This limitation in the 1972 recommendation does not counsel against recognition of a privilege for social workers practicing psychotherapy. In the quarter-century since the Committee adopted its recommendations, much has changed in the domains of social work and psychotherapy. See generally Brief for National Association of Social Workers et al. as Amici Curiae 5-13 (and authorities cited). While only 12 States regulated social workers in 1972, all 50 do today. See American Association of State Social Work Boards, Social Work Laws and Board Regulations: A State Comparison Study 29, 31 (1996). Over the same period, the relative portion of therapeutic services provided by social workers has increased substantially. See U. S. Dept. of Health and Human Services, Center for Mental Health Services, Mental Health, United States, 1994, pp. 85-87, 107-114.

42 See Ariz. Rev. Stat. Ann. Section(s) 32-3283 (1992); Ark. Code Ann. Section(s) 17-46-107 (1995); Cal. Evid. Code Section(s) 1010, 1012, 1014 (West 1995); Colo. Rev. Stat. Section(s) 13-90-107 (1987); Conn. Gen. Stat. Section(s) 52-146q (1991); Del. Code Ann., Tit. 24 Section(s) 3913 (1987); D. C. Code Section(s) 14-307 (1995); Fla. Stat. Section(s) 90.503 (1991); Ga. Code Ann. Section(s) 24-9-21 (1995); Idaho Code Section(s) 54-3213 (1994); Ill. Comp. Stat., ch. 225, Section(s) 20/16 (1994); Ind. Code Section(s) 25-23.6-6-1 (1993); Iowa Code Section(s) 622.10 (1987); Kan. Stat. Ann. Section(s) 65-6315 (Supp. 1990); Ky. Rule Evid. 507; La. Code Evid. Ann., Art. 510 (West 1995); Me. Rev. Stat. Ann., Tit. 32, Section(s) 7005 (1988); Md. Cts. & Jud. Proc. Code Ann. Section(s) 9-121 (1995); Mass. Gen. Laws Section(s) 112:135A (1994); Mich. Comp. Stat. Ann. 339.1610 (1992); Minn. Stat. Section(s) 595.02(g) (1994); Miss. Code Ann. Section(s) 73-53-29 (1972); Mo. Ann. Stat. Section(s) 337.636 (Supp. 1996); Mont. Code Ann. Section(s) 37-22-401 (1995); Neb. Rev. Stat. Ann. Section(s) 71-1,335 (1995); Nev. Rev. Stat. Ann. Section(s) 49.215, 49.225, 49.235 (Supp. 1995); N. H. Rev. Stat. Ann. Section(s) 330-A:19 (1995); N. J. Stat. Ann. Section(s) 45:15BB-13 (1995); N. M. Stat. Ann. Section(s) 61-31-24 (Supp. 1995); N. Y. Civ. Prac. Law Section(s) 4508 (1992); N. C. Gen. Stat. Section(s) 8-53.7 (1986); Ohio Rev. Code Ann. Section(s) 2317.02 (1995); Okla. Stat., Tit. 59, Section(s) 1261.6 (1991); Ore. Rev. Stat. Section(s) 40.250 (1991); R. I. Gen. Laws Section(s) 5-37.3-3, 5-37.3-4 (1995); S. C. Code Ann. Section(s) 19-11-95 (Supp. 1995); S. D. Codified Laws Section(s) 36-26-30 (1994); Tenn. Code Ann. Section(s) 63-23-107 (1990); Tex. Rule Civ. Evid. 510; Utah Rule Evid. 506; Vt. Rule Evid. 503; Va. Code Ann. Section(s) 8.01-400.2 (1992); Wash. Rev. Code Section(s) 18.19.180 (1994); W. Va. Code Section(s) 30-30-12 (1993); Wis. Stat. Section(s) 905.04 (1993-1994); Wyo. Stat. Section(s) 33-38-109 (Supp. 1995).

43 51 F. 3d, at 1358, n. 19

44 See, e.g., Me. Rev. Stat. Ann., Tit. 32, Section(s) 7005 (1964); N. H. Rev. Stat. Ann. Section(s) 330-A:19 (1995); N. C. Gen. Stat. Section(s) 8-53.7 (1986); Va. Code Ann. Section(s) 8.01-400.2 (1992).

we explained in Upjohn, if the purpose of the privilege is to be served, the partici-pants in the confidential conversation "must be able to predict with some degree of certainty whether particular discussions will be protected. An uncertain privilege, or one which purports to be certain but results in widely varying applications by the courts, is little better than no privilege at all."[45]

These considerations are all that is necessary for decision of this case. A rule that authorizes the recognition of new privileges on a case-by-case basis makes it appropriate to define the details of new privileges in a like manner. Because this is the first case in which we have recognized a psychotherapist privilege, it is neither necessary nor feasible to delineate its full contours in a way that would "govern all conceivable future questions in this area."[46]

V. The conversations between Officer Redmond and Karen Beyer and the notes taken during their counseling sessions are protected from compelled disclosure under Rule 501 of the Federal Rules of Evidence. The judgment of the Court of Appeals is affirmed. *It is so ordered.*

Dissent

Justice Scalia, with whom The Chief Justice joins as to Part III, dissenting.

The Court has discussed at some length the benefit that will be purchased by creation of the evidentiary privilege in this case: the encouragement of psychoana-lytic counseling. It has not mentioned the purchase price: occasional injustice. That is the cost of every rule which excludes reliable and probative evidence-or at least every one categorical enough to achieve its announced policy objective. In the case of some of these rules, such as the one excluding confessions that have not been properly "Mirandized,"[47] the victim of the injustice is always the impersonal State or the faceless "public at large." For the rule proposed here, the victim is more likely to be some individual who is prevented from proving a valid claim-or (worse still) prevented from establishing a valid defense. The latter is particularly unpalatable for those who love justice, because it causes the courts of law not merely to let stand a wrong, but to become themselves the instruments of wrong.

In the past, this Court has well understood that the particular value the courts are distinctively charged with preserving-justice-is severely harmed by contraven-tion of "the fundamental principle that `"the public . . . has a right to every man's evidence."[48] Testimonial privileges, it has said, "are not lightly created nor expan-sively construed, for they are in derogation of the search for truth."[49] Adherence to that principle has caused us, in the Rule 501 cases we have considered to date, to reject new privileges.[50] The Court today ignores this traditional judicial preference

---

45 449 U.S., at 393

46 *Id.,* at 386. Although it would be premature to speculate about most future developments in the federal psychotherapist privilege, we do not doubt that there are situations in which the privilege must give way, for example, if a serious threat of harm to the patient or to others can be averted only by means of a disclosure by the therapist.

47 see Miranda v. Arizona, 384 U.S. 436 (1966)

48 Trammel v. United States, 445 U.S. 40, 50 (1980) (citation omitted)

49 United States v. Nixon, 418 U.S. 683, 710 (1974) (emphasis added)

50 see University of Pennsylvania v. EEOC, 493 U.S. 182 (1990) (privilege against disclosure of academic peer review materials); United States v. Gillock, 445 U.S. 360 (1980) (privilege against disclosure of "legislative acts" by member of state legislature), and even to construe narrowly the scope of existing privileges, see, e.g., United States v. Zolin, 491 U.S. 554, 568 -570 (1989) (permitting in camera review of documents alleged to come within crime-fraud exception to attorney-client privilege); Trammel, supra (holding that voluntary testimony by spouse is not

for the truth, and ends up creating a privilege that is new, vast, and ill-defined. I respectfully dissent.

I. The case before us involves confidential communications made by a police officer to a state-licensed clinical social worker in the course of psychotherapeutic counseling. Before proceeding to a legal analysis of the case, I must observe that the Court makes its task deceptively simple by the manner in which it proceeds. It begins by characterizing the issue as "whether it is appropriate for federal courts to recognize a 'psychotherapist privilege,'" and devotes almost all of its opinion to that question. Having answered that question (to its satisfaction) in the affirmative, it then devotes less than a page of text to answering in the affirmative the small remaining question whether "the federal privilege should also extend to confidential communications made to licensed social workers in the course of psychotherapy."[51]

Of course the prototypical evidentiary privilege analogous to the one asserted here-the lawyer-client privilege-is not identified by the broad area of advice-giving practiced by the person to whom the privileged communication is given, but rather by the professional status of that person. Hence, it seems a long step from a lawyer-client privilege to a tax advisor-client or accountant-client privilege. But if one recharacterizes it as a "legal advisor" privilege, the extension seems like the most natural thing in the world. That is the illusion the Court has produced here: It first frames an overly general question ("Should there be a psychotherapist privilege?") that can be answered in the negative only by excluding from protection office consultations with professional psychiatrists (i.e., doctors) and clinical psychologists. And then, having answered that in the affirmative, it comes to the only question that the facts of this case present ("Should there be a social worker-client privilege with regard to psychotherapeutic counseling?") with the answer seemingly a foregone conclusion.

At that point, to conclude against the privilege one must subscribe to the difficult proposition, "Yes, there is a psychotherapist privilege, but not if the psychotherapist is a social worker." Relegating the question actually posed by this case to an afterthought makes the impossible possible in a number of wonderful ways. For example, it enables the Court to treat the Proposed Federal Rules of Evidence developed in 1972 by the Judicial Conference Advisory Committee as strong support for its holding, whereas they in fact counsel clearly and directly against it. The Committee did indeed recommend a "psychotherapist privilege" of sorts; but more precisely, and more relevantly, it recommended a privilege for psychotherapy conducted by "a person authorized to practice medicine" or "a person licensed or certified as a psychologist,"[52] which is to say that it recommended against the privilege at issue here. That condemnation is obscured, and even converted into an endorsement, by pushing a "psychotherapist privilege" into the center ring. The Proposed Rule figures prominently in the Court's explanation of why that privilege deserves recognition, and is ignored in the single page devoted to the sideshow which happens to be the issue presented for decision.[53]

This is the most egregious and readily explainable example of how the Court's misdirection of its analysis makes the difficult seem easy; others will become apparent

covered by husband-wife privilege)
51 ante, at 13
52 Proposed Rule of Evidence 504, 56 F. R. D. 183, 240 (1972)
53 ante, at 13-14

when I give the social-worker question the fuller consideration it deserves. My initial point, however, is that the Court's very methodology-giving serious consideration only to the more general, and much easier, question-is in violation of our duty to proceed cautiously when erecting barriers between us and the truth.

II. To say that the Court devotes the bulk of its opinion to the much easier question of psychotherapist-patient privilege is not to say that its answer to that question is convincing. At bottom, the Court's decision to recognize such a privilege is based on its view that "successful [psychotherapeutic] treatment" serves "important private interests" (namely those of patients undergoing psychotherapy) as well as the "public good" of "[t]he mental health of our citizenry." I have no quarrel with these premises. Effective psychotherapy undoubtedly is beneficial to individuals with mental problems, and surely serves some larger social interest in maintaining a mentally stable society. But merely mentioning these values does not answer the critical question: are they of such importance, and is the contribution of psychotherapy to them so distinctive, and is the application of normal evidentiary rules so destructive to psychotherapy, as to justify making our federal courts occasional instruments of injustice? On that central question I find the Court's analysis insufficiently convincing to satisfy the high standard we have set for rules that "are in derogation of the search for truth."[54]

When is it, one must wonder, that the psychotherapist came to play such an indispensable role in the maintenance of the citizenry's mental health? For most of history, men and women have worked out their difficulties by talking to, inter alios, parents, siblings, best friends and bartenders-none of whom was awarded a privilege against testifying in court. Ask the average citizen: Would your mental health be more significantly impaired by preventing you from seeing a psychotherapist, or by preventing you from getting advice from your mom? I have little doubt what the answer would be. Yet there is no mother-child privilege.

How likely is it that a person will be deterred from seeking psychological counseling, or from being completely truthful in the course of such counseling, because of fear of later disclosure in litigation? And even more pertinent to today's decision, to what extent will the evidentiary privilege reduce that deterrent? The Court does not try to answer the first of these questions; and it cannot possibly have any notion of what the answer is to the second, since that depends entirely upon the scope of the privilege, which the Court amazingly finds it "neither necessary nor feasible to delineate," ante, at 16. If, for example, the psychotherapist can give the patient no more assurance than "A court will not be able to make me disclose what you tell me, unless you tell me about a harmful act," I doubt whether there would be much benefit from the privilege at all. That is not a fanciful example, at least with respect to extension of the psychotherapist privilege to social workers.[55]

Even where it is certain that absence of the psychotherapist privilege will inhibit disclosure of the information, it is not clear to me that that is an unacceptable state of affairs. Let us assume the very worst in the circumstances of the present case: that to be truthful about what was troubling her, the police officer who sought counseling would have to confess that she shot without reason, and wounded an innocent

---

54 Nixon, 418 U.S., at 710
55 See Del. Code Ann., Tit. 24, Section(s) 3913(2) (1987); Idaho Code Section(s) 54-3213(2) (1994)

man. If (again to assume the worst) such an act constituted the crime of negligent wounding under Illinois law, the officer would of course have the absolute right not to admit that she shot without reason in criminal court. But I see no reason why she should be enabled both not to admit it in criminal court (as a good citizen should), and to get the benefits of psychotherapy by admitting it to a therapist who cannot tell anyone else. And even less reason why she should be enabled to deny her guilt in the criminal trial-or in a civil trial for negligence-while yet obtaining the benefits of psychotherapy by confessing guilt to a social worker who cannot testify. It seems to me entirely fair to say that if she wishes the benefits of telling the truth she must also accept the adverse consequences. To be sure, in most cases the statements to the psychotherapist will be only marginally relevant, and one of the purposes of the privilege (though not one relied upon by the Court) may be simply to spare patients needless intrusion upon their privacy, and to spare psychotherapists needless expenditure of their time in deposition and trial. But surely this can be achieved by means short of excluding even evidence that is of the most direct and conclusive effect.

The Court confidently asserts that not much truth-finding capacity would be destroyed by the privilege anyway, since "[w]ithout a privilege, much of the desirable evidence to which litigants such as petitioner seek access . . . is unlikely to come into being." If that is so, how come psychotherapy got to be a thriving practice before the "psychotherapist privilege" was invented? Were the patients paying money to lie to their analysts all those years? Of course the evidence-generating effect of the privilege (if any) depends entirely upon its scope, which the Court steadfastly declines to consider. And even if one assumes that scope to be the broadest possible, is it really true that most, or even many, of those who seek psychological counseling have the worry of litigation in the back of their minds? I doubt that, and the Court provides no evidence to support it.

The Court suggests one last policy justification: since psychotherapist privilege statutes exist in all the States, the failure to recognize a privilege in federal courts "would frustrate the purposes of the state legislation that was enacted to foster these confidential communications." This is a novel argument indeed. A sort of inverse pre-emption: the truth-seeking functions of federal courts must be adjusted so as not to conflict with the policies of the States. This reasoning cannot be squared with Gillock, which declined to recognize an evidentiary privilege for Tennessee legislators in federal prosecutions, even though the Tennessee Constitution guaranteed it in state criminal proceedings.[56] Moreover, since, as I shall discuss, state policies regarding the psychotherapist privilege vary considerably from State to State, no uniform federal policy can possibly honor most of them. If furtherance of state policies is the name of the game, rules of privilege in federal courts should vary from State to State, a la Erie.

The Court's failure to put forward a convincing justification of its own could perhaps be excused if it were relying upon the unanimous conclusion of state courts in the reasoned development of their common law. It cannot do that, since no State has such a privilege apart from legislation.[57] What it relies upon, instead, is "the fact

---

56   Gillock, 445 U.S., at 368

57   The Court observes: "In 1972 the members of the Judicial Conference Advisory Committee noted that the common law `had indicated a disposition to recognize a psychotherapist-patient privilege when legislatures began moving into the field.' Proposed Rules, 56 F. R. D., at 242 (citation omitted)." Ante, at 12. The sole support the Committee invoked was a student Note entitled Confidential Communications to a Psychotherapist: A New Testimonial Privilege, 47 Nw. U. L. Rev. 384 (1952). That source, in turn, cites (and discusses) a single case recognizing a

that all 50 States and the District of Columbia have 1) enacted into law 2) some form of psychotherapist privilege." Let us consider both the verb and its object: The fact 1: that all 50 States have enacted this privilege argues not for, but against, our adopting the privilege judicially. At best it suggests that the matter has been found not to lend itself to judicial treatment-perhaps because the pros and cons of adopting the privilege, or of giving it one or another shape, are not that clear; or perhaps because the rapidly evolving uses of psychotherapy demand a flexibility that only legislation can provide. At worst it suggests that the privilege commends itself only to decision making bodies in which reason is tempered, so to speak, by political pressure from organized interest groups (such as psychologists and social workers), and decision making bodies that are not overwhelmingly concerned (as courts of law are and should be) with justice.

And the phrase 2: "some form of psychotherapist privilege" covers a multitude of difficulties. The Court concedes that there is "divergence among the States concerning the types of therapy relationships protected and the exceptions recognized."[58] To rest a newly announced federal common-law psychotherapist privilege, assertable from this day forward in all federal courts, upon "the States' *unanimous judgment* that some form of psychotherapist privilege is appropriate," *ibid.* (emphasis added), is rather like announcing a new, immediately applicable, federal common law of torts, based upon the States' "unanimous judgment" that some form of tort law is appropriate. In the one case as in the other, the state laws vary to such a degree that the parties and lower federal judges confronted by the new "common law" have barely a clue as to what its content might be.

III. Turning from the general question that was not involved in this case to

common-law psychotherapist privilege: the unpublished opinion of a judge of the Circuit Court of Cook County, Illinois, Binder v. Ruvell, No. 52-C-2535 (June 24, 1952)-which, in turn, cites no other cases. I doubt whether the Court's failure to provide more substantial support for its assertion stems from want of trying. Respondents and all of their amici pointed us to only four other state-court decisions supposedly adopting a common-law psychotherapist privilege. See Brief for the American Psychiatric Association et al. as Amici Curiae 8, n. 5; Brief for the American Psychoanalytic Association et al. as Amici Curiae 15-16; Brief for the American Psychological Association as Amicus Curiae 8. It is not surprising that the Court thinks it not worth the trouble to cite them: (1) In In re "B", 482 Pa. 471, 394 A. 2d 419 (1978), the opinions of four of the seven Justices explicitly rejected a nonstatutory privilege; and the two Justices who did recognize one recognized, not a common-law privilege, but rather (mirabile dictu) a privilege "constitutionally based," "emanat[ing]" from the penumbras of the various guarantees of the Bill of Rights, . . . as well as from the guarantees of the Constitution of this Commonwealth." *Id.,* at 484, 394 A. 2d, at 425. (2) Allred v. State, 554 P. 2d 411 (Alaska 1976), held that no privilege was available in the case before the court, so what it says about the existence of a common-law privilege is the purest dictum. (3) Falcon v. Alaska Pub. Offices Comm'n, 570 P. 2d 469 (1977), a later Alaska Supreme Court case, proves the last statement. It rejected the claim by a physician that he did not have to disclose the names of his patients, even though some of the physician's practice consisted of psychotherapy; it made no mention of Allred's dictum that there was a common-law psychiatrist-patient privilege (though if that existed it would seem relevant), and cited Allred only for the proposition that there was no statutory privilege, id., at 473, n. 12. And finally, (4) State v. Evans, 104 Ariz. 434, 454 P. 2d 976 (1969), created a limited privilege, applicable to court-ordered examinations to determine competency to stand trial, which tracked a privilege that had been legislatively created after the defendant's examination.

In light of this dearth of case support-from all the courts of 50 States, down to the county-court level-it seems to me the Court's assertion should be revised to read: "The common law had indicated scant disposition to recognize a psychotherapist-patient privilege when (or even after) legislatures began moving into the field."

58 Ante, at 12, n. 13

the specific one that is: The Court's conclusion that a social-worker psychotherapeutic privilege deserves recognition is even less persuasive. In approaching this question, the fact that five of the state legislatures that have seen fit to enact "some form" of psychotherapist privilege have elected not to extend any form of privilege to social workers,[59] ought to give one pause. So should the fact that the Judicial Conference Advisory Committee was similarly discriminating in its conferral of the proposed Rule 504 privilege, see supra. The Court, however, has "no hesitation in concluding . . . that the federal privilege should also extend" to social workers, ante, at 13-and goes on to prove that by polishing off the reasoned analysis with a topic sentence and two sentences of discussion, as follows (omitting citations and non-germane footnote):

> *"The reasons for recognizing a privilege for treatment by psychiatrists and psychologists apply with equal force to treatment by a clinical social worker such as Karen Beyer. Today, social workers provide a significant amount of mental health treatment. Their clients often include the poor and those of modest means who could not afford the assistance of a psychiatrist or psychologist, but whose counseling sessions serve the same public goals."[60]*

So much for the rule that privileges are to be narrowly construed.

Of course this brief analysis-like the earlier, more extensive, discussion of the general psychotherapist privilege-contains no explanation of why the psychotherapy provided by social workers is a public good of such transcendent importance as to be purchased at the price of occasional injustice. Moreover, it considers only the respects in which social workers providing therapeutic services are similar to licensed psychiatrists and psychologists; not a word about the respects in which they are different. A licensed psychiatrist or psychologist is an expert in psychotherapy-and that may suffice (though I think it not so clear that this Court should make the judgment) to justify the use of extraordinary means to encourage counseling with him, as opposed to counseling with one's rabbi, minister, family or friends. One must presume that a social worker does not bring this greatly heightened degree of skill to bear, which is alone a reason for not encouraging that consultation as generously. Does a social worker bring to bear at least a significantly heightened degree of skill-more than a minister or rabbi, for example? I have no idea, and neither does the Court. The social worker in the present case, Karen Beyer, was a "licensed clinical social worker" in Illinois, a job title whose training requirements consist of "master's degree in social work from an approved program," and "3,000 hours of satisfactory, supervised clinical professional experience."[61] It is not clear that the degree in social work requires any training in psychotherapy. The "clinical professional experience" apparently will impart some such training, but only of the vaguest sort, judging from the Illinois Code's definition of "[c]linical social work practice," viz., "the providing of mental health services for the evaluation, treatment, and prevention of mental and emotional disorders in individuals, families and groups based on knowledge and theory of psychosocial development, behavior, psychopathology, unconscious motivation, interpersonal relationships, and environmental stress."[62] But the rule the Court announces today-like the Illinois evidentiary privilege which

59 see ante, at 15, n. 17
60 Ante, at 13-14
61 Ill. Comp. Stat., ch. 225, Section(s) 20/9 (1994)
62 Ch. 225, Section(s) 20/3(5)

that rule purports to respect[63] -is not limited to "licensed clinical social workers," but includes all "licensed social workers." "Licensed social workers" may also provide "mental health services" as described in Section(s) 20/3(5), so long as it is done under supervision of a licensed clinical social worker. And the training requirement for a "licensed social worker" consists of either (a) "a degree from a graduate program of social work" approved by the State, or (b) "a degree in social work from an undergraduate program" approved by the State, plus "3 years of supervised professional experience."[64] With due respect, it does not seem to me that any of this training is comparable in its rigor (or indeed in the precision of its subject) to the training of the other experts (lawyers) to whom this Court has accorded a privilege, or even of the experts (psychiatrists and psychologists) to whom the Advisory Committee and this Court proposed extension of a privilege in 1972. Of course these are only Illinois' requirements for "social workers." Those of other States, for all we know, may be even less demanding. Indeed, I am not even sure there is a nationally accepted definition of "social worker," as there is of psychiatrist and psychologist. It seems to me quite irresponsible to extend the so-called "psychotherapist privilege" to all licensed social workers, nationwide, without exploring these issues.

Another critical distinction between psychiatrists and psychologists, on the one hand, and social workers, on the other, is that the former professionals, in their consultations with patients, do nothing but psychotherapy. Social workers, on the other hand, interview people for a multitude of reasons. The Illinois definition of "[l]icensed social worker," for example, is as follows:

"Licensed social worker" means a person who holds a license authorizing the practice of social work, which includes social services to individuals, groups or communities in any one or more of the fields of social casework, social group work, community organization for social welfare, social work research, social welfare administration or social work education."[65]

Thus, in applying the "social worker" variant of the "psychotherapist" privilege, it will be necessary to determine whether the information provided to the social worker was provided to him in his capacity as a psychotherapist, or in his capacity as an administrator of social welfare, a community organizer, etc. Worse still, if the privilege is to have its desired effect (and is not to mislead the client), it will presumably be necessary for the social caseworker to advise, as the conversation with his welfare client proceeds, which portions are privileged and which are not.

Having concluded its three sentences of reasoned analysis, the Court then invokes, as it did when considering the psychotherapist privilege, the "experience" of the States-once again an experience I consider irrelevant (if not counter-indicative) because it consists entirely of legislation rather than common-law decision. It says

---

63 Ch. 225, Section(s) 20/16. Section 20/16 is the provision of the Illinois Statutes cited by the Court to show that Illinois has "explicitly extend[ed] a testimonial privilege to licensed social workers." Ante, at 15, and n. 17. The Court elsewhere observes that respondent's communications to Beyer would have been privileged in state court under another provision of the Illinois Statutes, the Mental Health and Developmental Disabilities Confidentiality Act, Ill. Comp. Stat., ch. 740, Section(s) 110/10 (1994). Ante, at 14, n. 15. But the privilege conferred by Section(s) 110/10 extends to an even more ill-defined class: not only to licensed social workers, but to all social workers, to nurses, and indeed to "any other person not prohibited by law from providing [mental health or developmental disabilities] services or from holding himself out as a therapist if the recipient reasonably believes that such person is permitted to do so." Ch. 740, Section(s) 110/2.
64 Ch. 225, Section(s) 20/9A
65 Ch. 225, Section(s) 20/3(9)

that "the vast majority of States explicitly extend a testimonial privilege to licensed social workers."[66] There are two elements of this impressive statistic, however, that the Court does not reveal.

First-and utterly conclusive of the irrelevance of this supposed consensus to the question before us-the majority of the States that accord a privilege to social workers do not do so as a subpart of a "psychotherapist" privilege. The privilege applies to all confidences imparted to social workers, and not just those provided in the course of psychotherapy.[67] In Oklahoma, for example, the social-worker-privilege statute prohibits a licensed social worker from disclosing, or being compelled to disclose, "any information acquired from persons consulting the licensed social worker in his or her professional capacity."[68] The social worker's "professional capacity" is expansive, for the "practice of social work" in Oklahoma is defined as:

> "[T]he professional activity of helping individuals, groups, or communities enhance or restore their capacity for physical, social and economic functioning and the professional application of social work values, principles and techniques in areas such as clinical social work, social service administration, social planning, social work consultation and social work research to one or more of the following ends: Helping people obtain tangible services; counseling with individuals families and groups; helping communities or groups provide or improve social and health services; and participating in relevant social action. The practice of social work requires knowledge of human development and behavior; of social economic and cultural institutions and forces; and of the interaction of all of these factors. Social work practice includes the teaching of relevant subject matter and of conducting research into problems of human behavior and conflict."[69]

Thus, in Oklahoma, as in most other States having a social-worker privilege, it is not a subpart or even a derivative of the psychotherapist privilege, but rather a piece of special legislation similar to that achieved by many other groups, from accountants[70] to private detectives.[71]. These social-worker statutes give no support,

66 Ante, at 15
67 See Ariz. Rev. Stat. Ann. Section(s) 32-3283 (1992); Ark. Code Ann. Section(s) 17-46-107 (1995); Del. Code Ann., Tit. 24, Section(s) 3913 (1987); Idaho Code Section(s) 54-3213 (1994); Ind. Code Section(s) 25-23.6-6-1 (1993); Iowa Code Section(s) 154C.5 and Section(s) 622.10 (1987); Kan. Stat. Ann. Section(s) 65-6315 (Supp. 1990); Me. Rev. Stat. Ann., Tit. 32, Section(s) 7005 (1988); Mass. Gen. Laws Section(s) 112:135A (1994); Mich. Comp. Laws Ann. Section(s) 339.1610 (1992); Miss. Code Ann. Section(s) 73-53-29 (1995); Mo. Rev. Stat. Section(s) 337.636 (1994); Mont. Code Ann. Section(s) 37-22-401 (1995); Neb. Rev. Stat. Section(s) 71-1,335 (Supp. 1994); N. J. Stat. Ann. Section(s) 45:15BB-13 (1995); N. M. Stat. Ann. Section(s) 61-31-24 (1993); N. Y. Civ. Prac. Section(s) 4508 (McKinney 1992); N. C. Gen. Stat. Section(s) 8-53.7 (1986); Ohio Rev. Code Ann. Section(s) 2317.02(G)(1) (1995); Okla. Stat., Tit. 59 Section(s) 1261.6 (1991); Ore. Rev. Stat. Section(s) 40.250 (1991); S. D. Codified Laws Section(s) 36-26-30 (1994); Tenn. Code Ann. Section(s) 63-23-107 (1990); Wash. Rev. Code Section(s) 18.19.180 (1994); W. Va. Code Section(s) 30-30-12 (1993); Wyo. Stat. Section(s) 33-38-109 (Supp. 1995).
68 (with certain exceptions to be discussed infra). Okla. Stat., Tit. 59, Section(s) 1261.6 (1991) (emphasis added)
69 Tit. 59, Section(s) 1250.1(2) (1991)
70   see, e.g., Miss. Code Ann. Section(s) 73-33-16(2) (1995) (certified public accountant "shall not be required by any court of this state to disclose, and shall not voluntarily disclose" client information)
71 see, e.g., Mich. Comp. Laws Section(s) 338.840 (1979) ("Any communications . . . furnished by a professional man or client to a [licensed private detective], or any information secured in con-

therefore, to the theory (importance of psychotherapy) upon which the Court rests its disposition.

Second, the Court does not reveal the enormous degree of disagreement among the States as to the scope of the privilege.[72] It concedes that the laws of four States are subject to such gaping exceptions that they are "'little better than no privilege at all,'" so that they should more appropriately be categorized with the five States whose laws contradict the action taken today. I would add another State to those whose privilege is illusory.[73] In adopting any sort of a social worker privilege, then, the Court can at most claim that it is following the legislative "experience" of 40 States, and contradicting the "experience" of 10.

But turning to those States that do have an appreciable privilege of some sort, the diversity is vast. In Illinois and Wisconsin, the social-worker privilege does not apply when the confidential information pertains to homicide,[74] and in the District of Columbia when it pertains to any crime "inflicting injuries" upon persons.[75] In Missouri, the privilege is suspended as to information that pertains to a criminal act,[76] and in Texas when the information is sought in any criminal prosecution.[77] In Kansas and Oklahoma, the privilege yields when the information pertains to "violations of any law"[78]; in Indiana, when it reveals a "serious harmful act"[79]; and in Delaware and Idaho, when it pertains to any "harmful act."[80] In Oregon, a state-employed social worker like Karen Beyer loses the privilege where her supervisor determines that her testimony "is necessary in the performance of the duty of the social worker as a public employee."[81] In South Carolina, a social worker is forced to disclose confidences "when required by statutory law or by court order for good cause shown to the extent that the patient's care and treatment or the nature and extent of his mental illness or emotional condition are reasonably at issue in a proceeding."[82] The majority of social-worker-privilege States declare the privilege inapplicable to information relating to child abuse.[83] And the States that do not fall

---

nection with an assignment for a client, shall be deemed privileged with the same authority and dignity as are other privileged communications recognized by the courts of this state")

72 These ever-multiplying evidentiary-privilege statutes, which the Court today emulates, recall us to the original meaning of the word "privilege." It is a composite derived from the Latin words "privus" and "lex": private law.

73 See Wash. Rev. Code Section(s) 18.19.180 (1994) (disclosure of information required "[i]n response to a subpoena from a court of law")

74 see Ill. Comp. Stat., ch. 740, Section(s) 110/10(a)(9) (1994); Wis. Stat. Section(s) 905.04(4)(d) (1993-1994)

75 see D. C. Code Section(s) 14-307(a)(1) (1995)

76 see Mo. Rev. Stat. Section(s) 337.636(2) (1994)

77 compare Tex. Rule Civ. Evid. 510(d) with Tex. Rule Crim. Evid. 501 et seq

78 see Kan. Stat. Ann. Section(s) 65-6315(a)(2) (Supp. 1990); Okla. Stat., Tit. 59, Section(s) 1261.6(2) (1991)

79 see Ind. Code Ann. Section(s) 25-23.6-6-1(2) (1995)

80 see Del. Code Ann., Tit. 24, Section(s) 3913(2) (1987); Idaho Code Section(s) 54-3213(2) (1994)

81 See Ore. Rev. Stat. Section(s) 40.250(5) (1991)

82 See S. C. Code Ann. Section(s) 19-11-95(D)(1) (Supp. 1995)

83 See, e.g., Ariz. Rev. Stat. Ann. Section(s) 32-3283 (1992); Ark. Code Ann. Section(s) 17-46-107(3) (1995); Cal. Evid. Code Ann. Section(s) 1027 (West 1995); Colo. Rev. Stat. Section(s) 19-3-304 (Supp. 1995); Del. Rule Evid. 503(d)(4); Ga. Code Ann. Section(s) Code Evid. Ann., Art. 510(B)(2)(k) (West 1995); Md. Cts. & Jud. Proc. Code Ann. Section(s) 9-121(e)(4) (1995); Mass. Gen. Laws, Section(s) 119:51A (1994); Mich. Comp. Laws Ann. Section(s) 722.623 (1992 Supp. Pamph.); Minn. Stat. Section(s) 595.02.2(a) (1988); Miss. Code Ann. Section(s) 73-53-29(e) (1995); Mont. Code Ann. Section(s) 37-22-401(3) (1995); Neb. Rev. Stat. Section(s) 28-711 (1995); N. M. Stat. Ann. 4508(a)(3) (McKinney 1992); Ohio Rev. Code Ann. Section(s) 2317.02(G)(1)(a) (1995); Ore. Rev. Stat. Section(s) 40.250(4) (1991); R. I. Gen. Laws Section(s)

into any of the above categories provide exceptions for commitment proceedings, for proceedings in which the patient relies on his mental or emotional condition as an element of his claim or defense, or for communications made in the course of a court-ordered examination of the mental or emotional condition of the patient.[84]

Thus, although the Court is technically correct that "the vast majority of States explicitly extend a testimonial privilege to licensed social workers," that uniformity exists only at the most superficial level. No State has adopted the privilege without restriction; the nature of the restrictions varies enormously from jurisdiction to jurisdiction; and 10 States, I reiterate, effectively reject the privilege entirely. It is fair to say that there is scant national consensus even as to the propriety of a social-worker psychotherapist privilege, and none whatever as to its appropriate scope. In other words, the state laws to which the Court appeals for support demonstrate most convincingly that adoption of a social-worker psychotherapist privilege is a job for Congress.

The question before us today is not whether there should be an evidentiary privilege for social workers providing therapeutic services. Perhaps there should. But the question before us is whether (1) the need for that privilege is so clear, and (2) the desirable contours of that privilege are so evident, that it is appropriate for this Court to craft it in common-law fashion, under Rule 501. Even if we were writing on a clean slate, I think the answer to that question would be clear. But given our extensive precedent to the effect that new privileges "in derogation of the search for truth" "are not lightly created,"[85] the answer the Court gives today is inexplicable.

In its consideration of this case, the Court was the beneficiary of no fewer than 14 amicus briefs supporting respondents, most of which came from such organizations as the American Psychiatric Association, the American Psychoanalytic Association, the American Association of State Social Work Boards, the Employee Assistance Professionals Association, Inc., the American Counseling Association, and the National Association of Social Workers. Not a single amicus brief was filed in support of petitioner. That is no surprise. There is no self-interested organization out there devoted to pursuit of the truth in the federal courts. The expectation is, however, that this Court will have that interest prominently, indeed, primarily in mind. Today we have failed that expectation, and that responsibility. It is no small matter to say that, in some cases, our federal courts will be the tools of injustice rather than unearth the truth where it is available to be found. The common law has identified a few instances where that is tolerable. Perhaps Congress may conclude that it is also tolerable for the purpose of encouraging psychotherapy by social workers. But that conclusion assuredly does not burst upon the mind with such clarity that a judgment in favor of suppressing the truth ought to be pronounced by this honorable Court. I respectfully dissent.

5-37.3-4(b)(4) (1995); S. D. Codified Laws Section(s) 36-26-30(3) (1994); Tenn. Code Ann. Section(s) 63-23-107(b) (1990); Vt. Rule Evid. 503(d)(5); W. Va. Code Section(s) 30-30-12(a)(4) (1993); Wyo. Stat. Section(s) 14-3-205 (1994).

84 See, e.g., Fla. Stat. Section(s) 90.503(4) (Supp. 1992) (all three exceptions); Ky. Rule Evid. 507(c) (all three); Nev. Rev. Stat. Section(s) 49.245 (1993) (all three); Utah Rule Evid. 506(d) (all three); Conn. Gen. Stat. Section(s) 52-146q(c)(1) (1995) (commitment proceedings and proceedings in which patient's mental condition at issue); Iowa Code Section(s) 622.10 (1987) (proceedings in which patient's mental condition at issue).

85 United States v. Nixon, 418 U.S., at 710

DUTY TO WARN/PROTECT

(THAPAR VS. ZEZULKA)[1]

BACKGROUND

The primary issue in this case is whether a mental-health professional can be liable in negligence for failing to warn the appropriate third parties when a patient makes specific threats of harm toward a readily identifiable person. In reversing the trial court's summary judgment, the court of appeals recognized such a cause of action.[2] Because the Legislature has established a policy against such a common-law cause of action, we refrain from imposing on mental-health professionals a duty to warn third parties of a patient's threats. Accordingly, we reverse the court of appeals' judgment and render judgment that Zezulka take nothing.

Because this is an appeal from summary judgment, we take as true evidence favorable to Lyndall Zezulka, the nonmovant.[3] Freddy Ray Lilly had a history of mental-health problems and psychiatric treatment. Dr. Renu K. Thapar, a psychiatrist, first treated Lilly in 1985, when Lilly was brought to Southwest Memorial Hospital's emergency room. Thapar diagnosed Lilly as suffering from moderate to severe post-traumatic stress disorder, alcohol abuse, and paranoid and delusional beliefs concerning his stepfather, Henry Zezulka, and people of certain ethnic backgrounds. Thapar treated Lilly with a combination of psychotherapy and drug therapy over the next three years.

For the majority of their relationship, Thapar treated Lilly on an outpatient basis. But on at least six occasions Lilly was admitted to Southwest Memorial Hospital, or another facility, in response to urgent treatment needs.

Often the urgency involved Lilly's problems in maintaining amicable relationships with those with whom he lived. Lilly was also admitted on one occasion after threatening to kill himself. In August 1988, Lilly agreed to be admitted to Southwest Memorial Hospital. Thapar's notes from August 23, 1988, state that Lilly "feels like killing" Henry Zezulka. These records also state, however, that Lilly "has decided

---

1   Thapar vs. Zezulka, 994 S.W.2d 635 (Tex. 1999)
2   961 S.W.2d 506.
3   See Science Spectrum, Inc. v. Martinez, 941 S.W.2d 910, 911 (Tex. 1997).

not to do it but that is how he feels." After hospitalization and treatment for seven days, Lilly was discharged. Within a month Lilly shot and killed Henry Zezulka.

Despite the fact that Lilly's treatment records indicate that he sometimes felt homicidal, Thapar never warned any family member or any law enforcement agency of Lilly's threats against his stepfather. Nor did Thapar inform any family member or any law enforcement agency of Lilly's discharge from Southwest Memorial Hospital.

Lyndall Zezulka, Henry's wife and Lilly's mother, sued Thapar for negligence resulting in her husband's wrongful death. Zezulka alleged that Thapar was negligent in diagnosing and treating Lilly and negligent in failing to warn of Lilly's threats toward Henry Zezulka. It is undisputed that Thapar had no physician-patient relationship with either Lyndall or Henry Zezulka. Based on this fact, Thapar moved for summary judgment on the ground that Zezulka had not stated a claim for medical negligence because Thapar owed no duty to Zezulka in the absence of a doctor-patient relationship. The trial court overruled Thapar's motion.

Thapar filed a motion for rehearing of her summary judgment motion based largely on our decision in Bird v. W.C.W, in which we held that no duty runs from a psychologist to a third party to not negligently misdiagnose a patient's condition.[4] In light of Bird, the trial court reconsidered and granted summary judgment for Thapar. Zezulka appealed.

After concluding that Zezulka was not stopped from complaining about the trial court's judgment by her agreement to resolve the duty question through summary judgment, a conclusion with which we agree, the court of appeals reversed the trial court's judgment.[5] The court of appeals held that the no-duty ground asserted in Thapar's motion for summary judgment was not a defense to the cause of action pleaded by Zezulka.[6]

To decide this case we must determine the duties a mental-health professional owes to a nonpatient third party. Zezulka stated her claims against Thapar in negligence. Liability in negligence is premised on duty, a breach of which proximately causes injuries, and damages resulting from that breach.[7] Whether a legal duty exists is a threshold question of law for the court to decide from the facts surrounding the occurrence in question.[8] If there is no duty, there cannot be negligence liability.[9]

In her second amended petition Zezulka lists seventeen particulars by which she alleges Thapar was negligent. But each allegation is based on one of two proposed underlying duties: *(1) a duty to not negligently diagnose or treat a patient that runs from a psychiatrist to nonpatient third parties;* or *(2) a duty to warn third parties of a patient's threats.* In her motion for summary judgment Thapar asserted that she owed Zezulka no duty. Thus, we must determine if Thapar owed Zezulka either of these proposed duties.

NEGLIGENT DIAGNOSIS AND TREATMENT

First, we consider Zezulka's allegations that Thapar was negligent in her

---

4   868 S.W.2d 767 (Tex. 1994).
5   See 961 S.W.2d at 510-11.
6   See id. at 511.
7   See Bird, 868 S.W.2d at 769 (citing Greater Houston Transp. Co. v. Phillips, 801 S.W.2d 523, 525 (Tex. 1990)).
8   See St. John v. Pope, 901 S.W.2d 420, 424 (Tex. 1995); Bird, 868 S.W.2d at 769.
9   See Van Horn v. Chambers, 970 S.W.2d 542, 544 (Tex. 1998); St. John, 901 S.W.2d at 424; Graff v. Beard, 858 S.W.2d 918, 919 (Tex. 1993).

diagnosis and treatment of Lilly's psychiatric problems. Among other claims, Zezulka alleged that Thapar was negligent in releasing Lilly from the hospital in August 1988, in failing to take steps to have Lilly involuntarily committed, and in failing to monitor Lilly after his release to ensure that he was taking his medication. All of these claims are based on Thapar's medical diagnosis of Lilly's condition, which dictated the treatment Lilly should have received and the corresponding actions Thapar should have taken.[10] The underlying duty question here is whether the absence of a doctor-patient relationship precludes Zezulka from maintaining medical negligence claims against Thapar based on her diagnosis and treatment of Lilly.

In Bird we held that no duty runs from a psychologist to a third party to not negligently misdiagnose a patient's condition.[11] Since Bird, we have had occasion to consider several permutations of this same duty question.[12] Bird and our post-Bird writings answer definitively the first duty question presented by the facts before us: Thapar owes no duty to Zezulka, a third party nonpatient, for negligent misdiagnosis or negligent treatment of Lilly.[13] Accordingly, Thapar was entitled to summary judgment on all of the claims premised on Zezulka's first duty theory.

FAILURE TO WARN

Second, we consider Zezulka's allegations that Thapar was negligent for failing to warn either the Zezulkas or law enforcement personnel of Lilly's threats. We are not faced here with the question of whether a doctor owes a duty to third parties to warn a patient of risks from treatment which may endanger third parties.[14] Instead, we are asked whether a mental-health professional owes a duty to directly warn third parties of a patient's threats.

The California Supreme Court first recognized a mental-health professional's duty to warn third parties of a patient's threats in the seminal case Tarasoff v. Regents of University of California.[15] The court of appeals here cited Tarasoff in recognizing a cause of action for Thapar's failure to warn of her patient's threats.[16] But we have never recognized the only underlying duty upon which such a cause of action could be based -- a mental-health professional's duty to warn third parties of a

10 See, e.g., Van Horn, 970 S.W.2d at 545.

11 Bird, 868 S.W.2d at 769-70 (citing Vineyard v. Kraft, 828 S.W.2d 248, 251 (Tex. App._Houston [14th Dist.] 1992, writ denied); Wilson v. Winsett, 828 S.W.2d 231, 232-33 (Tex. App._Amarillo 1992, writ denied); Fought v. Solce, 821 S.W.2d 218, 220 (Tex. App._Houston [1st Dist.] 1991, writ denied); Dominguez v. Kelly, 786 S.W.2d 749 (Tex. App._El Paso 1990, writ denied)).

12 See Van Horn, 970 S.W.2d at 543; Edinburg Hosp. Auth. v. Trevino, 941 S.W.2d 76, 77-79 (Tex. 1997); Krishnan v. Sepulveda, 916 S.W.2d 478, 482 (Tex. 1995); see also Praesel v. Johnson, 967 S.W.2d 391, 392 (Tex. 1998); Cathey v. Booth, 900 S.W.2d 339, 342 (Tex. 1995).

13 See Van Horn, 970 S.W.2d at 545; Trevino, 941 S.W.2d at 79; Krishnan, 916 S.W.2d at 482; Bird, 868 S.W.2d at 770.

14 See Gooden v. Tips, 651 S.W.2d 364, 365-66 (Tex. App._Tyler 1983, no writ) (holding doctor owed duty to third party to warn patient not to drive after prescribing the drug Quaalude to patient); see also Flynn v. Houston Emergicare, Inc., 869 S.W.2d 403, 405-06 (Tex. App._Houston [1st Dist.] 1994, writ denied) (holding doctor owed no duty to third party to warn patient not to drive after patient was treated for cocaine use because doctor did not create impairment that resulted in injury).

15 551 P.2d 334, 345-47 (Cal. 1976).

16 961 S.W.2d at 511 n.2. The court of appeals also cited four Texas cases that considered whether to adopt a Tarasoff duty but did not. See 916 S.W.2d at 511 n.2 (citing Limon v. Gonzaba, 940 S.W.2d 236, 238-41 (Tex. App._San Antonio 1997, writ denied); Kehler v. Eudaly, 933 S.W.2d 321, 329-32 (Tex. App._Fort Worth 1996, writ denied); Kerrville State Hosp. v. Clark, 900 S.W.2d 425, 435-36 (Tex. App._Austin 1995), rev'd on other grounds, 923 S.W.2d 582 (Tex. 1996);Williams v. Sun Valley Hosp., 723 S.W.2d 783, 785-86 (Tex. App._El Paso 1987, writ ref'd n.r.e.)).

patient's threats. Without considering the effect of differences in the development of California and Texas jurisprudence on the outcome of this issue, we decline to adopt a duty to warn now because the confidentiality statute governing mental-health professionals in Texas makes it unwise to recognize such common-law duty.

The Legislature has chosen to closely guard a patient's communications with a mental-health professional. In 1979, three years after Tarasoff issued, the Legislature enacted a statute governing the disclosure of communications during the course of mental-health treatment.[17] The statute classifies communications between mental-health "professional[s]" and their "patient[s]/client[s]" as confidential and prohibits mental-health professionals from disclosing them to third parties unless an exception applies.[18]

Zezulka complains that Thapar was negligent in not warning members of the Zezulka family about Lilly's threats. But a disclosure by Thapar to one of the Zezulkas would have violated the confidentiality statute because no exception in the statute provides for disclosure to third parties threatened by the patient.[19] We considered a similar situation in Santa Rosa Health Care Corp. v. Garcia,[20] in which we concluded there is no duty to disclose confidential information when disclosure would violate the confidentiality statute.[21] The same reasoning applies here. Under the applicable statute, Thapar was prohibited from warning one of his patient's potential victims and therefore had no duty to warn the Zezulka family of Lilly's threats.

Zezulka also complains that Thapar was negligent in not disclosing Lilly's threats to any law enforcement agency. There is an exception in the confidentiality statute that provides for disclosure to law enforcement personnel in certain circumstances.[22] The statute, however, permits these disclosures but does not require them:

(b) Exceptions to the privilege of confidentiality, in other than court proceedings, allowing disclosure of confidential information by a professional, exist only to the following:...

(2) to medical or law enforcement personnel where the professional determines that there is a probability of imminent physical injury by the patient/client to himself or to others, or where there is a probability of immediate mental or emotional injury to the patient/client....[23]

The term "allowing" in section 4(b), quoted above, makes clear that disclosure of confidential information under any of the statute's exceptions is permissive but not mandatory. Imposing a legal duty to warn third parties of patient's threats would conflict with the scheme adopted by the Legislature by making disclosure of such threats mandatory.

17 See Act of May 9, 1979, 66th Leg., R.S., ch. 239, 1979 Tex. Gen. Laws 512 (amended 1991) (current version at Tex. Health & Safety Code § 611.002 (1996)).
18 See § 2(a), 1979 Tex. Gen. Laws at 513.
19 See § 4, 1979 Tex. Gen. Laws at 514.
20 964 S.W.2d 940, 941 (Tex. 1998) (involving disclosure of HIV test under Tex. Rev. Civ. Stat. art. 4419b-1, § 9.03).
21 Id. at 944.
22 See § 4(b), 1979 Tex. Gen. Laws at 514.
23 See § 4, 1979 Tex. Gen. Laws at 514 (emphasis added). Current Tex. Health & Safety Code § 611.004(a)(2) adopts the same standard: (a) A professional may disclose confidential information only:... (2) to medical or law enforcement personnel if the professional determines that there is a probability of imminent physical injury by the patient to the patient or others or there is a probability of immediate mental or emotional injury to the patient...

We consider legislative enactments that evidence the adoption of a particular public policy significant in determining whether to recognize a new common-law duty.[24] For example, in recognizing the existence of a common-law duty to guard children from sexual abuse, we found persuasive the Legislature's strongly avowed policy to protect children from abuse.[25] The statute expressing this policy, however, makes the reporting of sexual abuse mandatory[26] and makes failure to report child abuse a crime.[27] Further, under the statute, those who report child abuse in good faith are immune from civil and criminal liability.[28] Thus, imposing a common law duty to report was consistent with the legislative scheme governing child abuse.

The same is not true here. The confidentiality statute here does not make disclosure of threats mandatory nor does it penalize mental-health professionals for not disclosing threats. And, perhaps most significantly, the statute does not shield mental-health professionals from civil liability for disclosing threats in good faith. On the contrary, mental-health professionals make disclosures at their peril.[29] Thus, if a common-law duty to warn is imposed, mental-health professionals face a Catch-22. They either disclose a confidential communication that later proves to be an idle threat and incur liability to the patient, or they fail to disclose a confidential communication that later proves to be a truthful threat and incur liability to the victim and the victim's family.

The confidentiality statute here evidences an intent to leave the decision of whether to disclose confidential information in the hands of the mental-health professional. In the past, we have declined to impose a common-law duty to disclose when disclosing confidential information by a physician has been made permissible by statute but not mandatory.[30] We have also declined to impose a common-law duty after determining that such a duty would conflict with the Legislature's policy and enactments concerning the employment-at-will doctrine.[31] Our analysis today is consistent with the approach in those cases.

Because of the Legislature's stated policy, we decline to impose a common law duty on mental-health professionals to warn third parties of their patient's threats. Accordingly, we conclude that Thapar was entitled to summary judgment because she owed no duty to Zezulka, a third-party nonpatient. We reverse the court of appeals' judgment and render judgment that Zezulka take nothing.

---

24 See Gibbs v. Jackson, ___ S.W.2d ___, ___ (Tex. 1999); Smith v. Merritt, 940 S.W.2d 602, 604-05 (Tex. 1997) (citing Graff, 858 S.W.2d at 919).
25 See Golden Spread Council, Inc. v. Akins, 926 S.W.2d 287, 291 (Tex. 1996).
26 Tex. Fam. Code § 261.101(a) states: "A person having cause to believe that a child's physical or mental health or welfare has been adversely affected by abuse or neglect by any person shall immediately make a report as provided by this subchapter."
27 See Tex. Fam. Code § 261.109.
28 See Tex. Fam. Code § 261.106.
29 See § 5, 1979 Tex. Gen. Laws at 514.
30 See Praesel, 967 S.W.2d at 396-98.
31 See Austin v. HealthTrust, Inc._The Hosp. Co., 967 S.W.2d 400, 403 (Tex. 1998); see also Winters v. Houston Chronicle Pub. Co., 795 S.W.2d 723, 724-25 (Tex. 1990).

DERIVED JUDICIAL IMMUNITY & DUTY TO REPORT

(B.K. vs. Cox)[1]

BACKGROUND

Appellant Barbara K., individually and as next friend of T.K., C.K., P.K., and N.K., filed this negligence suit against the independent executrix of the estate of Michael Dennis Cox and Baylor College of Medicine[2] based on their alleged failure to report suspected child abuse of her children that they allegedly discovered while performing psychological examinations ordered by a Harris County district court. The trial court granted appellees' motion for summary judgment based on derived judicial immunity. Although the claims Barbara raises are slightly different from those raised in Delcourt, we affirm because the case is controlled by the absolute immunity doctrine we discussed in Delcourt.[3] This doctrine includes both judicial immunity and derived judicial immunity.[4]

I. FACTUAL AND PROCEDURAL BACKGROUND

Barbara filed for divorce from her husband, Larry. The case was assigned to the 257th District Court. Initially Larry was allowed unsupervised visits with his children; however, at some point Barbara petitioned the court to suspend Larry's unsupervised contact with the children because she was concerned about possible sexual misconduct by Larry. In response to Barbara's concerns, the judge ordered Dr. Michael Cox of the Baylor College of Medicine to perform psychological evaluations and examinations of Barbara and Larry and their children. The court's order stated that Cox and Baylor were to act as an extension of the court in performing these evaluations and examinations:

It is ORDERED that Dr. Michael Cox, Baylor Pilot Program, Baylor College

1 B.K. v. COX, 116 S.W.3d 351 (Tex. App. Houston [14th Dist.] 2003)
2 They were not the only defendants, but they are the only defendants relevant to this appeal.
3 See Delcourt v. Silverman, 919 S.W.2d 777, 781-83 (Tex. App.-Houston [14th Dist.] 1996, writ denied).
4 See Dallas County v. Halsey, 87 S.W.3d 552, 554 (Tex.2002).

of Medicine, [sic] Department of Psychiatry, 1 Baylor Plaza, Houston, [sic] Texas 77030 ... is appointed as an extension of the Court as the evaluating psychologist for evaluation and examination of Larry ... Barbara ... and the children the subject of this suit. ...

It is ORDERED that all written reports prepared by Dr. Michael Cox setting out his findings, including results from all tests made, if any, diagnosis, conclusions and observations shall be submitted directly to the Court.

In an affidavit the judge of the 257th District Court filed in connection with this lawsuit, the judge testified as follows: (1) Baylor College of Medicine created the Baylor Pilot Program in cooperation with the Court to provide "lower-cost mental health evaluations"; (2) the Court and the Baylor Pilot Program intended to have Ph.D psychology interns at Baylor College of Medicine perform evaluations with Dr. Cox's oversight, with Dr. Cox and these interns functioning as an arm of the Court and under the Court's order; (3) the Court appointed Dr. Cox and the Baylor Pilot Program to assist it in investigating, evaluating, and assessing the mental and emotional condition, including allegations of sexual abuse, of this family; and (4) Dr. Cox and the employees, agents, or servants of Baylor College of Medicine involved in the evaluation of the family did so to assist the Court in the integral judicial process of investigating, evaluating, and assessing the family members' mental and emotional condition.

Dr. Cox assigned intern Suman Rao to help him evaluate Barbara, Larry, and the children. In the summer of 1998, Rao interviewed all members of the family. During these interviews, two of the children told Rao about events which led her to believe that Larry was behaving inappropriately with the children. Rao prepared a report to the judge recommending that Larry have no visits with T.K. and only supervised visitation with the other three children. However, Rao left Baylor suddenly, and the draft report was never sent to the court.

About eight months later, in March of 1999, Barbara notified Dr. Cox that at least two of her children had made outcries that Larry had sexually assaulted them. After interviewing the children, Dr. Cox made his first report to Children's Protective Services ("CPS") and told the court about the situation, recommending that Larry be ordered not to see the children until the matter was investigated. The court followed the recommendation, ordering Larry not to see the children. CPS investigated the reports and concluded that there was reason to believe that the sexual abuse had occurred.

Because of the long delay between the time Rao first became aware of Larry's inappropriate behavior and the time that Barbara informed the experts that Larry was abusing their children, Barbara sued the independent executrix of Dr. Cox's estate ("Cox Estate"), Baylor College of Medicine, Suman Rao, and Larry. She alleged that Dr. Cox and Baylor were negligent because they did not report Larry's suspected child abuse to CPS.[5] Barbara alleged that Rao told Dr. Cox in the summer of 1998 convincing evidence existed that Larry had committed various acts of sexual abuse against the children. Barbara alleged that Dr. Cox ordered Rao to call CPS, but that Rao left Baylor College of Medicine without contacting CPS. Barbara alleged that these acts by Cox and Baylor caused the children to continue to be subjected to their father's sexual abuse from the summer of 1998 through March

---

5   Barbara alleged that this failure to act violated sections 33.008 and 261.101 of the Texas Family Code.

of 1999. In her petition, she did not assert that the defendants knowingly failed to report any suspected child abuse, and she did not allege they violated any criminal statute.

The Cox Estate and Baylor moved for summary judgment, alleging that they were entitled to absolute immunity from suit because the conduct in issue occurred while they were functioning as an arm of the court. The trial court granted this motion and entered a final judgment.

II. Issues Presented for Review

On appeal, Barbara asserts the following issues for review:

(1) Did the trial court err in granting summary judgment based on judicial immunity?

(2) Is the failure to report suspected child abuse a judicial act?

(3) Is the statutory duty to report suspected child abuse mandatory or discretionary?

(4) If mandatory, are appellees entitled to judicial immunity as a matter of law such that they are exempt from their mandatory statutory and professional duties to report suspected child abuse?

(5) If discretionary, does a fact issue exist as to whether appellees acted reasonably and in good faith so as to defeat summary judgment?

(6 Does judicial immunity extend to criminal acts and omissions?

(7) Does the existence of statutory immunity (which does not apply to the failure to report suspected child abuse) preclude the application of judicial immunity?

III. Standard of Review

The trial court granted summary judgment based on the affirmative defense of derived judicial immunity. The summary judgment was proper only if the movants conclusively established each element of this defense.[6] In reviewing this summary judgment, we take as true all evidence favorable to Barbara and indulge every reasonable inference in her favor.

IV. Analysis

A. Did the Trial Court Err in Granting Summary Judgment Based on Derived Judicial Immunity?

1. Rao, Baylor, and Cox were entitled to derived judicial immunity.

Barbara's first issue is that Rao, Baylor, and Cox were not entitled to derived judicial immunity. She recognizes the significance of the court appointing Cox and Baylor and recognizes that at least some of what they did was "intimately associated with the judicial process." Thus, Barbara acknowledges that Texas protects non-judges who have been appointed by a court as an arm of the court when (1) their function is intimately associated with the judicial process, and (2) they exercise discretionary judgment like a judge.[7] This approach to immunity is called the

---

6   See Science Spectrum, Inc. v. Martinez, 941 S.W.2d 910, 911 (Tex.1997)
7   See Dallas County v. Halsey, 87 S.W.3d 552, 554 (Tex.2002)

functional approach.[8] But Barbara claims Cox and Baylor are not protected--even though appointed by the court to function as an arm of the court--because they strayed from their judicial function when they failed to report suspected child abuse.[9] This argument reveals a fundamental misunderstanding of the functional approach to absolute immunity.

Generally, once an individual is cloaked with derived judicial immunity because of a particular function being performed for a court, every action taken with regard to that function—whether good or bad, honest or dishonest, well-intentioned or not—is immune from suit. [10]Once applied to the function, the cloak of immunity covers all acts, both good and bad.[11] The whole either is protected or it is not. See id. at 554-55. So, here, if Cox and Baylor were entitled to derived judicial immunity for any part of their psychological evaluations, they were entitled to it for all parts.

We have already held that a psychiatrist appointed to evaluate members of a family was entitled to derived judicial immunity.[12] We concluded this for the following reason:

> When a court appoints a mental health professional to examine the child and the parents in a custody proceeding, the professional is acting as a fact finder for the court. The court relies on the professional to provide information essential to the decision-making process. Without the protection of absolute immunity, such professionals would be, at the very least, reluctant to accept these appointments. This would in turn inhibit judges from performing their duties.

In Delcourt,[13] to determine whether the court-appointed psychiatrist was entitled to immunity, we looked to affidavit testimony from the appointing judge and affidavit testimony from the psychiatrist. Here, we have the same type of testimony.[14] The trial judge testified by affidavit that "Dr. Cox, Dr. Rao, and the employees, agents, or servants of Baylor College of Medicine who aided them in their evaluation of [the family] did so for the purpose of assisting the Court in the integral judicial process of investigating, evaluating, and assessing the [family members'] mental and emotional condition pursuant to the Court's order." In short, Dr. Cox, Dr. Rao, and their colleagues were to help the trial judge perform a judicial function of evaluating this family in an effort to determine custody issues. The only other question to ask in determining if immunity attaches was if Rao, Cox, and Baylor were acting within the scope of this appointment when they allegedly neglected to report suspected child abuse. Rao's affidavit establishes that they were within the scope of the order

---

8 See id.; Delcourt v. Silverman, 919 S.W.2d 777, 781-83 (Tex.App.-Houston [14th Dist.] 1996, writ denied).

9 Barbara separates her argument into two parts, first that their failure to report was not a judicial act and second that Cox and Baylor do not receive immunity simply because they are "court appointed." We answer both of these claims in our discussion below.

10 Halsey, 87 S.W.3d at 554

11 See id. at 555 (stating that "as applied in Texas, the functional approach in applying derived judicial immunity focuses on the nature of the function performed, not the identity of the actor, and considers whether the court officer's conduct is like that of the delegating or appointing judge")

12 See Delcourt, 919 S.W.2d at 781-83

13 Id. at 783. In fact, Delcourt involved the very same judge and a similar order to the one we have in this case. See id. at 779, 781-83

14 We have no affidavit from Dr. Cox because he died between the time of the events in this case and the lawsuit.

because their acts—whether negligent or not—related to the family's evaluation.[15] Barbara did not controvert this evidence in the trial court. Therefore, the trial court did not err in holding that the Cox Estate and Baylor were immune from suit.

Thus, the Cox Estate's and Baylor's summary-judgment evidence conclusively proved that they were entitled to absolute immunity. We overrule issues one, two, and five.

2. POSSIBLE VIOLATION OF STATUTES IMPOSING CRIMINAL LIABILITY DOES NOT NEGATE DERIVED JUDICIAL IMMUNITY IN A SUIT BY A PRIVATE CITIZEN.

In spite of this evidence of immunity, Barbara claims that the doctrine of judicial immunity did not shield the Cox Estate and Baylor from suit because (1) Cox and Rao violated statutory duties—which impose criminal liability—by not reporting suspected child abuse, (2) the duty to report suspected child abuse is mandatory and not discretionary, and (3) the statutory immunity given in section 261.106 of the Texas Family Code overrides judicial immunity. As with her earlier assault on the doctrine of judicial immunity, these arguments misinterpret and misapply the doctrine.

Barbara's first issue, whether judicial immunity continues to protect court-appointed psychiatrists when they have violated a statute imposing criminal liability for a failure to act, is flawed because she applies a general rule—no judicial immunity from criminal liability—to a specific situation to which it does not apply—a suit brought by a private citizen.

The broadest rule that controls our decision was announced in Pruitt v. Turner in a dissenting opinion approved by the Texas Supreme Court.[16] There, the dissent announced the guiding rule:

> *"It was a settled principle at the very foundation of well-ordered jurisprudence that every judge, whether of a higher or lower court, in the exercise of the jurisdiction, conferred on him by law, had the right to decide according to his own free and unembarrassed convictions, uninfluenced by any apprehension of private prosecution."*[17]

For this case, the key point in this quote is that the judge is free from private prosecution. Therefore, in Pruitt, a litigant could not sue the judge for failing to empanel a jury in a case.[18] That is a mandamusable act, not subject to private suit. This same concept adheres when criminal acts are alleged. So, a judge accused of conspiring with others to issue an injunction in violation of a plaintiff's civil rights cannot be sued in a civil rights action; however, the private individuals who allegedly conspired with the judge—and who were not engaged in a judicial function and merely acted as private citizens—could be sued in a civil rights action by the individuals.[19] The judge, though immune from private suit, is not immune from criminal prosecution by a state or federal agency.[20] Applying the rule here, the trial judge below—and the court-appointed psychiatrists who proved that they were functioning as an arm of the court—are immune from private prosecution by a

15 See Delcourt, 919 S.W.2d at 783
16 See Pruitt v. Turner, 336 S.W.2d 440, 444 (Tex.Civ.App.-Waco 1960) (Wilson, J., dissenting), rev'd 161 Tex. 532, 342 S.W.2d 422 (1961) (approving Justice Wilson's dissenting opinion)
17 Pruitt, 336 S.W.2d at 444 (Wilson, J., dissenting)
18 See Turner v. Pruitt, 161 Tex. 532, 342 S.W.2d 422, 423 (1961)
19 See Dennis v. Sparks, 449 U.S. 24, 26-29, (1980)
20 See Dennis, 449 U.S. at 27-31

private citizen. However, if they violated a criminal law, they are not immune from criminal prosecution by the government.

Some cases using the functional approach have held that certain administrative functions of judges are not part of the judicial function and therefore are outside the scope of judicial immunity.[21] However, the case before us today does not involve nonjudicial, administrative functions, and cases such as Forrester only reinforce the principle that judges or those whom they appoint are entitled to absolute immunity for alleged acts and omissions during the performance of functions intimately associated with the judicial process.[22]

Common law derived immunity might be unavailable if a statute provided Barbara with a statutory claim for damages against the Cox Estate and Baylor. We have not found—and Barbara has not cited us to—any authority holding that section 261.101of the Texas Family Code or any other statute provides Barbara with a statutory damage claim against the Cox Estate and Baylor on the facts of this case. In short, even if Cox and Baylor violated sections 33.008 and 261.101 of the Texas Family Code, Barbara has not shown that these statutes override the common law immunity to which Cox and Baylor have shown themselves to be entitled.

3. POSSIBLE VIOLATION OF A MANDATORY DUTY DOES NOT NEGATE DERIVED JUDICIAL IMMUNITY.

We now turn to the second reason Barbara claims immunity does not shield the Cox Estate and Baylor—the duty to report suspected child abuse is mandatory, not discretionary. In support of this claim, Barbara cites numerous "official immunity" cases. Official immunity cases do not apply to judicial immunity; judicial immunity and official immunity are two completely different doctrines.

Judicial immunity lends immunity for acts taken in a case before a court. [23] Judicial immunity is an absolute immunity from private action for all acts—good or bad—in a case. It applies to judges and those appointed by judges to perform judicial, discretionary functions. For those appointed by a court to assist it, immunity attaches only if they are performing judicial, discretionary tasks.

Official immunity applies to government officials. Official immunity is not absolute; the actor must act in good faith, and the act must be discretionary.[24]

Courts also use different analyses to determine if the judge or government official is immune from suit. As we explained earlier, when judicial immunity is claimed, Texas courts use the functional approach to decide if immunity attaches. That approach looks to the task the individual is assigned by the court. If the task is intimately involved with the judicial process and involves judicial decision-making and discretion, immunity attaches. We do not parse the individual acts—interviewing the individuals, deciding that an issue of abuse exists and allegedly failing to report suspected abuse—within the general assignment and scrutinize them for

---

21 See, e.g., Forrester v. White, 484 U.S. 219 (1988) (holding judge not able to invoke judicial immunity in § 1983 damages action against him for employment decision made in the exercise of his administrative functions)

22 See id., 484 U.S. at 224-26

23 Typically it is described as immunity in cases over which the court has jurisdiction. But, if a case was filed in a court, even if the court ultimately decided it had no jurisdiction over a case, judicial immunity would protect the judge's actions before the case was dismissed.

24 Obviously, a judge qualifies as a governmental official, but judges need not resort to official immunity because judicial immunity is broader..

proper behavior. Any general assignment or function intimately related to the judicial process is protected; any part of the general assignment, or function, that is part and parcel of the function is protected. We do not inquire about reasonableness; we do not inquire about good faith. We do not ask whether the alleged wrongful conduct was discretionary.[25] As we said before, once an individual is cloaked with derived judicial immunity because of a function being performed for a court, all the actions intimately connected with that process—whether good or bad, honest or dishonest, well-intentioned or not, criminal or not—are cloaked with immunity.

The inquiry in official immunity cases is quite different. There the focus is not the actor's general function, but the specific act in question. It delves into the specific act at issue and asks if it was discretionary. It looks at the alleged wrongful conduct and asks if the actor was well-intentioned and acted in good faith.[26]

Although at some point in the inquiry both types of immunity ask if the act (for official immunity) or function (for judicial immunity) was discretionary, or involved discretion, the similarity stops there. Thus, official immunity cases do not apply to a judicial immunity case because they employ the wrong analysis. Therefore, we overrule issues three, four, and six, all based on an assumption that official immunity cases apply to derived judicial immunity.

B. Does the Statutory Immunity under Section 261.106 of the Texas Family Code Override the Common-Law Derived Judicial Immunity?

In her seventh issue Barbara argues that the existence of statutory immunity under section 261.106 of the Texas Family Code shows that the Legislature intended to abolish common-law derived judicial immunity and replace it with this statutory immunity.[27] We disagree. Section 261.106 grants immunity from civil or criminal liability to a person acting in good faith who reports or assists in the investigation of a report of alleged child abuse or neglect or who testifies or otherwise participates in a judicial proceeding arising from a report, petition, or investigation of alleged child abuse or neglect.[28] This statutory immunity also extends to an authorized volunteer of the Department of Protective and Regulatory Services or a law enforcement officer who participates at the request of that department in an investigation of alleged or suspected child abuse or neglect or in an action arising from an investigation if the person was acting in good faith and in the scope of the person's responsibilities.[29]

In construing a statute, our objective is to determine and give effect to the

---

25 See Forrester, 484 U.S. at 224 (stating that "under [the functional] approach, we examine the nature of the functions with which a particular official or class of officials has been lawfully entrusted, and we seek to evaluate the effect that exposure to particular forms of liability would likely have on the appropriate exercise of those functions"); Halsey, 87 S.W.3d at 555 (stating that "as applied in Texas, the functional approach in applying derived judicial immunity focuses on the nature of the function performed, not the identity of the actor, and considers whether the court officer's conduct is like that of the delegating or appointing judge"); Delcourt, 919 S.W.2d at 782 ("[u]nder the functional approach, courts determine whether the activities of the party seeking immunity are intimately associated with the judicial process ... [i]n other words, a party is entitled to absolute immunity when the party is acting as an integral part of the judicial system or an 'arm of the court' ")

26 See City of Lancaster v. Chambers, 883 S.W.2d 650, 653 (Tex.1994)

27 See TEX. FAM CODE § 261.106

28 TEX. FAM CODE 261.106(a)

29 TEX. FAM CODE § 261.106(b)

Legislature's intent.[30] If possible, we must ascertain that intent from the language the Legislature used in the statute and not look to extraneous matters for an intent the statute does not state. If the meaning of the statutory language is unambiguous, we adopt the interpretation supported by the plain meaning of the provision's words.[31] We must not engage in forced or strained construction; instead, we must yield to the plain sense of the words the Legislature chose.

Barbara cites no authorities directly on point. She does cite a Texas Supreme Court case in which the court held that the Medical Liability and Insurance Improvement Act intended to abolish the common-law discovery rule regarding the claims to which it applies.[32] We find that the language of section 261.106 of the Texas Family Code unambiguously provides statutory immunity for certain persons who assist in the investigation of a report of alleged child abuse or neglect or who participate in a judicial proceeding arising from a report, petition or investigation of child abuse; however, we find no intent in the unambiguous language of this statute to abolish common-law derived judicial immunity.[33] We conclude that the statutory privilege granted by section 261.106 serves a different purpose than derived judicial immunity and that the Legislature, by enacting this statute, did not intend to abolish derived judicial immunity.[34] Accordingly, we overrule Barbara's seventh issue.

V. Conclusion

The Cox Estate and Baylor conclusively proved facts showing their entitlement to derived judicial immunity under Texas common law, and Barbara did not raise a genuine issue regarding any of the facts material to this defense. The focus of our derived-judicial-immunity analysis is on the nature of the function performed by Dr. Cox and Baylor, not on the alleged criminality of a specific act or omission allegedly committed while performing that function. The existence of a duty to report suspected child abuse under section 261.101(b) of the Texas Family Code and criminal sanctions for the knowing violation of this duty do not prevent Dr. Cox and Baylor from asserting derived judicial- immunity from civil liability in this case. We conclude that the statutory immunity provided by section 261.106 does not abolish common-law derived judicial immunity. Under the functional approach, we hold that the trial court correctly granted summary judgment based on derived judicial immunity.[35] Accordingly, we overrule Barbara's first global issue challenging this judgment and all sub-issues.

---

30 See Nat'l Liab. & Fire Ins. Co. v. Allen, 15 S.W.3d 525, 527 (Tex. 2000) ·
31 St. Luke's Episcopal Hosp. v. Agbor, 952 S.W.2d 503, 505 (Tex.1997)
32 See Morrison v. Chan, 699 S.W.2d 205, 208 (Tex.1985)
33 See TEX. FAM CODE § 261.106
34 See Laub v. Pesikoff, 979 S.W.2d 686, 690 n. 2. (Tex.App.-Houston [1st Dist.] 1998, pet. denied) (holding that section 261.106 of the Texas Family Code does not abolish or modify the absolute, common-law, judicial-communications privilege because the statute serves different purposes)
35 See Halsey, 87 S.W.3d at 554-57; Delcourt, 919 S.W.2d at 781-83

CONFIDENTIALITY OF A CHILD'S MENTAL HEALTH RECORDS

(ABRAMS VS. JONES)[1]

This case presents issues of statutory construction. We are called upon to determine if either section 153.072 of the Family Code or section 611.0045 of the Health and Safety Code allows a parent to demand access to detailed notes of his or her child's conversations with a mental health professional when that parent is not acting on behalf of the child or when the mental health professional believes that releasing the information would be harmful to the child's physical, mental, or emotional health. The Legislature has balanced a child's need for effective treatment and a parent's rights and has imposed some limits on a parent's right of access to confidential mental health records. Accordingly, we reverse the judgment of the court of appeals and render judgment that Jones take nothing.

BACKGROUND

The child whose records are at issue is Karissa Jones. Her parents, Donald and Rosemary Jones, divorced when she was about seven years old. Both parents remarried sometime before the present controversy erupted, and Rosemary Jones is now Rosemary Droxler. In the original decree, Karissa's parents were appointed joint managing conservators of her and her younger sister. Two years after the divorce, her father initiated further court proceedings to become the sole managing conservator of his daughters. Litigation ensued for two more years. Karissa's parents ultimately agreed to a modification of the original order, but both parents were retained as joint managing conservators. The modified decree gave Jones certain rights of access to his children's psychological records.

Several months after the modification proceedings were concluded, Rosemary Droxler sought the professional services of a psychologist, Dr. Laurence Abrams, for Karissa. The uncontroverted evidence is that Karissa, who by this time was eleven years old, was agitated and showed signs of sleeplessness and worry. At the time the trial court heard this case, Abrams had seen Karissa six times for about fifty minutes

1   Abrams vs. Jones, 35 S.W.3d 620 (Tex. 2000)

328 TEXAS LAW FOR THE SOCIAL WORKER

on each occasion.

At the beginning of Abrams's first consultation with Karissa, she was reluctant to talk to him. When Abrams explored that reluctance with her, she told him that she was concerned that he would relate what she had to say to her parents. Abrams responded that he would have to provide a report to her parents, but that he could give them a general description of what was discussed without all the specifics. Abrams and Karissa reached an understanding about what he would and would not tell her parents, and he was thereafter able to establish a rapport with her.

Shortly after Karissa began seeing Abrams, her father (Jones) and his legal counsel met with Abrams and requested that he release all of her records. Abrams gave Jones and his counsel a verbal summary of information, sharing with them the basic subject matter of his consultations with Karissa. Abrams related that Karissa had told him that Jones's new wife (who formerly was Karissa's nanny) had said to Karissa that when she turned twelve, she would have to choose where she lived. Karissa told Abrams that she was afraid there would be more conflict in court between her parents because of this choice. Abrams described Karissa as in a "panic" when he first saw her over what she believed to be her impending decision and an ensuing battle between her parents. Abrams also told Jones that Karissa had said that she leaned toward choosing to live with her father and that she was at times unhappy living with her mother because her mother was away from home more than Karissa liked.

After Abrams had related this information about his sessions with Karissa, Jones told Abrams that no conversations of the nature Abrams had described had occurred between Jones and Karissa or between Karissa and her stepmother. At some point in the dialogue among Abrams, Jones, and Jones's attorney, Abrams either agreed with Jones's counsel or said in response to a question from counsel that Karissa's mother had taken Karissa to see Abrams "to get a leg up on" Jones in court.

A few days after the meeting among Jones, his counsel, and Abrams, Jones's counsel again pressed for Abrams's records in two letters to Abrams. Abrams responded verbally and in writing that releasing the detailed notes about his conversations with Karissa would not be in her best interest. Abrams offered to give his notes to any other psychologist that Jones might choose to replace Abrams as Karissa's counselor, and Abrams explained that Karissa's new psychologist could then determine whether it was in Karissa's best interest to give Abrams's notes to Jones. Jones did not seek another counselor for Karissa, and Abrams did not release his notes to Jones. Abrams continued to treat Karissa until this suit was filed by Jones to compel Abrams to release his notes. The record is silent as to whether Abrams was to continue treatment after this suit was resolved.

Droxler, Karissa's mother, entered an appearance in the suit against Abrams, and she agreed with Abrams that neither parent should have access to his notes of conversations with Karissa. A hearing was held before the trial court. Abrams testified that a sense of protection and closeness is an integral part of psychotherapy and that without some expectation of confidentiality, Karissa would not have opened up to him. He said that Karissa had several discussions with him about the confidentiality of their sessions. Abrams testified that in his opinion the release to either parent of his detailed notes of what Karissa had said was not in her best interest.

Jones took the position in the trial court that as a parent, he was unconditionally entitled to see all of Abrams's records regarding his daughter. He further represented to the trial court that based on his conversations with Karissa, he was of the opinion that she did not object to the release of her records. Abrams testified, however, that Karissa had asked him not to reveal the details of their conversations, and that during the week before the hearing, her mother delivered a note which Karissa had written to Abrams again asking that he maintain the confidentiality of their discussions.

Abrams's detailed notes about what Karissa had told him during his professional consultations with her were provided to the trial court. The court, however, stated on the record at the conclusion of the hearing that it had not reviewed them and did not intend to. There is no indication that it ever did so.

The trial court held that Jones was entitled to Abrams's notes. Abrams appealed, and Karissa's mother (Droxler) filed briefing in the court of appeals in support of Abrams's position. The court of appeals affirmed the trial court's judgment with one justice dissenting.[2] We granted Abrams's petition for review, which was supported by Karissa's mother.

DECISION

There are three questions of statutory construction that we must decide. They are (1) whether section 153.073 of the Family Code gives a divorced parent greater rights of access to mental health records than parents in general have under chapter 611 of the Texas Health and Safety Code, (2) whether section 611.0045(b) of the Health and Safety Code allows a professional to deny a parent access to portions of mental health records if the professional concludes that their release would harm the child, and (3) whether a parent is always deemed to be acting on behalf of his or her child when requesting mental health records.

RIGHTS OF DIVORCED PARENTS FOR ACCESS TO RECORDS

Do divorced parents have greater rights of access to records than parents in general? As indicated above, the first question that we must resolve is whether section 153.073 of the Family Code or chapter 611 of the Health and Safety Code governs this matter.[3] We conclude that chapter 611 provides the framework within which this case must be decided.

Section 153.073 of the Family Code addresses parental rights upon dissolution of the parents' marriage to one another. It provides that unless a court orders otherwise, a parent who is appointed a conservator "has at all times the right... as specified by court order... of access to medical, dental, psychological, and educational records of the child."[4] Jones contends that this section of the Family Code mandates that a parent who is appointed a conservator has access at all times to all psychological records of the child. We disagree.

We interpret section 153.073 to ensure that a court may grant a parent who is divorced and who has been named a conservator the same rights of access to his or her child's psychological records as a parent who is not divorced. We do not interpret section 153.073 to override the provisions of chapter 611 of the Health and Safety Code that specifically address parents' rights to the mental health records of their children. The legislative history of section 153.073 indicates that it was

2   Abrams v. Jones, 983 S.W.2d 377 (Tex. App.-Houston [14th Dist.] 1999)
3   TEX. FAM. CODE § 153.073; TEX. HEALTH & SAFETY CODE §§611.001 to 611.008
4   TEX. FAM. CODE §153.073(a)(2).

enacted to equalize the rights of nonmanaging-conservator parents in comparison to managing-conservator parents.[5] The Legislature did not intend in section 153.073 to give greater rights to divorced parents than to parents who are not divorced. We turn to chapter 611 of the Health and Safety Code.

DENYING PARENTAL ACCESS TO RECORDS

Can a professional deny parents access to a child's mental health records if such access is harmful? The Legislature has determined that a patient's right of access to his or her own mental health records is not absolute. Section 611.0045 of the Health and Safety Code says that a "professional may deny access to any portion of a record if the professional determines that release of that portion would be harmful to the patient's physical, mental, or emotional health."[6]

There are, however, checks and balances on a professional's decision not to disclose portions of a mental health record to a patient. A patient may select another professional for treatment of the same or related condition, and the professional denying access must allow the newly retained professional to examine and copy the records that have not been released to the patient.[7] The newly retained professional may then decide whether to release the records to the patient.

There are provisions in chapter 611 of the Health and Safety Code that deal specifically with the mental health records of a minor. Section 611.0045(f) provides that the "content of a confidential record shall be made available to a [parent] who is acting on the patient's behalf." Jones contends that a parent necessarily acts on behalf of his or her child when seeking access to a child's mental health records under section 611.0045(f). The court of appeals agreed. It held that "by requesting that Abrams turn over Karissa's mental health records, Jones was necessarily 'acting on behalf' of Karissa as contemplated by section 611.0045(f) of the Code."[8]

In construing a statute, we must attempt to give effect to every word and phrase if it is reasonable to do so. [9] If the Legislature had intended for a parent to have access to all aspects of a child's mental health records by simply proving that he or she is indeed the child's parent, the Legislature would not have needed to add the phrase "who is acting on the patient's behalf" in section 611.0045(f).

We agree with the dissent in the court of appeals that, unfortunately, parents cannot always be deemed to be acting on the child's behalf.[10] An obvious example is when a parent has sexually molested a child and later demands access to the child's mental health treatment records. A court would not presume that the parent is acting on the child's behalf in such circumstances. Similarly, parents embroiled in a divorce or other suit affecting the parent/child relationship may have motives of their own for seeking the mental health records of the child and may not be acting "on the

---

5   See HOUSE COMM. ON JUDICIAL AFFAIRS, BILL ANALYSIS, Tex. H.B. 1630, 73d Leg., R.S. (1993) (explaining that this provision was needed to remedy (1) previous limitations on nonmanaging conservators during periods of possession, when the child might need health care, and (2) the fact that managing conservators were not required to consult with the other parent about important decisions affecting the child's health, education, or welfare).

6   TEX. HEALTH & SAFETY CODE § 611.0045(b).

7   Id. § 611.0045(e).

8   Abrams v. Jones, 983 S.W.2d 377, 381 (Tex. App.-Houston [14th Dist.] 1999).

9   See City of Amarillo v. Martin, 971 S.W.2d 426, 430 (Tex. 1998); see also TEX. GOV'T CODE § 311.021(2) (stating that in enacting a statute, it is presumed that the entire statute is intended to be effective).

10 See Abrams, 983 S.W.2d at 382 (Edelman, J., dissenting)

patient's [child's] behalf."[11] We therefore conclude that a mental health professional is not required to provide access to a child's confidential records if a parent who requests them is not acting "on behalf of" the child.

Request for Records and "Acting on Behalf of the Child"

Is a parent always deemed to be acting on behalf of his or her child when requesting mental health records? When a parent is acting on behalf of his or her child, the question that then arises is whether, under section 611.0045(b), a professional may nevertheless deny access to a portion of a child's records if their release would be harmful to the patient's physical, mental, or emotional health.[12] Jones contends that subsection (b) only applies when "the patient" seeks his or her own records and not when a parent seeks a child's records. We disagree.

Section 611.0045(f) contemplates that when a parent seeks a child's mental health records "on the patient's behalf," the parent steps into the shoes of the patient. Subsection (f) affords third parties, including a parent, no greater rights than those of the patient. This is evident when section 611.0045(f) is considered in its entirety. It applies not only to parents, but to "a person who has the written consent of the patient."[13] It would be unreasonable to construe subsection (f) to allow a patient to obtain through a third person a record that a mental health professional has determined under subsection (b) would be harmful if released to the patient. Because subsection (b) may limit a patient's rights to his or her own records, subsection (b) can also limit a parent's or third party's right to a patient's records when the third party or parent stands in the patient's stead.

In construing a statute or code provision, a court may consider, among other matters, the (1) object sought to be attained by the statute, (2) circumstances under which the statute was enacted, (3) legislative history, (4) consequences of a particular construction, and (5) laws on similar subjects.[14] This Court has recently recognized that, through Chapter 611, "the Legislature has chosen to closely guard a patient's communications with a mental-health professional." [15] One purpose of confidentiality is to ensure that individuals receive therapy when they need it.[16] Although a parent's responsibilities with respect to his or her child necessitate access to information about the child, if the absence of confidentiality prevents communications between a therapist and the patient because the patient fears that such communications may be revealed to their detriment, neither the purposes of confidentiality nor the needs of the parent are served.

If a professional does deny a parent access to part of a child's records, the parent has recourse under section 611.0045(e).[17] First, the professional denying access must allow examination and copying of the record by another professional selected by the parent acting on behalf of the patient to treat the patient for the same or a related condition. Second, a parent denied access to a child's records has judicial recourse. We therefore conclude that the court of appeals erred in construing

---

11 Tex. Health & Safety Code § 611.0045(f)

12 Tex. Health & Safety Code § 611.0045(b)

13 Id. §§ 611.004(a)(4), 611.0045(f)

14 See Tex. Gov't Code § 311.023

15 Thapar v. Zezulka, 994 S.W.2d 635, 638 (Tex. 1999)

16 See R.K. v. Ramirez, 887 S.W.2d 836, 840 (Tex. 1994) (describing the purposes of the physician-patient privilege under the Texas Rules of Evidence)

17 Tex. Health & Safety Code §611.0045(e)

sections 611.0045(b) and (f) of the Health and Safety Code as giving a parent totally unfettered access to a child's mental health records irrespective of the child's circumstances or the parent's motivation.

We turn to the facts of this case and the interplay between section 611.045 and section 611.005 of the Health and Safety Code, which provides a remedy to a parent if a child's mental health records have been improperly withheld.

RECOURSE WHEN A CHILD'S RECORDS IMPROPERLY WITHHELD

What recourse is there for a parent when a child's mental health records have been improperly withheld? As already indicated above, a person who is aggrieved by a professional's improper "failure to disclose confidential communications or records" may petition a district court for appropriate relief.[18] A professional who denies access has "the burden of proving that the denial was proper."[19] Accordingly, Abrams bore the burden of proving in these proceedings that he properly denied access to his notes about his conversations with Karissa.

The trial court ruled against Abrams. Abrams did not request and the trial court did not make any findings of fact or conclusions of law. But because the reporter's record is part of the record on appeal, the legal sufficiency of the trial court's implied finding in support of the judgment, which was that Abrams failed to meet his burden of proof, may be challenged in the same manner as jury findings.[20] We must examine the entire record to determine whether Abrams established as a matter of law that his denial of access was proper either because Abrams established that (1) Jones was not acting on Karissa's behalf, or (2) access to the notes would be harmful to Karissa's mental or emotional health.

Jones never indicated that he was seeking the notes on behalf of Karissa, as distinguished from his own behalf. At the hearing, Jones testified that his motivation for obtaining Abrams's notes was in part the indication that Karissa's mother had hired Abrams "to get a leg up on me in court." Although this is some evidence that Jones was not acting on behalf of Karissa but was acting in his own interest, it is not conclusive. Jones's testimony that he was "partially" motivated by what he perceived to be his former wife's custody tactics indicated that there were additional reasons for seeking Karissa's records. Abrams did not prove conclusively that Jones was not acting on behalf of Karissa.

But even if Jones were acting on behalf of Karissa, Abrams testified that in his professional opinion it would be harmful to her to release his notes detailing their conversations. When Abrams first saw Karissa, she would not talk to him. He was unable to establish a rapport with her until they discussed confidentiality. Abrams asked her "what it would take to get her to talk," and he explained at the hearing that "it came down to, she needed protection.... She needed protection against anyone knowing what she said. She simply couldn't talk if there was a chance either parent would know what she said." Abrams made the decision during the first session with Karissa not to give his notes to either of her parents. He testified, "I had to in order to be able to treat the girl." He told Karissa at that session that he would not disclose his notes to her parents unless required to do so by a court. Karissa thereafter opened up to Abrams. Abrams explained at the hearing that an integral part of psychotherapy is that the patient have a sense of protection and security and

18 TEX. HEALTH & SAFETY CODE §611.005(a)
19 Id. § 611.005(b)
20 See Roberson v. Robinson, 768 S.W.2d 280, 281 (Tex. 1989)

that she drop defensive mechanisms. Abrams continued to treat Karissa after he had denied her father access to the notes, and she responded positively to treatment after Abrams assured her that the details of her conversations would be confidential. Treatment continued until this suit was filed. None of this testimony was contradicted or even challenged.[21] This testimony, in the absence of contrary evidence, is sufficient to establish as a matter of law that release of Karissa's records would have been harmful to her.

Jones's testimony that in his opinion, Karissa did not object to the release of Abrams's notes does not raise a fact question of whether their release would be harmful to her. Karissa was a layperson—an eleven-year-old layperson. She was not qualified to make a determination of whether release of her records would be harmful to her physical, mental, or emotional health.[22] The uncontradicted evidence established as a matter of law that Abrams's denial of access to his detailed notes was proper.

CONCLUSION AND DISSENTING OPINIONS

The trial court erred in holding that Jones was entitled to the detailed notes about his daughter's conversations with her mental health professional under the facts of this case. Accordingly, we reverse the judgment of the court of appeals and render judgment that Jones take nothing.

—Priscilla R. Owen, Justice

DISSENT: JUSTICE BAKER, dissenting.

I believe that the court of appeals majority correctly construed the statutory scheme and properly applied the law to the facts to reach the result it reached. Accordingly, I respectfully dissent from the Court's decision in this case.

—James A. Baker, Justice

JUSTICE HECHT, dissenting.

In this Term's decisions construing the Parental Notification Act,[23] the Court has exhibited a disturbing lack of regard for the rights of parents to raise and care for their children;[24] This case continues in that vein, holding that under chapter 611 of the Texas Health and Safety Code, mental health care professionals — who, as defined by statute,[25] include everyone from physicians to pretenders — have broad discretion to deny parents access to their children's mental health records, broader discretion than even a district judge has to order disclosure. As eager as the Court has been to find justification for allowing a child to have an abortion without telling

21 See Allright, Inc. v. Strawder, 679 S.W.2d 81, 82 (Tex. App.-Houston [14 Dist.] 1984, writ ref'd n.r.e.) (observing that "uncontroverted testimony, even from a witness categorized as an expert, may be taken as true as a matter of law if it is clear, direct and positive, and is free from contradictions, inconsistencies, inaccuracies and circumstances tending to cast suspicion thereon")

22 See TEX. HEALTH & SAFETY CODE § 611.0045(b)

23 TEX. FAM. CODE §§ 33.001-.011.

24 In re Doe 1(I), 19 S.W.3d 249, 2000 Tex. LEXIS 21 (Tex. 2000); In re Doe 2, 19 S.W.3d 278, 2000 Tex. LEXIS 25 (Tex. 2000); In re Doe 3, 19 S.W.3d 300, 2000 Tex. LEXIS 26 (Tex. 2000); In re Doe 4(I), 19 S.W.3d 322, 2000 Tex. LEXIS 27 (Tex. 2000); In re Doe 4(II), 19 S.W.3d 337, 2000 Tex. LEXIS 34 (Tex. 2000); In re Doe 1(II), 19 S.W.3d 346, 2000 Tex. LEXIS 67 (Tex. 2000).

25 TEX. HEALTH & SAFETY CODE § 611.001(2) ("'Professional' means: (A) a person authorized to practice medicine in any state or nation; (B) a person licensed or certified by this state to diagnose, evaluate, or treat any mental or emotional condition or disorder; or (C) a person the patient reasonably believes is authorized, licensed, or certified as provided by this subsection.").

her parents, contrary to a trial court's view of the evidence, it will come as no surprise that the Court has no difficulty keeping parents ignorant of their children's mental health records, contrary to the trial court's conclusion. As in the parental notification cases, the Court casts responsibility for its decision in this case on the Legislature. But this steady erosion of parental authority is judicial, not legislative; it results from the Court's view of statutory language through a prism of presumed diminution in parental authority. I respectfully dissent.

It should go without saying that parents generally need to know information contained in their children's health records in order to make decisions for their well-being. To remove any doubt that this is true, even after divorce, for any parent with custodial responsibility for a child, section 153.073(a)(2) of the Texas Family Code states that "unless limited by court order, a parent appointed as a conservator of a child has at all times the right... of access to medical, dental, psychological, and educational records of the child...." A parent's right to this information is not an insignificant matter and should not be restricted absent compelling reasons.

Section 611.0045 of the Texas Health and Safety Code, the pertinent parts of which are quoted in the margin,[26] permits a mental health care "professional", broadly defined as stated above, to deny a patient access to his own mental health records if disclosure would harm the patient's physical, mental, or emotional health. For the same reason, access may be denied to a patient's representative, including a parent if the patient is a child.[27] In a suit to obtain the records, the professional has the burden of proving that denial of access is proper.[28] Nothing in the statute suggests that this burden should be anything but substantial. Certainly, a patient should not be denied access to his own mental health records absent solid, credible evidence that disclosure will cause him real, demonstrable harm. A general concern that disclosure to the patient would not be in his best interest should not be enough to deny him access. The statute sets no different harm standard for denying a parent access to a child's records. Denial of access cannot be based on some general concern

---

26 Section 611.0045. Right to Mental Health Record: (a) Except as otherwise provided by this section, a patient is entitled to have access to the content of a confidential record made about the patient; (b) The professional may deny access to any portion of a record if the professional determines that release of that portion would be harmful to the patient's physical, mental, or emotional health; (c) If the professional denies access to any portion of a record, the professional shall give the patient a signed and dated written statement that having access to the record would be harmful to the patient's physical, mental, or emotional health and shall include a copy of the written statement in the patient's records. The statement must specify the portion of the record to which access is denied, the reason for denial, and the duration of the denial; (d) The professional who denies access to a portion of a record under this section shall redetermine the necessity for the denial at each time a request for the denied portion is made. If the professional again denies access, the professional shall notify the patient of the denial and document the denial as prescribed by Subsection (c); (e) If a professional denies access to a portion of a confidential record, the professional shall allow examination and copying of the record by another professional if the patient selects the professional to treat the patient for the same or a related condition as the professional denying access; (f) The content of a confidential record shall be made available to a person listed by Section 611.004(a)(4) or (5) who is acting on the patient's behalf; (h) If a summary or narrative of a confidential record is requested by the patient or other person requesting release under this section, the professional shall prepare the summary or narrative.

27 The persons referred to in section 611.0045(f) who can act on behalf of a patient are "a person who has the written consent of the patient, or a parent if the patient is a minor, or a guardian if the patient has been adjudicated as incompetent to manage the patient's personal affairs", id. §611.004(a)(4), or "the patient's personal representative if the patient is deceased", id. §611.004(a)(5).

28 Id. § 611.005(b) ("In a suit contesting the denial of access under Section 611.0045, the burden of proving that the denial was proper is on the professional who denied the access.").

that the child may be displeased or discomfited, even severely, about the disclosure. Rather, denial must be grounded on evidence of actual impairment to the child's health.

As the parental notification cases recently demonstrate, the meaning the Court gives a statutory standard is best demonstrated not by the words used to describe it but by its application in specific circumstances. This case illustrates how little evidence the Court believes is necessary not simply to raise the issue of whether a parent should be denied a child's mental health records but to conclusively establish -- so that no court can rule otherwise -- that a parent is not entitled to the records. The Court's decision to deny access to the records in this case rests entirely on the testimony of Abrams, a licensed clinical psychologist, who stated at a hearing in the district court: that Jones's former wife brought their eleven-year-old daughter, Karissa, to him in February 1996 because Karissa was agitated and showed signs of worry and sleeplessness; that Karissa refused to open up to him until he promised her that he would not reveal the details of their conversations to her parents, even though she understood that a judge might later order disclosure; that Karissa then told him she was troubled that if when she turned twelve in October she had to express a preference for living with one parent or the other, as her stepmother (her former nanny) had suggested she might,[29] it would provoke more hostility between her parents; that after meeting with Karissa six times in five months, she seemed much better; that Karissa had reiterated her desire for confidentiality in their last meeting four months earlier in June 1996, and in a note her mother had brought to him a few days before the October 15 hearing; and that he had told Karissa's father, Jones, that his former wife had hired him to "get a leg up on" Jones in their continuing court proceedings. On the specific issue of whether disclosing Karissa's records to Jones would harm Karissa's health, Abrams's testimony in its entirety is as follows:

> Q: *Is it your opinion at this time that the release of those records would be physically or emotionally harmful to Karissa?*
>
> A: Yes, sir.
>
> Q: *And what is that opinion?*
>
> A: That would have harmed her, as a matter of fact. It would be the very essence, it would make her get better, to give her protection.
>
> Q: *As we sit here on October 15th of 1996, is it still your opinion that it would be harmful to her mental or emotional health if these records are released?*
>
> A: Yes, sir.
>
> Q: *And can you tell the Judge why you believe that?*
>
> A: I've had no communications from her to be otherwise. I asked her the last

---

29 Cf. TEX. FAM. CODE § 153.134(a)(6) ("If a written agreement of the parents is not filed with the court, the court may render an order appointing the parents joint managing conservators only if the appointment is in the best interest of the child, considering the following factors:... (6) if the child is 12 years of age or older, the child's preference, if any, regarding the appointment of joint managing conservators...."); id. § 153.008 ("If the child is 10 years of age or older, the child may, by writing filed with the court, choose the managing conservator, subject to the approval of the court."); id. § 153.009(b) ("When the issue of managing conservatorship is contested, on the application of a party, the court shall interview a child 10 years of age or older and may interview a child under 10 years of age.").

time I saw her, in June about it, she reaffirmed her need for it. I received a note from her last week asking for it again.

The Court holds that this testimony, which did not persuade the district judge, conclusively established that Karissa's health would be harmed by disclosing her records to her father. The Court not only denies the trial court any meaningful role in determining credibility and weighing evidence, it reaches a conclusion, as a matter of law, on evidence that is inconclusive. Assuming that Abrams's testimony established that Karissa's health would have been harmed in February 1996 if he could not have promised her a measure of confidentiality because she would not have opened up to him and he could not have counseled her, the only evidence that disclosure of the records would harm Karissa's health in October 1996, when Abrams was no longer seeing her, was that she continued to request confidentiality. Jones disputed whether Karissa still wanted Abrams's records kept from him, testifying that based on his conversations with his daughter, his opinion was that she wanted him to have the records.

The Court concludes that Jones's testimony is no evidence that disclosure would not harm Karissa because an eleven-year-old is not qualified to say what would be harmful to her health. But if that is true, as I agree it is, then Abrams's testimony that Karissa continued to request confidentiality must likewise be disregarded. Karissa is no more qualified to say that disclosure of her records to her father would harm her health than that it would not. If Abrams's opinion cannot be based on Karissa's wishes, then it has no basis at all. Asked why he believed that disclosure would harm Karissa's health, Abrams answered, "I've had no communications from her to be otherwise."

Surely the Court does not think that a need for confidentiality at one point in time precludes disclosure of information forever. Nothing in the evidence before us suggests that Abrams would ever see Karissa again. Her twelfth birthday was three days after the hearing, and her anxieties about any choices she would have to make at that point were soon to be resolved one way or the other. No reason that Abrams gave for denying Jones access to his daughter's records remained valid. Had the trial judge found from this evidence that there might yet be some lingering need for nondisclosure, I could understand this Court's deference to that finding. But I do not understand how this Court can conclude that no reasonable trial judge could find from this evidence that Karissa's health would not be harmed by allowing her father access to her records.

It is no answer to say, as the Court seems to, that section 611.0045 allows a parent to take a child to other professionals until one is found who will release the records. True, Jones could simply have taken his daughter to one professional or another until he found one willing to turn over her records, and the statute gives Abrams no way to object. But the statute is not a full-employment guarantee for mental health care professionals, and no parent should be forced to shop a child as a patient merely to obtain the child's records. More importantly, I see no justification for applying section 611.0045 to permit one professional to trump another, regardless of their relative qualifications, and yet let any professional trump a district judge.

The Court's determination to restrict parental access to mental health records despite and not because of the statute is further demonstrated by its conclusion that section 611.0045 authorizes nondisclosure not only when the child's health may be harmed but when a parent is not "acting on the patient's behalf" as provided in subsection (f) of the statute. These words cannot, in my view, be sensibly read to create a separate standard for access to records. One might think that a parent could easily meet such a standard by stating that his or her request for a child's records was motivated out of love and concern for the child, but the Court concludes that evidence that parents are hostile to one another is enough by itself to support an inference that they are selfishly motivated and therefore not acting on their child's behalf.

The evidence the Court points to in this case is especially problematic. Abrams told Jones — Jones did not merely have his suspicions — that he believed he had been hired by Karissa's mother to counsel Karissa in order to give the mother "a leg up" in her ongoing disputes with Jones over custody of Karissa and her sister. The Court is troubled by Jones's frank admission in the October hearing that Abrams's statement to him was part of his motivation for obtaining Karissa's records, even though it could not have been important to Jones when he first went to meet with Abrams the preceding February — which was before Abrams had expressed the view that he himself was being used by Karissa's mother. It is difficult to imagine any reasonable, candid parent who would not acknowledge a similar motivation under the circumstances; indeed, one might have been less inclined to believe Jones if he had denied any such motivation. To rest denial of access to a child's medical records merely on inferences drawn from disputes between the parents conflicts with their rights under section 153.073(a)(2) of the Texas Family Code.

By construing section 611.0045 as establishing an acting-on-behalf-of standard for gaining access to a child's mental health records, the Court requires inquiry into, and inevitable disputes over, a parent's subjective motivations, instead of focusing on the more objective harm-to-the-patient's-health standard. I do not read section 611.0045 to require such an inquiry, which will almost always exacerbate difficulties between divorced parents.

While Abrams appears to have been professional in his dealings with the parties, and the district court did not suggest the contrary, the court was not bound by Abrams's views. Today's decision, coming as it does four years after the events at issue, cannot be of much importance to these parties. Karissa will soon be sixteen. Its importance lies in the difficulties it will cause future parties and in its further deterioration of parents' rights to raise their children.

—Justice Hecht

HIPAA

Texas Law and the Federal Health Insurance Portability and Accountability Act

The Health Insurance Portability and Accountability Act (HIPAA) was signed into law in 1996 as a surviving vestige of the Clinton Administration effort to overhaul the health care system. HIPAA was intended to create a more cost efficient health care system by facilitating electronic communication of health information among health care providers, health plans (including employer-sponsored group plans, Medicaid, Medicare, etc.), health care clearinghouses, and a variety of business associates that are indirectly involved in the health care enterprise (accountants, billing services, attorney's, etc.). In order to encourage the use of electronic transmission of health care information, Congress approved the bill, acknowledged that patient privacy would be of paramount concern in the electronic era of health care, and shifted responsibility to the Department of Health and Human Services (HSS) for promulgating certain rules for protecting privacy and to assume ultimate regulatory authority for enforcement. HIPAA became effective in 2001, though compliance implementation did not begin until two years later.

As of this writing, actual enforcement of HIPAA in regards to an individual health care provider practice has been limited to one case involving Medicare fraud by a non-psychologist. It seems reasonable, on the short term, to assume HHS will likely engage in more educative rather than legal intervention with individual practitioners, with the exception of those cases involving egregious crimes or serious fraudulent events. Further, it is more likely that HHS will devote its policing activity to larger health care entities, such as insurance companies and managed care companies, where protected health care information may be compromised on a large scale. For the independent psychologist or small group practice, HIPAA will serve as the "standard of practice" in civil court actions initiated against service providers by disgruntled patients. Nevertheless, it is worth noting that violation of HIPAA carries civil penalties of not more than $100 for each violation, not to exceed $25,000 in a calendar year, fines of up to $250,000, and imprisonment for up to 10 years, or both.

There are three basic HIPAA rules germane to the typical Texas social worker engaged in health care practice: the Privacy, Transaction, and Security Rules. Please note that HIPAA is not intended to address forensic or other forms of non-health service related psychological records or communications. Briefly, the HIPAA Privacy Rule describes in some considerable detail when and to whom individually identifiable health information can be disclosed. The electronic transmission of protected health information (PHI) triggers the Privacy Rule and requires that the psychologist's entire health care practice be in compliance with HIPAA regulations. Therefore, a clinician may not segment or segregate certain patient files as being non-HIPAA compliant simply because there has been no electronic transmission of patient health care information.

There is little about the Privacy Rule that has dramatically changed the practice of social work in Texas. With patient confidentiality serving as a cornerstone to the profession and firmly underscored in the APA and NASW ethics codes, Texas law, and Texas licensure regulations, most social workers are practicing well above the minimum standards established by the HIPAA Privacy Rule. One important provision of the Privacy Rule that has been of considerable importance and assistance to social workers and their clients has been the federal mandate limiting the information that third party payers may require for payment of services. Specifically, the release of psychotherapy process notes may not be demanded as a condition for payment of services. However, clinicians are cautioned that a court ordered subpoena will likely open these records for review in a court of law and that patient access to their personal health care records was one of the specific aims of HIPAA. We strongly suggest adherence to the standards for record keeping outlined by the American Psychological Association and the National Association of Social Workers. It is also important to note that HIPAA specifies that health care records be preserved for a period of six years, however, for psychological records Texas law specifies ten years, and for another ten years past age of majority for health care records for minors. As HIPAA was intended to establish a minimal floor for protected patient information, the federal act specifically indicates that when the various health care entities, including practitioners, determine a conflict or inconsistency exists between this federal law and state statue, adherence to the "higher standard" should be followed. In the case of maintenance of patient records, Texas law prevails.

The Transaction Rule with a compliance date of October 16, 2003, addresses more technical aspects of the electronic health care transaction process and requires the use of standardized formats relevant to health care claims when sent electronically. There appears to be two primary aspects of this HIPAA rule impacting clinical practice. First, HIPAA specifies use of a standard diagnostic code set, the IDC of Diseases, 9th edition (ICD-9 CM) Vol. 1 & 2. Hence, social workers may have to use a billing service or clearinghouse to convert DSM codes to ICD codes. Second, as part of the transaction standards, the Current Procedural Terminology (CPT) must be used but will not otherwise require a conversion. Currently, there is no regulatory address of these "transaction" issues in Texas law.

The HIPAA Security Rule was the last of the three primary rules to be finalized, largely because it is the most complex due to the constantly changing world of technology. The reader should note that compliance with the HIPAA Privacy and Transaction Rules *does not* ensure compliance with the HIPAA Security Rule. The Security Rule requires assurance that confidential electronic patient health information (EPHI) is kept secure from inappropriate or incidental disclosure. The rule addresses administrative, physical, and technical procedures and processes regarding office space, files (hardcopy and electronic), computers and other electronic gadgetry (PDA'S , cell phones, electronic tablets). Compliance with the Security Rule requires a process called a "risk analysis." This risk analysis is painstaking, will likely involve at least several hours of time to complete by the typical private practitioner, and must be thoroughly documented. Essentially, a risk analysis requires social workers to determine the physical, procedural, and administrative security risks inherent in their maintenance and communication of protected health information. We anticipate that the HIPAA Security Rule will effectively define the minimally acceptable standards of practice in this regard.

Finally, it is also important to underscore that the HIPAA Privacy, Transaction and Security Rules do not require social workers to use electronic means for the communication of health care information, including billing. Indeed, some clinicians have made effort to arrange an electronic–free practice in order to dodge HIPAA regulatory authority. Unfortunately for these technologically defiant clinicians, they may soon find that most third party payers will require them to submit billings electronically. As well, as discussed earlier, the HIPAA security rule will likely define the appropriate standard of care regarding the protection of patient records, whether or not they are stored or communicated electronically. Social workers are encouraged to become more familiar with these HIPAA rules with understanding that HIPAA may at least set standards for the security and accessibility of patient records.

Much of the material presented here was derived directly from materials provided by the American Psychological Association's Practice Directorate and the National Association of Social Workers. A more thorough description of HIPAA rules and its implications for clinical practice, as well as helpful web-based products designed to facilitate compliance with HIPAA, may be found at *http://www.apapractice.org* and at *http://www.socialworkers.org.*

See also:

http://www.socialworkers.org/hipaa/default.asp

http://www.socialworkers.org/practice/behavioral_health/mbh0101.asp

OPINIONS
FROM THE
ATTORNEY GENERAL

ATTORNEY GENERAL OPINION LETTERS

AND OPEN RECORD OPINIONS

This section contains selected letters from the archive of Attorney General Opinions and Open Records Opinions that are relevant to the practice of social work. These opinions are relatively difficult to research because of the way they are indexed on the website of the Texas Attorney General. We hope that this archive will assist practitioners who have questions related to these decisions, such as: whether there is a conflict of interest when agency employees provide services to the general public outside of departmental work hours (LO 90-043); whether the Texas Department of Human Resources may prohibit workers from performing court ordered social studies on their own time (JM-188); what political activities are permissible for social workers (MW-243); whether social workers who are providing treatment to sex offenders have discretion in reporting information regarding possible child abuse (DM-458); what issues are relevant in disclosing confidential information in response to a subpoena (LO 96-102); clarification regarding patient access to social workers' school counseling records (JC-0438) and grandparent access to children and records (GA-260); whether parents may use the services of an advocate in dealing with matters of their child's education (GA-0813); whether a mental health professional is required by chapter 261, Family Code, to report abuse or neglect that occurred during the childhood of a now-adult patient (GA-0944); whether a law enforcement agency is required to furnish information about alleged child abuse by a person responsible for the child's care, custody, or welfare to the Department of Family and Protective Services (GA-0879); what must be included in school counseling records kept by social workers (JC-0538); and on whether a licensed social worker must also be licensed by the Council on Sex Offender Treatment to provide rehabilitation services or be a treatment provider for sex offenders (GA-423).

Services Outside of Agency—Conflict of Interest?

OFFICE OF THE ATTORNEY GENERAL

STATE OF TEXAS

JIM MATTOX
ATTORNEY GENERAL

July 11, 1990

Mr. Ron Lindsey
Commissioner
Department of Human Services
P.O. Box 149030
Austin, Texas 78714-9030

Letter Opinion No. 90-043

Re: *Possible conflict of interest when agency employees provide services to the general public outside of departmental work hours.*

Dear Mr. Lindsey:

You express concern that conflicts of interest may exist when employees of the Department of Human Services (the department) provide counseling services to the general public outside of their department work hours. You ask whether the department "could adopt a personnel policy prohibiting its employees from engaging in social work counseling activities with the general public in a private capacity." If not, you ask if the department could prohibit such activity for employees who provide counseling services for the department?

An administrative agency "may only exercise those powers granted by statute, together with those necessarily implied from the statutory authority conferred or duties imposed."[1] The department may establish "reasonable personnel policies for which there is an adequate showing of need" pursuant to its implied statutory authority.[2]

In Attorney General Opinion JM-188, this office upheld the validity of a rule adopted by your agency that prohibited child protective service workers from performing court-ordered social studies on their own time, because such activity "would compete with the department for court appointments and revenue under [certain specified] sections of the Family Code or would ... have other adverse affects on the department."[3] In contrast, Attorney General Opinion H-1317 (1978) determined that a department rule prohibiting all departmental personnel from being licensed as real estate brokers or salesmen was overbroad.

---

1 *City of Sherman v. Public Util. Comm'n*, 643 S.W.2d 681, 686 (Tex.1983)
2 Attorney General Opinion JM-188 (1984), at 2; accord Attorney General Opinion JM-93 (1983), at 2. *See also Bishop v. Wood*, 426 U.S. 341 (1976); *Perry v. Sindermann*, 408 U.S. 593 (1972); *Schware v. Bd. of Bar Examiners*, 353 U.S. 232 (1957) (right to work may be curtailed for legitimate state interest)
3 *Id*

You have not suggested any basis for prohibiting department employees, regardless of their job classification or duties, from conducting counseling services on their own time. Nor have you offered any basis to support a rule prohibiting department counselors from performing private counseling services. Absent a showing that the prohibitions are reasonably related to some interest of the department, the department may not adopt the suggested prohibitions.

SUMMARY

In summary, the Department of Human Services may not prohibit employees, regardless of their job classification or duties, from conducting counseling services on their own time unless it can show that there would be an adverse affect on the department.

Very truly yours,

Karen C. Gladney
Assistant Attorney General
Opinion Committee

APPROVED
    Rick Gilpin, Chairman
    Opinion Committee

    Sarah Woelk, Chief
    Letter Opinion Section

Court-Ordered Social Studies on Personal Time

OFFICE OF THE ATTORNEY GENERAL
STATE OF TEXAS

JIM MATTOX
ATTORNEY GENERAL

August 13, 1984

Honorable Lloyd Doggett
Texas State Senate
P.O. Box 12068, Capitol Station
Austin, Texas 78711

Opinion No. JM-188

Re: *Whether the Texas Department of Human Resources may prohibit workers from performing court ordered social studies on their own time*

Dear Senator Doggett:

You have requested an opinion on the validity of a policy of the Texas Department of Human Resources under which its child protective service workers are prohibited from performing court ordered social studies on their own time in disputed custody suits, even though the department has no official relationship with the parties involved in the proposed study. The existence of a conflict of interest in dual employment is a question of fact which ordinarily must be determined by the agency on a case-by-case basis, but we believe the department may find that a conflict of interest exists for all of its employees who would compete with the department for appointments and revenue under sections 11.12 and 11.18(c) of the Family Code or would perform services which may have other adverse affects on the department.

Section 11.12 of the Family Code provides, in pertinent part:

> (a) In a suit affecting the parent-child relationship, the court may order the preparation of a social study into the circumstances and condition of the child and of the home of any person seeking managing conservatorship or possession of the child.

> (b) The social study may be made by any state agency, including the Texas Department of Human Resources, or any private agency, or any person appointed by the court ..... .

House Bill No. 642 of the Sixty-eighth Legislature amended section 11.18 of the Family Code by adding subsection (c), which reads as follows:

> (c) If the court orders the Texas Department of Human Resources to prepare the social study prescribed by Section 11.12 of this code, the court shall award a reasonable fee for the preparation of the study to the department. The department's fee shall be taxed as costs, and shall be paid directly to the department. The department may enforce the order

for the fee in its own name. (Emphasis added).

A conference committee for House Bill No. 642 intentionally determined that the language of section 11.18(c) is mandatory instead of permissive. The conference committee bill analysis and the bill's fiscal note estimate that the bill will result in sizeable revenue gains to the department's Welfare Administration Operating Fund, with corresponding reductions in the state and federal funds required for the operation of the department.

The Department of Human Resources has the powers expressly granted to it by statute together with those necessarily implied from the authority conferred or duties imposed.[1] The Texas Board of Human Resources is responsible for the adoption of policies and rules for the government of the department.[2] The commissioner of Human Resources may employ personnel necessary for the administration of the department's duties.[3] We believe that reasonable personnel policies for which there is an adequate showing of need are authorized under the department's implied powers. Attorney General Opinion JM-93 (1983) expressed the opinion that a necessary concomitant of the authority to employ persons needed by an agency to perform its duties is the power to adopt reasonable employment policies calculated to insure the achievement of its objectives.

A public employee is not prohibited per se from simultaneously holding two different state employments or from simultaneously holding both state and private employments.[4] Under the Department of Human Resources' policy for dual employment, activity presenting a possible conflict of interest with the employee's job duties must be reviewed and approved by the department. Rule 7200 of the department's personnel procedures prescribes the following:

7200 OTHER EMPLOYMENT

Department employees may wish to become involved with employment or activities outside the department. This practice is generally acceptable to the department as long as the additional employment or activity is compatible with the department's work. Employees must not participate in employment or activity that violates the standards of conduct as prescribed in TEX.REV.CIV.STAT.ANN., art. 6252-9b, Section 8, known as the ethics code.

....

All requests for participation in dual employment or activities are considered on an individual basis except that:

1. Employees of the department may not hold positions in both county and state protective services programs.

2. Employees may not participate in those political activities listed in Item 7112, Political Activities Prohibited.

All other requests for participation in dual employment or activities are carefully reviewed to determine if they are compatible with the employee's assigned responsibilities in the department. The dual employment or

1   *See Stauffer v. City of San Antonio,* 344 S.W.2d 158, 160 (Tex.1961)
2   Human Resources Code, § 21.003(a)
3   Sec. 21.005(c)
4   *See* Attorney General Opinions JM-22 (1983); MW-415 (1981)

activity may not conflict with the employee's relationship with depart-ment clients, contractors, providers, persons regulated by the Licensing Branch, or the employee's job in the department. Employees approved to participate in dual employment or activities must not use clients' or licensees' names or other information from any department files in con-nection with the part-time employment or activity. Employees must not use their official position or identification to influence, threaten, or coerce any person in connection with part-time employment. Employees approved to engage in off-duty employment or activities must not con-duct any non-departmental business activity during duty hours. The only way an employee may conduct business for an outside activity during duty hours is for the activity to be department-related, such as councils of government, child welfare boards, or various advisory boards. The activity must be approved at the regional or state office level. Employees who violate these instructions may be subject to dismissal.

Personnel committees responsible for approving dual employment or activity requests should carefully consider the following outside activities:

....

9. Engaging in the independent activity of providing court-ordered social studies. (This type of request should be referred to the state office Personnel Committee.)

It is not suggested that Rule 7200 is per se an unreasonable procedure for screening dual employment activity that may involve conflicts of interest. The ques-tion is its present application to certain of the department's employees. We under-stand that since the effective date of section 11.18(c), the department has held that a conflict of interest exists in all cases involving child protective service workers who wish to perform court-ordered social studies on their own time.

Whether a conflict of interest exists is a question of fact which ordinarily must be determined by the agency on a case-by-case basis in light of the specific duties performed by the employee. However, *we cannot say* that the department may not validly determine that a conflict of interest exists in every instance in which a child protective service worker in his individual capacity competes with his employer, the Department of Human Resources, for court appointments and revenue anticipated by the department and the legislature under the recently enacted section 11.18(c) of the Family Code or adversely affects other aspects of the department, such as its anticipated workload or its credibility if the courts confuse the source of studies prepared by workers in their individual capacities.

One's right to work and earn an income, whether characterized as a liberty or a property interest, is a valuable right which should not be curtailed without legiti-mate state interest.[5] It is our opinion that a prohibition against outside employment will be upheld by the courts inasmuch as the prohibition is reasonably related to the legitimate interest of the state in prohibiting outside employment that creates a conflict of interest.[6]

5   See *Bishop v. Wood*, 426 U.S. 341 (1976); *The Board of Regents of State Colleges v. Roth*, 408 U.S. 564 (1972); *Perry v. Sindermann*, 408 U.S. 593 (1972); *Schware v. Board of Bar Examiners of the State of New Mexico*, 353 U.S. 232 (1957); Attorney General Opinion H-1317 (1978)

6   See *Gosney v. Sonora Independent School District*, 603 F.2d 522 (5th Cir.1979); Attorney Gen-

SUMMARY

The Texas Department of Human Resources may prohibit workers from performing court-ordered social studies on their own time when the workers' dual employment creates a conflict of interest by competing with the department for court appointments and revenue under sections 11.12 and 11.18(c) of the Family Code or by adversely affecting other aspects of the department.

Very truly yours,

Jim Mattox
Attorney General of Texas

TOM GREEN
First Assistant Attorney General

DAVID R. RICHARD
Executive Assistant Attorney General

Prepared by NANCY SUTTON
Assistant Attorney General

Political Activities of State Social Workers

OFFICE OF THE ATTORNEY GENERAL

STATE OF TEXAS

MARK WHITE
ATTORNEY GENERAL

September 22, 1980

Honorable James B. Adams
Director
Department of Public Safety
5805 N. Lamar Boulevard
Austin, Texas 78773

Opinion No. MW-243

Re: *Political activities of Department of Public Safety officers (or other state employees), including bumper stickers, badges, yard signs*

Dear Mr. Adams:

You ask whether commissioned officers of the Texas Department of Public Safety are eligible for appointment as a judge, clerk, or watcher of an election under article 3.04 of the Election Code. Article 3.04 provides, in pertinent part:

> *Except as otherwise provided herein, no one who holds an office of profit or trust under . . . this state . . . shall act as judge, clerk, or watcher of any election, general, special, or primary. . . .*

Courts have held that policemen are public officers.[1] Along with deputy sheriffs and constables, they hold offices of trust or profit.[2] Article 2.12 of the Code of Criminal Procedure provides that rangers and officers commissioned by the Department of Public Safety are peace officers. Accordingly, we think it is clear that commissioned officers of the Department of Public Safety hold an 'office of trust or profit' within the meaning of article 3.04 of the Election Code. They are therefore ineligible to serve as a judge, clerk, or watcher of a general, special, or primary election.

You also ask whether employees and officers of the department may place bumper stickers endorsing political candidates on their personal automobiles, place campaign signs in their yards, or wear badges endorsing political candidates while on or off duty.

Article 4413(9), section (2), V.T.C.S., provides that:

---

1   Sawyer v. City of San Antonio, 234 S.W. 2d 398 (Tex. 1950)
2   Attorney General Opinion H-1027 (1977)

No person in the Department shall . . . engage in political activities or campaign for or against any candidate for any public office in this State. Any person violating any provision of this subsection shall forfeit his position with the Department.

Attorney General Opinion MW-149 (1979) held that section (2) is constitutional, provided that it is construed 'so as not to infringe upon areas of protected conduct.'[3] The purpose of prohibitions like those found in article 4413(9) is to promote the efficiency and integrity of public service.[4] Attorney General Opinion MW-149 noted that article 4413(9) does not necessarily prohibit membership in a political organization or a group which supports such an organization, but held that employees may not legally work in a political candidate's campaign by giving speeches, making contributions and telephone calls, or engaging in similar activities.

The display of yard signs and bumper stickers and the wearing of badges endorsing political candidates may be political activities within the meaning of section (2), article 4413(9), but they may also be expressions of personal opinion protected by the First Amendment. The Supreme Court has not considered whether a state may constitutionally prohibit its employees from wearing political buttons or displaying bumper stickers. In Broadrick v. Oklahoma, 413 U.S. 601 (1973), the court suggested that a rule banning political buttons or bumper stickers might be impermissible, but did not reach this issue.[5] The employee in question had engaged in fund raising, which the state could constitutionally prohibit. See also Connealy v. Walsh, 412 F. Supp. 146 (W.D. Mo. 1976).

The Hatch Act reserves to federal employees the right to vote and to express opinions on political subjects and candidates. 5 U.S.C. s 7324(b). Federal regulations interpret this provision as permitting employees to display a political picture, sticker, badge or button. 5 CFR s 733.111.

In our opinion, section (2) of article 4413(9) should not be construed as prohibiting an employee from wearing a political button while off duty, placing a campaign sign in his yard, or displaying a bumper sticker in his private automobile which is not used on state business. Broadrick raises a question as to whether these activities constitute protected conduct. Such private and passive expressions of political opinion would seem, moreover, to have only a minimal effect, if any, on the efficiency and integrity of the public service. Finally, a prohibition against bumper stickers and yard signs in many cases would reach political expressions by a state employee's spouse who owns a community property interest in the house or car. We will avoid construing article 4413(9) to prohibit conduct which appears to be protected by the First Amendment. Accordingly, employees of your agency may legally display partisan political emblems while off duty.

The wearing of a political button while on duty, and the display of a bumper sticker on an automobile used on state business, raise different questions. Courts have found valid state interests in forbidding this kind of conduct on the job. In Smith v. United States, 502 F. 2d 512 (5th Cir. 1974), a psychologist challenged his

---

3   See also Attorney General Opinion M-1099 (1972) (construing similar provision applicable to Department of Public Welfare)

4   United States Civil Service Commission v. National Association of Letter Carriers, 413 U.S. 548, 555 (1973); United Public Workers v. Mitchell, 330 U.S. 75 (1947); Gray v. Toledo, 323 F. Supp. 1281 (N.D. Ohio 1971)

5   413 U.S. at 617, 622

dismissal from the staff of a Veterans Administration hospital for wearing a peace button while treating veterans. The court upheld the firing because display of the button, although symbolic speech protected by the First Amendment, resulted in substantial interference with the employee's duties. In another case, a social worker who counseled juvenile probationers at their homes and schools was dismissed for displaying a partisan bumper sticker on the personal car she drove to these interviews.[6] The court held that this expression of opinion could be forbidden because it would interfere with her job effectiveness.

We believe that section (2) of article 4413(9) should be construed to prohibit the display of political buttons while on duty and of bumper stickers on cars used in connection with work when such activities will interfere with the effectiveness of your employees.

Your last question is whether officers and employees of the department may serve as officers of local, state or national conventions. Article 13.34(h) of the Election Code provides that:

> No person shall be ineligible to serve as a delegate to any county, senatorial district, state or national convention of any political party by reason of his holding any public office.

You advise that the department has interpreted article 13.34(h) as applying to employees as well as to officers. We believe this is a reasonable construction. We can think of no reason why the legislature would have intended to permit public officers to participate in conventions as delegates but not allow employees to do so, and we do not think article 13.34(h) should be construed in that manner.

A literal construction of article 13.34(h) would also produce the rather odd result that individuals could serve as delegates to conventions but not be eligible for any of the offices which convention delegates hold. Convention officers are chosen from the body of delegates, and we do not think the legislature intended to permit individuals to serve as delegates but then limit them strictly to that role. Accordingly, we conclude that although article 13.34(h) refers to 'delegates,' that provision creates an exception to the general prohibition against participation in political activity set forth in article 4413(9), V.T.C.S., which should be liberally construed to permit individuals to perform any functions and be eligible for any positions which convention delegates typically hold. Thus, the answer to your question is that officers and employees of the department may serve as officers of local, state and national conventions.

---

6   Connealy v. Walsh, 412 F. Supp. 146 (W.D. Mo. 1976)

SUMMARY

Commissioned officers of the Department of Public Safety are ineligible to serve as a judge, clerk, or watcher of a general, special, or primary election under article 3.04 of the Election Code. Section (2) of article 4413(9), V.T.C.S., does not prohibit officers and employees of the department from placing bumper stickers endorsing candidates for political office on their personal automobiles, placing campaign signs in their yards, or wearing badges endorsing political candidates while off duty, but does prohibit them from displaying partisan bumper stickers or political buttons while on duty when such conduct would interfere with their effectiveness as public employees. Officers and employees of the department may serve as officers of political party conventions.

Very truly yours,

Mark White
Attorney General Of Texas

JOHN W. FAINTER, Jr.
First Assistant Attorney General

Prepared by JON BIBLE & SUSAN GARRISON
Assistant Attorneys General

Discretion for Reporting Sexual Abuse

OFFICE OF THE ATTORNEY GENERAL
STATE OF TEXAS

DAN MORALES
ATTORNEY GENERAL

November 26, 1997

Ms. Grace L. Davis, L.M.S.W.-A.C.P
Executive Director
Council on Sex Offender Treatment
1100 West 49th Street
Austin, Texas 78756-3183

Opinion No. DM-458

Re: *Whether Family Code section 261.101(a) permits a registered sex-offender-treatment provider discretion to report information regarding possible child abuse (RQ-944)*

Dear Ms. Davis:

Family Code section 261.101(a) requires a person who suspects that a child has been abused or neglected immediately to report the suspicion to the appropriate authorities. You ask whether, in the event a registered sex-offender-treatment provider obtains from a client dated or incomplete information suggesting that the client has abused a child, the treatment provider may use his or her "good judgment" in determining whether to report the information. The plain language of section 261.101(a) compels us to conclude that a treatment provider must report the information immediately if the information causes the treatment provider to believe that a child has been abused.

We understand that in the course of a sex-offender-treatment program, a treatment provider or affiliated-treatment provider (collectively, "treatment provider") may obtain information, through a client's statements or otherwise, that leads the treatment provider to believe the client may have abused a child (other than a child whom the client was convicted of abusing, we assume). You aver that your agency, the Council on Sex Offender Treatment, interprets the Family Code generally to require a treatment provider to report any allegation or statement of child abuse perpetrated by the client and disclosed to the treatment provider, as well as any suspicion the provider has of child abuse perpetrated by the client. You suggest, however, that the council has established an exception with respect to "incomplete or dated" information a treatment provider receives from a client. In that situation, the council apparently encourages a treatment provider to use his or her "good judgment" in deciding whether to report the information to the appropriate authorities.

You ask if the council's exception is consistent with Family Code section 261.101. We assume, for purposes of our analysis, that the information, although it is incomplete or dated, causes the treatment provider to suspect that a child has been abused.

Family Code section 261.101(a) mandates immediate reporting of suspected child abuse: "A person having cause to believe that a child's physical or mental health or welfare has been or may be adversely affected by abuse or neglect by any person *shall immediately make a report* as provided by this subchapter." (Emphasis added.) When the legislature originally enacted the substance of this requirement in 1971, it indicated its desire "to protect children . . . by providing for the *mandatory* reporting of suspected cases [of child abuse or neglect]."[1] Thus, the reporting requirement expressly applies *without exception* to any individual whose personal communications normally are privileged. The report should reflect the reporter's belief that a child has been abused and must identify the child if the child's identity is known.

We conclude that the council's interpretation, permitting a treatment provider to decide whether to report suspected child abuse where the suspicion is premised upon incomplete or dated information, is contrary to section 262.101(a).[2] As section 261.101(a) says, a person who suspects that a child has been abused *shall* report the suspicion, and shall do so *immediately*. The term "shall" ordinarily signals a mandate,[3] and the term "immediately" underscores the mandate with a sense of urgency. Conversely, we find no language in section 261.101(a) indicating that reporting suspected child abuse is discretionary[4] or establishing an exception where the suspicion is premised on information that is incomplete or dated. Indeed, a person who knowingly fails to report suspected child abuse in accordance with Family Code chapter 261 commits a class B misdemeanor.[5]

Moreover, chapter 261 appears to contemplate that, in some situations, the

---

1   Act of May 24, 1971, 62d Leg., R.S., ch. 902, sec. 1, § 1, 1971 Tex. Gen. Laws 2790, 2790 (emphasis added).

2   A court will not give weight to an agency's construction of an unambiguous statute if the construction is contrary to the statute's plain meaning. Attorney General Opinion JM-1149 (1990) at 2; *see also Calvert v. Kadane, 427 S.W.2d 605, 607 (Tex. 1968)*.

3   *See Wright v. Ector Indep. Sch. Dist., 867 S.W.2d 863, 868 (Tex. App.--El Paso 1993, no writ)* (citing *Inwood North Homeowners' Ass'n v. Meier, 625 S.W.2d 742, 743 (Tex. Civ. App.--Houston [1st Dist.] 1981, no writ)*).

4   Your letter to this office suggests that you believe Family Code section 261.101(b) might apply because you seek clarification of section 261.101 as it requires all "professionals" to report suspected child abuse or neglect. Subsection (b) requires a professional to report suspected child abuse within 48 hours after the suspicion arises. By its terms, however, subsection (b) applies only to a professional who has direct contact with children in the normal course of his or her official duties. We do not understand a treatment provider to have direct contact with children in the normal course of his or her official duties; we therefore need not consider whether a treatment provider is a "professional" in the word's broader sense.

5   Fam. Code § 261.109. We note that, under Family Code section 261.107, a person who knowingly or intentionally makes a report that the person knows is false or lacks factual foundation commits a class B misdemeanor. We do not in this opinion determine what a false report is or what a report that lacks a factual foundation is. In addition, whether in a particular situation treatment provider knows information is false or lacks a factual foundation is a fact question that cannot be resolved in the opinion process. *See, e.g.,* Attorney General Opinions DM-98 (1992) at 3; H-56 (1973) at 3; M-187 (1968) at 3; O-2911 (1940) at 2. We do not believe, however, that a treatment provider who reports a suspicion of child abuse based on incomplete or dated information ordinarily may be convicted of making a false report or a report lacking a factual foundation under section 261.107.

reporter will not know all of the details. Section 261.104 implies, for example, that the reporter may not know the child's name or the identity of the child's caregiver. According to the statute, the report must reflect only the reporter's belief that a child has been abused. So long as the reporter acts in good faith, he or she is immune from civil or criminal liability.

In our opinion, Family Code chapter 261 confers discretion in whether to file charges of child abuse upon the investigating authority, the court, and the prosecutor, but confers no discretion upon the person who originally suspects that a child has been abused, e.g., a treatment provider. Once a treatment provider has reported the suspicion to an appropriate authority, the authority will investigate the claim. If, upon completing the investigation, the authority believes the claim of child abuse is substantiated, the authority may recommend to the court, the district attorney, and a law-enforcement agency that a petition should be filed against the alleged perpetrator. The court then may direct a prosecuting authority to file appropriate charges.

SUMMARY

Under Family Code section 261.101(a), a person who suspects that a child has been abused or neglected must report that suspicion immediately to the appropriate authorities. The Council on Sex Offender Treatment may not interpret section 261.101(a) to permit a registered sex-offender-treatment provider or affiliated sex-offender-treatment provider to decide whether to report a suspicion where the suspicion is based on dated or incomplete information.

Very truly yours,

Dan Morales
Attorney General of Texas

JORGE VEGA
First Assistant Attorney General

SARAH J. SIRELY
Chair, Opinion Committee

Prepared by KYMBERLY K. OLTROGGE
Assistant Attorney General

Disclosure under Subpoena

OFFICE OF THE ATTORNEY GENERAL

STATE OF TEXAS

DAN MORALES
ATTORNEY GENERAL

September 23, 1996

Ms. Rebecca E. Forkner
Executive Director
Texas State Board of Examiners of
    Psychologists
333 Guadalupe, Suite 2-450
Austin, Texas 78701

Letter Opinion No. 96-102
Re: *Effect of provision of chapter*
    611, Health and Safety Code,
    authorizing mental health
    professional to disclose confidential
    information about a patient in
    response to a subpoena (ID#
    38823)

Dear Ms. Forkner:

On behalf of the Texas State Board of Examiners of Psychologists ("the board"), you inquire about a recent amendment to chapter 611 of the Health and Safety Code, which establishes the confidentiality of the mental health records of a patient that are created or maintained by a psychologist[1] and sets out exceptions to the confidentiality provision. Senate Bill 667 of the 74th Legislature addressed the disclosure of health and mental health care information by hospitals, physicians, and mental health professionals. Among other provisions, it adopted section 611.006 of the Health and Safety Code, which provides for disclosure of mental health information in judicial and administrative proceedings. Section 611.006 states as follows:

> *(a) A professional may disclose confidential information in:*
>
> > *(1) a judicial or administrative proceeding brought by the patient or the patient's legally authorized representative against a professional, including malpractice proceedings;*
> >
> > *(2) a license revocation proceeding in which the patient is a complaining witness and in which disclosure is relevant to the claim or defense of a professional;*
> >
> > *(3) a judicial or administrative proceeding in which the patient waives the patient's right in writing to the privilege of confidentiality of information or when a representative of the patient acting on the patient's behalf submits a written waiver to the confidentiality privilege;*

---

1   Chapter 611 defines "professional" to include a licensed physician, "a person licensed or certified by this state to diagnose, evaluate, or treat any mental or emotional condition or disorder," or "a person the patient reasonably believes" to hold the required license or certificate. Health & Safety Code § 611.001(2).

> *(4) a judicial or administrative proceeding to substantiate and collect on a claim for mental or emotional health services rendered to the patient;*
>
> *(5) a judicial proceeding if the judge finds that the patient, after having been informed that communications would not be privileged, has made communications to a professional in the course of a court-ordered examination relating to the patient's mental or emotional condition or disorder,... [exception omitted];*
>
> *(6) a judicial proceeding affecting the parent-child relationship;*
>
> *(7) any criminal proceeding, as otherwise provided by law;*
>
> *(8) a judicial or administrative proceeding regarding the abuse or neglect, or the cause of abuse or neglect, of a resident of an institution, as that term is defined by Chapter 242;*
>
> *(9) a judicial proceeding relating to a will if the patient's physical or mental condition is relevant to the execution of the will;*
>
> *(10) an involuntary commitment proceeding for court-ordered treatment or for a probable cause hearing...;*
>
> *(11) a judicial or administrative proceeding where the court or agency has issued an order or subpoena.*
>
> *(b) On granting an order under Subsection (a)(5), the court, in determining the extent to which disclosure of all or any part of a communication is necessary,* SHALL IMPOSE APPROPRIATE SAFEGUARDS AGAINST UNAUTHORIZED DISCLOSURE. *[Emphasis added.]*

You state that psychologists typically receive numerous subpoena duces tecum[2] for psychological records of present and former patients, and you ask how a psychologist should respond to receiving such a subpoena. You believe that subsection 611.006(a)(11) conflicts with a board rule governing the release of patient records, 465.22(d)(3), which provides as follows:

> *An individual licensed and/or certified by this Board shall release information about a patient or client only upon written authorization by the patient, client, or appropriate legal guardian; pursuant to a proper court order, or as required by applicable state or federal law.*

22 T.A.C. § 465.22(d)(3). The board interprets the quoted rule as requiring a psychologist to refuse to honor a subpoena unless it is accompanied by an authorization for release signed by the client or his or her legal guardian.

Because the rules for issuing subpoenas in civil cases[3] are relevant to your question about the effect of subsection 611.006(a)(11) on the board's rule, we will review them before answering it. The Texas Rules of Civil Procedure authorize various forms of discovery, including requests and motions for production, examination, and copying of documents. Rule 176 provides for issuing subpoenas to witnesses in

---

2   A subpoena duces tecum issued pursuant to rule 177a of the Texas Rules of Civil Procedure requires a witness to produce documentary evidence.

3   We will not review rules for issuing subpoenas in administrative proceedings under the Administrative Procedure Act, Gov't Code ch. 2001, because discovery in a contested case under that act is governed by the Rules of Civil Procedure. Gov't Code § 2001.091; Attorney General Opinion JM-1075 (1989) at 2. See also Gov't Code § 2001.089 (state agency authorized to issue subpoenas for witnesses and records in contested case).

civil suits:

> The clerk of the district or county court, or justice of the peace,[4] as the case may be, at the request of any party to a suit pending in his court, or of any agent or attorney, shall issue a subpoena for any witness or witnesses who may be represented to reside within one hundred miles of the courthouse of the county in which the suit is pending....

A subpoena may also command a witness to produce books, papers, and documents.

A witness summoned in any suit "shall attend the court... until discharged by the court or party summoning such witness." If a witness fails to attend after being summoned, the witness "may be fined by the court as for contempt of court, and an attachment may issue against the body of such witness to compel the attendance of such witness." "Any witness refusing to give evidence may be committed to jail, there to remain without bail until such witness shall consent to give evidence." Thus, the rules provide for enforcing a subpoena. They also provide a way for the witness to raise a claim of privilege. Rule 177a allows a witness to move to quash or modify a subpoena that is "unreasonable and oppressive." Rule 166b of the Rules of Civil Procedure authorizes a person from whom discovery is sought to seek a protective order limiting discovery.

Rules of civil procedure are promulgated by the Texas Supreme Court pursuant to article V, section 31(b) of the Texas Constitution, which states in part that "[t]he Supreme Court shall promulgate rules of civil procedure for all courts not inconsistent with the laws of the state...." If a rule of civil procedure conflicts with a statute, the rule must yield.[5] However, we find no conflict between subsection 611.006(a)(11) and rules 176 and 177a. Subsection 611.006(a)(11) in fact makes it clear that a psychologist may comply with a subpoena.[6]

Subsection 611.006(a)(11) does not expressly condition a psychologist's compliance with a subpoena upon a written release signed by the patient or guardian.

---

4   Section 611.006(11) authorizes a professional to disclose confidential information in "a judicial or administrative proceeding where the court or agency has issued an order or subpoena." (Emphasis added.) You suggest that a "subpoena" within this provision means a subpoena issued only after a review by a court or agency as to whether the person requesting the records has a need for the information that overrides the patient's general right to confidentiality. It appears that you equate "court" with "judge" in reading this statute. Your argument is not consistent with procedures for issuing and contesting subpoenas established in the Rules of Civil Procedure. Moreover, the term "court" does not necessarily mean "judge." It has been defined more broadly, as "an instrumentality of sovereignty, the repository of its judicial power, with authority to adjudge as to the rights of person or property between adversaries." The phrase "court or agency" in section 611.006(a)(11) appears to refer to the legal entity that has jurisdiction of a matter, and not to the individual officers or employees who perform its functions.

5   Attorney General Opinion DM-308 (1994) at 2. See Gov't Code § 22.004(c) (rule adopted by supreme court repeals all conflicting laws and parts of laws governing practice and procedure in civil actions, but substantive law is not repealed).

6   Subsection 611.006(a) states that a professional "may disclose confidential information" in various circumstances, and you suggest that the use of the word "may" means that the psychologist has discretion to comply or not comply with the subpoena, so that he may refuse compliance unless it is accompanied by a written release. We disagree with your argument. The bill analysis to Senate Bill 667 states that section 611.006 "[s]ets forth conditions under which a professional is authorized to disclose confidential information in a judicial or administrative proceeding." House Public Health Committee, Bill Analysis, Tex. S.B. 667, 74th Leg., R.S. (1995) at 3 (emphasis added). Moreover, your suggested construction of section 611.006 ignores the mandatory nature of a subpoena.

To read subsection 611.006(a)(11) as requiring a written release would render it superfluous, because subsection 611.006(a)(3) authorizes a psychologist to disclose confidential information about a patient in a judicial or administrative proceeding if a written waiver is provided by the patient or the patient's representative. It is presumed that the legislature intended the entire statute to be effective. Moreover, the overall purpose of Senate Bill 667 was to "define the appropriate disclosure of patient health and mental health care information by hospitals, doctors, and mental health professionals." Its legislative history states that it adopted provisions authorizing " professionals" to disclose mental health records in judicial or administrative proceedings.[7]

To the extent that an administrative rule is inconsistent with a statute, the rule must yield. This well-established standard is incorporated into the provision defining the board's rule-making power: the board "may make all rules not inconsistent with the Constitution and laws of this state, which are reasonably necessary for the proper performance of its duties...." Rule 465.22(d)(3), as interpreted by the board, is inconsistent with subsection 611.006(a)(11) and is invalid to the extent of the inconsistency. Accordingly, a psychologist's duty to comply with a subpoena for patient records is not contingent on receiving a written waiver from the patient or patient's representative.[8]

You also suggest that section 611.006(a)(11) conflicts with rule 510 of the Texas Rules of Civil Evidence, which establishes the confidentiality of communications between a patient and a mental health professional, subject to exceptions permitting disclosure of such communications in court proceedings.[9] Several of the exceptions in rule 510 are similar to exceptions in section 611.006. For example, disclosure is authorized if the proceedings are brought by the patient against a professional, if the patient or his or her representative signs a waiver, or if the purpose of the proceeding is to collect on a claim for mental or emotional health services rendered to the patient. Rule 510 also provides the following broad exception in court proceedings as to a communication or record relevant to an issue of the physical, mental or emotional condition of a patient in any proceeding in which any party relies upon the condition as a part of the party's claim or defense.

A psychologist may claim the rule 510 privilege on behalf of the patient, and the authority to do so is presumed in the absence of evidence to the contrary. The Rules of Civil Procedure provide methods for a witness to claim that records are privileged and to have the question resolved by the court. If a psychologist believes that he or she has received a subpoena for records that are privileged and not within

---

7   Id.; see also House Public Health Committee, Bill Analysis, Tex. S.B. 667, 74th Leg., R.S. (1995) at 1 ("Background" statement cites expense and delay involved in obtaining medical records for a court case). Senate Bill 667 also added to the provisions of article 4495b, V.T.C.S. that authorize a physician to disclose medical records in court or administrative proceedings..

8   We do not consider whether a psychologist was authorized to disregard a subpoena for patient records in the absence of a written waiver prior to the effective date of section 611.006(a)(11), Health and Safety Code.

9   On November 23, 1982, the Texas Supreme Court entered an order adopting the Texas Rules of Civil Evidence. Under this order, former article 5561h, V.T.C.S. (1925), now codified as Health and Safety Code, chapter 611, was deemed repealed with respect to civil actions and replaced by rule 510 of the Texas Rules of Evidence. see List of Repealed Statutes and Enumeration, 641-642 S.W.2d at LXVIII (Sept. 1, 1983); Health & Safety Code § 611.001 historical note (Vernon 1992) [Act of May 7, 1979, 66th Leg., R.S., ch. 239, § 1, 1979 Tex. Gen. Laws 512, 513]. Section 611.006 of the Health and Safety Code relates to a psychologist's authority to disclose otherwise confidential information in an administrative or judicial proceeding and thus appears to reflect provisions of the Rules of Civil Evidence.

an exception to rule 510, he or she should avail himself of the protections found in the Rules of Civil Procedure. Thus, section 611.006(a)(11) and rule 510 of the Texas Rules of Civil Evidence may be construed in harmony.[10]

You also ask the following questions about the psychologist's obligation upon receiving a subpoena that is not accompanied by a signed release:

> *Must the psychologist contact the patient to give the patient the opportunity to file a motion to quash before releasing the records? If the psychologist fails to contact the patient or cannot locate the patient and it is later determined that the records were not subject to being subpoenaed, is the psychologist then liable under [chapter 611 of the] Health and Safety Code[11]... to the patient for releasing the records? Does the psychologist bear the responsibility of hiring an attorney to determine if the records are privileged from being subpoenaed? If the psychologist delays in producing the records while attempting to contact the patient, can the psychologist be sanctioned for the delay?*

Section 611.006(11) authorizes a psychologist to provide confidential information in "a judicial or administrative proceeding where the court or agency has issued an order or subpoena." However, as we have already pointed out, a particular subpoena might seek records that are privileged and not within an exception to rule 510. You wish to know what the psychologist's responsibility would be in such a case. We are able to address these questions only in the most general way, by pointing out that courts of various states have found a mental health professional may be liable in tort to a patient for the unauthorized disclosure of confidential patient information,[12] but we have found no case addressing the psychologist's duty at the point of receiving a *subpoena duces tecum* for patient records that may or may not be privileged from disclosure in a judicial proceeding. Moreover, the question of liability must be decided on the basis of the relevant facts and circumstances of each case. Although it may be advisable for a psychologist to notify a patient that his records have been subpoenaed, we cannot determine that the action would be either necessary or sufficient to protect the psychologist from liability to the patient should privileged information from the patient's records be disclosed. We believe that the individual psychologist should consult a private attorney if such issues arise in connection with his or her practice.

---

10 You have asked us to consider the recent decision in Jaffee v. Redmond, 116 S. Ct. 1923 (1996), in which the United States Supreme Court, exercising its authority under Federal Rule of Evidence 501 to define new evidentiary privileges, recognized the existence of a psychotherapist-patient privilege. Jaffee v. Redmond is not relevant to the question before us, because a privilege for psychotherapist-patient communications already exists in Texas, see Rule of Civil Evidence 510, and because Texas courts, unlike federal courts, lack authority to establish new privileges, see Tex. R. Civ. Evid. 501.

11 Section 611.005 of the Health and Safety Code provides that "[a] person aggrieved by the improper disclosure of or failure to disclose confidential... records in violation of this chapter may petition the district court of the county in which the person resides for appropriate relief, including injunctive relief."

12 See generally 24 AM. JUR. Proof of Facts 3d, 123, Proof of Unauthorized Disclosure of Confidential Patient Information by a Psychotherapist (1994); Judy E. Zelin, J.D., Annotation, Physician's Tort Liability for Unauthorized Disclosure of Confidential Information About Patient, 48 A.L.R. 4th 668 (1986). These authorities relate to disclosures of confidential information in a wide variety of circumstances, not limited to disclosures in judicial proceedings.

SUMMARY

A psychologist is authorized to disclose confidential information about a patient in a judicial or administrative proceeding where the court or agency has issued an order or subpoena without receiving a written waiver of confidentiality from the patient or patient's representative. A rule of the Board of Examiners of Psychologists interpreted by the board as requiring such a waiver is invalid to the extent of inconsistency with the exception to the confidentiality requirement found in section 611.006(a)(11) of the Health and Safety Code. If a psychologist has received a subpoena for patient mental health records he or she believes are privileged by rule 510 of the Rules of Evidence, he or she may raise the claim of privilege under applicable provisions of the Rules of Civil Procedure. Although it may be advisable for a psychologist to notify a patient that his records have been subpoenaed, we cannot determine that the action would be either necessary or sufficient to protect the psychologist from liability in tort in the event that the patient's privileged mental health information is disclosed in a judicial proceeding.

Yours very truly,

Susan L. Garrison
Assistant Attorney General
Opinion Committee

Parent's Access to School Counseling Records

OFFICE OF THE ATTORNEY GENERAL - STATE OF TEXAS

JOHN CORNYN

August 7, 2002

Mr. Felipe T. Alanis   Opinion No. JC-0538
Commissioner of Education   Re: *Whether a parent has an unrestricted*
Texas Education Agency   *right of access to the school*
1701 North Congress Avenue   *counseling records of his or her*
Austin, Texas 78701-1494   *minor child (RQ-0506-JC)*

Dear Mr. Alanis:

Your predecessor in office requested our opinion as to whether a parent has an unrestricted right of access to the school counseling records of his or her minor child. The question arises because of an apparent conflict between section 26.004 of the Education Code, which grants to a parent access "to all written records of a school district concerning the parent's child," and section 611.0045 of the Health and Safety Code, which authorizes a mental health professional, under certain circumstances, to deny access to a patient's record "if the professional determines that release . . . would be harmful to the patient's physical, mental, or emotional health." In addition, federal law generally grants to a parent a right of access to all "education records" concerning his or her child. We conclude that only under very narrow and unusual circumstances may such records be withheld from the parent.

Section 26.004 of the Education Code provides, in relevant part:[1]

A parent is entitled to access to all written records of a school district concerning the parent's child, including: . . . . (5) counseling records; (6) psychological records; . . . . (9) teacher and counselor evaluations; . . . .

This statute requires that a school district provide access to a child's parent of "all written . . . counseling records."[2]

On the other hand, you suggest that section 611.0045 of the Health and Safety Code may, under particular circumstances, permit a school counselor to deny such records to the parent. That statute provides, in relevant part:

(a) Except as otherwise provided by this section, a patient is entitled to have access to the content of a confidential record made about the patient.

(b) The professional may deny access to any portion of a record if the

---

1   Tex. Educ. Code Ann. § 26.004 (Vernon 1996).
2   *See also* Tex. Fam. Code Ann. § 153.073(a)(2) (Vernon 1996) ("Unless limited by court order, a parent appointed as a conservator of a child has at all times the right . . . of access to medical, dental, psychological, and educational records of the child.")

professional determines that release of that portion would be harmful to the patient's physical, mental, or emotional health.

(c) If the professional denies access to any portion of a record, the professional shall give the patient a signed and dated written statement that having access to the record would be harmful to the patient's physical, mental, or emotional health and shall include a copy of the written statement in the patient's records. The statement must specify the portion of the record to which access is denied, the reason for denial, and the duration of the denial. . . . .

(e) If a professional denies access to a portion of a confidential record, the professional shall allow examination and copying of the record by another professional if the patient selects the professional to treat the patient for the same or a related condition as the professional denying access.[3]

"Professional" is defined as:

(A) a person authorized to practice medicine in any state or nation;

(B) a person licensed or certified by this state to diagnose, evaluate, or treat any mental or emotional condition or disorder; or

(C) a person the patient reasonably believes is authorized, licensed, or certified as provided by this subsection.[4]

The term "patient" means "a person who consults or is interviewed by a professional for diagnosis, evaluation, or treatment of any mental or emotional condition or disorder, including alcoholism or drug addiction."[5]

Section 611.004 states that "[a] professional may disclose confidential information only . . . to a person who has the written consent of the patient, or a parent if the patient is a minor."[6] In *Abrams v. Jones*, the Texas Supreme Court held that, "[b]ecause subsection (b) [of section 611.0045] may limit a patient's rights to his or her own records, subsection (b) can also limit a parent's or third party's right to a patient's records when the third party or parent stands in the patient's stead."[7] Furthermore, "[i]f a professional does deny a parent access to part of a child's records, the parent has recourse under section 611.0045(e). . . . First, the professional denying access must allow examination and copying of the record by another professional selected by the parent acting on behalf of the patient to treat the patient for the same or a related condition. Second, a parent denied access to a child's records has judicial recourse," which provides that "[a] person aggrieved by the improper disclosure of or failure to disclose confidential communications or records in violation of this chapter may petition the district court of the county in which the person resides for appropriate relief, including injunctive relief").[8]

Thus, on the one hand, section 26.004 of the Education Code grants a parent access to all school "counseling records" regarding his or her child.[9] On the other hand, under section 611.0045 of the Health and Safety Code, a "professional" may

3   Tex. Health & Safety Code Ann. § 611.0045 (Vernon Supp. 2002)
4   *Id.* § 611.001(2) (Vernon 1992)
5   *Id.* § 611.001(1)
6   *Id.* § 611.004(a)(4) (Vernon Supp. 2002)
7   35 S.W.3d 620 (Tex. 2000), *Abrams*, 35 S.W.3d at 626.
8   *See* TEX. HEALTH & SAFETY CODE ANN. § 611.005 (Vernon Supp. 2002)
9   TEX. EDUC. CODE ANN. § 26.004 (Vernon 1996)

deny such access if he or she "determines that release . . . would be harmful to the patient's physical, mental, or emotional health."[10]

Before we attempt to reconcile these statutes, we note that section 611.0045 does not necessarily apply to every individual designated a "school counselor." We must consequently inquire into the nature of that designation.

Chapter 21 of the Education Code creates the State Board for Educator Certification (the "Board"), whose duty it is to "regulate and oversee all aspects of the certification, continuing education, and standards of conduct of public school educators."[11] The Board is required to "propose rules that," *inter alia*, "specify the classes of educator certificates to be issued, including emergency certificates," and "specify the requirements for the issuance and renewal of an educator certificate." [12] In addition, "[t]he board shall propose rules establishing the training requirements a person must accomplish to obtain a certificate, enter an internship, or enter an induction-year program," and "shall specify the minimum academic qualifications required for a certificate." Rules adopted by the Board must, in general, be approved by the State Board of Education.[13]

With regard to school counselors, the Board has adopted specific requirements:

These specific requirements are applicable in addition to the under-graduate criteria outlined in Subchapter G of this chapter (relating to Certification Requirements for Classroom Teachers).

(1) The guidance program (at least three semester hours). This area provides an understanding of the principles, philosophy, organization, and services of the guidance program.

(2) The pupil served (at least six semester hours). This area is devoted to intensive study that develops an understanding of the physical, intellectual, social, and emotional development of children and youth, and the influences of the school program on development.

(3) Resource areas (at least 21 semester hours).

(A) The preparation program shall help the prospective counselor achieve a balanced program of teacher education by giving attention to related resource areas. The amount of emphasis given to an area shall depend on the student's undergraduate preparation and experience.

(B) These advanced level studies are not necessarily represented by a sequence of semester hour courses. They are planned programs to meet the needs of the individual student. They are intended to ensure professional competence.

(C) Upon completion of the program, the prospective counselor shall have developed skills in guidance techniques that assure an ability to use the instruments of measurement and evaluation necessary for understanding, appraising, and counseling individuals and groups. The student shall be skilled in the use of occupational and educational information and materials appropriate for the guidance of youths. Also, the student shall have developed, through study and supervised practice, an ability to

---

10 TEX. HEALTH & SAFETY CODE ANN. § 611.0045 (Vernon Supp. 2002)
11 TEX. EDUC. CODE ANN. § 21.031 (Vernon 1996).
12 *Id.* § 21.041(b)(2), (4)
13 *Id.* § 21.042

work with groups of youths and adults and to counsel with individuals.

(4) The certificate. The counselor certificate shall require:

(A) a valid provisional or standard teaching certificate; and

(B) three creditable years, as defined in Subchapter Y of this Chapter (relating to Definitions), of classroom teaching experience.[14]

It is significant, however, that these rules do not require an individual designated a "school counselor" to obtain any other professional license issued by the State of Texas.

Chapter 503 of the Occupations Code applies to a "licensed professional counselor," which is **defined as "a person who holds a license issued under this chapter"** and who:

(A) represents the person to the public by any title or description of services incorporating the words "licensed counselor" and offers to provide professional counseling services to any individual, couple, family, group, or other entity for compensation, implying that the person offering the services is licensed and trained, or expert in counseling; or

(B) engages in any practice of counseling.[15]

The "practice of professional counseling" is defined as "the application of mental health, psychotherapeutic, and human development principles to:

(1) facilitate human development and adjustment through life;

(2) prevent, assess, evaluate, and treat mental, emotional, or behavioral disorders and associated distresses that interfere with mental health;

(3) conduct assessments and evaluations to establish treatment goals and objectives; and

(4) plan, implement, and evaluate treatment plans using counseling treatment interventions that include: (A) counseling; (B) assessment; (C) consulting; and (D) referral.[16]

Moreover, to qualify for a license under chapter 503 of the Occupations Code, a person must have a master's or doctoral degree in counseling or a related field, complete 36 months or 3,000 hours of supervised experience working in a counseling setting, and meet other rigorous requirements set forth in section 503.302 of the Occupations Code. Although section 503.051 states that "[t]his chapter does not apply to an activity, service, or use of an official title by a person employed as a counselor by a . . . public or private educational institution if the person is performing counseling or counseling-related activities within the scope of the person's employment," section 503.059 declares that "[a] person otherwise exempt under this subchapter who obtains a license under this chapter is subject to this chapter to the same extent as any other person licensed under this chapter."[17]

It cannot reasonably be argued that a person who is merely certified as a "school counselor" by the State Board for Educator Certification is "a person licensed or certified by this state to diagnose, evaluate, or treat any mental or emotional condition

---

14 19 Tex. Admin. Code § 230.307 (2001).

15 Tex. Occ. Code Ann. § 503.002(4) (Vernon 2002) (emphasis added).

16 *Id.* § 503.003(a).

17 *Id.* §§ 503.051, .059.

or disorder." If an individual holds both a "school counselor" certification *and* a license as a "professional counselor," he or she may be entitled to claim the benefit of section 611.0045 of the Health and Safety Code. If the person holds *only* a certificate from the Board designating him or her as a "school counselor," the person is not so entitled.

On the other hand, it seems clear that a "licensed professional counselor" fits within the definition of "professional" for purposes of section 611.001 of the Health and Safety Code, as "a person licensed or certified by this state to diagnose, evaluate, or treat any mental or emotional condition or disorder." Thus, if a person licensed as a "professional counselor" in the State of Texas serves as a "school counselor," he or she may be entitled, under section 611.0045, to deny access to the parent of a student's counseling records if he or she "determines that release . . . would be harmful to the [student's] physical, mental, or emotional health."

As to those individuals who are both certified school counselors and licensed "professionals" under chapter 611 of the Health and Safety Code, we must attempt to reconcile section 26.004 of the Education Code, which grants to a parent access to all "written . . . counseling records," with subsection 611.0045(b) of the Health and Safety Code, which permits a "professional," as defined therein, to deny such access. Rules of statutory construction require that statutes be harmonized if there is any reasonable way to do so[18]. In our view, these two seemingly conflicting statutes may be harmonized by construing section 611.0045 as an exception to section 26.004, in the relatively narrow circumstance in which the school counselor also happens to fall within the definition of "professional" in section 611.001 of the Health and Safety Code. The result is that, under Texas law, a parent has an unrestricted access to all written counseling records regarding his or her child, except when the records are those created by a "professional" as defined in section 611.001.

We must also address the Federal Family Educational and Privacy Rights Act of 1974, often referred to as the Buckley Amendment. That statute provides, in relevant part:

> (a)(1)(A) No funds shall be made available under any applicable program to any educational agency or institution which has a policy of denying, or which effectively prevents, the parents of students who are or have been in attendance at a school of such agency or at such institution, as the case may be, the right to inspect and review the education records of their children.[19]

"Education records" are defined as "those records, files, documents, and other materials which - (i) contain information directly related to a student; and (ii) are maintained by an educational agency or institution or by a person acting for such agency or institution." The term does not include, *inter alia*, "(i) records of instructional, supervisory, and administrative personnel and educational personnel ancillary thereto which are in the sole possession of the maker thereof and which are not accessible or revealed to any other person except a substitute." Regulations adopted under this provision have slightly modified this exception:

> Education records. . . . . (b) The term does not include:
>
> (1) Records that are kept in the sole possession of the maker, are used

---

18 *See La Sara Grain Co. v. First Nat'l Bank*, 673 S.W.2d 558, 565 (Tex. 1984); *Acker v. Tex. Water Comm'n*, 790 S.W.2d 299, 301 (Tex. 1990).

19 20 U.S.C. § 1232g(a)(1)(A) (1994)

only as a personal memory aid, and are not accessible or revealed to any other person except a temporary substitute for the maker of the record.[20]

If an educational institution under 20 U.S.C. § 1232g "wishes to continue receiving federal funding, it must permit its students [or parent or guardian if the student is under the age of 18] to inspect and review their education records."[21] Thus, to the extent a school district receives federal funding, the Buckley Amendment is paramount in the matter of parental access to education records of a minor child. It is clear that, under federal law, a public school that receives federal funds may withhold counseling records from a parent of a minor student only if those records "are kept in the sole possession of" the counselor, "are used only as a personal memory aid, and are not accessible or revealed to any other person except a temporary substitute" for the counselor.[22]

We may now summarize our answer to your question. Generally, all student records are available to parents. Because federal law, to the extent a school district receives federal funding, is paramount in the matter of parental access to education records of a minor child, a public school may withhold counseling records from a parent only if the records are kept in the sole possession of the counselor, are used only as the counselor's personal memory aid, and are not accessible or revealed to any other person except a temporary substitute for the counselor. Within this circumscribed category, state law permits the counselor to withhold the records only if the counselor is a "professional," as defined in section 611.001(2) of the Health and Safety Code, and further, if the counselor "determines that release" of such record "would be harmful to the patient's physical, mental, or emotional health." If the counselor does not fall within the category of licensed professional under section 611.001 of the Health and Safety Code, section 26.004 of the Education Code prevails, and the parent "is entitled to access to all written records" of the school district "concerning the parent's child, including . . . counseling records."

Finally, we note that section 261.101 of the Family Code provides that "[a] person having cause to believe that a child's physical or mental health or welfare has been adversely affected by abuse or neglect by any person shall immediately make a report as provided by this subchapter."[23] Subsection (b) thereof declares:

> *If a professional has cause to believe that a child has been abused or neglected or may be abused or neglected, or that a child is a victim of an offense under Section 21.11, Penal Code, and the professional has cause to believe that the child has been abused as defined by Section 261.001, the professional shall make a report not later than the 48th hour after the hour the professional first suspects that the child has been or may be abused or neglected or is a victim of an offense under Section 21.11, Penal Code. A professional may not delegate to or rely on another person to make the report. . . .[24]*

"Professional" is defined for purposes of subsection (b) as "an individual who is licensed or certified by the state or who is an employee of a facility licensed,

---

20 34 C.F.R. § 99.3 (2001)
21 Tex. Att'y Gen. ORD-431 (1985) at 2. *See also* Tex. Att'y Gen. Op. No. JM-154 (1984) (private school may lose federal funds if it fails to accord inspection rights under Family Educational and Privacy Rights Act).
22 *See* 34 C.F.R. § 99.3 (2001)
23 TEX. FAM. CODE ANN. § 261.101(a) (Vernon Supp. 2002)
24 *Id.* § 261.101(b)

certified, or operated by the state and who, in the normal course of official duties or duties for which a license or certification is required, has direct contact with children. The term includes teachers, nurses, doctors, day-care employees, employees of a clinic or health care facility that provides reproductive services, juvenile probation officers, and juvenile detention or correctional officers." Furthermore, "[t]he requirement to report" under section 261.101 "applies without exception to an individual whose personal communications may otherwise be privileged, including an attorney, a member of the clergy, a medical practitioner, a social worker, a mental health professional, and an employee of a clinic or health care facility that provides reproductive services."[25] It is clear that, because any school counselor is necessarily "certified by the state," the requirements of section 261.101 apply to any school counselor.

SUMMARY

Generally, all student records are available to parents. Only under very narrow and unusual circumstances may a minor child's school counseling records be withheld from a parent. Under the Federal Family Educational and Privacy Rights Act, a public school may withhold a minor child's counseling records from a parent only if the records are kept in the sole possession of the counselor, are used only as the counselor's personal memory aid, and are not accessible or revealed to any other person except a temporary substitute for the counselor. Within this circumscribed category, state law permits the counselor to withhold a minor child's records only if the counselor is a "professional," as defined in section 611.001(2) of the Health and Safety Code, and further, if the counselor "determines that release" of such record "would be harmful to the patient's physical, mental, or emotional health." If the counselor does not fall within the category of licensed professional under section 611.001(2) of the Health and Safety Code, section 26.004 of the Education Code prevails, and the parent "is entitled to access to all written records" of the school district "concerning the parent's child, including . . . counseling records."

Yours very truly,

JOHN CORNYN
Attorney General of Texas

HOWARD G. BALDWIN, JR., *First Assistant Attorney General*
NANCY FULLER, *Deputy Attorney General - General Counsel*
SUSAN DENMON GUSKY, *Chair, Opinion Committee*
Rick Gilpin, *Assistant Attorney General, Opinion Committee*

---

25 *Id.* § 261.101(c)

Sex Offender Treatment License Necessary?

ATTORNEY GENERAL OF TEXAS

GREG ABBOTT

April 18, 2006

The Honorable D. Matt
  Bingham
Smith County Criminal
  District Attorney
Smith County Courthouse
100 North Broadway, Fourth
  Floor
Tyler, Texas 75702

Opinion No. GA-0423
Re: *Whether a physician, psychiatrist,
licensed professional counselor, licensed
marriage and family therapist, or social
worker must be licensed by the Council
on Sex Offender Treatment to provide
rehabilitation services or act as a sex
offender treatment provider (RQ-0405-
GA*

Dear Mr. Bingham:

You ask whether a physician, psychiatrist, licensed professional counselor, licensed marriage and family therapist, or social worker may provide rehabilitation services or act as a sex offender treatment provider without being licensed by the Council on Sex Offender Treatment (the "Council").[1] You also ask about the discretion of counselors concerning the scope of the terms "rehabilitation service" and "sex offender" as defined in chapter 110 of the Occupations Code.

As background, we observe that chapter 110 of the Occupations Code generally governs sex offender treatment providers. Under the chapter, a sex offender treatment provider is:

> *a person, licensed or certified to practice in this state, including a physician, psychiatrist, psychologist, licensed professional counselor, licensed marriage and family therapist, or social worker, who provides mental health or medical services for rehabilitation of sex offenders.*[2]

Prior to 2005, the Council maintained a voluntary registry of sex offender treatment providers who (1) met the Council's criteria for the treatment of sex offenders and (2) provided mental health or medical services for the rehabilitation of sex offenders.[3] During the legislature's last regular session in 2005, it changed the Council's mission from registering sex offender treatment providers on a voluntary

---

1 See Letter from Honorable D. Matt Bingham, Smith County Criminal District Attorney, to Honorable Greg Abbott, Attorney General of Texas (Oct. 13, 2005) (on file with the Opinion Committee, also available at http://www.oag.state.tx.us) [hereinafter Request Letter]

2 Tex. Occ. Code Ann. § 110.001(7) (Vernon Supp. 2005)

3 Act of May 20, 2003, 78th Leg., ch. 1276, § 14.005(a), 2003 Tex. Gen. Laws 4158, 4309 (formerly codified as Tex. Occ. Code Ann. § 110.001(4))

basis to mandatory licensing.[4] Thus, chapter 110 now provides:

(a) A person may not provide a rehabilitation service or act as a sex offender treatment provider unless the person is licensed under this chapter.[5]

You state that Smith County currently provides counseling to juveniles in the juvenile justice system through several counselors of different backgrounds: a licensed psychologist and diplomat in forensic psychology, a person licensed as a clinical social worker and as a professional counselor, a licensed master social worker, a licensed professional counselor intern, and a graduate student at the University of Texas at Tyler. You ask whether the health care licenses that qualify a person as a sex offender treatment provider in section 110.001(7) constitute the license required in section 110.301(a).

We must construe statutes in context.[6] Consequently, we must consider section 110.301 in light of other sections of chapter 110 governing the Council and sex offender treatment providers, particularly those that pertain to licensing. ("We should not give one provision a meaning out of harmony or inconsistent with other provisions . . . ."). Chapter 110 charges the Council with setting the standards that sex offender treatment providers must meet to be eligible for a license under the chapter.[7] The Council has broad authority to adopt rules consistent with chapter 110 and has the specific duty to develop and implement license requirements by rule. Under section 110.301, a person must be licensed "under" chapter 110 either to "provide a rehabilitation service" or to "act as a sex offender treatment provider." A "rehabilitation service" is "a mental health treatment or medical intervention program designed to treat or remedy a sex offender's mental or medical problem that may relate or contribute to the sex offender's criminal or paraphiliac problem." A person "act[s] as a sex offender treatment provider" when the person provides "mental health or medical services for rehabilitation of sex offenders." A person who does not have a license under chapter 110 and who provides a rehabilitation service or acts as a sex offender treatment provider may be liable criminally.

You state that several of the licensed professionals who are counseling juveniles for Smith County Juvenile Services meet the definition of a sex offender treatment provider in section 110.001(7) but do not possess any additional license under chapter 110. You suggest that the legislature likely did not intend to "provide an exclusive licensing program, to the exclusion of other licensing as provided for in section 110.001(7) of the Occupations Code." Also, while you acknowledge that section 110.302 as revised "seems to contemplate the issuance of a license by the Council," you note that the Council had not promulgated licensing rules as of the date of your request. For these reasons, you perceive a conflict among sections 110.001(7) (defining a sex offender treatment provider), section 110.301 (requiring a license), and 110.302 (requiring the Council to promulgate licensing rules). You propose that the conflict may be resolved by construing the provision in 110.301 that requires a person to be "licensed under this chapter" as referring to any of the health care licenses listed in section 110.001(7).[8] However, the plain language of the statutes does not support your construction.

4 Act of May 25, 2005, 79th Leg., R.S., ch. 1089, 2005 Tex. Gen. Laws 3579
5 Tex. Occ. Code Ann. § 110.301(a) (Vernon Supp. 2005)
6 See Tex. Gov't Code Ann. § 311.011(a) (Vernon 2005)
7 See Tex. Occ. Code Ann. § 110.151(2) (Vernon Supp. 2005)
8 Id. at 4-5

Sections 110.001(7), 110.301 and 110.302 do not conflict. Section 110.001(7) defines a person who is a sex offender treatment provider, not a licensed sex offender treatment provider.[9] The license required in section 110.301 is the sex offender treatment provider license, not any of the various health care licenses listed in section 110.001(7). Physicians, psychiatrists, psychologists, professional counselors, marriage and family therapists, and social workers do not receive their respective professional licenses "under" chapter 110.[10] Chapter 110 requires a person to have both a professional license and a sex offender treatment provider license before the person may render rehabilitation services or provide mental health or medical services for the rehabilitation of sex offenders.

We note that persons who held a registration issued under Chapter 110, Occupations Code, on the effective date of the 2005 legislation, September 1, 2005, are to be "considered to hold a license under Chapter 110, Occupations Code, as amended." Thus, if any of the Smith County Juvenile Services professionals were registered with the Council on September 1, 2005, they are automatically deemed to be licensed sex offender treatment providers. For further guidance concerning the implementation of chapter 110, you should keep apprised of any rules as they are promulgated by the Council.[11]

You suggest that if chapter 110 requires a separate license, it poses practical problems for professional counselors not licensed by the Council due to the scope of terms such as "rehabilitation service" and "sex offender." A "rehabilitation service" is a "mental health treatment or medical intervention program designed to treat or remedy a sex offender's mental or medical problem that may relate or contribute to the sex offender's criminal or paraphiliac problem."[12] A "sex offender" is not only a person who has been convicted of or received deferred adjudication for a sex crime, but also a person who admits to violating a state or federal law regarding sexual conduct or who "experiences or evidences a paraphiliac disorder as defined by the Revised Diagnostic and Statistical Manual." Thus, you conjecture that a professional counselor who is not licensed by the Council and is treating a condition such as substance abuse may have to terminate treatment if the patient admits a past sex crime or evidences a paraphiliac disorder. You also suggest that such a counselor should be granted a measure of discretion to determine if treatment for a problem such as substance abuse should continue.

We agree that the respective definitions of the terms "rehabilitation service" and "sex offender" are markedly broad, but the "wisdom or expediency of the law is the Legislature's prerogative." Under section 110.001(5), a person must be licensed under chapter 110 to provide mental health treatment or administer a medical intervention program to treat or remedy a sex offender's mental or medical problem if it "may relate or contribute to the sex offender's criminal or paraphiliac problem."[13] Whether the patient is a "sex offender" as defined, and whether the treatment or program is for a problem that "may relate or contribute to" the offender's criminal or paraphiliac problem is a matter for the treating professional's determination in

---

9 See Tex. Occ. Code Ann. § 110.001(7) (Vernon Supp. 2005)

10 See, e.g., id. §§ 155.001 (license to practice medicine); 501.251 (psychologist license); 503.301 (professional counselor license) (Vernon 2004)

11 We note that the Council has proposed rules concerning various categories of licenses and licensing requirements. See 31 Tex. Reg. 209, 234-64 (proposed Dec. 30, 2005) (Council on Sex Offender Treatment).

12 Tex. Occ. Code Ann. § 110.001(5) (Vernon Supp. 2005) (emphasis added)

13 Tex. Occ. Code Ann. § 110.001(5) (Vernon Supp. 2005)

the first instance. But the professional must exercise the discretion to make that determination within the confines of chapter 110's express terms and the rules promulgated by the Council. .

SUMMARY

Chapter 110 of the Occupations Code requires a person to have one of the professional licenses listed in section 110.001(7) as well as a sex offender treatment provider license under section 110.301(a) before the person may render rehabilitation services or provide mental health or medical services for the rehabilitation of sex offenders. A person who was registered as a sex offender treatment provider as of September 1, 2005, is considered to hold a license under chapter 110. Whether the patient is a "sex offender" as defined and whether the treatment or program is for a problem that "may relate or contribute" to the offender's criminal or paraphiliac problem is a matter for the treating professional's determination within the bounds of chapter 110's express terms and the rules of the Council on Sex Offender Treatment.

Very truly yours,

GREG ABBOTT
Attorney General of Texas

BARRY MCBEE
First Assistant Attorney General

ELLEN L. WITT
Deputy Attorney General for Legal Counsel

NANCY S. FULLER
Chair, Opinion Committee

William A. Hill
Assistant Attorney General, Opinion Committee

Grandparent Access to Children and Records

ATTORNEY GENERAL OF TEXAS

GREG ABBOTT

October 13, 2004

The Honorable Jeff Wentworth
Chair, Senate Jurisprudence Committee
Texas State Senate
Post Office Box 12068
Austin, Texas 78711-2068

Opinion No.GA-260

Re: *Constitutionality of the Texas grandparent access statute, section 153.433, Family Code, in light of the United States Supreme Court's decision in Troxel v. Granville, 530 U.S. 57 (2000) (RQ-0215-GA)*

Dear Senator Wentworth:

You ask about the constitutionality of the Texas grandparent access statute, section 153.433 of the Family Code, in light of the United States Supreme Court's decision in Troxel v. Granville, 530 U.S. 57 (2000).

I. THE STATUTE

Section 153.433 of the Family Code provides:

The court shall order reasonable access to a grandchild by a grandparent if:

1. at the time the relief is requested, at least one biological or adoptive parent of the child has not had that parent's parental rights terminated; and

2. access is in the best interest of the child, and at least one of the following facts is present:

    (A) the grandparent requesting access to the child is a parent of a parent of the child and that parent of the child has been incarcerated in jail or prison during the three-month period preceding the filing of the petition or has been found by a court to be incompetent or is dead;

    (B) the parents of the child are divorced or have been living apart for the three-month period preceding filing of the petition or a suit for the dissolution of the parents' marriage is pending;

    (C) the child has been abused or neglected by a parent of the child;

    (D) the child has been adjudicated to be a child in need of supervision or a delinquent child under Title 3 [ch. 51, Texas Family Code];

    (E) the grandparent requesting access to the child is the parent of a person whose parent-child relationship with the child has been terminated by court order; or

    (F) the child has resided with the grandparent requesting access to the child for at least six months within the 24-month period preceding the filing of the petition.

In 2000, the United States Supreme Court held a Washington grandparent access statute to be unconstitutional on the ground that it contravened the Due Process Clause of the Fourteenth Amendment to the United States Constitution.[1] The Washington statute provided, in pertinent part, that

[a]ny person may petition the court for visitation rights at any time including, but not limited to, custody proceedings. The court may order visitation rights for any person when visitation may serve the best interest of the child whether or not there has been any change of circumstances.

You note that, although the Court's holding is limited to the application of the Washington statute to the facts of that case, the constitutionality of the Texas statute is now in question. We begin with an analysis of Troxel v. Granville.

II. TROXEL V. GRANVILLE

The Troxel case involved the application of a state statute to a dispute over grandparent visitation rights. "Tommie Granville and Brad Troxel shared a relationship that ended in June 1991. The two never married, but they had two daughters . . . ." After Tommie and Brad separated, Brad lived with his parents and regularly brought his daughters to his parents' home for weekend visitation. Brad committed suicide in May 1993, and although the Troxels initially continued to see their granddaughters on a regular basis, Tommie informed the Troxels in October 1993 that she wished to limit the grandparents' access to one short visit per month. The Troxels responded by filing suit in December 1993 to obtain extended visitation rights. At trial, Tommie, rather than opposing all visitations, asked the court to order one day of visitation per month with no overnight stay. The Troxels requested two weekends of visitation per month and two weeks each summer. The trial court took a middle position, ordering one weekend visitation per month, one week during the summer, and four hours on each of the grandparents' birthdays. The trial court based its decision on the "best interest of the children."

The intermediate appellate court reversed the trial court's decision on the basis that the Troxels lacked standing to seek visitation. The Supreme Court of Washington disagreed with the appellate court on the standing issue, but held that under the federal constitution the Washington statute "unconstitutionally infringes on the fundamental right of parents to rear their children." The United States Supreme Court granted certiorari, specifically to determine whether the Washington visitation "violates the federal constitution."

Justice O'Connor, in a plurality opinion joined by three other justices, first affirmed that "[t]he liberty interest at issue in this case - the interest of parents in the care, custody, and control of their children - is perhaps the oldest of the fundamental liberty interests recognized by this Court." The opinion then reviewed the statute in question, noting in particular the following language, which Justice O'Connor described as "breathtakingly broad": "'[a]ny person may petition the court for visitation rights at any time,' and the court may grant such visitation rights whenever 'visitation may serve the best interest of the child.'". The opinion noted that this language

effectively permits any third party seeking visitation to subject any

1   See Troxel v. Granville, 530 U.S. 57 (2000)

decision by a parent concerning visitation of the parent's children to state-court review. Once the visitation petition has been filed in court and the matter is placed before a judge, a parent's decision that visitation would not be in the child's best interest is accorded no deference. Section 26.10.160(3) contains no requirement that a court accord a parent's decision any presumption of validity or any weight whatsoever. Instead, the Washington statute places the best-interest determination solely in the hands of the judge. Should the judge disagree with the parent's estimation of the child's best interests, the judge's view necessarily prevails. Thus, in practical effect, in the State of Washington a court can disregard and overturn any decision by a fit custodial parent concerning visitation whenever a third party affected by the decision files a visitation petition, based solely on the judge's determination of the child's best interests. The Washington Supreme Court had the opportunity to give § 26.10.160(3) a narrower reading, but it declined to do so.

Justice O'Connor observed that "[t]he problem here is not that the Washington Superior Court intervened, but that when it did so, it gave no special weight at all to Granville's determination of her daughters' best interests." Moreover, "the judge placed on Granville, the fit custodial parent, the burden of disproving that visitation would be in the best interest of her daughters." As a result, "the court's presumption failed to provide any protection for Granville's fundamental constitutional right to make decisions concerning the rearing of her own daughters." Furthermore, the court observed, there existed no evidence that Tommie Granville "ever sought to cut off visitation entirely." The trial court "gave no weight to Granville's having assented to visitation even before the filing of any visitation petition or subsequent court intervention."

Justice O'Connor concluded that

the combination of these factors demonstrates that the visitation order in this case was an unconstitutional infringement on Granville's fundamental right to make decisions concerning the care, custody, and control of her two daughters. The Washington Superior Court failed to accord the determination of Granville, a fit custodial parent, any material weight. In fact, the Superior Court made only two formal findings in support of its visitation order. First, the Troxels "are part of a large, central, loving family, all located in this area, and the [Troxels] can provide opportunities for the children in the area of cousins and music." . . . Second, "[t]he children would be benefited from spending quality time with the [Troxels], provided that that time is balanced with time with the childrens' [sic] nuclear family." . . . These slender findings, in combination with the court's announced presumption in favor of grandparent visitation and its failure to accord significant weight to Granville's already having offered meaningful visitation to the Troxels, show that this case involves nothing more than a simple disagreement between the Washington Superior Court and Granville concerning her children's best interests.

But the plurality added a caveat:

Because we rest our decision on the sweeping breadth of § 26.10.060(3) and the application of that broad, unlimited power in this case, we do not consider the primary constitutional question passed on by the

Washington Supreme Court - whether the Due Process Clause requires
all nonparental visitation statutes to include a showing of harm or poten-
tial harm to the child as a condition precedent to granting visitation.
We do not, and need not, define today the precise scope of the parental
due process right in the visitation context. . . . Because much state-court
adjudication in this context occurs on a case-by-case basis, we would be
hesitant to hold that specific nonparental visitation statutes violate the
Due Process Clause as a per se matter.

The message of Troxel may thus be summarized: state statutes that infringe upon a parent's right to control the care and custody of his or her children are subject to strict scrutiny. A court may not, in visitation cases, substitute its own judgment in such a way as to infringe upon this fundamental liberty. The Washington statute is deficient per se on grounds of overbreadth, and its application to the facts of Troxel indicate a deficiency in its overall structure. Nevertheless, while any particular nonparental visitation statute may not as a matter of law violate the Fourteenth Amendment, the ultimate determination of any visitation statute's constitutionality requires a fact-intensive case-by-case analysis.

III. THE TEXAS CASES

At least seven Texas appellate cases since Troxel have addressed the constitutionality of section 153.433 of the Family Code. None of them have concluded that that provision is facially unconstitutional.

A. CLARK V. FUNK

The first decision,[2] was issued less than three months after the Supreme Court's decision in Troxel. Although Clark involved a conservatorship battle, the trial court had ruled that, if the divorced parents were unable to agree about their rights under the joint managing conservatorship, the paternal grandparents would make the final decision. The court, in referring to the recent Troxel decision, noted that

[t]he Texas statute . . . is, unlike the Washington visitation statute . . .
very limited in its application and does not simply depend upon a best
interest of the child finding . . . and again . . . the record before us clearly
reflects that the trial court's order was based, not merely on its singu-
lar determination of the best-interest question, but was firmly grounded
upon special factors that justify the imposition of a tie breaking role for
the grandparents that imposes a limited restriction of both parents' fun-
damental right to make decisions concerning the raising of their children.

B. LILLEY V. LILLEY

The next Texas case to reach the appellate level, Lilley v. Lilley, involved facts remarkably similar to those of Troxel, in that the paternal grandfather sought scheduled visitation with his granddaughter after the girl's father had committed suicide. Unlike the situation in Troxel, the Lilleys had been married but had subsequently divorced. Like Tommie Granville, however, Wendy Lilley asserted that the trial court's order granting access to her former father-in-law infringed on her fundamental right to make child-rearing decisions. The trial court awarded visitation rights to William Lilley, the paternal grandfather, and the court of appeals affirmed.

The court of appeals first distinguished the Texas statute from the Washington

2   Clark v. Funk, (Aug. 24, 2000)

statute held invalid in Troxel. According to the court, section 153.433 of the Family Code is not, unlike the Washington statute, "breathtakingly broad." Rather, it "allows only grandparents, under particular circumstances, to petition for access to a child, provided it is in the child's best interest." Thus, section 153.433 is sufficiently distinguishable from the Washington statute that it cannot be said to be unconstitutional on its face. Furthermore, the court found, the statute had not been unconstitutionally applied to the facts at issue. The trial court, unlike the trial court in Troxel, did not place on Wendy Lilley the burden of proving that her daughter would be harmed by visitation with her grandfather. The Lilleys had themselves "sought the State's intervention into their family's relationships when they filed to dissolve their marriage." Most significantly, Wendy Lilley had, unlike Tommie Granville, "taken inconsistent positions" about the grandfather's access to her daughter. The court of appeals concluded that "[t]he district court balanced Wendy's varying positions and rights" as a mother with the grandfather's "request for visitation and the child's interest in having a continuing relationship with her deceased father's family."

C. SAILOR V. PHILLIPS

In Sailor v. Phillips, the court of appeals affirmed its holding in Lilley that section 153.433 is facially constitutional, noting that it "defines certain circumstances when grandparent [visitation] may be ordered if it is in the children's best interest." Moreover, the mother in Sailor had severed all contact between her children and her former mother-in-law, even blocking "a final visit or even telephone contact with the boys' terminally ill grandfather when they were ages twelve and fourteen." Under these circumstances, the court of appeals affirmed the trial court's order allowing the children to visit their grandmother.

D. ROBY V. ADAMS

The fourth case, Roby v. Adams, is one of only two post-Troxel Texas cases to deny visitation rights to grandparents. The court did not reach the issue of the facial constitutionality of section 153.433. Rather, it emphasized that portion of Troxel requiring that "special weight" be accorded a fit parent's determination about visitation. On the basis of the facts presented at trial, the court of appeals found that the trial court was not justified in "finding that granting grandparent access would be in the best interest of the Roby children, against Roby's decision as a parent." The court distinguished the facts before it from those in Lilley, on the ground that

> *Roby never declared it would be in the best interest of his children to allow the Adams['] access to the children and Roby was consistent in his position on the Adams' access to them. Furthermore, the holding in Lilley appears to place the burden of persuasion upon the parent to prove the best interest of the child. This goes against the presumption so strongly enunciated in Troxel, that a fit parent acts in the best interest of his or her child. A grandparent seeking access under Tex. Fam. Code Ann. § 153.433 has the burden to overcome the presumption that a fit parent acts in the best interest of the parent's child in order to establish the "best interest of the child" prong of the statute.*

This language evidences a fundamental disagreement between the Austin and El Paso Courts of Appeal on the application of the Troxel standard to section 153.433. Roby in no way, however, questions the facial constitutionality of the Texas statute.

E. IN RE MARRIAGE OF BLACK

After an interval of more than a year, yet another Texas appellate court entered the fray regarding Troxel and its application to Texas law. In In re Marriage of Black, Crystal Dawn Black appealed a trial court decision awarding, as part of a divorce decree, grandparent access to her child. Ms. Black raised on appeal for the first time the issue of the constitutionality of section 153.433. The court of appeals, although holding that the issue of constitutionality could not be raised for the first time on appeal, approvingly quoted the court's language in Lilley.

F. IN RE C.P.J. AND S.B.J.

In the last two cases, both from 2003, the Dallas and San Antonio Courts of Appeal have struck a balance between what might be considered the two approaches previously taken by the Texas appellate courts: the embracing standard of Lilley and the narrower test applied in Roby.

In the case of In re C.P.J. and S.B.J., Marshall Jackson had married Stephanie Adams in May 1989, a union that produced two daughters. Stephanie died in October 1994, and until May 1997, Stephanie's parents, Ronnie and Cheryl Adams, cared for the children during the daytime hours while their father worked. In July 1997, the Adamses filed a petition for grandparent access, and after mediation, the parties agreed on a schedule of regular visits, which schedule was approved by the trial court. In October 2000, Jackson filed a petition to modify the Adamses' visitation order in light of the Troxel decision. In September 2002, the trial court denied Jackson's request to terminate visitation, but modified the visitation schedule to reduce the time the children spent with the Adamses. Jackson appealed, citing Troxel for the proposition that section 153.433 is unconstitutional.

The court's analysis focused primarily on the argument that section 153.433 is unconstitutional on its face. The court noted initially that the "holding in Troxel is clearly limited to the application of the Washington statute to the facts of that case. Accordingly, we cannot apply Troxel as a sweeping indictment of all non-parental visitation statutes in general or as to the Texas statute in particular. Further, the United States Supreme Court expressly declined to define the precise scope of the parental due process right in the visitation context." The court then discussed the different approaches taken by the courts in Lilley and Roby:

> Several Texas courts have addressed the grandparent visitation statute since the Troxel decision was delivered. However, no decision has directly held that the statute is unconstitutional. In Lilley v. Lilley, . . . the court held specifically that section 153.433 is "not unconstitutional on its face or in the district court's application to the facts at hand." . . . Differing somewhat with the Lilley holding, the El Paso court of appeals, in Roby v. Adams . . . stated that it was "[h]eeding the holding in Troxel," but it did not declare the statute to be unconstitutional either facially or as applied. . . . Instead, the El Paso court engrafted upon the statute a presumption that the parent is fit, that a fit parent is presumed to act in the best interests of the child, and that without a finding of parental unfitness, no grandparent visitation can be allowed over the parent's objection.

The court then presented its own resolution of these two cases:

> Because these cases dealing with a challenge of section 153.433 were

narrowly decided under the facts before the respective courts, we view them as describing a path under those facts. They are not controlling in the case we now consider. However, we are mindful that the court in Lilley resolved against the appellant an attack on the facial constitutionality of the statute.

In reconciling these varying standards with the case before it, the court of appeals first declined "to take the position that the statute is facially unconstitutional." In applying the Troxel standard to the circumstances presented, the court found that "there are at least several pivotal facts which show that the trial court did not deny due process to Jackson respecting his parental rights. First, Jackson agreed to the 1999 visitation order, which specifically found that visitation was in the 'best interests of the children.' . . . By reducing the visitation schedule and excluding Sunday visitation, the trial court's judgment plainly resolved any . . . conflict. Further, Jackson testified that he was not refusing visitation by the Adamses." Finally, the court concluded that "the relief ordered by the trial court respecting Jackson's motion and the application of the grandparent access statute to Jackson does not violate his due process rights as described in Troxel. It is apparent that the trial court was able to craft its decision by according 'at least some special weight to the parent's own determination.'".

G. In re Pensom

The final Texas appellate decision thus far, In re Pensom, issued less than a year ago, takes, like In re C.P.J., a balanced and reflective approach to the question of the facial unconstitutionality of section 153.433, and its application to particular circumstances. In that case, Keith Pensom and his wife, Melanie, had been divorced and granted joint managing conservatorship of their two children. After Melanie's death, her mother and stepfather, Maria and James Weaver, filed a petition to be appointed temporary sole managing conservators, or alternatively, to be granted reasonable access to the children. The trial court entered temporary orders granting access to Maria Weaver. Keith Pensom then filed a mandamus action, alleging first, that section 153.433 is unconstitutional on its face, and, in the alternative, that "the trial court abused its discretion in granting Maria access because it did not find him to be an unfit parent."

The court of appeals noted first that the parental interest in the care, custody, and control of their children is "a fundamental right protected by the Due Process Clause of the Fourteenth Amendment to the United States Constitution," and as a result, a "strict scrutiny" test must be applied. The court then summarized the Texas grandparent access statute as follows:

The Grandparent Access Statute allows grandparents to petition for access only under circumstances where the family unit has already, to some degree, been disrupted. A grandparent may request access if the parent is incarcerated, incompetent, or dead; the parents are divorced or living apart; the child is a delinquent or has been abused by its parents; the parent-child relationship has been terminated with one parent; or the child has resided with the grandparents for a statutorily-required length of time. . . . These provisions evidence the Legislature's recognition that cessation of contact with a grandparent may have a dramatic, and even traumatic, effect upon the child's well-being. Under such circumstances the State has a compelling interest in providing a forum for those grandparents having a significant existing relationship with their grandchildren.

The court continued:

Because the statute allows only grandparents to petition for access, the jurisdictional prerequisite of standing serves to ensure that the statutory scheme is narrowly tailored so that a parent's personal affairs are not needlessly intruded upon or interrupted by the trauma of litigation by any third party seeking access. However, more than a narrow standing requirement is necessary to satisfy the due process concerns raised in Troxel. . . . [T]he Troxel court refused to define the precise scope of the parental due process right in the access context . . . . The Court did not issue a per se holding that non-parental visitation statutes violate the Due Process Clause. The underlying logic of abstaining from such a decision was that states, in ruling on the constitutionality of their own non-parental visitation statutes, have made these determinations in the past on a case-by-case basis . . . . Accordingly, the Grandparent Access Statute is constitutional if its application protects parents' fundamental rights under the Due Process Clause. To achieve that goal, we construe the Grandparent Access Statute narrowly and in a manner consistent with the constitutional principles stated in Troxel.

The Pensom court thus reached the heart of the matter of the facial constitutionality of section 153.433: how to construe that provision in a manner consistent with Troxel. To do so, the court required that section 153.433 be construed narrowly. The court then spelled out exactly how a narrow construction of the statute would read:

[I]n order to satisfy the "best interest of the child" prong of the Grandparent Access Statute, a grandparent must overcome the presumption that a fit parent acts in the best interest of his or her child. To overcome this presumption, a grandparent has the burden to prove, by a preponderance of the evidence, either that the parent is not fit, or that denial of access by the grandparent would significantly impair the child's physical health or emotional well-being. Our holding that grandparents meet this burden is consistent with other provisions of the Family Code that require a higher degree of proof when a non-parent files a Suit Affecting the Parent-Child Relationship. When interpreted and applied in light of the framework established in Troxel, the Grandparent Access Statute is narrowly drawn to serve a compelling state interest and therefore is facially constitutional.

In applying this standard to the facts at hand, the court of appeals held that "a constitutional application of the Grandparent Access Statute requires the trial court to find either that relator is not fit, or that denial of access by the grandparent would significantly impair the child's physical health or emotional well-being. Here, the trial court did not make any such findings because, in granting access, it did not have the benefit of this court's guidance on applying the statute in light of Troxel." As a result, the court of appeals set aside the trial court's order granting Maria Weaver access to her two grandchildren.

IV. ANALYSIS AND CONCLUSION

More than four years have elapsed since the United States Supreme Court's decision in Troxel. Seven intermediate Texas appellate courts have attempted to formulate a test for applying the Troxel standard to section 153.433 of the Family Code. Each court that has considered the issue has held that provision to be constitutional on its face. Like those courts, we must begin with the presumption that the legislative enactment is constitutional. . A facial invalidation of a statute is appropriate only if it can be shown that under no circumstances can the statute be constitutionally applied. On the basis of this presumption of constitutionality, the holding of these Texas appellate cases, and on the clearly limiting language of Troxel, we conclude that section 153.433 is facially constitutional.

The Texas appellate cases have traced an arc from the relative permissiveness of Lilley to the strict standard of Roby and on to the more subtle analyses of In re C.P.J. and In re Pensom. Each of these decisions was of course circumscribed by its particular facts, but in our view, the latter two cases, and especially In re Pensom, reflect a reasoned and thoughtful attempt to harmonize section 153.433 of the Family Code with the Supreme Court's standard in Troxel. Thus, while section 153.433 is facially constitutional, it may, under particular circumstances, be unconstitutionally applied. In order to avoid an unconstitutional application of the statute, a court must require a grandparent to "overcome the presumption that a fit parent acts in the best interest of his or her child." To overcome the presumption, "a grandparent has the burden to prove, by a preponderance of the evidence, either that the parent is not fit, or that denial of access by the grandparent would significantly impair the child's physical health or emotional well-being." Such an approach has the virtue both of adopting the test of the most recent Texas appellate case on the matter in question, and of most closely complying with the caveats imposed by Troxel. We conclude therefore that section 153.433 is facially constitutional, but is constitutional in application only if construed in light of the limitations imposed by Troxel.

SUMMARY

Section 153.433 of the Family Code, the Texas Grandparent Access Statute, is constitutional on its face. It may be constitutionally applied, however, only in light of the limitations imposed by Troxel v. Granville. In order to avoid an unconstitutional application of the statute, a court must require a grandparent to "overcome the presumption that a fit parent acts in the best interest of his or her child." To overcome the presumption, "a grandparent has the burden to prove, by a preponderance of the evidence, either that the parent is not fit, or that denial of access by the grandparent would significantly impair the child's physical health or emotional well-being."

Very truly yours,

GREG ABBOTT
Attorney General of Texas

BARRY MCBEE, *First Assistant Attorney General*

DON R. WILLETT, *Deputy Attorney General for Legal Counsel*

NANCY S. FULLER, *Chair, Opinion Committee*

Rick Gilpin, *Assistant Attorney General, Opinion Committee*

Reporting Abuse during Childhood of Now-Adult

Attorney General of Texas

Greg Abbott

May 30, 2012

Tim F. Branaman, Ph.D.
Chair, Texas State Board of Examiners
of Psychologists
333 Guadalupe, Suite 2-450
Austin, Texas 78701

Opinion No.GA-0944

Re: *Whether a mental health*
professional is required by chapter
261, Family Code, to report abuse
or neglect that occurred during the
childhood of a now-adult patient

Dear Dr. Branaman:

You ask"[w]hether a mental health professional who is treating an adult patient must report any abuse or neglect, as those terms are defined in Chapter 261 of the Texas Family Code, that the mental health professional has cause to believe occurred during the adult patient's childhood."[1] You pose several additional questions about what information must be included in the report in the event we conclude that a report is required. See Request Letter at 1 (asking additional questions "if such a report is required").

Chapter 261 of the Family Code establishes the statutory requirements for reporting and investigating child abuse or neglect.[2] Section 261.101 requires professionals with "cause to believe that a child has been abused or neglected or may be abused or neglected"[3] or is the victim of specified offenses, to make a report within 48 hours.[4] You suggest the term "child" in the phrase "a child that has been abused or neglected" is ambiguous and raises the question of whether under subsection 261.101 (b) the professional's duty to report includes only an at-present child or extends to an individual who is now an adult but was a child when abused.[5]

When construing a statute, our objective is to determine and give effect to the Legislature's intent.[6] "We look first to the plain and common meaning of the statute's

1 Letter from Tim F. Branaman, Ph.D. , Chair, Tex. State Bd . of Exam'rs of Psychologists, to Honorable Greg Abbott, Tex. Att ' y Gen. at 1 (Dec. 11, 2011) , http ://www.texasattorneygeneral. gov/opin ("Request Letter").
2 See generally TEX. FAM. CODE ANN.§§ 261.001-.410 (West 2008 & Supp. 2011).
3 See TEX.FAM. CODE ANN.§ 261.001(1) (West Supp. 2011) (providing comprehensive definition of "abuse," including sexual abuse), 261 .001 (4) (defining "neglect"). Because the definition of abuse includes sexual abuse, we do not in this opinion separately discuss nonsexual abuse and sexual abuse.
4 Id. § 261.101(b) (West 2008); see also id. § 261.101(a) (requiring a person to immediately report a belief that a "child's physical or mental health or welfare has been adversely affected by abuse or neglect")
5 See Request Letter at 1-3
6 See City of Waco v. Kelley, 309 S.W.3d 536, 542 (Tex. 2010)

words."[7] And we determine legislative intent from the statute as a whole and not from isolated provisions.[8]

Based upon the plain language of the statute enacted by the Texas Legislature, the term "child" in subsection 261.101 (b) is not ambiguous. The Legislature specifically defined the term "child" for purposes of chapter 261 as: "a person under 18 years of age who is not and has not been married or who has not had the disabilities of minority removed for general purposes."[9] As the Texas Supreme Court has explained, "If the Legislature provides definitions for words it uses in statutes, then we use those definitions ...."[10]

We thus conclude that the term "child" used in chapter 261 refers to a person who at-present satisfies the definition and is under eighteen.

Language in other provisions of chapter 261 supports the view that an at-present child is chapter 261's focus. Subsection 261.101 (b) defines "professional" as "an individual who is licensed or certified by the state or who is an employee of a facility licensed, certified, or operated by the state and who, in the normal course of official duties ... has direct contact with children."[11] On its face, the term "children" here cannot be construed to include adults or former children, and instead can mean only those who are currently children. Further, subsequent uses of the term child in chapter 261 are preceded by the definitive article "the," which limits the term "child" to a definite or particular child.[12] Thus, to be consistent in meaning and use throughout chapter 261, the term "child" when used in subsection 261.101(b) must be construed as an at-present child.[13]

For these reasons, we believe that the term "child" used in chapter 261 refers to only an at-present child. Accordingly, a professional is not required by subsection 261.101 (b) to report the abuse or neglect the professional believes occurred during an adult patient's childhood. Because your additional questions are contingent upon an alternative conclusion, we need not address them.

---

7   Harris Cnty. Hasp. Dist. v. TomballReg'lHosp., 283 S.W.3d 838, 842 (Tex. 2009).
8   See Kelley, 309 S.W.3d at 542
9   TEX. FAM. CODE ANN.§ 101.003(a) (West 2008); see also id. § lOl.OOl(a) (providing that definitions apply to Family Code, title 5, including chapter 261).
10 Kelley, 309 S.W.3d at 542
11 TEX. FAM. CODE ANN. § 261.101(b) (West 2008) (emphasis added)
12 See, e.g., id. §§ 261.101(b) (providing that the reporting period commences "the hour the professional first suspects that the child has been or may be abused or neglected"), 261.1 04(1)-(2) (specifying that report ofchild abuse contain information pertaining to "the child"), 261.301 (d) (stating that primary purpose of investigation of report of child abuse is the "protection of the child"), 261.302(a)-(c) (providing for conduct of investigation of "the child" and "the subject child"); see also Town of Flower Mound v. Teague, 111 S.W.3d 742,764 (Tex. App.-Fort Worth 2003, pet. denied) ("'The' is a function word used to indicate that a following noun ... is definite or has been previously specified by context or circumstance, or is a unique or particular member of its class.")
13 See Tex. Dep't of Transp. v. Needham, 82 S.W.3d 314, 318 (Tex. 2002) ("Statutory terms should be interpreted consistently in every part of an act.")

SUMMARY

Under subsection 261.101 (b) of the Family Code, a professional is not required to report abuse or neglect that the professional believes occurred during an adult patient's childhood.

Very truly yours,

GREG ABBOTT
Attorney General of Texas

DANIEL T. HODGE, *First Assistant Attorney General*

JAMES D. BLACKLOCK, *Deputy Attorney General for Legal Counsel*

JASON BOATRIGHT ,*Chair, Opinion Committee*

Charlotte M. Harper, *Assistant Attorney General, Opinion Committee*

Reporting of Alleged Child Abuse

ATTORNEY GENERAL OF TEXAS

GREG ABBOTT

August 12, 2011

Ms. Anne Heiligenstein, Commissioner
Texas Department of Family and
 Protective Services
701 West 51st Street
Austin, Texas   78751

Opinion No.GA-0879

Re: *Whether a law enforcement agency is required to furnish information about alleged child abuse or neglect by a person responsible for the child's care, custody, or welfare to the Department of Family and Protective Services (RQ-0957-GA)*

Dear Commissioner Heiligenstein:

You ask whether a law enforcement agency is required to furnish information about alleged child abuse or neglect by a person responsible for the child's care, custody, or welfare to the Department of Family and Protective Services (the "Department,,).[1]

You indicate that in January 2011 a special investigator of the Department requested information from a municipal police department (the "City"). Request Letter at 1. Subsequently, the City referred the request to its open records division, which sought an open records letter ruling from the Office of Attorney General, contending that the requested information was excepted from disclosure under section 552.101, Government Code, as (I) information deemed confidential by section 261.201 of the Family Code; and (2) information implicating common-law privacy.[2] You argue that a law enforcement agency is statutorily required to furnish the information to the Department. Request Letter at 1.

Section 261.105 of the Family Code provides, in relevant part:

(a) All reports received by a local or state law enforcement agency that allege abuse or neglect by a person responsible for a child's care, custody, or welfare shall be referred immediately to the department or the designated agency.

(b) The department or designated agency shall immediately notify the appropriate state or local law enforcement agency of any report it receives, other than a report from a law enforcement agency, that concerns the suspected abuse or neglect

---

1   lLetter from Anne Heiligenstein, Commissioner, Texas Department of Family and Protective Services, to Honorable Greg Abbott, Attorney General ofTexas at 1 (Mar. 15,2011), https:l!www.oag.state.tx.us!opinlindexjq.shtml ("Request Letter'").

2   'See Letter fromB. Chase Griffith, Brown & Hofmeister, L.L.P., to Honorable Greg Abbott, Attorney General of Texas (Jan. 24, 2011) (attached to Request Letter as Exhibit B). This office responded to the City with an Open Records Letter Ruling. See Tex. Att'y Gen. OR2011-04507, https:!!www.oag.state.tx.us!openlindex_orl.php.

of a child or death. of a child from abuse or neglect.[3]

In chapter 261, the word "Department" means "the Department ofFamily and Protective Services."[4] Independently of the requirements of the Public Information Act, section 261.105 mandates cooperation between the Department and a local law enforcement agency by specifically requiring that a report alleging abuse or neglect by a person responsible for a child's care, custody, or welfare must be referred immediately to the Department or a designated agency after it is received by a local law enforcement agency.[5]

Moreover, another statute complements the policy established under section 261.105. Section 261.301(a) provides:

(a) With assistance from the appropriate state or local law enforcement agency as provided by this section, the department or designated agency shall make a prompt and thorough investigation of a report of child abuse or neglect allegedly committed by a person responsible for a child's care, custody, or welfare.[6]

These two statutes, taken together, contemplate a complete and total sharing of information between the Department and a local law enforcement agency so long as the alleged child abuse or neglect is "committed by a person responsible for a child's care, custody, or welfare." Id. We conclude that a law enforcement agency is therefore required to furnish information about alleged child abuse or neglect by a person responsible for the child's care, custody, or welfare to the Department of Family and Protective Services.

SUMMARY

Pursuant to sections 261.105 and 261.301 of the Family Code, a law enforcement agency is required to furnish information about alleged child abuse or neglect by a person responsible for the child's care, custody, or welfare to the Texas Department of Family and Protective Services.

Very truly yours,

GREG ABBOTT
Attorney General of Texas

DANIEL T. HODGE, *First Assistant Attorney General*

DAVID J. SCHENCK, *Deputy Attorney General for Legal Counsel*

JASON BOATRIGHT, *Chair, Opinion Committee*

Rick Gilpin, *Assistant Attorney General, Opinion Committee*

---

3   TEX. FAM. CODE ANN. § 261.1 05 (West Supp. 2010)
4   Id. § 261.001(2) (West 200S)
5   Id. § 261.105(a) (West Supp. 2010)
6   Id. § 261.301(a) (West 200S).

Using Advocates in School for Counseling

ATTORNEY GENERAL OF TEXAS

GREG ABBOTT

October 27, 2010

The Honorable Yvonne Davis
Chair, Committee on Urban Affairs
Texas House of Representatives
Post Office Box 2910
Austin, Texas 78768-2910

Opinion No.GA-0813
Re: *Whether parents may use the
services of an advocate in dealing
with matters of their child's
education (RQ-0871-GA)*

Dear Representative Davis:

You write to inquire generally "whether school districts can prohibit a parent from having an advocate to act on their behalfon matters pertaining to their child's education."[1] You appear to use the term "advocate" as a term with a particular meaning, yet there is no definition ofthe term in your letter. Similarly, you do not provide any context for your question, nor do you ask us to opine about the scope of any particular statute.[2] Accordingly, we can advise you only generally.

We find only one provision in the Education Code that uses the noun "advocate" in the context of parental involvement in their child's education.[3] Without defining the term "advocate," §29.306 of the Education Code provides that "a student who is deafor hard of hearing must have an education in which the student's parents ... and advocates for the student's parents ... are involved in determining the extent, content, and purpose of programs." This provision expressly provides that parents may have an "advocate" involved in the education of their deaf or hard-of-hearing child. Accordingly, a school district may not prohibit a parent from having

---

1 'Request Letter at I (available at http://www.texasattomeygeneral.gov).

2 See Request Letter at 1 'You offer a provision of the Education Code and a Texas Education Agency ("TEA") rule as examples of "proactive provisions" that encourage parental participation in their child's education. Request Letter at I; see also TEX. EDUC. CODE ANN. § 29.005 (West 2006); 19 TEX. ADMIN. CODE § 89.1050(c)(I)(F) (2010) (TEA, The Admission, Review, and Dismissal (ARD) Committee). Both section 29.005 and the TEA rule pertain specifically to education for children with disabilities under the federal Individuals with Disabilities Education Improvement Act (IDEA). See TEX. EDUC. CODE ANN. § 29.001 (West 2006) (requiring development of a statewide plan for the delivery of services to children with disabilities that includes rules for a "special education program so that a free appropriate public education is available to all of those children between the ages of three and 21"); 19 TEX. ADMIN. CODE § 89.1001 (2010) (TEA, Scope and Applicability) (providing that "[s]pecial education services shall be provided to eligible students in accordance with all applicable federal law ... and the State Plan Under Part B ofthe Individuals with Disabilities Education Act"); see also 20 U.S.C.A. § 1412(a)(l)(A) (West 2010) (providing that a state is eligible for funding assistance for a fiscal year if the state submits a plan assuring that the state complies with IDEA provisions). Becauseneither provision uses the term "advocate," and because we do not understand you to ask us about the IDEA, we do not address these provisions in depth.

3 See TEX. EDUC. CODE ANN. § 29.306 (West2006).

an advocate within the scope of §29.306.[4]

None of the briefing we received raised a relevant state law provision, and we find no provision in the Education Code that expressly authorizes a school district either to allow or prohibit an advocate for all purposes. We thus can not opine on the authority of a school district with respect to a parent's use of an advocate in all circumstances.[5]

Briefing we received from the TEA[6] advises that the IDEA's guarantee of a free appropriate public education for children with disabilities includes the development of an individualized education program ("IEP").[7] In general, an IEP is designed by a team of participants that includes, "at the discretion of the parent or the [school district], other individuals who have knowledge or special expertise regarding the child."[8] The TEA's brief suggests this individual with specialized knowledge or expertise is an "advocate" within the scope of your question. Though you do not ask our opinion about this specific provision, we nevertheless advise that we believe a school district may not prohibit a parent from inviting a person with "knowledge or special expertise regarding the child" to participate in the development of their disabled child's IEP.[9]

You also ask whether a "legislative remedy [is] necessary for granting the use of an advocate in every circumstance that a parent may face with regard to their child's education[.]" To the extent the Legislature seeks to expressly permit or prohibit the involvement of an "advocate" in particular circumstances, other than those discussed herein, a legislative remedy may be necessary.

SUMMARY

A school district may not prohibit a parent from having an advocate as authorized by section 29.306 of the Education Code. Similarly, a school district may not prohibit a parent from inviting an individual with specialized knowledge or expertise to participate in a disabled child's individual education program pursuant to the Individuals with Disabilities Education Act.

---

4 Cf Benavides Indep. Sch. Dist. v. Guerra, 681 S.W.2d 246,249 (Tex. App.-SanAntonio 1984, writ refd n.r.e.) (recognizing that a school board's act done in contravention of a statute is void)
5 Cf Tex. Att'y Gen. Op. No. JM-1267 (1990) at 7-8 (declining to answer speculative question)
6 'Brief from Mr. David Anderson, General Counsel, TEA, at 1-2 (Apr. 20, 2010) [hereinafter TEA Brief].
7 See also 20 U.S.C.A. §§ 1400(d) (West 2010) (providing purposes of IDEA), 1414(d) (providing for individualized education program); 34 C.F.R. § 300.323(c) (2009) (When IEPs must be in effect - Initial IEPs; provision of services); 19 TEx. ADMIN. CODE § 89.1001 (20 I0) (TEA, Scope and Applicability) (providing for special education services in accordance with applicable federal law)
8 20 U.S.C.A. § 1414(d)(1)(B)(vi) (West 2010); 34 C.F.R. § 300.321(a)(6) (2009) (IEP Team); see also 19 TEx. ADMIN. CODE § 89.l050(c)(1)(F) (2010) (TEA, The Admission, Review, and Dismissal (ARD) Committee) (providing for an ARD Committee as the individualize deducation program)
9 See 20 U.S.C.A. § 1414(d)(I)(B)(vi) (West 2010); 34 C.F.R. § 300.321(a)(6)(2009); see also 19 TEX. ADMIN. CODE § 89.l050(c)(I)(F) (2010) (TEA, The Admission, Review, and Dismissal (ARD) Committee) (providing for an ARD Committee as the individualized education program); see also Benavides Indep. Sch. Dist., 681 S.W.2d at 249 (recognizing that a school board's act done in contravention of a statute is void)

To the extent the Legislature seeks to expressly permit or prohibit the involvement of an "advocate" in particular circumstances, other than those discussed herein, a legislative remedy may be necessary

Very truly yours,

GREG ABBOTT
Attorney General of Texas

DANIEL T. HODGE, *First Assistant Attorney General*

DAVID J. SCHENCK, *Deputy Attorney General for Legal Counsel*

NANCY S. FULLER, *Chair, Opinion Committee*

Charlotte M. Harper, *Assistant Attorney General, Opinion Committee*

APPENDIX A

CODE OF ETHICS

CODE OF ETHICS OF THE NATIONAL ASSOCIATION OF SOCIAL WORKERS[1]

PREAMBLE

The primary mission of the social work profession is to enhance human well-being and help meet the basic human needs of all people, with particular attention to the needs and empowerment of people who are vulnerable, oppressed, and living in poverty. A historic and defining feature of social work is the profession's focus on individual well-being in a social context and the well-being of society. Fundamental to social work is attention to the environmental forces that create, contribute to, and address problems in living.

Social workers promote social justice and social change with and on behalf of clients. "*Clients*" is used inclusively to refer to individuals, families, groups, organizations, and communities. Social workers are sensitive to cultural and ethnic diversity and strive to end discrimination, oppression, poverty, and other forms of social injustice. These activities may be in the form of direct practice, community organizing, supervision, consultation, administration, advocacy, social and political action, policy development and implementation, education, and research and evaluation. Social workers seek to enhance the capacity of people to address their own needs. Social workers also seek to promote the responsiveness of organizations, communities, and other social institutions to individuals' needs and social problems.

The mission of the social work profession is rooted in a set of core values. These core values, embraced by social workers throughout the profession's history, are the foundation of social work's unique purpose and perspective:

- service
- social justice
- dignity and worth of the person
- importance of human relationships
- integrity
- competence

This constellation of core values reflects what is unique to the social work profession. Core values, and the principles that flow from them, must be balanced within the context and complexity of the human experience.

PURPOSE OF THE *NASW* CODE OF ETHICS

Professional ethics are at the core of social work. The profession has an obligation to articulate its basic values, ethical principles, and ethical standards. The *NASW Code of Ethics* sets forth these values, principles, and standards to guide social workers' conduct. The *Code* is relevant to all social workers and social work students, regardless of their professional functions, the settings in which they work,

---

1 *Approved by the 1996 NASW Delegate Assembly, revised by the 1999 and the 2008 NASW Delegate Assembly,; Updated April 23, 2009*

or the populations they serve.

The *NASW Code of Ethics* serves six purposes:

1. The *Code* identifies core values on which social work's mission is based.

2. The *Code* summarizes broad ethical principles that reflect the profession's core values and establishes a set of specific ethical standards that should be used to guide social work practice.

3. The *Code* is designed to help social workers identify relevant considerations when professional obligations conflict or ethical uncertainties arise.

4. The *Code* provides ethical standards to which the general public can hold the social work profession accountable.

5. The *Code* socializes practitioners new to the field to social work's mission, values, ethical principles, and ethical standards.

6. The *Code* articulates standards that the social work profession itself can use to assess whether social workers have engaged in unethical conduct. NASW has formal procedures to adjudicate ethics complaints filed against its members.[2] In subscribing to this *Code*, social workers are required to cooperate in its implementation, participate in NASW adjudication proceedings, and abide by any NASW disciplinary rulings or sanctions based on it.

The *Code* offers a set of values, principles, and standards to guide decision making and conduct when ethical issues arise. It does not provide a set of rules that prescribe how social workers should act in all situations. Specific applications of the *Code* must take into account the context in which it is being considered and the possibility of conflicts among the *Code*'s values, principles, and standards. Ethical responsibilities flow from all human relationships, from the personal and familial to the social and professional.

Further, the *NASW Code of Ethics* does not specify which values, principles, and standards are most important and ought to outweigh others in instances when they conflict. Reasonable differences of opinion can and do exist among social workers with respect to the ways in which values, ethical principles, and ethical standards should be rank ordered when they conflict. Ethical decision making in a given situation must apply the informed judgment of the individual social worker and should also consider how the issues would be judged in a peer review process where the ethical standards of the profession would be applied.

Ethical decision making is a process. There are many instances in social work where simple answers are not available to resolve complex ethical issues. Social workers should take into consideration all the values, principles, and standards in this *Code* that are relevant to any situation in which ethical judgment is warranted. Social workers' decisions and actions should be consistent with the spirit as well as the letter of this *Code*.

In addition to this *Code*, there are many other sources of information about ethical thinking that may be useful. Social workers should consider ethical theory and principles generally, social work theory and research, laws, regulations, agency policies, and other relevant codes of ethics, recognizing that among codes of ethics

2   For information on NASW adjudication procedures, see *NASW Procedures for the Adjudication of Grievances.*

social workers should consider the *NASW Code of Ethics* as their primary source. Social workers also should be aware of the impact on ethical decision making of their clients' and their own personal values and cultural and religious beliefs and practices. They should be aware of any conflicts between personal and professional values and deal with them responsibly. For additional guidance social workers should consult the relevant literature on professional ethics and ethical decision making and seek appropriate consultation when faced with ethical dilemmas. This may involve consultation with an agency-based or social work organization's ethics committee, a regulatory body, knowledgeable colleagues, supervisors, or legal counsel.

Instances may arise when social workers' ethical obligations conflict with agency policies or relevant laws or regulations. When such conflicts occur, social workers must make a responsible effort to resolve the conflict in a manner that is consistent with the values, principles, and standards expressed in this *Code*. If a reasonable resolution of the conflict does not appear possible, social workers should seek proper consultation before making a decision.

The *NASW Code of Ethics* is to be used by NASW and by individuals, agencies, organizations, and bodies (such as licensing and regulatory boards, professional liability insurance providers, courts of law, agency boards of directors, government agencies, and other professional groups) that choose to adopt it or use it as a frame of reference. Violation of standards in this *Code* does not automatically imply legal liability or violation of the law. Such determination can only be made in the context of legal and judicial proceedings. Alleged violations of the *Code* would be subject to a peer review process. Such processes are generally separate from legal or administrative procedures and insulated from legal review or proceedings to allow the profession to counsel and discipline its own members.

A code of ethics cannot guarantee ethical behavior. Moreover, a code of ethics cannot resolve all ethical issues or disputes or capture the richness and complexity involved in striving to make responsible choices within a moral community. Rather, a code of ethics sets forth values, ethical principles, and ethical standards to which professionals aspire and by which their actions can be judged. Social workers' ethical behavior should result from their personal commitment to engage in ethical practice. The *NASW Code of Ethics* reflects the commitment of all social workers to uphold the profession's values and to act ethically. Principles and standards must be applied by individuals of good character who discern moral questions and, in good faith, seek to make reliable ethical judgments.

ETHICAL PRINCIPLES

The following broad ethical principles are based on social work's core values of service, social justice, dignity and worth of the person, importance of human relationships, integrity, and competence. These principles set forth ideals to which all social workers should aspire.

Value: *Service*

Ethical Principle: *Social workers' primary goal is to help people in need and to address social problems.*

Social workers elevate service to others above self-interest. Social workers draw on their knowledge, values, and skills to help people in need and to address social problems. Social workers are encouraged to volunteer some portion of their professional skills with no expectation of significant financial return (pro bono service).

Value: *Social Justice*

Ethical Principle: *Social workers challenge social injustice.*

Social workers pursue social change, particularly with and on behalf of vulnerable and oppressed individuals and groups of people. Social workers' social change efforts are focused primarily on issues of poverty, unemployment, discrimination, and other forms of social injustice. These activities seek to promote sensitivity to and knowledge about oppression and cultural and ethnic diversity. Social workers strive to ensure access to needed information, services, and resources; equality of opportunity; and meaningful participation in decision making for all people.

Value: *Dignity and Worth of the Person*

Ethical Principle: *Social workers respect the inherent dignity and worth of the person.*

Social workers treat each person in a caring and respectful fashion, mindful of individual differences and cultural and ethnic diversity. Social workers promote clients' socially responsible self-determination. Social workers seek to enhance clients' capacity and opportunity to change and to address their own needs. Social workers are cognizant of their dual responsibility to clients and to the broader society. They seek to resolve conflicts between clients' interests and the broader society's interests in a socially responsible manner consistent with the values, ethical principles, and ethical standards of the profession.

Value: *Importance of Human Relationships*

Ethical Principle: *Social workers recognize the central importance of human relationships.*

Social workers understand that relationships between and among people are an important vehicle for change. Social workers engage people as partners in the helping process. Social workers seek to strengthen relationships among people in a purposeful effort to promote, restore, maintain, and enhance the well-being of individuals, families, social groups, organizations, and communities.

Value: *Integrity*

Ethical Principle: *Social workers behave in a trustworthy manner.*

Social workers are continually aware of the profession's mission, values, ethical principles, and ethical standards and practice in a manner consistent with them. Social workers act honestly and responsibly and promote ethical practices on the part of the organizations with which they are affiliated.

Value: *Competence*

Ethical Principle: *Social workers practice within their areas of competence and develop and enhance their professional expertise.*

Social workers continually strive to increase their professional knowledge and skills and to apply them in practice. Social workers should aspire to contribute to the knowledge base of the profession.

ETHICAL STANDARDS

The following ethical standards are relevant to the professional activities of all social workers. These standards concern (1) social workers' ethical responsibilities to clients, (2) social workers' ethical responsibilities to colleagues, (3) social workers' ethical responsibilities in practice settings, (4) social workers' ethical responsibilities as professionals, (5) social workers' ethical responsibilities to the social work profession, and (6) social workers' ethical responsibilities to the broader society.

Some of the standards that follow are enforceable guidelines for professional conduct, and some are aspirational. The extent to which each standard is enforceable is a matter of professional judgment to be exercised by those responsible for reviewing alleged violations of ethical standards.

1. SOCIAL WORKERS' ETHICAL RESPONSIBILITIES TO CLIENTS

1.01 COMMITMENT TO CLIENTS

Social workers' primary responsibility is to promote the well-being of clients. In general, clients' interests are primary. However, social workers' responsibility to the larger society or specific legal obligations may on limited occasions supersede the loyalty owed clients, and clients should be so advised. (Examples include when a social worker is required by law to report that a client has abused a child or has threatened to harm self or others.)

1.02 SELF-DETERMINATION

Social workers respect and promote the right of clients to self-determination and assist clients in their efforts to identify and clarify their goals. Social workers may limit clients' right to self-determination when, in the social workers' professional judgment, clients' actions or potential actions pose a serious, foreseeable, and imminent risk to themselves or others.

1.03 INFORMED CONSENT

(a) Social workers should provide services to clients only in the context of a professional relationship based, when appropriate, on valid informed consent. Social workers should use clear and understandable language to inform clients of the purpose of the services, risks related to the services, limits to services because of the requirements of a third-party payer, relevant costs, reasonable alternatives, clients' right to refuse or withdraw consent, and the time frame covered by the consent. Social workers should provide clients with an opportunity to ask questions.

(b) In instances when clients are not literate or have difficulty understanding the primary language used in the practice setting, social workers should take steps to ensure clients' comprehension. This may include providing clients with a detailed verbal explanation or arranging for a qualified interpreter or translator whenever possible.

(c) In instances when clients lack the capacity to provide informed consent, social workers should protect clients' interests by seeking permission from an appropriate third party, informing clients consistent with the clients' level of understanding. In such instances social workers should seek to ensure that the third party acts in a manner consistent with clients' wishes and interests. Social workers should take reasonable steps to enhance such clients' ability to give informed consent.

(d) In instances when clients are receiving services involuntarily, social workers should provide information about the nature and extent of services and about the extent of clients' right to refuse service.

(e) Social workers who provide services via electronic media (such as computer, telephone, radio, and television) should inform recipients of the limitations and risks associated with such services.

(f) Social workers should obtain clients' informed consent before audiotaping or videotaping clients or permitting observation of services to clients by a third party.

1.04 COMPETENCE

(a) Social workers should provide services and represent themselves as competent only within the boundaries of their education, training, license, certification, consultation received, supervised experience, or other relevant professional experience.

(b) Social workers should provide services in substantive areas or use intervention techniques or approaches that are new to them only after engaging in appropriate study, training, consultation, and supervision from people who are competent in those interventions or techniques.

(c) When generally recognized standards do not exist with respect to an emerging area of practice, social workers should exercise careful judgment and take responsible steps (including appropriate education, research, training, consultation, and supervision) to ensure the competence of their work and to protect clients from harm.

1.05 CULTURAL COMPETENCE AND SOCIAL DIVERSITY

(a) Social workers should understand culture and its function in human behavior and society, recognizing the strengths that exist in all cultures.

(b) Social workers should have a knowledge base of their clients' cultures and be able to demonstrate competence in the provision of services that are sensitive to clients' cultures and to differences among people and cultural groups.

(c) Social workers should obtain education about and seek to understand the nature of social diversity and oppression with respect to race, ethnicity, national origin, color, sex, sexual orientation, gender identity or expression, age, marital status, political belief, religion, immigration status, and mental or physical disability.

1.06 CONFLICTS OF INTEREST

(a) Social workers should be alert to and avoid conflicts of interest that interfere with the exercise of professional discretion and impartial judgment. Social workers should inform clients when a real or potential conflict of interest arises and take reasonable steps to resolve the issue in a manner that makes the clients' interests primary and protects clients' interests to the greatest extent possible. In some cases, protecting clients' interests may require termination of the professional relationship with proper referral of the client.

(b) Social workers should not take unfair advantage of any professional relationship or exploit others to further their personal, religious, political, or business interests.

(c) Social workers should not engage in dual or multiple relationships with clients or former clients in which there is a risk of exploitation or potential harm to the client. In instances when dual or multiple relationships are unavoidable, social workers should take steps to protect clients and are responsible for setting clear, appropriate, and culturally sensitive boundaries. (Dual or multiple relationships occur when social workers relate to clients in more than one relationship, whether professional, social, or business. Dual or multiple relationships can occur simultaneously or consecutively.)

(d) When social workers provide services to two or more people who have a relationship with each other (for example, couples, family members), social workers should clarify with all parties which individuals will be considered clients and the nature of social workers' professional obligations to the various individuals who are receiving services. Social workers who anticipate a conflict of interest among the individuals receiving services or who anticipate having to perform in potentially conflicting roles (for example, when a social worker is asked to testify in a child custody dispute or divorce proceedings involving clients) should clarify their role with the parties involved and take appropriate action to minimize any conflict of interest.

1.07 PRIVACY AND CONFIDENTIALITY

(a) Social workers should respect clients' right to privacy. Social workers should not solicit private information from clients unless it is essential to providing services or conducting social work evaluation or research. Once private information is shared, standards of confidentiality apply.

(b) Social workers may disclose confidential information when appropriate with valid consent from a client or a person legally authorized to consent on behalf of a client.

(c) Social workers should protect the confidentiality of all information obtained in the course of professional service, except for compelling professional reasons. The general expectation that social workers will keep information confidential does not apply when disclosure is necessary to prevent serious, foreseeable, and imminent harm to a client or other identifiable person. In all instances, social workers should disclose the least amount of confidential information necessary to achieve the desired purpose; only information that is directly relevant to the purpose for which the disclosure is made should be revealed.

(d) Social workers should inform clients, to the extent possible, about the disclosure of confidential information and the potential consequences, when feasible before the disclosure is made. This applies whether social workers disclose confidential information on the basis of a legal requirement or client consent.

(e) Social workers should discuss with clients and other interested parties the nature of confidentiality and limitations of clients' right to confidentiality. Social workers should review with clients circumstances where confidential information may be requested and where disclosure of confidential information may be legally required. This discussion should occur as soon as possible in the social worker-client relationship and as needed throughout the course of the relationship.

(f) When social workers provide counseling services to families, couples, or groups, social workers should seek agreement among the parties involved concerning each individual's right to confidentiality and obligation to preserve the confidentiality of information shared by others. Social workers should inform participants in family, couples, or group counseling that social workers cannot guarantee that all participants will honor such agreements.

(g) Social workers should inform clients involved in family, couples, marital, or group counseling of the social worker's, employer's, and agency's policy concerning the social worker's disclosure of confidential information among the parties involved in the counseling.

(h) Social workers should not disclose confidential information to third-party payers unless clients have authorized such disclosure.

(i) Social workers should not discuss confidential information in any setting unless privacy can be ensured. Social workers should not discuss confidential information in public or semipublic areas such as hallways, waiting rooms, elevators, and restaurants.

(j) Social workers should protect the confidentiality of clients during legal proceedings to the extent permitted by law. When a court of law or other legally authorized body orders social workers to disclose confidential or privileged information without a client's consent and such disclosure could cause harm to the client, social workers should request that the court withdraw the order or limit the order as narrowly as possible or maintain the records under seal, unavailable for public inspection.

(k) Social workers should protect the confidentiality of clients when responding to requests from members of the media.

(l) Social workers should protect the confidentiality of clients' written and electronic records and other sensitive information. Social workers should take reasonable steps to ensure that clients' records are stored in a secure location and that clients' records are not available to others who are not authorized to have access.

(m) Social workers should take precautions to ensure and maintain the confidentiality of information transmitted to other parties through the use of computers, electronic mail, facsimile machines, telephones and telephone answering machines, and other electronic or computer technology. Disclosure of identifying information should be avoided whenever possible.

(n) Social workers should transfer or dispose of clients' records in a manner that protects clients' confidentiality and is consistent with state statutes governing records and social work licensure.

(o) Social workers should take reasonable precautions to protect client confidentiality in the event of the social worker's termination of practice, incapacitation, or death.

(p) Social workers should not disclose identifying information when discussing clients for teaching or training purposes unless the client has consented to disclosure of confidential information.

(q) Social workers should not disclose identifying information when discussing clients with consultants unless the client has consented to disclosure of confidential information or there is a compelling need for such disclosure.

(r) Social workers should protect the confidentiality of deceased clients consistent with the preceding standards.

1.08 ACCESS TO RECORDS

(a) Social workers should provide clients with reasonable access to records concerning the clients. Social workers who are concerned that clients' access to their records could cause serious misunderstanding or harm to the client should provide assistance in interpreting the records and consultation with the client regarding the records. Social workers should limit clients' access to their records, or portions of their records, only in exceptional circumstances when there is compelling evidence that such access would cause serious harm to the client. Both clients' requests and the rationale for withholding some or all of the record should be documented in clients' files.

(b) When providing clients with access to their records, social workers should take steps to protect the confidentiality of other individuals identified or discussed in such records.

1.09 SEXUAL RELATIONSHIPS

(a) Social workers should under no circumstances engage in sexual activities or sexual contact with current clients, whether such contact is consensual or forced.

(b) Social workers should not engage in sexual activities or sexual contact with clients' relatives or other individuals with whom clients maintain a close personal relationship when there is a risk of exploitation or potential harm to the client. Sexual activity or sexual contact with clients' relatives or other individuals with whom clients maintain a personal relationship has the potential to be harmful to the client and may make it difficult for the social worker and client to maintain appropriate professional boundaries. Social workers—not their clients, their clients' relatives, or other individuals with whom the client maintains a personal relationship—assume the full burden for setting clear, appropriate, and culturally sensitive boundaries.

(c) Social workers should not engage in sexual activities or sexual contact with former clients because of the potential for harm to the client. If social workers engage in conduct contrary to this prohibition or claim that an exception to this prohibition is warranted because of extraordinary circumstances, it is social workers—not their clients—who assume the full burden of demonstrating that the former client has not been exploited, coerced, or manipulated, intentionally or unintentionally.

(d) Social workers should not provide clinical services to individuals with whom they have had a prior sexual relationship. Providing clinical services to a former sexual partner has the potential to be harmful to the individual and is likely to make it difficult for the social worker and individual to maintain appropriate professional boundaries.

1.10 PHYSICAL CONTACT

Social workers should not engage in physical contact with clients when there is a possibility of psychological harm to the client as a result of the contact (such as cradling or caressing clients). Social workers who engage in appropriate physical contact with clients are responsible for setting clear, appropriate, and culturally sensitive boundaries that govern such physical contact.

1.11 SEXUAL HARASSMENT

Social workers should not sexually harass clients. Sexual harassment includes sexual advances, sexual solicitation, requests for sexual favors, and other verbal or physical conduct of a sexual nature.

1.12 DEROGATORY LANGUAGE

Social workers should not use derogatory language in their written or verbal communications to or about clients. Social workers should use accurate and respectful language in all communications to and about clients.

1.13 PAYMENT FOR SERVICES

(a) When setting fees, social workers should ensure that the fees are fair, reasonable, and commensurate with the services performed. Consideration should be given to clients' ability to pay.

(b) Social workers should avoid accepting goods or services from clients as payment for professional services. Bartering arrangements, particularly involving services, create the potential for conflicts of interest, exploitation, and inappropriate boundaries in social workers' relationships with clients. Social workers should explore and may participate in bartering only in very limited circumstances when it can be demonstrated that such arrangements are an accepted practice among professionals in the local community, considered to be essential for the provision of services, negotiated without coercion, and entered into at the client's initiative and with the client's informed consent. Social workers who accept goods or services from clients as payment for professional services assume the full burden of demonstrating that this arrangement will not be detrimental to the client or the professional relationship.

(c) Social workers should not solicit a private fee or other remuneration for providing services to clients who are entitled to such available services through the social workers' employer or agency.

1.14 CLIENTS WHO LACK DECISION-MAKING CAPACITY

When social workers act on behalf of clients who lack the capacity to make informed decisions, social workers should take reasonable steps to safeguard the interests and rights of those clients.

1.15 INTERRUPTION OF SERVICES

Social workers should make reasonable efforts to ensure continuity of services in the event that services are interrupted by factors such as unavailability, relocation, illness, disability, or death.

1.16 TERMINATION OF SERVICES

(a) Social workers should terminate services to clients and professional relationships with them when such services and relationships are no longer required or no longer serve the clients' needs or interests.

(b) Social workers should take reasonable steps to avoid abandoning clients who are still in need of services. Social workers should withdraw services precipitously only under unusual circumstances, giving careful consideration to all factors in the situation and taking care to minimize possible adverse effects. Social workers should assist in making appropriate arrangements for continuation of services when necessary.

(c) Social workers in fee-for-service settings may terminate services to clients who are not paying an overdue balance if the financial contractual arrangements have been made clear to the client, if the client does not pose an imminent danger to self or others, and if the clinical and other consequences of the current nonpayment have been addressed and discussed with the client.

(d) Social workers should not terminate services to pursue a social, financial, or sexual relationship with a client.

(e) Social workers who anticipate the termination or interruption of services to clients should notify clients promptly and seek the transfer, referral, or continuation of services in relation to the clients' needs and preferences.

(f) Social workers who are leaving an employment setting should inform clients of appropriate options for the continuation of services and of the benefits and risks of the options.

2. SOCIAL WORKERS' ETHICAL RESPONSIBILITIES TO COLLEAGUES

2.01 RESPECT

(a) Social workers should treat colleagues with respect and should represent accurately and fairly the qualifications, views, and obligations of colleagues.

(b) Social workers should avoid unwarranted negative criticism of colleagues in communications with clients or with other professionals. Unwarranted negative criticism may include demeaning comments that refer to colleagues' level of competence or to individuals' attributes such as race, ethnicity, national origin, color, sex, sexual orientation, gender identity or expression, age, marital status, political belief, religion, immigration status, and mental or physical disability.

(c) Social workers should cooperate with social work colleagues and with colleagues of other professions when such cooperation serves the well-being of clients.

2.02 CONFIDENTIALITY

Social workers should respect confidential information shared by colleagues in the course of their professional relationships and transactions. Social workers should ensure that such colleagues understand social workers' obligation to respect confidentiality and any exceptions related to it.

2.03 INTERDISCIPLINARY COLLABORATION

(a) Social workers who are members of an interdisciplinary team should participate in and contribute to decisions that affect the well-being of clients by drawing on the perspectives, values, and experiences of the social work profession. Professional and ethical obligations of the interdisciplinary team as a whole and of its individual members should be clearly established.

(b) Social workers for whom a team decision raises ethical concerns should attempt to resolve the disagreement through appropriate channels. If the disagreement cannot be resolved, social workers should pursue other avenues to address their concerns consistent with client well-being.

2.04 DISPUTES INVOLVING COLLEAGUES

(a) Social workers should not take advantage of a dispute between a colleague and an employer to obtain a position or otherwise advance the social workers' own interests.

(b) Social workers should not exploit clients in disputes with colleagues or engage clients in any inappropriate discussion of conflicts between social workers and their colleagues.

2.05 CONSULTATION

(a) Social workers should seek the advice and counsel of colleagues whenever such consultation is in the best interests of clients.

(b) Social workers should keep themselves informed about colleagues' areas of expertise and competencies. Social workers should seek consultation only from colleagues who have demonstrated knowledge, expertise, and competence related to the subject of the consultation.

(c) When consulting with colleagues about clients, social workers should disclose the least amount of information necessary to achieve the purposes of the consultation.

2.06 REFERRAL FOR SERVICES

(a) Social workers should refer clients to other professionals when the other professionals' specialized knowledge or expertise is needed to serve clients fully or when social workers believe that they are not being effective or making reasonable progress with clients and that additional service is required.

(b) Social workers who refer clients to other professionals should take appropriate steps to facilitate an orderly transfer of responsibility. Social workers who refer clients to other professionals should disclose, with clients' consent, all pertinent information to the new service providers.

(c) Social workers are prohibited from giving or receiving payment for a referral when no professional service is provided by the referring social worker.

2.07 SEXUAL RELATIONSHIPS

(a) Social workers who function as supervisors or educators should not engage in sexual activities or contact with supervisees, students, trainees, or other colleagues over whom they exercise professional authority.

(b) Social workers should avoid engaging in sexual relationships with colleagues when there is potential for a conflict of interest. Social workers who become involved in, or anticipate becoming involved in, a sexual relationship with a colleague have a duty to transfer professional responsibilities, when necessary, to avoid a conflict of interest.

2.08 SEXUAL HARASSMENT

Social workers should not sexually harass supervisees, students, trainees, or colleagues. Sexual harassment includes sexual advances, sexual solicitation, requests for sexual favors, and other verbal or physical conduct of a sexual nature.

2.09 IMPAIRMENT OF COLLEAGUES

(a) Social workers who have direct knowledge of a social work colleague's impairment that is due to personal problems, psychosocial distress, substance abuse, or mental health difficulties and that interferes with practice effectiveness should consult with that colleague when feasible and assist the colleague in taking remedial action.

(b) Social workers who believe that a social work colleague's impairment interferes with practice effectiveness and that the colleague has not taken adequate steps to address the impairment should take action through appropriate channels established by employers, agencies, NASW, licensing and regulatory bodies, and other professional organizations.

2.10 INCOMPETENCE OF COLLEAGUES

(a) Social workers who have direct knowledge of a social work colleague's incompetence should consult with that colleague when feasible and assist the colleague in taking remedial action.

(b) Social workers who believe that a social work colleague is incompetent and has not taken adequate steps to address the incompetence should take action through appropriate channels established by employers, agencies, NASW, licensing and regulatory bodies, and other professional organizations.

2.11 UNETHICAL CONDUCT OF COLLEAGUES

(a) Social workers should take adequate measures to discourage, prevent, expose, and correct the unethical conduct of colleagues.

(b) Social workers should be knowledgeable about established policies and procedures for handling concerns about colleagues' unethical behavior. Social workers should be familiar with national, state, and local procedures for handling ethics complaints. These include policies and procedures created by NASW, licensing and regulatory bodies, employers, agencies, and other professional organizations.

(c) Social workers who believe that a colleague has acted unethically should seek resolution by discussing their concerns with the colleague when feasible and when such discussion is likely to be productive.

(d) When necessary, social workers who believe that a colleague has acted unethically should take action through appropriate formal channels (such as contacting a state licensing board or regulatory body, an NASW committee on inquiry, or other professional ethics committees).

(e) Social workers should defend and assist colleagues who are unjustly charged with unethical conduct.

3. SOCIAL WORKERS' ETHICAL RESPONSIBILITIES IN PRACTICE SETTINGS

3.01 SUPERVISION AND CONSULTATION

(a) Social workers who provide supervision or consultation should have the necessary knowledge and skill to supervise or consult appropriately and should do so only within their areas of knowledge and competence.

(b) Social workers who provide supervision or consultation are responsible for setting clear, appropriate, and culturally sensitive boundaries.

(c) Social workers should not engage in any dual or multiple relationships with supervisees in which there is a risk of exploitation of or potential harm to the supervisee.

(d) Social workers who provide supervision should evaluate supervisees' performance in a manner that is fair and respectful.

3.02 EDUCATION AND TRAINING

(a) Social workers who function as educators, field instructors for students, or trainers should provide instruction only within their areas of knowledge and competence and should provide instruction based on the most current information and knowledge available in the profession.

(b) Social workers who function as educators or field instructors for students should evaluate students' performance in a manner that is fair and respectful.

(c) Social workers who function as educators or field instructors for students should take reasonable steps to ensure that clients are routinely informed when services are being provided by students.

(d) Social workers who function as educators or field instructors for students should not engage in any dual or multiple relationships with students in which there is a risk of exploitation or potential harm to the student. Social work educators and field instructors are responsible for setting clear, appropriate, and culturally sensitive boundaries.

3.03 PERFORMANCE EVALUATION

Social workers who have responsibility for evaluating the performance of others should fulfill such responsibility in a fair and considerate manner and on the basis of clearly stated criteria.

3.04 CLIENT RECORDS

(a) Social workers should take reasonable steps to ensure that documentation in records is accurate and reflects the services provided.

(b) Social workers should include sufficient and timely documentation in records to facilitate the delivery of services and to ensure continuity of services provided to clients in the future.

(c) Social workers' documentation should protect clients' privacy to the extent that is possible and appropriate and should include only information that is directly relevant to the delivery of services.

(d) Social workers should store records following the termination of services to ensure reasonable future access. Records should be maintained for the number of years required by state statutes or relevant contracts.

3.05 BILLING

Social workers should establish and maintain billing practices that accurately reflect the nature and extent of services provided and that identify who provided the service in the practice setting.

3.06 CLIENT TRANSFER

(a) When an individual who is receiving services from another agency or colleague contacts a social worker for services, the social worker should carefully consider the client's needs before agreeing to provide services. To minimize possible confusion and conflict, social workers should discuss with potential clients the nature of the clients' current relationship with other service providers and the implications, including possible benefits or risks, of entering into a relationship with a new service provider.

(b) If a new client has been served by another agency or colleague, social workers should discuss with the client whether consultation with the previous service provider is in the client's best interest.

3.07 ADMINISTRATION

(a) Social work administrators should advocate within and outside their agencies for adequate resources to meet clients' needs.

(b) Social workers should advocate for resource allocation procedures that are open and fair. When not all clients' needs can be met, an allocation procedure should be developed that is nondiscriminatory and based on appropriate and consistently applied principles.

(c) Social workers who are administrators should take reasonable steps to ensure that adequate agency or organizational resources are available to provide appropriate staff supervision.

(d) Social work administrators should take reasonable steps to ensure that the working environment for which they are responsible is consistent with and encourages compliance with the NASW *Code of Ethics*. Social work administrators should take reasonable steps to eliminate any conditions in their organizations that violate, interfere with, or discourage compliance with the *Code*.

3.08 CONTINUING EDUCATION AND STAFF DEVELOPMENT

Social work administrators and supervisors should take reasonable steps to provide or arrange for continuing education and staff development for all staff for whom they are responsible. Continuing education and staff development should address current knowledge and emerging developments related to social work practice and ethics.

3.09 COMMITMENTS TO EMPLOYERS

(a) Social workers generally should adhere to commitments made to employers and employing organizations.

(b) Social workers should work to improve employing agencies' policies and procedures and the efficiency and effectiveness of their services.

(c) Social workers should take reasonable steps to ensure that employers are aware of social workers' ethical obligations as set forth in the NASW *Code of Ethics* and of the implications of those obligations for social work practice.

(d) Social workers should not allow an employing organization's policies, procedures, regulations, or administrative orders to interfere with their ethical practice of social work. Social workers should take reasonable steps to ensure that their employing organizations' practices are consistent with the *NASW Code of Ethics*.

(e) Social workers should act to prevent and eliminate discrimination in the employing organization's work assignments and in its employment policies and practices.

(f) Social workers should accept employment or arrange student field placements only in organizations that exercise fair personnel practices.

(g) Social workers should be diligent stewards of the resources of their employing organizations, wisely conserving funds where appropriate and never misappropriating funds or using them for unintended purposes.

3.10 LABOR-MANAGEMENT DISPUTES

(a) Social workers may engage in organized action, including the formation of and participation in labor unions, to improve services to clients and working conditions.

(b) The actions of social workers who are involved in labor-management disputes, job actions, or labor strikes should be guided by the profession's values, ethical principles, and ethical standards. Reasonable differences of opinion exist among social workers concerning their primary obligation as professionals during an actual or threatened labor strike or job action. Social workers should carefully examine relevant issues and their possible impact on clients before deciding on a course of action.

4. SOCIAL WORKERS' ETHICAL RESPONSIBILITIES AS PROFESSIONALS

4.01 COMPETENCE

(a) Social workers should accept responsibility or employment only on the basis of existing competence or the intention to acquire the necessary competence.

(b) Social workers should strive to become and remain proficient in professional practice and the performance of professional functions. Social workers should critically examine and keep current with emerging knowledge relevant to social work. Social workers should routinely review the professional literature and participate in continuing education relevant to social work practice and social work ethics.

(c) Social workers should base practice on recognized knowledge, including empirically based knowledge, relevant to social work and social work ethics.

4.02 DISCRIMINATION

Social workers should not practice, condone, facilitate, or collaborate with any form of discrimination on the basis of race, ethnicity, national origin, color, sex, sexual orientation, gender identity or expression, age, marital status, political belief, religion, immigration status, or mental or physical disability.

4.03 PRIVATE CONDUCT

Social workers should not permit their private conduct to interfere with their ability to fulfill their professional responsibilities.

4.04 DISHONESTY, FRAUD, AND DECEPTION

Social workers should not participate in, condone, or be associated with dishonesty, fraud, or deception.

4.05 IMPAIRMENT

(a) Social workers should not allow their own personal problems, psychosocial distress, legal problems, substance abuse, or mental health difficulties to interfere with their professional judgment and performance or to jeopardize the best interests of people for whom they have a professional responsibility.

(b) Social workers whose personal problems, psychosocial distress, legal problems, substance abuse, or mental health difficulties interfere with their professional judgment and performance should immediately seek consultation and take appropriate remedial action by seeking professional help, making adjustments in workload, terminating practice, or taking any other steps necessary to protect clients and others.

4.06 MISREPRESENTATION

(a) Social workers should make clear distinctions between statements made and actions engaged in as a private individual and as a representative of the social work profession, a professional social work organization, or the social worker's employing agency.

(b) Social workers who speak on behalf of professional social work organizations should accurately represent the official and authorized positions of the organizations.

(c) Social workers should ensure that their representations to clients, agencies, and the public of professional qualifications, credentials, education, competence, affiliations, services provided, or results to be achieved are accurate. Social workers should claim only those relevant professional credentials they actually possess and take steps to correct any inaccuracies or misrepresentations of their credentials by others.

4.07 SOLICITATIONS

(a) Social workers should not engage in uninvited solicitation of potential clients who, because of their circumstances, are vulnerable to undue influence, manipulation, or coercion.

(b) Social workers should not engage in solicitation of testimonial endorsements (including solicitation of consent to use a client's prior statement as a testimonial endorsement) from current clients or from other people who, because of their particular circumstances, are vulnerable to undue influence.

4.08 ACKNOWLEDGING CREDIT

(a) Social workers should take responsibility and credit, including authorship credit, only for work they have actually performed and to which they have contributed.

(b) Social workers should honestly acknowledge the work of and the contributions made by others.

5. SOCIAL WORKERS' ETHICAL RESPONSIBILITIES TO THE SOCIAL WORK PROFESSION

5.01 INTEGRITY OF THE PROFESSION

(a) Social workers should work toward the maintenance and promotion of high standards of practice.

(b) Social workers should uphold and advance the values, ethics, knowledge, and mission of the profession. Social workers should protect, enhance, and improve the integrity of the profession through appropriate study and research, active discussion, and responsible criticism of the profession.

(c) Social workers should contribute time and professional expertise to activities that promote respect for the value, integrity, and competence of the social work profession. These activities may include teaching, research, consultation, service, legislative testimony, presentations in the community, and participation in their professional organizations.

(d) Social workers should contribute to the knowledge base of social work and share with colleagues their knowledge related to practice, research, and ethics. Social workers should seek to con-tribute to the profession's literature and to share their knowledge at professional meetings and conferences.

(e) Social workers should act to prevent the unauthorized and unqualified practice of social work.

5.02 EVALUATION AND RESEARCH

(a) Social workers should monitor and evaluate policies, the implementation of programs, and practice interventions.

(b) Social workers should promote and facilitate evaluation and research to contribute to the development of knowledge.

(c) Social workers should critically examine and keep current with emerging knowledge relevant to social work and fully use evaluation and research evidence in their professional practice.

(d) Social workers engaged in evaluation or research should carefully consider possible consequences and should follow guidelines developed for the protection of evaluation and research participants. Appropriate institutional review boards should be consulted.

(e) Social workers engaged in evaluation or research should obtain voluntary and written informed consent from participants, when appropriate, without any implied or actual deprivation or penalty for refusal to participate; without undue inducement to participate; and with due regard for participants' well-being, privacy, and dignity. Informed consent should include information about the nature, extent, and duration of the participation requested and disclosure of the risks and benefits of participation in the research.

(f) When evaluation or research participants are incapable of giving informed consent, social workers should provide an appropriate explanation to the participants, obtain the participants' assent to the extent they are able, and obtain written consent from an appropriate proxy.

(g) Social workers should never design or conduct evaluation or research that does not use consent procedures, such as certain forms of naturalistic observation and archival research, unless rigorous and responsible review of the research has found it to be justified because of its prospective scientific, educational, or applied value and unless equally effective alternative procedures that do not involve waiver of consent are not feasible.

(h) Social workers should inform participants of their right to withdraw from evaluation and research at any time without penalty.

(i) Social workers should take appropriate steps to ensure that participants in evaluation and research have access to appropriate supportive services.

(j) Social workers engaged in evaluation or research should protect participants from unwarranted physical or mental distress, harm, danger, or deprivation.

(k) Social workers engaged in the evaluation of services should discuss collected information only for professional purposes and only with people professionally concerned with this information.

(l) Social workers engaged in evaluation or research should ensure the anonymity or confidentiality of participants and of the data obtained from them. Social workers should inform participants of any limits of confidentiality, the measures that will be taken to ensure confidentiality, and when any records containing research data will be destroyed.

(m) Social workers who report evaluation and research results should protect participants' confidentiality by omitting identifying information unless proper consent has been obtained authorizing disclosure.

(n) Social workers should report evaluation and research findings accurately. They should not fabricate or falsify results and should take steps to correct any errors later found in published data using standard publication methods.

(o) Social workers engaged in evaluation or research should be alert to and avoid conflicts of interest and dual relationships with participants, should inform participants when a real or potential conflict of interest arises, and should take steps to resolve the issue in a manner that makes participants' interests primary.

(p) Social workers should educate themselves, their students, and their colleagues about responsible research practices.

6. SOCIAL WORKERS' ETHICAL RESPONSIBILITIES TO THE BROADER SOCIETY

6.01 SOCIAL WELFARE

Social workers should promote the general welfare of society, from local to global levels, and the development of people, their communities, and their environments. Social workers should advocate for living conditions conducive to the fulfillment of basic human needs and should promote social, economic, political, and cultural values and institutions that are compatible with the realization of social justice.

6.02 PUBLIC PARTICIPATION

Social workers should facilitate informed participation by the public in shaping social policies and institutions.

6.03 PUBLIC EMERGENCIES

Social workers should provide appropriate professional services in public emergencies to the greatest extent possible.

6.04 SOCIAL AND POLITICAL ACTION

(a) Social workers should engage in social and political action that seeks to ensure that all people have equal access to the resources, employment, services, and opportunities they require to meet their basic human needs and to develop fully. Social workers should be aware of the impact of the political arena on practice and should advocate for changes in policy and legislation to improve social conditions in order to meet basic human needs and promote social justice.

(b) Social workers should act to expand choice and opportunity for all people, with special regard for vulnerable, disadvantaged, oppressed, and exploited people and groups.

(c) Social workers should promote conditions that encourage respect for cultural and social diversity within the United States and globally. Social workers should promote policies and practices that demonstrate respect for difference, support the expansion of cultural knowledge and resources, advocate for programs and institutions that demonstrate cultural competence, and promote policies that safeguard the rights of and confirm equity and social justice for all people.

(d) Social workers should act to prevent and eliminate domination of, exploitation of, and discrimination against any person, group, or class on the basis of race, ethnicity, national origin, color, sex, sexual orientation, gender identity or expression, age, marital status, political belief, religion, immigration status, or mental or physical disability.

APPENDIX B

RULES & REGS[1]
TEXAS STATE BOARD OF SOCIAL WORKER EXAMINERS[2]

ALERT: Rules guiding the social work profession can be changed at any time. It is the licensee's responsibility to visit the Texas State Board of Social Worker Examiners website on a regular basis to check for any changes to the rules.
http://www.dshs.state.tx.us/socialwork/default.shtm

SUBCHAPTER A.
GENERAL PROVISIONS

§781.101. PURPOSE AND SCOPE

(a) This chapter implements the provisions in the Social Work Practice Act (Act), Texas Occupations Code, Chapter 505, concerning the licensure and regulation of social workers.

(b) The Act restricts the use of the titles "social worker," "licensed master social worker," "licensed social worker," "licensed baccalaureate social worker," "licensed clinical social worker" or any other title that implies licensure or certification in social work.

(c) This chapter covers the organization, administration, and general procedures and policies of the Texas State Board of Social Worker Examiners.

(d) The Act and this chapter apply to every licensee even if the licensee is involved in activities or services exempt under the Act, §505.003.

§781.102. DEFINITIONS

The following words and terms, when used in this chapter, shall have the following meanings, unless the context clearly indicates otherwise.

(1) Accredited colleges or universities--An educational institution that is accredited by an accrediting agency recognized by the Council on Higher Education Accreditation.

---

1   Title 22 (Examining Boards), Texas Administrative Code, Part 34, Chapter 781, Rules Relating to the Licensing and Regulation of Social Workers, Adopted by the Texas State Board of Social Worker Examiners, Effective on August 24, 2005, 30 TexReg 4836; amended to be effective May 4, 2006, 31 TexReg 3537; amended to be effective March 4, 2007, 32 TexReg 890; amended to be effective February 21, 2008, 33 TexReg 1336; amended to be effective January 27, 2011, 36 TexReg 242; amended to be effective June 12, 2011, 36 TexReg 3410; amended to be effective **March 28, 2013**, 38 TexReg 1977.

2   Texas State Board of Social Worker Examiners Department of State Health Services P.O. Box 149347 - Mail Code 1982 Austin, Texas 78714-9347 512/719-3521 800/232-3162 Fax: 512/834-6677 lsw@dshs.state.tx.us http://www.dshs.state.tx.us/socialwork/ DSHS Publication #77-10804 Rev. 3/2013

(2) Act--The Social Work Practice Act, Texas Occupations Code, Chapter 505, concerning the licensure and regulation of social workers.

(3) ALJ--An Administrative Law Judge within the State Office of Administrative Hearings who conducts hearings under this chapter.

(4) Agency--A public or private employer, contractor or business entity providing social work services.

(5) AMEC--Alternative method of examining competency, as referenced in Texas Occupations Code, §505.356(3), regarding reexamination.

(6) APA--The Administrative Procedure Act, Government Code, Chapter 2001.

(7) Assessment--An on-going process of gathering information about and reaching an understanding of the client or client group's characteristics, perceived concerns and real problems, strengths and weaknesses, and opportunities and constraints; assessment may involve administering, scoring and interpreting instruments designed to measure factors about the client or client group.

(8) Association of Social Work Boards (ASWB)--The international organization which represents regulatory boards of social work and administers the national examinations utilized in the assessment for licensure.

(9) Board--Texas State Board of Social Worker Examiners.

(10) Case record--Any information related to a client and the services provided to that client, however recorded and stored.

(11) Client--An individual, family, couple, group or organization that receives social work services from a person identified as a social worker who is either licensed or unlicensed by the board.

(12) Clinical social work--A specialty within the practice of master social work that requires applying social work theory, knowledge, methods, ethics, and the professional use of self to restore or enhance social, psychosocial, or bio-psychosocial functioning of individuals, couples, families, groups, and/ or persons who are adversely affected by social or psychosocial stress or health impairment. Clinical social work practice involves using specialized clinical knowledge and advanced clinical skills to assess, diagnose, and treat mental, emotional, and behavioral disorders, conditions and addictions, including severe mental illness and serious emotional disturbances in adults, adolescents and children. Treatment methods may include, but are not limited to, providing individual, marital, couple, family, and group psychotherapy. Clinical social workers are qualified and authorized to use the Diagnostic and Statistical Manual of Mental Disorders (DSM), the International Classification of Diseases (ICD), Current Procedural Terminology (CPT)   codes, and other diagnostic classification systems in assessment, diagnosis, and other practice activities. The practice of clinical social work is restricted to either a Licensed Clinical Social Worker, or a Licensed Master Social Worker under clinical supervision in employment or under a clinical supervision plan.

(13) Confidential information--Individually identifiable information relating to a client, including the client's identity, demographic information, physical

or mental health condition, the services the client received, and payment for past, present, or future services the client received or will receive. Confidentiality is limited in cases where the law requires mandated reporting, where third persons have legal rights to the information, and where clients grant permission to share confidential information.

(14) Completed application--The official social work application form, fees and all supporting documentation which meet the criteria set out in this chapter.

(15) Conditions of exchange--Setting reimbursement rates or fee structures, as well as business rules or policies involving issues such as setting and cancelling appointments, maintaining office hours, and managing insurance claims.

(16) Contested case--A proceeding in accordance with the APA and this chapter, including, but not limited to, rule enforcement and licensing, in which the board determines the party's legal rights, duties, or privileges after the party has an opportunity for a hearing.

(17) Counseling, clinical--The use of clinical social work to assist individuals, couples, families or groups in learning to solve problems and make decisions about personal, health, social, educational, vocational, financial, and other interpersonal concerns.

(18) Counseling, supportive--The methods used to help individuals create and maintain adaptive patterns. Such methods may include, but are not limited to, building community resources and networks, linking clients with services and resources, educating clients and informing the public, helping clients identify and build strengths, leading community groups, and providing reassurance and support.

(19) Consultation--Providing advice, opinions and conferring with other professionals regarding social work practice.

(20) Continuing education--Education or training aimed at maintaining, improving, or enhancing social work practice.

(21) Council on Social Work Education (CSWE)--The national organization that accredits social work education schools and programs.

(22) Department--Department of State Health Services.

(23) Direct practice--Providing social work services through personal contact and immediate influence to help clients achieve goals.

(24) Dual or multiple relationship--A relationship that occurs when social workers interact with clients in more than one capacity, whether it be before, during, or after the professional, social, or business relationship. Dual or multiple relationships can occur simultaneously or consecutively.

(25) Electronic practice--Interactive social work practice that is aided by or achieved through technological methods, such as the web, the Internet, social media, electronic chat groups, interactive TV, list serves, cell phones, telephones, faxes, and other emerging technology.

(26) Endorsement--The process whereby the board reviews licensure requirements a professional has completed while under another jurisdiction's

regulatory authority. The board may accept, deny or grant partial credit for requirements completed in a different jurisdiction.

(27) Examination--A standardized test or examination, approved by the board, which measures an individual's social work knowledge, skills and abilities.

(28) Exploitation--Using a pattern, practice or scheme of conduct that can reasonably be construed as primarily meeting the licensee's needs or benefitting the licensee rather than being in the best interest of the client. Exploitation involves the professional taking advantage of the inherently unequal power differential between client and professional. Exploitation also includes behavior at the expense of another practitioner. Exploitation may involve financial, business, emotional, sexual, verbal, religious and/or relational forms.

(29) Field placement--A formal, supervised, planned, and evaluated experience in a professional setting under the auspices of a CSWE-accredited social work program and meeting CSWE standards.

(30) Formal hearing--A hearing or proceeding in accordance with this chapter, including a contested case as defined in this section to address the issues of a contested case.

(31) Fraud--A social worker's misrepresentation or omission about qualifications, services, finances, or related activities or information, or as defined by the Texas Penal Code or by other state or federal law.

(32) Full-time experience--Providing social work services thirty or more hours per week.

(33) Group supervision for licensure or for specialty recognition--Providing supervision to a minimum of two and a maximum of six supervisees in a designated supervision session.

(34) Health care professional--A licensee or any other person licensed, certified, or registered by the State of Texas in a health related profession.

(35) Impaired professional--A licensee whose ability to perform social work services is impaired by the licensee's physical health, mental health, or by medication, drugs or alcohol.

(36) Independent clinical practice--The practice of clinical social work in which the social worker, after having completed all requirements for clinical licensure, assumes responsibility and accountability for the nature and quality of client services, pro bono or in exchange for direct payment or third party reimbursement. Independent clinical social work occurs in independent settings.

(37) Independent non-clinical practice--The unsupervised practice of non-clinical social work outside the jurisdiction of an organizational setting, in which the social worker, after having completed all requirements for independent non-clinical practice recognition, assumes responsibility and accountability for the nature and quality of client services, pro bono or in exchange for direct payment or third party reimbursement.

(38) Independent Practice Recognition--A specialty recognition related to unsupervised non-clinical social work at the LBSW or LMSW category of licensure, which denotes that the licensee has earned the specialty recognition,

commonly called IPR, by successfully completing additional supervision which enhances skills in providing independent non-clinical social work.

(39) Individual supervision for licensure or specialty recognition--Supervision for professional development provided to one supervisee during the designated supervision session.

(40) Investigator--A department employee or other authorized person whom the board uses to investigate allegations of professional misconduct.

(41) LBSW--Licensed Baccalaureate Social Worker.

(42) LCSW--Licensed Clinical Social Worker.

(43) License--A regular or temporary board-issued license, including LBSW, LMSW, and LCSW. Some licenses may carry an additional specialty recognition, such as LMSW-AP, LBSW-IPR, or LMSW-IPR.

(44) Licensee--A person licensed by the board to practice social work.

(45) LMSW--Licensed Master Social Worker.

(46) LMSW-AP--Licensed Master Social Worker with the Advanced Practitioner specialty recognition for non-clinical practice.

(47) Non-clinical social work--Professional social work which incorporates non-clinical work with individuals, families, groups, communities, and social systems which may involve locating resources, negotiating and advocating on behalf of clients or client groups, administering programs and agencies, community organizing, teaching, researching, providing employment or professional development non-clinical supervision, developing and analyzing policy, fund-raising, and other non-clinical activities.

(48) Peer assistance program--A program designed to help an impaired professional return to fitness for practice.

(49) Person--An individual, corporation, partnership, or other legal entity.

(50) Psychotherapy--Treatment in which a qualified social worker uses a specialized, formal interaction with an individual, couple, family, or group by establishing and maintaining a therapeutic relationship to understand and intervene in intrapersonal, interpersonal and psychosocial dynamics; and to diagnose and treat mental, emotional, and behavioral disorders and addictions.

(51) Recognition--Authorization from the board to engage in the independent or specialty practice of social work services.

(52) Rules--Provisions of this chapter specifying how the board implements the Act, how the board operates, and how individuals are affected by the Act.

(53) Social work case management--Using a bio-psychosocial perspective to assess, evaluate, implement, monitor and advocate for services on behalf of and in collaboration with the identified client or client group.

(54) Social worker--A person licensed under the Act.

(55) Social work practice--Services which an employee, independent practitioner, consultant, or volunteer provides for compensation or pro bono to effect changes in human behavior, a person's emotional responses, interpersonal relationships, and the social conditions of individuals, families,

groups, organizations, and communities. Social work practice is guided by specialized knowledge, acquired through formal social work education. Social workers specialize in understanding how humans develop and behave within social environments, and in using methods to enhance the functioning of individuals, families, groups, communities, and organizations. Social work practice involves the disciplined application of social work values, principles, and methods including, but not limited to, psychotherapy; marriage, family, and couples intervention; group therapy and group work; mediation; case management; supervision and administration of social work services and programs; counseling; assessment, diagnosis, treatment; policy analysis and development; research; advocacy for vulnerable groups; social work education; and evaluation.

(56) Supervisor, board-approved--A person meeting the requirements set out in §781.402 of this title (relating to Clinical Supervision for LCSW and Non-Clinical Supervision for LMSW-AP and Independent Practice Recognition), to supervise a licensee towards the LCSW, LMSW-AP or Independent Practice Recognition, or as a result of a board order.

(57) Supervision--Supervision includes:

(A) administrative or work-related supervision of an employee, contractor or volunteer that is not related to qualification for licensure, practice specialty recognition, a disciplinary order, or a condition of new or continued licensure;

(B) clinical supervision of a Licensed Master Social Worker in a setting in which the LMSW is providing clinical services; the supervision may be provided by a Licensed Professional Counselor, Licensed Psychologist, Licensed Marriage and Family Therapist, Licensed Clinical Social Worker or Psychiatrist. This supervision is not related to qualification for licensure, practice specialty recognition, a disciplinary order, or a condition of new or continued licensure;

(C) clinical supervision of a Licensed Master Social Worker, who is providing clinical services and is under a board-approved supervision plan to fulfill supervision requirements for achieving the LCSW; a Licensed Clinical Social Worker who is a board-approved supervisor delivers this supervision;

(D) non-clinical supervision of a Licensed Master Social Worker or Licensed Baccalaureate Social Worker who is providing non-clinical social work service toward qualifications for independent non-clinical practice recognition; this supervision is delivered by a board-approved supervisor;

(E) non-clinical supervision of a Licensed Master Social Worker who is providing non-clinical social work service toward qualifications for the LMSW-AP; this supervision is delivered by a board-approved supervisor;

(F) supervision of a probationary Licensed Master Social Worker or Licensed Baccalaureate Social Worker providing non-clinical services by a board-approved supervisor toward licensure under the AMEC program; or

(G) board-ordered supervision of a licensee by a board-approved supervisor pursuant to a disciplinary order or as a condition of new or continued licensure.

(58) Supervision hour--A supervision hour is a minimum of 60 minutes in length.

(59) Termination--Ending social work services with a client.

(60) Texas Open Meetings Act--Government Code, Chapter 551.

(61) Texas Public Information Act--Government Code, Chapter 552.

(62) Waiver--The suspension of educational, professional, and/or examination requirements for applicants who meet the criteria for licensure under special conditions based on appeal to the board.

SUBCHAPTER B

CODE OF CONDUCT AND PROFESSIONAL STANDARDS OF PRACTICE

§781.201. CODE OF CONDUCT

(a) A social worker must observe and comply with the code of conduct and standards of practice set forth in this subchapter. Any violation of the code of conduct or standards of practice will constitute unethical conduct or conduct that discredits or tends to discredit the profession of social work and is grounds for disciplinary action.

(1) A social worker shall not refuse to perform any act or service for which the person is licensed solely on the basis of a client's age; gender; race; color; religion; national origin; disability; sexual orientation; gender identity and expression; or political affiliation.

(2) A social worker shall truthfully report her or his services, professional credentials and qualifications to clients or potential clients. A social worker shall not advertise or claim a degree from a college or university which is not accredited by the Council on Higher Education Accreditation.

(3) A social worker shall only offer those services that are within his or her professional competency, and shall provide services within accepted professional standards of practice, appropriate to the client's needs.

(4) A social worker shall strive to maintain and improve her or his professional knowledge, skills and abilities.

(5) A social worker shall base all services on an assessment, evaluation or diagnosis of the client.

(6) A social worker shall provide the client with a clear description of services, schedules, fees and billing at the initiation of services.

(7) A social worker shall safeguard the client's rights to confidentiality within the limits of the law.

(8) A social worker shall be responsible for setting and maintaining professional boundaries.

(9) A social worker shall not have sexual contact with a client or a person who has been a client.

(10) A social worker shall refrain from providing services while impaired by physical health, mental health, medical condition, or by medication, drugs or alcohol.

(11) A social worker shall not exploit his or her position of trust with a client or former client.

(12) A social worker shall evaluate a client's progress on a continuing basis to guide service delivery and will make use of supervision and consultation as indicated by the client's needs.

(13) A social worker shall refer a client for those services that the social worker is unable to meet, and shall terminate services to a client when continuing to provide services is no longer in the client's best interest.

(b) The grounds for disciplinary action of a social worker shall be based on the code of conduct or standards of practice in effect at the time of the violation.

§781.202. THE PRACTICE OF SOCIAL WORK

(a) Practice of Baccalaureate Social Work--Applying social work theory, knowledge, methods, ethics and the professional use of self to restore or enhance social, psychosocial, or bio-psychosocial functioning of individuals, couples, families, groups, organizations and communities. Baccalaureate Social Work is generalist practice and may include interviewing, assessment, planning, intervention, evaluation, case management, mediation, counseling, supportive counseling, direct practice, information and referral, problem solving, supervision, consultation, education, advocacy, community organization, and policy and program development, implementation, and administration.

(b) Practice of Independent Non-Clinical Baccalaureate Social Work--An LBSW recognized for independent practice, known as LBSW-IPR, may provide any non-clinical baccalaureate social work services in either an employment or an independent practice setting. An LBSW-IPR may work under contract, bill directly for services, and bill third parties for reimbursements for services. An LBSW-IPR must restrict his or her independent practice to providing non-clinical social work services.

(c) Practice of Master's Social Work--Applying social work theory, knowledge, methods and ethics and the professional use of self to restore or enhance social, psychosocial, or bio-psychosocial functioning of individuals, couples, families, groups, organizations and communities. An LMSW may practice clinical social work in an agency employment setting under clinical supervision, under a board-approved supervision plan, or under contract with an agency when under a board-approved clinical supervision plan. Master's Social Work practice may include applying specialized knowledge and advanced practice skills in assessment, treatment, planning, implementation and evaluation, case management, mediation, counseling, supportive counseling, direct practice, information and referral, supervision, consultation, education, research, advocacy, community organization and developing, implementing and administering policies, programs and activities. An LMSW may engage in Baccalaureate Social Work practice.

(d) Advanced Non-Clinical Practice of LMSWs--An LMSW recognized as an Advanced Practitioner (LMSW-AP)   may provide any non-clinical social work services in either an employment or an independent practice setting. An

LMSW-AP may work under contract, bill directly for services, and bill third parties for reimbursements for services. An LMSW-AP must restrict his or her practice to providing non-clinical social work services.

(e) Independent Practice for LMSWs--An LMSW recognized for independent practice may provide any non-clinical social work services in either an employment or an independent practice setting. This licensee is designated as LMSW-IPR. An LMSW-IPR may work under contract, bill directly for services, and bill third parties for reimbursements for services. An LMSW-IPR must restrict his or her independent practice to providing non-clinical social work services.

(f) Practice of Clinical Social Work--The practice of social work that requires applying social work theory, knowledge, methods, ethics, and the professional use of self to restore or enhance social, psychosocial, or bio-psychosocial functioning of individuals, couples, families, groups, and/or persons who are adversely affected by social or psychosocial stress or health impairment. The practice of clinical social work requires applying specialized clinical knowledge and advanced clinical skills in assessment, diagnosis, and treatment of mental, emotional, and behavioral disorders, conditions and addictions, including severe mental illness and serious emotional disturbances in adults, adolescents, and children. The clinical social worker may engage in Baccalaureate Social Work practice and Master's Social Work practice. Clinical treatment methods may include but are not limited to providing individual, marital, couple, family, and group therapy, mediation, counseling, supportive counseling, direct practice, and psychotherapy. Clinical social workers are qualified and authorized to use the Diagnostic and Statistical Manual of Mental Disorders (DSM), the International Classification of Diseases (ICD), Current Procedural Terminology (CPT) Codes, and other diagnostic classification systems in assessment, diagnosis, treatment and other practice activities. An LCSW may provide any clinical or non-clinical social work service or supervision in either an employment or independent practice setting. An LCSW may work under contract, bill directly for services, and bill third parties for service reimbursements.

(g) A licensee who is not recognized for independent practice or who is not under a board-approved non-clinical supervision plan must not engage in any independent practice that falls within the definition of social work practice in §781.102 of this title (relating to Definitions) without being licensed and recognized by the board, unless the person is licensed in another profession and acting solely within the scope of that license. If the person is practicing professionally under another license, the person may not use the titles "licensed clinical social worker," "licensed master social worker," "licensed social worker," or "licensed baccalaureate social worker," or any other title or initials that imply social work licensure unless one holds the appropriate license or independent practice recognition.

(h) An LBSW or LMSW who is not recognized for independent practice may not provide direct social work services to clients from a location that she or he owns or leases and that is not owned or leased by an employer or other legal entity with responsibility for the client. This does not preclude in-home services such as in-home health care or the use of electronic media to provide services in an emergency.

(i) An LBSW or LMSW who is not recognized for independent practice may

422   TEXAS LAW FOR THE SOCIAL WORKER

practice for remuneration in a direct employment or agency setting but may not work independently, bill directly to patients or bill directly to third party payers, unless the LBSW or LMSW is under a formal board-approved supervision plan.

§781.203. GENERAL STANDARDS OF PRACTICE

This section establishes standards of professional conduct required of a social worker. The licensee, following applicable statutes:

(1) shall not knowingly offer or provide professional services to an individual concurrently receiving professional services from another mental health services provider except with that provider's knowledge. If a licensee learns of such concurrent professional services, the licensee shall take immediate and reasonable action to inform the other mental health services provider;

(2) shall terminate a professional relationship when it is reasonably clear that the client is not benefiting from the relationship. If continued professional services are indicated, the licensee shall take reasonable steps to facilitate transferring the client to an appropriate source of service;

(3) shall not evaluate any individual's mental, emotional, or behavioral condition unless the licensee has personally interviewed the individual or the licensee discloses with the evaluation that the licensee has not personally interviewed the individual;

(4) shall not persistently or flagrantly over treat a client;

(5) shall not aid and abet the unlicensed practice of social work by a person required to be licensed under the Act;

(6) shall not participate in any way in falsifying licensure applications or any other documents submitted to the board;

(7) shall ensure that, both before services commence and as services progress, the client knows the licensee's qualifications and any intent to delegate service provision; any restrictions the board has placed on the licensee's license; the limits on confidentiality and privacy; and applicable fees and payment arrangements;

(8) if the client must barter for services, it is the professional's responsibility to ensure that the client is in no way harmed. The value of the barter shall be agreed upon in advance and shall not exceed customary charges for the service or goods; and

(9) shall ensure that the client or a legally authorized person representing the client has signed a consent for services, when appropriate. Prior to commencement of social work services with a minor client who is named in a Suit Affecting Parent Child Relationship (SAPCR), the licensee shall ensure that all legally authorized persons representing the client have signed a consent for services, if applicable. A licensee shall maintain these documents in the client's record.

§781.204. RELATIONSHIPS WITH CLIENTS

(a) A social worker shall inform in writing a prospective client about the nature of the professional relationship, which can include but is not limited to office procedures, after-hours coverage, services provided, fees, and arrangements for payment.

(b) The social worker shall not give or receive a commission, rebate, or any other form of remuneration for referring clients. A licensee shall not intentionally or knowingly offer to pay or agree to accept any remuneration directly or indirectly, overtly or covertly, in cash or in kind, to or from any person, firm, association of persons, partnership, corporation, or entity for securing or soliciting clients or patronage for or from any health care professional. In accordance with the provisions of the Act, §505.451, a licensee is subject to disciplinary action if the licensee directly or indirectly offers to pay or agrees to accept remuneration to or from any person for securing or soliciting a client or patronage. Payment of credentialing or other fees to insurance companies or other third party payers to be part of an approved provider list shall not be considered as a violation of this chapter.

(c) A social worker shall not enter into a business relationship with a client. This rule does not prohibit a professional social work relationship with a client, as described in this subchapter.

(d) A social worker shall not engage in activities that seek to primarily meet the social worker's personal needs or personal gain instead of the needs of the client.

(e) A social worker shall be responsible for setting and maintaining professional boundaries.

(f) A social worker shall keep accurate records of services to include, but not be limited to, dates of services, types of services, progress or case notes and billing information for a minimum of five years for an adult client and five years beyond the age of 18 years of age for a minor, or in compliance with applicable laws or professional standards. If the foregoing provision conflicts with the standards, requirements, or procedures for records generated in the course and scope of rendering services as a social worker, either directly or indirectly, for an educational institution, or a federal, state, or local governmental entity or political subdivision, the foregoing provision does not apply.

(g) A social worker shall bill clients or third parties for only those services actually rendered or as agreed to by mutual written understanding.

(h) A licensee shall not make any false, misleading, deceptive, fraudulent or exaggerated claim or statement about the effectiveness of the licensee's services; the licensee's qualifications, capabilities, background, training, experience, education, professional affiliations, fees, products, or publications; the type, effectiveness, qualifications, and products or services offered by an organization or agency; or the practice or field of social work.

(i) If the licensee learns that false, misleading, deceptive, fraudulent or exaggerated statements about the services, qualifications, or products have been made, the licensee shall take all available steps to correct the inappropriate claims, prevent their reoccurrence, and report the incident to the board.

(j) A licensee shall provide social work intervention only in the context of a professional relationship.

(k) Electronic practice may be used judiciously as part of the social work process and the supervision process. Social workers engaging in electronic practice must be licensed in Texas and adhere to provisions of this chapter.

(l) The licensee shall not provide social work services or intervention to previous or current family members; personal friends; educational or business associates; or individuals whose welfare might be jeopardized by a dual or multiple relationship.

(m) The licensee shall not accept from or give to a client any gift with a value in excess of $25. If the licensee's employer prohibits giving or receiving gifts, the licensee shall comply with the employer's policy.

(n) The licensee may not borrow or lend money or items of value to clients or relatives of clients.

(o) The licensee shall take reasonable precautions to protect individuals from physical or emotional harm resulting from interaction within individual and group settings.

(p) A licensee shall not promote the licensee's personal or business activities that are unrelated to the current professional relationship.

(q) A licensee shall set and maintain professional boundaries, avoiding dual or multiple relationships with clients. If a dual or multiple relationship develops, the social worker is responsible for ensuring the client is safe.

§781.205. SEXUAL MISCONDUCT

(a) Definitions.

(1) Sexual contact--Any touching or behavior that can be construed as sexual in nature or as defined by the Texas Penal Code, §21.01, relating to assault.

(2) Therapeutic deception--A licensee's act or statement representing that sexual contact or sexual exploitation between the licensee and a client or client group is a valid part of the treatment process.

(3) Sexual exploitation--A pattern, practice or scheme of exploitation, which may include, but is not limited to, sexual contact with a client.

(b) A licensee shall not engage in sexual contact or sexual exploitation with a client or former client; a supervisee of the licensee; or a student at an educational institution at which the licensee provides professional or educational services.

(c) A licensee shall not practice therapeutic deception of a client or former client.

(d) It is not a defense to a disciplinary action under subsections (a) - (c) of this section if the person was no longer emotionally dependent on the licensee when the sexual exploitation began, the sexual contact occurred, or the therapeutic deception occurred. It is also not a defense that the licensee terminated services with the person before the date the sexual exploitation began, the sexual contact occurred or the therapeutic deception occurred.

(e) It is not a defense to a disciplinary action under subsections (a) - (c) of this section if the sexual contact, sexual exploitation, or therapeutic deception with the person occurred with the client's consent; outside appointments with the client; or off the premises the licensee used for appointments with the client.

(f) Examples of sexual contact are those activities and behaviors described in the Texas Penal Code, §21.01, relating to assault.

(g) A licensee shall report sexual misconduct in accordance with Texas Civil Practice and Remedies Code, Chapter 81, relating to sexual exploitation by a mental health services provider. If a licensee has reasonable cause to suspect that a client has been the victim of sexual exploitation, sexual contact, or therapeutic deception by another licensee or a mental health services provider, or if a client alleges sexual exploitation, sexual contact, or therapeutic deception by another licensee or a mental health services provider, the licensee shall report the alleged conduct not later than the 30th day after the date the licensee became aware of the conduct or the allegations to:

   (1) the prosecuting attorney in the county in which the alleged sexual exploitation, sexual contact or therapeutic deception occurred; and

   (2) the board if the conduct involves a licensee and any other state licensing agency which licenses the mental health services provider.

   (3) Before making a report under this subsection, the licensee shall inform the alleged victim of the licensee's duty to report and shall determine if the alleged victim wants to remain anonymous.

   (4) A report under this subsection shall contain information necessary to identify the licensee; identify the alleged victim, unless the alleged victim has requested anonymity; express suspicion that sexual exploitation, sexual contact, or therapeutic deception occurred; and provide the alleged perpetrator's name.

(h) The following may constitute sexual exploitation if done for sexual arousal, sexual gratification, or sexual abuse of either the social worker or a person who is receiving or has received the licensee's professional services as a social worker:

   (1) sexual harassment, sexual solicitation, physical advances, verbal or nonverbal conduct that is sexual in nature;

   (2) any behavior, gestures, comments, or expressions which may reasonably be interpreted as inappropriately seductive or sexual, including making sexual comments about a person's body or making sexually demeaning comments about an individual's sexual orientation, or making comments about potential sexual performance except when the comment is pertinent to issues of sexual function or dysfunction in counseling;

   (3) initiating conversation about the licensee's sexual problems, preferences, or fantasies; or requesting details of sexual history or sexual likes and dislikes when those details are not necessary for counseling;

   (4) kissing or fondling, or making any other deliberate or repeated comments, gestures, or physical acts of a sexual nature, even if they are not sexually intimate;

   (5) making a request to date;

   (6) exposing genitals, anus or breasts; or

   (7) encouraging another person to masturbate in the licensee's presence; or the licensee masturbating in front of another person.

§781.206. PROFESSIONAL REPRESENTATION

(a) A social worker shall not misrepresent any professional qualifications or associations.

(b) A social worker shall not misrepresent the attributes of any agency or organization, or make unreasonable, misleading, deceptive, fraudulent, exaggerated, or unsubstantiated claims about the effectiveness of any services.

(c) A social worker shall not encourage, or within the social worker's power, allow a client to hold exaggerated ideas about the effectiveness of the social worker's services.

§781.207. TESTING

(a) A social worker shall inform clients about the purposes and explicit uses of any testing done as part of a professional relationship.

(b) A social worker shall not appropriate, reproduce, or modify published tests or parts thereof without the publisher's permission.

(c) A social worker shall not administer any test without the appropriate training and experience to administer the test.

(d) A social worker must observe the necessary precautions to maintain the security of any test administered by the social worker or under the social worker's supervision.

§781.208. DRUG AND ALCOHOL USE

A licensee shall not use alcohol or drugs in ways that compromise the licensee's ability to practice social work; use illegal drugs of any kind; or promote, encourage, or concur in the illegal use, distribution, sale, or possession of alcohol or drugs.

§781.209. CLIENT RECORDS AND RECORD KEEPING

Following applicable statutes, the licensee shall:

(1) keep accurate and legible records of the dates of services, types of services, progress or case notes, intake assessment, treatment plan, and billing information;

(2) retain and dispose of client records in ways that maintain confidentiality;

(3) in independent practice, establish a plan for the custody and control of the licensee's client records should the licensee die, become incapacitated, or cease offering professional services;

(4) keep client records for five years for adult clients and five years beyond the age of 18 for minor clients unless the record keeping provision of §781.204(f) of this title (relating to Relationships with Clients) conflicts with the standards, requirements, or procedures for records generated in the course and scope of rendering services as a social worker, either directly or indirectly, for an educational institution, or a federal, state, or local governmental entity or political subdivision, the foregoing provision in §781.204(f) of this title does not apply;

(5) provide a written explanation of the types of treatment and charges on a bill or statement to the client (this applies even if the charges are to be paid by a third party); and

(6) comply with the requirements of Texas Health and Safety Code, Chapters 161 and 611; Texas Family Code, Chapter 261; and other applicable state law concerning confidentiality of protected health information and the

release of mental health records.

§781.210. Billing and Financial Relationships

(a) A licensee shall not intentionally or knowingly offer to pay or agree to accept any remuneration directly or indirectly, overtly or covertly, in cash or in kind, to or from any person, firm, association of persons, partnership, corporation, or entity for securing or soliciting clients or patronage for or from any health care professional. In accordance with the provisions of the Act, §505.451, a licensee is subject to disciplinary action if the licensee directly or indirectly offers to pay or agrees to accept remuneration to or from any person for securing or soliciting a client or patronage. Payment of credentialing or other fees to insurance companies or other third party payers to be part of an approved provider list shall not be considered as a violation of this chapter.

(b) A licensee employed or under contract with a chemical dependency facility or a mental health facility, shall comply with the requirements in the Texas Health and Safety Code, §164.006, relating to soliciting and contracting with certain referral sources. Compliance with the Treatment Facilities Marketing Practices Act, Texas Health and Safety Code, Chapter 164, shall not be considered as a violation of state law relating to illegal remuneration.

(c) A licensee shall not knowingly or flagrantly overcharge a client, and shall bill clients and/or third parties for only those services that the licensee actually renders.

(d) Billing documents shall accurately reflect any collateral service the licensee uses to help serve the client.

(e) A licensee may not submit to a client and/or a third party payer a bill for services that the licensee knows were not provided, with the exception of a missed appointment, or knows were improper, unreasonable or unnecessary.

§781.211. Client Confidentiality

(a) Communication between a licensee and client, as well as the client's records, however created or stored, are confidential under the provisions of the Texas Health and Safety Code, Chapter 181, Texas Health and Safety Code, Chapter 611, and other state or federal statutes or rules, including rules of evidence, where such statutes or rules apply to a licensee's practice.

(b) A licensee shall not disclose any communication, record, or client identity except as provided in the Texas Health and Safety Code, the Health Insurance Portability and Accountability Act (HIPAA), and/or other applicable state or federal statutes or rules.

(c) A licensee shall comply with Texas Health and Safety Code, Chapter 611, concerning access to mental health records.

(d) To release information for or about clients, a licensee shall have written permission signed by the client or the client guardian. That permission, which must be dated, shall include the client's name and identifying information; the purpose for releasing the information; the individual or entity to which the information is released; the length of time the release is authorized; the signature of the client or guardian representative; and date of signature.

(e) The social worker shall maintain the written release of information in the permanent client record and shall review and update it at least every twelve months.

(f)   A licensee shall report information if required by any of the following statutes:

(1)   Texas Family Code, Chapter 261, concerning abuse or neglect of minors;

(2)   Texas Human Resources Code, Chapter 48, concerning abuse, neglect, or exploitation of elderly or disabled persons;

(3)   Texas Health and Safety Code, §161.131 et seq., concerning abuse, neglect, and illegal, unprofessional, or unethical conduct in an in-patient mental health facility, a chemical dependency treatment facility or a hospital providing comprehensive medical rehabilitation services; and

(4)   Texas Civil Practice and Remedies Code, §81.006, concerning sexual exploitation by a mental health services provider.

(g)   A licensee may take reasonable action to inform only medical or law enforcement personnel if the professional determines that a client or others are at imminent risk of physical injury, or a client is in immediate risk of mental or emotional injury, in accordance with the Texas Health and Safety Code, Chapter 611, concerning mental health records.

§781.212. LICENSEES AND THE BOARD

(a)   Any person licensed as a social worker is bound by the provisions of the Act and this chapter.

(b)   A social worker shall report alleged misrepresentations or violations of this chapter to the board.

(c)   The licensee shall report any and all name changes, address changes, or employment setting changes to the board within 30 days.

(d)   The board is not responsible for any lost or misdirected mail if sent to the address last reported by the licensee.

(e)   The board may ask any applicant for licensure as a social worker, whose file contains negative references of good moral character, to come before the board for an interview before the licensure process may proceed.

(f)   The board may consider a social worker's failure to respond to the board's request for information or other correspondence as unprofessional conduct and as indicative of lack of fitness for practice. It is grounds for disciplinary proceedings in accordance with this chapter.

§781.213. CORPORATIONS AND BUSINESS NAMES

(a)   An independent clinical practice or an independent non-clinical practice by a social worker may be incorporated in accordance with the Professional Corporation Act, or other applicable law.

(b)   When a licensee uses an assumed name in any social work practice, the social worker's name must be listed in conjunction with the assumed name. An assumed name or credential that the social worker uses shall not be false, deceptive, or misleading.

§781.214. CONSUMER INFORMATION

(a)   A licensee shall inform each client of the board's name, address, and telephone number for reporting violations of the Act or this chapter on one of the following: each registration form; each application; each written contract for services; a sign prominently displayed in each place of business; or a bill for services.

(b) The board shall make consumer information available to the public on the board's website or upon request.

§781.215. DISPLAY OF LICENSE CERTIFICATE

(a) A social worker shall display an original board-issued license certificate in a prominent place at each practice location.

(b) A social worker shall not alter a board-issued license certificate.

(c) A social worker shall not display a board-issued license certificate which has been reproduced or is expired, suspended, or revoked.

(d) A licensee who elects to copy a board-issued license certificate or certificate card takes full responsibility for the use or misuse of the reproduced license.

§781.216. ADVERTISING AND ANNOUNCEMENTS

(a) Social workers' advertisements and announcements shall not contain deceptive, inaccurate, incomplete, out-of-date, or out-of-context information about services or competence. Advertising includes, but is not limited to, any announcement of services, letterhead, business cards, commercial products, website entries, email, cell phone communications, social media communications, and billing statements.

(b) The board imposes no restrictions on the advertising medium a social worker uses, including personal appearances, use of personal voice, size or duration of the advertisement or use of a trade name.

(c) All advertisements or announcements of a licensee's professional services, including website pages, social media communications, or telephone directory listings, shall clearly state the social worker's licensure designation and any specialty recognition, if any.

(d) A social worker shall not announce or advertise any information or reference to the social worker's certification in a field outside of social work that is deliberately intended to mislead the public.

(e) A licensee who retains or hires others to advertise or promote the licensee's practice remains responsible for the statements and representations made.

§781.217. RESEARCH AND PUBLICATIONS

(a) In research with a human subject, a social worker is responsible for the subject's welfare throughout a project, shall obtain informed consent and take reasonable precautions so that the subject shall suffer no injurious emotional, physical or social effect.

(b) A social worker shall disguise data obtained from a professional relationship for the purposes of education or research to ensure full protection of the identity of the subject client.

(c) When conducting and reporting research, a social worker must recognize previous work on the topic, as well as observe all copyright laws.

(d) A social worker must give due credit through joint authorship, acknowledgment, footnote statements, Internet sources, or other appropriate means to those who have contributed significantly to the social worker's research or publication.

§781.218. PROVIDING SOCIAL STUDIES

Licensees shall comply with the Texas Family Code, Chapter 107, and other applicable laws when providing social studies.

§781.219. LICENSED SEX OFFENDER TREATMENT

A social worker who is licensed as a sex offender treatment provider by the Council on Sex Offender Treatment is not subject to disciplinary action by the board in relation to the social worker's provision of sex offender treatment. A social worker who is a sex offender treatment provider and who acts in conformance with the rules, policies, and procedures of the council is not subject to any administrative sanction by the board. If the Council on Sex Offender Treatment takes disciplinary action against a social worker who is a sex offender treatment provider, the board may consider the final order imposing such disciplinary action as grounds for disciplinary action by the board.

§781.220. PARENT COORDINATION

(a) In accordance with the Family Code, §153.601(3), "parenting coordinator" means an impartial third party:

   (1) who, regardless of the title by which the person is designated by the court, performs any function described in the Family Code, §153.606, in a suit; and

   (2) who:

      (A) is appointed under Family Code, Chapter 153, Subchapter K (relating to Parenting Plan, Parenting Coordinator, and Parenting Facilitator) by the court on its own motion, or on a motion or agreement of the parties, to assist parties in resolving parenting issues through confidential procedures; and

      (B) is not appointed under another statute or a rule of civil procedure.

(b) A licensee who serves as a parenting coordinator is not acting under the authority of a license issued by the board, and is not engaged in the practice of social work. The services provided by the licensee who serves as a parenting coordinator are not within the jurisdiction of the board, but rather the jurisdiction of the appointing court.

(c) A licensee who serves as a parenting coordinator has a duty to provide the information in subsection (b) of this section to the parties to the suit.

(d) Records of a licensee serving as a parenting coordinator are confidential under the Civil Practices and Remedies Code, §154.073. Licensees serving as a confidential parenting coordinator shall comply with the Civil Practices and Remedies Code, Chapter 154, relating to the release of information.

(e) A licensee shall not provide social work services to any person while simultaneously providing parenting coordination services. This section shall not apply if the court enters a finding that mental health services are not readily available in the location where the parties reside.

§781.221. Parenting Facilitation

(a) In accordance with House Bill 1012, 81st Legislature, Regular Session, 2009, and Family Code, Chapter 153, this section establishes the practice standards for licensees who desire to serve as parenting facilitators.

(b) In accordance with the Family Code, §153.601(3-a), a "parenting facilitator" means an impartial third party:

   (1) who, regardless of the title by which the person is designated by the court, performs any function described by the Family Code, §153.6061, in a suit; and

   (2) who:

      (A) is appointed under Family Code, Chapter 153, Subchapter K (relating to Parenting Plan, Parenting Coordinator, and Parenting Facilitator) by the court on its own motion, or on a motion or agreement of the parties, to assist parties in resolving parenting issues through procedures that are not confidential; and

      (B) is not appointed under another statute or a rule of civil procedure.

(c) Notwithstanding any other provision of this chapter, licensees who desire to serve as parenting facilitators shall comply with all applicable requirements of the Family Code, Chapter 153, and this section. Licensees shall also comply with all requirements of this chapter unless a provision is clearly inconsistent with the Family Code, Chapter 153, or this section.

(d) In accordance with the Family Code, §153.6102(e), a licensee serving as a parenting facilitator shall not provide other social work services to any person while simultaneously providing parenting facilitation services. This section shall not apply if the court enters a finding that mental health services are not readily available in the location where the parties reside.

(e) A licensee serving as a parenting facilitator utilizes child-focused alternative dispute resolution processes, assists parents in implementing their parenting plan by facilitating the resolution of disputes in a timely manner, educates parents about children's needs, and engages in other activities as referenced in the Family Code, Chapter 153.

(f) A licensee serving as a parenting facilitator shall assist the parties involved in reducing harmful conflict and in promoting the best interests of the children.

(g) A licensee serving as a parenting facilitator functions in four primary areas in providing services.

   (1) Conflict management function. The primary role of the parenting facilitator is to assist the parties to work out disagreements regarding the children to minimize conflict. To assist the parents in reducing conflict, the parenting facilitator may monitor the electronic or written exchanges of parent communications and suggest productive forms of communication that limit conflict between the parents.

   (2) Assessment function. A parenting facilitator shall review applicable court orders, including protective orders, social studies, and other relevant records to analyze the impasses and issues as brought forth by the parties.

   (3) Educational function. A parenting facilitator shall educate the parties

about child development, divorce, the impact of parental behavior on children, parenting skills, and communication and conflict resolution skills.

(4) Coordination/case management function. A parenting facilitator shall work with the professionals and systems involved with the family (for example, mental health, health care, social services, education, or legal) as well as with extended family, stepparents, and significant others as necessary.

(h) A licensee serving as a parenting facilitator shall be alert to the reasonable suspicion of acts of domestic violence directed at a parent, a current partner, or children. The parenting facilitator shall adhere to protection orders, if any, and take reasonable measures to ensure the safety of the participants, the children and the parenting facilitator, while understanding that even with appropriate precautions a guarantee that no harm will occur can be neither stated nor implied.

(i) In order to protect the parties and children in domestic violence cases involving power, control and coercion, a parenting facilitator shall tailor the techniques used so as to avoid offering the opportunity for further coercion.

(j) A licensee serving as a parenting facilitator shall be alert to the reasonable suspicion of substance abuse by parents or children, as well as mental health impairment of a parent or child.

(k) A licensee serving as a parenting facilitator shall not provide legal advice.

(l) A licensee serving as a parenting facilitator shall serve by written agreement of the parties and/or formal order of the court.

(m) A licensee serving as a parenting facilitator shall not initiate providing services until the licensee has received and reviewed the fully executed and filed court order or the signed agreement of the parties.

(n) A licensee serving as a parenting facilitator shall maintain impartiality in the process of parenting facilitation. Impartiality means freedom from favoritism or bias in word, action, or appearance, and includes a commitment to assist all parties, as opposed to any one individual.

(o) A licensee serving as a parenting facilitator:

(1) shall terminate or withdraw services if the licensee determines the licensee cannot act in an impartial or objective manner;

(2) shall not give or accept a gift, favor, loan or other item of value from any party having an interest in the parenting facilitation process;

(3) shall not coerce or improperly influence any party to make a decision;

(4) shall not intentionally or knowingly misrepresent or omit any material fact, law, or circumstance in the parenting facilitator process; and

(5) shall not accept any engagement, provide any service, or perform any act outside the role of parenting facilitation that would compromise the facilitator's integrity or impartiality in the parenting facilitation process.

(p) A licensee serving as a parenting facilitator may make referrals to other professionals to work with the family, but shall avoid actual or apparent conflicts of interest by referrals. No commissions, rebates, or similar remuneration shall be given or received by a licensee for parenting facilitation or other professional referrals.

(q) A licensee serving as a parenting facilitator should attempt to bring about resolution of issues by agreement of the parties; however, the parenting facilitator is not acting in a formal mediation role. An effort towards resolving an issue, which may include therapeutic, mediation, education, and negotiation skills, does not disqualify a licensee from making recommendations regarding any issue that remains unresolved after efforts of facilitation.

(r) A licensee serving as a parenting facilitator shall communicate with all parties, attorneys, children, and the court in a manner which preserves the integrity of the parenting facilitation process and considers the safety of the parents and children.

(s) A licensee serving as a parenting facilitator:

    (1) may meet individually or jointly with the parties, as deemed appropriate by the parenting facilitator, and may interview the children;

    (2) may interview any individuals who provide services to the children to assess the children's needs and wishes; and

    (3) may communicate with the parties through face-to-face meetings or electronic communication.

(t) A licensee serving as a parenting facilitator shall, prior to the beginning of the parenting facilitation process and in writing, inform the parties of:

    (1) the limitations on confidentiality in the parenting facilitation process; and

    (2) the basis of fees and costs and the method of payment, including any fees associated with postponement, cancellation and/or nonappearance, and the parties' pro rata share of the fees and costs as determined by the court order or written agreement of the parties.

(u) Information obtained during the parenting facilitation process shall not be shared outside the parenting facilitation process except for professional purposes, as provided by court order, by written agreement of the parties, or as directed by the board.

(v) In the initial session with each party, a licensee serving as a parenting facilitator shall review the nature of the parenting facilitator's role with the parents to ensure that they understand the parenting facilitation process.

(w) A licensee serving as a parenting facilitator:

    (1) shall comply with all mandatory reporting requirements, including but not limited to Family Code, Chapter 261, concerning abuse or neglect of minors;

    (2) shall report to law enforcement or other authorities if they have reason to believe that any participant appears to be at serious risk to harm themselves or a third party;

    (3) shall maintain records necessary to support charges for services and expenses, and shall make a detailed accounting of those charges to the parties and their counsel, if requested to do so;

    (4) shall maintain notes regarding all communications with the parties, the children, and other persons with whom they speak about the case; and

(5) shall maintain records in a manner that is professional, legible, comprehensive, and inclusive of information and documents that relate to the parenting facilitation process and that support any recommendations made by the licensee.

(x) Records of a licensee serving as a parenting facilitator are not mental health records and are not subject to the disclosure requirements of Health and Safety Code, Chapter 611. At a minimum, records shall be maintained for the period of time described in §781.209(4)   of this title (relating to Client Records and Record Keeping), or as otherwise directed by the court.

(y) Records of a licensee serving as a parenting facilitator shall be released on the request of either parent, as directed by the court, or as directed by the board.

(z) Charges for parenting facilitation services shall be based upon the actual time expended by the parenting facilitator, or as directed by the written agreement of the parties, and/or formal order of the court.

(aa) All fees and costs shall be appropriately divided between the parties as directed by the court order of appointment and/or as noted in the parenting facilitators' written fee disclosure to the parties.

(bb) Fees may be disproportionately divided fees if one parent is disproportionately creating a need for services and if such a division is outlined in the court order of appointment and/or as noted in the parenting facilitators' written fee disclosure to the parties.

(cc) Services and activities for which a licensee serving as a parenting facilitator may charge include time spent interviewing parents, children and collateral sources of information; preparation of agreements, correspondence, and reports; review of records and correspondence; telephone and electronic communication; travel; court preparation; and appearances at hearings, depositions and meetings.

(dd) The minimum training for a licensee serving as a parenting facilitator that is required by the Family Code, §153.6101(b), and is determined by the court is:

(1) eight hours of family violence dynamics training provided by a family violence service provider;

(2) 40 classroom hours of training in dispute resolution techniques in a course conducted by an alternative dispute resolution system or other dispute resolution organization approved by the court;

(3) 24 classroom hours of training in the fields of family dynamics, child development, family law; and

(4) 16 hours of training in the laws and board rules governing parenting coordination and facilitation, and the multiple styles and procedures used in different models of service.

(ee) A licensee serving as a parenting facilitator:

(1) shall complete minimum training as required by the Family Code, §153.6101, as determined by the appointing court;

(2) shall have extensive practical experience with high conflict or litigating parents;

(3) shall complete and document upon request advanced training in family dynamics, child maltreatment, co-parenting, and high conflict separation

and divorce; and

(4) shall regularly complete continuing education related to co-parenting issues, high-conflict families and the parenting coordination and facilitation process.

(ff) A licensee serving as a parenting facilitator shall decline an appointment, withdraw, or request appropriate assistance when the facts and circumstances of the case are beyond the licensee's skill or expertise.

(gg) Since parenting facilitation services are addressed under multiple titles in different jurisdictions nationally, acceptability of training to meet the requirements of subsection (bb)   of this section is based on functional skills taught during the training rather than the use of specific titles or names.

SUBCHAPTER C

THE BOARD

§781.301. BOARD RULES

(a) This subsection outlines the board's procedures for submitting, considering, and disposing of a petition to the board to adopt or change a rule.

(1) Any person may petition the board to adopt or change a rule. The petition, which must be in writing and shall be filed with the board office, shall state the petitioner's name, address, and phone number, and shall include a brief justification and explanation of the proposed rule; the proposed text of the rule, indicating the words to be added or deleted from the current text; the statutory or other authority under which the rule is to be promulgated; and the public benefit that adopting the proposed rule would create, or the anticipated injury or inequality which would result if the proposed rule is not adopted.

(2) The board office may determine the petition does not contain existing information described in this subsection and shall return the petition to the petitioner.

(3) Except as otherwise provided in this subsection, the executive director shall submit a completed petition to the board for consideration.

(4) At the first full board meeting after receiving the petition, the board shall either deny the petition or institute rulemaking procedures in accordance with the APA, the Government Code, Chapter 2001. If the board denies the petition, the board will explain to the petitioner, in writing, why the board denied. If the board initiates rulemaking procedures, the board may alter the wording of the rule from the petitioner's version.

(b) The board will consider and act on all petitions for rule adoption or changes in accordance with this section. If the board considered and acted on a proposed rule change within the previous six months, the board may decline to consider a subsequent petition for the same rule adoption.

§781.302. BOARD MEETINGS

(a) The board shall hold at least one meeting each year and additional meetings as necessary.

(b) The chairperson may call a meeting after consultation with board members or by a majority of members so voting at a meeting.

(c) Meetings shall be announced and conducted under the provisions of the Texas Open Meetings Act, Government Code, Chapter 551.

(d) The chairperson may invite comments or statements from non-board members on all agenda items, but may limit the time allotted to each individual. The board may not act on comments or statements related to issues not on the agenda.

(e) Interpreters and other reasonable accommodations necessary to facilitate public participation will be made available as requested. The executive director must receive notice that reasonable accommodations will be needed at least 10 days in advance of the board or committee meeting.

§781.303. BOARD TRAINING

A person who is appointed to and qualifies for office as a member of the board may not vote, deliberate, or be counted as a member in attendance at a meeting of the board until the person completes a training program that meets the requirements established in the Act.

§781.304. TRANSACTION OF OFFICIAL BOARD BUSINESS

(a) The board may transact official business only when in a legally constituted meeting with a quorum present. A quorum of the board necessary to conduct official business is five members.

(b) The board shall not be bound by any board member's or staff member's statement or action except when such statement or action results from the board's specific instructions. Board member or staff member opinions, except when a statement or action is in pursuance of specific instructions of the board, about ethical dilemmas or practice issues should never be substituted for appropriate professional consultation.

(c) Robert's Rules of Order Revised shall be the basis of parliamentary decisions except as otherwise provided in this chapter.

§781.305. BOARD AGENDAS

(a) The executive director is responsible for preparing and submitting an agenda to board members prior to each meeting; the agenda is subject to the chair's approval. The agenda shall include items requested by board members, items required by law, items previously tabled, and other matters of board business.

(b) Any individual, including a board member, may request an agenda item by submitting the written request and supporting documentation at least 30 days before the scheduled meeting. The board or committee chair and legal counsel must approve any item before it is placed on the agenda.

(c) The official board meeting agenda shall be filed with the Texas Secretary of State as required by law.

§781.306. BOARD MINUTES

(a) The minutes of a board meeting are official only when affixed with the original signature of the chairperson.

(b) Drafts of the meeting minutes shall be forwarded to each board member for review and comments or corrections prior to the board's approval.

(c) The official board meeting minutes shall be posted on the publicly-accessible board website.

§781.307. ELECTIONS

(a) At the first meeting following the last day of January of each year, the board shall elect a vice-chair.

(b) A vacancy which occurs in the office of vice-chair may be filled at any meeting.

§781.308. OFFICERS OF THE BOARD

(a) The chair, who is appointed by the governor, shall preside at all meetings which he or she attends. The chair performs all duties prescribed by law or this chapter and is authorized to make day-to-day decisions regarding board activities to make the board more effective and responsive.

(b) The vice-chair shall perform the duties of the chair in case the chair is absent or disabled. If the office of chair becomes vacant, the vice-chair shall serve until a successor is appointed.

§781.309. COMMITTEES OF THE BOARD

(a) The board and/or the board chair may establish board committees, advisory committees and task forces.

(b) The board chair shall appoint members of the board to serve on board committees and shall appoint the board committee chairs. The board chair shall assign board members and/or the executive director to serve on advisory committees and task forces. The board chair may invite others to serve on advisory committees and task forces.

(c) Only members of the board may be appointed to board committees.

(d) Committee chairs shall make regular reports to the board in interim written reports or at regular meetings.

(e) Committees shall meet when called by the committee chair or when so directed by the board or the board chair.

(f) Each committee shall consist of least one public member and one professional member, unless the board authorizes otherwise. At least one public member of the board shall be appointed to any board committee established to review a complaint filed with the board or review an enforcement action against a license holder related to a complaint filed with the board.

§781.310. EXECUTIVE DIRECTOR

(a) The executive director, who serves at the will of the board, is a department employee who administers board activities, such as keeping board meeting minutes and proceedings and serving as custodian of the board files and records.

(b) The executive director shall exercise general supervision over persons employed in the administration of the Act. The executive director may delegate responsibilities to other staff members when appropriate.

(c) The executive director shall be responsible for the investigation and presentation of complaints.

(d) The executive director manages board correspondence and obtains, prepares, and assembles reports and information as directed by the board, or as authorized by the department or other agency with appropriate statutory authority.

(e) The executive director is responsible for assembling and evaluating materials that applicants submit for licensure and renewal. The executive director's determinations are subject to the approval of the appropriate board committee or the full board.

§781.311. OFFICIAL RECORDS OF THE BOARD

(a) Public records may be reviewed by inspection or duplication, or both, in accordance with the Texas Public Information Act, Government Code, Chapter 552. Confidential records are not available.

(b) The requester shall pay the customary department charge for duplicating costs before or at the time the duplicated records are transferred to the requester.

(c) The procedural rules contained in the Texas Public Information Act for inspecting and duplicating public records apply to requests the board receives.

§781.312. IMPARTIALITY AND NON-DISCRIMINATION

(a) The board shall make all decisions in the discharge of its statutory authority without regard to any person's age; gender; race; color; religion; national origin; disability; sexual orientation; gender identity and expression; or political affiliation.

(b) Any board member who cannot be impartial in determining an applicant's eligibility for licensure or in a disciplinary action against a licensee shall so declare this to the board and shall not participate in any board proceedings involving that applicant or licensee.

§781.313. APPLICANTS WITH DISABILITIES

(a) The board shall comply with applicable provisions of the Americans with Disabilities Act.

(b) Applicants with disabilities shall inform the board in advance of any reasonable accommodations needed.

§781.314. THE LICENSE

(a) The board shall prepare and provide to each licensee a license certificate, which contains the licensee's name, license granted and license number. The license certificate will include any specialty recognition or supervisory status granted by the board to the licensee. The board shall have a method to indicate the expiration date of a new license and a license which has been renewed.

(b) The license shall display the chairperson's signature and the seal of the State of Texas.

(c) Temporary license certificates shall include an expiration date. A temporary license expires on the expiration date, the date that the first licensing examination is failed, or, if the first licensing examination is passed, the date that the board issues a regular license certificate, whichever is first.

(d) Provisional license certificates shall include an expiration date. A provisional license expires on the expiration date or the date that the board issues a regular license certificate, whichever is first.

(e)   All licenses issued by the board remain the property of the board and must be surrendered to the board on demand. The board maintains jurisdiction over a licensee until the license is returned to the board.

§781.315. ROSTER OF LICENSEES

The board, on its website, will make available to the general public a roster of licensees at its discretion.

§781.316. FEES

(a)   The following are the board's fees:

(1)   application fee for all licenses, approved supervisory status, or specialty recognition--$20;

(2)   license fee for LBSW, or LMSW--$60;

(3)   renewal fee for LBSW, or LMSW--$80 biennially;

(4)   license fee for LCSW--$100;

(5)   renewal fee for LCSW--$100 biennially;

(6)   additional license fee for AP or Independent Practice specialty recognition--$20 biennially;

(7)   additional or replacement license fee--$10;

(8)   fee for late renewal:

(A)   1 - 90 days--renewal fee plus fee equal to one-fourth of the renewal fee for an unexpired license (LMSW or LBSW fee - $20; LCSW, LBSW-IPR, LMSW-IPR, or LMSW-AP fee - $25); or

(B)   91 days, but less than one year--renewal fee plus fee equal to one-half of the renewal fee for an unexpired license (LMSW or LBSW fee - $40; LCSW, LBSW-IPR, LMSW-IPR, or LMSW-AP fee - $50);

(9)   conversion fee covering active to inactive status, or inactive to active status--$30;

(10) inactive status renewal fee--$30 biennially;

(11) returned check fee--$25;

(12) written license verification fee--$10 per verification copy;

(13) specialty license verification fee--$10 per verification copy;

(14) continuing education provider application fee--$50 annually;

(15) delinquent child support administrative fee--$35;

(16) legislatively mandated fees for the Office of Patient Protection;

(17) legislatively mandated fees related to administering www.texas.gov;

(18) board approved supervisor fee--$50 biennially;

(19) AMEC participant administrative fee--Fee equal to the current contract examination fee;

(20) Temporary license fee--$30; and

(21) Criminal history evaluation letter fee--$50.

(b)   Fees paid to the board by applicants are not refundable except in accordance with §781.405 of this title (relating to Application for Licensure).

(c)   A license which is issued by the board, but for which a check is returned (for example, insufficient funds, account closed, or payment stopped) is invalid. A license will be considered expired and the licensee in violation of board rules until the board receives and processes the renewal fee and returned check fee.

§781.317. CRIMINAL HISTORY EVALUATION LETTER

(a)   In accordance with Texas Occupations Code, §53.102, a person may request the department to issue a criminal history evaluation letter regarding the person's eligibility for a license if the person:

(1)   is enrolled or planning to enroll in an educational program that prepares a person for an initial license or is planning to take an examination for an initial license; and

(2)   has reason to believe that the person is ineligible for the license due to a conviction or deferred adjudication for a felony or misdemeanor offense.

(b)   A person making a request for issuance of a criminal history evaluation letter shall submit the request on a form prescribed by the department, accompanied by the criminal history evaluation letter fee and the required supporting documentation, as described on the form. The request shall state the basis for the person's potential ineligibility.

(c)   The department has the same authority to investigate a request submitted under this subsection and the requestor's eligibility that the department has to investigate a person applying for a license.

(d)   If the department determines that a ground for ineligibility does not exist, the department shall notify the requestor in writing of the determination. The notice shall be issued not later than the 90th day after the date the department received the request form, the criminal history evaluation letter fee, and any supporting documentation as described in the request form.

(e)   If the department determines that the requestor is ineligible for a license, the department shall issue a letter setting out each basis for potential ineligibility and the department's determination as to eligibility. The letter shall be issued not later than the 90th day after the date the department received the request form, the criminal history evaluation letter fee, and any supporting documentation as described in the request form. In the absence of new evidence known to, but not disclosed by, the requestor or not reasonably available to the department at the time the letter is issued, the department's ruling on the request determines the requestor's eligibility with respect to the grounds for potential ineligibility set out in the letter.

SUBCHAPTER D

LICENSES AND LICENSING PROCESS

§781.401. QUALIFICATIONS FOR LICENSURE

(a)   Licensure. The following education and experience is required for licensure as designated. If an applicant for a license has held a substantially equivalent license in good standing in another jurisdiction for at least five years immediately preceding the date of application, the applicant will be deemed to have met the experience requirement under this chapter. If the applicant has been licensed or certified in another jurisdiction for fewer than five years preceding the date of application, the applicant must meet current Texas licensing requirements.

(1) Licensed Clinical Social Worker (LCSW).

    (A) Has been conferred a master's degree in social work from a CSWE-accredited social work program, or a doctoral degree in social work from an accredited institution of higher learning acceptable to the board, and has documentation in the form of a university transcript of successfully completing a field placement in social work.

    (B) Has had 3000 hours of board-approved supervised professional clinical experience over a period of 24 to 48 months, or its equivalent if the experience was completed in another jurisdiction. Board-approved supervised professional experience must comply with §781.404 of this title (relating to Recognition as a Board-approved Supervisor and the Supervision Process)   and all other applicable laws and rules.

    (C) Has had a minimum of 100 hours of board-approved supervision, over the course of the 3000 hours of experience, with a board-approved supervisor. Supervised experience must have occurred within the five calendar years immediately preceding the date of LCSW application. If the social worker completed supervision in another jurisdiction, the social worker shall have the supervision verified by the regulatory authority in the other jurisdiction. If such verification is impossible, the social worker may request that the board accept alternate verification of supervision.

    (D) Has passed the Clinical examination administered nationally by ASWB.

(2) Licensed Master Social Worker (LMSW).

    (A) Has been conferred a master's degree in social work from a CSWE-accredited social work program, or a doctoral degree in social work from an accredited university acceptable to the board, and has documentation in the form of a university transcript of successfully completing a field placement in social work.

    (B) Has passed the Master's examination administered nationally by ASWB.

(3) Licensed Baccalaureate Social Worker (LBSW).

    (A) Has been conferred a baccalaureate degree in social work from a CSWE accredited social work program.

    (B) Has passed the Bachelors examination administered nationally by ASWB.

(b) Specialty Recognition. The following education and experience is required for specialty recognitions.

    (1) Licensed Master Social Worker-Advanced Practitioner (LMSW-AP).

        (A) Is currently licensed in the State of Texas or meets the current requirements for licensure as an LMSW.

        (B) While fully licensed as a social worker, has had 3000 hours of board-approved supervised professional non-clinical social work experience over a period of 24 to 48 months, or its equivalent if the experience was completed in another jurisdiction. Board-approved supervised professional experience must comply with §781.404 of this title and all other applicable laws and rules.

(C) Has had a minimum of 100 hours of board-approved supervision, over the course of the 3000 hours of experience, with a board-approved supervisor. Supervised experience must have occurred within the five calendar years immediately preceding the date of LMSW-AP application. If supervision was completed in another jurisdiction, the social worker must have the supervision verified by the regulatory authority in the other jurisdiction. If such verification is impossible, the social worker may request that the board accept alternate verification of supervision.

(D) Has passed the Advanced Generalist examination administered nationally by the ASWB.

(2) Independent Non-clinical Practice.

(A) Is currently licensed in the State of Texas as an LBSW or LMSW.

(B) While fully licensed as a social worker has had 3000 hours of board-approved supervised full-time social work experience over a minimum two-year period, but within a maximum five-year period or its equivalent if the experience was completed in another state. Board-approved supervised professional experience must comply with §781.404 of this title and all other applicable laws and rules.

(C) Has had a minimum of 100 hours of board-approved supervision, over the course of the 3000 hours of experience, with a board-approved supervisor. Supervised experience must have occurred within the 5 calendar years immediately preceding the date of application for IPR specialty recognition. If supervision was completed in another jurisdiction, the social worker shall have the supervision verified by the regulatory authority in the other jurisdiction. If such verification is impossible, the social worker may request that the board accept alternate verification.

(c) Applicants for a license must complete the board's jurisprudence examination and submit proof of completion at the time of application. The jurisprudence examination must have been completed no more than six months prior to the date of application.

§781.402. CLINICAL SUPERVISION FOR LCSW AND NON-CLINICAL SUPERVISION FOR LMSW-AP AND INDEPENDENT PRACTICE RECOGNITION

(a) A person who has obtained a temporary license may not begin the supervision process toward independent non-clinical practice or independent clinical practice until the regular license is issued.

(b) An LMSW who plans to apply for the LCSW must:

(1) within 30 days of initiating supervision, submit to the board one clinical supervisory plan for each location of practice for approval by the board or executive director/designee;

(2) submit a current job description from the agency in which the social worker is employed with a verification of authenticity from the agency director or his or her designee on agency letterhead. In order for a plan to be approved, the position description or other relevant documentation must demonstrate that the duties of the position are clinical as defined in this chapter;

(3) submit a separate supervision verification form for each location of practice to the board for approval within 30 days of the end of each supervisory plan with each supervisor. If the supervisor does not recommend that the supervisee is eligible to examine for LCSW, the supervisor must indicate such on the clinical supervision verification form and provide specific reasons for not recommending the supervisee. The board may consider the supervisor's reservations as it evaluates the supervision verification submitted by the supervisee;

(4) submit a new supervisory plan within 30 days of changing supervisors or practice location; and

(5) submit an application for re-categorizing his/her licensure to Licensed Clinical Social Worker.

(c) An LMSW who plans to apply for the advanced practitioner specialty recognition must:

(1) submit one non-clinical supervisory plan for each location of practice to the board for approval by the board or executive director/designee within 30 days of initiating supervision;

(2) submit a current job description from the agency in which the social worker is employed with a verification of authenticity from the agency director or his or her designee on agency letterhead. In order for a plan to be approved, the position description must demonstrate that the duties of the position are social work;

(3) submit a separate supervision verification form for each practice location to the board for approval within 30 days of the end of each supervisory plan with each supervisor. If the supervisor does not recommend that the supervisee is eligible to examine for advanced practice specialty recognition, the supervisor must indicate such on the non-clinical supervision verification form and provide specific reasons for not recommending the supervisee. The board may consider the supervisor's reservations as it evaluates the supervision verification that the supervisee submits;

(4) submit a new supervisory plan within 30 days of changing supervisors or practice location; and

(5) upon completing and submitting documentation of the required non-clinical supervision, the LMSW must apply for the advanced practitioner specialty recognition.

(d) An LBSW or an LMSW who plans to apply for the Independent Practice Recognition must:

(1) submit one supervisory plan to the board for each location of practice for approval by the board or executive director/designee within 30 days of initiating supervision;

(2) submit a current job description from the agency in which the social worker is employed with a verification of authenticity from the agency director or his or her designee on agency letterhead or submit a copy of the contract or appointment under which the LBSW or LMSW intends to work, along with a statement from the potential supervisor that the supervisor has reviewed the contract and is qualified to supervise the LBSW or LMSW in the setting;

(3) submit a separate supervision verification form for each practice location to the board within 30 days of the end of each supervisory plan with each supervisor. If the supervisor does not recommend that the supervisee is eligible for independent practice recognition, the supervisor must provide specific reasons for not recommending the supervisee. The board may consider the supervisor's reservations as it evaluates the supervision verification that the supervisee submits; and

(4) submit a new supervisory plan within 30 days of changing supervisors or practice location.

(e) A licensee who is required to be supervised as a condition of initial licensure, continued licensure, or disciplinary action must:

(1) submit one supervisory plan for each practice location to the board for approval by the board or executive director/designee within 30 days of initiating supervision;

(2) submit a current job description from the agency in which the social worker is employed with a verification of authenticity from the agency director or his or her designee on agency letterhead or submit a copy of the contract or appointment under which the licensee intends to work, along with a statement from the potential supervisor that the supervisor has reviewed the contract and is qualified to supervise the licensee in the setting;

(3) ensure that the supervisor submits reports to the board on a schedule determined by the board. In each report, the supervisor must address the supervisee's performance, how closely the supervisee adheres to statutes and rules, any special circumstances that led to the imposition of supervision, and recommend whether the supervisee should continue licensure. If the supervisor does not recommend the supervisee for continued licensure, the supervisor must provide specific reasons for not recommending the supervisee. The board may consider the supervisor's reservations as it evaluates the supervision verification the supervisee submits; and

(4) notify the board immediately if there is a disruption in the supervisory relationship or change in practice location and submit a new supervisory plan within 30 days of the break or change in practice location.

(f) An LBSW or an LMSW who has been approved for a probationary license under supervision while participating in the AMEC program must follow the application and supervision requirements in §781.413 of this title (relating to Alternate Method of Examining Competency (AMEC) Program).

§781.403. INDEPENDENT PRACTICE RECOGNITION (NON-CLINICAL)

(a) An LBSW or LMSW who seeks to obtain board approval for the specialty recognition of independent non-clinical practice shall meet requirements and parameters set by the board in §781.401 of this title (relating to Qualifications for Licensure).

(b) An individual supervising an LBSW for independent non-clinical practice recognition shall be an LBSW recognized for independent non-clinical practice; an LMSW recognized for independent non-clinical practice; an LMSW-AP; or an LCSW. The supervisor shall be board-approved.

(c) An individual supervising an LMSW for the independent non-clinical practice recognition shall be board-approved and shall be an LMSW recognized for independent non-clinical practice, an LMSW-AP, or an LCSW.

(d) A person who has obtained only the temporary license may not begin supervision until the board issues a regular license.

(e) The board may use the Internal Revenue Service (IRS) guidelines developed in 1996 to demonstrate whether a professional is an independent contractor or an employee. These guidelines revolve around the control an employer has in an employer-employee relationship, in which the employer has the right to control the "means and details" by which services are performed.

    (1) Behavioral control. The employer can control the employee's behavior by giving instructions about how the work gets done rather than simply looking at the end products of work. The more detailed the instructions, the more control the employer exercises. An employer requiring that employees be trained for the job is also an example of behavioral control, though contractors may also go through training.

    (2) Financial control. The employer determines the amount and regularity of payments to employees. A contractor is typically paid when he/she completes the work, and the contractor usually sets a timeframe for completing the work. The most important element of financial control is that a contractor has more freedom to make business decisions that affect the profitability of his/her work. A contractor, for instance, may invest in renting an office or buying equipment, while the employee does not. While employees are usually reimbursed for job-related expenses, the contractor may or may not be reimbursed, but lack of reimbursement usually signals that a worker is independent. An independent contractor often makes his or her services available to other potential clients, while an employee does not.

    (3) Relationship of the parties. The intent of the relationship is significant. The relationship is usually outlined in the written contract and gives one party more control than the other. If a company gives a worker employee benefits, the worker is an employee. The ability to terminate the relationship is another evidence of control in the relationship. If the employer-employee relationship appears to be permanent, it denotes an employee, not contractor, relationship. If a worker performs activities that are a key aspect of the company's regular business, that denotes an employee status.

(f) An LBSW or LMSW who plans to apply for the specialty recognition of non-clinical independent practice shall follow procedures set out in §781.402 of this title (relating to Clinical Supervision for LCSW and Non-Clinical Supervision for LMSW-AP and Independent Practice Recognition).

(g) An LBSW or LMSW may practice independently when the LMSW or LBSW holds the independent practice specialty recognition, or when under a supervision plan for independent practice that has been approved by the board.

§781.404. Recognition as a Board-approved Supervisor and the Supervision Process

(a)   Types of supervision include:

(1)   administrative or work-related supervision of an employee, contractor or volunteer that is not related to qualification for licensure, practice specialty recognition, a disciplinary order, or a condition of new or continued licensure;

(2)   clinical supervision of a Licensed Master Social Worker in a setting in which the LMSW is providing clinical services; the supervision may be provided by a Licensed Professional Counselor, Licensed Psychologist, Licensed Marriage and Family Therapist, Licensed Clinical Social Worker or Psychiatrist. This supervision is not related to qualification for licensure, practice specialty recognition, a disciplinary order, or a condition of new or continued licensure;

(3)   clinical supervision of a Licensed Master Social Worker, who is providing clinical services and is under a board-approved supervision plan to fulfill supervision requirements for achieving the LCSW; a Licensed Clinical Social Worker who is a board-approved supervisor delivers this supervision;

(4)   non-clinical supervision of a Licensed Master Social Worker or Licensed Baccalaureate Social Worker who is providing non-clinical social work service toward qualifications for independent non-clinical practice recognition; this supervision is delivered by a board-approved supervisor;

(5)   non-clinical supervision of a Licensed Master Social Worker who is providing non-clinical social work service toward qualifications for the LMSW-AP; this supervision is delivered by a board-approved supervisor;

(6)   supervision of a probationary Licensed Master Social Worker or Licensed Baccalaureate Social Worker providing non-clinical services by a board-approved supervisor toward licensure under the AMEC program; or

(7)   board-ordered supervision of a licensee by a board-approved supervisor pursuant to a disciplinary order or as a condition of new or continued licensure.

(b)   A person who wishes to be a board-approved supervisor must file an application and pay the applicable fee.

(1)   A board-approved supervisor must be actively licensed in good standing by the board as an LBSW, an LMSW, an LCSW, or be recognized as an Advanced Practitioner (LMSW-AP), or hold the equivalent social work license in another jurisdiction. An individual whose licensure status is emeritus may not serve as a board-approved supervisor. The person applying for board-approved status must have practiced at his/her category of licensure for two years. The board-approved supervisor shall supervise only those supervisees who provide services that fall within the supervisor's own competency.

(2)   The board-approved supervisor is responsible for the social work services

provided within the supervisory plan.

(3) The board-approved supervisor must have completed a supervisor's training program acceptable to the board.

(4) The board-approved supervisor must complete three hours of continuing education every biennium in supervision theory, skills, strategies, and/or evaluation.

(5) The board-approved supervisor must designate at each license renewal that he/she wishes to continue board-approved supervisor status.

(6) The board-approved supervisor must submit required documentation and fees to the board as listed in §781.316 of this title (relating to Fees).

(7) When a licensee is designated a board-approved supervisor, he or she may perform the following supervisory functions.

(A) An LCSW may supervise clinical experience toward the LCSW license, non-clinical experience toward the Advanced Practitioner specialty recognition, non-clinical experience toward the Independent Practice Recognition (non-clinical), a licensee under probationary initial or continued licensure, board-ordered probated suspension, and probationary license holders under the AMEC program.

(B) An LMSW-AP may supervise non-clinical experience toward the Advanced Practitioner specialty recognition; non-clinical experience toward the non-clinical Independent Practice Recognition; a licensee under probationary initial or continued licensure; board-ordered probated suspension for non-clinical practitioners; and probationary license holders under the AMEC program.

(C) An LMSW with the Independent Practice Recognition (non-clinical)   who is a board-approved supervisor may supervise an LBSW's or LMSW's non-clinical experience toward the non-clinical Independent Practice Recognition; an LBSW or LMSW under probationary initial or continued licensure; an LBSW or LMSW (non-clinical)   under board-ordered probated suspension; and a probationary license holder under the AMEC program; however, an LMSW who does not hold the independent practice recognition may only supervise probationary license holders under the AMEC program in an employment setting.

(D) An LBSW with the non-clinical Independent Practice Recognition who is a board-approved supervisor may supervise: an LBSW's non-clinical experience toward the non-clinical Independent Practice Recognition; an LBSW under probationary initial or continued licensure; an LBSW under board-ordered probated suspension; and a probationary LBSW license holder under the AMEC program; however, an LBSW who does not hold the independent practice recognition may only supervise probationary license holders under the AMEC program in an employment setting.

(8) On receiving the licensee's application to be a board-approved supervisor, as well as fee and verification of qualifications, the board will issue a letter notifying the licensee that the licensee is a board-approved supervisor.

(9) The approved supervisor must renew the approved supervisor status in conjunction with the biennial license renewal. The approved supervisor may surrender supervisory status by documenting the choice on the appropriate board renewal form and subtracting the supervisory renewal fee from the renewal payment. If a licensee who has surrendered supervisory status desires to regain supervisory status, the licensee must reapply and meet the current requirements for approved supervisor status.

(10) A supervisor must maintain the qualifications described in this section while he or she is providing supervision.

(11) A board-approved supervisor who wishes to provide any form of board-approved or board-ordered supervision must comply with the following.

(A) The supervisor is obligated to keep legible, accurate, complete, signed supervision notes and must be able to produce such documentation for the board if requested. The notes shall document the content, duration, and date of each supervision session.

(B) A social worker may contract for supervision with written approval of the employing agency. A copy of the approval must accompany the supervisory plan submitted to the board.

(C) A board-approved supervisor may not charge or collect a fee or anything of value from his or her employee or contract employee for the supervision services provided to the employee or contract employee.

(D) Before entering into a supervisory agreement, the supervisor shall be aware of all conditions of exchange with the clients served by her or his supervisee. The supervisor shall not provide supervision if the supervisee is practicing outside the authorized scope of the license. If the supervisor believes that a social worker is practicing outside the scope of the license, the supervisor shall make a report to the board.

(E) A supervisor shall not be employed by or under the employment supervision of the person who he or she is supervising.

(F) A supervisor shall not be a family member of the person being supervised.

(G) A supervisee must have a clearly defined job description and responsibilities.

(H) A supervisee who provides client services for payment or reimbursement shall submit billing to the client or third-party payers which clearly indicates the services provided and who provided the services, and specifying the supervisee's licensure category and the fact that the licensee is under supervision.

(I) If either the supervisor or supervisee has an expired license or a license that is revoked or suspended during supervision, supervision hours accumulated during that time will be accepted only if the licensee appeals to and receives approval from the board.

(J) A licensee must be a current board-approved supervisor in order to provide professional development supervision toward licensure or specialty recognition, or to provide board-ordered supervision to a licensee. Providing supervision without having met all requirements for current, valid board-approved supervisor status may be grounds for disciplinary action against the supervisor.

(K) The supervisor shall ensure that the supervisee knows and adheres to the Code of Conduct and Professional Standards of Practice of this chapter.

(L) The supervisor and supervisee shall avoid forming any relationship with each other that impairs the objective, professional judgment and prudent, ethical behavior of either.

(M) Should a supervisor become subject to a board disciplinary order, that person is no longer a board-approved supervisor and must so inform all supervisees, helping them to find alternate supervision.

(N) The board may deny, revoke, or suspend board-approved supervisory status following a fair hearing for violation of the Act or rules, according to the department fair hearing rules. Continuing to supervise after the board has denied, revoked, or suspended board-approved supervisor status, or after the supervisor's supervisory status expires, may be grounds for disciplinary action against the supervisor.

(O) If a supervisor's board-approved status is expired, suspended, or revoked, the supervisor shall refund all supervisory fees the supervisee paid after the date the supervisor ceased to be board-approved.

(P) A supervisor is responsible for developing a well-conceptualized supervision plan with the supervisee, and for updating that plan whenever there is a change in agency of employment, job function, goals for supervision, or method by which supervision is provided.

(Q) All board-approved supervisors shall have taken a board-approved supervision training course by January 1, 2014 in order to renew board-approved supervisor status. The board recognizes that many licensees have had little, if any, formal education about supervision theories, strategies, problem-solving, and accountability, particularly LBSWs who may supervise licensees toward the IPR. Though some supervisors have functioned as employment supervisors for some time and have acquired practical knowledge, their practical supervision skills may be focused in one practice area, and may not include current skills in various supervision methods or familiarity with emerging supervisory theories, strategies, and regulations. Therefore, the board values high-quality, contemporary, multi-modality supervision training to ensure that all supervisors have refreshed their supervisory skills and knowledge in order to help supervisees practice safely and effectively.

(12) A board-approved supervisor who wishes to provide supervision towards licensure as an LCSW or towards specialty recognition in Independent Practice (IPR) or Advanced Practitioner (LMSW-AP), which is supervision for professional growth, must comply with the following.

(A) Supervision toward licensure or specialty recognition may occur in one-on-one sessions; in a combination of individual and group sessions; or in board-approved combinations of supervision in the same geographical location, supervision via audio and visual web technology, and other electronic supervision techniques.

(B) Supervision groups shall have no fewer than two members and no more than six.

(C) Supervision shall occur in proportion to the number of actual hours worked, with a base line of one hour of supervision for every 40 hours worked. If the supervisee works full-time, supervision shall occur on average at least twice a month and for no less than four hours per month; if the supervisee works part-time (at least 20 hours per week), supervision shall occur on average at least once a month and no less than two hours per month. Supervisory sessions shall last at least one hour and no more than two hours per session. No more than 10 hours of supervision may be counted in any one month, or 30-day period, as appropriate, towards satisfying minimum requirements for licensure or specialty recognition.

(D) The board considers supervision toward licensure or specialty recognition to be supervision which promotes professional growth. Therefore, all supervision formats must encourage clear, accurate communication between the supervisor and the supervisee, including case-based communication that meets standards for confidentiality. Though the board favors supervision formats in which the supervisor and supervisee are in the same geographical place for a substantial part of the supervision time, the board also recognizes that some current and future technology, such as using reliable, technologically-secure computer cameras and microphones, can allow personal face-to-face, though remote, interaction, and can support professional growth. Supervision formats must be clearly described in the supervision plan, explaining how the supervision strategies and methods of delivery meet the supervisee's professional growth needs and ensure that confidentiality is protected. The plan must be approved by the board.

(E) Supervision toward licensure or specialty recognition must extend over a full 3000 hours over a period of not less than 24 full months and a period of not more than 48 full months for LCSW or LMSW-AP or not more than 60 full months for Independent Practice Recognition (IPR). Even if the individual completes the minimum of 3000 hours of supervised experience and minimum of 100 hours of supervision prior to 24 months from the start date of supervision, supervision which meets the board's minimum requirements shall extend to a minimum of 24 full months. A month is a 30-day period or the length of the actual calendar month, whichever is longer.

(F) The supervisor and the supervisee bear professional responsibility for the supervisee's professional activities.

(G) If the supervisor determines that the supervisee lacks the professional skills and competence to practice social work under a regular license, the supervisor shall develop and implement a written remediation plan for the supervisee.

(H) Board-approved supervised professional experience towards licensure must comply with §781.401 of this title (relating to Qualifications for Licensure)   and §781.402 of this title (relating to Clinical Supervision for LCSW and Non-Clinical Supervision for LMSW-AP and Independent Practice Recognition)   of this title and all other applicable laws and rules.

(13) A board-approved supervisor who wishes to provide supervision required as a result of a board order must comply with relevant provisions of §781.413 of this title (relating to Alternate Method of Examining Competency (AMEC)   Program), §781.610 of this title (relating to Due Process Following Violation of an Order) and §781.806 of this title (relating to Probation)   of this title, all other applicable laws and rules, and/or the following.

(A) A licensee who is required to be supervised as a condition of initial licensure, continued licensure, or disciplinary action must:

    (i) submit one supervisory plan for each practice location to the board for approval by the board or executive director/designee within 30 days of initiating supervision;

    (ii) submit a current job description from the agency in which the social worker is employed with a verification of authenticity from the agency director or his or her designee on agency letterhead or submit a copy of the contract or appointment under which the licensee intends to work, along with a statement from the potential supervisor that the supervisor has reviewed the contract and is qualified to supervise the licensee in the setting;

    (iii) ensure that the supervisor submits reports to the board on a schedule determined by the board. In each report, the supervisor must address the supervisee's performance, how closely the supervisee adheres to statutes and rules, any special circumstances that led to the imposition of supervision, and recommend whether the supervisee should continue licensure. If the supervisor does not recommend the supervisee for continued licensure, the supervisor must provide specific reasons for not recommending the supervisee. The board may consider the supervisor's reservations as it evaluates the supervision verification the supervisee submits; and

    (iv) notify the board immediately if there is a disruption in the supervisory relationship or change in practice location and submit a new supervisory plan within 30 days of the break or change in practice location.

(B) The supervisor who agrees to provide board-ordered supervision of a licensee who is under board disciplinary action must understand the board order and follow the supervision stipulations outlined in the order. The supervisor must address with the licensee those professional behaviors that led to board discipline, and must help to remediate those concerns while assisting the licensee to develop strategies to avoid repeating illegal, substandard, or unethical behaviors.

(C) Board-ordered and mandated supervision timeframes are specified in the board order.

(c) A licensee who submits one of the following: a Clinical Supervision Plan, a Non-Clinical Supervision Plan, or a Board-Ordered Supervision Plan, to the board for approval, shall receive a written response from the board of either approval or deficiency related to the plan. If no written response is received by the licensee within four weeks of submission of the plan, it is the responsibility of the licensee who has submitted the plan to follow-up with the board office related to receipt and/or status of the plan within 60 days of submission. If written approval or deficiency is sent to the last known address of the licensee, a board response related to acceptance of the plan shall be considered to have been sent. Supervision and supervised experience hours are not acceptable to meet minimum requirements towards licensure or specialty recognition or to satisfy the terms of a board order if not accrued under a board-approved plan without explicit authorization from the board.

§781.405. APPLICATION FOR LICENSURE

(a) A licensure application must be on the official form designated by and available from the board.

(b) The application process begins when the board office receives the completed application form and fee.

(c) The department will acknowledge in writing receiving the application and fee within 15 working days of receipt. The letter will include the requested licensing or specialty recognition category; any documented deficiencies in qualifications; and any additional documentation, such as transcripts or supervisory references, required for the examination approval.

(d) The board will mail a letter approving the applicant to sit for the examination within 15 working days after the board office receives all required documentation.

(e) If an applicant fails to fully document his or her qualifications and/or fails to pass the examination within 12 months after filing the application, his or her application shall be voided, and the applicant will be required to reapply.

(f) When the applicant passes the examination, the department shall mail an approval notice stating the initial licensure fee.

(g) Under no circumstances may a license applicant falsify any application materials. If the board determines that false information has been submitted, the applicant shall be determined unfit for licensure.

(h) When the applicant has met all other qualifications for licensure or specialty recognition, and when the board office receives the applicant's license fee payment, the board will grant the license or specialty recognition.

(i) In the event an application is not processed in the time periods stated in this section, the applicant has the right to request, in writing, reimbursement of all fees paid in that particular application process. The applicant shall address the reimbursement request to the executive director, who will respond within 30 days. The director may find that good cause existed for exceeding the time period and may deny the request. In that event, the applicant may appeal in writing to the board chairperson, addressed to the board office. The chairperson shall review the executive director's report of the situation and may approve or deny, in writing, the applicant's request for reimbursement of fees.

§781.406. REQUIRED DOCUMENTATION OF QUALIFICATIONS FOR LICENSURE

(a) Application form. An applicant for licensure must submit a completed official application form with all requested information.

(b) Education verification.

   (1) The applicant's education must be documented by official college transcripts from social work educational units accredited by CSWE.

   (2) Degrees for licensure as an LBSW or LMSW must be from programs accredited or in candidacy for accreditation by CSWE. (Current written verification of a program's CSWE candidacy status must be on file with the board.) College or university degrees from outside of the United States and its territories must be from programs judged by the CSWE to be equivalent to a CSWE accredited program in the United States.

(c) Experience verification.

   (1) An applicant's experience for licensure or for specialty recognition must meet the requirements of §781.401 of this title (relating to Qualifications for Licensure), §781.402 of this title (relating to Clinical Supervision for LCSW and Non-Clinical Supervision for LMSW-AP and Independent Practice Recognition), and §781.404 of this title (relating to Recognition as a Board-approved Supervisor and the Supervision Process). The applicant must document the names and addresses of supervisors; beginning and ending dates of supervision; job description; and average number of hours of social work activity per week. The applicant must further document the appropriate supervision plan and verification form, both approved by the board, for each practice location. If any elements described in the supervision plan change, including but not limited to work hours, full- or part-time work status, location of supervision, or name of supervisor, the applicant must submit the appropriate verification form within 30 days of the change or supervision termination. The applicant must submit a new, complete supervision plan for board approval within 30 days of beginning the new supervision agreement.

   (2) The applicant's experience must have been in a position providing social work services, under the supervision of a qualified supervisor, with written evaluations to demonstrate satisfactory performance.

   (3) Supervised experience must have occurred within the five calendar years immediately preceding the date of application.

   (4) The applicant must maintain and upon request, provide to the board documentation of employment status, pay vouchers, or supervisory evaluations.

(d) References. An applicant must list on the official application the names and addresses of three individuals familiar with the applicant's professional qualifications. The board may contact the references for verification of the applicant's qualifications and fitness.

(e) Jurisprudence examination. Applicants for a license must complete the board's jurisprudence examination and submit proof of completion at the time of application. The jurisprudence examination must have been completed no more than six months prior to the date of application.

§781.407. Fitness of Applicants for Licensure

(a) To determine the applicant's fitness, the board shall consider the applicant's skills and abilities to provide adequate social work services to clients; the applicant's ethical behavior in relationships with other professionals and clients; and the applicant's worthiness of public trust and confidence.

(b) The board may consider a person, who has committed any act that would have been a violation of the Act or this chapter had the person been licensed at the time the act was committed, as unworthy of public trust and confidence.

(c) Surrender or revocation of a social work license within the previous five years while under investigation or under a board order for professional misconduct shall be considered evidence that the person is unworthy of public trust and confidence.

(d) In determining fitness, the board may also consider a surrender, revocation, or violation of a board order which occurred more than five years before application.

§781.408. Materials Considered in Determination of Fitness of Applicants

In determining the fitness of applicants, the board shall consider evaluations and assessments of supervisors, employers, instructors, and other individuals who can attest to the applicant's fitness for practice; transcripts or findings from official court, hearing, or investigative proceedings; and other relevant information.

§781.409. Finding of Non-fitness

(a) The board may deny a license, license renewal, or specialty recognition if it substantiates that the applicant lacks the necessary skills and abilities to provide adequate social work services; has misrepresented any materials in the licensure application or renewal application, or any materials submitted to the board; has violated any provision of the Act in effect when the applicant applied; or has violated the Code of Conduct, Standards of Practice, or any other section of this chapter which would have applied had the applicant been licensed when he/she committed the violation.

(b) The board may require an applicant for licensure or licensure renewal to obtain a criminal background check from a board-designated agency and to provide the board an official copy of that report. The board may consider the report in determining the applicant's eligibility for licensure or renewal. Failure to obtain the background check within 30 days of the board's request is grounds for denying the application.

§781.410. Provisional Licenses

The board may grant a provisional social work license to a person who holds, at the time of application, a social work license or certificate issued by another jurisdiction acceptable to the board, and who applies for the provisional license in writing and submits all required academic and experience documentation required for licensure. The applicant must have passed an equivalent licensing test as accepted by the board. If granted a provisional license, the individual must use the appropriate licensing title followed by the word "provisional." If the board deems that the applicant meets the requirements for licensure set forth in this Act, the board will issue a regular license. If the board determines that the applicant does not meet this state's licensing requirements, the board will deny the application, and the provisional license will no longer be valid.

§781.411. TEMPORARY LICENSE

(a) Prior to examination, a licensure applicant may obtain a temporary social work license as long as the applicant meets all the requirements, except the licensing examination, for the license category the applicant seeks.

(b) A person holding a temporary license must take the designated examination within six months of issuance of the temporary license.

(c) The temporary license is valid until the licensee attempts the appropriate examination or the end of the six-month issuance of the temporary license.

(d) A person holding a temporary license must display the license at the licensee's place of business and must use the appropriate licensed title or initials followed by the word "Temporary" in all professional use of the licensee's name.

(e) Should the applicant take and fail the examination, the temporary license is no longer valid. The applicant must immediately cease and desist from using the temporary license and title, and return the license certificate and certificate card to the board.

(f) Should the applicant pass the examination, the board will issue the license or specialty recognition in accordance with §781.405(g) of this title (relating to Application for Licensure). A temporary license holder who has passed the licensing examination continues to be temporarily licensed until the board issues a regular license or the temporary license expires.

(g) A person who failed the examination and is without a valid temporary license may retake the examination under §781.412 of this title (relating to Examination Requirement).

(h) A temporary license will not be granted to an applicant who has held a temporary license for the same license category previously within his/her lifetime.

(i) An applicant for LCSW or specialty recognition is not eligible for a temporary or provisional license.

(j) Applicants requesting a temporary license must submit the application form and temporary fee required by the board.

§781.412. EXAMINATION REQUIREMENT

(a) An applicant for licensure or specialty recognition must pass an examination designated by the board.

(b) When an applicant passes the examination, the individual has no more than one year from the date of passing the examination to complete the requirements for licensure, completing all documentation and paying all fees or the passing examination score will not longer count towards licensure.

(c) If an applicant fails the examination on the first attempt of his/her lifetime, the individual may retake the examination no more than two additional times. An applicant who has failed the examination on the first, second, and third attempts must request in writing to the board to retake the examination a fourth time. The board may order the applicant to complete one or more social work educational courses as a prerequisite to retaking the examination.

(d) An applicant who fails the examination must wait the required timeframe between examination administrations. The board or executive director may waive the waiting period if the applicant petitions in writing, justifying the waiver in accordance with board policy.

(e)   If an applicant fails the examination on the fourth attempt, the person's application will be voided. The applicant will not be permitted to reapply for licensure for one year. Each subsequent attempt must be approved by the appropriate committee of the board.

(f)   The board may waive the examination for an applicant with a valid certificate or license from another state if the certificate or license was issued before January 1, 1986, if petitioned in writing.

(g)   On the basis of a verified report from ASWB that an applicant has cheated on the examination, the application shall be denied.

§781.413. Alternate Method of Examining Competency (AMEC) Program

(a)   An applicant who has taken an examination within the previous 12 months and who has failed the examination on two or more occasions by no more than five points may submit a written petition to the board for an LBSW or LMSW license. It is also the applicant's responsibility to contact ASWB and secure the test scores to submit to the board. The applicant must apply, pay the administrative fee, and submit the memorandum of understanding and the findings of facts documentation to the board to be considered for AMEC.

(b)   The board will consider the public interest in reviewing the petition and will issue its written decision after the next full board meeting at which the petition and the applicant's required materials are reviewed.

(c)   The written decision will explain why the board has denied AMEC participation, or outline the terms of participation under which the AMEC license is granted.

(d)   The participant must complete the professional portfolio, quarterly reports and other requirements within the board's required timeframe.

(e)   The participant must complete the AMEC program in no less than 12 and no more than 24 consecutive calendar months from the date of board's agreed order unless the board gives prior approval.

(f)   An AMEC participant remains under the supervision of a board-approved supervisor until the board has reviewed the required documents and issued a final order regarding the board's issuance of a regular license. The board may require continued supervision reports.

(g)   The board may grant a regular license to an applicant who successfully completes the AMEC participation terms.

§781.414. Issuance of License Certificates

(a)   The board issues license certificates and license cards indicating the social work title, whether LBSW, LMSW or LCSW, granted to applicants who have met all of the board's qualifications. The board-issued license cards will indicate the license expiration date. The board shall indicate the new expiration date of a renewed license on the board-issued cards. The license certificate will also include any applicable specialty recognition or supervisory status.

(b)   The licensee must include the license title or associated initials in all professional uses of the licensee's name as required by the Act, §505.351, as in Licensed Clinical Social Worker - LCSW; Licensed Master Social Worker - LMSW; or Licensed Baccalaureate Social Worker - LBSW. If the licensee holds a specialty recognition, he or she shall use the specialty recognition initials as well: Licensed Master Social Worker with non-clinical Independent Practice Recognition - LMSW-IPR; Licensed Baccalaureate Social Worker with non-clinical Independent Practice Recognition - LBSW-IPR; or Licensed Master Social Worker with Advanced Practitioner Recognition - LMSW-AP.

(c) A licensee shall display an original board-issued license certificate, a current license card, and a copy of the Code of Conduct in a prominent place in all practice locations.

(d) The board will post its client information brochure on the board's website.

(e) A licensee who offers social work services on the Internet must include a statement that the licensee is licensed by the State of Texas and provide a copy of the Code of Conduct with the information on how to contact this board by mail or telephone.

(f) Upon a client's request, a licensee shall provide information regarding his or her license category and how to contact the board.

§781.415. APPLICATION DENIAL

(a) The board may deny an application if the applicant does not meet all requirements for licensure or specialty recognition.

(b) A person whose application for licensure or specialty recognition is denied is entitled to a formal hearing as set out in Subchapter G of this chapter (relating to Formal Hearings).

§781.416. REQUIRED REPORTS TO THE BOARD

(a) A licensee shall make written reports to the board office within 30 days of the following:

  (1) a change of mailing address, place of employment or business or home phone number;

  (2) the licensee's arrest, deferred adjudication, or criminal conviction, other than a Class C misdemeanor traffic offense;

  (3) the filing of a criminal case against the licensee;

  (4) the settlement of or judgment rendered in a civil lawsuit filed against the licensee and relating to the licensee's professional social work practice; or

  (5) complaints, investigations, or actions against the licensee by a governmental agency or by a licensing or certification body.

(b) The board may use information received under subsection (a) of this section to determine whether a licensee remains fit to hold a license.

(c) Failure to make a report as required by subsection (a) of this section is grounds for disciplinary action by the board.

§781.417. SURRENDER OF LICENSE

(a) Surrender by licensee.

  (1) A licensee may at anytime voluntarily offer to surrender his or her license

for any reason, without compulsion.

(2) The license may be delivered to the board office by hand or mail. The licensee must cease practice as a social worker pending action from the board on the surrender of the licensee's license.

(3) If there is no complaint pending, the board office may accept the surrender and void the license.

(b) Formal disciplinary action.

(1) When a licensee has offered the surrender of his or her license after a complaint has been filed, the board shall consider whether to accept the surrender of the license.

(2) When the board has accepted such a surrender, the surrender is deemed to be the result of a formal disciplinary action and a board order shall be prepared accepting the surrender.

(3) In order to accept a surrender, the board may require the licensee to agree to certain findings of fact and conclusions of law, including admitting to a violation of the Act or this chapter.

(4) When the board does not accept an offer of surrender or when the licensee fails to renew the license, the board is not deprived of jurisdiction against the licensee under the Act or any other statute.

(c) Reinstatement. A license, which has been surrendered by the licensee and accepted by the board, may not be reinstated; however, a person may apply for a new license in accordance with the Act and this chapter.

§781.418. ISSUANCE OF LICENSES TO CERTAIN OUT-OF-STATE APPLICANTS

(a) Notwithstanding any other licensing requirement of this chapter or the Act:

(1) The board may not require an applicant who is licensed in good standing in another state to retake a licensing examination conducted by the board under the Act if the applicant has passed the same examination in another jurisdiction.

(2) The board may issue a license to an applicant who is currently licensed in another jurisdiction to independently practice social work if the board determines that the applicant demonstrates sufficient experience and competence; has passed the licensing examination appropriate to the category of licensure the applicant seeks; has passed the jurisprudence examination conducted by the board under the Texas Occupations Code, §505.3545; and is in good standing with the regulatory body of the licensing jurisdiction at the time the applicant applied in Texas.

(b) When assessing the applicant's experience and competence, the board may consider any supervision the applicant received in another jurisdiction if the board determines that the supervision would be considered for licensing or certification in the jurisdiction in which the applicant received the supervision.

§781.419. MILITARY SPOUSE

(a) This section sets out the alternative license procedure for military spouse required under Texas Occupations Code, Chapter 55 (relating to License While on Military Duty and for Military Spouse).

(b)   The spouse of a person serving on active duty as a member of the armed forces of the United States who holds a current license issued by another state that has substantially equivalent licensing requirements shall complete and submit an application form and fee. In accordance with Texas Occupations Code, §55.004(c), the executive director may waive any prerequisite to obtaining a license after reviewing the applicant's credentials and determining that the applicant holds a license issued by another jurisdiction that has licensing requirements substantially equivalent to those of this state.

(c)   The spouse of a person serving on active duty as a member of the armed forces of the United States who within the five years preceding the application date held the license in this state that expired while the applicant lived in another state for at least six months is qualified for licensure based on the previously held license, if there are no unresolved complaints against the applicant and if there is no other bar to licensure, such as criminal background or non-compliance with a board order. Board approval of a new application, including submission of all required fees and attachments, is required prior to issuance of a license.

SUBCHAPTER E

LICENSE RENEWAL AND CONTINUING EDUCATION

§781.501. GENERAL

(a)   A license must be renewed biennially.

(b)   A licensee must have fulfilled any continuing education requirements that this chapter prescribes in order to renew a license.

(c)   Each person who holds a license is responsible for renewing the license and shall not be excused from paying penalty fees for late renewal. Failure to receive notice from the board does not waive payment of penalty fees.

(d)   The board may deny the license renewal of a licensee who is in violation of the Act, or this chapter, at the time of renewal application.

(e)   A person whose license has expired shall not use the terms or titles described in the Act, §505.351. The person shall return his or her license to the board.

(f)   The deadlines established for renewals, late renewals, and penalty fees are based on the postmarked date or electronic submission date by which the licensee submits documentation.

(g)   The board shall deny renewal if required by the Education Code, §57.491 (relating to Defaults on Guaranteed Student Loans).

(h)   The board upon receipt of a final court or attorney general's order will suspend a license due to failure to pay child support per the Family Code, Chapter 232, regarding suspension of licenses. The individual must pay the reinstatement fee set out in §781.316 of this title (relating to Fees).

(i)   A license must be renewed and in good standing prior to the licensee obtaining a different category of licensure.

§781.502. RENEWAL CYCLES

The license renewal date is the last day of the month of the licensee's birth month. The first renewal of licensure following issuance of the license will be valid for a period of 13 to 24 months, depending on the licensee's birth month. Subsequent to the first renewal period, licenses must be renewed every two years, and the renewal extends for two years.

§781.503. LICENSE RENEWAL

(a) At least 45 days prior to the expiration of a license, the board will send the licensee notice of the expiration date, schedule of renewal fees and penalties, and continuing education activities required for renewal. The licensee is responsible for renewing his/her license, regardless of whether or not the licensee receives a notification.

(b) The board will provide eligible licensees with renewal forms, soliciting the licensee's current address and contact numbers; completed continuing education; information regarding civil lawsuits and criminal complaints; any governmental agency or licensing body's action against the licensee; and a statement of continuing compliance with the Act and this chapter.

(c) When the board office receives the completed application, the executive director will respond within 15 working days to notify the applicant about the status of the application. Failure to process a renewal application in the time periods stated shall be governed by §781.405(h) of this title (relating to Application for Licensure).

(d) The board shall renew the license of a social worker who has met all renewal requirements, including fee payments, completed documentation, and evidence of completed continuing education requirements.

(e) If a licensee has made timely and sufficient application for license renewal, the license does not expire until the board has acted on the renewal. If the licensee claims to have made timely, sufficient application and is otherwise eligible for renewal, the license will remain current until the renewal is issued or until the board office determines that the application was not timely or sufficient.

(f) A licensee who has been recommended for disciplinary action must file a timely and complete license renewal application, pay all fees, and verify that required continuing education is complete. If he/she fails to do these things, the licensee must cease all social work practice until all renewal requirements are complete.

(g) The board may deny a license renewal if the licensee is a party to a formal disciplinary action. A formal action commences when the board mails notice described in §781.602(c) of this title (relating to Disciplinary Action and Notices).

(h) A license that is not revoked or suspended as a result of formal proceedings shall be renewed provided that all other requirements are met.

(i) In the case of delay in the license renewal process because of formal disciplinary action, penalty fees shall not apply.

(j) The board may refuse to renew the license of a person who fails to pay an administrative penalty imposed in accordance with the Act unless the enforcement of the penalty is stayed or a court has ordered that the administrative penalty is not owed.

§781.504. LATE RENEWAL

(a) A person who fails to meet all the requirements to renew his or her license by the renewal date ceases to be licensed.

(b) A person who renews a license after the expiration date but on or before 90 days after the expiration date shall pay the renewal fee and appropriate penalty fees.

(c) A person whose license was not renewed on or before 90 days from the expiration date may renew within one year of the expiration date by paying the appropriate renewal and penalty fees.

(d) A person whose license has expired must document that he/she completed all continuing education requirements in order to renew the license. A licensee who has not completed all required continuing education in the renewal period shall cease practice and must complete all continuing education before the board will allow the individual to renew. In that case, the board may impose late renewal fees and additional fees.

(e) On or after one year from the expiration date, a person may no longer renew the license and must reapply by submitting a new application, paying the required fees, and meeting the current requirements for the license including passing the licensure examination.

§781.505. INACTIVE STATUS

(a) A licensee who does not wish to practice social work in the State of Texas and whose license has not expired may request the board to grant inactive status anytime before the license expires. If a licensee requests conversion to inactive status within 45 days of the expiration date for the license, the individual must provide verification of completion of all continuing education requirements for the renewal.

(b) No continuing education is required of a licensee while on inactive status.

(c) The inactive status conversion fee and any applicable renewal fee and penalty fee for late renewal must be paid prior to the date the license expires.

(d) A licensee on inactive status must renew the inactive license and pay all applicable inactive renewal fees throughout the duration of the inactive status. A licensee on inactive status who fails to remit the biennial inactive status renewal fee or who otherwise fails to renew the inactive license timely ceases to be licensed and must reapply for licensure and meet all current minimum requirements for licensure in place at the time of submission of the new application for licensure.

(e) A license, if appropriately converted and renewed as inactive, may be on inactive status for no more than 48 consecutive months or for no more than 96 months total in a lifetime. There must be a minimum of 48 months of active licensure before subsequent inactive status may be requested and granted.

(f) A licensee on inactive status must notify the board in writing to reactivate the license, provide proof of completion of the Jurisprudence Exam completed within six months of the date of requesting reactivation of the license, and pay the conversion fee for inactive to active status. The reactivated license status shall begin seven days after the board receives the licensee's reactivation fee.

§781.506. EMERITUS STATUS

(a) A licensee who is at least 60 years of age or disabled, and who is not engaged in professional social work practice, may request emeritus status in writing to the board. An emeritus license must be renewed every two years but requires no renewal fee or continuing education.

(b) The emeritus licensee may only use his or her emeritus title while providing social work services as a volunteer without compensation. The emeritus licensee who volunteers social worker services is under the board's jurisdiction and must comply with the Code of Conduct and Professional Standards of Practice, as well as the Act and the rule requirements in this chapter.

(c) An emeritus licensee whose license is in good standing can be reinstated to an active license within 48 months of conversion to emeritus status. To be eligible for an active license through reinstatement of an emeritus license, the emeritus licensee shall submit an application for licensure at the appropriate category, as well as proof of completion of the Jurisprudence Exam within six months prior to requesting reactivation, and payment of the licensing fee. Verification of education, supervision, and examination score is not required.

(d) An emeritus licensee who reactivates his/her license within 48 months of conversion to emeritus status may not regain board-approved supervisor status upon activation without verification of completion of minimum requirements as a board-approved supervisor in place at the time of reactivation. An emeritus licensee who reactivates his/her license within 48 months may regain other specialty recognition(s)   without demonstration of meeting current minimum requirements for that specialty recognition.

(e) An emeritus licensee who does not reactivate his/her license within 48 months of conversion to emeritus status may not convert the license to active status except as follows. An emeritus licensee who did not reactivate his/her license within 48 months of conversion must reapply for active licensure and meet all current minimum requirements for licensure, specialty recognition, and board-approved supervisor status in place at the time of application. If all current minimum requirements for licensure are met, upon issuance of a new license and license number, the emeritus license will be null and void.

(f) A licensee who converts to emeritus status may only reactivate the license to active status once per lifetime.

§781.507. ACTIVE MILITARY DUTY

(a) A licensee on active duty with the Armed Forces of the United States who is not practicing in the State of Texas at the time of renewal is exempt from the renewal requirement and may, within one year of his or her return to Texas or release from active duty, whichever occurs first, request reinstatement of his or her license.

(b) The board will issue a license on receipt of the request for reinstatement, documentation of his or her active duty status at the time the license expired, and the fee for the current license. No continuing education will be required prior to reinstatement and no penalty fees will be charged.

§781.508. HOUR REQUIREMENTS FOR CONTINUING EDUCATION

(a) A licensee must complete a total of 30 clock-hours biennially of continuing education obtained from board-approved continuing education providers. A licensee must complete a total of 30 clock-hours of continuing education obtained from a board-approved continuing education provider including the first renewal of the licensure following issuance of the license, which is valid for a period of 13 to 24 months, depending on the licensee's birth month.

(b) As part of the required 30 biennial clock-hours, a licensee must complete a minimum of six clock-hours of continuing education in professional ethics and social work values.

(c) A clock-hour is defined as 60 minutes of standard time.

(d) A licensee may earn credit for ethics as a presenter or a participant.

(e) Upon a licensee's petition, the executive director may waive part, but not all, of the continuing education renewal requirements for good and just cause or may permit the licensee additional time to complete all continuing education requirements. If the director decides not to waive requirements, a licensee may appeal to the board, which may elect to waive the late fees accrued. Should the board not uphold the licensee's petition, all late fees accrued will apply.

§781.509. TYPES OF ACCEPTABLE CONTINUING EDUCATION

The board accepts continuing education in which the licensee learns by:

(1) participating in institutes, seminars, workshops, conferences, independent study programs, post graduate training programs, college academic or continuing education courses which relate to or enhance the practice of social work and are offered by a board-approved provider;

(2) teaching or presenting the activities described in paragraph (1) o f this section;

(3) writing a published work or presenting work applicable to the profession of social work;

(4) serving as a field instructor for social work interns attending a college or university accredited by or in candidacy status with CSWE;

(5) providing supervision to a social worker participating in the program in accordance with §781.413 of this title (relating to the Alternative Method of Examining Competency (AMEC) Program); or

(6) completing the board's jurisprudence training course no more than once per renewal period, unless the board directs otherwise.

§781.510. ACTIVITIES UNACCEPTABLE AS CONTINUING EDUCATION

The board will not give credit hours for:

(1) education incidental to the regular professional activities of a social worker such as learning occurring from experience or research;

(2) organizational activity such as serving on committees or councils or as an officer in a professional organization;

(3) meetings and activities such as in-service programs required as a part of one's job, unless the in-service training is acceptable continuing education under §781.509 of this title (relating to Types of Acceptable Continuing Education);

(4) college academic courses which are audited or not taken for credit; or

(5) any experience which does not fit the types of acceptable continuing education in §781.509 of this title.

§781.511. REQUIREMENTS FOR CONTINUING EDUCATION PROVIDERS

(a) A provider must be approved under this section to offer continuing education programs.

(b) A person seeking approval as a continuing education provider shall apply using board forms and include the continuing education provider application fee. Governmental agencies shall be exempt from paying this fee.

(c) Entities that receive automatic status as approved providers without applying or paying fees include accredited colleges and universities; a national or statewide association, board or organization representing members of the social work profession; nationally accredited health or mental health facilities; or a person or agency approved by any state or national organization in a related field such as medicine, law, psychiatry, psychology, sociology, marriage and family therapy, professional counseling, and similar fields of human service practice. Regarding entities that receive automatic status as approved providers under this section, the board will not provide documentation of board-approved status nor will the board include such entities in its roster of board-approved providers.

(d) The applicant shall certify on the application that all programs that the provider offers for board-approved credit hours will comply with the criteria in this section; and the provider will be responsible for verifying attendance at each program and provide an attendance certificate as set forth in subsection (k) of this section.

(e) A program the provider offers for board-approved credit hours shall advance, extend, and enhance the licensees' professional social work skills and knowledge; be developed and presented by persons who are appropriately knowledgeable in the program's subject matter and training techniques; specify the course objectives, course content, teaching methods, and number of credit hours; specify the number of credit hours in ethics and values separately and as part of the total hours credited.

(f) The provider must document each program's compliance with this section, maintaining that documentation for three years.

(g) Department staff shall review the continuing education provider application and notify the applicant of any deficiencies or grant approval, assigning the continuing education provider approval number which shall be noted on all certificates.

(h) Each continuing education program shall provide participants an evaluation instrument which may be completed on-site or returned via the web or by mail. The provider and the instructor shall review the evaluation outcomes and consider those outcomes in revising subsequent programs, keeping all evaluations for three years and allowing the board to review the evaluations on request.

(i) The provider will supply a list of subcontractors as part of the renewal process or upon request.

(j) To maintain continuing education provider approval, each provider shall annually apply to renew provider status and pay applicable fees.

(k) It is the provider's responsibility to provide each program participant with a legible certificate of attendance after the program ends. The certificate shall include the provider's name, approval number, and expiration date of the provider's approved status; the participant's name; the program title, date, and place; the credit hours earned, including the ethics hours credited; the provider's signature or that of the provider's representative; and the board contact information, which shall at a minimum, include the board's name and web address.

(l) The provider is responsible for assuring that the licensee receives credit only for time actually spent in the program.

(m) If the provider fails to comply with these requirements, the board, after notice to the provider and due process hearing, may revoke the provider's approval status.

(n) The board may evaluate any provider or applicant at any time to ensure compliance with requirements of this section.

(o) Complaints regarding continuing education programs offered by approved providers may be submitted in writing to the executive director.

(p) A program offered by a provider for credit hours in ethics shall meet the minimum course requirements for an ethics course approved by the board.

§781.512. Evaluation of Continuing Education Providers

(a) Department staff shall audit approved continuing education providers regularly, reporting audit results to the board. During the audit, staff shall request the provider's documentation regarding compliance with §781.511 of this title (relating to Requirements for Continuing Education Providers).

(b) Department staff shall notify a continuing education provider of the results of an audit. A continuing education provider who does not comply with these regulations shall implement a correction plan to address deficiencies, and will submit documentation of these corrective measures to the board within 30 days of the board's notice that corrective actions are necessary.

(c) The board shall review and may rescind the approval status of continuing education providers.

(d) If the board receives written complaints about continuing education offered by approved providers, the department may audit the provider and refer the matter to the board for appropriate action.

(e) A provider whose approval status has been rescinded may reapply for approval on or after the 91st day following the board action. The provider must document that corrective action has been taken and that the provider's programs will be presented in compliance with §781.511 of this title. The board shall review the reapplication.

(f) A licensee may not count hours to renew the license if those continuing education hours were received from a provider has failed to meet renewal requirements, or whose approval has been denied or rescinded by the board but is accepted by another approval entity.

(g) Fees paid by a provider whose approval has been rescinded or denied are non-refundable.

§781.513. ACCEPTANCE OF CONTINUING EDUCATION APPROVED BY ANOTHER LICENSING BOARD

(a)   A licensee may request in writing that the board approve continuing education hours provided by a non-approved provider. The licensee shall submit documentation as specified in §781.511(e) of this title (relating to Requirements for Continuing Education Providers) for the board to review and a fee equal to the continuing education provider application fee.

(b)   The executive director will review the documentation and notify the licensee in writing whether the program(s) are acceptable as credit hours. This decision may be appealed to the board.

§781.514. CREDIT HOURS GRANTED

The board will grant the following credit hours toward the continuing education requirements for license renewal.

(1)   One credit hour will be given for each hour of participation in a continuing education program by an approved provider.

(2)   Credit may be earned, post-licensure, through successfully completing postgraduate training programs (e.g., intern, residency, or fellowship programs) or successfully completing social work courses in a graduate school of social work at a rate of five credit hours per each semester hour or its equivalent not to exceed 10 hours per renewal period. A licensee may complete the ethics requirement in §781.508(a) of this title (relating to Hour Requirements for Continuing Education) only through a course specifically designated as an ethics course.

(3)   Credit may be earned for teaching social work courses in an accredited college or university. Credit will be applied at the rate of five credit hours for every course taught, not to exceed 15 hours per renewal period. A licensee may complete the ethics requirement in §781.508(a)of this title only through teaching a course specifically designated as an ethics course.

(4)   A field instructor for a social work intern will be granted five credit hours for each college semester completed, not to exceed 20 credit hours per renewal period.

(5)   A presenter of a continuing education program or an author of a published work, which imparts social work knowledge and skills, may be granted five credit hours for each original or substantially revised presentation or publication, not to exceed 20 credit hours per renewal period.

(6)   A licensee may carry over to the next renewal period up to 10 credit hours earned in excess of the continuing education renewal requirements. Continuing education earned during the licensee's birth month may be used for the current renewal or for the following year.

(7)   Completing the jurisprudence examination shall count as three hours of the continuing education requirement in ethics and social work values, as referenced in §781.508(b) of this title.

§781.515. CONTINUING EDUCATION DOCUMENTATION

(a)   Licensees must verify their credit hours on the board's license renewal form. Failing to submit the form with completed continuing education hours is grounds to deny the application for license renewal.

(b) Licensees must maintain documentation of their continuing education for three years.

(c) The board will review a random sample of applications for quality control. A licensee selected for review will be notified by mail and required to submit acceptable documentation of the continuing education listed on the continuing education report form. Documentation must specify the subject, date(s), credit hours, name of sponsor, board-issued sponsor approval number or other identifying sponsor information (if applicable) and board contact information. The licensee shall include such items as copies of attendance certificates or other attendance verification from the provider; grade reports or transcripts verifying that a college course is completed; letters from deans, directors, department chairs, or their representatives verifying a field instructor assignment; letters from program sponsors verifying the licensee presented continuing education; or copies of continuing education programs or other documentation verifying that the continuing education was relevant to social work when the program does not have an assigned provider number.

§781.516. REQUIREMENTS OF SUPERVISOR TRAINING COURSE PROVIDERS

(a) A supervisor training course provider must be an approved continuing education provider or exempt under §781.511 of this title (relating to Requirements for Continuing Education Providers) to apply for approval as a supervisor training course provider. A provider shall apply on board forms.

(b) A supervisor training course provider must be approved under this section to offer supervisor training courses. The board shall maintain a list of supervisor training course providers on the board's website.

(c) The applicant shall certify on the application that all supervisor training courses that the provider offers for board credit will comply with the criteria in this section; and that the supervisor training course provider will be responsible for verifying attendance at each program and provide an attendance certificate as set forth in this section.

(d) A supervisor training course offered for board credit shall enhance recipients' professional knowledge and skills about supervision so that they can successfully fulfill the supervision duties the board expects board-approved supervisors to complete. The course shall be developed and presented by persons who are appropriately knowledgeable in supervision theories, strategies, and techniques. It shall specify the course objectives, course content, and teaching methods.

(e) The supervisor training course provider must document that each course complies with this section and maintain that documentation for a period of three years.

(f) To be approved, an applicant must demonstrate compliance with the board's course content guidelines. The board will review the supervisor training course provider application and notify the applicant of any deficiencies or grant approval. If the applicant is not already a board-approved continuing education provider, the applicant will be notified of the deficiency of this requirement. Once minimum requirements are met, the board-approved supervisor training course provider shall indicate the supervisor training course provider approval number all attendance certificates.

(g)   Each supervisor training course shall allow participants to formally evaluate the course using an evaluation instrument. The provider and the instructor shall review the evaluation outcomes and revise subsequent programs accordingly. The supervisor training course provider shall keep all evaluations for three years and allow the board to review the evaluations on request.

(h)   A supervisor training course provider must submit updated curricula every six years in order to maintain approval as a provider.

(i)   The supervisor training course provider is responsible for providing each training participant with a legible attendance certificate when the training ends, verifying the name, date, and place of the training; the provider's name, approval number, and signature; and board contact information.

(j)   The supervisor training course provider shall maintain attendance records for not fewer than three years.

(k)   The supervisor training course provider is responsible for assuring that only licensees who attend the complete training and have demonstrated that they met training objectives receive credit for the training.

§781.517. EVALUATION OF SUPERVISOR TRAINING COURSE PROVIDERS

(a)   The board may evaluate any approved supervisor training provider at any time to ensure compliance with requirements of this section.

(b)   Department staff shall audit approved supervisor training course providers regularly, reviewing the supervisor training provider's documentation regarding compliance with §781.516 of this title (relating to Requirements of Supervisor Training Course Providers), and report audit results to the appropriate board committee.

(c)   Department staff shall notify supervisor training providers of the audit results. If the provider is not compliant, the provider shall implement a correction plan to address audit deficiencies, and will submit documentation verifying corrective action to the board within 30 days of the date of the board's notice that corrective action is necessary.

(d)   The board shall review the approval status of supervisor training providers who are not in compliance and who have not taken corrective action.

(e)   The board may rescind the approval status of a supervisor training provider.

(f)   Complaints regarding supervisor training courses offered by approved providers may be submitted in writing to the executive director. Complaints may result in an audit and may be referred to the board for appropriate action.

(g)   A supervisor training course provider whose approval status has been rescinded by the board may reapply on or after the 91st day following the board action. The provider must document corrective action and demonstrate that the provider's courses will be presented in compliance with §781.516 of this title.

(h)   In order to get board credit of supervisor training to meet requirements of §781.404 of this title (relating to Recognition as a Board-approved Supervisor and the Supervision Process), a licensee must take that training from a provider approved in good standing with the board.

SUBCHAPTER F

COMPLAINTS AND VIOLATIONS

§781.601. PURPOSE

This subchapter sets out grounds for denying an application or disciplining a licensee and procedures for reporting alleged violations of the Act or this chapter.

§781.602. DISCIPLINARY ACTION AND NOTICES

(a) The board shall revoke, suspend, suspend on an emergency basis, or deny a license or specialty recognition, place on probation a person whose license or specialty recognition has been suspended, or reprimand a person with a license or specialty recognition for:

    (1) violating any provision of the Act or any board rule;

    (2) failing to cooperate in a complaint investigation filed under this chapter's provisions;

    (3) failing to comply with any board-ordered action;

    (4) exhibiting physical or mental incompetency, as determined by the board, to perform social work;

    (5) providing false or misleading information to the board regarding qualifications for licensure or renewal or in response to a board inquiry;

    (6) violating any of the grounds described in the Act, §505.451;

    (7) violating the law or rules of another health or mental health profession resulting in disciplinary action by that profession's regulatory body;

    (8) violating the law, rules, or policies of a governmental agency related to social work practice resulting in disciplinary action by the governmental agency;

    (9) violating a board order; or

    (10) engaging in conduct that discredits or tends to discredit the social work profession.

(b) Prior to instituting formal disciplinary proceedings against a licensee, the board shall notify the licensee in writing by certified mail, return receipt requested or registered mail. The notice of violation letter will include the facts or conduct alleged to warrant revocation, suspension, or reprimand and the severity level from the sanction guide. The licensee shall be given the opportunity, as described in the notice, to show compliance with all requirements of the Act and this chapter, including the opportunity for an informal conference. A licensee's opportunity for an informal conference under this subsection shall satisfy the requirement of the APA, §2001.054(c).

(c) The licensee or applicant must request, in writing, a formal hearing within 10 days of receiving the notice, or the right to a hearing shall be waived and the license or specialty recognition shall be denied, revoked, suspended, probated, or reprimanded.

(d) Receipt of a notice under subsection (b) or (c) of this section is presumed to occur on the tenth day after the notice is mailed to the last address known to the board unless another date is reflected on a United States Postal Service return receipt or other official receipt.

(e) The licensee will be considered to have received notice of board disciplinary action if the notice is mailed to the last address provided in writing to the board by the licensee.

(f) If a notice is mailed to the last known address of the licensee, and the licensee fails to respond to the notice within 10 days from receipt of the notice, the licensee will be considered to have waived his or her right to a hearing in the matter.

(g) If it appears to the board that a person who is not licensed under this chapter is violating this chapter, a rule adopted under this chapter, or another state statute or rule relating to social work practice, the board, after notice and opportunity for a hearing as described in this section, may issue a cease and desist letter prohibiting the person from engaging in the activity. A violation of an order under this subsection constitutes grounds for the board to impose an administrative penalty.

§781.603. COMPLAINT PROCEDURES

(a) A person wishing to report that a licensee has allegedly violated the Act or this chapter may notify the department staff in writing, by telephone, by email or in person.

(b) The department staff is responsible for logging in complaints as they are received and investigating them.

(c) The board chairperson will appoint an Ethics Committee to review the department's investigations, determine if licensees have violated the law or rules, and decide what sanctions, if any, to impose.

(d) The board office shall not accept a complaint if the official form is not filed within five years of the date that the professional-client relationship involved in the alleged violations ended, or five years from the date the complainant learned that the behavior of the social worker violated the rules and/or law. If the client was a minor at the time of the alleged violation, this time limitation does not begin until the client reaches the age of 18 years. A complainant shall be notified of the non-acceptance of untimely complaints.

(e) The board may waive the time limitation in cases of egregious acts or continuing threats to public health or safety when presented with specific evidence that warrants such action.

(f) Department staff will acknowledge in writing that they have received the complaint.

(g) The executive director initially reviews the complaint to determine jurisdiction. If a complaint appears to be within the board's jurisdiction, the executive director shall decide whether to authorize sending a copy of the complaint to the respondent and requesting a response, which may include but not be limited to requesting that a copy of the client's records be attached to the response. If the executive director does not authorize written notification of the respondent, the complaint will be referred for an investigation and the assigned investigator will determine whether the respondent will be notified by letter, phone call, site visit, or some other appropriate means. If the complaint is against a person licensed by another board, the department staff will forward the complaint to that board not later than the 15th day after the date the agency determines that the information shall be referred to the appropriate agency as provided in Government Code, Chapter 774, relating to exchange of information between regulatory agencies.

(h) If the allegations clearly do not fall within the board's jurisdiction, the executive director may consult with both the attorney for the board as well as the board chair or his/her designee, and if all agree, the executive director may close the complaint and will present the case to the Ethics Committee at the committee's next meeting. The Ethics Committee retains the right to request full disclosure of any case closed and order a comprehensive hearing of the complaint.

(i) If the allegations in the complaint are within the board's jurisdiction and sufficient for investigation, the executive director shall:

(1) evaluate the threat to public health and safety documented by the complaint;

(2) establish an appropriate plan and schedule for its investigation to be noted in the complaint file;

(3) instruct agency staff to send a notice to the complainant acknowledging that the complaint was received, unless the complaint was anonymous; and

(4) report the status of all continuing investigations to the complainant and the licensee or applicant periodically.

(j) The department staff will begin investigating the complaint by requesting statements and evidence from all parties; by referring the investigation to a department investigator; or by enlisting the service of a private investigator. If using a private investigator is appropriate, department staff will so inform the board.

(k) If an investigation uncovers evidence of a criminal act, the executive director or the Ethics Committee will determine whether notifying law enforcement is appropriate, and if so, give such approval to the appropriate department staff for implementation. The complaint process will continue to its completion unless a law enforcement agency requests in writing that action be delayed, clarifying the reason for delay, and the date by which that agency plans to take action on the case. The executive director will request the law enforcement agency provide timely updates on the case progress.

(l) The executive director or the investigator assigned to the case will notify the subject of the complaint of the allegations either in writing, by phone or in person. The subject is required to provide a sworn response to the allegations within fifteen days of that notice. Failure to respond to the allegations within the 15 days is evidence of failure to cooperate with the investigation and subject to disciplinary action.

(m) The Ethics Committee will review complaints to ensure that complaint investigations are being handled in a timely manner and that complaints are not dismissed without appropriate consideration. The Ethics Committee will also ensure that any person who files a complaint has an opportunity to explain the allegations made in the complaint, and that any issues related to complaints which arise under the Act, or this chapter, are resolved.

(n) The Ethics Committee shall determine whether to dismiss a complaint as unsubstantiated, whether a violation exists, and what disciplinary action to take.

(o) The Ethics Committee may resolve pending complaints in which no violation is found or substantiated, or in which a violation is found, but the violation does not seriously affect the health and safety of clients or other persons, with actions which are not considered formal disciplinary actions. These include: issuance of an advisory notice, warning letter; or informal reminder; issuance of a "Conditional Letter of Agreement;" and/or other actions as deemed appropriate by the Ethics Committee. The licensee is not entitled to a hearing on the matters set forth in the notice, letter, reminder, "Conditional Letter of Agreement," or other action but may submit a written response to be included in the complaint record. Such actions by the Ethics Committee may be introduced as evidence in any subsequent disciplinary action involving acts or omissions after receipt of the notice, letter, reminder, "Conditional Letter of Agreement," a cease and desist letter, or other action which does not involve a formal disciplinary action.

(1) An advisory notice, warning letter or informal reminder. The Ethics Committee may resolve pending complaints by issuance of a formal advisory notice, warning letter, or informal reminder informing licensees of their duties under the Act or this chapter, whether the conduct or omission complained of appears to violate such duties, and whether the board has a concern about the circumstances surrounding the complaint.

(2) A "Conditional Letter of Agreement." The Ethics Committee may resolve pending complaints by issuance of a "Conditional Letter of Agreement" informing licensees of their duties under the Act or this chapter, whether the conduct or omission complained of appears to violate such duties, and creating board-ordered conditions for the long-term resolution of the issues in the complaint. This "Conditional Letter of Agreement" specifies the immediate disposition of the complaint. The licensee is issued the "Conditional Letter of Agreement" by the Ethics Committee, executive director, or designee; a signature of agreement by the licensee is not required. If the licensee fails to comply with all the board-ordered conditions in the specified time frame outlined in the "Conditional Letter of Agreement," the licensee will not have a right to a subsequent review of the issues in the original complaint by the Ethics Committee, but rather, a new complaint will be opened for the original violation(s), and notice of the violation(s) will be issued to the licensee, proposing to impose a formal disciplinary action as the resolution. The disciplinary action proposed for failure to comply with a "Conditional Letter of Agreement" will be a reprimand, unless otherwise specified by the Ethics Committee. "Procedures for Revoking, Suspending, Probating or Denying a License, or Reprimanding a Licensee" shall apply when a formal disciplinary action is proposed.

(3) Other actions. The Ethics Committee may resolve pending complaints with other actions, including issuance of a cease and desist letter, which are not considered formal disciplinary actions.

(p) If the complaint is not resolved by the committee, the committee may recommend that disciplinary action or other appropriate action as authorized by law be taken, including injunctive relief or civil penalties. If the investigation produces evidence of possible violations not described in the complaint, a separate complaint will be opened regarding such alleged violations. Notice will be given to the licensee that the new complaint will be heard at a subsequent meeting of the Ethics Committee. The committee may proceed with the action regarding the original complaint.

(q) If no violation exists or the complaint is dismissed as unsubstantiated, the department will notify the complainant and the licensee or applicant in writing of the finding. The notice may include a statement of issues and recommendations that the committee wishes the subject of the complaint to consider.

(r) If the executive director receives credible evidence that a licensee is engaging in acts that pose an immediate, significant threat of physical or emotional harm to the public, the executive director shall consult with the board chair or Ethics Committee members to authorize an emergency suspension of the license.

(s) Once a complaint has been dismissed by the committee, it cannot be reopened. If new significant information emerges about the circumstances of the dismissed complaint, a new complaint may be opened.

§781.604. ETHICS COMMITTEE MEETINGS AND POLICY

(a) The Ethics Committee will meet regularly to review and recommend action on complaints filed against social workers. Additionally, as requested by the respondent, the committee will hold informal conferences to review previous committee actions.

(b) Department staff will send an agenda and completed reports of complaint investigations to committee members approximately two weeks prior to each meeting. The agenda will list all items to be considered by the committee. Complaints will be listed on the agenda by the assigned complaint tracking number.

(c) Persons who are not committee members may observe committee work unless the committee enters into executive session for legal consultation. Committee members, staff, the licensee against whom the complaint is filed, and the person filing the complaint may participate in discussing a complaint before the committee. The committee chair or committee by vote may impose time limitations on discussion.

(d) Department staff will report on all completed investigations to committee members, including investigation results and a summary of staff recommendations for disposition.

(e) The committee will determine a complaint's validity based on the evidence and information. The committee may determine that the evidence does or does not support a finding of a violation of licensing law or rules, or the committee may request additional information for later review. If the committee finds that a social worker has violated licensing law or rules, the committee will consider the established policy guidelines and other relevant factors in recommending disciplinary action.

(f) All parties to a complaint will be notified of the committee's findings and recommendations.

§781.605. INFORMAL CONFERENCES

(a)   Informal conferences will be scheduled as needed.

(b)   The board's legal counsel or an attorney from the department's Office of General Counsel shall attend each informal conference.

§781.606. LICENSING OF PERSONS WITH CRIMINAL BACKGROUNDS

(a)   The board may take action against a licensee or deny a license pursuant to Texas Occupations Code, Chapter 53, concerning felony or misdemeanor convictions, or the Act, §505.451(12), concerning felony convictions.

(b)   The following felonies and misdemeanors relate to licensure as a social worker because these criminal offenses indicate a tendency to be unable to perform as a social worker: a violation of the Act; failure to report child abuse or neglect; a misdemeanor involving deceptive business practices; a conviction of assault or sexual assault, and the felony offense of theft. Further, the board will also consider other misdemeanors or felonies as possibly indicating an inability to perform appropriately as a social worker.

(c)   An applicant or licensee with a criminal background may provide or be requested to provide documentation of rehabilitation for the board's consideration.

(d)   A person may submit documentation of rehabilitation, including court records and a summary of the arresting event and the conditions which led to the arrest. Further, a person may submit documents related to a sentence imposed by the court, a sentence completed, or probation or parole successfully completed. It is also appropriate to submit information attesting to subsequent good behavior, letters from employers or others familiar with the person's accomplishments after being convicted, and any other information related to the applicant's qualifications for licensure.

(e)   The licensee may be referred to the appropriate board committee for review and determination of eligibility or monitoring requirements. Licensees referred to the board are afforded due process under the APA.

§781.607. SUSPENSION, REVOCATION, OR NON-RENEWAL

(a)   If the board suspends a license or specialty recognition, the suspension shall remain in effect for the period of time stated in the order or until the board determines that the reason for the suspension no longer exists.

(b)   While on suspension, the licensee shall comply with this chapter's renewal requirements, including paying fees and completing continuing education. However, the suspension remains in effect pursuant to subsection (a) of this section.

(c)   Upon revocation, suspension or non-renewal of a license, a licensee shall return his or her license to the board.

(d)   The board may refuse to renew the license of a person who fails to pay an administrative penalty imposed in accordance with the Act unless the enforcement of the penalty is stayed or a court has ordered that the administrative penalty is not owed.

§781.608. INFORMAL DISPOSITION

(a)   If a licensee agrees to the disciplinary action proposed by the Ethics Committee or recommended through an informal conference, the board office or board legal counsel shall prepare an agreed order, including agreed findings of fact and conclusions of law, and forward it to the licensee or applicant. An uncontested Notice of Violation executed and signed by the respondent may serve as the basis for a board order.

(1) The licensee or applicant shall execute the order and return the signed order to the board office within 10 days of receiving the order. If the licensee or applicant fails to return the signed order within 10 days, the inaction shall constitute rejection of the recommendations.

(2) If the licensee or applicant signs and accepts the recommendations, the agreed order shall be submitted to the entire board for its approval. Placing the agreed order on the board agenda constitutes only a recommendation for board approval.

(3) If the licensee or applicant rejects the proposed recommendations, the matter shall be referred to the executive director for appropriate action.

(b) The board shall notify the licensee or applicant of the date, time, and place of the board meeting at which the proposed agreed order will be considered. Attendance by the licensee or applicant is voluntary.

(c) Upon an affirmative majority vote, the board shall enter an agreed order approving the accepted recommendations. The board may not change the terms of a proposed order but may only approve or disapprove an agreed order unless the licensee or applicant is present at the board meeting and agrees to other terms proposed by the board.

(d) If the board does not approve a proposed agreed order, the licensee or applicant and the complainant shall be so informed. The matter shall be referred to the executive director for other appropriate action.

(e) A proposed agreed order is not effective until the full board has approved the agreed order. The order shall then be effective in accordance with the APA.

(f) The board may order a license holder to pay the consumer a refund as an informal conference agreement provides, instead of or in addition to imposing an administrative penalty. The amount of refund ordered in an informal conference agreement may not exceed the amount the consumer paid to the license holder for a service regulated by the Act and this title. The board may not require payment of other damages or estimate harm in a refund order.

§781.609. MONITORING OF LICENSEES

(a) The executive director shall maintain a disciplinary action tracking system.

(b) Each licensee who has had disciplinary action taken against his or her license or specialty recognition shall be required to submit regularly scheduled reports.

(c) The executive director shall review these monitoring reports resulting from formal disciplinary action and notify the Ethics Committee if the licensee is not meeting the disciplinary requirements. The Ethics Committee may consider more severe disciplinary proceedings if the licensee does not comply.

(d) Regardless of whether the board has received a formal complaint, the board may require monitoring of a licensee who may pose a potential threat to public health or safety because of drug or alcohol use, mental or physical health concerns, criminal activity or allegations, and other issues which may adversely affect the public. The board may require a licensee on monitoring status to comply with conditions the board specifies. Though such monitoring is not considered a formal disciplinary action, the licensee must comply fully with the board's order or face possible formal disciplinary action levied by the board.

(e) Participants of the AMEC program in accordance with §781.411 of this title (relating to Temporary License) shall be considered to be on monitoring status until released by the board and issued a regular license.

§781.610. DUE PROCESS FOLLOWING VIOLATION OF AN ORDER

(a) A licensee accused of violating the terms of an Order is not entitled to a formal hearing on the matter, but is entitled to a degree of due process, as follows.

(b) When it appears that the licensee has violated a term of the Order, the department will send a Notice of Violation of the Order to the licensee. The Notice shall include:

(1) a brief statement of the acts or omissions believed to constitute a violation, including information sufficient to apprise the licensee about the date and nature of the violation;

(2) a statement that, within 10 days of receiving the Notice, the licensee must respond in writing to explain why the licensee believes he or she did not violate the Order, or if such violations did occur, why the disciplinary action proposed in the Order should not be imposed; and

(3) a statement in large bold type that, if the licensee fails to respond, the disciplinary action described in the Order will be imposed, and further that additional disciplinary actions may be taken if the conduct constituting the violation of the Order also violates a board rule or statute: "FAILURE TO RESPOND. YOUR FAILURE TO RESPOND, WILL BE CONSIDERED A WAIVER OF YOUR RIGHT TO A HEARING. THE FACTUAL ALLEGATIONS IN THIS NOTICE WILL BE DEEMED ADMITTED AS TRUE AND THE PROPOSED DISCIPLINARY ACTION WILL BE IMPOSED BY DEFAULT. ADDITIONAL DISCIPLINARY ACTIONS MAY BE TAKEN."

(c) When the department receives the licensee's written response, the executive director and board chair will review the response and decide whether there are sufficient grounds to find that the Order was violated and, if so, whether the disciplinary action provided in the Order should be imposed.

(d) The executive director and the board chair shall write and submit their decision to the board for final action.

(e) A decision to impose or to forego imposing disciplinary action under the terms of the Order does not preclude the board from initiating disciplinary action independent of the Order if the alleged conduct may constitute a violation of statute or rules.

SUBCHAPTER G

FORMAL HEARINGS

§781.701. PURPOSE

These rules, which cover the hearing procedures and practices available to persons or parties who request formal board hearings, supplement the contested case provisions outlined in the Texas Government Code, Chapter 2001, Administrative Procedure Act (APA), and the hearing procedures of the State Office of Administrative Hearings (Texas Government Code, Chapter 2003, and Rules of Procedure, 1 Texas Administrative Code, Chapter 155).

§781.702. NOTICE

(a) Proper notice of contested case proceedings before the State Office of Administrative Hearings, means notice sufficient to meet the provisions of the Texas Government Code, Chapter 2001 and the State Office of Administrative Hearings, Rules of Procedure, 1 Texas Administrative Code, Chapter 155.

(b) For purposes of informal conferences, proper notice shall include the name and style of the case, the date, time, and place of the informal conference, and a short statement of the purpose of the conference.

(c) The following statement shall be attached to the notice of hearing or notice of informal conference, in bold, capital letters of at least 10 point type: "FAILURE TO APPEAR. YOUR FAILURE TO APPEAR, IN PERSON OR BY REPRESENTATIVE, ON THE ABOVE DATE, TIME, AND PLACE, WILL BE CONSIDERED A WAIVER OF YOUR RIGHT TO A HEARING. THE FACTUAL ALLEGATIONS IN THIS NOTICE WILL BE DEEMED ADMITTED AS TRUE AND THE PROPOSED DISCIPLINARY ACTION WILL BE GRANTED BY DEFAULT."

§781.703. DEFAULT

(a) In this section, "default" means the respondent's failure to appear in person, by legal representative, or by telephone on the day and at the time set for hearing in a contested case or informal conference, or in accordance with the notice of hearing or notice of informal conference.

(b) Remedies available upon default in a contested case before the State Office of Administrative Hearings (SOAH). The Administrative Law Judge (ALJ) shall proceed in the party's absence and such failure to appear shall entitle the department to seek informal disposition as provided by the Texas Government Code, Chapter 2001. The ALJ shall grant any motion by the department to remove the case from the contested hearing docket and allow for informal disposition by the board.

(c) Remedies available upon default in an informal conference. The board may proceed to make such informal disposition of the case as it deems proper, as if no request for hearing had been received.

(d) The board may enter a default judgment by issuing an order against the defaulting party in which the factual allegations in the notice of violation or notice of hearing are deemed admitted as true without the requirement of submitting additional proof, upon the offer of proof that proper notice was provided to the defaulting party.

(e)   Motion to set aside and reopen. The respondent's timely motion to set aside the default order and reopen the record may be granted if the respondent establishes that his/her failure to attend the hearing, rather than being intentional or the result of conscious indifference, was in fact due to mistake, accident, or circumstances beyond the respondent's control.

   (1)   A motion to set aside the default order and reopen the record shall be filed with the board prior to the board's order becoming final, pursuant to the provisions of the Texas Government Code.

   (2)   A motion to set aside the default order and reopen the record is not a motion for rehearing and is not considered a substitute for a rehearing motion. Filing a motion to set aside the default order and reopen has no effect on either the statutory time periods for filing a motion for rehearing, or on the time frame for ruling on a rehearing motion, as provided in the Texas Government Code.

(f)   This subsection also applies to cases where proof exists that notice of hearing was served at the defaulting party's last known address as shown on the department's records, with no evidence that the defaulting party or the defaulting party's agent actually received notice. In that situation, the default procedures described in subsection (c) of this section may be used.

§781.704. Action after Hearing

(a)   Reopening a hearing for new evidence. If new evidence is offered which was unobtainable or unavailable at the time of the hearing, and if the board deems that this evidence is necessary to make a fair, proper determination of the case, the board may reopen a hearing, including the new evidence as part of the record. The reopened hearing will be limited to only such new evidence. All previously designated parties will be served official notice of the new hearing.

(b)   Final orders or decisions. The board or its designee will render the board's final order or decision, in writing. The decision will state the findings of fact and conclusions required by law, either in the body of the order, by attachment, or by reference to an ALJ's proposal for decision. All final orders will be signed by the board chair, and his/her designee, unless otherwise permitted by statute or by these actions.

(c)   Motion for rehearing. A motion for rehearing shall be governed by the APA or other pertinent statute and shall be filed with the board.

(d)   Appeals. All appeals from final board orders or decisions shall be governed by the APA or other pertinent statute and shall be addressed to the board.

SUBCHAPTER H

SANCTION GUIDELINES

§781.801. Purpose

The schedule of sanctions is adopted by rule pursuant to the Act, §505.254. The schedule is intended to be used by the Ethics Committee as a guide in assessing sanctions for violations of the Act or this chapter. The schedule is also intended to serve as a guide to administrative law judges, and as a written statement of applicable rules or policies of the board pursuant to the Government Code. The failure of an administrative law judge (ALJ) to follow the schedule may serve as a basis to vacate or modify an order pursuant to the Government Code. No two disciplinary cases are the same. This schedule is not intended as a substitute for thoughtful consideration of each individual disciplinary matter.

§781.802. RELEVANT FACTORS

(a) When a licensee has violated the Act or this chapter, three general factors combine to determine the appropriate sanction: the licensee's degree of culpability; the harm caused or posed; and appropriate deterrence.

(b) The board and ALJ may consider special factors, but the licensee is responsible for bringing these exonerating factors to light for the board or ALJ to consider.

  (1) The seriousness of the violation can be a special factor. The board or ALJ may consider the nature and extent of harm caused or risk posed to the public health, safety, or welfare. How frequently the violation occurred and over what time period are also important factors.

  (2) The board and ALJ can also examine the nature of the violation, as determined by the relationship between the licensee and the person harmed or exposed to harm. The vulnerability of the person harmed or exposed to harm is an important factor. Determining the licensee's culpability is affected by whether the violation was intentional or premeditated; reflected the licensee's blatant disregard or gross neglect; resulted from error or inadvertence; and/or reflects the licensee's lack of character, integrity, trustworthiness, or honesty.

  (3) Another special set of factors deal with the licensee's personal accountability, including the licensee's capacity to admit wrong-doing and accept responsibility; whether the licensee shows an appropriate degree of remorse or concern; what efforts the licensee has taken to ameliorate harm or make restitution; how the licensee has instituted a plan to ensure that future violations do not occur; and how well the licensee cooperated with any investigations and requests for information.

  (4) How to prevent violations is another set of factors worthy of consideration. Determining the sanction(s) required to deter the licensee from engaging in similar violations and to ensure that the licensee abides by the other provisions of the Act or this chapter; and sanctions which can effectively deter other licensees from making similar violations are considerations that shed light on the appropriate sanction(s).

  (5) Other miscellaneous factors which affect decisions on sanctions include the licensee's professional experience at time of violation; whether the licensee has previously or subsequently violated the law and rules; how the licensee has conducted himself or herself, particularly in the work setting, prior to and following the violation; any character references; and any other factors justice may require.

§781.803. SEVERITY LEVEL AND SANCTION GUIDE

The following severity levels and sanction guides are based on the relevant factors in §781.802 of this title (relating to Relevant Factors):

  (1) Level One--Revocation of license. These violations evidence the licensee's intentional or gross misconduct, cause or pose a high degree of harm to

the public, and/or require severe punishment to deter the licensee, or other licensees. The fact that a license is ordered revoked does not necessarily mean the licensee can never regain licensure. The board may also impose an administrative penalty of not less than $250 or more than $5,000 for each Level One violation. Each day a violation continues or occurs is a separate violation for the purpose of imposing a financial penalty.

(2) Level Two--Extended suspension of license. These violations involve less misconduct, harm, or need for deterrence than Level One violations, but require termination of licensure for a period of not less than one year. The board may also impose an administrative penalty of not less than $250 or more than $4,000 for each Level Two violation. Each day a violation continues or occurs is a separate violation for the purpose of imposing a penalty.

(3) Level Three--Moderate suspension of license. These violations involve less misconduct, harm, or need for deterrence than Level Two violations, but require termination of licensure for some period of time. The board may also impose an administrative penalty of not less than $250 or more than $3,000 for each Level Three violation. Each day a violation continues or occurs is a separate violation for the purpose of imposing a penalty.

(4) Level Four--Probated suspension of license. These violations do not involve enough harm, misconduct, or need for deterrence to warrant termination of licensure, yet are severe enough to warrant monitoring of the licensee to ensure future compliance. Possible probationary terms are set out as in §781.806 of this title (relating to Probation)   and may be ordered as appropriate. The board may also impose an administrative penalty of not less than $250 or more than $2,000 for each Level Four violation. Each day a violation continues or occurs is a separate violation for the purpose of imposing a penalty.

(5) Level Five--Reprimand. These violations involve minor misconduct not directly involving the health, safety or welfare of the particular member of the public at issue. The board may also impose an administrative penalty of not less than $250 or more than $1,000 for each Level Five violation. Each day a violation continues or occurs is a separate violation for the purpose of imposing a penalty.

§781.804. OTHER DISCIPLINARY ACTIONS

The Ethics Committee or executive director, as appropriate, may resolve pending complaints by issuing formal advisory letters to inform licensees of their duties under the Act or this chapter, and whether the conduct or omission relevant to the complaint appears to violate such duties. Advisory letters may be introduced as evidence in any subsequent disciplinary action involving the licensee's acts or omissions after the licensee receives the advisory letters. The Ethics Committee or executive director, as appropriate, may also issue informal reminders to licensees regarding other licensing matters. The licensee is not entitled to a hearing on the matters addressed in the formal advisory letter or informal reminders, but may write a response to be included with such letters in the social worker's licensing records.

§781.805. STATE OFFICE OF ADMINISTRATIVE HEARINGS

In cases requiring a hearing, the Ethics Committee, through the executive director, will issue a notice of violation letter to the licensee, and state the severity level and the recommended sanction, which will reflect the Ethics Committee's judgment based on the information available at that time. The evidence presented at a hearing could indicate a greater or lesser sanction.

§781.806. PROBATION

If probation is ordered or agreed to, the following terms may be required.

(1) General conditions of probation.

    (A) The licensee shall obey all federal, state and local laws and rules governing social work practice in this state.

    (B) Under penalty of perjury, the licensee shall submit periodic reports as the board requests on forms provided by the board, stating whether the licensee has complied with all conditions of probation.

    (C) The licensee shall comply with the board's probation monitoring program.

    (D) The licensee shall appear in person for interviews with the board or its designee at various intervals and with reasonable notice.

    (E) If the licensee leaves this state to reside or to practice outside the state, the licensee must notify the board in writing of the dates of departure and return. Periods of practice outside this state will not count toward the time of this probationary period. The social work licensing authorities of the jurisdiction to which the licensee is moving or has moved must be promptly notified of the licensee's probationary status in this state. The probationary period will resume when the licensee returns to the state to reside or practice.

    (F) If the licensee violates probation in any respect, the board, after giving formal notice and the opportunity to be heard, may revoke the licensee's license and specialty recognition or take other appropriate disciplinary action. The period of probation shall be extended until the matter is final.

    (G) The licensee shall promptly notify in writing all settings in which the licensee practices social work of his or her probationary status.

    (H) While on probation, the licensee shall not act as a supervisor or gain any hours of supervised practice required for any board-issued license.

    (I) The licensee is responsible for paying the costs of complying with conditions of probation.

    (J) The licensee shall comply with the renewal requirements in the Act and the board rules.

    (K) A licensee on probation shall not practice social work except under the conditions described in the probation order.

    (L) A licensee who is required to be supervised as a condition of initial licensure, continued licensure, or disciplinary action must:

       (i) submit one supervisory plan for each practice location to the board for approval by the board or executive director/designee within 30 days of initiating supervision;

(ii) submit a current job description from the agency in which the social worker is employed with a verification of authenticity from the agency director or his or her designee on agency letterhead or submit a copy of the contract or appointment under which the licensee intends to work, along with a statement from the potential supervisor that the supervisor has reviewed the contract and is qualified to supervise the licensee in the setting;

(iii) ensure that the supervisor submits reports to the board on a schedule determined by the board. In each report, the supervisor must address the supervisee's performance, how closely the supervisee adheres to statutes and rules, any special circumstances that led to the imposition of supervision, and recommend whether the supervisee should continue licensure. If the supervisor does not recommend the supervisee for continued licensure, the supervisor must provide specific reasons for not recommending the supervisee. The board may consider the supervisor's reservations as it evaluates the supervision verification the supervisee submits; and

(iv) notify the board immediately if there is a disruption in the supervisory relationship or change in practice location and submit a new supervisory plan within 30 days of the break or change in practice location.

(2) Special Conditions. At the board's discretion, one or more special conditions of probation may appear in the board's disciplinary order that places a licensee on probation. Those special conditions and example wording are described in the following subparagraphs of this paragraph.

(A) Actual Suspension. As part of probation, the license is suspended for a period of (example: one) year beginning the effective date of this order.

(B) Drug/Medication Use. The licensee shall abstain completely from using or possessing controlled substances and dangerous drugs as defined by law, or any drugs requiring a prescription except those medications which a licensed physician lawfully prescribes for a bona fide illness or condition.

(C) Alcohol. The licensee shall abstain completely from using alcoholic beverages.

(D) Body Fluid or Hair Follicle Testing. The licensee shall immediately submit to appropriate testing, at the licensee's cost, upon the board's written request or order.

(E) Rehabilitation Program. Within (example: 30) days of the effective date of the order, the licensee shall submit to the board for its prior approval a rehabilitation program in which the licensee shall participate at least weekly for at least (example: 50) weeks of the calendar year for the duration of probation. In the periodic reports to the board, the licensee shall document continuing participation in this program, including the dates of the weekly meetings attended and the address of each meeting. At the end of the required period, the rehabilitation program director shall document to the board that the license has completed the program and has made arrangements for appropriate follow-up.

(F) Community Service. Within (example: 60)   days of the effective date of the order, the licensee shall submit to the board for its prior approval a community service program in which the licensee shall provide free regular social work services to a community or charitable facility or agency for at least (example: 20) hours a month for the first (example: 24) months of probation.

(G) Medical Evaluation Treatment. Within (example: 30) days of the effective date of the order, and periodically thereafter as the board or its designee may require, the licensee shall undergo a medical evaluation by a licensed physician who shall furnish a medical report to the board or its designee. If the board or its designee requires the licensee to undergo medical treatment, the licensee shall, within (example: 30) days of the requirement notice, submit to the board for its prior approval the name and qualifications of a physician of the licensee's choice. Upon the board's approval of the treating physician, the licensee shall undergo and continue medical treatment until further notice from the board. The licensee shall have the treating physician submit periodic reports to the board as the board directs. In cases where the evidence demonstrates that medical illness or disability was a contributing cause of the violations, the licensee shall not engage in the practice of social work until the board notifies the licensee that the board has determined that the licensee is medically fit to practice safely.

(H) Psychosocial/Psychological/ Psychiatric Evaluation. Within (example: 30) days of the effective date of the decision, and periodically thereafter as required by the board or its designee, the licensee shall undergo evaluation by a licensed professional (social worker, psychologist, or psychiatrist) selected by the board. The evaluator shall furnish a written report to the board or its designee regarding the licensee's judgment and ability to function independently and safely as a social worker and any other information the board may require. The licensee shall pay all evaluation costs. The licensee shall execute a release of information authorizing the evaluator to release all information to the board. The board will treat the evaluation as confidential. If the evidence demonstrates that physical illness or mental illness was a contributing cause of the violations, the licensee shall not engage in the practice of social work until the board determines that the licensee is medically fit to practice safely and so notifies the licensee.

(I) Ethics Course. Within (example: 60)   days of the effective date of the order, the licensee shall select and submit to the board or its designee for prior approval a course in (example: ethics), which the licensee shall take and successfully complete as directed by the board.

(J) Supervision of the Licensee's Practice. Within (example: 30) days of the effective date of this order, the licensee shall submit to the board for its prior approval the name and qualifications of three proposed supervisors. Each proposed supervisor shall be licensed in good standing and be a board-approved supervisor with expertise in the licensee's field of practice. The supervisor must review and maintain a copy of the board order and must ensure that the supervisory content relates to the licensee's rehabilitation and fitness for practice. The supervisor shall submit to the board quarterly written reports (or other time periods the board may specify), verifying that the supervisor and supervisee have met together in the same geographical location to engage in required supervision of at least one hour per week (or other time periods the board may specify), in individual face-to-face meetings, and including an evaluation of the licensee's performance. The licensee will bear all supervision costs and is responsible for assuring that the required reports are filed in a timely fashion. The licensee shall give the supervisor access to the licensee's fiscal and client records. The supervisor shall be independent, with no current or prior business, professional or personal relationship with the licensee. The licensee shall not practice until the board has approved the designated supervisor and so notified the licensee. If the supervisor ceases supervision, the licensee shall not practice until the board has approved a new supervisor. The supervisor and licensee shall inform the board in writing within 10 business days of supervision termination, or any substantive change to the supervision plan; these changes are subject to the board's approval. Board-ordered supervision shall comply with relevant requirements of §781.404 of this title (relating to Recognition as a Board-approved Supervisor and the Supervision Process) as well as all other laws and rules.

(K) Psychotherapy. Within (example: 60) days of the effective date of the order, the licensee shall submit to the board for its prior approval the name and qualifications of one or more therapists of the licensee's choice. The therapist shall possess a valid license and shall have had no current or prior business, professional or personal relationship with the licensee. Upon the board's approval, the licensee shall undergo and continue treatment, for which the licensee pays all costs, until the board determines that no further psychotherapy is necessary. The licensee shall execute a release of information authorizing the therapist to divulge information to the board, and will have the treating psychotherapist submit periodic reports as the board requires. If the therapist believes the licensee cannot safely continue to render services, the therapists will notify the board immediately.

(L) Education. The licensee shall successfully complete any remedial education the board requires.

(M) Take and Pass Licensure Examinations. The licensee shall take and pass the licensure examination currently required of new applicants for the license possessed by the licensee. The licensee shall pay the established examination fee.

(N) Peer Assistance Program. Within (example: 30) days of the effective date of the order, the licensee shall participate in a board-approved Peer Assistance Program in which the licensee shall participate at least (example: weekly) for at least (example: 50)   weeks of the calendar year for the duration of probation. In the periodic reports to the board, the licensee shall document continuing participation in this program, including the dates of the meetings attended and the address of each meeting. The program shall also submit periodic progress reports and a final disposition report concerning whether the licensee completed the program and has made arrangements for appropriate follow-up. If a licensee does not complete the program, the board or board committee will determine an appropriate sanction.

(O) Other Conditions. The board may order other terms of probation as may be appropriate.

§781.807. RELEASE FROM PROBATION

(a) If the executive director believes that a licensee has satisfied the terms of probation, the executive director shall report to the Ethics Committee the status of the licensee's probation.

(b) If the executive director does not believe that the licensee has successfully completed probation, the executive director shall so notify the licensee and shall refer the matter to the Ethics Committee for review and recommendations. The licensee shall continue supervision and all requirements set forth in the board order, including periodic reports, until the Ethics Committee reviews and disposes of the case.

§781.808. PEER ASSISTANCE PROGRAM

(a) The board shall establish criteria for a peer assistance program to help impaired professionals. Any peer assistance program wishing to serve licensees will submit evidence to the board that the program meets board criteria. The board may approve a peer assistance program, and may rescind such approval.

(b) The board has the authority to request that a licensee be evaluated by an appropriate substance abuse or mental health provider, and reserves the right to choose the provider. The licensee will pay the costs of such evaluation directly to the provider. The board may use the evaluation results in determining the licensee's fitness to practice.

(c) The board will recognize a board-approved peer assistance program to serve an impaired licensee if the board or a board committee approves such intervention or makes such intervention a condition of board-ordered sanction, as a condition of continued licensure, or if the licensee acknowledges impairment and requests peer assistance services.

(d) The board does not waive authority to conduct ethics investigations or impose sanctions against a licensee who is in a peer assistance program.

(e) Any licensee who enters evaluation, treatment, or monitoring by a board-approved peer assistance program is obligated to pay the costs incurred by this intervention directly to the peer assistance program. Neither the board nor the department will collect such costs from the licensee, nor serve as an intermediary for such payments.

(f) The board-approved peer assistance program shall submit reports of the licensee's progress in a time frame that the board specifies. The program shall also submit a final disposition report concerning whether the licensee completed the program. If the licensee does not complete the program, the board or board committee will determine an appropriate sanction.

(g)   A licensee who knows or suspects that another licensee under the board's jurisdiction is impaired by alcohol, chemical, or mental illness is required to report this information to the board within 30 days for investigation.

Appendix C

NASW/TX Resources

General Counsel Law Note Series

The General Counsel Law Note Series provides information to social workers about legal topics of concern to the social work profession. The Law Notes are developed with the support and financial assistance of the NASW Legal Defense Fund (LDF). The topics addressed in the Law Note series include the following:

❏ **Social Workers and the Legal Rights of Students**
   <https://www.socialworkers.org/ldf/lawnotes/studentLegal.asp>
   It is the position of the National Association of Social Workers (NASW) that the nation's school systems are responsible for providing "all students with free, appropriate, quality education" to prepare them for full, productive, and intelligent participation in society upon reaching adulthood. The U.S. Constitution does not protect the right to an education; however, denying children an education would deny them "the ability to live within the structure of our civil institutions, and [would] foreclose any realistic possibility that they will contribute... to the progress of our nation."

   School social workers are significant contributors to the formative years of children in America's schools. In many school systems across the country, school social workers are among a select group of professionals who are able to address the "personal and social problems that inhibit a student's ability to learn." Furthermore, the role of the school social worker has evolved into a link between the family, the school, and the community.

   This law note reviews a number of the legal issues that affect the practice of social workers within the schools and under the multitude of jurisdictions that exercise control over public and private schools. (Part II in the Series, Social Workers and the Legal Rights of Children)

❏ **Client Confidentiality and Privileged Communications**
   <https://www.socialworkers.org/ldf/lawnotes/confidentiality.asp>
   Many problems arise in the application of the concepts of confidentiality and privilege to the professional services provided by social workers. This paper

discusses the two principles and outlines some of the exceptions applicable to them, particularly in the context of clinical social work practice.

❏ **Social Workers and Subpoenas**
<https://www.socialworkers.org/ldf/lawnotes/subpoenas.asp>
Social workers are becoming involved in clients' lawsuits more frequently than they would like. Domestic relations matters, drunk driving accidents, and sexual harassment or other work-related problems can lead to litigation for clients who are in family counseling, therapy, or employee assistance programs. In addition, social workers are required to report acts or suspicions of child or elder abuse and may have to testify about these reports. Further, troubled clients may be involved in legal proceedings such as child custody contests, workers' compensation hearings, civil damage suits, or criminal matters including domestic violence and violation of probation orders.

These and similar matters may result in litigation involving social workers and the subpoena of their records. The type of subpoena, whether it must be obeyed, whether the client has provided a valid written release of information, and whether original records must be provided are some issues that must be addressed. The first step in sorting out how to treat a subpoena is to understand the concepts and rules on which a subpoena is based. Armed with some information about the purpose of a subpoena and the legal and ethical rules that generally apply, social workers can analyze how to respond and also can formulate legal questions for an attorney.

❏ **Social Workers and Alternative Dispute Resolution**
<https://www.socialworkers.org/ldf/lawnotes/dispute.asp>
An important part of a social worker's professional responsibility is to manage conflict in a productive manner. "Whether advocating for clients, dealing with conflict within organizations, or helping people learn more-effective ways of coping with conflict in their lives, . . ." resolving conflict in employment settings or related to the delivery of services to clients, social workers are involved with conflict resolution daily. Social workers are increasingly compelled to follow disputes into court, whether as fact witnesses, expert witnesses, or parties to lawsuits. The many tensions and negative feelings associated with litigation leave social workers and others asking whether there is a better method for conflict resolution. The courtroom can be both costly and time consuming, sometimes taking years for the simplest case to go to trial. The process of resolving disputes in the courtroom is being replaced or assisted in many areas by alternative dispute resolution (ADR) processes. The courts, state and federal agencies, and employers have all begun providing private and less adversarial methods of dispute resolution than litigation. "ADR is perceived as the solution to problems of runaway jury verdicts, expensive discovery proceedings and protracted litigation. Accordingly, courts, legislatures, government agencies, and private organizations are endorsing various forms of ADR."

ADR is a process by which parties to a dispute resolve their differences without litigation. Social workers participate in ADR both as providers and as parties. This law note describes the three principle methods of voluntary alternative dispute resolution - negotiation, arbitration, and mediation - and discusses traditional and evolving uses for these processes within the social work profession.

❏   **Social Workers as Expert Witnesses**
       <https://www.socialworkers.org/ldf/lawnotes/expert.asp>
Courts of law rely upon information offered in evidence as the basis for decisions rendered. Evidence comes in many forms, including photographs, recordings, devices, forensic evidence, documents, and individual testimony. Oral testimony by witnesses is, however, often the major source of evidence at a trial.

Witnesses who testify as experts play an important role in interpreting data, explaining complex material, and drawing knowledgeable inferences based upon their training and experience. Social workers are called to testify as expert witnesses on a variety of subjects. This Law Note discusses the role of the expert witness and reviews case law confirming the role of social workers as expert witnesses in a variety of settings.

❏   **Social Workers, Managed Care and Antitrust Issues**
       <https://www.socialworkers.org/ldf/lawnotes/antitrust.asp>
Managed care organizations (MCOs), in conjunction with employers who provide employment-based health insurance programs, play a large and growing role in the health care options made available to health plan participants. MCOs have been placed in positions of bargaining strength vis-à-vis social workers as providers of mental health care or other covered services. Federal and state antitrust laws are being used by other health care professionals to challenge MCO practices that limit or interfere with the right to practice, to be members of provider panels, and to make appropriate decisions on behalf of their patients. Social workers should understand the issues and arguments raised in antitrust health care cases to be able to evaluate the business practices of the MCOs with which they are dealing.

To assist social workers in these efforts, this law note describes federal antitrust laws, the type of conduct that could be actionable under those laws, and health care cases in which MCO conduct is being challenged as violating antitrust laws. The note identifies the steps that might be taken by social workers to evaluate their own fact situation under antitrust laws, including obtaining assistance from federal and state antitrust authorities, state insurance regulators, state legislatures, and Congress. Finally, precautions that should be observed by social workers in their work and as NASW members to minimize their own risk of antitrust liability are reviewed. A sample protest letter to an MCO is also included.

❏   **The Social Worker and Protection of Privacy**
       <https://www.socialworkers.org/ldf/lawnotes/privacy.asp>
Clients receiving psychotherapy risk social stigma should their "private" mental health information be disclosed. Disclosures may affect many aspects of a client's life including the ability to obtain gainful employment or run for public office. Harm may be inflicted through the very fact of disclosure-that is, simply through other people's coming to know facts or feelings that a client and psychotherapist expected to be kept confidential. "The [client] may feel embarrassed, vulnerable, or otherwise violated, as well as feel betrayed by the [psychotherapist], and personal or other relationships may suffer." Access to medical and mental health records is currently "safeguarded" under a patchwork of case law, statutes, regulations, federal and state constitutional law, and

personal injury tort law. No overriding federal rule of law directly controls or protects the privacy of all persons in the United States, although some state constitutions guarantee privacy for citizens in a particular state. An invasion of privacy in the exposure of confidential mental health treatment records may have no legal recourse.

The purpose of this paper is to provide social workers with a brief overview of the current state of privacy law and how it impacts on the provision of mental health services and treatment. With an informed understanding of the many issues affecting privacy, social workers will be able to engage in the debate taking place regarding comprehensive federal legislation as well as recognize issues within their states that require response and appropriate action to ensure that client privacy is properly protected.

❑   **Social Workers and Child Abuse Reporting: A Review of State Mandatory Reporting Requirements**
<https://www.socialworkers.org/ldf/lawnotes/abuse.asp>
"Reporting [child abuse] frequently becomes an ethical dilemma as a result of complex interactions among several factors including diverse professional contexts, legal requirements, professional-ethical standards, and the circumstances of suspected abuse. The reporting dilemma also reflects the fact that breaching confidentiality and breaking the law both constitute unethical behavior." However, beyond the professional difficulties in dealing with child abuse and neglect, there is a distinct need to intervene on behalf of the children victimized by abuse. Currently, an estimated one million children are victims of child abuse and neglect each year. In 1996, child protective services in all states investigated more than two million reports and substantiated just under one million, child abuse victims. Approximately 1,000 victims, who were previously known by child protective services, died as a result of abuse and neglect. Because of legal requirements, over fifty percent of all investigated reports of child abuse came from professionals, including medical personnel, law enforcement, educators and social service workers.

This law note discusses issues social workers confront when dealing with child abuse and neglect situations. First, this note provides a brief history of the federal legislation that mandated child protective services and the reporting of suspected child abuse at the federal level then surveys state statutes and case law, providing an overview of the current state of mandatory reporting. Third, it identifies ethical considerations mandated reporters face. Finally, it provides practical steps in reporting child abuse and, in addition, an appendix summarizing each state's reporting requirements.

❑   **Social Workers and Managed Care Contracts**
<https://www.socialworkers.org/ldf/lawnotes/contracts.asp>
This law note was developed to aid clinical social workers who work in a managed care environment as independent practitioners in evaluating managed care agreements. For social workers new to managed care and for those who are assessing their provider status, it is helpful to have some understanding of the legal issues related to managed care contracts. Social workers involved in health policy development or legislative initiatives may also find the law note useful to identify particular aspects of managed care provider relationships in need of

state or national legislative reforms. A three-stage process for analyzing managed care concerns is presented. First, social workers are urged to evaluate fully, in advance, the organizations with which they will be doing business. Second, analytical tools are provided for social workers to review critically the language presented in managed care provider agreements. Social workers are directed to seek out other resources where appropriate, including the advice of legal counsel. Third, social workers are presented with some general considerations if a formal means of redress is necessary to resolve conflicts between the parties to the contract. In addition, a glossary of managed care terms and acronyms is provided. Finally, model contract provisions are offered for those who are in a position to revise provider agreements to form the strongest fit between social workers' ethical obligations and managed care restrictions. In some instances, this law note suggests options for social workers that may be available in only a few, optimal circumstances; however, consideration of how managed care companies and social workers "should" act is instructive and anticipates the future direction of public and private standards in the managed care industry.

A dynamic flow of ideas and information moves between legislatures, government agencies, the courts, and private standard-setting organizations. As the "best practices" of the managed care industry emerge in any one of these bodies, new measures are quick to be adopted by others. Options available to a few social workers one year may be widespread within five. Social workers need to be informed about the general trends in the world of managed care to make wise decisions about what reforms to support, when to litigate, and when to wait patiently for the storm to pass.

❑ **Social Workers and Clinical Notes**
<https://www.socialworkers.org/ldf/lawnotes/notes.asp>
This law note reviews legal issues specifically germane to social workers' clinical notes or "psychotherapy notes." However, a discussion of clinical notes takes place under various categories of guiding principles, including the NASW Code of Ethics, state medical records acts, social work licensing laws, specific federal and state psychotherapy privacy protection statutes, and state regulations applicable to social work case records in general. The definition and even the existence of clinical notes as distinct from medical or case records has been a matter of some disagreement among states, while recently issued federal regulations recognize psychotherapy notes as a distinct part of the mental health record accorded special privacy protection. This law note reviews legal opinions, statutory and regulatory language, and ethical principles that control the creation, handling, protection, and release of clinical notes within social work practice. It provides guideposts for professional practice, but does not aim to resolve particular legal problems. Consultation with an attorney, a social work licensing board representative, and other mental health professionals is necessary to resolve particular issues related to clinical notes.

The legal precedent and statutory support discussed in detail in this law note should cement social workers' understanding that it is essential to maintain accurate and timely clinical notes. Clinical notes facilitate the delivery of mental health services, ensure continuity of care, protect clients' privacy, and ensure reasonable future access to client treatment history. Contemporaneous clinical notes are an important part of the client record, as are evaluations, treatment plans, prognoses, collateral contacts, contact dates, and payment plans. Clinical notes often contain the most private client information as well as the therapist's observations, clinical concerns, and relevant anecdotal information. Social workers sometimes hold the view that the obligation to keep such records is a discretionary one. Although discretion is required when determining what to include and how to phrase comments, this law note provides abundant support for the proposition that clinical notes are necessary to create an accurate treatment record and demonstrate commitment to professional practice standards.

❑   **Social Workers and Work Issues**
<https://www.socialworkers.org/ldf/lawnotes/workIssues.asp>
This law note surveys various work-related legal problems faced by social workers who provide professional services. Some of the issues discussed are specific to social workers as a class of employees, and others apply to social workers as independent contractors. Problems common to both groups are also examined. This law note will also highlight potential legal remedies for addressing work-related problems.

LEGAL ISSUE OF THE MONTH

The "Legal Issue of the Month" provides an overview of a specific legal topic of relevance to social workers from the perspective of a particular legal decision. Topics are updated monthly and previous topics remain available for viewing.

Jan 2014   **A Legal Standard for Diagnosing Intellectual Disability**
<https://www.socialworkers.org/ldf/legal_issue/2014/working-wiht-children.asp>

Feb 2014   **Legal Issues That Can Trip Social Workers Working With Children**
<https://www.socialworkers.org/ldf/legal_issue/2014/January2014.asp>

Nov 2013   **A Managed Care Toolkit for NASW Clinical Social Workers**
<https://www.socialworkers.org/ldf/legal_issue/2013/nov2013.asp>

Oct 2013   **HIPAA Highlights for Social Workers**
<https://www.socialworkers.org/ldf/legal_issue/2013/oct2013.asp>

Sep 2013   **A Review of the 2013 NASW Sample HIPAA Privacy Forms**
<https://www.socialworkers.org/ldf/legal_issue/2013/sep2013.asp>

July 2013   **Social Workers and the Recent Decisions of the Supreme Court**
<https://www.socialworkers.org/ldf/legal_issue/2013/jul2013.asp>

June 2013   **Social Workers and Drug Testing of Public Benefits Applicants**
<https://www.socialworkers.org/ldf/legal_issue/2013/jun2013.asp>

May 2013   **Criminalization of Psychotherapist Sexual Misconduct**
<https://www.socialworkers.org/ldf/legal_issue/2013/may2013.asp>

Apr 2013   **Selling a Clinical Social Work Practice**
<https://www.socialworkers.org/ldf/legal_issue/2013/apr2013.asp>

Mar 2013   **Social Workers and the 2013 Omnibus HIPAA Rule**
<https://www.socialworkers.org/ldf/legal_issue/2013/mar2013.asp>

Feb 2013   **Health Care Privacy Exceptions to Avert Harm and Duty to Warn**
<https://www.socialworkers.org/ldf/legal_issue/2013/feb2013.asp>

Jan 2013   Social Workers and Labor Strikes
<https://www.socialworkers.org/ldf/legal_issue/2013/jan2013.asp>

Nov 2012   Client Records and the Death of a Social Worker
<https://www.socialworkers.org/ldf/legal_issue/2012/Nov2012.asp>

Oct 2012   Access to Records by Social Workers' Clients
<https://www.socialworkers.org/ldf/legal_issue/2012/Oct2012.asp>

Sep 2012   Social Work Ethics and Non-Compete Clauses in Employment
Contracts and Independent Contractor Agreements
<https://www.socialworkers.org/ldf/legal_issue/2012/Sep2012.asp>

July 2012   Social Workers and Advance Directives
<https://www.socialworkers.org/ldf/legal_issue/2012/Jul2012.asp>

June 2012   The Defense of Marriage Act DOMA
<https://www.socialworkers.org/ldf/legal_issue/2012/June2012.asp>

May 2012   Social Workers, Smartphones and Electronic Health Information
<https://www.socialworkers.org/ldf/legal_issue/2012/May2012.asp>

Apr 2012   Social Workers and Skype—Part II, Telemental Health Law
<https://www.socialworkers.org/ldf/legal_issue/2012/Apr2012.asp>

Mar 2012   LDF's Third Prong in its Mission: Providing Legal Information
tNASW Members
<https://www.socialworkers.org/ldf/legal_issue/2012/Mar2012.asp>

Feb 2012   LDF: Defending NASW Members for 40 Years
<https://www.socialworkers.org/ldf/legal_issue/2012/Feb2012.asp>

Jan 2012   LDF: Forty Years of Legal Advocacy for Social Work
<https://www.socialworkers.org/ldf/legal_issue/2012/022012.asp>

Nov 2011   Social Workers and Skype: Part I
<https://www.socialworkers.org/ldf/legal_issue/2011/112011.asp>

Oct 2011   Release of Records and Client Privacy
<https://www.socialworkers.org/ldf/legal_issue/2011/102011.asp>

Sep 2011   Legal Developments in LGBT Family Rights
<https://www.socialworkers.org/ldf/legal_issue/2011/092011.asp>

July 2011   Health Insurance, HIPAA and Client Privacy
<https://www.socialworkers.org/ldf/legal_issue/2011/072011.asp>

June 2011   Closing a Social Work Private Practice
<https://www.socialworkers.org/ldf/legal_issue/2011/062011.asp>

May 2011   Provider Refusal and Conscience Clause Controversies
<https://www.socialworkers.org/ldf/legal_issue/2011/052011.asp>

Apr 2011   Social Workers and Health Care Reform
<https://www.socialworkers.org/ldf/legal_issue/2011/042011.asp>

Mar 2011   Identity Theft "Red Flags Rule" Exclusion for Social Workers
<https://www.socialworkers.org/ldf/legal_issue/2011/032011.asp>

Feb 2011   **Confidentiality of Drug and Alcohol Abuse Treatment Records**
<https://www.socialworkers.org/ldf/legal_issue/2011/022011.asp>

Jan 2011   **Social Workers and Child Protection Investigations**
<https://www.socialworkers.org/ldf/legal_issue/2011/201101.asp>

Nov 2010   **Social Workers and Record Retention Requirements**
<https://www.socialworkers.org/ldf/legal_issue/2010/201011.asp>

Oct 2010   **Privacy Protections for Deceased Clients' Records**
<https://www.socialworkers.org/ldf/legal_issue/2010/201010.asp>

Sep 2010   **Preventing And Responding TElectronic Privacy Breaches**
<https://www.socialworkers.org/ldf/legal_issue/2010/201009.asp>

July 2010   **Social Workers and the Supreme Court**
<https://www.socialworkers.org/ldf/legal_issue/2010/201007.asp>

June 2010   **Children's Treatment Records: Parental Access and Denial**
<https://www.socialworkers.org/ldf/legal_issue/2010/201006.asp>

May 2010   **Social Workers and Conscience Clauses**
<https://www.socialworkers.org/ldf/legal_issue/2010/201005.asp>

Apr 2010   **Mental Health Parity and Addiction Equity Act Interim Final Rules**
<https://www.socialworkers.org/ldf/legal_issue/2010/201004.asp>

Mar 2010   **Disclosing Confidential Information to Social Workers' Business Associates**
<https://www.socialworkers.org/ldf/legal_issue/2010/March2010.asp>

Feb 2010   **HIPAA Amendments for a New Decade: 2010 and Beyond**
<https://www.socialworkers.org/ldf/legal_issue/2010/201002.asp>

Jan 2010   **Social Workers, Immigration Policies and State Benefits**
<https://www.socialworkers.org/ldf/legal_issue/2010/201001.asp>

Nov 2009   **Social Workers and Continuing Education Requirements**
<https://www.socialworkers.org/ldf/legal_issue/2009/200911.asp>

Oct 2009   **Social Workers and Confidentiality for Court-Ordered Juvenile Treatment**
<https://www.socialworkers.org/ldf/legal_issue/2009/200910.asp>

Sep 2009   **Social Workers and Accommodations for Deaf and Hearing Impaired Clients**
<https://www.socialworkers.org/ldf/legal_issue/2009/200909.asp>

July 2009   **Confidentiality and Minors' Reproductive Rights: A Case Example from Ohio**
<https://www.socialworkers.org/ldf/legal_issue/2009/200907.asp>

June 2009   **Social Workers and Identity Theft: The FTC "Red Flags" Rule**
<https://www.socialworkers.org/ldf/legal_issue/2009/200906.asp>

May 2009   **Social Work Supervision for State Licensure**
<https://www.socialworkers.org/ldf/legal_issue/2009/200905.asp>

April 2009   **Responding to a Subpoena**
<https://www.socialworkers.org/ldf/legal_issue/2009/200904.asp>

March 2009   **HITECH HIPAA for Social Workers**
<https://www.socialworkers.org/ldf/legal_issue/2009/200903.asp>

Feb 2009   **The Social Worker and the Home Office**
<https://www.socialworkers.org/ldf/legal_issue/2009/200902.asp>

Jan 2009   **Social Workers and the Mental Health Parity Act of 2008**
<https://www.socialworkers.org/ldf/legal_issue/2009/200901.asp>

Nov 2008   **Social Workers and the Kennedy v. Louisiana Death Penalty Case**
<https://www.socialworkers.org/ldf/legal_issue/2008/200811.asp>

Oct 2008   **Recent Cases on Child Welfare Workers' Liability for Removal of Children**
<https://www.socialworkers.org/ldf/legal_issue/2008/200810.asp>

Sep 2008   **School Social Workers and Student Strip Searches**
<https://www.socialworkers.org/ldf/legal_issue/2008/200809.asp>

July 2008   **Social Workers and the California Same-Sex Marriage Cases**
<https://www.socialworkers.org/ldf/legal_issue/2008/200807.asp>

June 2008   **Social Workers and the Genetic Information Nondiscrimination Act (GINA)**
<https://www.socialworkers.org/ldf/legal_issue/2008/200806.asp>

May 2008   **Social Workers and Coaching**
<https://www.socialworkers.org/ldf/legal_issue/2008/200805.asp>

Apr 2008   **School Social Workers and Confidentiality**
<https://www.socialworkers.org/ldf/legal_issue/2008/200804.asp>

Mar 2008   **Social Workers and Legal Policy Development**
<https://www.socialworkers.org/ldf/legal_issue/2008/200803.asp>

Feb 2008   **Social Workers and "Duty to Warn" State Laws**
<https://www.socialworkers.org/ldf/legal_issue/2008/200802.asp>

Jan 2008   **Legal and Ethical Issues in Social Worker/Lawyer Collaborations**
<https://www.socialworkers.org/ldf/legal_issue/2008/200801.asp>

Nov 2007   **Social Workers and Confidentiality for Couples Counseling**
<https://www.socialworkers.org/ldf/legal_issue/200711.asp>

Oct 2007   **Social Workers and Child Custody Evaluations**
<https://www.socialworkers.org/ldf/legal_issue/200710.asp>

Sep 2007   **A Review of the Supreme Court's 2007 Affirmative Action Decision**
<https://www.socialworkers.org/ldf/legal_issue/200709.asp>

July 2007   **A Review of the Supreme Court's Abortion Ruling**
<https://www.socialworkers.org/ldf/legal_issue/200707.asp>

June 2007   **The NASW Code of Ethics and State Licensing Laws**
<https://www.socialworkers.org/ldf/legal_issue/200706.asp>

May 2007   Social Workers and the National Provider Identifier
               <https://www.socialworkers.org/ldf/legal_issue/200705.asp>

Apr 2007   Social Workers and e-Therapy
               <https://www.socialworkers.org/ldf/legal_issue/200704.asp>

Mar 2007   Social Workers and Non-custodial Parents' Requests for Records
               <https://www.socialworkers.org/ldf/legal_issue/200703.asp>

Feb 2007   Social Workers and Fee Collection
               <https://www.socialworkers.org/ldf/legal_issue/200702.asp>

Jan 2007   Current Issues in Health Privacy
               <https://www.socialworkers.org/ldf/legal_issue/200701.asp>

Nov 2006   Social Workers and Same-Sex Marriage and Adoption
               <https://www.socialworkers.org/ldf/legal_issue/200611.asp>

Oct 2006   Social Workers as Volunteers
               <https://www.socialworkers.org/ldf/legal_issue/200610.asp>

Sep 2006   Social Workers and Student Loan Forgiveness
               <https://www.socialworkers.org/ldf/legal_issue/200609.asp>

July 2006   HIPAA Help for Social Workers
               <https://www.socialworkers.org/ldf/legal_issue/200607.asp>

June 2006   Social Workers and Psychotherapy Notes
               <https://www.socialworkers.org/ldf/legal_issue/200606.asp>

May 2006   Children's Rights to Confidentiality
               <https://www.socialworkers.org/ldf/legal_issue/200605.asp>

Apr 2006   Social Workers and the CIGNA Managed Care Settlement
               <https://www.socialworkers.org/ldf/legal_issue/200604.asp>

March 2006   Overview of the LDF Amicus Brief Database
               <https://www.socialworkers.org/ldf/legal_issue/200603.asp>

Feb 2006   Social Workers and End-of-Life Decisions
               <https://www.socialworkers.org/ldf/legal_issue/200602.asp>

Jan 2006   Social Workers and Post-Disaster Record Keeping Questions
               <https://www.socialworkers.org/ldf/legal_issue/200601.asp>

Nov 2005   Parental Rights and Responsibilities for Lesbian and Gay Parents
               <https://www.socialworkers.org/ldf/legal_issue/200511.asp>

Oct 2005   Social Workers and Record Retention Requirements
               <https://www.socialworkers.org/ldf/legal_issue/200510.asp>

Sep 2005   Social Workers and Disaster Relief Services
               <https://www.socialworkers.org/ldf/legal_issue/200509.asp>

July 2005   Psychotherapist-Patient Privilege in the Military
               <https://www.socialworkers.org/ldf/legal_issue/200507.asp>

June 2005   **Social Work Licensure: Practice and Title Protection Reviewed**
<https://www.socialworkers.org/ldf/legal_issue/200506.asp>

May 2005   **Social Workers, Medication, and Scope of Practice**
<https://www.socialworkers.org/ldf/legal_issue/200505.asp>

April 2005   **Social Workers and HIPAA Security Standards**
<https://www.socialworkers.org/ldf/legal_issue/200504.asp>

March 2005   **Social Workers and Psychotherapist-Patient Privilege: Jaffee v. Redmond Revisited**
<https://www.socialworkers.org/ldf/legal_issue/200503.asp>

Feb 2005   **Social Workers and the Duty to Warn**
<https://www.socialworkers.org/ldf/legal_issue/200502.asp>

Jan 2005   **Review of State Balloting on Marriage for Same-Sex Couples**
<https://www.socialworkers.org/ldf/legal_issue/200501.asp>

Nov 2004   **Are Public Social Workers Liable for Failing to Prevent Child Abuse?**
<https://www.socialworkers.org/ldf/legal_issue/200411.asp>

Oct 2004   **What Do the Courts Say about Same-Sex Marriage?**
<https://www.socialworkers.org/ldf/legal_issue/200410.asp>

Sep 2004   **Social Workers and the USA PATRIOT Act**
<https://www.socialworkers.org/ldf/legal_issue/200409.asp>

July 2004   **Legal Developments in Treating and Prosecuting Pregnant Substance Abusers**
<https://www.socialworkers.org/ldf/legal_issue/200407.asp>

June 2004   **Business Expense Deductions for Psychotherapy**
<https://www.socialworkers.org/ldf/legal_issue/200406.asp>

May 2004   **HIPAA for Social Work Employers and Administrators**
<https://www.socialworkers.org/ldf/legal_issue/200405.asp>

April 2004   **Social Workers and International Human Rights**
<https://www.socialworkers.org/ldf/legal_issue/200404.asp>

March 2004   **Social Workers' Rights as Probationary Employees**
<https://www.socialworkers.org/ldf/legal_issue/200403.asp>

Feb 2004   **Social Workers and Civil Liability for Failure to Report Child Abuse**
<https://www.socialworkers.org/ldf/legal_issue/200402.asp>

Jan 2004   **Social Workers and Capital Punishment for Juveniles**
<https://www.socialworkers.org/ldf/legal_issue/200401.asp>

Nov 2003   **Social Workers and Legal Developments in Gay Rights**
<https://www.socialworkers.org/ldf/legal_issue/200311.asp>

Oct 2003   **Megan's Law: Protecting the Public or Branding Offenders?**
<https://www.socialworkers.org/ldf/legal_issue/200310.asp>

Sep 2003   **Social Workers as Death Penalty Mitigation Specialists**
<https://www.socialworkers.org/ldf/legal_issue/200309.asp>

July 2003   **Social Workers, HIPAA, and Subpoenas**
<https://www.socialworkers.org/ldf/legal_issue/200307.asp>

June 2003   **Is it Necessary for Protective Services Social Workers to Obtain a Warrant to Investigate a Child Abuse or Neglect Complaint**
<https://www.socialworkers.org/ldf/legal_issue/200306.asp>

May 2003   **Social Workers and "Any Willing Provider" Laws**
<https://www.socialworkers.org/ldf/legal_issue/200305.asp>

April 2003   **A First Look at the HIPAA Security Regulations**
<https://www.socialworkers.org/ldf/legal_issue/200304.asp>

March 2003   **HIPAA Compliance Toolkit**
<https://www.socialworkers.org/ldf/legal_issue/200303.asp>

Feb 2003   **Social Work Ethics and Non-Compete Clauses in Employment Contracts and Independent Contractor Agreements**
<https://www.socialworkers.org/ldf/legal_issue/200302.asp>

INDEX

A

Abrams v. Jones 28, 33, 294, 327, 329, 330,
    365
absence
    of a formal application 228, 315, 316, 331,
        333, 361
    of a written waiver 361
    of confidentiality 331
    of contrary evidence 228, 333, 361
    of doctor-patient relationship 315–317
    of evidence against privilege 124
abuse
    access to records of 141
    confidentiality in reporting 135
    contents of report 133
    definition of 130, 233
    examination without consent 109
    failure to report 134
    false report 133
    investigation of 139
    matters to be reported 133
    minor seeking treatment in 109
    of elder 233, 234
    penalty for failure to report 235
    persons required to report 132
    reporting of
        in chemical dependency treatment facilities
            197
        in children 130, 488
        in convalescent/nursing homes 187
        in elders 233, 235, 488
    reporting own 236
    reporting to agency 133
    suspected 132
access to mental health records
    and conservatorship/possession 125
    denying parents 330
    harmful to child 331
    improperly withheld 332
    limits on parents' rights 327
    of parents suspected of child abuse 141
    rights of divorced parents 329
    standards set by HIPAA 342
access to practitioners 243
accidental exposure to HIV
    consent to test 154
Accident and Health Insurance Policy 245
acting on behalf of the child 331
acupuncturist
    definition of 243
administrative hearing 222
admission
    as a voluntary patient 199
    of evidence 75
    request for 198, 199
    to inpatient facility 200
adoption
    excluded witness 77, 81
    of public policy 299, 313, 318, 348
adoption counseling 129
adoptive parents 136
adult
    definition of 76
advance directives 169
advanced practice nurse
    definition of 243
    selection of 247
advertising
    and Treatment Facilities Marketing Practices
        Act 172
    definition of 172
    of mental health services 172
    prohibited acts 177
age
    10 years of age 335
    14 - 16 years of age
        affirmative defense for sexual assault 271,
            292
    15 years of age
        issues regarding sexual activity of 275
    16 - 17 years of age
        issues regarding reporting sexuality 277

"living together as husband and wife" *274*
parental consent for marriage *273*
16 years of age
  consenting for treatment *108*
  refusing consent for treatment *109*
  refusing psychoactive medication *218*
18 years of age
  "disability" and abuse issues *234*
  qualifying as adult *76*
21 years of age and under
  special education eligibilitiy *95*
under 13 years of age
  reporting HIV status *269*
under 14 years of age
  eligibility for marriage *273*
  reporting all instances of sexual activity *292*
  reporting pregnancy of *270, 271, 274, 292*
  reporting STD with *270, 271, 274, 292*
under 17 years of age
  issues in reporting sexual abuse *270*
under 18 years of age
  court-ordered divorce counseling *106*
  evaluating all allegations of abuse *164*
agency employees *344, 345*
AIDS. *See HIV*
alcohol abuse *314*
alcoholism *227, 230*
alternate delivery site *155*
alternative dispute resolution (ADR) *488*
alternative method of examining competency *50*
AMEC. *See Alternative Method of Examining Competency*
"Any Willing Provider" Laws *498*
apprehension
  application for *204*
  by peace officer *203*
arbitration *488*
assessment
  definition of *200*
  for inpatient facility *200*
attending physician
  definition of *76*
Attorney General Opinion Letters
  DM-458 (11/26/97) *344, 355*
  GA-260 (10/13/04) *344, 375, 384, 387, 389*
  GA-423 (3/18/06) *371*
  JC-0049 (5/17/99) *364*
  JC-438 (8/7/02) *344*
  JM-188 (8/13/84) *344, 345, 347*
  LO 90-043 (7/11/90) *345*
  LO 96-102 (9/23/96) *344, 358*

MW-243 (11/22/80) *344, 351*
audiologist
  definition of *243*
  selection of *247*

B

Baker, James *333*
behavior management *63, 64, 65, 66, 98, 99*
beneficiary
  under a health insurance policy *245*
bereavement services *155*
best interest of child *125*
B.K. vs Cox *28, 294*
Board of Protective and Regulatory Services *131*
business expense deductions
  for psychotherapy *497*

C

California Supreme Court *316*
capital punishment for juveniles *497*
career classes *94*
case law
  B.K. vs Cox *28, 294*
  Jaffee vs. Redmond *295*
  Thapar vs. Zezulka *314, 319*
catch-22 *318*
Centers for Disease Control of the United States Public Health Service *152*
certified home health services *155*
chemical dependency
  counselor *71, 172*
    definition of *244*
    selection of *247*
  definition of *172*
  facility *172*
  minor seeking treatment for *109*
  treatment facilities
    reports of abuse *197*
child abuse
  confidentiality of report *136*
  contents of report *133*
  definition of *130*
  failure to report *497*
  immunities in reporting *133*
  interference with investigation *140*
  investigation of report *139*
  mandatory reporting requirements *490*
  penalty of false report *133*
  reporting of *488, 490*
  reporting to appropriate agencies *133*
  warrant for investigation *498*
child abuse reporting by DSHS providers
  acceptable basis for NOT reporting abuse

270
and conflict with confidentiality 269
and HIV partner notification program 269
and sexually transmitted disease 273
Child Abuse Reporting Form 292
contradicting anonymous reporting 273
defining "any other pertinent information"
   271
DSHS Child Abuse Reporting Form 272
FAQs regarding 268
general reporting issues 271
interfering with professional patient relationship 270
monitoring by DSHS 279, 289
monitoring under age 14 family planning
   271
plan for implementing 283
policies and procedures for 284
quality management and compliance issues
   289
questions regarding acceptable teen relationships 275
reporting, general issues of 267, 285
reporting same incident twice 278
reporting suspected sexual abuse 272, 288
reporting under age 17 sexual activity 268
training of evaluators 289
training of non-professional staff 278
with emancipated minors 273
Child Abuse Reporting Form. *See DSHS Child*
   Abuse Reporting Form
child custody 488
   interference with 260
child neglect
   definition of 130
children with disabilities
   coordination of services to 97
   definition of 97
   procedures for identifying 98
   statewide plan for services to 93, 98
chiropractor
   definition of 244
   selection of 247
CIGNA Managed Care Settlement 496
civil damage suits 488
civil liability
   for social workers 497
civil penalty 153, 183
Civil Practice and Remedies Code. *See Texas*
   Codes and Statutes
clear and convincing evidence 207, 208, 209
client confidentiality 487
clinical notes 491
Code of Ethics 301, 491, 495
collaborative law
  agreement 126

in determining conservatorship 125
   procedures 125, 126
commitment
   content of patients records in 229
   involuntary 206
   order of 210
   to private facility 212
commitment proceeding
   involuntary 231, 359
common-law principles 298, 299
compensability denial 240
compensation
   for guardianship evaluation 263
   for patient revenues 173
competency
   to stand trial 86
comprehensive assessment 95
confidential
   communications 229, 230, 296, 298, 299,
      300, 301, 302, 305, 307, 332
   information 363
   network-carrier contract 241
   network-provider contract 239
confidentiality
   absence of 331
   and privileged communication 487
   and protection of privacy 490
   authorized disclosure 228
   breach of in reporting HIV for minors 268
   children's rights to 496
   claiming privilege 228
   disclosure of information 135, 227
   disclosure under subpoena 363
   exceptions to 361, 488
   exeptions with genetic information 254
   general issues of 225
   in child abuse proceedings 137
   in HIV testing 152
   in response to a subpoena 358
   of child's mental health records 327
   of conversations 296, 298, 300
   of genetic information 254
   of mental health information in civil cases
      123
   of past services 227
   of psychotherapy notes 295
   of records 216, 295
   with clients 487
confinement
   use of 98
conflict of interest 344, 345, 347, 348, 349,
     350
conflict resolution 488
consent
   criteria for 220

examination without consent 109
for mental health treatment 80
general 154
incapable of giving 80
legally adequate 220
minor refusing examination 109
revocation of 231
to counseling by child 109
to release HIV test results 152
to test for HIV accidental exposure 154
to treatment by child
  authorized instances 108
  general issues 108
  purposes 109
to treatment of child by non-parent 107
  consent form 107
  written form 107
conservator
  administration of psychoactive medication
    218
  consenting to treatment of child 108
  counseling of child without permission 109
  denying access to child's psychological
    records 327, 329
  disclosure of information to 136
  duties of parents not appointed conserva-
    tor 127
  informed of patient's rights 201
  inpatient rights 217
  neglect by 131
  parenting plan for 128
  public policy regarding 125
  reasonable discipline by 130
  required consent for marketing 178
  responsible for a child's care and welfare
    131
  rights and duties during period of posses-
    sion 126
  rights and duties of possessory conservator
    129
  rights and duties of sole managing conserva-
    tor 127
  rights of parents at all times 126
  right to independent evaluation 220
  right to list of medications 220
conservatorship
  history of conflict regarding 127
  parenting plan for joint managing conserta-
    borship 128
  possession and access 125
  public policy regarding 125
contempt of court 360
continuity of care 239, 242
  requested in writing by provider 239
continuity of treatment 239
  clause in network provider contract 239

contract
  for network providers 239
  provisions for contracting 239
contracting
  with certain referral sources 173
convalescent/nursing homes
  social worker in administrative role 197
convulsive treatment 76, 79, 80
COPSD. (Also referred to as Co-Occurring
    Psychiatric & Substance Use Disorder)
  definition of 66
  screening and assessment 70
  service provider competencies 69
  services to individuals 68
  treatment plan 70
copying of documents 359
Cornyn, John 370
counseling
  in adoption 129
court-ordered
  counseling
    in divorce 106
  emergency services 203
    application for 204
    apprehension by peace officer 203
    appropriate facilities 203
    physician statement 205
    release from 206
    rights in 206
    temporary mental health services 207
  examination 90–92
  family counseling 127
  investigation
    interfering with 140
  outpatient services 211
  release of records of abuse investigation 198
  treatment 202, 231, 359
    outpatient services 211
    rights of patient 212
    voluntary admission 215
criminal court 110

D

damages 109, 134, 153, 155, 230, 315
  employer responsibility 73
  for sexual expoitation of patient 72
  immunity from for consenting to treatment
    107
  immunity from liability for 109
dating violence 114
death penalty mitigation specialists
  role of social worker 497
Declaration for Mental Health Treatment
  conflicting provisions in 79
  definition of 76

discrimination in 78
disregard of 79
eligibility of 77
eligible persons 77
execution and witness 77
general issues in 76
guidelines for health care provider 77
health care provider 77
limitation on liability 78
notice to person signing 82
period of validity 77
revocation of 79
sample form of 80–81
special form 80
use of 78
defendant 134
denial of payment 240
dentist
definition of 244
selection of 247
Department of Human Resources 344, 347, 348, 349, 350
Department of Human Services 345, 346
Department of Protective and Regulatory Services 130, 234
deviate sexual activity 257
definition of 257
homosexual conduct 258
indecency with a child 259
indecent exposure 259
public lewdness 258
deviate sexual intercourse
definition of 71, 257
diagnosis-related group (DRG) 250
dietitian
definition of 244
selection of 247
disabilities with children
coordination of services 97
definition of 94
eligibility criteria 95
individualized education plan (IEP) 97
in educational setting 93
psychotropic drugs 102
statewide plan for 93
use of confinement, restraint, time-out 98
disabled person 233, 235, 236
definition of 234
disaster relief services 496
discharge
24 hour time period 201
after court-ordered evaluation 202
from emergency detention 202
from voluntary inpatient facility 201
with medication list 220
written request for 198, 201, 202

written withdrawal of request for 202
discipline management 66, 98, 99
disclosure
and confidentiality 135
by referral source to person seeking treatment 176
consent to 225
damages for 153
date regarding sexual exploitation 72
excepted from 180, 361
exceptions to privilege 135, 358, 361
in judicial proceedings 362
limitations of 226
of abuse report 135
of confidential information 228, 230
of mental health records 358, 361
of patient-child information 345
of sexual abuse report 74
ordered by court 136
under subpoena 358, 359
discounted fee 243
disruption of care 239
divorce
counseling 106
court-ordered counseling 106
testimony by marriage counselor 106
divorced parents
rights to access records 329
doctor-patient relationship 315–317
domestic relations 488
domestic violence 488
drug addiction 71, 109, 227, 230
drunk driving accidents 488
DSHS Child Abuse Reporting Form 292
DSHS Rider 23 267
duties and powers
of guardian 265
duty to protect 27, 294
duty to warn 27, 294, 295, 314, 315, 316, 317, 318, 319, 497

E

educational records 180
effective psychotherapy 296
elder abuse. See abuse of elder
reporting of 488
elderly person
definition of 233
Election Code 353
electronic transmission of health care information 340
emergency
definition of in declaration for mental health treatment 76
definition of in school 63
emergency admission 205

emergency detention
  and court-ordered mental health services
    202
  application for *204*
  criteria for *201, 205*
  release from *206*
  rights in *206*
emergency mental health treatment
  declaration for *76*
  form to use *80*
  notice to person *82*
  preferences for *81*
emotional injury to child *130*
end-of-life decisions *496*
evidence
  Texas rules of. *(See Texas rules of evidence*
    and privileges)
examination
  court-ordered *140*
  for emergency detention *202*
  limitation of liability of *198*
  not interfering with mandated examination
    140
  of abuse without consent *109*
  of patient records by another professional
    229, 331
  of patient records by patient *231*
  of requested documents in subpoena *359*
exchange of records *227*
excluded provisions for use of restraint *66*
exempt facility *173*
exemption from fees *141*
expert
  court appointed
    for incompetency to stand trial *88–89*
    for insanity defence *90–92*
expert testimony *206*
expert witness *489*
  social workers *489*
exploitation
  definition of *234*
  failure to report *235*
  protection from *221*

F

failure to report *235*
failure to warn *314, 316*
faith-based organizations *147*
false report *133, 236*
family
  definition of *114*
Family Code *106, 197, 218, 329*
family counseling
  court ordered *127*
family health history *252*
family violence

and protective order *115*
  counseling for *173, 175*
  definition of *114, 116*
  documentation of *116*
  information provided by medical profession-
    als *116*
  notice to victims *117*
  reporting of *116*
  service provider dynamics training *119*
  written notice of *116*
federal antitrust laws *489*
federal privilege *296, 301, 302, 305, 309*
Federal Rules of Evidence *295, 296, 297, 298,*
    300, 302, 304, 305
fees
  for medical records
    exemption from *141*
financial incentive
  prohibited to limit services *239*
force, use of
  on child by parent *256*
  on incompetent by guardian *256*
  on student by educator *256*
frivolous claims
  against person reporting *134*

G

gay rights *497*
General Counsel Law Note series *487*
genetic information
  authorized disclosure of *255*
  confidentiality of *254*
  definition of *252*
  disclosure of *254*
  exceptions to confidentiality *254*
  prohibited uses *253*
  use and retention of *253*
  use of by mental health professionals *252*
good faith report *198*
Government Code *114, 135, 234, 239, 241*
grievances *224*
guardianship
  court initiated *262*
  court proceedings *262*
  duties and powers *265*
  examinations and reports *264*
  expiration of letters *262*
  for a ward *262*
  general duties and powers of guardians *265*
  information letter *263*
  issuance of letter *262*
  law *262*
  letters of *262*
  of ward's estate *266*
  persons appointed guardians *265*
  renewal of letter *262*

required findings 263
transportation of ward 266
Guardianship Law 262

H

harm 205, 208, 210
Hays, J. Ray 35
healing art practitioners
  definition of 249
  fradulent claims 250
  niche hospital referral payback 250
  required identification 249
health care networks
  acceptance of providers 239
  contracts with providers 239
health care practitioners
  access to 243
  definition of 243
  designation of 245
  designation of under HIPAA 245
  nondiscriminatory reimbursement 246
  selection of 245
  selection of clinical social worker 247
  terms for 245
  terms used to designate 245
health care provider
  definition of 76
  guidelines for declaration for mental health
    treatment 77
  out-of-network 240
health insurance policy 245
  definition of 245
Health Insurance Portability and Accountability Act. *See HIPAA*
health policy development 490
HIPAA. *See Health Insurance Portability and
  Accountability Act*
  and medical records privacy 178
  and the practice of social work 340, 341,
    342
  appropriate standard of care 342
  compliance toolkit 498
  creation of 340
  for Social Work Employers & Administra-
    tors 497
  privacy rule 341
  security rule 341, 342
  transaction rule 341
HIV
  accidental exposure to 154
  confidential report 152
  content of post-test counseling 154
  damages for unauthorized release of test
    results 155
  general consent for test 154
  informed consent in testing 153

partner notification program 269
refusing post-test counseling 155
releasing test results to partner 152
reporting for minors 268
required counseling 154
required post-test counseling 154, 155
testing issues 152
test results released to 152
hold-harmless clause 239
hold-harmless provision 241
home and community support services
  agency 156
  license 155
home health service 156
homosexual conduct 258
hospice 156
hospice services 156

I

imminent danger of serious impairment 263
immunity
  in reporting child abuse 133
  in reporting elder abuse 236
improper disclosure 230
incapacitated
  definition of 76
  person 262
incompetency
  admissibility of statements 87
  appointed evaluation expert 87–88
  determination of 87
  examination factors 89
  examination of 87–89
  expert report 89
  issue raised 86
  qualification of experts 88
  to stand trial 86, 87
incompetency to stand trial 86
  admissibility of statements 87
  appointment of expert examiner 87
  compansation of experts 92
  court-ordered examination 90
  determining 87
  examination 87
  examiner qualifications 88
  expert report 89
  expert's qualifications 91
  factors considered 89
  order compelling examination 91
  presumptions of 86
  raising the issue of 86
  report deadline 90
  reports submitted 92
indecency with a child 259
indecent exposure 233, 259

independent living environment 157
independent psychiatric evaluation 206, 219
individualized education program 94, 95, 97
individualized habilitation plan 223
inducement to limit medically necessary ser-
     vices 239
information letter 262, 263
informed consent
     guiding health care provider actions 77
     in creating Declaration for Mental Health
          Treatment 80
     in HIV testing 153
     regarding convulsive treatment 80
     regarding psychoactive medications 80
     vs. Declaration for Mental Health Treat-
          ment 77
injunctive relief 183, 230
inpatient treatment facility
     discharge from 201
inpatient unit 157
insanity 256
insanity defense 90, 91, 92
     appointed evaluation expert 90
     compensation for evaluation of 92
     concurrent appointment 91
     expert report 92
     experts qualifications 91
insurance carrier 34, 239, 240, 241, 243
Insurance Code 243
insured
     definition of 245
insurer 245
     definition of 245
intake
     definition of 201
     for voluntary inpatient treatment 200
     yearly inservice regarding 200
integrated assessment 67
interagency coordinating group 149
interdisciplinary team 157
interference
     with child abuse investigation 140
     with child custody 260
international human rights 497
internet
     and health care 251
     use of by health care practitioners 251
investigation of report 139, 197

J

Jaffee v. Redmond 27, 33, 294, 295, 497
joint managing conservatorship 128
Judicial Conference Advisory Committee 299,
     300, 301, 303, 305, 307, 309
juvenile
     capital punishment 497

     court 107

L

law case
     Abrams v. Jones 327
     Allright, Inc. v. Strawder 333
     Bird v. W.C.W 315
     City of Amarillo v. Martin 330
     Jaffee v. Redmond 295
     R.K. v. Ramirez 331
     Roberson v. Robinson 332
     Santa Rosa Health Care Corp. v. Garcia
          317
     Tarasoff v. Regents of University of Califor-
          nia 316
     Thapar v. Zezulka 331
Law Note Series
     from NASW General Counsel 487
lawsuits 488
LBSW. See Licensed Baccalaureate Social
     Worker
LCSW. See Licensed Clinical Social Worker
     (LCSW)
LDF. See NASW Legal Defense Fund
LDF Amicus Brief Database 496
least restrictive alternative 223, 236
least restrictive environment 94, 221
legal domicile 265
legal holiday
     definition of 234
legally adequate consent 220
legally authorized representative (LAR) 67
legal remedies 230
letters of guardianship 262
lewdness
     definition of 258
liability
     for unauthorized disclosure of records 362
     of employer if patient harmed 72
Licensed Clinical Social Worker (LCSW) 244
     definition of 244
licensed marriage and family therapist. See
     also LMFT
Licensed Marriage and Family Therapist
     (LMFT) 71, 173
licensed professional counselor. See also LPC
     as "mental health services provider" 71
Licensed Professional Counselor (LPC)
     as "mental health services provider" 172
licensed social worker. See also LMSW
     as "mental health services provider" 71,
          173
Licensed Specialist in School Psychology. See
     also LSSP
Licensing
     of social workers 62, 251

licensure
  relicensure without examination *364, 371, 375*
life-threatening condition *239*
Lilly, Freddy Ray *314, 316, 317*
limitations *106, 230*
limited immunity from liability *75*
litigation
  involving social workers *488*
LMSW. *See Licensed Master Social Worker*
LMSW-AP. *See Licensed master social worker-advanced practitioner*
local mental health authority (LMHA) *67*

M

managed care contracts
  with social workers *490*
managed care organizations *489*
  and federal antitrust laws *489*
management contractor *241, 242*
managing conservator
  advised of treatment given to child *108*
  and administration of psychoactive medication *218*
  child choosing managing conservator *335*
  consenting to treatment of child *108*
  information regarding child abuse investigation *136*
  informed of inpatient restrictions *217*
  informed of inpatient's rights *201*
  not obligated to pay for treatment without consent *109*
  parent appointed as "sole managing conservator" *127*
  prohibited solicitation without consent *178*
  provided list of medications *220*
  rights and duties of *127*
  sole managing conservator *327*
  when consent not needed for counseling *109*
  when consent not needed for treatment of child *108*
marketing mental health services *172*
  prohibited acts *177*
marriage
  for same-sex couples *497*
  same-sex *497*
marriage and family therapist *244. See licensed marriage and family therapist*
MCOs. *See Managed Care Organizations*
mediation *488*
medical examination *198, 203, 208, 210, 220*
Medical Liability and Insurance Improvement Act of Texas *229*
medical professional

definition of *116*
medical records privacy *178*
medical society *175*
medications
  administration of *218*
  freedom from unnecessary meds *224*
  information on *212*
  information to inpatients *199*
  providing list of *220*
Megan's Law *497*
mental health facility *172*
mental health professional *172*
mental health records *227*
mental health referral service
  1-900 telephone number *176*
  definition of *175*
  full disclosure *178*
  open access *176*
  staffing of *175*
  standards for *175*
  termination of *176*
mental health services
  court-ordered *201, 202, 203, 215, 218*
  definition of *71, 72, 173*
  extended *206, 208, 210*
  inpatient *215*
  involuntary *217*
  outpatient *207, 208*
  provider *71*
  temporary *207*
  voluntary *198*
mental health treatment *76, 77, 78, 79, 80, 82, 330*
  definition of *76*
mental illness *173*
mental retardation
  confidentiality of records *225*
  determination of *222*
  freedom from mistreatment *224*
  general issues *221*
  grievances *224*
  individualized habilitation plan *223*
  least restrictive living environment *221*
  rights *221*
  rights guaranteed *221*
  right to education *221*
  treatment *222*
mistreatment *224*
Morales, Dan *358*

N

NASW Legal Defense Fund (LDF) *487*
National Association of Social Workers *2, 34, 35, 303, 313, 341, 342, 514*
neglect

confidentiality of report *135*
contents of report *133*
court-ordered disclosure of report *135*
definition of for child *130*
definition of regarding child *130*
definition of regarding elders *234, 235*
disclosing information in judicial hearing *231*
disclosure of report information *136*
examination without consent *109*
failure to report *235*
false report penalty *133, 236*
general issues of *130*
immunity from liability for reporting *133, 236*
in chemical dependency treatment facility *198*
in regulated facility *136*
interference with investigation *140*
investigation of report *139*
of child
　reporting issues *130*
of elders
　reporting issues *233, 235*
persons required to report *132*
privileged communication regarding evidence *137*
reporting issues *133*
reporting of *131, 197*
report made to appropriate agency *133*
negligence
　criminal *153*
　liability for *107, 108, 109, 110*
　practicing without *198*
negligent diagnosis *315*
negotiation *488*
network-carrier contract *241*
　hold-harmless provision *241*
　necessary provisions *241*
network provider *240*
　contract
　　hold-harmless clause *239*
　denial of payment *240*
　reimbursement rate *240*
niche hospital *250*
non-parent
　consent to treatment *107*
not-for-profit organization *173, 175*
notification
　of release *217*
　of rights *217*
nurse first assistant
　definition of *245*
nursing facility administrator *196*
nursing home residents

required mental health services in *195*
requiring mental health or mental retardation services *195*

O

occupational therapist *244*
Occupations Code
　Mental Health Service Provider *71*
　Social Workers *39*
offenders with mental impairments
　records of *180*
Open Record Opinions *344*
optometrist *244*
oral testimony *489*
out-of-network providers *240*
Owen, Priscilla *333*

P

palliative care *157*
parental notification *335*
Parental Notification Act *333*
parental rights and responsibilities
　for gay and lesbian parents *496*
parent-child relationship *106, 107, 125, 126, 134, 139, 231, 347, 359*
patient
　definition of *71, 123, 227*
　rights of. *See rights — of patients*
peace officer
　apprehension without warrant *203*
peauthorized health care service *240*
Penal Code. *See Texas Codes*
penalty
　for failure to report *235*
　for failure to report abuse *134*
　for false report *133, 236*
periodic examination *218*
personal care *157*
physical injury to child *130*
physical restraint *218*
physical therapist *244*
physician *71, 172, 244*
podiatrist *244*
political activities *352*
political opinion *352*
possession
　and conservatorship *125*
　by state of adoptive study report *136*
　determining best interest of child in *125*
　modified based on false report *134*
　of mental health record *230*
　rights and duties during *107, 126, 129*
post-disaster record keeping *496*
power of attorney *79, 263*

pregnant substance abusers
    treatment of *497*
preliminary examination *199, 204, 206*
presumption of competency *216, 222*
principal
    definition of *76*
privacy
    of information *28, 294*
    of therapist-client records *28, 294*
    protection of *489*
    rights in psychotherapy notes *27, 294*
privilege
    federal *296, 301, 302, 305, 309*
    of confidentiality *228, 230, 317, 358*
    psychotherapist-patient *295*
    testimonial *295*
    touchstones for acceptance of *295, 297*
privileged
    communication *487*
        regarding child abuse *137*
    information *74, 362*
Probate Code. *See Texas Codes & Statutes*
probationary employees *497*
    social workers *497*
professional
    definition of *123, 227*
    disclosing mental health records *361*
professional counselor. *See licensed profes-
    sional counselor*
prospective adoptive parents *136*
protected health information
    excluding educational records *180*
    reidentified information *181*
protection of privacy *489*
protective order *115*
protective services
    definition of *234*
    voluntary *236*
    withdrawal from *224*
protective services agency
    definition of *234*
provider contracts
    necessary provisions *239*
provider reimbursement *240*
    and discounted fees *243*
    compensability denial *240*
    restrictions on *243*
prudent management *266*
psychoactive medication
    administering without patient consent *219*
    administration of with voluntary mental
        health services *218*
    and Declaration for Mental Health Treat-
        ment Form *80, 82*
    consent for not valid under court order *215*
    consent to administration of *218*

documenting patient refusal of *219*
in declaration for mental health treatment
    76, 80
informed consent regarding *80*
in medication-related emergency *219*
prescribing *219*
psychological associate *244*
psychological extenders. *See extenders*
psychologist *244*
    as a "mental health professional" *172*
psychotherapist-patient privilege *295, 297,
    298, 299, 301, 302, 306, 307, 308,
    497*
    in the military *496*
psychotherapist privilege *296, 298, 300, 301,
    302, 303, 304, 305, 306, 307, 308,
    309, 310, 311, 313*
psychotherapy notes *491*
psychotropic drug
    definition of in school *102*
    recommendation by school staff *102*
Public Education Information Management
    System *94*
public good *296, 300, 302, 306, 309*
public interest *226, 296, 300*
public schools *174*

Q

quality of care *242*

R

"reason and experience"
    privilege touchstone *295, 297, 298, 299,
        301*
recognized member of the clergy *347*
records
    post-disaster *496*
    retention requirements *496*
referral service *175*
referral source *173*
regional education service centers *93, 98*
registered nurse *172*
reidentified information *181*
reimbursement *88, 207, 240, 243, 246*
related services *93, 95*
relicensure without examination *364, 371, 375*
report
    duty to report abuse *132*
    failure to *134*
    limitations of *75*
    limited immunity from liability *75*
    of abuse *197*
    of elderly abuse *235*
    of family violence *116*
    of suspected abuse *131*

of therapist-client sexual relationship 74
required persons 132
time to with abuse 132
to appropriate agency 133
residential unit 158
respite services 158
restraint
    clarification regarding 64
    definition of 63, 98
    documentation of 64
    notification of 64
    training on use of 63
    use of 63
rights
    information about 224
    in general 223
    in inpatient facility 216
    in mental retardation 221
    in voluntary inpatient treatment 215
    of detained person 206
    of divorced parents for access to records
        329
    of parent 126
    of patients 201, 212, 213
    of person with mental retardation 222
    relating to treatment 217
    to mental health record 229
Rule 176 359
Rule 510 361
Rules of Civil Procedure 361

S

school counselor
    certification required 93
seclusion
    definition of 98
    use of 98, 99
Senate Bill 667 361
services outside of agency
    conflict of interest 345
sexual abuse 318
    guarding children from 318
    in elderly persons 233
    in sexual exploitation 72
    investigation of report of 140
sexual activity
    deviate. See deviate sexual activity
sexual contact
    definition of 71
sexual exploitation
    admission of evidence 75
    by mental health provider 71
    cause of action 72
    damages in 73
    defenses in 73
    definition of 71, 72

inadequate defenses 73
liability of employer 72
limitations of reporting 75
limited liability from 75
reporting of 74
sexual harassment 488
sexual intercourse
    definition of 71
sexually transmitted disease 272
site visits 94
Smith v. United States 352
social study 347
    adoptive report 123
    and special appointments 117
    definition of 117
    elements of 120
    evaluator bias 119
    evaluator conflict of interest 119
    evaluator qualifications 118
    for adoption 122
    general issues regarding 117
    general provisions 120
    order for 117
    post-placement adoptive 122
    pre-adoptive 122
    report preparation 120
social worker. See licensed social worker
    medication and license 497
    providing home and community support
        services 158
    scope of practice 497
    working in school setting 93
social work licensure
    practice and title protection 497
Social Work Practice Act 39
sole managing conservator 127, 327
soliciting 173
special appointments 117
special education 93
special services
    comprehensive assessment 95
    definition of 94
    eligibility criteria 95
speech-language pathologist 244
standards of practice of professional social
        work
    minimally acceptable 342
statewide plan for services to children with
        disabilities 93
subpoena
    and HIPAA 498
    authorized issuer 83
    disclosing confidential information in re-
        sponse to 358
    enforcement of 85
    for confidential information 362
    form of 82

for privileged records *361*
for records *360*
for witnesses in civil suits *359*
general issues for social workers *488*
in cival cases *82*
in civil cases *359*
in judicial proceedings *359*
issues for social workers *488*
limitations of *83*
manner of service *83*
move to quash *360*
of social work records *488*
protection under *84*
purpose of *488*
required response *83*
requiring disclosure of confidential information *231*
responding to *488*
types of *488*
suicide data *186*
suicide prevention
minor seeking treatment in *109*
superintendent *225*
support services
administrative penalty *169*
alternate delivery site license *164*
civil penalty *168*
compliance recored *163*
consumer complaints *164*
controlling person *159*
definitions of *155*
display of license *163*
exemptions from licensing requirement *160*
home and community *155*
license application *162*
license required *159*
request for hearing *171*
retaliation prohibited *167*
scope, purpose and implementation *158*
surveyor training *166*
suspension of license *168*
temporary license *160*
violation relating to advance directives *169*
surgical assistant *244*
surrogate parent *94*
suspicions *337*

T

telehealth *251*
telemedicine *251*
temporary and extended mental health services *206*
terminal illness *158*
termination
of provider status *239*
testify *488*

testimonial privilege *296, 303, 310, 311, 313*
testing for accidental exposures to the HIV virus *154*
Texas Code
Penal Code *256*
Texas Codes
Occupations Code - Other *249*
Penal Code *256*
Probate Code *262*
Texas Codes and Statutes
Civil Practice and Remedies Code *71*
Civil Practices and Remedies Code *71*
Code of Criminal Procedure *86, 90*
Education Code *93, 221*
Family Code *106*
Government Code *144*
Health and Safety Code *151*
Human Resources Code *232, 233*
Insurance Code *239*
Penal Code *256*
Probate Code *262*
Texas Administrative Code *63*
Texas Department of Health *108*
Texas Department of Mental Health and Mental Retardation *173, 174, 175, 195*
Texas Health and Safety Code *151, 235, 327*
Texas Human Resources Code *136, 139, 172, 232*
Texas Rules of Civil Procedure *359*
Texas Rules of Evidence and Privileges
exceptions *124*
general rule of privilege *124*
who may claim privilege *124*
Texas State Board of Examiners of Psychologists *35, 358*
Texas State Board of Social Worker Examiners *41, 62, 244*
Texas Supreme Court *360*
Texas Workers' Compensation Act *240, 241, 242*
Texas Youth Commission *133*
Thapar v. Zezulka *27, 33, 294, 331*
therapeutic deception
definition of *72*
liability for *72*
time-out *63*
definition of *63, 98*
documentation of *66*
documentation on use of *66*
training on use of *65*
use of *65, 98*
Trammel v. United States *295, 296, 299*
Treatment Facilities Markeing Practice Act
public safeguard against fraud *172*
Treatment Facilities Marketing Practice Act

conditioning employee relationship on
    patient revenue 173
legislative purpose 172
prohibited acts 177
qualified mental health referral service 175
soliciting certain referrals 173
treatment facility
    advertising for 172
    appropriate referrals to 175
    contracting 173
    definition of 173
    making referrals to 174
    marketing practices 172
    not paying employees based on referrals
        173
    prohibited acts 177
    prohibited from paying for referrals 174
    prohibited from solicity from patients 173
    referral service 176
treatment guidelines 239
treatment of child
    consent 107
treatment provider
    and referral service 176

U

unauthorized disclosure 226, 231, 359, 362
unprofessional conduct by health care provider
    250
USA PATRIOT Act 497
use of force. See force, use of
utilization review 242

V

violation of probation orders 488
violence
    and protective order 115
vocational nurse 173
voluntary admission
    for court-ordered services 215
voluntary alternative dispute resolution 488
voluntary inpatient treatment
    administration of psychoactive medication
        218
    admission to treatment facility 200
    independent evaluation 219
    list of medication 220
    notification of release 217
    notification of rights 217
    rights 215
    use of physical restraint 218
voluntary mental health services 198
volunteer
    definition of 234

W

waiver of jurisdiction
    and discretiionary transfer 110
    for child cases 110
ward
    care for 266
    eligibility for medical assistance 266
    treatment of 266
weapon
    use of confinement for 99
workers' compensation helath care networks
    239
work-related problems 492
written notice
    about family violence 116

Z

Zezulka, Henry 314

ORDERING INFORMATION

Additional copies of **Texas Law for the Social Worker—2016** are available from the publisher. Orders may be placed by phone, by mail, by FAX, or directly on the web. Purchase orders from institutions are welcome.

❏ *To order by mail:* Complete this order form and mail it (along with check or credit card information) to Bayou Publishing, 2524 Nottingham, Houston, TX 77005-1412.

❏ *To order by phone:* Call (800) 340-2034.

❏ *To order by FAX:* Fill out this order form (including credit card information) and fax to (713) 526-4342.

❏ *To place a secure online order:* Visit *http://www.bayoupublishing.com.*

Name: _____

Address: _____

_____

City: _____ ST: ___ Zip: _____

Ph: _____

FAX: _____

❏ VISA ❏ MasterCard ❏ American Express ❏ Discover

Charge Card #: _____

Expiration Date: _____

Signature: _____

Please send me ____ copies at $49.95 each _____

Sales Tax 8.25% (Texas residents) _____

plus $4.95 postage and handling *(per order)* _____ $4.95

Total $ _____

Bayou Publishing
2524 Nottingham, Suite 150
Houston, TX 77005-1412
Ph: (713) 526-4558/ FAX: (713) 526-4342
Orders: (800) 340-2034
http://www.bayoupublishing.com

NASW. TEXAS CHAPTER

National Association of Social Workers

For additional resources provided by the
National Association of Social Workers—Texas Chapter, visit the
NASW/TX website at http://www.naswtx.org,
or the national website at http://www.socialworkers.org.

National Association of Social Workers
Texas Chapter
810 West 11th Street
Austin, TX 78701-2010
(512) 474-1454

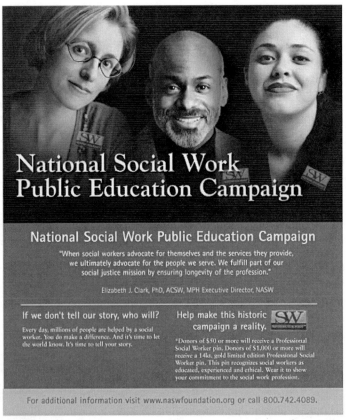

National Social Work Public Education Campaign

National Social Work Public Education Campaign

"When social workers advocate for themselves and the services they provide,
we ultimately advocate for the people we serve. We fulfill part of our
social justice mission by ensuring longevity of the profession."

Elizabeth J. Clark, PhD, ACSW, MPH Executive Director, NASW

If we don't tell our story, who will?

Every day, millions of people are helped by a social
worker. You do make a difference. And it's time to let
the world know. It's time to tell your story.

**Help make this historic
campaign a reality.**

*Donors of $50 or more will receive a Professional
Social Worker pin. Donors of $1,000 or more will
receive a 14kt. gold limited edition Professional Social
Worker pin. This pin recognizes social workers as
educated, experienced and ethical. Wear it to show
your commitment to the social work profession.

For additional information visit www.naswfoundation.org or call 800.742.4089.

National Association of Social Workers

750 First Street NE, Suite 700
Washington, DC 2002-4241

NASW foundation